The Emil and Kathleen Sick Lecture-Book Series
in Western History and Biography

Under the provisions of a Fund established by the children of Mr. and Mrs. Emil Sick, whose deep interest in the history and culture of the American West was inspired by their own experiences in the region, distinguished scholars are brought to the University of Washington to deliver public lectures based on original research in the fields of Western history and biography. The terms of the gift also provide for publication by the University of Washington Press of the books resulting from the research upon which the lectures are based.

The Emil and Kathleen Sick Lecture-Book Series
in Western History and Biography

Henry M. Jackson

A LIFE IN POLITICS

Robert G. Kaufman

UNIVERSITY OF WASHINGTON PRESS

SEATTLE AND LONDON

Publication of this book was supported in part by a generous grant from
the Henry M. Jackson Foundation.

Library of Congress Cataloging-in-Publication Data
Kaufman, Robert Gordon.
   Henry M. Jackson : a life in politics / Robert G. Kaufman.
     p.   cm. — (Emil and Kathleen Sick lecture-book series in western history
   and biography ; 9)
   Includes bibliographical references (p.   ) and index.
   ISBN 0-295-97962-3 (alk. paper)
     1. Jackson, Henry M. (Henry Martin), 1912–1983.   2. United States—
   Politics and government—1945–1989.   3. Washington (State)—Politics
   and government—1951–   4. Legislators—United States—Biography.
   5. United States. Congress—Biography.   6. Presidential candidates—United
   States—Biography.   I. Title.   II. Series.
   E840.8.J33 K38   2000   328.73'092 — dc21   [B]   00-030235

Contents

Contents

Acknowledgments

I HAVE INCURRED many debts in writing this book. A grant from the Henry M. Jackson Foundation allowed me to spend a year as a Visiting Assistant Professor at the University of Washington doing archival research in the Henry M. Jackson papers located there. The Jackson family cooperated with me patiently throughout the project, even when sometimes disagreeing with my analysis and conclusions. The generosity and sage advice of Professors Nicholas Lardy, the Director of the Jackson School of International Studies, Kenneth Pyle, and Donald Hellmann made my stay at the University of Washington a particularly productive one. Karyl Winn and her fine staff of librarians at the Jackson archives also facilitated my research. I thank Leila Charbonneau and Jill Nason for their splendid editing, and Julidta Tarver, Managing Editor of the University of Washington Press, and Candace Smith for their invaluable assistance on many aspects of this project. Naomi Pascal, Editor-in-Chief of the University of Washington Press, has earned high praise for ensuring the book's publication despite some rocky moments.

I have benefited greatly, too, from the penetrating insights and advice of a number of friends and colleagues who kindly took the time out of their busy schedules to read the manuscript: Michael G. Franc, Marshall Wittman, Douglas Macdonald, John Burke, F. Gregory Gause, Bill Van Ness, Douglas Glant, Charles Horner, John Cremeans, Lee Edwards, and my anonymous reviewers at the University of Washington Press. Special thanks are owed Herbert J. Ellison, Director of Eurasia Policy at the National Bureau of Asian Research and Professor of Russian and East European Studies at the University of Washington, for his unwavering commitment and indispensable assistance on behalf of this project.

I can never repay my family for their love, support, and generosity, which made this book possible. My in-laws, Janet and John Cremeans, showed me great hospitality during my frequent visits to Washington, D.C., where I conducted many of my interviews. My hearty thanks also go to my parents, Morton and Dorothy Kaufman, and to my sister, Dr. Julie Kaufman, for their timely financial assistance that helped enormously to defray the costs I incurred working on the book. My children—Caroline, Natalie, Rebecca, and Molly—not only patiently endured their father's immersion in this project, but provided a joyous respite from it. No one deserves more credit for whatever merit this book has than my wife Anne, who read the manuscript with penetrating insight and served cheerfully throughout as my sounding board. She is indeed a marvelous woman, and irresistible too.

Henry M. Jackson

Prologue

Henry Jackson ranks high in the pantheon of great American legislators.[1] His congressional career, including twelve years in the House of Representatives and thirty-one in the Senate, spanned the tenures of nine presidents: Roosevelt, Truman, Eisenhower, Kennedy, Johnson, Nixon, Ford, Carter, and Reagan. He not only served during watershed times in foreign and domestic politics, but also had a decisive impact on the most crucial foreign policy and defense issues of the Cold War era: Soviet-American relations, national defense policy, human rights, arms control, China policy, the Arab-Israeli conflict, and the oil crisis.

Jackson achieved his greatest prominence and influence between 1968 and 1981. During those tumultuous years, he led the fight and offered the most compelling arguments against the policy of détente as Presidents Richard Nixon, Gerald Ford, and Jimmy Carter practiced it; at the same time, he waged an increasingly lonely battle against the isolationist impulse then regnant in the national Democratic Party.[2] This book argues that Jackson played a pivotal role during the 1970s, laying the basis for America's successful foreign and defense policies in the 1980s. Jackson himself and former Jackson Democrats devised many of the major initiatives of President Reagan that, confounding the fears of his critics, contributed mightily to winning the Cold War. This defeat of Soviet totalitarianism will likely be the most significant political event of our lifetime. Also, Jackson's failure to win the presidency, an office he ran for twice, underscored the transformation of the Democratic Party from the Cold War vision of Harry Truman to the New Politics of antiwar and other protest movements. This aspect of Jackson's career provides an excellent vantage point from which to reappraise the major political debates of his era that have profound implications for our own.

Why, then, is there no comprehensive biography of Henry Jackson? Owen Harries, editor of *The National Interest*, suggests one important reason for this neglect in his laudatory review of Randall Bennett Woods's recent biography of Senator J. William Fulbright, Democrat of Arkansas:

the literature dealing with the Cold War has focused almost exclusively on the executive branch. This book on Jackson thus serves as a needed corrective for the tendency to slight the importance of major legislators in the making of American foreign and national security policy.[3]

After 1968, Henry Jackson emerged as an intellectual and political leader in the perennial struggle of U.S. foreign policy to reconcile ideals with self-interest. His approach to the dilemma defied easy classification. Specifically, his career demonstrates the need to go beyond traditional realism and idealism as paradigms for the study of American foreign policy.[4] Although both paradigms provide some insight, neither offers an adequate framework to understand Jackson or American foreign policy in general. Jackson's active support for promoting democracy and human rights abroad put him at odds with classical realists such as George Kennan, who lamented America's legalistic and moralistic tradition of foreign policy. Yet Jackson's emphasis on the importance of power and the eternally lurking danger of international conflict often put him at odds with traditional idealists, who tended to exaggerate harmony of interest among peoples and states. Although sharing with idealists the desire to spread liberty and democracy throughout the world, Jackson stressed that the survival of the United States was a necessary condition for achieving those worthy objectives. Power, force, and the willingness to use them would remain necessary, in his view, for sustaining a tolerable international order. On this subject, he frequently quoted Reinhold Niebuhr, the eminent theologian whose outlook he largely shared:

> There has never been a scheme of justice in history which does not have the balance of power as its foundation. If the democratic nations fail, their failure must be partly attributed to the faulty strategy of idealists who have too many illusions when they face realists who have too little conscience.[5]

Unlike many liberals and conservatives, Jackson considered American ideals and self-interest not mutually exclusive, but largely complementary. He opposed the Nixon administration, on the one hand, for trying to define America's self-interest too narrowly without reference to either American ideals or the ideological dimensions of the communist threat. As Jackson saw it, the duty of the American government to safeguard and encourage human rights in the Soviet Union arose from both moral and practical considerations. Nations, especially geopolitically powerful ones, that systematically repress their citizens at home, he insisted, would likely commit or threaten aggression abroad. His relentless battle for human rights and the Jackson-Vanik Amendment of 1974 on freedom of emigration established human rights as a central focus of U.S. foreign policy. He opposed the Carter administration, on the other hand, for slighting the imperatives of geopolitics, military preparedness, and historical realities in pursuit of its ideals. He considered President Carter's human rights policy well meaning but deeply flawed in theory and practice. For Jackson, the Carter administration selectively applied human rights sanctions against rightist governments while downplaying the more systematic human rights violations of America's more dangerous communist adversaries.[6]

Jackson also figured prominently in American domestic politics. He was a pioneer in environmentalism and energy policy. He was a strong and early champion of civil rights. As a freshman senator he stood up to Senator Joseph McCarthy, helping to bring about his censure during the Army-McCarthy hearings of 1954.[7] In committees and on the Senate floor, Jackson distinguished himself for his diligence, effectiveness, and capacity to build winning coalitions. More broadly, his failure to attain the presidency sheds much light on why the Democratic Party had such difficulty winning presidential elections from 1968 until the end of the Cold War.[8] Elected to the Senate in 1952, he began his tenure there firmly in the mainstream of the Democratic Party—a liberal on domestic affairs and a vigilant anticommunist who believed in the necessity of American power to promote the values of decency around the world. His presidential prospects seemed initially promising. In 1960, Jackson was John Kennedy's first choice for vice president, but lost out to Lyndon Johnson because of the perceived need for a more conservative, Southern running mate. In both 1968 and 1972, Richard Nixon considered Jackson his most formidable potential opponent. President Nixon even offered Jackson his choice of being secretary of defense or secretary of state partly in the hope of neutralizing him as a political rival. In 1976, Gerald Ford considered Jackson his strongest potential opponent.[9]

Jackson performed poorly, however, as a presidential candidate. The growing importance of electronic media, the political impact of the Vietnam War, and the increasing rifts in American politics radically altered the political landscape in the late 1960s and early 1970s. Together they spelled the demise of the New Deal coalition, and the Democratic Party, in presidential politics for nearly twenty-five years. Unswerving in his belief in the compatibility of liberalism at home and anticommunism abroad, by 1972 Jackson was in an increasingly lonely position on the political spectrum. His ideology was not the only problem. A formidable legislator but a man of little charisma, he lacked the inclination or the skill to develop a style of campaigning appropriate in an age of mass media.[10] Politically, he became not only the last of the 1940s liberals but a transitional figure. Many Reagan Democrats—blue-collar workers and Cold War Democrats alienated by the coalition that gave George McGovern the nomination in 1972—began as Jackson Democrats.[11]

Even Jackson's detractors concede the magnitude of his impact. Henry Kissinger called Jackson his most persuasive and effective critic. Senator William Fulbright excoriated Jackson for sabotaging détente as practiced by the Nixon, Ford, and Carter administrations—a policy Fulbright believed might otherwise have succeeded. In his widely acclaimed study of the Nixon administration's foreign policy, William Bundy, another critic of Jackson's approach, stressed nevertheless that his "effect on attitudes and events must rank him among the top American public figures concerned with foreign policy in the 1970s."[12]

Indeed, the views that Jackson personified continue to encounter two lines of criticism. As revisionists see it, advocates of military preparedness and ideological hostility toward Soviet communism, such as Jackson, prolonged the Cold War at great cost and risk to both sides.[13] Strobe Talbott, a journalist before he became deputy secretary of state in the Clinton administration, distilled this outlook to its essence when he wrote in *Time* that the United States won the Cold War because it need not have been fought in the first place.[14] As declinists see it, Jackson's approach culminated in imperial overreach, excessive military spending, and a gross neglect of the economic underpinnings of our security, the staggering cost of which the United States will continue to pay for decades to come.[15]

Yet neither of these lines of criticism is persuasive. Jackson's synthesis of power and principle—a blend of geopolitics, a Judeo-Christian conception of morality, and a belief in the possibility if not the inevitability or irreversibility of evolutionary progress toward democracy—offered the best practicable framework for a remarkably successful American foreign policy during the Cold War era. Without succumbing to either utopian idealism or amoral realpolitik, the United States prevailed against a Soviet empire that was not only truly malignant but truly dangerous.

Events have belied the pessimistic prognostications of the declinists who argued that America could not afford the robust foreign policy that Jackson championed. The Cold War ended and the post–Cold War era has begun with the United States not in decline, but in ascendance—technologically, militarily, economically, and politically. In large measure, the collapse of Soviet communism accounts for why U.S. defense spending has declined 38 percent since 1985. This peace dividend has generated hundreds of billions of dollars for reducing the U.S. budget deficit that so alarmed declinists.[16]

To be sure, Jackson was hardly infallible. China's brutal suppression of democracy since 1989 suggests that his strategic attraction to China, which predated even Nixon's, blinded him to the human rights violations there. Also, the implacable consistency of his convictions and the irrepressibility with which he advocated them—his outstanding virtues in foreign affairs—became his outstanding liabilities in domestic affairs. Jackson unduly mistrusted private markets. He never relinquished a sanguine belief, forged during his formative years, in the efficacy of government intervention in the economy and the need for and practicability of a massive welfare state. His response to the oil crisis of the 1970s illustrated in bold relief his misunderstanding of markets, which flowed from his lack of experience in the private sector, from his passionate commitment to cheap public electric power for Washington State, and from his hostility toward private power companies (which he later transferred to the large oil companies). As chairman of the Energy Committee, Jackson rightly worried about America's excessive dependence on foreign oil, but his attempts to reduce that dependence through policies such as price controls on oil and natural gas only made shortages worse and gas lines longer.

Notwithstanding these shortcomings, Jackson left behind what Owen Harries calls "an adoring band to celebrate his legacy."[17] Senator Daniel Patrick Moynihan, the liberal Democrat from New York, hailed him as proof of the "old belief in the Judaic tradition that at any moment in history goodness in the world is preserved by the deeds of 36 just men who do not know that this is the role the Lord has given them. . . . Henry Jackson was one of those men." Similarly, George F. Will, the nation's pre-eminent conservative commentator, called him the "finest public servant I have known." In his judgment, Jackson "mastered the delicate balance of democracy, the art of being a servant to a vast public without being servile to any part of it." Former United Nations ambassador Jeane Kirkpatrick also emphasized approvingly that many informed advocates of vigilant internationalism continue to invoke Jackson's name on behalf of their positions.[18]

Finally, Jackson's career refutes the cynical but prevalent view that good character and politics are mutually exclusive. He personified integrity and decency in all aspects of his life. He also possessed in abundance the cardinal virtue of political courage: a willingness to maintain unpopular positions he thought were right. As much as anybody, observed James H. Billington, a renowned historian of Russia and the librarian of Congress, "Jackson vindicated the Founding Fathers' hope that the Senate might be a place for genuine deliberation about the broad, long-term interest of the Republic."[19]

The time is right for a full-scale biography of Henry Jackson. What we have learned from the Soviet archives has roundly confirmed his views on the nature of the Soviet threat and how to respond to it.[20] There is also an abundant archival record. In writing this book, I have had full access to Senator Jackson's papers, located at the University of Washington, where I plowed through more than fifteen hundred boxes of written materials and hundreds of tapes collected for an oral history project on the senator. Although this is not an official biography, Mrs. Helen Jackson and many of Senator Jackson's closest advisers have cooperated fully by granting me extensive interviews. Many of his political rivals have also given me lengthy interviews. Altogether, I have conducted more than one hundred interviews for the book, with subjects spanning the wide range of Jackson's career.

Two main themes run through this chronological study of Jackson's life and times: his career offers a prism through which to view the transformation of the Democratic Party and American liberalism; more important, he had a decisive impact on the seminal struggle of our lifetime—the Cold War.

Chapter 1

The Everett Years, 1912–1940

Henry Martin Jackson, the youngest of five children, was born May 31, 1912, in the back bedroom of his family's home at 3602 Oakes Street in Everett, Washington. He always took great pride in the Norwegian heritage on both sides of his family. His father, born Peter Gresseth on an island near the village of Aure, in western Norway, grew up on a farm. Before leaving Norway for the United States in 1885, he anglicized his family name to Jackson: a combination of his Uncle Jack's name and the traditional Scandinavian suffix. The course of his journey to Everett reflected the experiences of thousands of Scandinavians who migrated to the Pacific Northwest. After arriving in Minnesota, Peter Jackson moved to Montana, where he worked briefly before continuing west to Washington in 1888, a year before it achieved statehood.[1]

Henry Jackson's mother, born Marine Anderson in Alvenes, a remote Norwegian village north of the Arctic Circle, was the youngest of twelve children. She also grew up on a farm where life was rigorous. The devoutly religious Andersons weekly traveled seventeen miles each way to get to Roerstad Lutheran Church, the one where Marine was confirmed. The only way to get there was by rowing across a fjord exposed to the North Sea, then walking several miles. In summer, they set out early on Sunday morning to reach church on time; in winter, they had to start on Saturday because the crossing was even rougher and more dangerous, with just four or five hours of daylight in which to make it. Marine came to the United States in 1891 to join her oldest brother, Konrad, who had settled in Gig Harbor, Washington. In 1893, she moved to Everett, where she became a charter member of the local Lutheran church, the first meeting place of many of the early immigrants from Norway, among them Peter Jackson. In 1897, Marine and Peter married in that church.[2]

During the early years of their marriage, the Jacksons moved back to

Montana in search of work for Peter. Their stay, however, was unhappy and brief. Toiling at a hot, strenuous, and dreary job in the Anaconda smelter, Peter, characteristically reticent and stoic, objected volubly to "the damn company town's" exploitation of him and the many poor, unskilled Scandinavians employed in similar circumstances.[3] He and Marine thus returned to Everett, which remained their home for the rest of their lives.

Founded in 1888 on a peninsula thirty miles north of Seattle, Everett has never lived up to the lofty expectations of its first generation of civic leaders. They had nicknamed this port town the "City of Smokestacks," anticipating that the arrival of the railroads and the promise of huge profits from mining gold, silver, and lead from the hills east of town would transform it into the major industrial center of the Pacific Northwest. Although the railroads came to Everett, they also came to Seattle, which emerged instead as the major economic and population center of the region. Nor did mining pan out. By the time Henry Jackson was born, Everett had truly become the city of smokestacks: a mill town with a population of roughly thirty thousand, dependent on lumber and shingle mills that noisily spewed smoke and cinders over the entire metropolitan area. When the Everett Pulp and Paper Company opened its plant early in Henry's boyhood, the sulfate process added a noxious odor to the town's mill-induced haze.[4]

The Everett of Jackson's youth had a simple social structure: a tiny elite of eastern-born lumber barons, almost no middle class, and a vast working class, many of whom were Scandinavian immigrants like Peter and Marine. The town had its share of labor unrest and radicalism, especially rife in the Pacific Northwest during those years. The worst episode, known as the Everett Massacre, occurred in 1916, when Jackson was just four years old and too young to remember. Local vigilantes and other leaders of the Everett establishment, led by an overly aggressive Sheriff Donald McRae, confronted a force of 250 Industrial Workers of the World protesters (Wobblies) as they disembarked from the ship *Verona* coming from Seattle. A source never identified fired a single shot, which unleashed a panic. The ensuing gunfire killed two vigilantes and five Wobblies and wounded fifty others, including the sheriff, who was shot in the leg. Bitter memories of this episode lingered for years.[5]

Everett had a well-deserved reputation as a rough and tumble town, full of bars, gambling, and houses of prostitution for the loggers and seamen who came there periodically for recreation. Yet neither labor radicalism nor licentiousness had any place in the Jackson home. Residents of Everett admired the Jacksons for their prudence and probity. Peter played no part in any of the labor violence that culminated in the Everett Massacre. Tall, lean, and physically powerful, he worked first as a policeman, then as a laborer in the Sumner Iron Works, manufacturing logging equipment, then for several more years as a laborer working with concrete. Eventually, he established his own business as a small independent contractor, pouring concrete basements and foundations. When Everett later became a union town, he became a union man. The members of the Plasterers and Cement Masons Local 190 elected him as their treasurer for twenty-six consecutive years. Peter Jackson did not belong to the Democratic Party, which in Washington State and in Everett until the 1930s was a minority party whose leadership was largely dominated by Irish Catholics. Like most non-Catholics in Snohomish County, Peter and Marine Jackson voted Republican before the Great Depression. People knew Pete, the name his friends called him, as a quiet, hardworking, and thoughtful man who laid the finest basement in town.[6]

Arthur Jackson, ten years older than his brother Henry, resembled his father physically and worked with him. Contemporaries remember him as intelligent and a fine athlete. "No one threw the ball as well," according to Jack Dootson, a neighborhood friend of both Jackson boys. Arthur could not finish high school because he had to help support his family, as the oldest siblings of many immigrant families did. Severe arthritis incapacitated him in his thirties. Thereafter he lived a painful, sad life; he was frequently in hospitals for operations or therapy, and during one such stay his brief marriage ended. For a long time, he remained estranged from his entire family.[7] What caused the estrangement remains unclear. Some locals speculate that Arthur may have resented Henry's success and the advantages Henry had that were denied to him.[8] Whatever the cause, the records indicate that Henry Jackson always behaved honorably toward his older brother. During the 1940s, he paid for all of Arthur's expenses at the Mayo Clinic, including surgery to have both hips replaced with artificial ones. Correspondence between them also reveals Henry's generosity and empathy for his older brother's suffering.[9] Despite his legendary thrift, Henry continually implored Arthur to ask for and accept all the spending

money he needed. Arthur's twenty-year career as a bookkeeper for Pacific Foundry and Light ended when he suffered a series of debilitating
strokes during the 1960s. He languished for the rest of his life in nursing
homes, first in Renton and then in north Seattle. During the mid-1970s,
with Arthur so incapacitated that he could barely speak, the Jackson
brothers reconciled. Henry paid for all of Arthur's care until his death in
1979.[10]

Henry's mother and his sister Gertrude, who jointly reigned supreme
in the Jackson matriarchy, exerted the most powerful influence on his development. Physically, he resembled his mother more than his father:
shorter, broader, stockier, with a head that seemed slightly oversized for
his body. Friends recall Mrs. Jackson as a proud and gentle woman, determined to promote her children, particularly Henry, her favorite, whom
she had identified early as the most gifted member of the family with the
greatest potential for worldly success. By the time she gave birth to Henry, she was forty-three years old and the financial situation of the family
had improved considerably. Although they lived modestly and never became wealthy, the Jacksons were somewhat better off than most families
in their circle. The house at 3602 Oakes was not outstanding, but was respectable and substantial by the standards of the town's working class. The
downstairs had three large rooms: a bedroom for the parents; a living
room, with ample pieces of comfortable, overstuffed furniture; and a
huge, well-stocked kitchen. Upstairs were three large bedrooms for Henry and his sisters, Gertrude and Marie. Over the garage, there was also an
apartment that the Jacksons rented out. So the family had the resources
for Marine to indulge Henry more than she had her other children.[11]

The loss of a third daughter, Agnes, to infantile paralysis when she was
fourteen and Henry barely three, only magnified Marine's propensity to
shower him with attention and affection. By all accounts she was a marvelous cook and took special delight in lavishing Henry with quantities of
delicious but fattening delicacies. The sweet tooth his mother cultivated
exacerbated his genetic predisposition, inherited from her, to put on
weight, a problem he struggled with all his life with varying degrees of
success.[12]

Marine and Peter Jackson encouraged Henry to assimilate as quickly
and completely as possible. Like other Scandinavians of their generation,
the Jacksons came to the United States to become Americans. They took

great pride in their Norwegian heritage, but regarded assimilation as complementing that sentiment. The Jacksons insisted on speaking English around the children, both inside and outside the home. Marine remained an active member of Our Savior's Lutheran Church, where the towering Reverend Karl Norgaard, known for his severity and keen intellect, conducted his services in both English and Norwegian. Although Henry was baptized and started Sunday School in that church, Marine supported his decision to join the more socially prominent Presbyterian church closer to home, where most of his neighborhood friends attended. He belonged to that Presbyterian church until he died.[13]

Marine also insisted that her children judge people as individuals rather than imputing negative group characteristics to them, an ethic that Henry practiced and preached faithfully with the sole but deplorable exception of his attitude toward Japanese Americans during the Second World War. His mother particularly abhorred anti-Semitism in any form, perhaps the first clue to understanding Jackson's fervent devotion to Israel and Jewish causes generally.[14] Henry recalled his normally placid mother displaying uncharacteristic anger toward neighborhood children who yelled "Kike" at a Jewish junkman. "My mother was a Christian who believed in a strong Judaism," Henry observed. "She taught me to respect the Jews, help the Jews! It was a lesson I never forgot."[15]

Henry's sister Gertrude, fourteen years his senior, had an equally profound effect on his character and career. Tall like her father, with a slightly oversized head like her mother, Gertrude taught for thirty-nine years at the Garfield Elementary School, whose students came mostly from poorer, working-class homes. Blunt, strict, determined, and outspoken, not reluctant to offer her neighbors advice about everything from politics to the behavior of their children. Gert also had a reputation for being a splendid teacher, the best educator in Everett. She inspired large numbers of young people, including Henry, to whom she was devoted. Without boasting or ostentatious sentimentality, she had a way of getting good things done, often providing clothing or giving money to children acutely in need.[16]

Gert was the one, struck by her brother's aptitude for avoiding household chores, who nicknamed him Scoop, after a comic strip character adept at persuading others to do his jobs for him. She also was the person who advised him from his childhood through much of his career in the

Senate. From his first campaign for office, she was his most dedicated supporter, his eyes and ears in Everett, someone on whom he often called for information about the local political scene. She helped, too, to pay for his college and law school education. Her descriptions of the plight of her most impoverished students kindled in Henry an empathy for the less fortunate that became a trademark of his political philosophy. She never married. She lived at the Oakes Street house until she died in February 1969, after suffering several months with pancreatic cancer. Henry reciprocated Gert's devotion. For his entire Senate career, he donated all of his honoraria to provide scholarships for Everett children, through an anonymous fund until Gert's death and to a scholarship fund in her name thereafter.[17]

Marie Jackson, five years older than Henry, was the most socially inclined and physically attractive member of the family. Like Gert, she never married or moved away from the Oakes Street house. She spent most of her life working at home, cooking and caring for her mother until Mrs. Jackson died in 1957. Sadly, she developed a dependency on alcohol that she never fully overcame. In December 1969, just months after Gert's death, Marie died at home in a fire that she apparently ignited when she fell asleep addressing Christmas cards.[18]

SCHOOL DAYS

Henry Jackson's friends and acquaintances in Everett remember him as a model youth: "a serious and hardworking kid, a super achiever. . . . Teachers liked him. . . . He was on time, neat, clean, prepared, but in a way that did not alienate his classmates." "He was a teacher's pet but without the liabilities." There were, of course, the occasional bouts of mischief typical of young boys. When he was five or six, according to boyhood friend Jack Dootson, they set fire to an open field in their neighborhood, full of dry grass, hoping that the fire trucks would come. They got more than they reckoned on: "The fire grew rather fast toward the house down the street. . . . Scoop and I ran down an alley around the block. When I got home, my mother was waiting for me and took me down to the Jackson house. Mrs. Jackson looked for Scoop, found him under the bed, and hauled him out." Helen Sievers, a classmate of Scoop's at the Longfellow Elementary School, remembered him putting pennies on the trolley car tracks on Broadway. "We all did it," she said. She added, however, that

"that was probably the most illegal thing Scoop did in his life. He was as square as they come." Strong but a poor athlete with terrible hand-eye coordination, Henry avoided sports and concentrated on other activities. He was a good student in grammar school, a particularly good speller. The most memorable episode from his Longfellow school days occurred one day in third grade when Mrs. Dootson, his third-grade teacher, asked her students what they wanted to be. Henry answered, "President of the Untied States," provoking much ribbing from his family and classmates.[19]

Although usually successful in escaping the grueling physical labor of helping his father pour cement, Henry worked hard nonetheless, which he considered the norm for young people of the time. "Working was a way of life, and the work ethic was very important," recalled Jackson to his daughter Anna Marie. "All youngsters had jobs of one kind or another. Some worked in groceries and others in garages." What distinguished Henry from his peers was his diligence and thrift. He managed to save most of what he earned, a habit he retained throughout his life. He got his first job at age nine selling the *Saturday Evening Post*. He had a newspaper route at age ten delivering the *Everett Daily Herald*, the course of which made him aware of the rough, seedy bars and houses of ill repute that made up the dark side of life in Everett. Later, he worked at the newspaper office on weekends, helping to put out a Sunday edition. In high school, he delivered the Sunday edition in an old Model T Ford he purchased because the load was too big to carry on his bicycle. He also worked in the sawmills during some summers and the fish canneries during others.[20]

Henry's performance as a newspaper boy won him a national award for carrying 74,880 newspapers without a single complaint, a story that made the front page of the *Everett Herald* of July 2, 1927. In attaining this feat, the young Jackson displayed a shrewdness essential for any successful politician: "I had a little system I used. . . . We would give the customer a receipt when they paid for the paper. I had on the receipt: don't call me at the Everett office. Call me at home if you have a complaint. So I managed to develop and build a good organization." Even after he became a senator, he reminisced with evident pride about how he always managed to toss the newspaper from his bicycle right to the front door of his customers.[21]

Henry really began to distinguish himself in junior high and high school. He excelled as a member of the debate team, with the help and encouragement of Ellen Repp, his junior high school debate coach and teacher. Miss Repp explained that he "was a very good debater because he was extremely thorough and was sure that he had his facts before he would say anything." Miss Repp also stimulated her students' interest in politics: "To make them aware of the world at large and their own community, I used to have them impersonate foreign newscasters. So you were practically a citizen of the world. It gave them an understanding that the world was much larger than just Everett." Studious, logical, and deliberate, he won almost all his debates in high school. Fred Moore, a high school friend, recounted the circumstances of one of his rare losses, a debate with him over the Smoot-Hawley tariff act. Henry defended it, suggesting that his political inclinations leaned then to the Republican side: "He worked hard on that. . . . He could have filled a volume. . . . He was heart-crushed when he got a B. His big mistake was not knowing that Isabel Carlyle was a Democrat."[22]

Besides debating, Jackson's main extracurricular activities included writing articles for the newspapers, working on the yearbook staff, and participating actively in De Molay, a Masonic organization very popular among Everett males of his generation. Academically, he was smart, not brilliant, a good student, not an excellent one, who liked and did best in history, a subject for which he retained a lifelong passion.[23] In his relations with others, he was cautious and morally upright. Not every adolescent or adult male would have displayed the forbearance that he did in circumstances such as those that Dr. Edwin Chase, Jackson's De Molay sponsor and lifetime friend, witnessed in admiration:

> At a De Molay initiation ceremony when Scoop was a freshman in high school, both of us were on the drill team. We were put up in Spokane in the Coeur d'Alene Hotel. Scoop and I shared one room. I guess we did not lock the door . . . because a lady came in who said she was a nurse. She jumped in bed with Scoop, saying "I am going to take care of you." Scoop kicked her out. He was a very moral character. He kicked her out. But I think one of our fellow De Molays didn't.[24]

Jackson had girlfriends. His most steady was Dorothy White, who later became a physician in Oregon, but he did not date anyone seriously. Even in high school his thoughts were often on politics. "We used to kid about it," said Les Cooper, a close friend, remembering that "Scoop could not take a girl out on a date without talking about politics." Scoop told Fred Moore that he intended to be a senator as they prepared for their Smoot-Hawley debate. Moore considered him somewhat obsessed about the threat of invasion from Japan, which Henry would "expound on until it became a rather tiresome subject." He had no sense of humor about such things, according to Moore, who once needled him not to worry because he could count on the longshoremen, then on strike, to prevent the Japanese from landing. "Scoop was not amused. He didn't speak to me for a couple of weeks."[25]

The young Henry Jackson did not exhibit a great sense of adventure. There was, however, one exception, which acquainted him with the joys of the wilderness and perhaps played some part in his later incarnation as the major sponsor of landmark environmental legislation while in the Senate. In the summer between the eighth and ninth grades, he and friends Bob Humphrey and Ivan Ramsted took a seven-day trip into the mountains, around Glacier Peak in the North Cascades. The boys carried homemade backpacks, filled with homemade sleeping bags of heavy canvas which "weighed a ton." They brought their own food (pancake flour, canned milk, eggs in a jar), which they supplemented with fish caught in the river. However much Henry may have marveled at the splendor of the mountains, he was not eager to do his share of the chores. Humphrey recalled wryly that when it came to his day to light the fire and cook breakfast, "Scoop did not want to do it. It ties in to this talent he had to manipulate. . . . You have someone else do the yard work or cut the grass. . . ."[26]

Although Henry did not finish high school at the top of his class, his teachers selected him for his overall academic and debating achievements to deliver one of the four commencement speeches at graduation, held in the Everett Theater in the spring of 1930. His topic was law enforcement: the importance of respecting the law, about which he spoke with great gravitas and at excessive length. Bob Humphrey summed up best the local consensus about what set the young Henry Jackson apart:

He had a fixidity of purpose, received good advice, and uniquely he followed it. He never took the detours that others of us took. He never messed around and was more dedicated than anybody I met. He did not go out looking for girls. He did not drink. He did not smoke. These things take time when you are young. . . . You do not meet many people like Jackson today. He was a very honorable man.

OFF TO THE UNIVERSITY

Jackson entered the University of Washington in the fall of 1930 just as the Depression had begun to hit Washington State severely. Thousands were out of work. In Everett, most of the major businesses had to close down. The Everett Pulp and Paper Company, the only plant running in the city, eventually cut back to three days a week. From the money he earned working, Henry had managed to save $2,000, enough to pay for much of his first two years of college. His sister Gert, making $1,200 a year as a schoolteacher, contributed significantly to defray his tuition and expenses. Nonetheless, he had to struggle financially to make it through college and law school.[27]

When he arrived on campus, he did not cut a dashing figure. Lloyd Shorett, Jackson's sponsor at Delta Chi fraternity and later a roommate in law school, portrays him as a young freshman "equipped with an old red sweater and with hair that stuck straight up in the air all the way around his head." Luckily, Jackson did not pay a social price for his awkwardness, for the Depression had caused a significant drop in the number of pledges to fraternities. So Delta Chi took him, according to Shorett, because the members "thought this young fellow had a lot of possibilities—and besides that we needed pledges."[28]

Jackson lived at the fraternity house only during his first quarter. Thereafter he commuted from Everett by car, driving several other students, to save money. He obtained the car thanks to the generosity of Abe Kosher, a Jewish family friend from Everett with a thick Yiddish accent, who ran an auto-wrecking yard and scrap metal business. When Jackson told him he planned to commute by bus because he could not afford a car, Kosher insisted he take the used car sitting out on the lot. "But I have no money," said Jackson. "Do not worry," replied Kosher, "you can pay me back someday when you are a success." When Jackson returned after graduating to repay him, Kosher did not want to accept any money, but Jackson insisted. Kosher set the price at $150, substantially less than the car was worth. Jackson never forgot his kindness and generosity.[29]

When he entered law school in the fall of 1932, Jackson moved back to the fraternity house, making up for the added expense by washing dishes and waiting on tables. He described his typical day as follows:

> I used to get up at 5:00 A.M. to help set up tables and assist the cook. Then I would attend classes from 8:00 A.M. to 12:00 P.M. I would rush back to wait on tables at noon and worked part of the afternoon. Then I studied part of the afternoon and worked again in the evening and studied until 12:00 A.M. or 1:00 A.M. or so.[30]

Jackson's persona in college and law school evoked much the same reaction as it did during his adolescent years in Everett. Friends and acquaintances described him as temperate, friendly, studious, and honest, with little interest in sports or recreation. In college, he performed solidly, but not brilliantly, with history again his best and most beloved subject. His studies and his need to make money left him little time to pursue his interest in politics, with just two known exceptions. Although never a socialist, he led the fight to allow Norman Thomas to speak on campus, because he believed strongly in free speech.[31] Also, he joined the League for Industrial Democracy (LID), a moderate organization of intellectuals and professionals that supported trade unions and social democratic principles generally. His years at the University of Washington do, however, mark one of the major turning points in his life.

At the end of his freshman year, Jackson spent the summer at Stanford, taking a full academic load in the hope of transferring there permanently. He wanted to pursue a career in the foreign service but feared that with thousands out of work the chances for employment after college were not good. Dr. Graham Stuart, a professor of international relations at Stanford who acted as a mentor, recommended that he study law. A law degree would ensure that he could support himself in private practice if necessary, and would also provide him with the best entry to politics, while preserving the option of joining the foreign service later if the employment situation improved. Finding that he could not afford the vastly higher cost of Stanford, Jackson returned to the University of Washington and followed Stuart's advice.[32] He graduated from law school just making the top third of his class, a respectable finish that owed as much to hard work as to his natural ability. Stan Golub, a class behind Henry, then an acquaintance and later his best friend, recalled him as "not one to have a good time as so many of us did at law school. He really concentrated on the law, came from a family where they didn't have the money to waste on education frivolously. He really was a good student and very determined."[33]

Events rather than theories largely determine the political philosophy of most successful statesmen. Henry Jackson was no exception. Perhaps he might have become a Republican but for the Depression, as several of his Everett contemporaries surmised. But his days at the frat house exposed him to the real hunger and suffering that the Depression had inflicted on Seattle, an experience that was the genesis of his mature views about the need for a strong, active federal government. He watched in anguish as mothers came by to salvage for their families the leftover food in the fraternity's garbage cans. He talked and commiserated with these women. He also encountered the Depression at his family dinner table, where Marine Jackson frequently fed men in Everett who were down on their luck. An ardent believer in the importance of the rule of law, the subject of his high school commencement address, he not only empathized with those suffering but feared the social consequences if the government did not help them.[34] As he later remembered:

> There was not a welfare program nor a Works Projects Administration (WPA) program. The people were in desperate shape. In addition, they were being evicted from their homes. So it was a difficult period in our country's history. We almost had a revolution in the United States. In many instances, people who were hungry and desperate raided food chains. Several Safeways in Washington were raided. They would clean out the store and distribute the food among the needy. There was only limited food distribution, a limited amount of sugar, flower, salt, limited items. There was no means of properly feeding the people. People were literally starving. The patience of the American people during this period was hard to believe.[35]

COMING HOME

After graduating from law school in the spring of 1935, Henry returned to Everett. He took a temporary job with the local office of the Federal Emergency Relief Administration (FERA) for several months while awaiting the results of his bar exam. Times were not as bad as in the early 1930s, but they were still not good. Jackson had the responsibility of looking after 180 needy families living in the vicinity of Lake Stevens. He also talked regularly with local merchants to identify needy people too proud to ask for relief, and would go out and interview them so he could get them help. In the fall of 1935, he helped place the first people of Snohomish County on the WPA and referred young people to the Civilian Conservation Corps (CCC).[36]

His stint at FERA reunited him with John Salter, who worked with him there. They had first met as twelve-year-olds at Providence Hospital in Everett, lying in adjacent beds while recuperating from having their tonsils out. Afterward they had gone their separate ways, despite living just blocks apart. Except for his senior year at Everett High School, Salter had gone to Catholic schools. Then he attended the seminary, but left just months before he would have been ordained. It was a good thing for both the Catholic Church and Salter, because he liked women too much for the priesthood, and his real vocation was politics. Small, wiry, acerbic, irreverent, a poor administrator but a superb strategist, Salter was an effective alter ego for Jackson, who in the early stages of his political career needed someone endowed with the qualities he lacked. Gerald Hoeck, in charge of Jackson's media operations for all his Senate campaigns and an intimate of both men, regarded Salter as essential for Jackson's early political success: "Without Salter, Jackson would never have achieved what he did for the first fifteen to twenty years of his career. Jackson developed into a skillful politician. Salter was born one."[37]

Equally, Salter needed someone like Jackson to further his political ambitions. The economic crisis of the 1930s precipitated a political revolution in Washington State that the young Jackson's political odyssey epitomized. From the Civil War until 1932, the Republic Party had dominated the state's presidential, state, and local politics. At one point during the early 1920s, only two Democrats served in the state legislature. The Depression and the New Deal changed all that. Historians Robert Ficken and Charles LeWarne have illustrated the swiftness and totality of this realignment. In 1932, Franklin Roosevelt won 57 percent of the vote, doubling Al Smith's percentage of 1928. The Democratic trend extended beyond the presidency. In 1932, Washington State elected Clarence D. Martin, a Democrat, as governor and Homer Bone, a Democrat, to the Senate, denying the incumbent Republican senator a fifth term. The Democrats also increased from eight to seventy the number of seats held in the Washington State House of Representatives, giving them a three-to-one majority in that chamber. The fortunes of labor unions in Washington also improved dramatically after 1932, foreshadowing the transformation of Washington State into one of the most powerful bastions of organized labor for much of the post–World War II era. By the late 1930s, Washington had become one of the most liberal, Democratic states in the nation. James A. Farley, President Roosevelt's postmaster general, quipped that the nation consisted of forty-seven states and the Soviet of Washington.[38]

Salter exemplified the political tradition of Irish Catholics who formed the backbone of the Democratic Party during its pre–New Deal lean years. Salter, Ed Hennessee, and Harold Walsh, mainstays of the Snohomish County Democratic Party, would seize upon the electoral potential of Henry Jackson in this new era: a New Deal liberal, scrupulously honest, Protestant, with a Norwegian ancestry, which would have wide appeal in a county where Scandinavians made up a quarter of the electorate. In 1936, Jackson and Salter collaborated politically for the first time. They formed a local chapter of the Roosevelt First Voter's League, then persuaded the established Young Democrats to merge with them. Jackson became the president and Salter the treasurer of this combined organization.[39]

In December 1936, Jackson received notice that he had passed the bar exam. The law firm of Black and Rucker hired him. Lloyd Black, one of the most prominent attorneys in Everett, had always taken an interest in mentoring young people. He saw great promise in young Henry, whose father he also knew and admired. Jackson venerated Black, a longtime Democrat noted for his integrity, who advised Jackson that "if he wanted to be a businessman, be a Republican, but if he wanted a career in politics, be a Democrat." For nearly two years, Jackson practiced law: first with Black and his partner, Jasper Rucker, together; then, with Rucker alone after Black became a judge in 1937. His responsibilities ran the gamut of legal issues typical of private practice in a large town: trust and estates, family law, partnerships and corporations, insurance work, personal injury. Jackson liked practicing law. He was good at it. This was, nonetheless, the last time he would have a job in the private sector or outside of politics. Although he probably would have had a fine career in private practice and might have wanted one in other circumstances, good fortune intervened.[40]

JACKSON'S FIRST CAMPAIGN

The young attorney practiced law in a town where breaking the law had proliferated rampantly. During Prohibition, Everett had become a prime locale for bootlegging, with a corrosive influence that also spread to law enforcement and the political establishment. The repeal of Prohibition in 1933 had not diminished corruption significantly. Illegal gambling, drinking, and prostitution still ran wide open in Snohomish County. Many restaurants and bars had slot machines. Frequently, men would get drunk, gamble their paychecks away, and have no money to provide their family with essentials. A man named Joe Hart, who arrived in Everett in 1934, had a particularly notorious reputation as the king of gambling in Snohomish County. Although Tom Hart, his son, has insisted that his father was not a gangster, most of those in Everett who recall those days disagree. "Joe Hart was the big guy in the county," according to Les Cooper, who succeeded Jackson as county prosecutor. "He controlled the Teamsters Union. If you wanted to have a slot machine in your restaurant and it wasn't his, you would not get delivery. He had a monopoly." Worse, Snohomish County seemed to tolerate the lawlessness. Ellen Allen, not implicated herself, witnessed payoffs of some public officials with money disguised in Lucky Strike cigarette packages.[41]

The prosecuting attorney, Al Swanson, the incumbent Democrat up for reelection in the fall of 1938, had assumed office as a popular figure. In 1936, he had lost by only 2,000 votes in his bid to become state attorney general. He had since, however, descended into debilitating alcoholism. Many locals construed his failure to stop corruption as evidence that he, too, was on the take.[42] Jackson took maximum advantage of this opportunity. With the encouragement of Lloyd Black, he decided to run for prosecuting attorney, not only because he abhorred gambling and corruption, but also because he believed that he could win against Swanson in the primary and that he stood a better chance of beating the Republican than such a vulnerable incumbent did. He chose Salter as his campaign manager. What his first political campaign lacked in money it more than made up for in diligence and energy. He ran against Swanson in the primary as a reform candidate, stressing his integrity and eliciting the enthusiasm of many of the town's young people, who came out and volunteered for him. His sister Gert was one of his most effective campaigners. Osa Nurmi, a friend of the Jackson family and one of those youthful volunteers, later reminisced that the campaign of 1938 was wonderful, different from modern campaigns: "It was all footwork . . . house to house, with pep rallies, parades."[43]

Henry Jackson excelled, then and always, as a practitioner of this labor-intensive, retail politics. He possessed a remarkable memory, giving him total recall of names, places, and events, even years later. Also, he had boundless energy for campaigning. Although as a public speaker he was always indifferent at best, on a face-to-face basis people found him an appealing combination of thoughtfulness, confidence, empathy, and integrity. His ability to project that image was a tremendous asset in that era when those attributes mattered more and media magnetism mattered less.[44] Despite Swanson's liabilities, Jackson would never take an election for granted. He always campaigned indefatigably. In the morning, he would be at the Weyerhaeuser mill by 8:00 greeting workers and shaking hands. During lunch hour, he would stand on the corner of Wetmore and Hewitt in downtown Everett, shaking more hands. In the evening, he returned to the mills for even more handshaking with men going to work or heading for home. He also campaigned in the rural parts of the county. Jackson realized that Snohomish County was between 23 and 25 percent Scandinavian, many of whom lived outside Everett. With his Norwegian name (despite the anglicization, locals recognized it as such), they knew he was one of theirs. John Salter and friend Mary Claus drove him to coffee klatches everywhere: "Scandinavian ones, where the food was extremely rich and the conversation was extremely boring."[45]

On primary election night in September 1938, Jackson and Salter awaited the results at the Everett County Courthouse, where officials tallied the votes as they came in on huge blackboards with the names of candidates on them. Jackson won by the largest margin in the history of the contested elections in Snohomish County, receiving 14,582 votes to Swanson's 4,407.[46] Tom Stiger, Jackson's Republican opponent, did not stand a chance: "Republicans were not popular in Snohomish County," recalled Stiger. "At rallies, Jackson would get roundly cheered and I would get booed."[47] Jackson trounced Stiger in the November election, winning more than three-quarters of the vote. He was just twenty-six years old.

SODA POP JACKSON

From his first day in office, January 9, 1939, Henry Jackson demonstrated that he meant what he had said about cracking down on corruption in Snohomish County. He initiated and sustained a series of raids against houses of prostitution and operations selling bootleg liquor. One of his prime targets was the Ranch, a nightclub on Highway 99, close enough to Seattle to attract customers from there but just within the Snohomish County line. This establishment reputedly had the most wide-open gambling, the best entertainment, and some of the best food and liquor in the entire Pacific Northwest.[48]

Joe Hart offered Jackson a bribe to relent on his crackdown, but to no avail. On April 15, 1939, Jackson defied Hart by issuing an ultimatum requiring the removal of all slot and pinball machines from the county by June 15. Justifying this action, he said that "school children were spending their luncheon money on pinball games." He added that "many wives complained to me that they had never received any support from their husband due to this fact that all their pay checks were spent either on slot machines, or on the speakeasies, or both."[49] Jackson then left Everett on his first trip to the East Coast in order to lower the temperature of the debate that his ultimatum had sparked among municipal officials reluctant to lose the revenues that licensing slot and pinball machines had generated.[50]

Alarmed at the prospect of losing those revenues, the mayors of several of the county's cities and towns challenged Jackson at a public meeting about the legality and practicality of his ultimatum. Some union officials chimed in that ousting the machines would result in a loss of jobs in restaurants and taverns. Jackson did not budge. He replied that the state attorney general had sustained his interpretation that pinball machines were gambling devices that municipal corporations could not license. He rejoined, too, that the state's increased appropriation of money for cities and towns would more than compensate for the loss of licensing fees. Above all, he deemed pinball machines and the way that they were handled a "corruptive influence." When some city officials asked him what he meant by corruptive influence, he answered that "the syndicate handling the machines was too powerful," and that he had been offered money to "keep still." Mayor A. C. Edwards of Everett revealed that he had received similar offers. Hart backed down. He had all the machines removed from the county by the June 15 deadline. By then, people in Everett had started to refer to Henry as "Soda Pop Jackson," a tribute both to the zeal with which he pursued bootleggers and to his conspicuous abstemiousness.[51]

Contemporaries of Jackson disagree about whether he envisaged the prosecutor's office as the stepping stone to a political career. Those who believe that he stumbled into politics by accident point to his effort to replace Lloyd Black on the Snohomish County Superior Court after President Roosevelt appointed Black to the federal court in the fall of 1939. The record leaves no doubt that Jackson wanted that appointment and felt disappointed when he did not get it.[52] That is not incompatible, however, with the possibility that he always harbored national political ambitions. Having just turned twenty-seven when the vacancy on the court arose, he could not afford to count on having the chance to run for Congress any time soon. Mon Wallgren, a jeweler from Everett who represented Jackson's Second District in the House of Representatives, showed no inclination to relinquish his safe seat; at Jackson's age, the Senate was out of the question. He thought it prudent, therefore, to capitalize on the name he had established as an incorruptibly tough crime-fighting prosecutor by becoming a judge, not only a more prestigious position, but also one that he reasoned could enhance his electability should the opportunity for national office arise.

Governor Martin had other ideas. He selected Charles E. Denney, a Republican, to fill the vacancy instead of Jackson, whom he presumably considered too young and inexperienced. Even though his decision irritated Jackson at the time, the governor did him a huge favor.[53] As it turned out, 1940 proved to be a very bad year for the world but a very good one for Henry Jackson's political career, as a favorable confluence of events propelled him into the United States Congress.

Jackson became immersed in two sensational trials—of Vivian Reeves, a Tulalip housewife, and of Edward Bouchard, a homicidal grifter—that gave him months of front-page headlines in the local newspapers. The

Reeves trial occurred first. On December 23, 1939, the car Mrs. Reeves was driving south on Pacific Highway near Marysville had swayed, then overturned into the lane for northbound traffic, causing a crash that killed seven people. The state charged her with negligent homicide on March 6, 1940. In the ensuing trial, Prosecutor Jackson seemed to build an impressive case. The results of the blood alcohol test showed that Mrs. Reeves was highly intoxicated. Several police officers testified that she had admitted to them in the hospital that she had been drinking. Two nurses who had treated her for injuries testified to smelling liquor on her breath. Sheriff Ray Ryan had found an empty bottle of whiskey in the car, which the court admitted as evidence. Several eyewitnesses testified to seeing Mrs. Reeves's car swerving dangerously at Island Crossing, just a mile north of the accident site. She conceded, under Jackson's cross-examination, that one of those eyewitnesses had attempted unsuccessfully to flag her down just minutes before the crash.[54]

Jackson was sure he would win based on the evidence. He did not. John C. Richards, Mrs. Reeves's counsel and a colorful personality, was the most successful defense attorney in the county. Richards typically won acquittals for his clients by relying less on the law and more on manipulating the emotions of the jury. Tom Stiger, the Republican Jackson had defeated for prosecutor, recalled Richards as someone who "knew his way around a jury. He would put on an old shoe act. Juries would feel sorry for his client because he was such a rotten lawyer. He murdered the king's English. He was clever, smart, and a gifted conniver." Richards played on the jury's sympathy for Mrs. Reeves, a shy, attractive Native American woman apparently coerced into driving the night of the accident by her fellow passengers, who were also intoxicated.[55]

The blood alcohol test—then brand new—figured prominently in the outcome. The court established its legal standing for the first time in Washington State by denying Richards's motion to strike and suppress all testimony relative to the test. Richards convinced the jury, however, to ignore the results. In defiance of the overwhelming evidence to the contrary, he argued that cough syrup rather than whiskey accounted for Mrs. Reeves's intoxication. The jury accepted the cough syrup defense, acquitting her on all counts. The verdict stunned Jackson, who had lost what appeared to be an open-and-shut case. Afterward he called Fred Moore and suggested they go for a walk. "Is there anything I am doing in the courtroom that I should not be doing?" Jackson asked. "Yes," Moore answered, "get the chewing gum out of your mouth. You look like an ass."[56]

Jackson was lucky he did not suffer any political fallout by losing a highly publicized case that he was expected to win. The Bouchard case gave him a chance immediately to redeem himself. On March 25, 1940, officers had discovered in the woods southeast of Arlington the bodies of two men who had been missing since fall. It was obvious from their condition and placement that someone had murdered them in a particularly gruesome fashion, with an ax found leaning against a tree nearby. One victim's skull was smashed. The other had a cord tied tautly around his neck. Although five months had elapsed between the murder and the discovery of the bodies, the mystery began to unravel a day later, when the police traced the car of one of the victims to a Portland garage. The police established that Edward Bouchard had driven the car there from Seattle, represented himself as its owner, left it for repairs, then abandoned it without paying the bill.[57]

On March 31, as the jury deliberated the fate of Vivian Reeves, Jackson filed first-degree murder charges against Bouchard. He and Sheriff Ray Ryan conducted a nine-day investigation in Los Angeles during the month of April that uncovered enough evidence to link Bouchard to the victims and to demolish his alibis. The trial, which began June 24, lasted just eight days. Jackson succeeded in exposing the inconsistencies in Bouchard's stories. Despite having no eyewitnesses, he persuaded the jury, with an impressive array of circumstantial and forensic evidence derived from extensive FBI laboratory work, that the defendant had lured the victims to the murder site with the promise of logging work, then murdered them for money. On July 2, 1940, the jury found Bouchard guilty and sentenced him to death, a punishment he received with apparent calm on September 6, 1940.[58]

THE MAKINGS OF A YOUNG CONGRESSMAN

Prosecutor Jackson received glowing headlines for the Bouchard verdict just as events began to unfold that would leave the congressional race in his Second District wide open. On July 10, 1940, Clarence Martin surprised everyone by announcing he would run for a third term as governor instead of for the U.S. Senate seat that Lewis Schwellenbach was relinquishing to become a federal judge. His decision had a domino effect. With Martin out of the race, Congressman Mon Wallgren announced on August 9 that he would run for the Senate, throwing the Second District's seat up for grabs just a week before the filing deadline.[59]

Although Jackson had long wished for such a moment, he needed to act fast. The Second District, then predominantly rural, encompassed the northwest corner of Washington State. It spanned from the Canadian border in the north through Bellingham to the south of Everett and included the San Juan Islands in the west. Jackson's record as prosecutor had generated him wide and positive visibility; in a multicandidate field with no clear front-runner, however, he would need all the help he could get. Howard Bargreen, the well-known owner of the Bargreen Coffee Company, also Scandinavian and a resident of Bellingham, loomed as his toughest opponent. Verne Sievers, also from Everett, contemplated entering the race. Sievers had no chance of winning, but he might have drawn just enough support away from Jackson to elect Bargreen. At Jackson's behest, Frank Cooper, an active Democrat in the county, persuaded Sievers to forgo running during a lunch in downtown Everett that Jackson also attended. "We talked it over," Sievers recounted. "Scoop was single. I was married. He could hack it better than I." With that hurdle overcome, Phil Sheridan, Jackson's deputy and one of his closest friends, rushed him down to Olympia where he just managed to beat the filing deadline, which expired at noon that day.[60]

The *Everett Herald* carried Jackson's announcement of his candidacy on August 16, 1940, on page 2. Candidate Jackson stressed his credentials as a prosecuting attorney, his experience practicing with Lloyd Black, and the recommendation for the superior court judgeship he had received from the Snohomish County Bar Association. He said that "the immediate problem before the country is the preparation of an adequate national defense," although "we should also not lose sight of our continued desire to also better the standard of living of our people during these perilous times." He promised, as well, to support public ownership of power utilities and to work for an adequate and uniform federal old-age pension law.[61]

Jackson and Salter employed the same strategy and tactics that had worked so well in Jackson's successful race for prosecutor: a heavy reliance on youthful volunteers and intense door-to-door campaigning with a message that focused on Jackson's integrity. His most popular campaign ad during the primary read: "Vote for Henry M. Jackson for Congress. Vote for a Man who has the Courage of his Convictions." In the September 10 primary, Jackson finished first, more than 3,000 votes ahead of Howard Bargreen and 4,000 votes ahead of Pat Hurley, his closest rival in a six-candidate field. Jackson had an even easier race in the general election against Republican Payson Peterson, a perennial candidate who would run against and lose to him several more times. Jackson's slogan: "Henry M. Jackson, Democrat for Congress: He kept his word as your prosecuting attorney. He will keep his word as congressman." His campaign even attracted some notice from the national Democratic Party. Senator Claude Pepper, the fiery New Deal Democrat from Florida, came out to campaign for him and appeared with him on October 30 at a campaign rally in the Everett Auditorium. Riding the coattails of President Roosevelt's decisive victory and emphasizing his Scandinavian background, his support of the New Deal, and his integrity, Jackson defeated Peterson with more than 57 percent of the vote. The Second District now had a twenty-eight-year-old congressman-elect.[62]

Chapter 2

Member of the House, 1941–1953

HENRY JACKSON entered the Seventy-seventh Congress as its youngest and certainly not its most worldly member. It was the first time he had ever been to Washington, D.C. After arriving by train at Union Station on January 2, 1941, he and John Salter, now his administrative assistant, could not even find the way to their destination, just three blocks away. "Where's the Capitol?" they asked an astonished cab driver. "Right over there, you dummies," he replied, pointing to the Capitol dome directly ahead.[1] Neither the cab driver nor Jackson had any clue that this inauspicious start would inaugurate a forty-two-year career in the Congress of the United States.

Jackson's main concerns between 1941 and 1949 reflected a parochialism typical, in that era, of new members of Congress. Despite his long-standing interest in foreign affairs, his campaign of 1940 had focused almost entirely on domestic issues, especially those significant for the livelihood of his largely rural constituents: fishing, logging, and farming. He requested and received an appointment to the House Merchant Marine and Fisheries Committee, where he served until his appointment in January 1949 to the more powerful and prestigious Appropriations Committee (Interior Subcommittee). Later, as chair of the Indian Affairs Committee, he achieved one of his first significant legislative accomplishments: cosponsorship and passage of the Indian Claims Commission Act of 1946. This measure provided Native Americans the legal remedy to seek financial redress for treaty violations, a right that an 1863 law had denied them. Jackson's other committee assignments also had a strong local orientation: the Flood Control, Rivers and Harbors, and Civil Service Standing Committees; and the Small Business and Conservation and Wildlife Resources Select Committees.[2]

JACKSON AND PUBLIC POWER

Nothing during Jackson's early House years reveals more clearly his priorities or philosophy of government than his unbridled advocacy of public power. The issue of public versus private power had dominated the politics of the Northwest since the 1920s. Both sides of this bitter dispute realized the enormous potential of the Columbia River to generate cheap electric power, on which the industrial development of the region depended. But they disagreed about means and consequences. Proponents of public power such as Jackson believed that only government could undertake the comprehensive development of the river, entailing not just the generation of power but the construction and management of huge multiple-use projects—agricultural, irrigation, and flood control—that crossed state and, in some cases, international boundaries. Public power could provide abundant electricity at less cost and with greater equity, according to its proponents, who believed that private power companies lacked the resources and incentives to bring their power lines to rural areas. Most of Washington State's farms had no electricity until the public power movement began in earnest. As a representative of a predominantly rural district with a strong local grange movement, Jackson knew that his support for public power also made good politics. Public power also appealed to his Norwegian sensibilities: Scandinavian countries had pioneered the type of large projects that he advocated for Washington State.[3]

The private power companies equated public power with creeping socialism. They had opposed public utility districts (PUDs), the rural equivalent of municipal power authorities, which in 1930 the states of Washington and Oregon established the right of local communities to create. They had fought furiously but unsuccessfully President Roosevelt's decision to build the Bonneville and Grand Coulee Dams, which came on line in 1939, and Congress's decision in 1937 to create the Bonneville Power Administration (BPA), a government entity chartered to supply power to both the private utilities and the PUDs. Private power companies favored the government paying for and operating facilities to ensure flood control, navigation, and farm reclamation, and leaving the construction of power plants and their ownership to the private sector. Jackson and other leading proponents of public power found this scheme unacceptable. Although not aiming to supplant private power companies entirely, they did consider them rapacious and shortsighted, obtuse to the reality that energy was a public good. They opposed leaving the profits generated from Columbia River power exclusively in private hands while government shouldered the burden of paying for costly multiple-use projects without reaping the revenues and social benefits of cheap electricity.[4]

In 1949, Jackson introduced bills to create a Columbia Valley Authority, modeled in part on the Tennessee Valley Authority, although not identical to it, that would have consolidated the activities of at least twenty federal agencies with overlapping jurisdictions in the Columbia Valley. The bill failed. Like similar legislation that Washington's Democratic Senators Warren Magnuson and Hugh Mitchell had pushed previously, it died in committee, defeated by a powerful coalition of private utilities that decried the CVA as a "vehicle for socialism" and federal water and power agencies—most prominently the Interior Department and the army— that opposed CVA as an intrusion on their prerogatives.[5]

WORLD WAR II AND THE MAKING OF AN INTERNATIONALIST

Jackson served his first four years of Congress during World War II, which he could do little to influence but which tremendously influenced him. His core convictions about foreign policy and national security affairs derived largely from the lessons of World War II as Winston Churchill rendered them in his magisterial account of that war: the folly of isolationism and appeasement, the importance of democracies remaining militarily strong and standing firm against totalitarianism, and the need for the United States to accept and sustain its pivotal role as a world power.[6] Nevertheless, Henry Jackson never reached his ultimate views with alacrity or ease. He formulated them by a cumulative process of observation and deliberation, the slow pace of which sometimes exasperated friends who wished for more expeditious decisions on his part. Once he made up his mind, though, he was difficult to move.[7] His views on foreign policy evolved in this emblematic fashion. Despite the horror of the Nazi invasion of his beloved Norway in March 1940, Jackson came to the Congress inclined to isolationism, a position popular in his district. It took time and the weight of cataclysmic events to budge him from the view that the United States must stay out of war.

On a bitter cold day in early January 1941, Jackson sat in the fourth row of a special section of the Capitol steps as President Roosevelt exhorted the Seventy-seventh Congress to pass the lend-lease program of military aid for Great Britain. The international situation looked dismal. Hitler dominated all of Europe west of the Soviet border. Since the Nazi-Soviet pact of August 23, 1939, the Soviet Union had continued to collaborate with the Nazi regime, providing Germany with a steady supply of food, oil, and raw materials. Thanks to the convergence of Churchill's indomitable will, an insular position, radar, and the strength of the Royal Navy and Air Force, Britain managed to fight on, but desperately needed American resources to survive. The British had no plausible theory of victory without Soviet and American intervention against Germany. Their Middle Eastern lifeline was vulnerable to Germany's overwhelming military power if Hitler chose to move in that direction, their Asian empire vulnerable to the Imperial Japanese Army and Navy. Having begun to rearm belatedly, the United States would not have substantial and properly equipped armed forces until 1943, at the earliest. President Roosevelt believed, in January 1941, that Great Britain's collapse would result in the inevitable encirclement and defeat of the United States. Jackson voted against lend-lease anyway. As he saw it, the British needed to put up more collateral—transferring their bases in the Western Hemisphere to the United States, supplying critical raw materials such as tin and rubber—before he would support the sale and transfer of war materials to Great Britain. As late as June 9, 1941, Jackson still assured his constituents that he was "unalterably opposed to our country entering the European conflict, and will do all in my power to prevent it."[8]

By October 1941, he had begun to change his mind, voting for massive military and economic aid to Great Britain. The Japanese attack on Pearl Harbor on December 7, and Hitler's declaration of war against the United States four days later, dispelled the last vestiges of Jackson's isolationism. The House's December 8th resolution endorsing the declaration of war on Japan was one of the few critical votes that he missed in his entire congressional career. Flying west on December 7 to conduct a series of local hearings, he learned about the bombing on Pearl Harbor as he got off the plane in Seattle. He left for Washington, D.C., immediately, but was not in time for the House vote. Boarding that return flight to D.C., he warned of the danger of a Japanese attack on Washington's poorly defended coast, with the Boeing plant in Seattle an inviting target.[9] He also worried that the Japanese might attack Alaska, a threat that he complained his constituents did not take seriously enough.[10] His statement for the House record left no doubt that he considered Japan a dangerous and treacherous foe, which the United States must do everything in its power to defeat. Ultimately, the Second World War stimulated and refined Jackson's best instincts as a statesman. In the case of Japan, however, it brought out an atypical disregard for the rights and dignity of Japanese Americans.

Retrospectively, the outcome of the war with Japan has appeared to many commentators as a foregone conclusion. The situation did not appear that way in December 1941 as panic gripped the nation, particularly in the Pacific Northwest, where residents feared a Japanese attack and internal subversion from some of the many Japanese Americans in the area. Succumbing to the intense political pressure from West Coast voters and politicians, President Roosevelt signed Executive Order 9066, authorizing the military to designate war zones where certain categories of persons could be excluded. Although the language was neutral, singling out no particular ethnic group, its target was clear: Japanese Americans.

Henry Jackson endorsed the wartime relocation of all persons of Japanese descent from the coastal areas, including Washington State west of the Cascades. Of course, he was hardly alone. Most, though not all, of the major politicians from the West Coast catered to and sometimes incited anti-Japanese hysteria. Even Earl Warren, then attorney general of California and later the most liberal chief justice of the U.S. Supreme Court in history, defended the deportation. So did Governor Arthur Langlie, Senator Mon Wallgren, and then Congressman Warren Magnuson of Washington. The Supreme Court upheld the constitutionality of the evacuation order. Justice William O. Douglas, a native of Washington State whom liberals would come to revere as a paladin of their cause, joined in the decision, ruling that the matter did not involve racial discrimination.[11]

Although racial prejudice against Japanese Americans had a long tradition in the Pacific Northwest and accounts for much of the anti-Japanese sentiment during the Second World War, it did not account for Jackson's, whose animosity toward the Japanese arose mainly from his empathy for China's plight. He was philo-Chinese (i.e., favorably disposed to the Chinese) just as he was philo-Semitic, the antithesis of being anti-Semitic: He admired, and at times romanticized, the Chinese and Jews for their emphasis on hard work, strong families, and education, the very qualities he admired most about his own Norwegian background. His positive image of China stemmed largely from the mesmerizing novels of Pearl Buck, which engrossed a generation of Americans, particularly residents of the West Coast. Jackson viewed the Japanese enemy of his Chinese friends as an enemy of the United States.[12]

Senator Daniel Inouye, Democrat from Hawaii, and one of Jackson's closest friends in the Senate, later assessed Jackson's record on wartime internment with magnanimity. A Japanese American who lost his right arm in combat and won the Distinguished Service Cross for his valor on the battlefield, Inouye cautioned against judging Jackson and others too harshly, because of the unprecedented threats the United States had faced.[13] He is, however, too magnanimous. Jackson was not just an advocate of internment, but an enthusiast, and he justified his attitude with a logic and rhetoric that still makes chilling reading:

> We first heard much of Japanese infiltration tactics on Bataan and in the Philippines, but the Japanese had for many years practiced a different type of infiltration—infiltration into the vitals of our economic, political, and domestic structure. The principles of Bushido, by insidious and indirect means inserted themselves in a great many organizations in much the same fashion as the Nazis have utilized their front organizations. In our great Pacific coast cities, they controlled much of the hotel and restaurant business although always there was a white manager who would front for them with the general public. They lowered the prices to their own countrymen in the fresh produce and vegetable field, forcing out their white competition, only to raise prices as soon as they had monopolized that sphere of business. Always they had prominent civic leaders as their attorneys, paying them on a retainer basis. Whenever a situation came up in which they were interested, they had only to contact these individuals with their specious reasons to have them immediately come forward in their interest. Investigations will show that the Japanese counsels in our large cities lavished expensive and sumptuous gifts on a great number of prominent citizens at Christmas and other appropriate occasions.[14]

Jackson here also expressed reservations about establishing a Japanese American unit in the armed forces. Even when the tide of the war had turned irrevocably to America's favor, in a draft of a speech he never delivered Jackson not only opposed ending internment but expressed doubts about whether Japanese Americans ever should be allowed to return to their homes on the Pacific Coast:

> What is to be the eventual disposition of the Japanese alien and native
> . . . is the second aspect of this problem in the Pacific. Are we to return
> them to their former homes and businesses on the Pacific Coast to face
> the active antagonism of their neighbors? Shall they again, as happened
> in World War I, compete economically for jobs and businesses with re-
> turning war veterans?[15]

Not all of Jackson's constituents appreciated the virulence of his wartime hostility toward the Japanese. On May 7, 1943, E. Harriet Gipson wrote him this withering critique:

> There is no better way that you could play into Hitler's hands than by
> continuing your present fascist attitude toward Americans of Japanese
> ancestry. It is Hitler's belief that one race is superior to another, that
> blood rather than education and training make a man what he is. No rep-
> resentative of the American people should be allowed to flout the Con-
> stitution of the United States, the Bill of Rights, or the Declaration of
> Independence as you have done in upholding General DeWitt's con-
> tention that a Jap is a Jap, whenever born, however raised.[16]

The plight of his ancestral homeland brought out the better angel of Jackson's nature. On March 1, 1942, he delivered a stirring (for him, especially) radio address in Boston, carried by shortwave to Norway. Addressing the House on April 9, 1942, the anniversary of the German invasion of Norway, Jackson hailed the courage of the Norwegian clergy for their defiance of Hitler and pilloried the Nazis for their remorseless persecution of religion.[17]

The war also aroused in Jackson conflicting emotions about whether he ought to enlist in the military. Speaker of the House Sam Rayburn, Democrat from Texas, tried to discourage him. Replying to Jackson's letter of March 25, 1942, expressing his desire to enlist, Rayburn informed him that both the secretary of the navy and the secretary of war did not think "any more members of Congress should be taken into the Armed Forces as they are of the opinion as I am that a Member of Congress can be of more service to his people by serving in Congress than he can by serving in the Armed Forces." He added, "the President has strongly expressed himself to me (his agreement) on this subject."[18]

Even so, Jackson agonized over the matter, soliciting the advice of Fred Moore and Bob Humphrey, who both urged him to volunteer. There was grumbling in the Second District that a young bachelor ought not to remain in Washington, D.C., while other boys had to fight. Congressman Warren Magnuson had taken an officer's commission in the navy. In September 1943, Jackson underwent his induction into the army at Fort Lewis, in Washington State.[19] His brief military stint brought neither danger nor glory. He endured boot camp at Fort McClellan, Alabama, where he met George Wallace, the future governor of Alabama and his rival for the Democratic presidential nomination in 1972 and 1976. "The next time we met," Jackson recalled, "all we could remember was how we all got chiggers."[20] Jackson served three months as a buck private at Fort McClellan before President Roosevelt ordered all congressmen out of the service, just days before Jackson's unit shipped off for combat in Italy. His correspondence with his parents during his army days reveals a touching concern for their welfare and an extraordinary naïveté: He had the idea that, as a congressman, he received the same treatment as any other buck private.[21] While Jackson was away, Salter ran the congressional office, keeping him apprised.

By the spring of 1944, Jackson had moved from isolationism to the belief that the United States must remain engaged in the world to preserve the peace. "The United States cannot live separate and apart from the rest of the world," he wrote a constituent, Mrs. Elizabeth C. Kerr. "We can have the strongest Army, Navy, and Air Force in the world and still that alone will not completely protect us from an aggressor nation or nations. It is therefore to our own self-interest, if nothing else, to do our part in ensuring a just and lasting peace when the war is over."[22] In 1945, Jackson made two trips to Europe that transformed his internationalism from instinct into ardent conviction. What he witnessed there—the breakdown of law and civilization—convinced him that the United States must prevent totalitarianism in any form from devastating free societies in the future.

On April 22, 1945, Jackson and seven other congressmen visited

Buchenwald at the invitation of General Dwight Eisenhower, eleven days after General Patton's Third Army had liberated the death camp. Jackson reacted with outrage and revulsion:

> The atrocities are the most sordid I have ever imagined. . . . It is almost impossible to describe adequately in words the condition of these prisoners. Most of them stayed in their bunks at all times because they were too weak for proper nourishment. . . . The mortality rate at the time the camp was liberated approximated 100 per day due to malnutrition alone. These men lived like animals penned up in a cage without food. In addition to death by starvation, these prisoners were treated in the most brutal manner, receiving every form of punishment one could imagine.

Previously, he had doubted what he had heard about the conditions in Nazi prison camps, recalling the false propaganda about German atrocities in Belgium during World War I. He left Buchenwald "completely convinced that the Nazis were engaged in the systematic destruction of peoples who opposed their form of government and all peoples who they believed belonged to so-called inferior races. I also thought of how easily it could have happened to us if their program of world conquest had reached our shores."[23]

Jackson's close friends and political associates refer to his experience at Buchenwald as the genesis of his intense, unwavering support for the state of Israel and Jewish causes generally. This explanation is true, but incomplete. Several other experiences and attitudes inclined him in the same direction, including his philo-Semitism; his close friendship with Jews in Washington State (Stan Golub and Paul Friedlander among others); and his empathy for Jews arising from Norway's oppression by the Nazis.[24]

Jackson returned to Europe in November 1945 as President Truman's choice for U.S. delegate to the International Labor Organization meeting in Copenhagen. On his way home, he stopped in Norway in early December. Three hours after arriving in Oslo, he suddenly became terribly sick. After he spent a miserable night in the hotel room, the Norwegian government summoned Dr. H. A. Salvesen, one of the country's leading internists, who arrived to find Jackson running a temperature of 105 degrees. He was so feverish that they had to peel the paper bed sheets off his body. He did not respond to sulfa drugs, the only treatment on hand; at that time, penicillin was unavailable in Norway and largely unknown. So Jackson contacted Major Leslie Johnson, a boyhood acquaintance and distant cousin stationed in Germany, who immediately commandeered a plane, flew to Frankfurt for penicillin, and delivered it to Jackson in Norway, saving Jackson's life but barely averting a court-martial for his actions. The Norwegians impressed Jackson by treating him as a national of the country and a participant in their national health care program. He received a bill of only $15.44 for his entire treatment and ten-day stay in the hospital. From that moment, Jackson championed the cause of such a health care plan for the United States. His doctor in Washington, D.C., gave him a clean bill of health upon his return, admonishing him only that he should lose some weight.[25]

Jackson's observations and conversations in Norway while recuperating raised his concern about the Soviet danger. The great lesson of the 1930s, he concluded, was the imperative for democracies to understand and respond firmly to the totalitarian threat. Although his views on the Soviet Union would crystallize slowly, the fears Norwegians expressed about their Soviet neighbors planted the seed in Jackson's mind that Soviet totalitarianism had replaced the defeated, discredited Nazi version as the primary threat to civilization. A war-ravaged and demoralized Western Europe was not strong enough, from what he observed, to defend itself against the Soviet Union. If the democracies hoped to deter and eventually defeat this malevolent empire, he began to believe that there was no substitute for American power and a commitment to vigilant, enlightened internationalism.[26]

The Second World War reinforced rather than transformed Henry Jackson's fundamental principles of domestic politics. He had entered the Congress in 1941 an avowed supporter of the New Deal. The results of the war strengthened his belief in the necessity of a strong federal government to promote economic growth and ensure social justice resting on the ethic of common provision. Not only had Roosevelt saved freedom by defeating Hitler; big government also had ended the Depression, vindicating, in Jackson's eyes, the vitality of democracy, a form of government that had seemed so imperiled during the 1930s under the combined assaults of fascism, communism, and worldwide economic collapse. In Washington State the billions of dollars the federal government poured in stimulated a veritable boom in the economy.

Largely because of the vast quantities of hydroelectric power available from the Grand Coulee and Bonneville Dams, federal projects that Jackson and Magnuson had supported and private power had opposed, the state of Washington contributed mightily to and benefited mightily from the war effort. The Aluminum Company of America (ALCOA) relocated a substantial part of its exponentially expanding production facilities to the Pacific Northwest, an ideal location because the plants required prodigious amounts of cheap electricity to produce a finished product. Most of that aluminum—a metal essential for airplanes because of its felicitous combination of strength, lightness, and resistance to decay—found its way to the Boeing Company in Seattle. Wartime demand transformed Boeing into a national enterprise, one that built thousands of aircraft a year, including the B-17 Flying Fortress, the mainstay of the U.S. bomber fleet in the strategic bombing campaign against Germany, and the B-29, the most advanced long-range bomber of the war employed against Japan. In the Puget Sound area, employment at Boeing increased by a factor of more than twelve: 4,000 in 1939 to more than 50,000 by the war's end. The navy's demand for warships also invigorated the state's dormant shipyards, whose employment exceeded 100,000, including 36,000 at the Bremerton Naval Shipyard alone.[27]

In 1942, the Roosevelt administration located the plutonium manufacturing plant, one of the three major facilities for building the atomic bomb, in Hanford, Washington, a site that offered easy access to the enormous quantities of electric power and fresh water that nuclear reactors required. The giant atomic research complex created 20,000 federal jobs and a metropolis of 50,000 people in the middle of desolate sagebrush country. Scientists and engineers flocked, as federal military research money flowed, to an area that flourished only because of government.[28] No wonder an enthusiastic New Dealer from Washington State interpreted the experience of World War II as demonstrating the effectiveness of Big Government.

POSTWAR DOMESTIC POLITICS

Jackson's standing in the House of Representatives rose significantly during his first eight years in Congress. From the outset he had a natural affinity with Southern congressmen, even though he voted with Northern Democratic liberals on the three great issues most dear to conservative Southern Democrats: civil rights, retention of the Taft-Hartley Act curtailing the rights of organized labor, and securing tideland oil deposits for the states. Jackson found the affable manner of the southerners, their modest demeanor, the studiousness of their approach to national security issues, and their reverence for Congress as an institution more congenial than the style and attitude of northeastern Democrats. Southerners found him equally appealing for these same qualities, despite their differences. Estes Kefauver, a champion of public power from the Tennessee Valley, became one of his earliest and closest friends. Jackson's diligence and seriousness of purpose also attracted the attention of Speaker of the House Sam Rayburn.[29]

Typically, senior Southern congressmen had served as mentors of younger members. Rayburn followed in this tradition. Lyndon Johnson, Wilbur Mills, Hale Boggs, and Carl Albert were Rayburn's proteges. So was Henry Jackson. Although Jackson's hostility toward the oil depletion allowance (a provision that greatly benefited Texas and Texas politicians) exasperated the Speaker, both men cultivated the friendship. Jackson declined Rayburn's request in 1945 that he chair the House Un-American Activities Committee (HUAC), because he had voted against funding the committee repeatedly. He did not dismiss the danger of domestic subversion but considered the external threat posed by the combination of Soviet communism and Soviet power by far the greater menace. The conduct of the committee had offended his insistence on due process, which he envisaged as a complement to his equally strong commitment to law and order evident as early as his Everett days. He believed that HUAC's previous chairman, Martin Dies, Democrat from Texas, had used the committee for a wild and irresponsible witch-hunt to ferret out domestic communists.[30]

His refusal to serve on HUAC had no adverse effect on his relationship with Rayburn. The Republican victory in the congressional election in 1946 slowed Jackson's rise within the House, but only temporarily. When the Democrats recaptured Congress in 1948, Rayburn appointed him to the Appropriations Committee (Interior Subcommittee), a plum position that helped him deepen and broaden his statewide base by channeling public works projects, and great sums of money to pay for them, to Washington State. Rayburn also appointed him in January 1949 to the Joint

Committee on Atomic Energy, the launching pad for establishing his reputation as an expert on defense and foreign policy issues.[31]

Jackson's political position back home had also improved significantly by the mid–1940s. Although he had not yet built the broad coalition that would make him the most successful politician in the history of Washington State, there were signs that he was on his way. He easily defeated Payson Peterson, his perennial Republican challenger, in 1942 and 1944, winning over 60 percent of the vote each time. He had a more difficult time defeating him in 1946, with 53 percent of the vote, the smallest margin in his congressional career. Under the circumstances, he did remarkably well to win at all, for 1946 was a terrible year for Democrats. The Republicans promised what voters wanted: an end to wage and price controls; lower taxes; and restrictions on labor unions, a major constituency of the Democratic Party, which was blamed for making 1946 the most strike-plagued year in American history. In Washington State, Republican Harry Cain, a paratrooper during the war, defeated liberal Democratic senator Hugh Mitchell. In the Pacific Northwest, Republicans won every congressional seat but one: Henry Jackson's. The *Seattle Times* editorial of November 4, 1946, attributed the exception of Jackson's victory to "his personal popularity and, in a larger part, by the nature of his service he had given the district, the state, and the interests of Alaska. Always a stout Democrat, that circumstance has never been circumscribed by narrow politics."[32]

Jackson would never run a close race for Congress again. His approach to campaigning had changed little since he ran for county prosecutor of Snohomish County. He returned to his district frequently, visited with his constituents perpetually, and always remembered names, faces, and previous discussions with those he met. He continued to relish and excel at the retail politics of small-group and one-on-one encounters. Immediately after each election, he toured the district to thank the voters, a practice he continued statewide when he went to the Senate. His political success in Washington State during his House years remained largely due to John Salter's talent for making and sustaining connections with local Democratic politicians throughout the state. Joe Miller, a longtime friend and professional associate of both men, put it best: "John was the politician. Jackson was the workhorse. John was the man to see. If Jackson had anything called charm, it was not visible to the naked eye. Salter had a wicked tongue. He kept Jackson tuned in to the politics of the state."[33]

Jackson had a very liberal voting record on domestic matters during the 1940s. His opposition to HUAC could have spelled trouble for a different type of politician, especially in the charged political atmosphere of Washington State, with its history of radicalism that extended to large segments of both the labor movement and the Democratic Party. In 1947, the Canwell Committee, the Washington State analogue to HUAC, chaired by conservative Spokane Republican Al Canwell, had just started its own hunt for subversives, which ended up focusing on professors at the University of Washington. Although Jackson and his family in Everett periodically received threatening phone calls accusing him of being a communist during the height of the postwar Red scare, his standing with voters did not suffer. Jackson's conservative personal demeanor, his strong support for national defense, his unremitting call for vigilance against the external communist threat, and his conspicuous dissociation from the more radical wing of the Democratic Party in Washington State insulated him from the types of attacks that threatened liberals who were less hard-line on national security issues. Voters also appreciated the extraordinary attention and effort Jackson and his staff devoted to constituent services, a trademark of his office by the middle 1940s. In the early days, Jackson read all the mail and personally signed all the letters in reply, often crossing out the formal salutation and writing in the first name or nickname of the addressee. No legitimate constituent problem was too small for him.[34]

SHAPING OF A COLD WAR LIBERAL

For American foreign policy, for the Democratic Party, and for Henry Jackson, 1948 was a pivotal year. By then, most Americans realized that the Cold War had begun, and that the United States would have to renounce its traditional isolationism and assume unprecedented global responsibilities to meet the Soviet threat, changing the nation's role in the world forever. This recognition, to be sure, did not arise instantaneously or spontaneously, but was the culmination of events and trends dating back to the end of the Second World War. American anger and apprehension had mounted steadily as Stalin methodically tightened his grip on

Eastern Europe in defiance of his pledge at Yalta in February 1945 to allow genuinely free elections.[35]

In his famous Fulton, Missouri, speech of March 1946, Churchill proclaimed that an "iron curtain" had descended across the Continent and warned of worse to come if the West did not rouse itself to prevent communism from spreading across Western Europe. Stalin had also refused to withdraw Soviet troops from northern Iran, occupied during the war, until President Truman pressured him to do so. In February 1947, following a debilitating coal strike during a terribly cold winter, the British government announced that it could no longer protect the anticommunist governments of Greece and Turkey. American statesmen had become increasingly worried that communist victories in either of those countries could have a domino effect in Western Europe. In France and Italy, particularly, strong local communist parties appeared to have a genuine chance to win the impending elections. By all appearances, a defeated, demoralized, economically devastated Western Europe had neither the will nor the capability to defend itself unaided against the looming threat of the Red Army.[36]

The first major American response came in March 1947. With the indispensable support of Republican Senator Arthur Vandenberg from Michigan, chairman of the Foreign Relations Committee, who thereby forever abandoned his previous isolationism, President Truman issued his famous Truman Doctrine, a pledge to support not only Greece and Turkey, but also "free peoples everywhere who are resisting attempted subjugation by armed minorities or by outside pressure." The administration soon followed with the Marshall Plan to assist Western Europe's economic recovery, which General Marshall laid out as a concept at the June 1947 Harvard commencement.

It was not until 1948, however, that the full dimensions of the Cold War in Europe revealed themselves unambiguously. In February, local communists acting on Moscow's orders took control of Czechoslovakia's government, then murdered Czech Foreign Minister Jan Masaryk. In April, a bipartisan coalition of Democrats and internationalist Republicans voted to fund the Marshall Plan substantially. In June, this same coalition passed Vandenberg's resolution authorizing the United States to enter into an alliance beyond the Western Hemisphere—a precursor to the

North Atlantic Treaty and the North Atlantic Treaty Organization (NATO) of 1949, committing the United States to defend Western Europe against any Soviet attack. In July, several months after walking out of the Four Power Talks over the future of Germany, the Soviets began their blockade of Berlin.[37]

The intensification of the Cold War in 1948 catalyzed a major debate among Democrats over the future direction of the party. Truman's victory in the November presidential election settled the issue for two decades, but for much of the year he encountered attacks from all sides. One challenge came from the Left, much of which supported the independent candidacy of Henry Wallace, who blamed Truman's hard-line policies rather than Soviet aggression for provoking the Cold War. During the Cold War, both political parties, albeit the Republicans less frequently or sharply, experienced internal divisions over the gravity of the Soviet danger and the most appropriate response to it. Had the Soviet Union replaced Nazi Germany as a mortal threat to the United States—tactically more cautious but relentlessly striving for domination of Eurasia—propelled by an insidious combination of messianic ideology and totalitarian control? Or was the Soviet Union, a traditional authoritarian empire, dangerous and expansionist perhaps, but with limited aims? Or was the Soviet Union inherently defensive—vulnerable and insecure—provoked to aggression by U.S. belligerence but amenable to cooperation were the United States to pursue more conciliatory policies? The argument within the Democratic Party between the Truman and Wallace wings foreshadowed the more cataclysmic internal divisions in the party from 1968 until the collapse of communism in 1991.[38]

The outcome of the party's internal struggles in 1948 was more congenial to Henry Jackson than the outcome after 1968. In 1947, eminent theologian Reinhold Niebuhr, historian Arthur Schlesinger, and hero of the farm labor movement Hubert Humphrey (elected to the Senate from Minnesota the next year) led the successful fight against Wallace supporters, who were advocating conciliatory policies toward the Soviet Union, by having the newly created Americans for Democratic Action (ADA) make opposition to communism and totalitarianism the litmus test for mainstream liberal thinking. Niebuhr's brand of melioristic anti-utopian liberalism, rooted in a biblical conception of human fallibility, appealed powerfully to Jackson, who also shared Neibuhr's view that any scheme of provisional justice in international relations depended on American power and willingness to use it. By 1948, the Truman administration's foreign policy attracted strong and wide support, including that of most liberals who, like Jackson, considered Wallace's view of the Soviet Union dangerously naive and Truman's vigilant internationalism a brave, enlightened response to Soviet aggression. Seventy-seven percent of Americans believed that the Soviets sought to be "the leading power of the world," according to a Gallup Poll taken after the communist coup in Czechoslovakia.[39]

Another challenge to Truman came from the right wing of the Democratic Party—proponents of states' rights, mainly from the South, who were hostile to labor unions, opposed to greater federal involvement in managing the economy, and defenders of segregation. Reacting to the strong civil rights plank liberal Democrats introduced at the 1948 convention with Truman's approval, a large part of this constituency rallied to the presidential candidacy, as an independent Dixiecrat, of Governor Strom Thurmond, Democrat from South Carolina.[40]

An interplay of strategic calculation and first principles inspired President Truman to define his candidacy, the mainstream of his party, and the meaning of postwar liberalism in much the same way Henry Jackson came to define himself: vigilantly internationalist and anticommunist abroad but statist at home, committed to realizing the New Deal–Fair Deal vision of a strong, active federal government presiding over the economy, preserving and enhancing welfare protection, and extending civil rights. Truman campaigned in 1948 as an intrepid defender of the liberal Democratic platform: repeal of the Taft-Hartley Act, which organized labor considered a fundamental assault on the right of workers to organize; support for additional Social Security and a program of national health insurance; advocacy for increasing the minimum wage, federal aid to education, and federal support for public housing; and support for a Columbia Valley Authority in the Pacific Northwest, analogous to the TVA.[41]

What Truman and Jackson stood for reveals striking similarities. The evolution of Jackson's thinking about the Soviet danger closely paralleled Truman's.[42] Jackson had voted enthusiastically in support of the key measures of Truman's foreign policy program: aid to Greece and Turkey, the Marshall Plan, and Vandenberg's resolution authorizing the creation of an alliance outside the Western Hemisphere.[43] He construed the Berlin blockade, the effects of which he observed on his trip to Europe in December 1948, as confirmation of his somber assessment that American power must contain the Soviet Union. Naturally, he welcomed Truman's decision to support a Jewish state in Palestine and recognize Israel almost immediately after it declared independence in May 1948. By so doing, Truman had set an example that Jackson would later follow: he defied the advice of his secretary of state, George Marshall, and the Arabists in the State Department, who opposed the creation of Israel because they believed Arab hostility to its existence would undermine America's position in the Middle East.[44]

Although Jackson revered Franklin Roosevelt, he had more in common with Harry Truman, especially in foreign affairs. Neither man ever entertained high hopes for the United Nations or for the prospect of making Stalin a responsible statesman in world affairs through a combination of incentives, redressing legitimate grievances, and the force of personal charm the way FDR did. Whereas FDR was the quintessential eastern patrician, Truman and Jackson were westerners, men of modest origins who succeeded mainly through a combination of hard work, resoluteness, and a moral compass fixed in the ethics of small-town America. They not only shared a passion for reading history, but also advised other statesmen to learn from it. As Jackson himself later put it: "The man I most admired for his inner toughness, compassion, and his ability to make decisions was Harry Truman. He did not go to college, but read a lot of history. He really saved Western Europe from utter ruin and going Communist. He was the architect of containment and the building of Europe that prevented the Russians from dominating Europe. Truman also did the right thing on Korea, because Japan would not otherwise have survived."[45]

Jackson's record on domestic issues also put him firmly in the mainstream of the liberal consensus of Northern Democrats. He supported virtually all of the major domestic initiatives contained in the 1948 platform, which President Truman would recast as a sweeping legislative program in January 1949. Representing a state with one of the most powerful organized labor movements in the nation, coming from a union family himself, believing that the right to bargain collectively protected the legitimate rights of working people and inoculated them against the lure of communist radicalism, Jackson surpassed even Truman in his support for the political agenda of organized labor. He served as an American representative to five International Labor Organization meetings during his House years. When the International Maritime Conference convened in Seattle in 1946, representatives of fifty-six nations elected Jackson to chair the proceedings, which mainly espoused the outlook of the strongly anticommunist International Maritime Union.[46] Jackson had opposed the Taft-Hartley Act in 1947 and later spoke for its repeal with a zeal that displayed why he would finish his congressional career with the highest COPE rating (compiled by the political arm of the AFL-CIO) of any congressional figure of the postwar era.[47] Throughout his career, Jackson also embraced wage and price controls as his favorite remedy for a wide array of economic difficulties. His first radio address as a congressman (November 1941) emphasized the pressing need to impose controls and the dire inflationary consequences of the failure to do so. After the war, he unsuccessfully urged that the United States maintain them even as the Republican Congress, with the reluctant acquiescence of the Truman administration, phased them out.[48] All of that showed one revealing aspect of a man aware of the importance of free enterprise but skeptical of the workings of purely private markets and confident in government's ability to stimulate economic growth equitably. Jackson warned, however, that domestic liberalism was not enough. Above all, the survival of political freedom and economic prosperity hinged, in his view, on the ability of free societies to defend and preserve their way of life against the challenge of communist states:

> You cannot talk about a better United States if the country can be destroyed. Look at what happened to Norway. Norway had a thousand years of political freedom. The Norwegians had clean air, clean water, clean land, a great environment. They had one of the highest standards of living in the world. They had one of the first national health programs, dating back to the turn of the century. What good did it do them when the hobnail boot took over in the spring of 1940?[49]

JACKSON AND THE DEMOCRATS

Jackson demonstrated his prowess more as a vote getter than as a social lion. The Democratic Party of Washington State experienced its own version of the Truman-Wallace debate during the election cycle of 1948. Although the Truman forces prevailed, it was a tougher fight locally than nationally. The strength of the left wing of the Democratic Party in Washington State exceeded that of any in the nation, with the possible exceptions of Minnesota and New York. The combination of Henry Wallace's soft line on the Soviet Union and his statist, redistributionist economics appealed powerfully not only to that constituency, but even to many Democrats who ultimately cast their lot with Truman. Nevertheless, Jackson proved that his close race in 1946 was an aberration. Receiving help from the ADA, he easily swept aside a primary challenge the Wallacites mounted because they considered him too strident an anticommunist, having voted for Truman's foreign policy right down the line. Running in the general election for the fourth time against Republican Payson Peterson, who accused him of being too soft on communism, Jackson won nearly two-thirds of the vote.[50]

In January 1949, Jackson returned to Washington, D.C., with the Democrats in control of the presidency and the Congress. But liberal exhilaration soon turned to frustration. For the remainder of Truman's term, a coalition of Northern Republicans and conservative Southern Democrats succeeded in stifling almost all of the president's ambitious and liberal legislative agenda, which had Jackson's enthusiastic backing: a strong civil rights bill, establishment of national health insurance, repeal of the Taft-Hartley Act, increases in Social Security, and creation of Jackson's cherished Columbia Valley Authority.

Alaska statehood, a cause for which Jackson and Magnuson, elected to the Senate from Washington State in 1944, became early enthusiasts, also went nowhere during Truman's second term. Most Republicans still feared that Alaska, once admitted, would vote perpetually Democratic, adversely affecting the balance in Congress against them. Many legislators of both parties also rejected Jackson's argument that Alaska had attained levels of population and economic development to justify immediate statehood.[51]

MATURING OF A YOUNG CONGRESSMAN

The year 1948 also marked a watershed for Jackson in his personal life and for what it adumbrated about his political future in Washington State. Following a short illness, Peter Jackson died in 1948 at the age of eighty. The loss of his father inspired Henry Jackson to become even more serious about his work and more determined to attain national stature as a statesman. Now in his middle thirties, Jackson was still a very unsophisticated young congressman. He devoted practically all his time to politics, spending most evenings reading and doing his work in Congress. During congressional recesses, he campaigned ceaselessly. Sterling Munro, who met him in 1948 and later served with distinction as his administrative assistant in the Senate (1961 to 1977), remembered politics dominating the conversation even at the Jackson home in Everett. When he did take a rare vacation—maybe a fishing or hiking trip in Washington State or a weekend with Estes Kefauver and Bob Low at a Westchester estate owned by friends of Low's family—he hardly relaxed, spending most of his time talking on the telephone about politics.[52]

It was not that he lacked opportunities for a more active social life. As a nice-looking, eligible-bachelor congressman, he was a prime catch in a city teeming with attractive, educated young women drawn to the power and excitement of politics. For nearly a decade he roomed with John Salter, who was not reluctant to indulge his taste for liquor and women, in a small apartment on northeast Capitol Hill whose modesty attested to Jackson's vaunted thriftiness with his own money. For a time, Kefauver, who enjoyed having a fine time himself, joined them as a roommate. Salter even acquainted Jackson with a young Democratic congressman from Massachusetts named John Kennedy, not known for an aversion to the opposite sex. During 1947–48, Kennedy had an apartment in the same building as Jackson, just behind the Supreme Court.[53]

None of this rubbed off on Jackson, "who twitched when he had to spend more than five minutes in a saloon." When Salter got dates for him, Jackson often forgot them. When, in January 1947, locals in Everett speculated erroneously, based on a misprinted announcement, that Jackson had married, he set the record straight with vehemence. He was "not now married, never has been married, has no plans to be married." Joe Miller provided the most reliable version of one dating episode, the encapsulation of Jackson's romantic side at that time:

Martha Wright, from Duval, Washington, in Scoop's old district, was an aspiring musical comedy actress around Seattle. Then she went to New York in 1947 or 1948 and did very well. Scoop had known her around Seattle. He went up to New York to take her out. Martha had familiarity with show business mores, which were not strict about sex. Scoop wanted to take her back to her apartment. She was intrigued that straight arrow Scoop was interested. When they got to the apartment, Scoop said he wanted to watch the eleven o'clock news. He did and then left.[54]

There was nothing mysterious about Jackson's lack of interest in romance and marriage until later in life, no hidden meaning, no repressed sexuality or psychological disorder. There was, indeed, no contradiction between the public and private sides of Henry Jackson, no wrenching tension or dark paradox in his personality or political outlook. His personal and political lives meshed seamlessly. In the case of his decision to defer romance and marriage, his straightforward explanation rings true. His dedication to politics did not leave him time for much else, especially for the time-consuming obligations of family life that he was determined to take seriously when his time for marriage did come. His upbringing magnified his cautious social instincts. In ethnic families with strong mothers and siblings who marry either late or not at all, the course Jackson took was not unusual. Nor was it unusual for the Washington, D.C., of his time, where lifelong bachelors Sam Rayburn in the House and Richard Russell in the Senate also considered marriage incompatible with their political responsibilities.

The most remarkable aspect of Jackson's private life was the absence of flair or any hint of impropriety. His rectitude and predictability irritated the acerbic, more colorful Salter, who complained, among other things, that Jackson ate the "same god damn prunes for breakfast every morning." Driving was the one area where Jackson's reverence for law and order lapsed, whether behind the wheel or dispensing backseat advice on how fast to go and which route to take. Friends found him to be a harrowing driving companion. Traffic laws, physical obstacles such as median strips, and elementary geography did not deter him, especially when he was in a hurry.[55]

Chapter 3

The Cold War Becomes Colder

D URING HIS LAST four years in the House, Jackson fared better at influencing America's defense and atomic policies. In January 1949 he became a member of the Joint Committee on Atomic Energy, an appointment he sought initially to fortify and broaden the base of his popularity back home. The massive Hanford nuclear complex in central Washington gave him an enormous political incentive for advocating expansion of America's nuclear program, which his boundless enthusiasm for the peaceful use of atomic energy inclined him to support anyway.[1]

His membership on the Joint Committee, which was responsible for overseeing the national atomic energy program, soon thrust him into the heart of a pivotal debate about how to contain Soviet power. In July 1949, the Soviet Union stunned the world by exploding its first atomic bomb, years sooner than most experts expected. David Lilienthal, chairman of the Atomic Energy Commission, had earlier predicted that the Soviets might never attain the capability to build an atomic bomb. The Soviet detonation also surprised Henry Jackson. With the Soviet test just weeks away, Jackson had said that he did not take "any stock in the possibility of the Russians actually exploding the bomb." He, too, had relied on the CIA's top secret estimate of the Soviet nuclear program, issued July 1, 1949, assuring that the first Soviet atomic bomb could not be completed before 1951.[2]

THE HYDROGEN BOMB AND THE ARMS RACE

The Truman administration responded vigorously. It secured congressional approval, including Jackson's, to supplement the North Atlantic Treaty with the North Atlantic Treaty Organization, thus establishing the infrastructure to make America's commitment to the security of Western Europe operationally credible. The president also revived the issue of whether the United States should build a hydrogen bomb, a program dormant since the end of World War II. Jackson became a member of a special subcommittee to determine the technical feasibility and military desirability of such a weapon, infinitely more destructive than the atomic bomb. For the first time, he played a significant role in deciding a crucial national security issue, consulting regularly during the course of the subcommittee's fall 1949 meetings with experts of national rank: Ernest O. Lawrence, Nobel Prize-winning physicist, and Dr. Edward Teller and Dr. Robert Oppenheimer, fathers of the atomic bomb.

There was sharp disagreement about how to proceed. The majority of the members of the Atomic Energy Commission, along with the commission's advisory committee, opposed developing the hydrogen bomb immediately. So did Oppenheimer, the most prominent and forceful opponent, who raised both technical and political objections. Even if the United States could build such a weapon—no sure thing, according to Oppenheimer—he did not believe that we could develop a system capable of delivering it. Even if we could deliver it, he did not believe there were targets in the U.S.S.R. large enough to justify using such awesome weapons. He also made the political argument that if the United States did not build an H-bomb, the Soviets would refrain from building one. If the United States did, the Soviet Union would have no choice but to respond, setting off an escalating spiral of arms building that would leave both sides less secure.[3]

Jackson reached the opposite conclusion. Teller and Lawrence convinced him, always a buoyant optimist about the potential of American technology, that the H-bomb could be built. His assessment of the Soviet Union convinced him that the bomb should be built. He respected Oppenheimer as a man of integrity, never doubting his loyalty, as some anticommunists more preoccupied than Jackson with the danger of internal subversion would do during the height of the Red scare. For Jackson, the problem with Oppenheimer was not his patriotism but his political judgment. Jackson gave no credence to the idea that American forbearance from building the H-bomb would induce the Soviet Union to reciprocate. As he read history, arms races did not cause political conflicts; political conflicts caused arms races. The Soviet-American atomic arms race was to him a symptom of the Cold War for which relentless Soviet expansionism should bear exclusive responsibility. If the United States built the

H-bomb, he conceded that the Soviets would eventually match it. He believed, however, that the Soviets would try to build an H-bomb regardless of what the United States did. So there was no choice but to go forward rapidly with the H-bomb program; or else the United States would lose its position of nuclear superiority essential to deter the Soviet Union:

> Until now, our atomic superiority has held the Kremlin in check. The ground troops of Stalin vastly outnumber those of the free world. The Red air force is far larger than the combined air fleets of the free peoples. In only one field of endeavor—the field of atomic weapons—have we maintained a commanding lead over the Soviets. Yet this trump card alone—the fearful retribution that would be visited upon the men of the Politburo if the dictators struck—has served to keep Stalin from beginning the third world war.
>
> Falling behind in the atomic armaments competition will mean national suicide. The latest Russian explosion means that Stalin has gone all out in atomic energy. It is high time that we go all out.[4]

Jackson's approach triumphed, a success for which he received considerable credit. As Ernest Lawrence observed, "Jackson saw the urgency of working on the H-bomb long before many and helped it become a crash program." Proponents of the H-bomb had the added advantage that President Truman had grown steadily more receptive to the logic of their arguments. On July 26, 1949, Jackson attended the Blair House meeting at which the president told the assembled leaders, "since we can't obtain international control we must be strongest in atomic weapons."[5] The Soviet detonation of an A-bomb moved Truman further in the direction of building the H-bomb, a decision that the arguments of the Jackson faction on the Joint Committee on Atomic Energy clinched.

In this case, Jackson demonstrated not only his capacity to influence events but also his gift of foresight. The Soviet archives have revealed that Stalin had Soviet scientists working feverishly on building an H-bomb, a program he determined to keep on an all-out basis even had the United States delayed its program. If Oppenheimer's approach had won out, the Soviet Union would have had a monopoly on hydrogen bombs, leaving the United States in a dangerous position of conventional and strategic nuclear inferiority.[6] The lessons Jackson drew from his participation in the H-bomb decision conditioned his responses to the great national debates over arms control, national security, and détente during the 1970s, on which he had a decisive impact. He never forgot the experience of well-meaning but naive scientists arguing against building the H-bomb, according to Richard Perle, Jackson's most important national security adviser between 1969 and 1979:

> His enthusiasm for building missile defense, his skepticism about détente and the Strategic Arms Limitations Talks (SALT), all stemmed from his previous experiences and the lessons he drew from it: that had we listened to the scientists who had opposed the Hydrogen Bomb, Stalin would have emerged with a monopoly and we would have been in deep trouble.[7]

Jackson's position on the Joint Committee on Atomic Energy, a position he later retained in the Senate, also gave the young congressman a marvelous opportunity to learn about such critical issues of national security as the H-bomb program, arms control, production of fissionable material, the nuclear submarine program, and the land-based ballistic missile program, not to exhaust the list. With a Q clearance, giving them access to the most sensitive and restricted data about nuclear weapons, Jackson and other members of the committee received great deference from their congressional colleagues on matters of national security. This was his first major opportunity to cultivate a technique of drawing on the advice and counsel of the best experts, both inside and outside of government. Endowed with an impervious self-confidence, Jackson respected intellectuals without being one himself or being in awe of them. He established enduring relationships throughout his Senate career with a wide range of scholars and scientists of the first rank. While on the Joint Atomic Energy Committee in the House, he previewed his ability to attract such auspicious talent by befriending Captain Hyman Rickover and Dr. Edward Teller, two brilliant men with difficult personalities that others found daunting. Yet his experience with Oppenheimer and scientists of similar perspective ingrained in him a wariness of specialists who viewed problems from what he saw as a narrow perspective. What he valued most was the foreign policy generalist: a man or woman exhibiting steadiness and strength of character, steeped in a knowledge of history, broadly trained by study and experience to approach issues from a larger context. There was no substitute, he thought, for sound judgment.[8]

Four men personified Jackson's conception of the foreign policy generalist in the best sense of the term: Dean Acheson, a powerful Maryland and District of Columbia lawyer who became Truman's secretary of state and a prime architect of the policy of vigilant containment that Jackson expounded; Robert Lovett, a successful investment banker, who served with distinction as Truman's undersecretary of state and secretary of defense; Paul Nitze, another Wall Street banker turned strategist, later a close friend and political ally, who served as the director of the State Department's Policy and Planning Staff among other things; and James Schlesinger, an academic who later served in various government capacities, most prominently as director of the Central Intelligence Agency, secretary of defense, and the first secretary of energy.

Paul Nitze first won Jackson's trust and admiration for his role in composing National Security Council (NSC) 68, a reexamination of American grand strategy for which the Soviet A-bomb and Truman's decision to proceed with the hydrogen bomb provided the impetus. This document, sent to the president in April 1950, laid down the main lines of American foreign and defense policy for much of the Cold War: in the long term "to foster fundamental change in the nature of the Soviet system," in the short term to thwart the Soviet Union's grand geopolitical design to achieve dominance of the Eurasian landmass. The first principle underpinning NSC 68 was that the United States, as the most powerful liberal democratic nation in the world, had a moral, geopolitical, and ideological imperative to preserve free institutions throughout the world. Noting that the Soviet Union devoted 13.8 percent of its GNP to defense, twice the U.S. allocation, the document urged that the United States equip itself with the military means to protect large areas of the world for the long haul, especially now that the U.S. atomic monopoly had ended. It argued that the American economy could bear the burden of devoting up to 20 percent of the GNP to defense, if necessary. Jackson agreed completely with NSC 68's conceptual framework of a long-term struggle between American freedom and Soviet totalitarianism, and with the expensive means that it called for to combat the Soviet threat: a vast military buildup in conventional and nuclear arms, the alternative to which was the enslavement of the free world.[9]

Secretary of State Dean Acheson, Nitze, Lovett, and others like Jackson who endorsed the recommendations of NSC 68, faced the task of persuading a reluctant President Truman. Although he agreed with the document's stark depiction of the Soviet threat, he did not want to increase military spending substantially for fear of jeopardizing the ambitious Fair Deal legislation before Congress. Also, his secretary of defense, Louis Johnson, determined to establish a reputation as a budget cutter, opposed a full-scale rearmament program.[10] For George Kennan and other experts in the State Department who had a more modest vision of what containment should entail and the burdens it need impose, NSC 68 had wildly inflated the military dimension of the Soviet threat.[11] In Kennan's view, the United States needed merely to keep Western Europe and Japan, centers of industrial capability, out of Soviet hands. He opposed the NATO alliance as unnecessary and the idea of incorporating a liberal democratic West Germany into it as unduly provocative.[12] Assuming that ideology did not determine alignment decisions in international politics, he also believed that the United States could even tolerate a communist Germany or Japan so long as they were not satellites of the Soviet Union. He urged that the United States take a relatively relaxed view toward unfriendly regimes outside the vital power centers of Eurasia and the Middle East, because, however undesirable, such regimes lacked the capacity to menace vital American interests.[13] Ultimately, President Truman found the arguments of Acheson, Nitze, and the experts they arrayed in support of NSC 68 more compelling than those of its critics. Accepting that defense spending should increase, Truman deferred the question of how much until the outbreak of the Korean War in June 1950 intervened to create a political climate conducive to transforming NSC 68 from a paper doctrine to a tangible program. Defense spending tripled between 1950 and 1951 as the president judged the North Korean invasion a prelude to an attack on Japan and a test of America's reliability to its new European allies.[14]

Again, Jackson supported resolutely the president's decisive response to North Korean aggression. His instincts corresponded with the president's, too, about how to deal with Red China, a bitterly divisive issue in American politics, inextricably linked with the Korean conflict. Since the turn of the century, many Americans, including Jackson, had maintained a romantic attachment to China, which its brave resistance to Japanese aggression during World War II intensified. President Roosevelt had admired Chiang Kai-shek, head of the Kuomintang party (KMT), and insisted on making China a permanent member of the United Nations, en-visaging it as an architect of postwar stability in East Asia.[15] Much of the press, most notably Henry Luce, proprietor of *Time, Life,* and *Fortune* magazines, shared Roosevelt's vision of Chiang and China's role in the postwar world. So did Asia Firsters, led by Senator Robert Taft, Republi-can from Ohio; Senator William Knowland, Republican from California; and Congressman Walter Judd, Republican from Minnesota, who be-lieved that America's destiny lay not in Europe, but in the Pacific, with Chiang's China as a linchpin of the U.S. position in the region.[16]

It was unrealistic, however, to think that Chiang's China would emerge as a pillar of stability. China was neither stable nor united. Civil war had ravaged the country for most of the century. A poor administrator, an indifferent general, and corrupt, Chiang never effectively controlled more than half of the country. He had always faced stiff internal resistance from rival warlords and the Communists. After the Second World War, the Chinese civil war entered its final phase. Truman sent General Mar-shall to China to mediate the conflict between the KMT and the Com-munists. In January 1946, Marshall arranged a truce that held only inter-mittently and briefly. In June 1946, the civil war between the KMT and the Communists escalated, despite U.S. efforts to mediate, which the United States abandoned in the spring of 1947, blaming both sides for their intransigence. Between 1945 and 1948, the Truman administra-tion provided Chiang with generous amounts of aid: a total of $2 bil-lion. Thereafter, U.S. aid ceased as the Truman administration, viewing Chiang's cause as hopeless, determined to cut its losses. By October 1949, Mao Zedong's Communist forces had crossed south of the Yangtze, cap-turing Nanking. By December, Mao controlled all of Mainland China.[17] In August 1949, the State Department issued a White Paper explaining the victory of the Chinese Communists as a result of the weakness of the Chinese Nationalists, an interpretation that later events largely con-firmed. This White Paper precipitated ferocious criticism of Secretary of State Acheson by Asia Firsters, however, outraged that the United States had lost China, ostensibly because the Truman administration refused to render military aid to the Nationalists.[18]

Like Truman, Jackson was "wholly in opposition to our troops in Chi-na taking sides in an internal civil war." He considered the defense of South Korea essential lest the United States lose Japan, for which Korea was a vital interest, to neutralism or communism. Like the president, moreover, he concluded that the Chinese military intervention in the Korean War during the winter of 1950–51 required the United States to scale back its objectives from uniting the entire Korean peninsula to preserving the independence of South Korea below the 38th parallel.[19] He not only applauded President Truman for his courage in firing General MacArthur, but also excoriated the insubordinate general's willingness to escalate the war as the height of strategic folly:

> It is important that we not be diverted into a long war of attrition with the Chinese. It would be nothing short of colossal stupidity to be successfully maneuvred by the Russians into an impossible war with our traditional friends and allies, the Chinese people, leaving the real antagonist, Russia, free to continue to build up their strength. This is not appeasement. This should be common, ordinary horse sense. Our objective in the meantime, therefore, must be to preserve as much American strength as possible for what now seems to be an inevitable struggle with our primary antagonist, Russia.[20]

For his remaining two years in the House, Jackson vigorously defended the Truman administration's foreign and national security policies. He called for a "real all-out atomic program" instead of "our half-way program." He urged concentration on both strategic and tactical nuclear weapons for use on the battlefield, delivered by "airpower, guided missiles, nuclear submarines, artillery shells, and other weapons that can deliver atomic ammunition." This offered, he thought, the most promising, cost-effective way to bolster the confidence of European allies and to deter Soviet aggression. Atomic weapons offered no panacea, however, in Jackson's eyes. The United States would still need to increase the size of its navy and other conventional forces substantially. "The day is not in sight, and never will be," he declared, "when we can win wars without the loss of American lives." He did not regard the atomic bomb, "as a miracle weapon, which need not conform to grand strategy." Nevertheless, he urged that ordinary common sense required the United States to give top priority to its atomic program:

> It is simple logic to stress the one field in which we can remain ahead of the Soviets. Unless we make ourselves into a garrison state, it is truly dif-

ficult to imagine matching the Red Army division by division. In raw
quantitative power—power measured by the yardstick of foot soldiers
and ordinary weapons—the Soviets have an actual and potential advantage. But in qualitative military power—in the power of laboratories, scientific skills, and specialized brains—the advantage is overwhelmingly
on our side.[21]

Jackson was no warmonger. He denounced proposals for preventive
war as reckless and "plain foolish."[22] He advocated devoting more of the
vastly superior industrial potential of Western Europe and the United
States to military programs not to start a war with the Soviet Union but
to deter the Soviets from starting one—"to make it unmistakably clear to
the men in the Kremlin that an aggressive war against the West will not
pay off." For Jackson, the Cold War was more than a military confrontation between two superpowers: it was, above all, an ideological and moral
struggle that the United States must wage relentlessly because the "one
thing that Stalin fears more than our atomic stockpile" was the truth.
"Godless Communism and the Soviet system," Jackson said, were "based
from beginning to end upon monstrous falsehoods. Let men come to understand that our free way of life offers them both infinitely more material wealth and infinitely more freedom than the way of the Kremlin—
and Communism can never win out."[23] Jackson always hoped that the
United States and the Soviet Union could reach a verifiable arms accord
conducive to American interests that would cut weapons in all categories
significantly. In 1950 and again in 1951, he introduced a resolution in the
House calling for across-the-board arms cuts. There was, however, no evidence that Stalin had any interest in good faith arms reduction of the kind
Jackson proposed. So Jackson recommended hoping for the best, but
preparing for the worst. The Soviet detonation of the atomic bomb had
underscored his conviction that the prime danger lay in underestimating,
not overestimating, Soviet capabilities and ambitions.[24]

LIBERALISM ON THE DEFENSIVE, 1950–1952

The vision of containment that the Truman administration pursued and
that Jackson embraced provided the framework for winning the Cold War
with minimal cost and risks compared to any of the plausible alternatives.[25] What we have since learned from the Soviet archives indicates

that the Soviet Union was neither a defensive nor a traditional imperial entity.[26] It was indeed engaged in a relentless quest to achieve hegemony in Eurasia, a hegemony incompatible with the fundamental security interests of the United States and its democratic allies in Western Europe. The Cold War spread to the underdeveloped world not because American statesmen desired that result, but because a combination of opportunism and Leninist ideology impelled Moscow to rely on proxy wars as a preferred strategy for draining Western resources and undermining Western resolve.[27] Stalin aimed to control all of Europe, not just part of it, beginning with a unified communist Germany.[28] The cooperation of Western European democracies so conducive to their welfare and that of the United States did presuppose a strong, liberal, democratic Germany, anchored to the West, lest the Germans return to the militaristic and aggressive courses that were largely responsible for two world wars.[29] The Truman administration also made a prudent decision to fight in Korea, despite the increase in Sino-American rivalry that resulted. Recent scholarship has revealed that North Korea initiated the war, with the active encouragement of Stalin and Mao, who were then still collaborators rather than rivals.[30] Without American intervention to save South Korea, U.S. efforts to create a stable, liberal Japan anchored to the American alliance system also might have failed. Yet the remarkable success of Truman's foreign policy emerged with clarity only later. During the final two years of his presidency, his popularity plummeted as the public grew increasingly frustrated over the loss of China, the fear of internal subversion, the stalemate in Korea, the failure to enact the Fair Deal, and the corruption that engulfed his administration.[31]

Most Americans agreed with the Truman administration's decision to stay out of the Chinese civil war. Not even the Asia Firsters endorsed American military intervention; they were, however, upset with the communist victory in China and ready to blame the Truman administration for it. What intensified the political firestorm that the loss of China ignited was Senator Joseph McCarthy's charges in February 1950 that 205 communists were working at and shaping the policy of the State Department. For the next four years, this obscure senator from Wisconsin became the scourge of American politics. A pathological liar, opportunist, and alcoholic, McCarthy did more to damage the honorable cause of principled anticommunism than any other figure during the Cold War. His reckless charges resonated so powerfully because they seemed to have some plausibility and semblance of truth. Although Truman was undoubtedly right that the United States could not save Chiang Kai-shek, some of the China experts in the State Department badly misjudged Mao, who was not a benign agrarian reformer but a totalitarian dictator responsible for the deaths of millions of Chinese.[32]

Much of the American public took McCarthy's charges seriously not just because of the loss of China to the communists, but because communist subversion was a serious problem. American communists pledged their allegiance to a totalitarian enemy of the United States whose line they followed slavishly.[33] There was a significant communist presence in American labor unions. As Allen Weinstein and Sam Tanenhaus have proved, Alger Hiss, who served in the State Department at high levels, was undoubtedly a communist agent. So probably was Harry Dexter White, who served in the upper echelons of the Treasury Department.[34] Soviet agents also had penetrated the Manhattan Project and America's postwar nuclear program, one reason the Soviets achieved nuclear capability so rapidly.[35] Ironically, the Truman administration's loyalty program, announced in March 1947, had largely succeeded in curbing the problem of communist subversion in government by the time McCarthy made his notorious accusations. But the president contributed to his own political misfortunes by dismissing the significance of the Hiss investigation, which culminated in a guilty verdict against Hiss for perjury in January 1950. Secretary of State Acheson made things worse by refusing to condemn Hiss, whose brother Donald was formerly a partner with Acheson in private law practice.[36]

The Korean War extended McCarthy's period of ascendancy. Acheson's honest mistake in January 1950—excluding South Korea from America's defense perimeter in Asia in a speech before the National Press Club in Washington, D.C.—fed the paranoia that McCarthy fanned when North Korea invaded South Korea. After the Chinese Army intervened in Korea in November 1950, Truman abandoned, with Jackson's support, the goal of unifying the Korean peninsula in favor of the more limited goal of restoring South Korean independence south of the 38th parallel. Conservative Republicans, irate over the president's firing of General MacArthur in April 1951, favored the general's preferred course of fighting a land war with China, using nuclear weapons if necessary. Truman managed to convince Congress that an escalation of the Korean War would imperil U.S. ability to deter the Soviet Union, by far the greater danger. The administration insisted, correctly, that the Soviets would have relished the United States getting bogged down in a land war in China, leaving them free to intimidate Western Europe. Still, the protracted costly war of attrition in Korea, which promised nothing but a stalemate, made the president monumentally unpopular. The rampant corruption of his administration, not implicating the president personally but extending widely, added to his political woes. By early 1952, President Truman's job approval rating had dropped to 25 percent, and remained there until he left office. By March, he trailed Dwight Eisenhower, the eventual Republican presidential nominee, 64 percent to 27 percent in the polls, perhaps the decisive reason he decided not to run for reelection.[37]

THE 1952 SENATE CAMPAIGN

It was in this political climate that Henry M. Jackson, the consummate Truman Democrat, determined to run for the Senate in 1952. The announcement of his candidacy, on May 31, 1952, his fortieth birthday, came as no surprise. Since 1948 he had spent almost all of his time outside Congress canvassing Washington State and amassing contacts in preparation for a senatorial run. Since 1950 Salter, formally the regional director of the Office of Price Administration, had worked in Seattle making arrangements and formulating the strategy for the upcoming campaign. At the same time, Jackson's congressional office staff had compiled a painstakingly detailed dossier on the record of his prospective opponent, Republic Harry P. Cain, who had defeated Hugh Mitchell in the great Democratic debacle of 1946 in the Pacific Northwest.[38] In 1950, Jackson turned down President Truman's offer to become undersecretary of the interior, because he believed leaving Congress would imperil his chances for election to the Senate. His positions on the Interior Subcommittee of the House Committee on Appropriations and the Joint Committee on Atomic Energy gave him the forum and the influence to develop a statewide constituency. Running for reelection to the House in 1950, he had impressed Washington State Democrats with his popularity and his invulnerability to red baiting by defeating his Conservative Republican opponent Herb Wilson by a margin of two to one. Wilson's attempts to portray him as soft on communism fell flat even though this tactic had exposed the vulnerability of liberal Democrats elsewhere.[39] Facing a conservative challenger, Warren Magnuson, more flamboyantly liberal than Jackson in temperament and less credible as a hawk on national defense, had won reelection to the Senate in 1950 by just 60,000 votes. Magnuson attributed his slender margin of victory to the fear McCarthy had instilled in the American people. An exaggerated sense of McCarthy's political clout inspired dread and reticence in many liberal Democratic politicians, especially after the defeat in 1950 of Magnuson's friend Senator Millard Tydings from Maryland, a four-term incumbent and an outspoken critic of the Wisconsin senator.[40]

In his quest for the Democratic nomination for the Senate, Jackson actually benefited from the dismal expectations of the Democratic Party's prospects in the 1952 elections. The Republicans appeared headed for a smashing victory in the nation and the state, with Eisenhower at the top of the ticket and domestic anticommunism a potent campaign issue. To stave off a clean Republican sweep in the Pacific Northwest, Washington State Democrats needed to nominate the strongest possible candidate, which doomed the chances of Hugh Mitchell, Jackson's main rival for the nomination. Mitchell had served for fourteen years as Mon Wallgren's chief of staff: two years in the House and twelve in the Senate. When Wallgren was elected governor in 1944, he chose Mitchell to fill out his unexpired term in the Senate, where Mitchell made his mark as a liberal reformer and an unsuccessful proponent of establishing a Columbia Valley Authority. He had become the sentimental favorite of many Washington State liberals who might have thrown their support to him rather than Jackson in more favorable political circumstances. He was, however, an indifferent campaigner in a year the Democrats could not afford indifference. He had already lost decisively to Harry Cain in 1946, while Jackson alone survived the Republican congressional onslaught in the Pacific Northwest. In 1950, running for his second term in Congress, Mitchell had proved politically vulnerable to charges of being soft on communism, winning by only 4,000 votes. He also had offended mainstream Democrats by calling on Truman early in 1948 to forgo a run for reelection and head the movement to draft Eisenhower to run as a Democrat.[41]

There was a widespread perception that Jackson was a more skillful and effective legislator than Mitchell. In 1952, *Liberty* magazine had selected

Jackson as one of the ten most effective congressmen, distinguished for his "honesty, independence, and leadership." One local editorial heralded him as "the best congressman the Peninsula has ever known." "Jackson and his staff knew how to get their press releases in the Seattle papers to influence the debate on the Columbia Valley Authority; Hugh Mitchell was ineffective in his advocacy," remembered Charles Luce, former chairman of Con Ed, then a lawyer in Walla Walla working as a consultant to the Truman administration on the unsuccessful legislation to establish a CVA. Bowing to the inevitable, Mitchell decided in 1952 to run for governor instead. After an acrimonious campaign, he lost to Republican Arthur B. Langlie, who succeeded in tarnishing him with being soft on communism.[42]

Jackson took a major risk running for the Senate against incumbent Harry Cain in a year that the Republican nominee for president, Dwight Eisenhower, appeared destined to win by a landslide over his Democratic opponent, Adlai Stevenson. Cain not only identified with Senator McCarthy but also attacked his political opponents in a similar fashion—with scant regard for veracity or civility. In 1949, Cain filibustered to block the appointment of Wallgren as chairman of the National Security Resources Board, accusing him of abetting communist control of the Democratic Party in Washington State. In 1950, he objected to the appointment of Anna Rosenberg as assistant secretary of defense, because she was "foreign born, a woman, and a member of a minority race" (i.e., a Jew).[43]

Nevertheless, Cain appeared to be politically vulnerable, especially against Jackson, whose record of integrity and effectiveness contrasted favorably with his. He had suffered through a messy public divorce that produced salacious material for gossip about his affair with a secretary.[44] *Time* had listed him as one of the eight most expendable men in the Senate. A poll of 128 Washington, D.C., correspondents rated him the seventh worst senator, "incompetent, lazy, without the capacity for high office," and a poll of the nation's top political scientists, taken in February 1952, listed him as one of the five worst senators.[45] For a series of poorly received filibusters on rent control, he had earned the dubious distinction of the "number one real estate lobbyist in America." His views on foreign policy oscillated wildly between isolationism and militancy. He was one of a handful of senators who had opposed creating a seventy-group air force, allowing NATO nations to render military assistance to other members under attack, and allowing the president to send more than four divisions to Europe in an emergency. He also had supported General MacArthur in his fight against President Truman, urging that "the United States hit China with everything we've got." On April 17, 1951, Senator Cain had introduced two resolutions that totally contradicted one another: one proposed all-out war with China; the other proposed a complete withdrawal from the Pacific. "Senator Harry P. Cain is endowed with a matchless ignorance of foreign affairs," wrote the nationally syndicated Alsop brothers in the *New York Herald Tribune*.[46]

During the campaign, Jackson pounded Cain for his weak record on national defense and his opposition to public power projects critical to the Pacific Northwest. "The Sorry Record of Harry P. Cain" became one of Jackson's major campaign slogans. He berated Cain across the state for a six-year voting record on both domestic and foreign policy that was a source of continuing embarrassment to the Republican Party. Jackson's positive message complemented his negative one: he stressed his integrity and independence, his position as spokesman for the West on power and reclamation issues, his leadership in the field of atomic energy, and his principled anticommunism, which "fought Communists effectively abroad without destroying civil liberties at home."[47] He demonstrated his typical vigor as a campaigner and retained his composure, even in difficult circumstances. Speaking at a sawmill in Centralia, Washington, he stood on a 25-foot-high platform with nothing but rocks beneath him when a plank suddenly gave way. He slipped through the hole to his hips, barely managing to stop. Although shaken, he pulled himself up, smiling! It reminded him, he told the crowd, "of Vice President Alben Barkley's description of the Republican platform—convenient to get in on but not to stand on."[48]

Judging by results, voters found Jackson's persona and message appealing. His campaign's media strategy, quite innovative by the standards of the time, also worked well for him. John Salter had assembled a first-rate team, including Gerry Hoeck, a young advertising executive who had handled the media work for Magnuson's reelection campaign in 1950. Hoeck's most decisive contribution to Jackson's first Senate run was "the billboard": a full-color portrait of Jackson leaning forward, looking like Jimmy Stewart in *Mr. Smith Goes to Washington*. The billboard's message read simply: "Jackson will make a great U.S. Senator." Joe Miller, who assisted Hoeck during the 1952 campaign, recalled: "Never in my subsequent campaign experience did I see a single media create the sensation that the Jackson posters did when unveiled across Washington state in August 1952. For days, it dominated the conversation of everyone in political circles because no one had seen anything like it." Democratic doorbell ringers found that voters accepted the Jackson brochures while they rejected others because they considered him a "fine-appearing man" who "will be a great credit to our state."[49]

In 1952, Magnuson and his staff lent critical assistance to Jackson's campaign, a practice that would continue and that Jackson would reciprocate for the rest of his Senate career. The remarkable collaboration between these two men would make them one of the most powerful tandems in Senate history, not because of their similarities but because of their fundamental and complementary differences. Usually two senators of the same party do not get along because they are in face-to-face competition for their own constituents. In the case of Jackson and Magnuson, their styles and policy interests did not produce friction. Magnuson specialized in commerce, appropriations, and fisheries; Jackson in armed services, the environment, and energy. Magnuson was an archpartisan Democrat, a Senate insider more comfortable on the left side of the party. Jackson's style was less confrontational, his interest in national security more bipartisan, his temperament more congenial to Southern Democratic titans such as Richard Russell than to the Senate leadership under Lyndon Johnson, where Magnuson thrived. In his personal life and habits, Jackson was the antithesis of the cigar-smoking, hard-drinking, womanizing Magnuson. Sometimes their staffs fought bitterly, because they were very competitive. For many years, however, the senators managed to enforce a discipline that chilled public confrontation and ensured cooperation on the major domestic issues affecting Washington State. Both believed in senatorial courtesy, decorum, a division of labor, and respecting each other's province. Both became first-rate players in the Senate game.[50]

Throughout the 1952 campaign, public opinion steadily moved Jackson's way. Cain countered by attacking him furiously. He accused Jackson of "being a coward who does not tell the truth." He threatened to make Jackson "eat his words if he would only say in my presence what he says behind my back." He implied that Jackson was not anticommunist enough by accusing him of voting often with far-left Representative Vito Marcantonio, a tactic that Richard Nixon had used with devastating effect in his first congressional race against Jerry Voorhis.[51]

In the waning days of the campaign, Cain even brought Senator McCarthy, whom Jackson had criticized, to Seattle. The visit ended in farce. The diversion of his airplane caused McCarthy to miss a Republican rally in Everett, where he planned to deliver a speech blistering Jackson. His scheduled television appearance never happened because he refused to submit his remarks for editing; so the station would not let him on the air. The press club dinner in Seattle that he did attend turned out even worse. The club had invited him to debate Vic Meyers, the bandleader who had become lieutenant governor of Washington State. Arriving surly and stern-faced, McCarthy encountered a hostile crowd that taunted him and did not let him speak. "He got madder and madder," according to Gerry Hoeck, an eyewitness to the event. "Finally, he pounded the lectern and said, God dammit, I did not come three thousand miles to be funny; Vic Meyers walked up to the podium and said, I did not walk six blocks to be serious." McCarthy stormed out of the dinner.[52]

Jackson defeated Cain decisively, a victory all the more impressive in light of the resounding Republican victory across the nation and elsewhere in Washington State. His 135,000-vote margin exceeded Eisenhower's in the state by 30,000 votes and Magnuson's in 1950 by more than a factor of two.

Jackson had backed his friend Estes Kefauver, winner of fourteen of the seventeen primaries, for the Democratic Party's presidential nomination. He feared that Adlai Stevenson, the eventual nominee, whose intellectual pretensions he disliked and whose foreign policy instincts he distrusted, would alienate the rank-and-file Democratic voter, the backbone of Roosevelt's New Deal coalition. At the Democratic Convention, he had attended a secret Stop Stevenson meeting of Kefauver, Averell Harriman of New York, also a presidential aspirant, and their top aides.[53] Adlai Stevenson presaged, in some ways, the liberal Democrats of the late 1960s and 1970s who would spurn Jackson. He was an elitist, a critic rather than a celebrator of the common man, and far more dovish than either Truman or Jackson in his instincts about foreign policy.[54] By venting his doubts about Stevenson, Jackson hoped to keep the Democratic Party squarely in line with the New Deal–Fair Deal policies of President Truman: assertively anticommunist abroad, aggressively activist at home.[55]

After the 1952 campaign, Jackson toured Washington State to thank the voters for their support. He had attained his intense ambition to become a senator, a position he had desired since his high school days in Everett. Just as his experience during the Depression forged his convictions about domestic affairs, his experience in the House between 1940 and 1952 forged his convictions about America's role in the world and the paramount threat of totalitarianism. He had entered the House as an isolationist skeptical of American involvement in the Second World War. He left in 1952 an ardent exponent of the policy of vigilant containment as President Truman envisaged it. It is impossible to understand his role in subsequent events without understanding the lessons he drew from World War II, the Holocaust, and Stalin's foreign policy during the formative period of the Cold War.

Chapter 4

The Eisenhower Years, 1953–1961

THE NEW DEMOCRATIC senator from Washington State returned to the nation's capital just before the Eighty-third Congress convened in early January 1953. On the surface, the political situation looked precarious for New Deal–Fair Deal Democrats like Henry Jackson. The American people had just elected their first Republican president in twenty years. The Eisenhower landslide also gave the Republicans control of Congress, albeit by just one vote in the Senate. After twenty years in the political wilderness, conservative Republicans not only savored their party's victory but also interpreted it as a mandate for rolling back much of the New Deal. Senator Joseph McCarthy, the new chairman of the Senate Committee on Government Operations and its investigating subcommittee, continued to pursue his reckless crusade against communists in government, real and imagined, that made even the most staunch Cold War liberals apprehensive.

Beneath the surface, the long-term situation for liberal Democrats looked much better. The Eisenhower landslide had not prevented the election of several young and talented Democrats to the Senate besides Jackson: John Kennedy in Massachusetts, Mike Mansfield in Montana, and Stuart Symington in Missouri. Demographically, the New Deal coalition remained strong during the 1950s, reflected in the percentage of labor union members in the work force, the population of America's central cities, and the numbers of self-identified ethnic voters.[1] The next eight years would disappoint conservatives who had anticipated the establishment of the Republicans as a permanent majority party. When Eisenhower left office on January 20, 1961, Cold War liberalism had experienced a resurgence as a potent political force. The Democrats had restored their sizable majorities in Congress and had also recaptured the White House.

Cold War liberalism's resurgence intersected with Jackson's growing prominence during the Eisenhower years. He achieved national recognition for his role in bringing about the fall of Senator McCarthy, which helped the Democrats regain control of the Congress in 1954. He took an active part in all the major defense debates of the 1950s. Increasingly he established himself as an expert on national security and foreign affairs. He popularized, as much as anyone, the idea of the missile gap that his friend John Kennedy stressed to great effect when he ran for president against Richard Nixon. After coming close to naming Jackson as his running mate, Kennedy made him the chairman of the Democratic Party, the national symbol of Cold War liberalism for the watershed campaign of 1960.

JACKSON AND JOSEPH MCCARTHY

Jackson started his Senate career, however, at the bottom of the institutional ladder. He entered a Senate that required long years of hard work within the system to attain power and influence. The institution rewarded seniority and the observance of strict traditions.[2] Normally, freshman senators could not expect the most desirable accommodations or the most coveted committee assignments, which usually went to their more established colleagues. Jackson received the same treatment. Along with his administrative assistant John Salter, his executive secretary Julia Cancio, and the rest of his staff of twelve, he moved into their cramped quarters—a three-room suite, number 1428, on the fourth floor, really the attic, of the Old Senate Office Building.[3]

Initially, Jackson failed to get the committee assignments he wanted: Armed Services, Foreign Relations, the Joint Committee on Atomic Energy. With fear of Senator McCarthy's political clout still running high, Lyndon Johnson, the new Senate minority leader from Texas, assigned Jackson and two other freshman senators—Stuart Symington and John Kennedy—to the Senate Committee on Government Operations. Johnson also assigned Jackson, Symington, and veteran senator John McClellan of Arkansas to represent the Democrats on McCarthy's investigating subcommittee of Government Operations.[4]

Jackson undertook these assignments with a reluctance bordering on aversion. He abhorred McCarthy and his methods. While in the House, he had spoken out against the paranoid fear of domestic subversion while others remained silent. He had publicly defended Paul Raver, director of the Bonneville Power Administration, and David Lilienthal, chairman of the Atomic Energy Commission, against charges of being soft on communism. On the House floor in July 1951, he delivered a spirited rebuttal to McCarthy's attack on George Marshall, the most indefensible of the Wisconsin senator's career.[5] Jackson also resented McCarthy for actively supporting his Republican opponent Harry Cain in the 1952 election. From his first days in the Senate, Jackson privately expressed his disdain for McCarthy's conduct, particularly his uncontrolled drinking. McCarthy often stopped by Jackson's office with his breath smelling of alcohol. Before one investigating subcommittee hearing, an appalled Jackson had even encountered McCarthy in the Senate men's room gulping down quantities of whiskey.[6]

Jackson hoped, however, to avoid an ugly and divisive fight, in which it appeared that McCarthy and his cohorts would have the upper hand in the Government Operations Committee and investigating subcommittee. Senate rules and traditions did not accord much prerogative to freshman senators. McCarthy still had abundant support across the country, including Washington State. He could count, too, on the loyal support of the Taft wing of the Republican Party, which formed a sizable block of the Senate. Also, McCarthy had reason to believe that Eisenhower would be supportive. Although the president detested McCarthy in private, he refused to criticize him in public, and said nothing even when McCarthy impugned the integrity and patriotism of George Marshall, the president's friend and former commanding officer. Nor did it appear that McCarthy would face formidable opposition from the Democrats in the Senate unless the Republicans initiated action against him. Senate Minority Leader Johnson considered it suicidal for the Democrats to take on McCarthy in 1953. Most Senate Democrats agreed. "For a Democrat to take the lead at this juncture would likely cause the Republicans to rally around McCarthy," confided J. William Fulbright of Arkansas, adding that "unless some leading Republican is willing to take the curse of partisanship off this matter, I doubt it is wise for Democrats to make a move."[7]

Now a member of McCarthy's committee, Jackson pondered how to discharge his responsibilities. It would not be easy. McCarthy raised fundamental issues in a way that divided the country terribly. Jackson never strayed from his position as the quintessential liberal anticommunist who identified Soviet totalitarianism as a clear and present danger to the American way of life. Although he took seriously the danger of communist efforts at espionage and subversion, he believed that the United States could deal with them without jettisoning fundamental constitutional principles or abridging civil liberties. His emphasis on the duty to obey the law extended to the government as well as to the governed. Addressing the Democratic Party of Washington State on September 1, 1951, he put it this way:

> If we are not strong at home, our efforts abroad cannot meet with success. One of these areas involves personal freedoms on which our country was founded. I am just as eager to make sure that our government is not in the hands of Communists as anyone else. But some people are letting their fear of Communism lead them down fruitless alleys of witch-hunting and character assassinations. As Bishop Oxnan has said: "Men who see political advantage in the headlines that follow the wildest charge are themselves contributing to the Communist cause, since they divide our people, create suspicion, and divert our energies from those constructive measures that, in realizing justice, make us impregnable to Communist attack."
>
>   . . . If we keep our feet on the ground about this business of Communists in America, and approach the problem of ferreting them out in a sane and sober fashion, we can rest assured that our liberties will be secure. If we don't, we will have no one but ourselves to thank for the campaigns of fear and intimidation against honest and decent public servants and citizens and the resulting restrictions, unwritten and otherwise, on our freedom.[8]

Jackson decided to adopt a firm but cautious approach to McCarthy: to take his time, to play it cool, to control his emotions. Remembering his days as Snohomish County prosecutor and lessons learned from the Vivian Reeves case, he did not want to take on McCarthy until the American people grasped the full malignity of his methods. This required patiently amassing the evidence and giving McCarthy sufficient exposure to undo himself. Some of Jackson's political foes criticized him for his caution. Senator Eugene McCarthy, Democrat from Minnesota, always one of Jackson's severest detractors, believed that Jackson and Symington should have acted sooner to rein in McCarthy. "Liberal Republicans started the move against Joe McCarthy," according to Eugene McCarthy. "Then the Southern Democrats came in, because he was not a gentleman in the Southern tradition. Then liberal Democrats such as Henry came in only when it was safe."[9]

Bob Low and other liberal friends also urged Jackson to do more. In the spring of 1950, Low and Jackson, roommates with Salter in a small apartment on Capitol Hill, moved to a house at 3407 O Street in Georgetown that Low's mother helped him purchase. When Salter returned to Washington in January 1953 as Jackson's administrative assistant following his stint as regional director of the Office of Price Administration in the Northwest, he and Jackson roomed together on the third floor. The newly married Low and his wife Frances, also on Jackson's staff, occupied the two floors below. Jackson told Low and other liberal friends appalled by McCarthy: "Just be patient. Give him enough rope, and he will hang himself."[10]

It would exaggerate Jackson's influence to credit him with a pivotal role in bringing down Joseph McCarthy, for in large measure McCarthy destroyed himself. His abusive use of the investigative committees and total disregard for the facts accumulated inexorably to alienate most of his colleagues in the Senate, even many who sympathized with him on the issue of domestic subversion.[11] His mounting feud with President Eisenhower and the Republican leadership in the Senate also contributed significantly to his fall. Nevertheless, Jackson did play a larger and more honorable role in this process than Eugene McCarthy would admit.

Jackson rarely challenged Joe McCarthy directly during the first six months of 1953, with a few notable exceptions. McCarthy's attack on James A. Wechsler, liberal editor of the *New York Post*, before the subcommittee of Government Operations in April 1953 spurred Jackson and Symington to come to Wechsler's defense. Jackson, Herbert Lehman, and Mike Mansfield issued a joint statement the same month calling on the Democratic Party to make McCarthy a major issue in the 1954 campaign. Jackson also spoke out publicly in June 1953, deploring McCarthy's committee-led assault on the Voice of America and the State Department to purge their overseas libraries of subversive books. Yet Jackson usually conveyed his objections to McCarthy's behavior during those early months on the committee more circumspectly than Symington did. Jackson acquiesced, for example, when McCarthy demanded that Wechsler give the subcommittee a list of everyone he could remember from his youth who had been a communist or Young Communist League member.[12] Instead, biding his time, Jackson waited for McCarthy to make a catastrophic blunder that he and his fellow Democrats on the committee could exploit.

On June 18, 1953, McCarthy committed the first in a series of such blunders. He hired J. B. Matthews, a veteran of the Dies Committee in the House, which Jackson had opposed for conducting a witch-hunt, as executive director of the investigating subcommittee of Government Operations. In early July, a few days before Matthews joined the subcommittee staff, the *American Mercury*, a magazine of the far right that mainline conservatives such as William F. Buckley later repudiated, published Matthews's "Reds and Our Churches." The article began with this incendiary passage: "The largest single group supporting the Communist apparatus in the United States today is composed of Protestant clergymen."[13]

The headline in the *Washington Post*, reporting what Matthews had written, caught Bob Low's eye as he, his wife Frances, and Jackson prepared for their regular morning drive to work "squeezed into the front seat of Jackson's ten-year old Chevrolet." "Did you see this, Scoop?" Low asked. "J. B. Matthews says that the largest single group supporting the communists is the Protestant clergy." Jackson said, "Let me have that," and Low tore the piece from the paper and handed it over. After dropping Low off at the State Department where he worked, an irate Jackson and Frances Low headed for Capitol Hill. Now, Jackson felt ready for a major confrontation with Senator McCarthy. He had company.[14]

The Matthews article provoked bipartisan denunciation of McCarthy from the president and the congressional leaders of both parties. The Clearing House, an anti-McCarthy task force of liberal Democrats, passed along the Matthews article to Symington and McClellan. On July 2, Jackson, Symington, and McClellan confronted McCarthy in his office, demanding that Matthews resign. McCarthy refused. On July 7, the three reiterated their demand during a contentious session of the investigating subcommittee. Again, McCarthy refused. On July 10, they angrily resigned from the subcommittee in protest immediately after McCarthy had won by a straight party vote of 4 to 3 the sole right to hire and fire subcommittee staff, including Matthews.[15] It took political courage for the three to defect from the committee in the atmosphere that prevailed in the summer of 1953. Although McCarthy did not curb his investigations, the Democratic boycott hurt him badly. Commentator William S. White called the boycott a fundamental attack on McCarthy's standing in the Senate. "Officially, publicly and studiously to boycott one's fellow Senator is about as grave a step as one can take. To lose one's face in the club that is the Senate, is sometimes actually to lose it all."[16]

For six months, Jackson, Symington, and McClellan declined McCarthy's repeated invitations to rejoin the subcommittee. They insisted that McCarthy must relinquish exclusive authority to choose staff and give them the right to hire a minority counsel. They also demanded that, should the subcommittee Democrats unanimously oppose a public hearing on an issue, the full Committee of Government Operations would decide by majority vote whether to proceed.[17] Finally, McCarthy relented, but not before Carl Hayden, Democrat from Arizona, threatened to cut off all the subcommittee's funds on the grounds that absent the Democrats, it lacked a majority. Alarmed at the bad press the boycott was generating, Republican Senators Karl Mundt and William Knowland, two of McCarthy's strongest supporters, interceded with McCarthy to accept the three Democrats' procedural demands.

Jackson, McClellan, and Symington returned to the subcommittee in January 1954. They selected Robert (Bobby) Kennedy as their minority counsel, based largely on Jackson's recommendation. From early January to late July 1953, Bobby had worked as an assistant counsel to the subcommittee for Senator McCarthy, a great favorite of the Kennedy clan and a frequent guest at their Hyannisport estate. McCarthy's message and personality had great appeal to Bobby's father, Joseph P. Kennedy, the conservative and isolationist former ambassador to Great Britain, whose strident advocacy of appeasing Hitler and abandoning Great Britain forced President Roosevelt to remove him from his post. In December 1952, Joe Kennedy had even asked McCarthy to name Bobby as chief counsel to the Subcommittee on Investigations. McCarthy declined but did offer Bobby a position on the subcommittee as assistant counsel. Sharing his father's enthusiasm for McCarthy's cause, Bobby accepted eagerly. There he stayed until three weeks after Jackson, McClellan, and Symington walked off the committee, and although his letter of resignation on July 29, 1953, expressed gratitude to McCarthy, he had begun to have serious doubts about the merits and political expediency of linking his fate with the Wisconsin senator's.

Jackson had helped sow those doubts. His friend Jack Kennedy, the freshman senator from Massachusetts, had introduced Jackson to his brother during one of the semiregular softball games that the staffs of Senators Jackson, Kennedy, and Mansfield convened on summer Sundays at the Georgetown University athletic fields. The famous photograph of Jackson and Kennedy taken at one of these reputed athletic encounters captures strikingly the vastly different backgrounds and sensibilities of the two young senators. Dressed in heavy work boots, an undershirt, and dark flannel trousers, Jackson looked awkward swinging a bat, as if he was a logger from Everett who had never played softball before and wished never to play again. Wearing a polo shirt, khaki shorts, and blue boat sneakers, Kennedy looked tanned and confident crouched behind home plate, as if he had just stepped off the family yacht after a sail to Nantucket. Kennedy staged such scenes to convey an image of physical robustness that his poor health belied. The back disease from which he suffered had so debilitated him that he could not even run to first base during these games; he needed a pinch runner even when batting.[18]

The relationship between Jackson and Kennedy blossomed despite their different styles and backgrounds. After getting to know Bobby, Jackson warned him to jettison McCarthy before the Wisconsin senator dragged him down. Bobby told Jackson, not quite truthfully, that he had worked for McCarthy only out of obligation to his father. Jackson offered a grateful Bobby Kennedy the job as minority counsel to the subcommittee. By accepting, he contributed enormously to rehabilitating his reputation among liberals, which his association with McCarthy had damaged. His work on the subcommittee impressed Jackson, who wrote to Joseph and Rose Kennedy: "I am proud of the fine job that Bobby is doing. I feel that I'm safe in getting into trouble as long as I can have him for a counsel."[19]

In February 1954, McCarthy committed his fatal blunder. President Eisenhower had thwarted his efforts to launch a full-scale investigation of the CIA by flatly refusing to allow any of its personnel to appear before his committee. So McCarthy announced that he was going to conduct hearings aimed at exposing communist subversion in the army. His investigators charged that the army had promoted and later discharged honorably Dr. Irving Peress, a left-wing dentist stationed at Fort Monmouth, New Jersey, even though the doctor had declined to sign a loyalty oath. The army responded with a devastating charge of its own: that McCarthy and Roy Cohn, his chief counsel, had put pressure on the army to secure special treatment for Cohn's friend former assistant G. David Schine, who had been drafted. The not so subtle subtext of the army's complaint was that the homosexual Cohn's illicit obsession with getting Schine exempted from regular military service prompted McCarthy's investigation of alleged subversion in the army.[20]

A ferocious public controversy erupted over these charges and countercharges. To resolve it, the investigating subcommittee decided to investigate itself. The resulting Army-McCarthy hearings that ran between April and June of 1954 proved to be a watershed experience for the country, a calamity for Joseph McCarthy, and an enormous boon to the political career of Henry Jackson. For only the second time (the first being the Kefauver Committee's investigation of crime), national network television broadcast a major congressional hearing. The Army-McCarthy hearings drew a large audience and elicited passionate interest, demonstrating the growing impact of television on American politics and foreshadowing its destiny largely to supplant other media of political communication.[21]

McCarthy self-destructed under the pressure of the publicity. By taking on the army on such spurious grounds, he had put himself in an impossible situation. He had incurred the irreconcilable enmity of President Eisenhower, of many Democrats and liberal Republicans in Congress, and of large segments of the press. He also came across terribly on television, looking bloated, paunchy, with a dark five-o'clock shadow. His dreadful television visage radiated the sinisterness that his liberal critics had long insisted he personified. During the hearings, Joseph Welch, counsel for the army, exposed him as a liar, a bully, and a buffoon. McCarthy reacted by becoming increasingly wild and reckless, behavior exacerbated no doubt by an intensification of his heavy drinking that Henry Jackson himself had witnessed.[22]

McCarthy's imbroglio with the army emboldened Jackson and his fellow Democrats on the committee. Even before the hearings entered their final and decisive phase, Jackson stepped up the number and sharpness of his challenges to McCarthy. During the committee hearings of February

24, 1954, for example, Jackson objected voluably to McCarthy's merciless bullying of Anna Lee Moss, a black civilian employee of the Army Signal Corps, for her alleged communist past. An outraged McCarthy lashed back, berating Jackson for his long absences from the subcommittee, a lie that Jackson's near perfect attendance record at the hearings refuted.[23]

During the hearings, Jackson, McClellan, and Symington intensified their challenges to McCarthy. The senators and their counsel met every morning to map out a strategy, and then spent hours sitting tensely under the hot lights as the spectacle unfolded. After each day's hearings, Jackson and his staff worked late into the night analyzing the testimony and preparing for the next day's strategy. Sterling Munro remembered that Jackson's office received so much mail—fifteen to twenty bags a day—that the staff could not open all of it: "We did not open the ones with invectives on the envelopes. We opened all the mail from Washington State. It took hours." Throughout the hearings, Jackson collaborated closely with Bobby Kennedy to identify and probe the weak links in McCarthy's case.[24]

Jackson's most dramatic moment during the hearings came on June 11, 1954, the day Ralph E. Flanders, Republican senator from Vermont, announced that he intended to introduce a resolution to remove McCarthy permanently from the committee. Earlier, Jackson and Bobby Kennedy had decided to concentrate their assaults on the qualifications of G. David Schine, for whom Cohn and McCarthy had fought to secure special treatment from the army. On June 2, Kennedy had written Jackson that he could make McCarthy and Cohn look "ridiculous" by approaching the matter of Schine's lack of expertise in an "incredulous way, if you known what I man." Jackson did precisely that. In the afternoon session on June 11, he homed in on Schine, who had instituted a plan to combat communism with "pinups, bumper stickers, and Elks clubs." Jackson's good-humored but probing questions brought laughs throughout the room, and McCarthy looked foolish.[25]

President Eisenhower telephoned Jackson to congratulate him on his performance.[26] Roy Cohn did not. He confronted Bobby Kennedy at the end of the hearings on June 11 and threatened to get Senator Jackson for ridiculing Schine's plan for anticommunist psychological warfare. Kennedy told Cohn that if he had any threat to make to Senator Jackson, he should go right to Jackson. Escalating the confrontation, Cohn asked

Kennedy if he wanted to "fight now." Kennedy shot back, "Don't warn me. Don't try it again Cohn!" When his staff informed him of Cohn's threat, Jackson declared that it was "not the first threat" Cohn had made during the Army-McCarthy hearings. "This is one senator that's not going to be intimidated by anybody," Jackson declared defiantly. He would "continue to go after all the facts."[27] In private, however, he did not dismiss Cohn's threat. He instructed his staff to go through all his files to see if there was anything McCarthy could use against him. With "a couple of cases of beer" in hand, Sterling Munro and five other Jackson staffers spent the weekend of June 12–13 in the attic of the Old Senate Office Building "going through Scoop's record line by line." They found nothing incriminating.[28]

The Army-McCarthy hearings ended on June 17, 1954, with McCarthy in disgrace and his cause in ruins. Michael Barone's careful study of polling data indicates that the majority of American voters had turned against McCarthy even before the hearings. Doubtless the two-month televised spectacle locked him into a downward spiral from which he could not recover. A July 1954 Gallup Poll reported that Americans favored his replacement as head of the investigating subcommittee by a margin of 46 percent to 34 percent. Correspondingly, McCarthy's antics during the hearings had eroded his support in the Senate to a core group of Republican Asia Firsters. On June 30, Senator Flanders introduced his motion to censure McCarthy. On September 27, the Watkins Committee, convened to investigate the Flanders resolution, recommended unanimously that the Senate censure McCarthy for his behavior toward General Ralph Zwicker during the Fort Monmouth hearings. On December 2, 1954, the Senate voted 67 to 22 to censure McCarthy. Jackson cast his vote with the majority.[29]

In the last resort, the publicity that served as McCarthy's most potent weapon destroyed him. It had the opposite effect on Jackson's career, elevating him to a national figure in the Democratic Party. He had attended the televised hearings for more than 160 hours, the most of any member of the committee except the chairman, Senator Karl Mundt, Republican of South Dakota.[30] His office received 21,000 telegrams in six weeks, two-thirds from outside Washington State, 80 percent of which were favorable. Many compared his appearance and demeanor to Jimmy Stewart in *Mr. Smith Goes to Washington*. Commentators also complimented him for his performance during the hearings. George Sokolsky, a prominent conservative columnist and one of McCarthy's great defenders in the media, wrote nevertheless that Senator Jackson appeared on television like the eternal collegian, "young, fresh, and buoyant." Jackson received excellent press even from editorialists who deplored the "circus atmosphere of the hearings" and blamed it on television. The *Springfield Daily News* rhapsodized that, unlike many of the participants, Jackson was no jester, "no specialist in cap and bell performance, but as conscientious a man as ever sat in the upper house of the U.S. legislature." Some even speculated that he should strive for higher office, starting with the vice presidency, possibly, in 1956.[31]

Physically, the Army-McCarthy hearings took a toll on Jackson. From sitting for hours through an ordeal fraught with tension, he developed fibromyositis, a chronic muscular condition causing cramps. An extremely painful attack hospitalized him in December 1954. His doctors recommended a strict regime of regular exercise to alleviate the frequency and the severity of such attacks. Jackson listened. He blocked out time daily in the early evening to work out in the Senate gym: swimming laps, riding the stationary bike, and occasionally lifting weights. For the rest of his life, he followed this regimen scrupulously when the Senate was in session, unless a president or a national emergency beckoned.[32]

With his political power at an end, McCarthy descended into obscurity and the final stages of the alcoholism that killed him. Jackson reacted to McCarthy's swift eclipse by proclaiming that "McCarthyism is no longer an issue."[33] In one sense, he was right. With McCarthy's fall, the salience of domestic subversion as a political issue fell, too. In another sense, however, Jackson underestimated the long-term impact of McCarthyism. McCarthy's irresponsible crusade did great damage to the cause of principled anticommunism that Jackson himself embodied, an anticommunism that gave primacy to confronting the external threat of Soviet expansion rather than the domestic threat of subversion. The backlash against McCarthy spawned, among an increasing number of liberals, the opposite fallacy of anti-anticommunism as paranoid and fundamentally dangerous.[34]

In the immediate aftermath of Joseph McCarthy's censure in December 1954, the prospects of the national Democratic Party and Henry Jackson looked bright. The Democrats had recaptured control of both the

House and the Senate in the off-year elections of November 1954. As a sign of Jackson's enhanced stature and visibility, many Democrats asked him to campaign for them in their home states. He made a trip to Illinois at the request of his friend, Senator Paul Douglas, who ran a close but successful race for reelection.[35] Jackson profited handsomely from the Democrats' recapturing the Senate. In January 1955, he secured assignments to the Armed Services Committee, the Joint Committee on Atomic Energy, and the Interior Committee. He also retained his position on the Government Operations Committee. Collectively, these four committees provided him with a powerful base from which to shape the course of policy in two areas he cared about the most. Through his positions on the Armed Services Committee, the Government Operations Committee, and the Joint Committee on Atomic Energy, Jackson attained a growing mastery and influence in national security and foreign affairs. Through his position on the Senate Interior Committee, he solidified and expanded his political base in Washington State by exerting mounting influence on issues dear to him and his constituents: public power projects, national parks, recreation, logging, mining, and water policy.

DOROTHY FOSDICK AND HYMAN RICKOVER

Jackson's felicitous committee assignments coincided with an equally felicitous addition to his staff: Dr. Dorothy Fosdick, the daughter of Harry Emerson Fosdick, the great pacifist preacher for whom John D. Rockefeller, Jr., had built the Riverside Church in New York. Dorothy Fosdick's personal and intellectual odyssey serves as a reminder that the generation of the 1960s had no monopoly on rebelling against the values of their parents. She rejected her father's pacifism and embraced the worldview of his colleague and rival Reinhold Niebuhr, whose biblically grounded liberal realism staked a persuasive middle ground between utopian idealists "who had too many illusions" and "realists who have too little conscience."[36]

After receiving her A.B. from Smith College and her Ph.D. from Columbia University, Fosdick taught at Smith for four years before joining the State Department in 1942. She came to Senator Jackson's staff after serving more than ten years in the State Department: first as a member of the American delegations to the Dumbarton Oaks and San Francisco Conferences of 1944–45; then as a member of the U.S. delegation to the United Nations between 1946 and 1948; and finally as a member of the

Policy Planning Staff of the Department of State between 1948 and 1953 during the chairmanships of George Kennan and Paul Nitze. By then, she had become a staunch Cold Warrior in the Truman tradition who envisaged the conflict between the Soviet Union and the United States largely as NSC 68 portrayed it. Fosdick also had written several major speeches for Adlai Stevenson, with whom she had an intense love affair that ended in her disappointment during the 1952 presidential campaign. Later, she found out that Stevenson had carried on a secret affair with Alicia Patterson at the same time as his with her. Beyond her feelings of betrayal, she grew increasingly skeptical about Stevenson's capacity as a leader. She thought, as Henry Jackson did, that he lacked the gumption to be president.[37]

Jackson first met Fosdick in 1954 at a dinner during which she impressed him with her considerable expertise and experience. Race, gender, religion, or previous patterns of association rarely inhibited Jackson from appreciating and cultivating gifted people of integrity. Rising above the standards of the times, he had absolutely no reservation about a woman as his principal foreign policy adviser, a role Fosdick would serve with distinction for the next twenty-eight years. Those who knew her best described her as a "dynamo" and "dedicated," someone who represented "incorruptibility."[38] They praised her, too, for her warmth, friendliness, and sense of humor even as she pursued "policy 97 percent of her waking hours." Some of Jackson's close associates have speculated that she may have had a romantic interest. If so, it went unrequited. The Jackson-Fosdick relationship was professional, platonic, and symbiotic. Although Jackson's church attendance had lapsed significantly since he had been in Congress, Fosdick's Niebuhrian liberalism struck a responsive chord in him. His upbringing and formative experiences had instilled in his bones instincts that mirrored hers, rooted in similar strains of Protestant Christianity.[39]

Fosdick did not change Jackson's approach to politics, for they thought alike. They shared a greater optimism than Niebuhr, as a matter of degree, about the innate good sense and decency of ordinary people. In Jackson's case, sober, anti-utopian faith in his fellow Americans to triumph over adversity reflected his background and self-conscious identification as a man of the West, a region where optimism about the fate of the nation has usually run higher than in other parts of the country.[40] Fosdick's major contribution to Jackson's career lay in broadening, deepening, and refining his political sensibilities. She deserves much credit for attracting and helping retain first-rate talent for his staff. Thanks largely to her connections with the academic world, which she diligently promoted, Jackson developed an extraordinary reservoir of unofficial advisers that made him one of the best informed men in the Senate on foreign and national security affairs. Alike in their basic convictions and the steadfastness with which they held them, Jackson and Fosdick also had complementary differences in style and temperament that "made them a perfect match," said Sterling Munro. "Jackson was scholarly and diplomatic; she was scholarly and not so diplomatic. . . . She never stopped being a teacher."[41]

Even before Dorothy Fosdick joined the staff, the freshman senator had begun to demonstrate his prowess in the realm of national security. He intervened to save the career of Captain Hyman Rickover, who was being forced into retirement by a narrow-minded navy promotions board. When he was passed over for promotion a second time in 1952, the law required that he would have to leave the navy. Rickover recounted his plight to then Representative Jackson just weeks after the 1952 election, as they flew out together to the Pacific to observe nuclear tests.[42] Their conversation not only kindled a lasting friendship, with Rickover and his wife frequent guests of the Jacksons in Everett, but also prompted Jackson to act immediately on Rickover's behalf.

An early and enthusiastic advocate of the nuclear submarine program while serving on the Joint Committee on Atomic Energy in the House, Jackson saw Rickover as the driving force in the navy's atomic power program and largely responsible for its progress, including the development of atomic submarines. He derided the navy for failing to recognize the importance of atomic power and the genius of Rickover.[43] Jackson thought the navy's archaic thinking on the nature of warfare bad enough. Worse, he suspected correctly that anti-Semitism was a motive for denying Rickover his promotion to rear admiral.[44] He began lobbying for Rickover even before being sworn into the Senate. On December 9, 1952, he wrote the secretary of the navy asking that the navy justify its decision. He received an unsatisfactory reply. He was "so incensed at the navy for having so flagrantly discriminated against Rickover" that he dropped most of his work for weeks in order to marshal the evidence and material he presented to the Senate Armed Services Committee on March 4,

1953.[45] He informed the Defense Department that he would scrutinize any other promotions the navy recommended with special care should it force Rickover into retirement: a polite but powerful threat that doubtless helped inspire the navy to rethink its position. Conceding that Rickover had an angular personality jarring to military etiquette, Jackson argued that genius must trump manners for the sake of national security. He proceeded to demolish the navy's case that Rickover was replaceable without seriously damaging the nuclear submarine program. For his testimony, he received acclaim from the national press, Rickover himself, and Senator John Stennis, Democrat from Mississippi and chairman of the Armed Services Committee, who thanked him for his "splendid presentation of the Rickover matter."[46] The technical result of Jackson's intervention was to postpone Rickover's retirement for one year to give him time to attain the promotion to rear admiral. In reality, however, it made Rickover's promotion and retention in active service a foregone conclusion for many years to come.

Saving Rickover was not Jackson's only contribution to America's nuclear submarine program. He pressed relentlessly for development and deployment of strategic nuclear submarines: overcoming the reluctance of a naval establishment oblivious to the potentials of this revolutionary technology, and the diffidence of the Eisenhower administration, which was then opposed to accelerating the program for budgetary reasons. Gerald Ford, a participant in the debate as a Republican member of the House Armed Services Committee, credited Jackson, above all others, for the expeditious completion of the nuclear submarine program that he still regards as the most important component of America's strategic nuclear deterrent for the Cold War. So did Admiral Rickover. After the trials of the *Nautilus* nuclear submarine in New London, Connecticut, in January 1955, he wrote Jackson: "I am deeply grateful for the help you gave when it was needed. . . . What we have been able to accomplish is due just as much to your efforts as to those who were more immediately concerned with the design and construction."[47]

THE NEW LOOK IS NOT ENOUGH

With Fosdick on his staff, Jackson grew steadily more assertive and influential on foreign policy and national security. He participated prominently in the stormy defense debate between the Eisenhower administration and the Democrats in Congress. What divided mainstream Republicans and Democrats during the 1950s did not involve the first principles of American foreign policy itself or the fundamental dimensions of the Soviet threat, issues that would create a major fault line in American politics from the late 1960s until the end of the Cold War. The defense debate of the 1950s occurred within the context of a widespread foreign policy consensus, uniting the Eisenhower administration with the vast majority of liberal and conservative Democrats in Congress. Despite his campaign rhetoric of supporting the rollback rather than the containment of communism, President Eisenhower largely accepted the merits of Truman's foreign policy priorities and his assessment of the Soviet threat that NSC 68 had set forth. He infuriated the Asia Firsters in his party by supporting the Europe First policy that President Truman had initiated. Similarly, he shared the postwar consensus that the Truman administration had established on the importance of NATO, the Marshall Plan, and free trade. He adhered to Truman's policy of limiting the war in Korea rather than pursuing total victory. When Red Army tanks rolled into Budapest in 1956 to crush the Hungarian revolt, Eisenhower did nothing to help the Hungarian freedom fighters, repudiating the Republican platform of 1952 that promised to liberate Eastern Europe.[48]

What President Eisenhower and his Democratic critics debated were the military and strategic requirements for meeting America's global responsibilities. Eisenhower's strategy, known as the New Look, departed from the NSC 68 program in several key aspects. Whereas the latter assumed that the economy could sustain a substantially larger defense program with no adverse consequences, Eisenhower did not. The unprecedented high levels of military spending necessary to implement NSC 68's recommendations, he feared, could lead to price controls, regimentation, and economic stagnation that could jeopardize the American way of life. Whereas NSC 68 aimed at a balanced military program of nuclear and conventional forces capable of responding effectively to any Soviet threat in a manner symmetrical to the level of provocation, the New Look placed greater emphasis on nuclear weapons and covert operations. It called for the United States to rely on the threat of using nuclear weapons to deter a wide range of threats to vital U.S. interests. By making this shift in strategy away from NSC 68, Eisenhower believed that the United States could cut back on expensive ground force commitments and reduce somewhat the size of conventional forces.

The president conceived of strategic (i.e., intercontinental) air power, then the principal means of delivering nuclear weapons, as the cornerstone of U.S. deterrence. Also, his administration accelerated the process of equipping ground forces with tactical nuclear weapons to offset the Soviet Union's significant advantage in conventional arms. Eisenhower's emphasis on nuclear weapons paralleled NATO's decision in 1954 to abandon the 1952 Lisbon program, which called for a large conventional ground force capable of defending Western Europe against a massive conventional Soviet attack. The nuclear component of the New Look strategy, otherwise known as the Doctrine of Massive Retaliation, depended heavily on maintaining great U.S. strategic nuclear superiority over the Soviet Union and China. In this way, argued the president, the United States could most cost-effectively deter not only a Soviet or Red Chinese nuclear threat but also conventional attacks on U.S. allies.[49]

Eisenhower's New Look strategy, particularly the Doctrine of Massive Retaliation, alarmed many defense experts, including recently retired General Maxwell Taylor, national security specialists in the civilian community, and a large number of Democrats on Capitol Hill. It was a dangerous gamble, they countered, to rely on nuclear weapons for deterring challenges to vital interests that entailed the use of force substantially below the nuclear threshold. Critics deemed the Doctrine of Massive Retaliation especially dangerous because it might trigger a nuclear war wholly disproportionate to the level of provocation. Also, many worried that once the Soviet Union developed the capacity to destroy American cities with nuclear weapons, it no longer made sense to adopt a defense posture requiring the United States to fight an unlimited nuclear war to meet a conventional or limited nuclear attack on vital interests. Professor Henry Kissinger made this case elegantly in *Nuclear Weapons and American Foreign Policy*, published in 1957, his first book on national security policy to have a seminal impact on the U.S. defense debate.[50]

The Eisenhower administration attempted to address these criticisms within the framework of the New Look by favoring deployment of large numbers of tactical nuclear weapons on the battlefield and devising a strategy of Graduated Deterrence for the use of such weapons. Instead of resorting to an all-out nuclear war, the administration assumed that the United States and its allies could defeat another attack on the scale of the Korean War by using a small number of these tactical weapons in the theater of combat without expanding the geography of the war. Critics replied, however, that this strategy depended on possessing superiority in tactical nuclear weapons. If the Soviet Union deployed such weapons in large numbers, this would render U.S. first use of nuclear weapons not credible, because of U.S. vulnerability to the same kind of attack.[51]

Critics of the New Look approach advocated a strategy of Flexible Response, calling for substantial conventional forces available at all times. Ideally, the United States and its allies should possess in combination forces large enough to deter the Soviet Union or Red China from using its own forces to threaten a vital interest. Like NSC 68, the Flexible Response assumed that deterring the Soviet Union would have to be accomplished in different ways at different levels of violence. Like NSC 68, too, it assumed that the United States could afford the increased spending that developing robust defense capabilities would entail. Proponents argued that Flexible Response would enhance deterrence by making the resort to force more credible. Even were deterrence to fail, the existence of large conventional forces would free the United States from the horrific choice of surrender or nuclear war.[52]

Henry Jackson emerged as an early, eminent, vocal, and severe critic of President Eisenhower's defense strategy and weapons procurement policy. Although Jackson had advocated an all-out expansion of America's atomic weapons program while in the House, he opposed relying "solely on atomic and hydrogen weapons as a means of deterring aggression." He warned that such a policy invited "a grave calculated risk and means the big war or no war," and he disagreed with the administration's program to cut American ground forces and the conventional arm of the air force substantially. He believed that the United States not only should, but could, spend significantly more on defense than the budget-conscious administration deemed prudent. By Jackson's reckoning, the United States could afford to spend up to 15 percent of its GNP on defense, if necessary, without jeopardizing American prosperity. He proclaimed himself "as much in favor of fiscal soundness as the next man" but disagreed with Eisenhower's conception of it. He contended that the United States could pay for the defense establishment it needed by expanding "our economy at an annual rate of 5 or 6 percent, not 1 or 2 percent."[53] Invoking the precedents of World War II and Korea, he assumed the compatibility of significantly higher defense spending with achieving higher rates of growth.

It was in the realm of nuclear preparedness—the heart of the New Look strategy—that Jackson was most relentless. Obsessed with achieving fiscal austerity, the Eisenhower administration, according to Jackson, had dangerously underestimated the pace and scope of the Soviet nuclear weapons program. Jackson warned particularly that the United States trailed in the race to develop intercontinental ballistic missiles (ICBMs), a revolutionary weapons system that threatened to overwhelm the American decisive advantage in strategic bombers (bombers of intercontinental range). On July 30, 1954, he wrote to Charles Wilson, secretary of defense, requesting an answer to the question whether "we have heretofore underestimated the magnitude and effectiveness of the Soviet long-range missile program." In the spring of 1955, as chairman of the Military Applications Committee of the Joint Committee on Atomic Energy, Jackson conducted a series of hearings on the prognosis for Soviet ICBM development and its implications for U.S. strategy. On June 30, 1955, he and the chairman of the Joint Committee, Clinton Anderson, Democrat from New Mexico, submitted to President Eisenhower the findings of these hearings in the form of a five-page classified memorandum entitled "Findings and Recommendations Concerning the International Continental Ballistic Missile." This memorandum exhorted the administration to accelerate its program to develop an ICBM before the Soviets did. Jackson and Anderson also met with Eisenhower to underscore the urgency of their recommendations. On November 14, 1955, Secretary of Defense Wilson assured Jackson that the Department of Defense was "treating the ICBM Program as one of highest priority."[54]

What the Eisenhower administration regarded as high priority did not satisfy Jackson. Throughout 1956, he repeatedly criticized budget cutbacks in the Department of Defense for impeding the progress of the American missile program as the Soviets raced ahead with their own. He warned that the Soviet Union might successfully develop an ICBM before the United States; he blamed the habitual U.S. underestimation of Soviet ballistic missile capabilities on an overconfidence in our technological edge that the record belied. If, he forecast, the Soviets won the race to develop ICBMs, the United States and the "free world would soon face the threat of nuclear blackmail."[55]

He continued to speak out boldly on the need for a "redoubling of the defense effort against the growing might of Soviet Russia" during the first session of the Eighty-fifth Congress, which began in January 1957. On May 27, Jackson delivered on the floor of the Senate a major address, entitled "Ballistic Seapower—Fourth Dimension of Warfare," calling for "the accelerated development of atomic submarines capable of launching nuclear missiles." Acknowledging the difficulties of building an effective missile force, he reasoned that "the arguments for a far greater emphasis on a sea based system are even more compelling." He referred to submarine-launched ballistic missiles (SLBMs) as the fourth dimension of warfare "because it would introduce a new element into military strategy and tactics." Anticipating that U.S. land-based ICBMs and strategic bombers would inevitably become vulnerable to Soviet attack, he worried about the possibility of a Soviet preemptive strike that would make effective retaliation impossible. Submarine-launched missiles offered, in his view, the most promising way to ward off this danger because submarine missiles, unlike land-based ICBMs or strategic bombers, were enormously difficult to locate and even more difficult to destroy:

> The problem faced by an aggressor would be like that of a man trying to find a black cat on a vast and empty plane on a dark, moonless, and starless night. If we rely on land based sites, an aggressor's first surprise blow may be the final blow which makes effective retaliation impossible.
>
> This is where the fourth dimension of warfare is crucial. No matter how fast the enemy missiles travel, they could not eliminate the underseas fleet in one massive assault. Enough submarines would remain intact to strike a crushing counterblow.[56]

Jackson considered interservice rivalry an obstacle to giving the SLBM program the priority it deserved. He lashed out again at "tradition-bound unimaginative carrier admirals" who gave insufficient thought to the striking power of the submarine. He compared their devotion to huge aircraft carriers to their misplaced ardor for battleships on the eve of Pearl Harbor.

Jackson's challenge to President Eisenhower's defense program found a receptive audience within his own party. In the 1950s, the Democratic

Party was generally more hawkish than the Republican Party. It was the Democrats who warned of missile gaps and wanted to spend more on nuclear and conventional forces. It was the Republicans, not just President Eisenhower but conservatives from the Taft wing of the party, who wanted to spend less and resisted Democratic pressure for significant increases in the defense budget. Other prominent Democrats echoed Jackson's critique of Eisenhower's defense strategy. In 1956, Senator Stuart Symington's subcommittee of the Armed Services Committee, on which Jackson served, issued a dire warning that the United States might also face a strategic bomber gap with the Soviet Union. Majority Leader Lyndon Johnson, who cooperated with President Eisenhower more than Republican conservatives did on most issues, criticized the president relentlessly for the inadequacy of his defense and missile program. So did Senator John Kennedy.[57]

The Soviet Union's successful launching of Sputnik, the earth's first artificial satellite, which went into orbit October 4, 1957, intensified the debate. That revelation deeply shook the American people and their leaders. The Soviet Union appeared to be on the threshold of being able to deliver a devastating nuclear attack on the United States with ballistic missiles, a revolutionary weapons system the United States did not yet possess. To Jackson, who called for a "national week of shame and danger," and other Democrats, Sputnik appeared to confirm warnings about the dangers of underestimating the Soviet missile program and proceeding too casually with their own.[58]

Public reaction to the Soviet satellite plus the huge Democratic gains in the off-year election of 1958 altered the political dynamics in favor of those calling for accelerating development and deployment of ICBMs and SLBMs. Until Sputnik, the Eisenhower administration had largely succeeded in fending off these demands. Thereafter, the president found it increasingly difficult to resist the mounting pressure to spend more on defense. Even the Gaither Commission, an advisory group the president himself had assembled to reevaluate his defense strategy, issued a top secret report in late 1957 recommending a substantial increase in U.S. nuclear capabilities similar to what Eisenhower's Democratic critics advocated. Lyndon Johnson said that the space program should be a top priority; John Kennedy called for a return to the principles of NSC 68, which required the U.S. to increase significantly strategic and conventional forces capable of "flexible response"; and Henry Jackson spoke repeatedly of the need for moving faster to develop and deploy the Minuteman ICBM and the Polaris SLBM launched from nuclear submarines.[59] To compensate for the Soviet advantage in ballistic missiles that he presumed would exist until U.S. ICBMs and SLBMs became operational, Jackson advocated building the B-52 strategic bomber. He also agreed with Kennedy and others that the United States must substantially increase its conventional forces, and he pushed "to strengthen education across the board, especially in sciences and languages" so the United States could compete more effectively with the Soviets.[60]

By 1960, these programs had become a reality. After a three-year fight, Jackson prevailed on a reluctant naval establishment that wanted more conventional warships, and a president who wanted fewer ships, to increase from four to nine the number of Polaris submarine platforms slated for early deployment.[61] He cosponsored the National Defense Education Act of 1958, this time with the president's acquiescence, which increased government support for scientific research, government spending on education, and emphasis on the teaching of science in schools.[62] Jackson's charge that a growing missile gap portended dire consequences for the United States also became a major issue for John Kennedy in his 1960 presidential campaign against Vice President Richard Nixon. Although one cannot know for sure how much the charge of a missile gap contributed to Kennedy's exceedingly close margin of victory over Nixon, it certainly helped Kennedy and hurt Nixon.

Immediately after President Kennedy's inauguration in January 1961, his administration asked for large increases in the defense budget to accelerate the missile programs and improve U.S. conventional forces along the lines Jackson advocated. Kennedy discovered just weeks after taking office, however, that the missile gap that he had run on so effectively, and that Jackson had warned about so ominously, did not exist. The Soviets had serious problems with the development of their missile program that American intelligence had failed to detect. Critics of Cold War hardliners such as Jackson have seized upon the "myth of the missile gap" as an object lesson illustrating the danger of overestimating the Soviet threat.[63] Jackson did not see it that way. He conceded, to be sure, that his assessment of the missile gap was mistaken. Based on the information he had at his disposal, however, his concerns were plausible. Recent scholarship has established that the Eisenhower administration worried less about the missile gap during the late 1950s than its Democratic critics, because of the secret intelligence about the Soviet missile program obtained from flights of the U-2 reconnaissance aircraft over the Soviet Union. Jackson was not privy to that information, notwithstanding his Q clearance. The Eisenhower administration withheld it from all of Congress for fear of exposing the source: U-2s overflying the Soviet Union.[64]

The behavior of Soviet Premier Nikita Khrushchev added plausibility to Jackson's concerns about a missile gap. From late 1957 until President Kennedy called the Soviet bluff during the Cuban missile crisis of 1962, Khrushchev engaged in a sustained and systematic campaign of deception claiming that the U.S.S.R. had in fact achieved superiority in ballistic missile technology. He brandished his phantom superiority in an effort to intimidate the West during a series of crises over the status of Berlin in 1958, 1959, and 1961 that culminated in the Soviets erecting the Berlin Wall in August 1961. Khrushchev claimed, too, that the Soviet Union's alleged advantage in ballistic missiles evidenced a dramatic shift in the correlation of forces toward the Soviet Union not only in Europe but also throughout the underdeveloped world, where Soviet support and encouragement of "wars of national liberation" accelerated dramatically.[65]

The myth of the missile gap also stands out as the exception to the general rule about the extent and scope of the Soviet military buildup. In the 1940s, the United States did underestimate the Soviet Union's ability and inclination to produce an atomic bomb. In the 1950s, the Soviet Union did succeed in building a hydrogen bomb and developing ballistic missiles sooner than many experts, though not Jackson, expected. In the late 1960s and 1970s, the CIA did seriously underestimate the Soviet Union's strategic nuclear buildup and resources devoted to defense, notwithstanding Jackson's more accurate assessments.[66]

Chapter 5

Khrushchev's Communism

JACKSON'S INTERESTS extended beyond the military dimensions of the Cold War. By the end of the Eisenhower administration, he had engaged increasingly in the broader issue of formulating and implementing U.S. grand strategy. A fundamental question in the missile gap debate was what the death of Stalin in March 1953 portended for the future of Soviet-American relations. During the Cold War, transitions in the Soviet leadership often stimulated high hopes in the Western democracies that Soviet foreign policy would become more cooperative and conciliatory. Nikita Khrushchev, who reached the pinnacle of his power only after 1957 and held it until his ouster in 1964, appeared fundamentally different from Stalin to many Americans. The initial actions of the post-Stalinist Soviet leadership encouraged the belief that Soviet-American relations had entered a new and more benign era. The year 1955 brought several hopeful developments: a summit meeting in Geneva at which the leaders of the Big Four—the Soviet Union, Great Britain, France, and the United States—spoke amiably to one another; Soviet willingness to withdraw its troops and agree to the neutralization of Austria; and Soviet encouragement of limited de-Stalinization at home and within the Eastern European satellites. Khrushchev's denunciation of Stalin at the Twentieth Party Congress in early 1956 and his frequent assertions of commitment to the policy of peaceful coexistence seemed to mark an even more promising step toward relaxed tensions between East and West.[1]

Within the year, however, Soviet words and deeds had deflated the most lofty expectations. The deterioration in Soviet-American relations stemmed from more than just the missile gap and Khrushchev's relentless attempts to exploit it. The process of de-Stalinization also proved more dangerous and uncontrollable than Khrushchev had expected. Events in Poland and Hungary demonstrated to the Soviet leaders that, left to their own devices, their Eastern European satellites would jettison not only Stalinism but also communism and alignment with the Soviet Union itself. With their Eastern European empire hanging in the balance, and fearful that reverberations of the democratic revolution in Eastern Europe could imperil the Soviet regime itself, Khrushchev determined to maintain Soviet control. In October 1956, the Soviet Union imposed on Poland by thinly veiled threat a political agreement that retained the substance of Soviet influence and ensured the primacy of the Communist Party.

But intimidation and subversion alone would not suffice to avert the democratic revolution unfolding in Hungary. On October 31, 1956, Hungarian Prime Minister Imre Nagy declared that Hungary would no longer be a one-party state and that he intended to withdraw it from the Warsaw Pact. On November 1, 1956, the Soviets responded with a massive invasion of Hungary that brutally restored the authority of Hungarian Communists compliant to Moscow, infuriating American public opinion.[2]

Soviet foreign policy also signified that peaceful coexistence as Khrushchev conceived it did not end the communist quest for victory over the West. Deterred from direct aggression in Europe and Japan by American defensive alliances, and faced with a ring of American-led alliances erected by the Eisenhower administration around the Soviet periphery in a conscious attempt to emulate NATO, Khrushchev and his successors decided to leapfrog these barriers. They revived Lenin's strategy of viewing the West's former colonial areas as ripe for Soviet exploitation. Communist victory, explained Khrushchev, would take place not by nuclear war but by wars of national liberation in Asia, Africa, and Latin America, "the centers of revolutionary struggle against imperialism."[3]

Although many of the militantly nationalistic regimes that proliferated throughout the world during this period of rapid decolonization began as uncompromisingly hostile to communism domestically, the Soviet Union initially possessed some considerable advantages over the United States as the Cold War shifted to this arena. Militant nationalists such as Nasser in Egypt usually directed their venom against the United States and the former imperial powers of the West, whom they tarred as their exploiters. The Soviet Union did not have to stir up trouble in such areas, although it did plenty of that. All that Soviet leaders had to do was exploit the turbulent expressions of nationalism that erupted with or without their involvement.[4]

The moral and productive superiority of market over command economies that the collapse of communism demonstrated in the late 1980s was not self-evident in the 1950s and early 1960s. The success stories of Taiwan, South Korea, and Singapore had not yet emerged to refute the myth of Marxian strategies of development. In those earlier days, the Soviet economic model was seductive because it seemed that perhaps the Soviet Union had succeeded in compressing into a single generation the process of elevating poor nations to the ranks of industrial powers. Also, Khrushchev predicted, and many in the West then feared, that the Soviet union would overtake the United States productively as well as militarily. For many elites in the underdeveloped world, some type of national socialism had the added bonus of justifying their retention of absolute political power in a way that Western-style regimes would not permit.[5]

The Suez crisis of 1956 illustrated how the Soviet Union could successfully exploit militant nationalism to penetrate the Middle East, a region vital to the United States and the Western allies because of its location and vast oil reserves. The main events of this crisis, coinciding with the Soviet invasion of Hungary, need only brief recapitulation. Disturbed by Egypt's growing dependence on the Soviet bloc following the overthrow of the monarchy in 1952, the United States and Great Britain withdrew their offer to finance the Aswan Dam. This precipitated the decision of Egyptian dictator Gamal Abdel Nasser, a militant proponent of Pan-Arab unity, to nationalize the Suez Canal in July 1956. Days after the Hungarian Revolt of 1956, the French, fearful of the repercussions of Nasser's actions on their control of Algeria; the Israelis, harassed by terrorist raids that the rabidly anti-Israeli Nasser sponsored from his territory; and the British, formerly the power of authority in the canal zone, launched a joint invasion that occupied the Sinai region of Egypt and seized the Suez Canal. President Eisenhower then surprised and humiliated his allies, who had not consulted him before acting, by forcing them to return to Egypt what they had captured. To the president's dismay, however, Arab nationalists credited rhetorical Soviet threats to the invaders, rather than American actions, for thwarting the design of the Western imperial powers and their Zionist ally.[6]

The upshot was that Khrushchev genuinely believed that communism was the way of the future.[7] With decolonization proceeding rapidly in Asia and Africa, and the former colonial powers of the West in retreat, great opportunities for Soviet advances seemed to beckon. Khrushchev also hoped that a policy of encouraging and supporting wars of national liberation would help forestall an open break with Communist China, with whom Soviet relations had deteriorated significantly since the mid-1950s. Increasingly disenchanted with Khrushchev's handling of de-Stalinization, with the levels of economic aid the Soviet Union provided China, and with Khrushchev's treatment of ideological questions, Mao had begun to reproach him severely for the Soviet Union's risk-averse approach to confrontation with the United States. The Soviet premier calculated that boldness in the underdeveloped world would help propitiate Mao by demonstrating that the Soviets had not abandoned their commitment to world revolution.[8]

Ultimately, Soviet-American summit diplomacy also did not progress as optimists had anticipated, notwithstanding the cosmetic improvement in superpower relations that 1959 seemed to bring. In August 1959, Vice President Nixon traveled to Moscow, where he engaged Khrushchev in a famous televised debate. During Khrushchev's ten-day tour of the United States in September 1959, the media and American celebrities lavished the Soviet premier with attention. But the U-2 incident of May 1960 precipitated a turn for the worse in Soviet-American relations. The Soviet Union initiated the incident by shooting down a U-2 reconnaissance plane flying over Soviet territory. When President Eisenhower first denied and then later refused to apologize for authorizing the U-2 flights, a practice the Soviets had long known about but chose not to make an issue of until that moment, Khrushchev used Eisenhower's reaction as a pretext for breaking up the summit and canceling the president's scheduled visit to Moscow.[9]

For Henry Jackson, the Soviet Union remained an evil empire bent on the destruction of the West. He dismissed Khrushchev's handling of the U-2 incident as "a ploy the Soviet premier seized upon to torpedo the conference. . . . After all, the Soviet Union, with its first Sputnik, was the first to fly over the airspace of other nations."[10] He warned that Khrushchev's policy of peaceful coexistence was also a dangerous ploy. Even before the Soviet invasion of Hungary, he had declared it "merely as a tactical maneuver, designed to lull the free world into complacency while the Kremlin continued its military buildup and developed a wide-swinging political and economic offensive." Jackson told his Senate colleagues on February 1, 1956:

> The basic aim of the Kremlin remains unchanged—a Moscow domi-nated world. The Soviet rulers stand ready and able to employ every last weapon in the Communist arsenal of conquest. These weapons are well known to you, Mr. President—diplomatic initiative, the smile, psycho-logical pressure, economic warfare, political infiltration, subversion, and military conquest on the installment plan through satellite forces. Beyond that, if the gains appeared worth the cost, the Soviets would not even shrink from an all-out nuclear attack against the American homeland.
>
> Let us pay the devil his due: The overlords of the Communist world are not stupid men. They are skillful practitioners of the art of conquest. They have read their Machiavelli and their Clausewitz, just as they have read their Mein Kampf. Moreover, the Soviets have profited from the mistakes of aggressors in ages past. Unlike Hitler, they might wait for years, or even decades, to achieve their ends. Unlike the rulers of Japan in 1941, they may refrain from acting rashly.
>
> The Kremlin knows that if the opponent can be relaxed, while the Communists are hard at work, time will run in their favor. As Khru-shchev said in India last November:
>
> We can wait. The wind is now blowing in our faces. We can wait for the better weather.[11]

In August 1956, Jackson made a 10,000-mile trip through the Soviet Union, his first and only visit there, taking his own interpreter from the Library of Congress with him. He then made a 5,000-mile trip to the Middle East, the first of many to that region, before returning home in late September. What he observed confirmed and deepened his convic-tions about the gravity of the Soviet threat. "It was easy for a visitor to underestimate the strength of the Soviet Union," he noted, because it seemed "a drab, unhappy land of burdened people." He found the peo-ple—"except for the chosen few" poorly clothed and inadequately housed. They existed on "a meager diet of staples with little variety at the dinner table." He also found Soviet transportation—highway, rails, and air—similarly poor. He cautioned, however, against underestimating the

U.S.S.R. or its people based on these superficial experiences. "By depriving its people of the goods and services Americans take for granted," he said, the Soviet Union had made impressive military and foreign policy strides: producing the H-bomb "before our experts thought it would"; leading the United States "in the race for ballistic missile power"; dispensing "foreign aid—despite the needs of its people—in a manner calculated to impress the more underprivileged areas of the world that the Soviet Union is a land of plenty and the communist method the best way to get things done."[12]

"There was no question," Jackson surmised, "that the present Soviet government was engaged in a large-scale program to destroy the myth of Stalin." Nevertheless, he deplored the repression and antipathy to freedom that he considered the essence of Khrushchev's Soviet Union, not just of Stalin's. He observed, too, that the Soviets kept him and their people under complete surveillance. He commented that most Soviet citizens needed an internal passport to travel in their own country, which gave the government "complete control over the citizenry." He also castigated the Soviets for their systematic repression of religion, a practice he regarded as emblematic of the regime's malignance. Jackson's trip to the U.S.S.R. redoubled his beliefs about the true object of Khrushchev's strategy of peaceful coexistence:

> The Kremlin's center of interest is still Western Europe, notably the military industrial potential of Germany. In time, Russian leaders hope to undermine the NATO alliance, win control of Germany, and exclude us from vital overseas bases.
>
> But the first round in Western Europe has gone against them. Adopting shrewd new techniques, the Kremlin has now turned its sight toward the billion peoples of Asia and Africa. The free world is confronted with an unprecedented threat.
>
> Soviet foreign policy, to state it another way, works something like a burglar going down a hotel corridor, trying each doorknob. When the door is open, in he goes quietly, but accomplishing the work without waking up the sleepers.

Jackson's journey also took him to Kabul, Afghanistan. What he saw there convinced him that the Soviet Union would eventually attempt to make that country a satellite:

By paving the streets of Kabul, and other things the Soviet Union has done in Afghanistan, points up to the fact that the Soviets know how to go about winning friends among the underprivileged areas—and then moving in to take over completely. The Soviets are busy building a highway through the tremendous mountain range—with some peaks as high as 20,000 feat—separating the U.S.S.R. and Afghanistan.

The road will continue across Afghanistan to the border of Pakistan. It will give the Russians a military highway right up to the border of Pakistan—and present the Free World with a grave threat.

From the Soviet Union, Jackson moved on to the Middle East.[13] "The hand of the Soviet Union," he perceived, was "stirring a witches' brew for the Free World in the Middle East." He considered Nasser's Egypt the Soviet Union's chief target and collaborator in the region: "If it isn't clear outside the U.S.S.R., it certainly is obvious that Egyptian dictator Nasser has the full backing of the men in the Kremlin." It was folly, he argued, to think that the West could lure Nasser away from his Soviet connection by propitiating him: "The goals of Nasser are the goals of the Kremlin. The Suez Canal is Nasser's first objective. His second objective is control of the oil-rich Middle East, including the destruction of Israel. His third objective is domination of all Africa."

The Soviet Union did not want all-out atomic war, assured Jackson. "The Kremlin rulers would rather inherit the world than obliterate it," and sought to use Nasser to avoid a shooting war. Similarly, "Nasser no doubt believes that he can use the men of the Kremlin to further his own goals." Either way, Jackson insisted that the West must stop Nasser, equating appeasement of the Egyptian dictator with appeasement of Hitler.

Jackson recommended that the United States pursue two main policies to counter Soviet machinations in the Middle East: first, fully publicize the suppression of religious freedom under communism ("Nothing influences the Arab peoples as much as their religion"); second, do everything possible to ensure that Israel remained strong and secure. In 1956, arriving in Israel for the first time, Jackson was already a firm defender of the Jewish state for moral reasons. His experience there now added a geopolitical rationale: "Israel, an oasis of civilized progress in the Arab World, is one of our main bulwarks against Nasser," he reported. "It is strong both economically and militarily." What especially impressed him was the prowess of the Israeli armed forces:

> The Israeli soldier, bronzed by the sun and hardened by everyday labor, . . . is without a doubt the toughest fighting man in the Middle East today.
>
> More important than the physical condition of the troops is their mental condition—the determination that they cannot and will not retreat from any military position they are given to hold.
>
> An Israeli officer told me that they had a secret weapon—every Israeli soldier or a member of his family has spent time in a concentration camp. The Israelis are determined to defend their new-found freedom with their lives if necessary.[14]

Thus, Jackson voted enthusiastically for the "Eisenhower Doctrine" passed in early 1957 declaring U.S. readiness to use its military force, when the president determined it necessary, to assist any nation in the Middle East requesting such assistance against armed aggression.[15]

Jackson devoted increasing attention during the Eisenhower years to other areas besides the Soviet Union and the Middle East. In late 1955 he made a major trip through East Asia, including a visit to South Vietnam, whose defense against communism he thought pivotal. "It was absolutely essential," he said, "that we be aware of the overwhelming importance of Indo-China in the fight to stop Communist domination of the Far East and the world." From 1956 through 1969, he served as a U.S. delegate to the NATO Parliamentary Conferences in Paris, where he developed an important set of contacts and friendships with members of the defense community in Western Europe. He chaired the special subcommittee that investigated how NATO might more effectively develop its technological talent, the genesis of his cosponsorship of the National Defense Education Act of 1958.[16]

By the end of the 1950s, Jackson's foreign policy views had crystallized into an overarching grand strategy for the United States, which he set forth in a series of speeches. He defined as the fundamental issue of the time whether "a free society can generate and sustain the great national endeavor required to outperform Soviet tyranny." The outcome of the Cold War, he declared, would "determine what kind of world system is to be created on this planet, a communist world system or a world system in which free institutions can survive and flourish." The communists, he insisted, aimed to demonstrate that their system represented the inevitable wave of the future, and "that our friends and allies have no realistic alternative except to join forces with them. Loss of the Cold War could be as final, and fatal, as defeat in an all-out war."[17]

Jackson remained confident about the capacity of the United States to win the Cold War. He predicted in a 1957 Boston speech that the Soviet Union's race to catch up to the United States contained the seeds of Soviet political failure:

> This is the essence of the Soviet dilemma: the Kremlin must grant some freedom in order to maintain technological growth but allowing freedom undermines communist ideology and discipline. Rule by more and more repression can work only at the expense of weakening Soviet standing in the industrial competition with the West. But in a system where there has been few freedoms, the introduction of new freedoms is perilous.[18]

Jackson never took victory for granted, however. The United States would have to persevere in the struggle, which he believed would take years and years of confrontation and discussions with Moscow. He always advocated talking with the Soviets: "I would be the last to suggest that we slam the door on communication." Yet the United States should never forget "that summitry is just another device in the Cold War arsenal. The Soviet rulers think in terms of power. Superior power, they believe, will eventually prevail."

Jackson's concerns about the adequacy of America's policy-making machinery arose from the widespread but erroneous assumption of Cold War liberals that President Eisenhower was a passive president, largely uninformed about critical detail and often a hostage of his staff.[19] Jackson's own experience with Eisenhower in 1955, during the preliminary phase of the missile-gap debate, had stimulated his concern that the National Security Council apparatus in particular might be badly flawed. Why, he wondered, "did it take a letter from the Congress as late as 1955 to induce the President to receive his first full-scale briefing on the status of our ballistic missile programs?"[20]

For the first six months of 1959, Jackson immersed himself in the study of the executive branch's policy-making process by consulting the foremost academic experts on that subject, among them Samuel Huntington, Richard Neustadt, and Warner Schilling of Columbia University, and Roberta Wohlstetter of the University of Chicago. In June 1959, Jackson proposed that his Subcommittee on National Policy Machinery of the Government Operations Committee undertake a comprehensive study of the national policy-making machinery. In July the Senate authorized funds, thus eliciting a cool reaction from the White House. President Eisenhower worried that the committee might infringe on executive prerogative and sensitive issues of specific National Security Council decisions. Also, a committee with too broad a mandate might uncover what Eisenhower may have wanted to conceal and what recent scholarship has revealed: that he was a hands-on, well-informed president who made virtually all major national security decisions by largely bypassing an NSC that was more form than substance. After weeks of negotiations, Jackson and the White House reached a compromise. The committee agreed not to delve into the substance of NSC policies. President Eisenhower agreed, in turn, to endorse the committee's study, which he did by letter to Jackson dated July 10, 1959.[21]

Jackson earned high praise for his conduct of the proceedings and the report the committee produced. Rejecting partisanship, he elicited the cooperation of conservative Karl Mundt of South Dakota, the ranking Republican member of the subcommittee. Before conducting public hearings, he directed his staff, whose key members were J. Kenneth Mansfield, the director; Dorothy Fosdick; and Professor Robert Tufts of Oberlin, to consult a wide range of experts.[22]

Robert A. Lovett, the former secretary of defense and undersecretary of state, one of the wise men of American foreign policy whom Jackson had revered since the late 1940s, led off the public phase of the inquiry with his testimony before the committee on February 23, 1960.[23] Over the next several months, an array of blue-ribbon witnesses followed: Robert Sprague, co-chairman of the Gaither Commission; Allen Dulles, director of the Central Intelligence Agency; Secretary of Defense Thomas Gates; Secretary of State Christian Herter; Thomas J. Watson, president of IBM; Governor Nelson Rockefeller, Republican from New York; General Maxwell Taylor; and George F. Kennan, among others. The committee eventually rejected the multitude of arguments for creating a first secretary or executive vice president to stand between the cabinet secretaries and the president. It called for the elimination of a significant number of interagency committees that it saw as clogging the foreign policy making process. It reaffirmed the secretary of state's right and responsibility to be the president's first adviser. It also emphasized that no government is better than the men and women who are in it. Having Dean Acheson, Robert Lovett, and Paul Nitze in mind, Jackson believed that people with experience and good judgment could surmount faulty organization, but not the reverse; no organizational gimmick could make up for the absence of public servants lacking these essential qualities.[24]

James Reston's front-page article in the *New York Times* of February 26, 1960, hailed Jackson's study as "inquiry at its best." David Broder marveled at the way Jackson conducted the hearings and the results:

> Unlike Capitol Hill extravaganzas that come readily to mind, this probe produced no stormy disputes between Democrats and Republicans. Its chairman was not one accused for trampling on the rights of witnesses or leaking confidential documents to the press. He did not use the investigation to build a political career or even a bureaucratic empire of his own. The staff of the investigation never outgrew a single room. . . . The Senate Committee on National Policy Machinery has won little publicity but it has proved, once again, that congressional investigations can yield more than headlines.[25]

On January 1, 1961, President-elect Kennedy announced that he, too, was "much impressed with the constructive criticism contained in the recent staff report by Senator Jackson's Subcommittee on National Policy Machinery."[26] One of his first executive orders abolished the Operations Coordinating Board of the National Security Council pursuant to the recommendation of the Jackson committee's report.

Chapter 6

Domestic Politics to 1961

Jackson also received high marks for helping break the logjam that had blocked Alaska and Hawaii from achieving statehood: a cause he had championed since the late 1940s along with Senator Magnuson and others from Washington State with longstanding ties to Alaska. As chairman of the Subcommittee on Territories of the Interior Committee of the Senate, he presided over the hearings that eventually produced the Alaskan and Hawaiian statehood bills of 1958 and 1959, respectively. He also deftly managed both bills through the Senate, according to a bipartisan consensus of those most intimately involved with the issue.[1]

Residents of Alaska and Hawaii had already voted by large majorities in favor of statehood. In 1945, President Truman had endorsed statehood for both, and polls indicated that the American public favored that action by a margin of more than three to one. Yet since 1948, the year Jackson introduced his first bill for Alaskan and Hawaiian statehood, several such bills had languished and died in committee, thwarted by a powerful coalition of interests. The Pentagon opposed statehood for fear of losing its free hand in Alaska and Hawaii. Many powerful Southern Democrats opposed Hawaiian statehood for racial reasons—the high proportion of Asian Americans living there. Other Democrats opposed it because they thought the Republicans would dominate in Hawaii, giving the GOP two more senators. Conversely, the Eisenhower administration initially opposed Alaska statehood for fear that the Democrats would dominate there. In both places, ironically, the reverse occurred. The president also had deep reservations about whether much of Alaska had developed sufficiently to justify statehood. Southern Democrats worried, too, that the addition of the two Northern Democratic senators they assumed Alaska would send to Washington would give Northern liberals the upper hand in the battle within the Democratic Party over civil rights.

Jackson worked closely to devise a successful legislative strategy with his friend Clinton Anderson, chairman of the Interior Committee; Thomas Kuchel, Republican senator from California; Fred Seaton, Eisenhower's secretary of the interior who favored statehood for both Alaska and Hawaii; and Seaton's legislative counsel Ted Stevens, who later became a Republican senator from Alaska and a protege of Jackson's. Whenever the issue had come up before, opponents of statehood had insisted on putting forward the two states together. Jackson and his cohorts calculated that they could get statehood through the Congress if Alaska was acted on first, but that the Republicans would never allow Alaska in if Hawaii came first. The "Alaska first strategy" created a major furor, remembered Gordon Culp, a longtime friend of Jackson's who worked on his committee staff to push through the Alaska and Hawaii statehood bills, "because Hawaii was far more developed than Alaska."[2]

Jackson persuaded a reluctant Jack Byrnes, the elected delegate from Hawaii and the territory's official lobbyist, to cooperate. If the Senate could proceed with Alaska first, Jackson pledged that Hawaii would get statehood in the next Congress. Jackson then sent Byrnes to Richard Russell of Georgia, the key senator controlling what the Southern bloc would do. Russell assured Byrnes, whose political future hinged on Hawaii obtaining early statehood, that he would support it in the next Congress and for that matter would "strangle anybody in the South who tried to oppose it." At Jackson's instigation, Lyndon Johnson of Texas, the majority leader, made Byrnes the same promise. Byrnes thus agreed not to object to Alaska going first.

There were still more hurdles for Jackson to clear. As Ted Stevens recalled, Section 10 of the Alaska Statehood Act lurked as the most serious obstacle. Section 10 granted the president of the United States special powers in a large area of northwestern Alaska, including the authority to declare martial law, normally a prerogative of the presidency only in wartime. Concerned that this region lacked the attributes to provide government for itself, Eisenhower had pushed for the inclusion of Section 10 in the House version of the bill. Those who opposed Alaska statehood attacked Section 10. Jackson also had doubts about the legality of this provision, but calculated that the pro-statehood coalition could not permit the Senate to amend the bill (identical to the House version) on the floor, lest it go to Conference Committee, where it was likely to die. There also was controversy over how much land should be granted to the state. In an effort to scuttle the bill by largesse, Representative Arthur Lewis Miller, Republican from Nebraska, kept increasing the land grant to Alaska in the House version of the bill, from the 20 million acres that Alaska delegate Bob Bartlett had asked for to 103.5 million acres. Miller calculated that this so-called giveaway of federal lands would cause major problems in the Senate.

Jackson managed, however, to keep his colleagues in the Senate on target. The Alaska Statehood Act passed by a wide margin. So did the Hawaiian Statehood Act in the next session of Congress. These were, according to Ted Stevens, among the great legislative achievements of Jackson's career. The discovery of oil in Cook Inlet, Gordon Culp speculated, may have had something to do with why Southern Democrats, particularly those from major oil-producing states such as Russell Long's Louisiana, had a positive change of heart about Alaska statehood at a critical juncture of the debate. The people eager to drill for oil believed that they would have a better chance getting the laws, land, and leasing permits they needed if Alaska became a state.

An apostle of nuclear power as a source of energy, Jackson also fought successfully during the 1950s for the authorization of two new reactors at Hanford, Washington—a plutonium recycle reactor designed to determine the feasibility of using plutonium for peacetime as well as for military purposes, and a convertible dual-purpose reactor capable of producing electric power as well as plutonium. He spoke throughout the country stressing the great potential of atomic power for peacetime use. He envisaged nuclear power supplementing hydroelectric power to maintain Washington State's comparative advantage in providing the abundant, low-cost energy on which the growth of the state's economy largely depended.[3]

Jackson had less success in his efforts to expand the federal government's role in providing cheap hydroelectric power. Philosophically committed to private enterprise, President Eisenhower wanted the federal government out of the public power business. Jackson and Eisenhower had their first face-to-face disagreement on the issue in late 1955 during the dedication of the McNary Dam on the Columbia River between Washington and Oregon. Flying out to a dam site on the president's plane, Jackson lectured White House correspondents on the importance of federally constructed dams as Eisenhower played bridge. But Eisenhower's speech made clear that he did not believe the federal government should have built the dam. He pointed to a privately built bridge as an example of the way such projects should be done.[4]

This disagreement previewed a larger debate. For two years, Jackson and other pro-public power Democrats from the West clashed with President Eisenhower over whether the federal government should build a dam at Hells Canyon along the Snake River in Idaho. Eisenhower favored leaving to the privately owned Idaho Power Company the responsibility for developing dams along the Snake River. As a compromise, the president proposed for Hells Canyon in particular and all major projects in general that the federal government would provide for flood control, navigation, and irrigation projects affected by these dams; the private utilities would build and finance the dams in partnership with the federal government.[5]

Jackson objected. What the president proposed contradicted his long-standing, passionately held philosophy on matters of public power. He favored a multipurpose program with all of these elements, including reclamation and public power, supporting the payment for a riverwide development plan that the federal government would administer. The division of responsibility that the president advocated, he complained, meant giving private interests the profitable part, leaving the federal government with the unprofitable part, and hence sticking the American taxpayer with the bill. Joined by his Democratic colleagues in the Senate from the Pacific Northwest, Jackson emphasized that Washington and Oregon had developed and prospered because of the cheap energy generated from large projects that only the federal government had the resources and public interest to undertake.[6]

Jackson's coalition was not strong enough to prevail. In 1957, the Senate voted 45 to 38 to support the Hells Canyon Dam, due largely to the support of Lyndon Johnson, who brought several powerful senators along with him. But the measure died in the House. The defeat of the Hells Canyon Dam signaled the end of an era. Henceforth, Jackson and Magnuson had to abandon their cherished goal of undertaking a truly comprehensive development of the Columbia River through a Columbia Valley Authority modeled after the TVA. For the remainder of the Eisenhower administration, federal involvement in major new public power projects virtually ceased. Meanwhile, local utility districts and private entities stepped in to fill the vacuum.[7]

The legislative battles over Alaska, Hawaii, and Hells Canyon all were linked to the conflict brewing in the Democratic Party over civil rights. This was the main fault line that threatened to divide the party and the nation during the 1950s as much as foreign policy and national security did from the late 1960s until the end of the Cold War. Racial considerations had a major influence on how Southern Democrats positioned themselves on Alaskan and Hawaiian statehood. Liberal critics have accused Jackson, Frank Church, Clinton Anderson, Warren Magnuson, and other Democratic liberals of accepting a watered-down civil rights bill, which the Congress passed in 1957, in exchange for the support of Southern Democrats for the Hells Canyon Dam.[8]

Throughout the 1950s and 1960s, Jackson voted with his fellow Northern Democratic liberals for virtually every piece of landmark civil rights legislation. Others, however, played a more prominent role in these battles. So the importance of understanding Jackson's record on civil rights lies primarily in what it reveals about the cleavages running through the Democratic Party. A combination of two circumstances accounted for Jackson's comparatively lower profile on this pivotal issue. In the first place, his committee assignments reflected and reinforced his legislative priorities: foreign policy, national security, natural resources, energy, the environment. In the second place, the Senate of the 1950s and 1960s operated much differently than it does today. Senators had much smaller staffs, tightly circumscribing their capacity to develop areas of expertise outside their committee jurisdictions. The institution rewarded seniority and knowledge. Senators who tried to lead on every issue would end up leading on none. Typically, senators would defer to other members whom they trusted in areas beyond their province. On civil rights, Jackson followed the lead of other Northern liberals, such as Senators Paul Douglas of Illinois and Hubert Humphrey of Minnesota, just as many others deferred to him on foreign policy and defense matters.

Jackson had excellent personal and working relationships with many of the leading Southern Democrats of his day, in spite of his abhorrence for their segregationist views. He particularly admired chairman of the Armed Services Committee Richard Russell of Georgia, and Russell's successor, John Stennis of Mississippi.[9] Yet his cooperation with Southern

Democrats never extended to civil rights. On the contrary, he joined with other Northern Democratic liberals to denounce the Southern Manifesto of March 1956 opposing desegregation, which all the national politicians of the South signed, except for majority leader Lyndon Johnson; Senator Albert Gore, Democrat from Tennessee; and Estes Kefauver, Jackson's closest friend in the Senate.[10]

Jackson's rationale for his vote on the Civil Rights Bill of 1957 proves the rule of his staunch liberalism on matters of race. Early that year, the House had passed a strong civil rights bill prepared by Herbert Brownell, Eisenhower's pro-civil rights attorney general.[11] The overwhelming support of the House Republicans—conscious of the legacy of Lincoln—and Northern Democratic liberals provided the margin of victory. In the Senate, however, the bill encountered powerful opposition from Southern Democrats who controlled the major committees and constituted a sufficiently large bloc to filibuster successfully. Torn between the northern and southern factions of his party, burning with ambition to get the Democratic presidential nomination in 1960, genuinely committed to civil rights but well aware of what the politics of the Senate would bear, Lyndon Johnson sought a compromise that was palatable to all sides. He secured an amendment to the bill requiring a jury trial in voting rights cases, the effect of which was essentially to neuter it, because white Southern juries would never cast the unanimous vote for conviction that civil rights cases required. Jackson joined several western liberals, southerners, and a few Republicans to support the amendment.[12] The evidence suggests that Johnson's promise to back the Hells Canyon Dam influenced Jackson less than his genuine but naive belief that the right to a jury trial was a fundamental American principle that white southerners would apply fairly in the era before desegregation.[13] Like his fellow liberals from the West, Jackson also believed that even a flawed civil rights bill was better than none at all—the likely outcome minus the jury trial amendment.

Jackson's approach to the major issues of the Eisenhower era reveals important aspects of his character that over the years would contribute mightily to his longevity, accomplishments, and legacy as a statesman. Utopianism held no allure for him. He was a meliorist, striving more modestly for gradual but significant improvement in people's lives and keeping in mind that the search for the perfect was the enemy of the good. For him, compromise was honorable and necessary so long as it did not conflict with his fundamental principles. As the relationship he forged with his constituents attests, he was attentive to public opinion without being a slave to it.

Jackson's run for reelection to the Senate in 1958 showed that he was continuing along the road to becoming the most popular politician in the history of Washington State. In the Democratic primary, he crushed his opponent Alice Franklin Bryant, a peace candidate whose criticism of his support for the military did not even register with the voters. Then Jackson trounced his Republican opponent, William "Big Bill" Bantz, in the general election, winning more than 67 percent of the vote.[14] Academics and political philosophers have generally employed two, dichotomous theories in explaining the political behavior of representatives in a democracy. The "agency" view holds that decisions should be based mainly on the convictions of the majority of constituents rather than on what an individual elected representative believes to be in the national interest. The "Burkean" model (named after the great British statesman Edmund Burke) holds that those who govern should base their decisions on their informed judgment of what best serves the nation rather than on what public opinion wants. In the case of American politics in general and Henry Jackson in particular, a more complex but interesting approach lies somewhere in the middle of the spectrum.[15]

What allowed Jackson after 1968 to defy the prevailing dovishness within his own party was the enormous political capital he had amassed in satisfying the interests of his constituents. In the 1950s, he believed fervently in what was then popular in Washington State: maintaining a vigilant deterrent to an evil and dangerous Soviet empire; spending more on the military to boost Boeing, the Bremerton Shipyard, and the Hanford nuclear complex; spending more on public power projects critical to the state's development; maintaining the federal government's protection of labor unions especially powerful in a state that ranked third in the number of workers per capita belonging to organized unions; and spending more on farm subsidies and irrigation projects important to the agricultural eastern part of the state.

Jackson's popularity arose from more than just the views he espoused. He could also deliver on what he promised, thanks to a felicitous combination of knowledge, diligence, committee assignments, and a close working relationship with Senator Magnuson, sitting on the powerful Appropriations Committee. From the fifties through the seventies, Washington State received so much federal money that Jackson and Magnuson became known as the "gold dust twins." Under their patronage, cooperation and coordination became a hallmark of the Washington State delegation in Congress.[16] Their close collaboration also encompassed the partisan politics of the state, where both exerted a powerful influence on the local Democratic Party. While the Senate was in session, Jackson and Magnuson met every morning to plot out how to provide assistance for the constituents they deemed most in need. Traditionally, each senator's administrative assistant served as titular chairman for the other's reelection campaign.

As one of the consummate insiders in the Senate, Magnuson wielded even greater influence there than Jackson until the 1960s, except on matters of foreign policy and national defense. Magnuson was "an archetypical man's man" who "loved the good life" but "was conscientious of his Senate duties," records Harry McPherson, a high-level aide to Lyndon Johnson during the 1950s. "Maggie knew the game well. . . . He and Lyndon Johnson were fast friends."[17] Magnuson could never approach Jackson's level of popularity in Washington State. While Magnuson's well-indulged taste for young, attractive women and good liquor and his softer views on national defense drove away many Republicans and independents, Jackson's record and personal demeanor attracted their support. This was a source of great strength, especially in a state with a weak party system that did not restrict voting eligibility in primaries to registered party members but permitted Republicans, Democrats, and independents to vote in the primary of their choice.

Washington voters not only agreed with Jackson, but liked, admired, and trusted him. "Running for reelection is like selling soap," he explained. "People have to believe in you; you have to convince them that you deserve their trust. They vote for you out of respect, not because of the way you vote in the Senate. If they think you are a damn fool, your vote isn't going to change their mind."[18] Public affection for Jackson ripened slowly but steadily the more people got to know him, and he made sure that almost everybody in the state did get to know him. What many politicians found tedious he found exhilarating: touring, meeting his constituents, and talking incessantly with local Democratic officials. He had boundless energy for it. Even when the Senate was in session, he would take a red-eye flight back to Seattle on weekends so he could listen and speak to gatherings of people across the state. When Congress was in recess, those activities consumed even more of his time. He frequently spent his lunch hour in the Senate entertaining constituents from the state, sometimes capping off a visit by giving them a personal tour of the Capitol. By the sheer force and number of all these one-on-one and small group encounters, he conveyed his genuine empathy for people and their problems. He did not talk down to or pander to people. The voters of Washington State appreciated his robust confidence in the American people's ability to understand and solve difficult and complex problems.[19]

There were, indeed, few men in politics who worked harder or longer at it than Henry Jackson. For him, politics was not everything; it was the only thing. He did not smoke. He did not drink. He did not go to the symphony or listen to music of any kind. He did not follow professional sports. He did not really have any hobbies. Nor did he socialize with many of his Senate colleagues except his friends Estes Kefauver and John Kennedy.[20]

Even though he had emerged as a prominent and knowledgeable critic of President Eisenhower's defense policy, Jackson had not become part of the Senate's inner club. Harry McPherson described him as "steady, serious, and ambitious, a hard-liner in military affairs . . . , but something of a loner interested in arcane matters like national security policy machinery."[21] Jackson and Lyndon Johnson had not yet developed the rapport with one another apparent during the late 1960s, when the controversy over the Vietnam War drew them together. The two men had a cool relationship during Johnson's tenure as Senate majority leader. Although Jackson respected Johnson for his legislative ability and praised him for his courageous decision not to sign the Southern Manifesto of 1956, he disliked his arm-twisting methods and overbearing personality. He also detested Johnson's majority whip, Senator Robert Kerr of Oklahoma, who equally detested Jackson. Kerr struck Jackson as a crass and unprincipled defender of oil interests, in which the state of Oklahoma and the senator, an oilman himself, had a stake.[22]

Newspapers and magazines often referred to Henry Jackson as one of Washington's most eligible bachelors. One year he even made the Ten Most Eligible Bachelors' list. But he seemed to have no clue to the boundless opportunities that surrounded him. "Eligible women who wanted to become Mrs. Scoop Jackson were omnipresent," remembered Peggy MacDonald Heily, who began working as an appointments secretary on his staff in 1956. "But Scoop was more interested in his job."[23] According to one story, typical of Jackson, two of his aides struck up a conversation with some young women in a bar at a Vancouver, Washington, hotel while the senator worked in his room. They mentioned not only that Jackson was their boss but that he was right upstairs. This news had the intended effect of impressing the young women tremendously. Hoping to lure the senator to join them, the less inhibited of the two aides phoned Jackson to tell him that there were some young women who were very interested in talking with him about politics. Jackson put aside his work, arrived at their table, and ordered an orange juice. After nearly an hour lecturing the young women about national affairs, oblivious to their adoring gazes, he returned to his room to resume his work.[24]

In the late 1950s, Alice Langer, daughter of Republican Senator William Langer of North Dakota, attracted more of Jackson's sporadic romantic interest than any of the other women he occasionally dated. He would regularly see Miss Langer in Seattle, where she lived, during his frequent trips home. There is no indication that they contemplated marriage. As Jackson himself put it in 1958, "I am not foreclosing the idea of marriage by a long shot, but I find it easy to postpone."[25] Shortly after Miss Langer accompanied Jackson to President Kennedy's inaugural ball in January 1961, their relationship ended amiably.

For as long as she lived, his mother, Marine, remained the most important woman in his life, his role model and source of inspiration. While in Washington State, he still lived with her and his two sisters, Gert and Marie, in his boyhood home in Everett. Marie assumed most of the cooking and housekeeping duties as Marine Jackson grew more elderly. Gert, still a third-grade teacher at the Garfield School, remained as devoted as ever to Henry, serving as an invaluable source of local information and gossip. She handled many of the practical aspects of his life—from car insurance to travel plans and taxes—for which he had little interest or aptitude. On February 19, 1957, Marine Jackson died at home, eight days before her ninetieth birthday.[26]

Jackson's life in Washington, D.C., revolved almost entirely around the office. He maintained a grueling pace, working twelve to fourteen hours a day, six and sometimes seven days a week. His idea of a fun evening was poring through classified documents (accessible via his Q clearance) that detailed the characteristics of new weapons systems. When John Salter married in 1955, Jackson moved from the third floor of Bob and Frances Low's house to a one-room apartment at 2500 Q Street in Georgetown, notable for the astonishing modesty of the decor and furnishings. He had stacks of newspapers piled all over the apartment. His one and only radio was so old that part of its cover had fallen off, exposing the tubes. He did not have a full set of dishes or silverware. When, occasionally, he did entertain, his guests would receive their cocktails in a jelly glass or other unconventional glassware. He never ate lunch or dinner at home. For a treat, he and his staffers would go to the cafeteria in the Old Methodist Building a few blocks away from his office in the Russell Building. Usually, he dined in the Senate cafeteria or dining room, where he indulged his taste for cornbread and towering hot fudge sundaes that he battled to work off with his daily swims, stationary bicycle riding, and weight lifting at 5:30 P.M. in the Senate gym.[27]

One of the most remarkable aspects of Jackson's character was the veneration he evoked from the hundreds of people who worked for him over the years, a subject to which this book will return periodically. His relationship with his then small staff of twelve during the 1950s illustrates why. He not only encouraged them to take the initiative in their jobs, but also treated them as part of his family. He was always accessible to his staff, sometimes too accessible, recalled Julia Cancio and Erna Miller: "It used to drive the administrative assistants crazy." Secretaries and committee staff streamed into his office for all sorts of advice that Jackson loved to dispense: career, personal, professional, and medical. There was one proviso, according to Bill Van Ness: "If you went to Scoop for advice, you had better be prepared to listen. He was relentless."[28]

From the hundreds of examples available, the following three exemplify the paternal side of Henry Jackson that those who worked for him found so endearing. Sterling Munro recalled having his commanding general summon him while serving as a buck private in basic training at Fort Sill, Oklahoma. Senator Jackson had called that morning because Munro's mother had complained to Jackson during a stop in Bellingham, Washington, that Sterling had not written home. Loathe to incur the senator's wrath, the general ordered Munro "to please write his mother" as Jackson admonished. For Peggy MacDonald Heily, his appointments secretary, "Jackson was a true friend whose reaction never disappointed me." She remembered Jackson returning from the Senate gym and finding her "crying, head down on the desk" because her date had insulted her terribly. "You know men are terrible creatures anyway," Jackson assured her. He consoled her until she felt better. Noreen Lydday Potts, a native of Everett who joined Jackson's staff in 1958, fondly recalled Jackson inviting her mother and aunt to lunch in the Senate dining room during their visit to Washington. As they were about to go, Dorothy Fosdick came up to ask Jackson to eat instead with her and "some important people with whom he should talk." Miss Potts and her relatives offered to postpone the lunch. Jackson would not hear of it. He spent the next two hours reminiscing with them about Everett and getting the latest update, interrupting the conversation only momentarily to pay a courtesy visit to the table of the perturbed Fosdick and her guests.[29]

Jackson's staff had only one activity they all wished avidly to avoid: driving with him. He remained a menace behind the wheel and a terrible backseat driver who blithely disregarded any obstacle in his path or traffic law on the books. Stuck in traffic outside National Airport in Washington, D.C., he once commanded John Salter to drive his sports car across the median strip so he would not miss his flight to Seattle.[30]

During his first eight years in the Senate, Jackson counted heavily on Salter, though Salter was not particularly conscientious about his administrative duties. Often he did not even return phone calls. He had a sarcastic, biting wit that would often amuse but sometimes antagonize, and he had no illusions about his personality. On the afternoon that the Congressional Class of 1958 took the oath of office, Joe Miller took Salter to the Carroll Arms, a favorite drinking spot near the Capitol, where they met Howard Cannon, the new Democratic senator from Nevada. "Salter asked Cannon how many votes he had won. 'Forty-six thousand,' answered the senator proudly. Salter replied, 'I would not be worth a damn in your state. I alienate that many people in a single day.'"[31]

Salter was, however, an excellent listener whom Jackson had not yet surpassed in political savvy. It was Salter as much as Jackson who developed and sustained the impressive array of organizational and personal ties in Washington State that made Jackson such a formidable political figure there by the late 1950s. It was Salter who served as Jackson's entrée to the Kennedy clan: first with John Kennedy and then with Bobby. It was

Salter who persuaded Jackson to become the first and only senator to endorse the Massachusetts senator for president before the Democratic
Convention of 1960. It was the combination of Salter's connections, far-
sightedness, and dogged determination, as much as anything, that nearly
persuaded John Kennedy to name Jackson as his vice presidential candidate. As Theodore White reported in his classic *The Making of the President, 1960,* Salter even attended the historic meeting at Hyannisport on
Wednesday morning, October 28, 1959, where the Kennedy entourage
mapped out the strategy that launched John Kennedy's 1960 campaign.[32]

Of course, Salter's courtship of the Kennedys does not account exclusively for Jackson's emergence as a serious vice-presidential contender.
Jackson's performance during the Army-McCarthy hearings of 1954 had
established his reputation across the nation as a man of thoughtfulness
and integrity, a reputation that his subsequent record in the Senate had
underscored. By 1960, Jackson had attained national recognition for his
record on national defense and foreign policy, issues that seemed to loom
large for the forthcoming presidential race between Kennedy and Vice
President Nixon. Also, Jackson and Kennedy respected one another despite vastly different temperaments which precluded a truly close personal connection. Kennedy had often cited and incorporated into the *Congressional Record* Jackson's statements on national security matters.[33]
Bobby Kennedy's high regard for and friendship with Jackson, dating back
to the Army-McCarthy hearings, inclined John Kennedy to be even more
favorably disposed. Politically, Jackson seemed to have the profile that the
Catholic, eastern, and patrician Kennedy would likely look for to balance
his ticket: he was a Protestant, a westerner, and a man of modest origins.
For his part, Jackson found Kennedy's political outlook and optimism
congenial. He also rated the Massachusetts senator as a much stronger
presidential candidate than any of the other likely Democratic alternatives
for 1960: the twice-defeated Adlai Stevenson, who had an unappealing
streak of irony and disdain for the common views of Americans; and Senate Majority Leader Lyndon Johnson, who had an abrasive personality
and limited appeal outside the South.[34]

Jackson pursued the Kennedy connection early and actively despite the
misgivings of some of his friends and advisers about John Kennedy's seriousness, electability, and competence. Kennedy received only a cool re-

The young Henry Jackson. (Henry M. Jackson Papers, University of Washington Libraries)

Congressman Jackson accompanying his parents, Peter and Marine Jackson, in the mid-1940s. (HMJ Papers, UW Libraries)

Congressman Henry M. Jackson in the early 1940s. (HMJ Papers, UW Libraries)

Congressman Jackson and Senator Warren G. Magnuson with President
Harry Truman at a White House bill signing, 1949. (HMJ Papers, UW
Libraries)

Senator Jackson playing softball on the Georgetown, D.C., playing fields in the mid-1950s, with catcher Senator John F. Kennedy and umpire Senator Mike Mansfield. (HMJ Papers, UW Libraries)

Senator Jackson and Dorothy Fosdick (kneeling) with the staff softball team. (HMJ Papers, UW

Senator Jackson with Senator Stuart Symington and Robert Kennedy
during the Army-McCarthy hearings in 1954. (HMJ Papers, UW
Libraries)

Senator Jackson and Rear-Admiral
Hyman Rickover behind the wheel of
the USS Nautilus. (HMJ Papers, UW
Libraries)

Senator Jackson with President Harry Truman and Senator John F. Kennedy in 1960. (HMJ Papers, UW Libraries)

Senator Jackson with Senator Warren G. Magnuson and President John F. Kennedy in the oval office. (HMJ Papers, UW Libraries)

Senator Jackson, Jacqueline Kennedy, and President John F. Kennedy at Kennedy's inauguration ball in January 1961. (HMJ Papers, UW Libraries)

The Jackson family in 1966: Henry, Peter, Helen, and Anna Marie.
(HMJ Papers, UW Libraries)

The Jacksons' home in Everett, to which they moved in 1967. (HMJ Papers, UW Libraries)

A mainstay of the Sunday morning television news programs, Jackson appears here on Face the Nation. (HMJ Papers, UW Libraries)

Senator Jackson inspecting American facilities in South Vietnam, 1966. (HMJ Papers, UW Libraries)

Senator Jackson inspecting the battlefield in Vietnam, 1966. (HMJ Papers, UW Libraries)

Senator Jackson conferring with President Lyndon B. Johnson, 1966.
(HMJ Papers, UW Libraries)

In the oval office with
President Lyndon B.
Johnson, 1966. (HMJ Papers,
UW Libraries)

Senator Jackson with Israeli Prime Minister Golda Meir, 1971. (HMJ Papers, UW Libraries)

(opposite page) Senator Jackson conferring at the White House with President Richard M. Nixon and his National Security Advisor, Henry A. Kissinger. (HMJ Papers, UW Libraries)

Henry and Helen Jackson. (HMJ Papers, UW Libraries)

Henry Jackson takes a stroll with his children, Anna Marie and Peter. (HMJ Papers, UW Libraries)

Dorothy Fosdick and Richard Perle. (HMJ Papers, UW Libraries)

Senator Jackson introduces Alexander Solzhenitsyn to Senate colleagues in July 1975 after President Ford decides against inviting Solzhenitsyn to the White House. (HMJ Papers, UW Libraries)

Senator Jackson on the stump during the 1976 Democratic Presidential primaries.
(HMJ Papers, UW Libraries)

A buoyant Senator Jackson brandishes the *Boston Herald* headline proclaiming his victory in the Massachusetts Democratic Presidential Primary, March 1976. (HMJ Papers, UW Libraries)

A working lunch at the White House, 1977: (from left) Senators Abraham Ribicoff and Henry M. Jackson, Vice President Walter Mondale, National Security Advisor Zbigniew Brzezinski, Senator Edmund Muskie, and President Jimmy Carter. (HMJ Papers, UW Libraries)

Senator Jackson meets with President Carter at the White House. (HMJ Papers, UW Libraries)

Senator Jackson with Henry Kissinger in the late 1970s. (HMJ Papers, UW Libraries)

Senator Jackson meets with
Egyptian President Anwar Sadat
and his wife, Jehan, at their villa
on the Nile. (HMJ Papers,
UW Libraries)

Senator Jackson and Senator Jacob Javits with Israeli Prime Minister
Menachem Begin. (HMJ Papers, UW Libraries)

Henry Jackson and Deng Xiaoping, the Great Hall of the People, Beijing, 1983.

In the rose garden of the White House, Helen Jackson accepts the Medal of Freedom from President Reagan, which the President awarded to Henry M. Jackson posthumously, June 1984.

Senator Jackson and President Ronald Reagan, the White House, 1983.
(HMJ Papers, UW Libraries)

Senator Jackson riding his bike no-hands in Everett, 1972. (HMJ Papers, UW Libraries)

ception at a gathering that Jackson held for him at the Rainier Club in Seattle during a visit to the state in 1959. Sterling Munro had an extremely negative reaction the previous year to a speech he heard Kennedy deliver to a meeting of Young Democrats in the District of Columbia: "Of all the speakers on the program, Kennedy was the worst. You would have never picked out Jack Kennedy as this glamorous and persuasive orator. That came later and very well. Even on the way to Los Angeles, Scoop was very concerned that they were going to make him look ridiculous."[35]

Jackson believed, however, that Jack Kennedy had a steep learning curve. After winning smashing victories in the Wisconsin, West Virginia, and Oregon primaries of 1960, he rolled to the nomination. Senator Hubert Humphrey's failure to carry Wisconsin, a neighboring state demographically similar to his own Minnesota, eliminated him as a plausible contender fro the nomination. His failure to defeat Kennedy in Protestant West Virginia killed the chance for a deadlocked convention, on which the hopes of Kennedy's other rivals—Lyndon Johnson, Stuart Symington, and Adlai Stevenson—depended. Henceforth, previously skeptical party bosses jumped on the Kennedy bandwagon. By the time the Democratic Convention convened in Los Angeles in July 1960, Kennedy not only had sewn up the nomination but seemed well positioned to run a strong campaign in the general election.[36]

The political tide, too, appeared to be running the Democrats' way. The recession of 1957–58 contributed significantly to the huge Democratic majorities in the House and the Senate that the off-year election of 1958 yielded. Kennedy would not have to run against Dwight Eisenhower, the popular incumbent probably no one could have beaten. Although everyone expected Vice President Nixon to be a formidable opponent, he had serious liabilities as a candidate, which Kennedy and the Democrats thought made him vulnerable. Unlike Eisenhower, who united the nation, Nixon polarized it. A large bloc of voters perceived him as expedient rather than principled, a political opportunist who did not really have core beliefs. Many also disliked him for his aggressive partisan style while serving in the House, Senate, and vice presidency, where he sometimes skirted dangerously close to the boundaries of truth.[37] By July 1960, the U-2 crisis also had eroded the Republican Party's edge over Democrats in the polls on the issue of which party could better keep the country out of a major war, a development that did not auger well for Nixon, who planned to make a major campaign issue of his experience in national security affairs and Kennedy's lack of it.[38]

So Jackson arrived in Los Angeles buoyant about his party's prospects and his own. His team had assembled an impressive organization to lobby all the state delegations to choose Jackson as the vice presidential candidate for Kennedy. John Salter, Sterling Munro, and Gerry Hoeck directed the overall effort from Jackson headquarters. They assigned Russ Holt, Jackson's speech writer, the responsibility for disseminating up-to-date information about the Jackson record and ensuring that Jackson met as many delegates as possible in their caucuses and business meetings. Publicly, Jackson downplayed his campaign. He announced that "he would accept the nomination," but that no one runs for it.[39] From his demeanor and the concerted campaign his organization mounted, however, it was obvious that he wanted very much to be John Kennedy's running mate.

Jackson's vice presidential bid seemed to gain momentum during the first week of July. The July 4 issue of *Time* listed him as a leading contender for the nomination. He was endorsed by the Alaska and Hawaii delegations, Senator Mike Mansfield of Montana, Senator Frank Moss of Utah, and Representative Stewart Udall of Arizona.[40] Governor Pat Brown of California also indicated that he leaned in Jackson's direction. By the eve of Kennedy's nomination on July 13, the national press had narrowed the field of viable candidates to Jackson, Symington, and Governor Orville Freeman of Minnesota. Jackson also had a powerful ally in Bobby Kennedy, who declared that day that Henry Jackson was his first choice to run with his brother.[41] Privately, Bobby promoted Jackson's candidacy to several delegations. The late Secretary of State Edmund Muskie, then a freshman senator from Maine, remembered one such visit from Bobby.[42]

There were still doubts, however, that Jackson had to overcome. Bobby Kennedy had carefully qualified his endorsement with the provision that Jackson would have to convince the delegations himself that he would be an asset to the ticket. Jackson's inability to deliver even his own delegation for JFK also troubled the Kennedys. The weak primary system of Washington State made it almost impossible to impose unanimity on delegates to a nominating convention. Magnuson came to the convention pledged to his close friend Lyndon Johnson, whose virulent attack on Kennedy and sarcasm toward Jackson before the Washington State delegation left many delegates cold. Governor Albert Rosellini, a Catholic running for reelection in 1960, also supported Johnson for president, fearful that two Catholics on the ticket would be too much for the voters of Washington State. In the end, a reluctant Magnuson relented to Jackson's pressure and switched his support to Kennedy, but the rest of the delegation remained split among Kennedy, Stevenson, Symington, and Johnson.[43]

Meanwhile, Stewart Alsop, perhaps the preeminent national columnist of his day, and much of the national press continued to report that Jackson had the inside track as Kennedy's running mate.[44] Kennedy himself fueled this speculation by his remarks to writer Jim Bishop during a car ride the morning of his nomination. Mentioning only one name as a prospective running mate, Kennedy said he needed a Protestant, someone from the West, someone like Scoop Jackson. Bishop told the Jackson entourage that "it looked like Jackson would get the nomination."[45] He spent the day of July 14 in Jackson's hotel suite as Sterling Munro and Russ Holt prepared Jackson's acceptance speech in anticipation of the eagerly awaited call from John Kennedy. The day before, Jackson's meeting with Kennedy had seemed to go well. Just after the delegates assembled in the Los Angeles Coliseum gave John Kennedy a first-ballot victory, Kennedy's chief strategists directed the Jackson people to designate someone to speak to them on Jackson's behalf. Salter, Hoeck, and Munro decided on Mike Mansfield. "Mike and I sat on a couple of damn hard benches in a waiting room in the Coliseum," remembered Gerald Hoeck. The meeting never occurred, however, because the Kennedy people were "probably celebrating or someone thought it was a bad idea," added Hoeck.

The Jackson staff also celebrated much of the night. Jackson himself did not get to sleep until the ungodly (for him) hour of 1:30 A.M. At 7:00 in the morning of July 14, Bobby summoned Salter to come to John Kennedy's suite. Talks between the Jackson and Kennedy staffs went on throughout the day. As Jackson and Salter prepared to leave John Kennedy's suite late in the afternoon, he told them that no matter what decision he was forced to make, "Jackson would always be a factor in his administration."[46] They then suspected that something was amiss. There was one adviser to John Kennedy who had even greater influence than Bobby: his father, Joseph Kennedy. After consulting with Speaker of the House Sam Rayburn, Joe Kennedy concluded that if his son was going to win he needed Lyndon Johnson on the ticket. Johnson surprised almost everybody by accepting the offer that John Kennedy extended. The decision to choose Johnson rather than Jackson enraged Bobby Kennedy, who loathed Johnson. Nevertheless, it was the right decision politically, as Henry Jackson himself recognized. The support Lyndon Johnson delivered to Kennedy in key southern states provided him with his razor-thin margin of victory over Richard Nixon. With anyone else as his running mate, including Jackson, Kennedy probably would have lost.[47]

Late in the afternoon of July 14, Jackson received the fateful call from Kennedy: Johnson would take the vice presidential nomination. Jackson maintained his composure and told Jack he "understood perfectly." But, terribly disappointed, he refused "under any circumstances" to take the position of chairman of the Democratic National Committee that Kennedy urged as a consolation prize. An agitated Salter forced Jackson to call back immediately and amend his refusal to maybe. At 4:00 P.M., Jackson ventured forth to face 250 members of the press. By almost all accounts, he made a gracious speech, one of the best of his career. The audience applauded heartily. Hours later, he showed that he was indeed a team player by reluctantly agreeing to become chairman of the national Democratic Party. He also made a gracious nominating speech that evening for Lyndon Johnson.[48]

There was just one dissenter to the widespread perception that Jackson handled his defeat with aplomb and dignity: Jim Bishop. Perhaps frustrated with Kennedy for his lack of candor during their car-ride conversations about the vice presidency, Bishop took it out on Jackson in "A Study in Defeat," which the *Boston Evening American* published on July 15:

> Any signs of levity in Henry Jackson are false. He is serious and ambitious. His eyes are always on the goal and the goal was the Vice Presidency. He can taste it . . .
>
> The vital statistics are unimpressive. The Senator is 48. He is a bachelor. He has two sisters back home who are spinsters. . . . Once, long ago, he had a girl. No one knows her name or what became of her. When he ran for county Prosecutor in Snohomish, politics became the romantic

side of his life. He goes on dates now and then, but he handles them gracelessly and with embarrassment.[49]

Jackson endured more frustration and disappointment as Kennedy's national chairman for the 1960 presidential campaign. Although Kennedy people had assured Jackson that he and deputy chairman John Salter would run the entire campaign, he soon discovered to his chagrin that the real power lay elsewhere: Bobby Kennedy and the group of advisers known as the Irish Mafia would have total control. Jackson's standing with the inner circle of the Kennedy campaign suffered, too, when John Kennedy received a poor turnout in Seattle at the outset of the fall campaign. The Kennedy people blamed Jackson despite ignoring his warning that early September was a terrible time to visit a city whose people valued outdoor recreation more than the opportunity to see a presidential candidate of any party. It irritated Jackson and infuriated Salter that the Kennedys had relegated them to a minor role in the strategic and tactical dimensions of the campaign.[50]

Jackson played a more significant role as DNC chairman, making the public case for the Democratic Party in general and John Kennedy in particular. In dozens of speeches across the nation and dozens of appearances on the major network news programs, he called for a more activist government at home and a more assertive foreign policy to get the country moving again. Jackson pronounced "his Democrats the best equipped to adapt to change and meet the new challenges" that the United States would face in the years ahead.[51]

In good partisan fashion, Jackson also attacked his Republican opponents and their presidential candidate, Richard M. Nixon. He chided the Republican Party for being "naturally allergic to change" and "trying to resist it."[52] He ripped Eisenhower for clamping a rigid and dangerously low budget ceiling on defense spending, which created "the missile gap" and imperiled the nation. "The richest country in the world," he said, "can afford whatever it needs for defense. We cannot afford less, for the next war must be stopped before it starts. Adequate defenses are the first essential of a policy to keep the peace." Speaking at the National Press Club in Washington, D.C., on October 18, he accused Vice President Nixon of "crossing the line of demagoguery" in his presidential debates and in his speeches across the country.[53] In the campaign of 1960 and throughout

his political career, Jackson rarely crossed the line of demagoguery himself. He believed deeply that free government depended on the civility of
the citizenry and its elected representatives. As election day approached,
he urged voters to remember that what united Americans was far more
important than what divided them:

> Although I am a Democrat and will work hard for the Democratic vic-
> tory in November, I respect my Republican friends and their views—and
> wish them well 364 days a year. On election day, it is a little harder.
>
> There is much, I am thankful to say, that our two parties have in com-
> mon. All of us, Republicans and Democrats, are patriots. All of us hold
> dear the values of our free society and would fight, if need be, to defend
> them. All of us believe in the proven worth of our economic system,
> which has given us the highest standard of living in the world. These
> things, which are fundamental, we share in common, and let us remem-
> ber during our campaign debates that our agreements are more impor-
> tant than our disagreements. We are Republicans or Democrats second,
> and Americans first.[54]

Jackson also believed deeply that Americans were Jews, Catholics, or
Protestants second and Americans first. During the 1960 campaign, the
headquarters of the Democratic National Committee received thousands
of hate letters expressing virulent opposition to Kennedy because of his
Roman Catholic faith. Any kind of religious bigotry appalled Henry Jackson. He did not think, however, that the anti-Catholic bigotry directed
against Kennedy would be effective, for two reasons: his confidence in the
basic decency of most Americans; and "the forthright way that Senator
Kennedy had handled all questions relating to church and state."[55] On
September 14, Jackson made perhaps his most important contribution to
the Kennedy campaign by taking on the popular Reverend Norman Vin-
cent Peale, who stated publicly that Kennedy might take his orders from
the pope and obliterate the proper separation of church and state. Jackson delivered a widely publicized address criticizing Peale "for employ-
ing religious hate and prejudice." As a Presbyterian and a Mason, Jackson
assured Americans that Kennedy's Catholicism would not interfere with
his constitutional responsibilities as president.[56]

Jackson spent election day of 1960 anxiously awaiting the results at
DNC headquarters in Washington, D.C. He would have to wait until ear-

ly Wednesday morning before it became definitively clear that Kennedy had defeated Nixon by an exceedingly narrow margin. Jackson had good reason for the exhilaration he felt over Kennedy's victory—despite his disappointment over not getting the vice presidential nomination, despite his embarrassment over Nixon winning Washington State, and despite his irritation over how the Kennedy campaign had treated him as head of the DNC, a post from which he resigned eagerly on December 1, 1960. Kennedy had won running as the kind of New Deal–Fair Deal liberal Jackson personified.[57] He had campaigned aggressively in particular for a more assertive foreign policy and higher defense spending: causes that Jackson not only championed but also had urged Kennedy to emphasize.

It was not unreasonable for Jackson to expect that he would have significant influence in the Kennedy administration and in the Democratic Congress. During his first eight years in the Senate, he had established a reputation as a national expert on foreign policy and defense. Correspondingly, he had established himself as the most popular politician in the history of Washington State. With his reelection to the Senate perpetually certain, he stood to benefit increasingly from the ample prerogatives that seniority conferred. His chairmanship of the party in 1960 and Kennedy's victory indicated that the agenda of the Northern liberal wing to which they belonged would increasingly dominate the national Democratic Party. If the nation and the party remained on the course that the election seemed to set, then the prognosis for Jackson someday becoming president seemed decent to good. He was still only forty-eight years old. His boyish appearance and inexhaustible energy made him seem even younger. His highly praised investigation of Eisenhower's national security apparatus had provided him a superb education on the ways the executive branch operated that few of his colleagues could match.

What is striking, in retrospect, is how much the 1960 presidential campaign truly marked a crossroad in American politics. It heralded changes that would transform the nature of American politics and the balance of power within the Democratic Party, all to the detriment of Jackson's future presidential aspirations. There was the increasing impact of television and telegenic charm, which Kennedy relied on so effectively, especially in the debates with Nixon. There was the increasing importance of political primaries, which presaged the diminution of party organizations and regulars in selection of presidential candidates. There was the slow but increasing shift in the alignment of the demographically dynamic West and South toward the Republican Party, which would make it steadily more difficult for Democrats to win the presidency after 1964 until the end of the Cold War.[58] In one respect, however, the 1960 election was not the first of its kind, but the last. Never again during the Cold War would the Democratic Party run as the more internationally aggressive and hawkish of the two political parties. There was no more fitting symbol of the party for this type of campaign than Henry Jackson.

Chapter 7

Henry Jackson and the New Frontier

SINCE HIGH SCHOOL, Henry Jackson had subordinated his social life to his professional and political ambitions. Friends wondered whether Jackson—now entrenched in his bachelor ways and still obtuse about the women who yearned for his attention—would ever find the time for serious romance or marriage. On January 4, 1961, the day the new Congress convened, a ride on the Senate elevator changed all that. Senator Clinton Anderson introduced him to his new receptionist from Albuquerque, New Mexico, whom Anderson had invited to attend the swearing-in ceremony for new senators. A slim, elegant, very attractive, well-educated, twenty-eight-year-old blonde, Helen Hardin had just arrived in Washington, D.C., after her five-year marriage to a physician had ended in divorce. Her father owned and operated the American Gypsum Company in Albuquerque; her mother, born in China, was the daughter of Protestant missionaries. Helen Hardin had started college at Vassar in upstate New York but longed to return west. She transferred to Scripps College in southern California, where she received her bachelor's degree in English. For graduate school, she decided to give the East Coast another try. She enrolled at Columbia University in New York, where she received a master's degree in contemporary literature, specializing in Virginia Woolf.[1]

Henry Jackson appealed to her immediately. She thought him handsome, with "a friendly, easy manner, a firm handshake, and a bright look." She made an equally striking impression on him. A few weeks later, he called to ask whether she would join him for a cup of tea in the Senate cafeteria. The tea date "swept" Helen off her feet, although Henry's friends stress that he did most of the pursuing during their courtship.

Throughout the spring and summer of 1961, the romance blossomed. Usually, Helen and Henry did not do "extravagant financial things because Scoop was thrifty." They liked to take long walks or bicycle rides along the C & O Canal. On special occasions, Henry would live it up by taking Helen and friends for barbecued ribs at Arbaugh's, a longtime favorite of Washingtonians, located on Connecticut Avenue near Cleveland Park. When Henry asked Helen to help pick out jewelry for his sisters' Christmas presents, the office staff knew he was smitten. The November 29, 1961, issue of *Roll Call*, the insiders guide to politics on Capitol Hill, reported the engagement of "the Hill's pre-eminent bachelor" to Helen Hardin.[2]

The wedding took place on December 16, 1961, in the Central Methodist Church in Albuquerque. It was a small affair. President Kennedy could not attend but did send a telegram "extending heartiest congratulations to you and your bride on this happy day." John Salter served as best man. Stan Golub, a law school classmate turned Seattle businessman; Bob Low; and Clarence Daniel Martin, one of Jackson's deputies at the Democratic National Committee, served as the ushers. Love and marriage mellowed but could not completely transform Jackson the workaholic. On their honeymoon in Hawaii, he could not resist talking to reporters on the beach about the need to resume atmospheric testing of nuclear weapons. He left Helen stranded days later to attend a briefing given by Rear Admiral Thach at Pearl Harbor on antisubmarine warfare and the communist submarine threat in the Pacific. When the honeymoon resumed, Helen noticed that there was little anonymity or privacy: "It seemed that the entire state of Washington was vacationing in Hawaii, and they all wanted to talk with Scoop."[3]

Helen Jackson took in stride her husband's inability to take a respite from politics. Having worked in the Senate, she came to the marriage with an understanding of what the life of an ambitious senator entailed. She became his anchor in life, a source of pride and joy. For his part, Jackson was always a devoted husband, easy to satisfy. He never complained about a meal, as long as the food was hot, which Helen found a "godsend" because she did not like to cook. Her tolerance had it limits, however. She was not going to live in Henry's bachelor apartment, "with a hodgepodge of furniture from previous tenants, the old broken radio, his box of bran flakes on the kitchen table, and newspapers stacked up to the arms of the couch." When they returned from their honeymoon to Washington, D.C., the Jacksons lived briefly in Helen's apartment in the Towers at 4201 Cathedral Avenue. When they moved back to 2500 Q Street, they combined two apartments into one by knocking out the wall that separated them. Henry Jackson got his old address back but not his old decor. Helen Jackson furnished the apartment elegantly. Muted beige and cream replaced the black and white of newspaper print as the prevailing color scheme. When Congress was out of session, the Jacksons lived with sisters Gert and Marie at the family home in Everett.

Still more domesticity lay in store for Jackson before long. On February 7, 1963, he became a father to daughter Anna Marie, given her middle name in honor of Jackson's beloved mother, Marine, who did not live to see the grandchildren.

JACKSON AND KENNEDY: CORDIAL BUT NOT CLOSE

Meanwhile, Jackson's relations with President Kennedy waned significantly from the high point reached at the Democratic Convention of 1960. Personal, temperamental, institutional, and philosophical considerations converged to cool their relationship. It still irritated the Kennedy insiders, according to Ted Sorensen's account, that Nixon had defeated Kennedy in Jackson's home state.[4] Friends of Jackson have speculated, too, that Kennedy insiders, though not the president himself, thought Jackson too old-fashioned and out of step with the telegenic whiz-kid image that the administration strove to project. The president also had little interest in the water and reclamation projects that were so important to Jackson and his constituents. It displeased Jackson, moreover, that the Kennedy people, with whom Salter had waged a losing battle for control of the 1960 presidential campaign, appeared to drag their feet in finding Salter a position in the new administration. When he finally received an offer, which he accepted in March 1961—deputy director for the Agency for International Development—he considered the position beneath what he had earned by his service to the Kennedy clan.[5]

As the careers of many illustrious legislators reveal, powerful senators often exert great influence in a situation of divided government, with their party controlling Congress and the other party controlling the presidency. Presidents must then work closely with them lest gridlock thwart their administration's policies. Powerful senators often exert less influence when their party controls the White House. Particularly in the areas of foreign policy and national security, where the Constitution gives the executive branch its broadest authority, presidents and their chief cabinet officers want to make the major decisions; correspondingly, they expect more deference from leading legislators of their own party. What accelerated and aggravated the inevitable institutional predilection in the Kennedy administration to treat Jackson less consequentially was the president's choice of Robert McNamara as secretary of defense. After "talking with Robert Lovett and Dean Acheson," Jackson had unsuccessfully recommended his friend Paul Nitze for the position. Jackson touted Nitze, whom he also "believed would be a strong candidate as secretary of state," as "toughminded, knowledgeable, and articulate." Instead, Kennedy appointed Nitze as secretary of the navy, partly as a consolation to Jackson.[6]

Inevitably, Henry Jackson and Robert McNamara would clash. The former president of the Ford Motor Company, renowned for his mathematical mind and managerial genius, McNamara epitomized the type of expert that Jackson disliked and distrusted: arrogant; self-confident; disdainful of knowledge and decisions based on history, experience, and intuition rather than quantification. McNamara had little patience for the judgment of leading members of the armed services or legislators invested with responsibility for overseeing America's national security policy, such as Senator Jackson. He believed in the efficacy of running the Department of Defense by the same techniques he had learned at Harvard Business School and applied at Ford. Instead of allowing interservice rivalry to determine America's defense program—his interpretation of what had occurred during the Eisenhower administration—McNamara proposed an alternative, based on the principles of economics and management accounting: a system of planning, programming, and budgeting (PPBS). PPBS aimed to identify what missions needed to be performed and the most cost-effective way for achieving them. He saw this method as the most reliable way to discern the military effectiveness of a program (the output) relative to its cost (the input), thereby avoiding costly redundancy and waste.[7]

PPBS aroused controversy within the military and in Congress because it promised to diminish their roles in the process of determining military budgets, procuring weapons, and formulating strategy. It encountered serious opposition from Henry Jackson, always wary of specialists who viewed problems from a narrow, technical perspective. Jackson extolled the virtues of the foreign policy and defense generalist, imbued with an appreciation of the larger context of their decisions. He considered it not only futile but dangerous to reduce the complexities of national security and foreign policy to a formula or technique the way McNamara proposed to do.[8] It took the cumulative weight of time and events for the clash between Jackson and McNamara to erupt full-blown.

Jackson and John Kennedy never drifted apart entirely or experienced a rupture in their relations. Jackson visited the president at the White House periodically. He supported enthusiastically the president's Keynesian tax-cutting plan, the administration's significant acceleration of America's nuclear buildup, and its ambitious agenda for securing the civil rights of black Americans—an agenda that had achieved considerable momentum by the fall of 1963 after a halting start. He heartily approved of the tone and content of Kennedy's inaugural address, devoted almost entirely to the subject of the Cold War and the need to wage it vigilantly. In the fall of 1963, Kennedy, Jackson, and Warren Magnuson stood shoulder to shoulder exuding genuine friendship and affection as large and enthusiastic crowds turned out for the charismatic president's visit to Washington State.[9]

President Kennedy's tragic assassination on November 22, 1963, stunned Jackson, who learned of it while eating lunch in the Senate dining room. Totally in shock, he reacted to the news by immersing himself in the details of his office routine. In the late afternoon, with the Senate office buildings nearly deserted, he went to the Senate payroll office to correct a mistake in his paycheck.[10] Later, some journalists raised the inevitable question about his feelings concerning Lyndon Johnson as president. Did he now think about what might have been if President Kennedy had followed Bobby's advice and named him as running mate? Jackson dismissed such hypotheticals without hesitation. As he reiterated frequently, Richard Nixon would have won the 1960 election if Kennedy had chosen him or anyone else but Lyndon Johnson.[11]

The Jackson-Kennedy connection continued even after the assassination. On August 27, 1964, Jackson introduced Bobby Kennedy at the Democratic National Convention with a moving tribute to his fallen brother:

He was a spirited man—and America is more vigorous today because he had a zest for life. He lived life to the full. He was a rational man—and America is a wiser country today because he helped us understand the need for restraint and for responsibility in the use of our great power. He was a compassionate man—and America and the world felt his deep concern for people, his commitment to the cause of justice, and we are better for it today. . . . The quality he admired above all was courage—and he was a courageous, gallant man in a world that never has too many. . . .[12]

The convention hall erupted in a roar of applause as Robert Kennedy stood at the podium. The crowd continued to cheer as he tried several times to bring the demonstration to an end by raising his arms to hush them. Arthur Schlesinger records that Jackson whispered to Kennedy as he began to raise his arms again: "Let it go on. . . . Just let them do it, Bob. . . . Let them get it out of their system." After the film *A Thousand Days* was shown to the delegates, Jackson concluded: "There is nothing to add. . . . We have our memory. . . . We will cherish it. Now it is for us, the living, to go on. Let us continue. . . . That is the way to build a memorial—that is the way we will keep faith with John Fitzgerald Kennedy."[13]

Despite their connections, the record reveals plainly that Jackson was never a close confidant of Kennedy's during his presidency. Kennedy did not solicit his advice when the Soviets erected the Berlin Wall or during the Cuban missile crisis, two of the major foreign policy crises of his administration during which he sought the advice of other senators. By the time Kennedy died, the approach of these two men to foreign and national security affairs had begun to diverge perceptibly, albeit as a matter of degree. Jackson opposed the administration on four key issues in 1962–63 that prefigured, in milder form, his later estrangement from post-1968 Northern Democratic liberals over the entire course of American foreign policy.

THE U.N. SPEECH

In a widely publicized speech to the National Press Club on March 20, 1962, Jackson ignited a debate over the United Nations. The speech coincided with congressional deliberations over whether to approve buying U.N. bonds to help finance two peacekeeping missions. Jackson had always believed that America's position in the world depended foremost on the strength and unity of the Atlantic community and the NATO alliance. He worried about trends and practices that would give excessive weight to the United Nations at the expense of U.S. vital interests in Western Europe. Specifically, he opposed the United Nations and the U.S. ambassador to the U.N. impinging on the roles of the secretary of state and the president. The United Nations, he warned, "was never intended to be a substitute for our own leaders as the makers and movers of American foreign policy."[14] Nor should "the UN delegation in New York . . . operate as a second foreign office," lest the United States weaken its allies "in deference to what is represented in New York as a world opinion." Although he emphasized that the United Nations "should continue to be an important avenue of American foreign policy," he also said that "the involvement of the United Nations has . . . at times hampered the wise definition of our national interest and the development of sound policies for their advancement." He advised that an exaggerated view of the U.N.'s role could imperil the ability of the United States to contain the Soviet Union, the paramount threat to America's interests:

> The Soviet Union was not and is not a peace-loving nation. Khrushchev has announced his support for "wars of national liberation." He has threatened to "bury" us. In their more agreeable moments, the Russians promise to bury us nicely, but whatever their mood, the earth will still be six feet deep above us. We must realize that the Soviet Union sees the UN not as a forum of cooperation but as one more arena of struggle. . . .
>
> The hope for peace with justice does not lie with the United Nations. Indeed the truth is almost exactly the reverse. The best hope for the United Nations lies in the maintenance of peace. . . . Peace depends on the power and unity of the Atlantic community and the skill of our direct diplomacy. . . .

American statesmen, he continued, needed to educate public opinion "in the direction of a more realistic appreciation of the [United Nation's] limitations, more modest hopes for its accomplishments, and a more mature sense of the burdens of responsible leadership."

The speech elicited a strong reaction. Jackson received the preponderance of his compliments from conservatives and his most severe criticisms from liberals. Richard Russell wrote Jackson that "no finer, saner or more historic speech on international relations has been made during my time in Washington. You are hereby nominated as my candidate for Secretary of State. It is refreshing to see someone admit that this country has rights that should be asserted out loud." Conservative Senator John Tower, Republican from Texas, also praised Jackson's speech. "The theory that the UN has preserved the peace is preposterous," proclaimed Tower. "We must not allow it to dictate our foreign policy." Several prominent liberals attacked Jackson for suggesting that the United States paid too much attention to the United Nations and should downgrade its policy-making role. Liberal Senator Jacob Javits, Republican from New York, called the speech unfortunate. Senator Hubert Humphrey said that Jackson's view revealed "a shocking lack of knowledge of the world in which we live and of the structure of the United Nations. . . ." Although U.S. Ambassador to the United Nations Adlai Stevenson did not attack Jackson by name publicly, he described the ideas of his speech as a "great mistake" and "very odd."[15]

Stevenson had inferred wrongly from Dorothy Fosdick's major role in drafting the speech that her resentments toward him for the way their love affair had ended influenced Jackson's critique of the United Nations. He intimated as much in a series of letters to Jackson and his staff, attempting to allay their concerns about the U.N.'s role in American foreign policy. To Dorothy Fosdick, he wrote: "I shall refrain from any talk of brickbats and retaliation which have never had a part in my dialogue with Democrats—let alone you!" To Robert Tufts, professor at Oberlin College and a consultant to Jackson who collaborated with Fosdick in drafting the U.N. speech, Stevenson wrote that he was "baffled" by its origins. Stevenson appealed to Senator Jackson for an early opportunity to reassure and enlighten him about America's role in the United Nations.[16]

Stevenson did not get the solicitous response he had anticipated. Tufts replied that Senator Jackson was "engaged in constructive criticism." He did not believe it was helpful for Stevenson to "distort" Jackson's statements or "impugn" his motives. Dorothy Fosdick replied with equal firmness. What Jackson had to say, she insisted, was "serious and constructive. . . . A strategy of distorting this concern . . . is no answer." The tone of her letter "grieved and surprised" Stevenson, who failed utterly to grasp that Jackson's speech reflected his deep convictions about the primacy of NATO and the danger of reorienting U.S. foreign policy too much in the direction of support for the underdeveloped countries in the United Nations.[17] Indeed, Jackson's speech marked a significant watershed in the perception of the U.N.'s proper role. The themes he laid out anticipated the neoconservative critique of the United Nations that Daniel Patrick Moynihan and others made during the 1970s: namely, that the U.N. served as a vehicle for a radical coalition of Soviet bloc and third world nations to undermine Western values and America's vital interests.[18]

Kennedy tried to play down the controversy between Jackson and Stevenson, reaffirming his support for NATO and the United Nations at his press conference the day after the speech. He said that "there was no fundamental disagreement" between himself and Jackson over the U.N.[19] This is not, however, what he wrote in a private letter to Stevenson. Kennedy assured his U.N. ambassador that he disagreed with Jackson on several points but did not "want to build up his criticism by too much notice—and I also have to bear in mind that he has been a strong and consistent supporter of our whole program in Congress."[20]

In his dealings with Soviet Premier Khrushchev, Kennedy displayed less resolution than Jackson favored or expected. The president was, to be sure, a Cold Warrior who viewed the world in those terms. Acutely aware of the political backlash against Democrats that ensued after the Communist takeover of China in 1949, he was loath to have Americans perceive him as having lost any country to communism. Thus the Kennedy administration deepened U.S. involvement in South Vietnam, notwithstanding the president's apprehensions about the survivability of the regime.[21]

The caution and restraint of Kennedy's foreign policy often belied the boldness of his public rhetoric. Fearing that American military action against Cuba would provoke hostility in Latin America and provide a pretext for the Soviets to launch retaliatory action against Berlin, Kennedy refused to provide decisive American support to the Bay of Pigs operation, which ended in fiasco in April 1961. He agreed to the neutralization of Laos in the summer of 1962, which, in the long run, effectively ceded this tiny Southeast Asian nation to communism.[22] By his own admission, he patiently endured too much of Khrushchev's bombastic presentations and blithe disregard for the president's conciliatory demeanor at the Vienna Summit in June 1961. The president acquiesced, too, when the Soviet Union erected the Berlin Wall in August 1961, a passivity that alarmed former Secretary of State Dean Acheson and former President Dwight Eisenhower, who both believed that a strong American action could have forced Khrushchev to back down without danger.[23]

Kennedy's ambivalence arose from the basic tension between two competing historical influences that shaped his outlook on foreign affairs. On the one hand, the lessons of Munich—so deeply ingrained in Henry Jackson—made Kennedy very conscious of the danger of appeasing the Soviets or relying on their good will as a substitute for American power. On the other hand, the revisionist views of Sidney Fay and Barbara Tuchman on the origins of World War I had more salience for the president than for Jackson, who considered World War I an inappropriate analogy for understanding the Cold War or the nature of the Soviet threat.[24] Fay and Tuchman blamed the outbreak of hostilities in 1914 not on the nature of German ambitions but on one nation's misinterpretation of another's intentions, which set off a spiral of escalation culminating in a destructive war that nobody wanted.[25] By summit diplomacy and measured responses to provocation, Kennedy hoped to educate Khrushchev on the virtues of mutual restraint and hence reduce the risk of war by miscalculation.[26]

THE CUBAN MISSILE CRISIS

The analogy of 1914 largely informed Kennedy's reactions during the Cuban missile crisis. By mid-October of 1962, pictures taken from U-2 surveillance flights had established incontrovertibly that the Soviets had introduced into Cuba surface-to-surface missiles (MRBMs) and undertaken construction of intermediate-range ballistic missiles (IRBMs), both with nuclear capability. With a range of 1,020 nautical miles, the MRBMs could strike most of the major cities in the southern and south-central region of the United States, as far north as Washington, D.C. With a range of 2,200 nautical miles, the IRBMs could strike every major U.S. city in the continental United States except Seattle. This discovery confronted Kennedy with a grave challenge. Previously, he had announced emphatically that his administration would not tolerate Soviet deployment of offensive nuclear missiles in Cuba. Since August 31, 1962, his administration also had dismissed the charges of New York Senator Kenneth Keating, a liberal pro-defense Republican in the Rockefeller tradition, that the Soviets had begun to install such missiles. The confirmation that Keating was right triggered a crisis of thirteen tension-filled days during which the Soviet Union and the United States appeared to be on the brink of nuclear war.[27] Scholars have proffered several rationales for Khrushchev's decision to take such an enormous risk. Although the desire to obtain leverage to pressure the Allies on Berlin and to force the removal of NATO nuclear missiles from Turkey probably had something to do with it, three motives stand out as paramount: the desire to defend Castro's Cuba, then a Soviet revolutionary outpost in the Caribbean; the opportunity to reduce the margin of America's nuclear superiority, which the Kennedy administration declared publicly, calling the bluff of the saber-rattling missile diplomacy that Khrushchev had engaged in since Sputnik; and the advantage in the underdeveloped world that a dramatic victory would confer in the U.S.S.R.'s struggle against China within the Communist bloc.[28]

What tempted Khrushchev to take an enormous risk that could have ended in Soviet humiliation or in a nuclear war that the Soviet Union would have lost was his assessment of Kennedy's likely reactions based on past performance. He persuaded his colleagues and himself that Kennedy would not use U.S. nuclear superiority and its equally overwhelming naval superiority in the Caribbean to reverse the dramatic change in the balance of power that the successful deployment of Soviet missiles in Cuba would achieve.[29]

Kennedy now sought advice about how to react. He established an advisory board known as the Executive Committee on National Security (ExCom). He also consulted with three of the wise men outside his administration whom Henry Jackson had long revered: Dean Acheson, John McCloy, and Robert Lovett. In addition, the president consulted with Senator Richard Russell, chairman of the Armed Services Committee, and Senator J. William Fulbright, chairman of the Foreign Relations Committee.[30] These advisers split into three groups.[31] Arguing that the deployment of nuclear weapons in Cuba had no significant effect on the military balance, Secretary of Defense Robert McNamara suggested that no action need be taken considering that long-range missiles deployed in the U.S.S.R. already made the United States vulnerable to devastating attack. Arguing that the missiles posed an acute danger to the United States and a major step toward Soviet nuclear parity, Nitze, Acheson, CIA director John McCone, Russell, Maxwell Taylor, and even Fulbright favored immediate and decisive military action to take out the missiles. This entire group recommended an air strike, at a minimum. Russell and some others were in favor of invading Cuba, too, if necessary.[32] Kennedy chose an intermediate option: establishing a naval quarantine around Cuba to block further Soviet weapons shipments and applying pressure on Khrushchev to remove the missiles already there. The hawks—Jackson included—believed that stopping the Soviet missiles at sea was even more dangerous than taking out the bases by air strike, because waiting increased the likelihood of the Soviet missiles becoming operational. Their logic did not persuade the president. He agreed not only with McNamara, who deemed a successful surgical strike impractical, but also with his brother Bobby, who considered that option immoral, the equivalent of Pearl Harbor.[33] Indeed, the president inclined toward McNamara's judgment that the Soviet deployment of IRBMs would have no significant effect on the military balance, a judgment that Henry Jackson disagreed with entirely. By the same token, Kennedy also feared that Congress and the American public would excoriate him for allowing the Soviet deployment of missiles to stand. So he counted on the quarantine making more vigorous action unnecessary.[34]

The president's strategy succeeded. Khrushchev agreed to remove the missiles, although not before the United States agreed in private to a quid pro quo: a public U.S. pledge not to invade Cuba; and a private pledge, which the administration denied in public, to withdraw nuclear missiles from Turkey. The public hailed Kennedy for his apparent deftness in resolving the crisis consistent with U.S. interests. The president received fulsome tributes from all quarters, including Henry Jackson. Subtle criticism, however, lurked beneath the surface of Jackson's tribute. He implied that the Kennedy administration had not taken Senator Keating's earlier warnings seriously enough. Although Jackson spent the missile crisis, which coincided with a congressional recess, campaigning for Warren Magnuson in Washington State, his instincts on how to respond corresponded with those whose judgment he most trusted: Acheson, Nitze, Lovett, and Russell. Jackson implied, too, that the United States may have conceded too much by pledging not to invade Cuba and tacitly agreeing to remove the missiles from Turkey.[35]

Jackson and leading figures in the Kennedy administration also disagreed fundamentally about the proper lessons to be learned from the Cuban missile crisis. For Secretary of Defense McNamara and for Kennedy, America's nuclear superiority did not contribute significantly to its successful resolution. Both had already gone a long way toward abandoning the assumption, axiomatic since the Truman administration, that the United States must maintain strategic nuclear superiority to offset the Soviet Union's sizable advantage in conventional power. Instead, McNamara championed the doctrine of mutual assured destruction (MAD), which eventually became the basis for U.S. strategic nuclear policy. MAD rested on the assumption that effective ballistic missile defense was beyond the technical capacity for either of the superpowers to achieve; hence, nuclear deterrence operated most robustly when both the United States and the Soviet Union possessed an assured second-strike capability to inflict unacceptable damage on the other. As McNamara and a generation of MAD devotees interpreted the successful resolution of the Cuban missile crisis, the source of American strength lay in the preponderance, not of nuclear power, but of conventional power in the Caribbean, an area where the United States had a more vital stake in the outcome than the Soviets. A generation of American arms controllers had postulated confidently that the Soviets reached the same conclusion about the futility of striving for nuclear superiority in an age when the missile would always get through.[36]

Henry Jackson drew the opposite conclusion. For him, the Cuban missile crisis confirmed the malevolence of Soviet intentions and the imperative of maintaining a U.S. strategic nuclear advantage. He inveighed against "the widespread assumption that our superiority in conventional forces was the decisive factor last October in the near-collision over Cuba." He thought it dangerous, too, to concede the Soviet Union nuclear parity: "An expansionist nation would never be satisfied with this state of affairs." As he "read history, international peace and security depend not on a balance of power, but on a certain imbalance of power favorable to the defenders of peace—in which the strength of the peacekeeper is greater than that of the peace upsetter."[37]

Chapter 8

The TFX Controversy and the "Senator from Boeing"

H ENRY JACKSON and Robert McNamara had their first major public
confrontation over the Defense Department's decision in November
1962 to award the multibillion-dollar contract for the TFX fighter plane,
today known as the F-111, to General Dynamics, headquartered in Fort
Worth, Texas, rather than to the Boeing Company, headquartered in
Seattle, which had planned to build the aircraft at its plant in Wichita,
Kansas. Civilian pentagon officials decided on General Dynamics despite
the repeated and nearly unanimous endorsement of the Boeing aircraft by
the military technical advisers and review boards.[1]

An angry Jackson suspected that political pressure from the Texas congressional delegation and Vice President Johnson had influenced the
decision, which on military grounds he found inexplicable. Jackson objected also to the decision-making process. McNamara's choice of the
General Dynamics version of the TFX displayed his managerial approach
to weapons procurement. For this new fighter-bomber, he had insisted on
a common design for navy and air force use, rather than allowing development of two distinct tactical planes as both branches of the armed forces
advocated.[2]

Reluctant to embarrass President Kennedy publicly, Jackson attempted to raise his concerns privately with those responsible for the decision.
In December 1962, he telephoned Roswell Gilpatric, the deputy secretary of defense, asking for a more detailed justification. He called for assurances that this award was decided on the merits, and the merits alone.
Then he met privately with McNamara to discuss his concerns. Their en-

counter went badly. Jackson left angrier and more offended than before. As Deborah Shapley, McNamara's biographer, tells it:

> According to one account, the defense secretary was shockingly rude to Jackson. McNamara insisted that the General Dynamics plane was chosen solely on its merits, that Boeing still did not understand what he wanted. McNamara acted as though congressmen had no business seeking defense contracts for their states and for their districts; such politicking was not in the national interest.[3]

Whereupon Jackson, a member of the Permanent Investigations Subcommittee of the Government Operations Committee, proposed to Senator John McClellan that it investigate the awarding of the TFX contract. Sharing Jackson's doubts about McNamara and the circumstances of the award, McClellan required little persuading. The Permanent Subcommittee commenced a series of major hearings on the TFX decision on February 26, 1963. President Kennedy defended McNamara repeatedly and predicted that the hearings would confirm the soundness of McNamara's judgment. On the morning of the day he died, Kennedy reiterated that the secretary of defense had handled the TFX decision properly.

The hearings never resolved definitively whether political considerations had determined the choice of General Dynamics rather than Boeing. This did not, however, allay the suspicions of some critics that the administration made the award to bolster the president's sagging popularity among those in the South upset by Kennedy's civil rights agenda, and to reward Vice President Johnson for delivering the critical state of Texas in the 1960 election. Jackson's and McClellan's investigation and questioning of Deputy Defense Secretary Roswell Gilpatric and Navy Secretary Fred Korth did reveal information that triggered a subsequent investigation over whether these two civilian subordinates of McNamara's had a conflict of interest: Gilpatric was previously a legal adviser to General Dynamics; Korth was president of a Fort Worth bank that had loaned money to General Dynamics. Both men resigned their positions shortly after the Justice Department cleared them of conflict-of-interest charges in the fall of 1963. The hearings uncovered absolutely no evidence of untoward political influence on McNamara's decisions.[4]

The grilling of Defense Department officials by Jackson and McClellan did disclose beyond a reasonable doubt, however, that McNamara had run roughshod over the advice of his professional military in awarding the TFX contract. Several disturbing findings emerged from their investigation: McNamara's decision contradicted four clear military evaluations endorsing the superiority of the Boeing design by a nearly unanimous margin. He reached his final decision without consulting either Admiral George W. Anderson, the chief of naval operations, or Curtis LeMay, the highest ranking general in the air force, both of whom believed that the Boeing design was superior to the General Dynamics design. McNamara also overruled the military's recommendation that Boeing could build the plane at a lower price, even though the bid from General Dynamics was $100 million higher than Boeing's. Further, the Boeing bid included an engine thrust-reverser to permit shorter runs after landing, a feature the General Dynamics proposal did not.[5]

In the hearing, McNamara said that he had discounted Boeing's cost estimates as unrealistically low. He said, too, that regardless of what the military thought, General Dynamics came much closer to his new approach to weapons procurement, which required that the air force and navy versions of the plane be as similar as possible in order to cut costs. General Dynamics better met this objective than Boeing, according to McNamara, who also told the senators that "the hearings would do nothing but harm."[6] During his appearance before the committee in executive session, he wept as he told the committee that his son, teased in the schoolyard over his father's role in the TFX controversy, asked plaintively whether he ever would be proved an honest man.[7]

Jackson found McNamara's demeanor appalling, an unsavory mix of arrogance and weakness unacceptable for a secretary of defense.[8] His weeping astonished and disgusted Jackson. Jackson also attacked McNamara's reasoning sharply. He called the Defense Department's appraisal of the Boeing Company's cost estimates on the TFX "an amazing operation in unrealism."[9] As his battles with the navy during the Eisenhower administration over Rickover and the Nuclear Submarine Program had demonstrated, Jackson never advocated absolute deference to the expertise of the professional military. He did not believe, however, in snubbing the military's input, as he felt McNamara had done. Nor did he accept McNamara's notion that there was a perfect correspondence between efficiency in business and sound military practice. He questioned, in particular, the wisdom of making commonality the supreme goal for weapons designs, a policy he feared could compromise the combat capabilities of American armed forces if pushed too far. There is usually a tradeoff, sometimes severe, between making weapons versatile and requiring optimum performance. Weapons designed for multiple uses cannot achieve the same level of capability as those designed for more specialized missions. Standardization of weapons also simplifies the task of adversaries striving to devise countermeasures. Diversification reduces the risk that an opponent's technical breakthrough may degrade the effectiveness of an entire category of weapons systems.[10]

THE BOEING CONNECTION

The hearings rolled on until November 1963, when the assassination of President Kennedy led McClellan to suspend them—for several years, as it turned out. The outcome satisfied neither McNamara nor Jackson. On the one hand, Jackson and McClellan had exposed significant shortcomings in McNamara's decision-making process—shortcomings that would spell great trouble for the country in the future. On the other hand, the investigations did not result in a reversal of the TFX award. Eventually, events proved Jackson right on the merits of the TFX dispute. From the beginning, all sorts of technical difficulties plagued the program. The plane ultimately cost much more than McNamara had estimated. Although the program survived outright cancellation, the magnitude of its problems greatly reduced the number of F-111s produced.[11]

Nevertheless, the hearings also hurt Jackson's reputation among some liberals, disturbed by his collaboration with Dixiecrats and conservative Republicans to set off the TFX investigation. As the hearings proceeded, the bitterness of their tone increased, leaving all the participants scathed. On March 5, 1963, Congressman Jim Wright, a Democrat representing the Fort Worth area of Texas, accused Jackson of trying to pressure the Defense Department in favor of the Boeing Company on the TFX fighter-bomber contract.[12] Similarly, McNamara and his civilian deputies launched a counterattack against Jackson and McClellan. In the middle of March 1963, several newspapers reported the claims of "anonymous" Defense Department officials that Henry M. Jackson helped start the Senate's TFX fighter plane investigation to further his political fortunes. These officials said that McNamara and Gilpatric inferred from their conversations with Jackson in December 1962 that "the main aim of the investigation was to help the Senator get off the hook with his constituents in the state of Washington." Accordingly, they professed surprise at the length and acrimony of the hearings. From what Jackson had told them, they expected the hearings to last only a few days, just long enough to appease disappointed voters.[13]

Although Henry Jackson usually engaged in political debate with equanimity, he could not abide a colleague or government official lying to him. Also, he reacted with the rage of a biblical prophet to anyone who impugned his integrity. So it was in the case of the TFX. To Jim Wright, Jackson responded with a mixture of anger and indignation:

> At no time did I ever call anyone or talk to anyone in behalf of the Boeing Co. I did call to be given definite assurance this award would be decided on the merits, and the merits alone. . . . Maybe Mr. Wright would be glad to testify under oath on his part and I would be glad to do so on mine.[14]

The allegations of the anonymous Defense Department officials, later identified as Gilpatric himself and Arthur Sylvester, assistant secretary of defense, made Jackson even more furious. Notified of these allegations just before delivering a speech in Wenatchee, Washington, Jackson said "it was just plain absurd" to suggest that he had described the inquiry to Gilpatric "as principally a face-saving affair."[15] The committee summoned McNamara, Gilpatric, and Sylvester to justify their allegations at a special session on March 21, 1963. Gilpatric apologized, conceding that Jackson "was perfectly proper in asking that this investigation be brought." Jackson forced McNamara to disavow the allegations of the anonymous sources, although the secretary of defense insisted he had nothing to do with disseminating them.[16]

The apologies and retractions of McNamara and his deputies undid some but not all of the damage the allegations inflicted on Jackson. The controversy over the TFX also produced some sharp exchanges between Jackson and his fellow Democratic liberals on the floor of the Senate, a foretaste of things to come. Stuart Symington complained that Jackson's attack on the civilian members of the defense establishment had lowered the morale of the armed forces, to the detriment "of the security of the United States." Noting that Boeing had "obtained nearly $11 billion in business in the last eleven years," Symington also rejected Jackson's claim that Boeing had been "treated unfairly." Jackson countered that Symington not only had his facts wrong, but also missed the main issue at stake: General Dynamics, not Boeing, was "the largest holder of defense contracts, excluding the TFX." For Jackson, moreover, the amount of business a company had was "certainly not a relevant basis for the consideration of a decision of whether an award of the contract should be made."[17]

Others also criticized Jackson's role in the TFX controversy. The sage of liberal journalists, Walter Lippmann, rebuked Jackson and other committee members, writing that "the Secretary of Defense was just doing his job." Syndicated columnist Drew Pearson condemned the subcommittee for using the same grueling tactics on Defense Department officials during the TFX hearings as they used on "labor racketeers, cheap hoods, and B girls." The editorials of several other national newspapers continued to defend McNamara, assailing Jackson for pursuing the investigation to ingratiate himself with Boeing, Washington State's largest employer.[18]

In the final analysis, the TFX controversy fueled the slowly but steadily burgeoning perception among those critical of Jackson's Cold War views that he was the "Senator from Boeing," in thrall to the so-called military-industrial complex.[19] This moniker did not correspond to the reality of Jackson's relationship with Boeing. True, he did what he could to promote the interests of the largest employer in his state when it did not conflict with his conception of the national interest. Doubtless, too, he tried to make Boeing's best case for a TFX project estimated to be worth over $6.5 billion, involving 20,000 jobs and 1,700 aircraft. Boeing also reciprocated by sometimes making the best case for Jackson to the electorate of Washington State. When Lloyd J. Andrews, Jackson's Republican opponent in the Senate race of 1964, circulated literature blaming Jackson for Boeing's loss of the TFX contract, William M. Allen, president of Boeing, issued a public statement defending Jackson. Allen called it "completely unjust" to "a man of integrity" such as Jackson in connection with the TFX.[20] Over the years, Jackson did maintain a close relationship with Allen and his successor, T. A. Wilson. Also, Jackson and Senator Magnuson allowed representatives from Boeing to use their Senate offices during 1970–71 to run a lobbying campaign for congressional funding of an SST (supersonic transport).[21] Yet no credible evidence exists that Jackson ever pushed for a Boeing project that clashed with his conception of the national interest. Boeing had a reputation for being one of the most reliable and honest defense contractors in the nation. Generally, officials of the company did not even have to lobby Jackson. He genuinely believed that Boeing built the best military aircraft in the world, and considered these weapons essential for preserving the credibility and effectiveness of America's armed forces so necessary to waging the Cold War.

Throughout the late 1970s and early 1980s, however, he adamantly opposed the sale of Boeing-built AWAC radar planes to Saudi Arabia because of his concern about the effect on Israel and American interests in the Middle East. Wilson explained that the company did not even attempt to persuade Jackson on AWACs, knowing it was hopeless, notwithstanding the huge size of the contract (equal to the TFX award) and its benefits for the economy of Washington State.[22] Even Senator Eugene McCarthy, who frequently mocked Jackson for his Cold War views and actively disliked him, defended him from the imputation that he was the senator from Boeing:

> They used to call him the Senator from Boeing. That was not really it. He would be for defense if it was all being produced by McDonnell Douglas or somebody else. He was continually and relentlessly an advocate of high defense expenditure and anti-Soviet policies. . . . If someone told him that the Russians had 3,000 cavalry, Henry would say that we are underdefended and that we need to build cavalry.[23]

Jackson had too much integrity to tailor his views to Boeing's, but he also had no need to do so politically. Contrary to what Roswell Gilpatric and others critical of his position on the TFX asserted, he had no fear about his prospects for reelection. In the 1964 election he swamped Andrews, winning by more than 538,000 votes, and more than 72 percent. His coattails and Lyndon Johnson's also contributed enormously to transforming the Washington State congressional delegation from one Democrat and six Republicans to six Democrats and one Republican. Unlike Magnuson, who won reelection in 1962 by just 4 percent of the vote, Jackson campaigned from such a commanding position of popularity that he could spend much of his time and resources helping other Democrats. Lloyd Meeds, Floyd Hicks, Brock Adams, and Tom Foley, future Speaker of the House, all gave Jackson much of the credit for their successful maiden runs for Congress in 1964.[24] In the Fourth Congressional District of Washington State, Democrat Mike McCormack's 1970 upset of the Republican incumbent, Congresswoman Catherine May, also owed largely to Jackson's active support raising money and appearing on McCormack's TV advertisements.[25]

Foley's association with Jackson went back to his father, who became a friend of Jackson's as a Democratic prosecutor of Spokane County. When Brock Adams—also elected to Congress from Seattle in 1964—beat out Foley in 1961 for a position as U.S. attorney from Washington State, Jackson invited Foley to join his staff on the Interior Committee. Foley served as Jackson's special counsel on the committee until July 1964. He also sometimes had the responsibility for driving Jackson around from reception to reception in the District of Columbia, marveling at his ability to attend several events an evening with record speed:

> Scoop was the fastest reception attender ever. He was in and out in 20 minutes. I discovered one of the things he did. . . . He took a drink and walked around as if he would spend the night there. He never said good-by, but left by the side door without notice. Then he was on to the next one. He could go through three receptions in an hour. Later on, the Jackson style became more common. But he was a record holder in those days.[26]

In 1962–63, Jackson suggested to Foley that he should someday run for Congress. Foley let the matter lie, however, until July 1964. While in the state of Washington recuperating from a bout of mononucleosis, he suddenly resigned his job on the Interior Committee and filed for a congressional run because nobody else had filed against Republican incumbent Walt Horan, representing a heavily Republican district that included Foley's hometown of Spokane. Foley recalled fondly that "Scoop was remarkably supportive, even though I had not advised him ahead of time, even though he thought I should wait, and even though I gave him a fait accompli that I was quitting." Jackson raised plenty of money for Foley and the other Democrats running for Congress in 1964. He also "devoted a significant part of his television time in eastern Washington" talking about Foley and urging people to vote for him. Jackson portrayed the Foley-Horan race as a referendum on him, a strategy that worked.[27]

Jackson's willingness to take on the Kennedy administration over the

TFX elevated his standing among Republicans, Southern Democrats, and Democrats in the West who valued his expertise, integrity, and independence. It lowered his standing among some of his northeastern liberal brethren in the Senate, who argued privately, according to columnists Roland Evans and Robert Novak, that Jackson "had stunted his chances for political advancement." In a reception room of the national Democratic headquarters where the pictures of all the former DNC chairmen hung on the wall, a Democratic politician had pointed to Jackson's and said: "That's one picture they ought to turn to the wall."[28]

THE TEST BAN TREATY

The Kennedy administration had no intention of ostracizing Jackson, a loyal supporter of most of the president's policies, whose criticism on some national security issues the president still considered friendly rather than adversarial. Nor, in the summer of 1963, could the president afford to antagonize Jackson with a vote pending on the administration's nuclear test ban treaty with the Soviet Union: an issue far more important, in the president's mind, than the TFX or the dispute over the United Nation's role. The president delivered a celebrated address at American University on June 10, 1963, to build support for the pending Limited Test Ban Treaty, which was signed August 5 and precluded the United States, the Soviet Union, and Great Britain from testing nuclear weapons in the atmosphere. The soaringly optimistic rhetoric of that address indicated that the president's public view of the Soviet Union had softened considerably since the campaign of 1960 and his vigilant inaugural address of January 1961. Refusing to place blame for the Cold War on either side, Kennedy laid out eloquently why both sides needed to find a way out of the conflict and improve Soviet-American relations for the interest of everyone:

> Some say that it is useless to speak of world peace or world law or world disarmament and that it will be useless until the leaders of the Soviet Union adopt a more enlightened attitude. I hope they do. But I also believe that we must reexamine our own attitude—as individuals and as a nation—for our attitude is as essential as theirs. . . .[29]

Historians attribute Kennedy's apparent change of heart to a mixture of idealism, experience, and political calculation. After the Cuban missile crisis demonstrated his resolve to the American people, the president had more political leeway to pursue less confrontational policies. The Cuban missile crisis and the tensions over Berlin convinced him simultaneously of the dangers of not ameliorating the Soviet-American rivalry.[30]

Kennedy anticipated, however, a bruising fight over the test ban treaty in the Senate. He worried that a coalition of Southern Democrats and conservative Republicans would unite to prevent it from obtaining the two-thirds majority necessary for ratification. He worried, too, that Jackson might oppose the treaty, leading to the defection of several additional senators from the West, who were deferential to Jackson on national security issues. Kennedy's ratification strategy hinged on having the Joint Chiefs of Staff testify first before the Senate Foreign Relations Committee, which the dovish William Fulbright chaired, rather than the Armed Services Committee or its Preparedness Investigating Subcommittee, which Richard Russell, Henry Jackson, and other hawks opposed to or skeptical about the treaty dominated. As the president confided to Senate Majority Leader Mike Mansfield on August 12:

> If we don't get the Chiefs just right, we can get blown out. I would like to get them on public record before they go to the Preparedness Committee. What they say in public would be more pro-treaty than what they will say under interrogation by (Senator Henry) Scoop Jackson with leading questions and Barry Goldwater and Strom Thurmond.[31]

Jackson's initial reaction to the treaty gave credence to Kennedy's concern. On August 4, 1963, the *New York Times Magazine* published an article by Jackson warning, with regard to the treaty and other aspects of East-West relations "to beware of believing things that are not necessarily so." Americans, he cautioned, should reject "the widespread assumptions" that the "arms race is leading to catastrophe" and that we can win our way with the Russians by a policy of inoffensiveness." Apprehensive that the treaty could generate a dangerous euphoria about Soviet intentions, he emphasized that Khrushchev's objective of world supremacy remained unchanged. His words directly contradicted the conciliatory spirit and letter of the president's June 10 address at American University:

> Khrushchev is adept, resourceful, and devious in his maneuvres. . . . He can turn it on and turn it off in short order. We can expect that Khrushchev will continue to twist and turn, thaw and freeze, agree and dis-

agree—in pursuit of his ultimate aim, which he openly admits is to bury us. (There is both a lesson from history and a warning for the future in Russia's sudden signing of the non-aggression pact with Hitler).

All Americans want peace. The debate is over means. The debates need to receive our most thoughtful, honest, tough-minded attention. But certainly the weight of responsible opinion lies with preparedness combined with restraint—what Theodore Roosevelt meant when he said we should speak softly but carry a big stick.

The only way to bargain successfully with expansionist states is to maintain the strength to make bargaining attractive to them.[32]

In the ratification fight over the test ban treaty, Jackson unveiled a legislative strategy that he would refine to great effect during the 1970s in the struggles over the Strategic Arms Limitation Talks (SALT) with the Soviets and the Jackson-Vanik Amendment. He did not oppose the treaty outright, as hawks such as Richard Russell and Barry Goldwater did, because he expected it to pass. Instead, he used the ratification process as a device to educate the American people about the nature of the Soviet threats, to toughen the provisions of the treaty, and to establish a legislative record as a litmus test by which to assess future Soviet behavior that he was sure would flaunt the optimistic expectations underlying the treaty.[33]

Jackson announced therefore that he would reserve judgment until "the Senate has received the full range of evidence in our hearings." He did say, however, that he thought "safeguards were needed under the treaty," because the Soviets might violate a test ban treaty that was not adequately verifiable.[34] Walter Lippmann criticized Jackson for his ambivalence over the treaty and for the belligerent tone of his *New York Times Magazine* article of August 4.[35] William L. Neuman, a professor of history at Goucher College, wrote the editors of the *New York Times* that Jackson's "faith in the get tough approach" evinces "the same type of primitive thinking found in those who feel that our current racial problems can be solved by punching noses and breaking heads."[36] Some of his constituents also expressed their dismay over his unwillingness to back Kennedy unequivocally on the test ban.

None of this deflected Jackson from pursuing his purpose with resolution. He wrote back to one such critic that it was "plain absurd" to think that he had become connected "with the lunatic fringe of Thurmond, Eastland, et al." or had drifted "into a pattern of consistent opposition to major administration programs." He insisted that it was "the constitutional obligation of the Senate to look at any agreement with the greatest care, to make sure that the possible gains are not overshadowed by the risks that are inevitably run."[37]

On August 9, the day after the *Washington Post* published Lippmann's editorial criticizing him, Jackson propounded on the Senate floor a number of questions that needed "frank and adequate" answers from the administration before the "Senate could prudently determine to give its advice and consent for ratification":

> Can the United States afford a position of parity or equality with the Soviet Union? . . . Can we make the progress necessary to protect and maintain our deterrent by underground testing within the limits of the proposed treaty? . . . What assurances will be given that all the experiments involving testing permissible under the treaty and required by our nuclear weapons research laboratories will go forward in a vigorous and sustained manner, and not be stifled by the qualified, half-hearted stop and go support characteristic of the recent past? What steps are being taken to deal with the possibility of a planned treaty by the Soviets—that is, the possible use of the treaty by Moscow to degrade our laboratory programs in nuclear research and our test organizations while secretly preparing to abrogate the treaty and carry out another massive atmospheric test series? . . . What assurances will we be given that our weapons laboratories will have full and wholehearted support, so that the budgets of the laboratories will be adequate, the morale in the laboratories will remain high, and the best men will not drift away to more attractive positions? What can and will be done to deal with the new difficulties in information-gathering which would reinforce the difficulties already imposed on a free world by a closed Soviet society? . . . What is the capability of our nuclear test detection systems for the atmosphere, high altitude, outer space, and underwater?[38]

Accordingly, Jackson convened a hearing of the Preparedness Investigating Subcommittee during the second week of August 1963 to address these concerns. His cross-examination elicited from the Joint Chiefs of Staff (JCS) four safeguards "which they believed would reduce the disadvantages and risks of the Treaty":

1. The conduct of a comprehensive, aggressive, and continuing underground nuclear test program. . . .

2. The maintenance of modern nuclear laboratory facilities and programs in theoretical and exploratory nuclear technology. . . .

3. The maintenance of facilities and resources necessary to institute promptly nuclear tests in the atmosphere should they be deemed essential for our national security. . . .

4. The improvement of our capability, within feasible and practicable limits, to monitor the terms of the treaty, to detect violations, and to maintain our knowledge of Sino-Soviet nuclear activities, capabilities, and achievements.[39]

On August 14, Jackson offered a motion that the subcommittee approved immediately and the Armed Services Committee subsequently adopted, both unanimously. It called for the Department of Defense to provide detailed assurances that those in the highest levels of government would recognize, accept, and promise to observe the safeguards by the JCS. The committees also approved Jackson's motion that the subcommittee review compliance with the test ban treaty and the JCS safeguards annually.[40] The Kennedy administration finally agreed to these conditions in September, and Jackson announced his support for the treaty on September 13.[41] It passed shortly thereafter by a vote of 80 to 19.

Jackson's endorsement may have bolstered the pro-treaty total by six or seven, according to some informed observers of the debate,[42] but that did not mean his assessment of the Soviet Union had softened. On the contrary, he made it a point to dispel that notion. Speaking on the floor of the Senate on behalf of the treaty, he admonished the administration not to lapse "into a state which the Senate has learned to call euphoria—which is, if I may play the same game, a state in which one believes that he has serendipity and is therefore likely to display velleity for vigorous action."[43] "No responsible official," he told his fellow senators, "had rested the case for the treaty on the belief that the Soviet government can be trusted." The Preparedness Investigating Subcommittee, he promised, would vigilantly monitor the implementation of the safeguards the administration had accepted. The Soviet Union, he reiterated, aimed "to dominate the world" and "to bury us"; hence, "peace and the prevention of nuclear catastrophe depended on the United States maintaining nuclear superiority . . . that the Soviet Union will do everything it can to overcome."

Some of the more dovish senators, such as Fulbright, bristled at Jackson's reservations to the treaty and circumspectly challenged his underlying analysis. This group considered any reservations not only unnecessary but contradictory to the spirit of Soviet-American cooperation that produced the treaty. With Jackson in mind, Fulbright said, "Our only trouble will be with people trying to tack on reservations to cripple the treaty."[44] Fulbright and company declined, however, to press their disagreements further, lest they jeopardize the ratification of the treaty.[45] Jackson's reservations survived intact.

VIETNAM

Henry Jackson accepted the judgment of a bipartisan consensus that the United States had a vital interest in preserving the independence of a noncommunist Vietnam. When President Kennedy took office, he inherited certain commitments and policy premises that generated powerful pressure to intensify America's involvement in South Vietnam. Although Presidents Truman and Eisenhower both declined to send American combat troops there, both administrations believed that a communist victory in Indochina could result in the rest of Southeast Asia and potentially the Middle East submitting to or aligning with communism, raising the danger that no coalition adequate to confront the Kremlin with greater strength could be assembled.[46] Their reasoning flowed logically from the premises of the "domino theory," which became the conventional wisdom of the Truman and Eisenhower administration (i.e., if one country fell to communism, others would soon follow, with a momentum that could menace gravely the favorable balance of power on which victory in the Cold War depended). Even with the experience of Tito's communist Yugoslavia breaking with the Soviet Union in the late 1940s, both administrations also embraced the corollary premise of the domino theory, which perceived any communist gain as a gain for the Soviet Union. Both the

Truman and the Eisenhower administrations therefore envisaged the Vietnamese communists led by Ho Chi Minh as proxies for the Chinese communists, and Chinese communists as proxies for the Soviet Union.[47]

The Truman administration had no intention of supporting continued French colonial domination of Indochina, a region French colonial authorities had divided into three units: Laos, Vietnam, and Cambodia. The JCS had persuaded the administration, however, that the simultaneous U.S. commitments to NATO and the defense of South Korea left no combat resources to spare for Indochina. So the United States would have to provide the French Army with the necessary logistical and financial support to defeat the Indochinese Communists while simultaneously pressing the French government to grant independence to Indochina after it achieved victory.[48]

Eisenhower's decision not to intervene in Indochina militarily after the French defeat at Dien Bien Phu in 1954 stemmed from his fear of a land war in Asia and his aversion to having the United States tainted with the legacy of French colonialism. Yet neither that decision nor his administration's reluctant de facto acceptance of the partition of Vietnam at the Geneva Conference of 1954, consolidating the communist victory in the North above the 17th parallel, altered its fundamental convictions about the importance of keeping Indochina out of the communist orbit. Eisenhower extended the newly created state of South Vietnam and its new ruler, Ngo Dinh Diem, an anticolonialist Catholic, with extensive financial and political support. He also committed the United States to building up South Vietnam's army so it could prevail in the guerrilla war, which had intensified during the last two years of his administration. Eisenhower had refused to intervene on behalf of French colonialism but had not ruled out military intervention in Indochina under different circumstances. He regarded the independence of Laos as critical to the U.S. position in Southeast Asia. During the transition period, he informed Kennedy of his opposition to any settlement accepting a coalition government in Laos that included the communists.[49]

President Kennedy did not question either the importance of the American commitment to South Vietnam's independence or the logic that justified it. He accepted the domino theory and its corollary premises about the monolithic nature of the communist threat. He also believed that Vietnam represented a decisive test of American credibility in the underdeveloped world. Khrushchev had avowed the Soviet Union's intent to bury the West by supporting wars of national liberation waged by guerrillas. Kennedy decided that Vietnam was the place to show that the United States could win such conflicts, and hence win the Cold War.[50] His administration sought not just to prevent the communist insurgents from winning on the battlefield, but also to create a more stable, more prosperous, and increasingly democratic society that would eradicate the poverty, repression, and injustice the insurgents exploited in their struggle to subvert the independence of South Vietnam. Enamored of theories of graduated response, and fearful, too, of provoking a repetition of the Chinese intervention that occurred during the Korean War, the Kennedy administration abjured the notion of a massive military intervention aimed at defeating communist North Vietnam decisively. Instead, the United States would fight a limited war, with limited means, by the calibrated, restrained use of force designed to convince the communist enemy that it could not win at tolerable cost and risk. Thus the United States would not invade North Vietnam about the 17th parallel, which had divided the two Vietnams, the way it had sent combat troops into North Korea about the 38th parallel in 1950. Through a combination of the proportionate, measured, gradual use of American military power and the implementation of internal political reforms, South Vietnam would remain independent and noncommunist.[51]

Events in Indochina soon revealed to the president that achieving his goals would be infinitely more difficult than he had imagined. South Vietnam possessed nearly none of the attributes conducive to establishing and maintaining the stable, liberal democracy that the Kennedy administration had in mind. This brand new country had no stable political institutions or traditions of pluralism. Civil unrest, insurrection, and conspiracies abounded. Diem was no democrat but an authoritarian steeped in the mandarin tradition who equated dissent with sedition. Despite American largesse, he never attained full control over South Vietnam. Nor did he attain the level of popularity that the Vietnamese communists enjoyed in North Vietnam.[52] There was only widespread discontent with Diem's regime, and he faced an enemy implacably determined to extend communist control throughout Vietnam, no matter what the cost.[53] Ho Chi

Minh and his North Vietnamese communists interpreted the American strategy of graduated response as evidence of American inhibition rather than resolve.[54]

By 1963 the situation in South Vietnam had deteriorated precipitously since the previous year, when the military trends had appeared to be improving. The agreement to neutralize Laos that Kennedy made in the summer of 1962, rather than fight as Eisenhower had advised, turned out to be a sham as the communists backed by North Vietnam imposed their rule. The loss of Laos made the defense of South Vietnam infinitely more difficult and probably prohibitive, given the self-imposed constraints on U.S. military strategy.[55] Thereafter, the North Vietnamese communists possessed a less dangerous route for infiltrating South Vietnam than crossing the 17th parallel, an area more vulnerable to effective American interdiction by air power. Through the dense jungle that spanned the hundreds of miles of border between Laos and South Vietnam, they built the Ho Chi Minh Trail, which largely sustained their war effort in the South.

Diem's position internally and his relationship with the Kennedy administration had also deteriorated. As discontent with his regime intensified, he resisted undertaking the domestic reforms that the Kennedy administration established as a precondition for increasing American assistance. The Buddhist uprising in May 1963 in the city of Hue precipitated an irrevocable break between Diem and the Kennedy administration. Diem's troops fired on the demonstrators, killing several of them. The uprising escalated in June as Buddhist monks immolated themselves in protest, horrific television images that millions of Americans witnessed with revulsion on the nightly news. Convinced that the United States could not win with Diem and morally averse to him, the Kennedy administration immersed the United States further into the conflict by encouraging Diem's removal. A group of dissident South Vietnamese generals overthrew and murdered Diem on November 1, 1963.[56]

Whether Kennedy would have sanctioned the massive American military intervention in Vietnam that occurred during the Johnson administration remains an open question. Some maintain that he had soured on the commitment by the end of his presidency and intended to withdraw American military personnel after the election of 1964.[57] Others maintain that Lyndon Johnson faithfully executed Kennedy's intentions by escalating American involvement in the war.[58] What we do know for certain is this: The Kennedy administration significantly raised the stakes of the American commitment to South Vietnam, making the choice of withdrawal much more difficult for his successors. Although he deferred the decision to introduce large numbers of American combat troops as some of his advisers recommended, he still approved a significant increase in the number of military personnel in South Vietnam from 900 to more than 16,000. His administration's complicity in the assassination of Diem implicated the United States further in the survival of the South Vietnamese regime. The unpopularity and incompetence of Diem's successors created intense pressure for the United States to assume a greater burden in conducting the war, lest the strife-ridden, beleaguered regime collapse.[59] When Lyndon Johnson escalated the war in 1965, he certainly believed that the decision was consistent with Kennedy's legacy. Indeed, he retained nearly all of Kennedy's principal foreign policy advisers, who, with the exception of Undersecretary of State George Ball, endorsed escalation in 1965.[60]

Henry Jackson also supported the Kennedy administration's commitment to South Vietnam, with one major qualification. He shared Eisenhower's fear that the loss of Laos to the communists would make the defense of South Vietnam untenable. As he observed in 1962: "We could free South-Vietnam of the Viet Cong and make it truly free and independent only to have it outflanked by a complete Communist takeover in Laos and Cambodia. If this should happen, it would be almost impossible to hold Viet-Nam and Southeast Asia in the free world."[61] The United States, Jackson insisted, must not only "restore freedom to Vietnam . . . we must also prevent South-Vietnam from later being encircled by the Communists from the North." He thought the neutralization scheme that the Kennedy administration had accepted for Laos in the summer of 1962 would facilitate rather than prevent communist domination. Convinced that "the so-called coalition government in Laos cannot succeed in maintaining any kind of honest neutrality," he urged the administration "to make a determined effort . . . to save that part of Laos vital to the security of South Vietnam": the area "along the Mekong River which extends from Burma along Thailand and Cambodia to Viet-Nam itself."

Jackson agreed with the president entirely, however, about the underlying premises that generated the commitment to Vietnam. Since the

1950s, he had conceived of the struggle there "as just as much a fight for freedom and our own security as the conflict in Berlin, Cuba, or elsewhere." He warned, too, that "if we lose Vietnam, we may well lose Laos, Cambodia, and eventually all of Southeast Asia to Communist domination." He did not yet conceive of the emerging Sino-Soviet split as an opportunity to play one superpower off against the other. Rather, he expected the split would exacerbate conflict and danger in the underdeveloped world by goading the Soviet Union and Red China to incite wars of national liberation even more relentlessly as a way of demonstrating their revolutionary credentials.

In December 1962, Jackson embarked on a two-week inspection of American facilities in Vietnam that only underscored his convictions. He found particularly rousing the courage of the Montagnard tribesmen whom he met in their tribal area of north central Vietnam. It was important, he wrote upon his return, "that we be successful in our efforts to stamp out guerrilla warfare and counterinsurgency, not just to save South Vietnam and Southeast Asia, but to demonstrate to the Communists that we can deal effectively with a kind of war that they hope to win in Asia, Africa, and Latin America. By doing this, we will be establishing a further deterrent to Sino-Soviet aggression." Vietnam, he said, was "the great testing area to determine whether we shall be successful in developing the deterrent to the kind of war that Khrushchev said he would wage and support."[62] He had no problem, either, with the Kennedy administration's decision to facilitate Diem's removal. In September 1963, two months before it happened, he declared to the Montesano Chamber of Commerce that a military coup to oust Diem could be a good thing. He "hoped U.S. intelligence officers in Vietnam would find a general favoring such a move." "We have reached a point," he stated, where "the present regime in South Vietnam had to go before continuing aid would be worthwhile."[63]

There is, of course, much to criticize legitimately about the U.S. role in the Vietnam War. Some American statesmen implemented their policy based on an exaggerated although not groundless fear that the loss of Vietnam could set off a chain of dominoes that would imperil the entire edifice of containment. The internal weakness of our South Vietnamese allies, the country's geographical vulnerability, and the tenacity of Ho Chi Minh made South Vietnam a very unpropitious place to draw the line against communist aggression in Southeast Asia. Hindsight confirms the instincts of the British at the time that Malaysia—more robust internally, more defensible, more amenable to the successful application of American military power—offered a better place to draw such a line. The strategy of graduated response gave the United States the worst of both worlds—a commitment large enough to invest American prestige heavily in the outcome, but not large enough to win. The Sino-Soviet split turned out to be deeper and more permanent than expected. Contrary to our original expectation, the victory of North Vietnam in 1975 did not dampen, but intensified, the rivalries between the Soviet Union and China on the one hand, and China and Vietnam on the other.

Yet the mistakes the United States committed in Vietnam do not invalidate the policy of vigilant containment that Cold Warriors such as Henry Jackson advocated. Nor do they invalidate much of the conventional wisdom underlying this policy.[64] Despite the caricature of it by many of its critics, the domino theory contained large elements of validity, properly qualified. History attests powerfully to the fact that dominoes sometimes do fall in international relations. Note the bleak history of the 1930s in Europe when Anglo-French appeasement of Hitler encouraged states to go along with or remain neutral toward Nazi Germany, with dire moral and practical consequences for the world. Note, too, the providential collapse of the Soviet empire during the 1990s after the Berlin Wall went down.[65] For Henry Jackson and his generation of American statesmen steeped in the lessons of Munich, prudence dictated that the United States should hedge against the real danger that newly independent countries of Asia, many of them fragile and beset with domestic problems, could fall in with the Soviet Union or China. Communism possessed enormous appeal to elites of the underdeveloped world, many of whom still considered it the wave of the future, as did both Khrushchev and Mao, for all their differences.[66]

Furthermore, Jackson and like-minded statesmen did not completely misread the dynamics of the Sino-Soviet split. At the outset, this split did goad both powers to pursue a more adventurous and belligerent policy toward the United States. Khrushchev undertook his Cuban gambit of October 1962 and stepped up his visible support for wars of national liberation partly to offset Chinese criticism that the Soviet Union had lost its revolutionary resolve.[67] As for Mao, American statesmen had ample grounds for worrying about a man who, in the name of his vision of communism, had just unleashed the catastrophic Great Leap Forward, resulting in the deaths of 30 million of his own citizens, and about a regime that allowed him to perpetrate this hideous crime.[68] Mao's rhetoric and his support for revolutionary wars in Asia gave plausibility to the fears of American statesmen that China was bent on applying those same fanatical ideological principles to the realm of international politics. It took the Cultural Revolution of 1966–69, another self-inflicted catastrophe in the name of ideology, before Mao was ready to consider as the lesser of two evils tacit collaboration with the United States against the surging power and expansionism of the Soviet Union.[69] For all the shortcomings of our South Vietnamese ally, the communists of North Vietnam proved to be infinitely more repressive and brutal than the Saigon government on its worst day.[70] American success in Vietnam would have averted the Cambodian holocaust; U.S. defeat made it possible.[71]

On November 22, 1963, however, the Vietnam War had not yet become controversial within the nation. It had barely registered in the consciousness of most Americans. Indeed, Cold War liberalism seemed more robust than ever. President Kennedy's death on that day produced an enormous reservoir of support for his ambitious domestic and civil rights agenda. In November 1964, President Lyndon Johnson, Henry Jackson, and the national Democratic Party won a landslide victory against the Republicans, whose presidential candidate, Senator Barry Goldwater from Arizona, campaigned to roll back the New Deal. President Johnson, the Democratic Congress, and the national media interpreted the results of the 1964 election as a resounding endorsement of Johnson's Great Society: the most expensive, most expansive liberal legislative initiative in American history, a program far more ambitious than the one Harry Truman proposed in his abortive Fair Deal. Before the Vietnam War triggered upheavals that would drive Johnson from office and move Jackson from the mainstream to an increasingly embattled position within his party, Cold War liberalism would achieve this one last triumph of epic proportions, a triumph that contained the seeds of its own demise.

Chapter 9

The Great Liberal Crackup,
1964–1969

HENRY JACKSON's relationship with President Johnson took the opposite course of his relationship with John Kennedy. Whereas he and Kennedy drifted slowly apart after the high point of their collaboration at the Democratic Convention of 1960, Jackson and Johnson grew steadily closer despite their initial reservations about one another dating back to their Senate days—reservations that the dispute over the TFX intensified because each suspected the other of exercising undue influence to win the contract for their home state.[1]

Jackson and Barry Goldwater, Johnson's Republican opponent in the presidential campaign of 1964, genuinely liked and respected each other. As plain speaking, bluntly honest men of the West, both elected to the Senate in 1953, they had worked harmoniously on the Territories Subcommittee of the Interior Committee. Goldwater regarded Jackson as one of the most knowledgeable and perspicacious men in the Senate on matters of foreign policy and national security.[2] He had opposed the Limited Test Ban Treaty of 1963 for reasons similar to Jackson's reservations. Unlike much of the national media and most liberal Democrats, Jackson refused to demonize Goldwater during the campaign. He came publicly to his defense, in fact, by clarifying what the Arizona senator meant rather than what he seemed to say about the possibility of using nuclear weapons to defoliate North Vietnam. The media had construed Goldwater's blustery and ill-advised rhetoric as advocating such use, although that is not what he intended.[3]

Jackson believed, however, that Goldwater lacked the qualifications to be president. He found Goldwater's work habits in the Senate lackadaisical and his domestic philosophy misguided. Goldwater had one of the worst attendance records in the Senate for roll-call votes.[4] He also opposed categorically most of the domestic legislation that Jackson supported devoutly. Ideologically averse to public power, Goldwater had unsuccessfully opposed Jackson's efforts in 1962 to secure congressional authorization for expanding the capacity of the Hanford nuclear complex to generate additional hydroelectric power for the Bonneville Power Administration (BPA) to market and distribute. He had opposed a measure Jackson introduced to allow the Northwest to recall any surplus power shipped to California, should the need for it arise at home. Goldwater was the only member of the Senate Interior Committee who opposed the Wilderness Bill of 1964, which Jackson co-sponsored and shepherded through the Senate in his capacity as chairman of the committee.[5] Goldwater opposed, as well, the Civil Rights Act of 1964, which Jackson thought long overdue and voted for with enthusiasm.[6]

Like Lyndon Johnson, Jackson saw robust activism on the part of the federal government as the key to making things better for all Americans. So did most liberals of their generation. In 1958, liberal Harvard economist John Kenneth Galbraith published *The Affluent Society*, whose arguments emerged as the conventional wisdom of 1960s liberals: that big business has such enormous power to set prices and control demand that only a combination of big government and big labor could countervail it; that advanced economies had solved the problem of producing abundance; that what remained was the political problem of distributing that abundance equitably; and that the state must take strong action to reduce dangerous disparities of wealth and to eliminate squalor in the midst of affluence. Neither Jackson nor John Kennedy nor Lyndon Johnson ever went as far as Galbraith's embrace of a corporate state resting on the trinity of big government, big business, and big labor.[7] Jackson and Johnson had supported Kennedy's decision in 1962 to stimulate the economy by cutting taxes rather than by increasing government spending as Galbraith recommended.[8] In large measure, however, Johnson's War on Poverty reflected the conventional wisdom of Galbraith and a growing number of liberals that the federal government could eradicate human misery without adversely affecting the prosperity of the nation or the moral virtues necessary to sustain it.[9] Henry Jackson staunchly supported Johnson's Great Society program and the landmark civil rights legislation that Congress passed in 1964 and 1965. He co-sponsored, too, the bill that established Medicare through Social Security.

Furthermore, Jackson and Johnson shared a common agenda in areas involving the jurisdiction of the Interior Committee, which Jackson chaired. Unlike Kennedy, who cared little about dams, public power, or reclamation projects, Johnson had an intense interest in and philosophy similar to Jackson's on these issues. Jackson and Stewart Udall, Johnson's secretary of the interior, whom the president had retained from the Kennedy administration, collaborated closely to produce and secure congressional approval of a plethora of landmark legislation that presaged the emergence of environmentalism as a critical issue in American politics.[10]

What most inspired Johnson's growing appreciation of Jackson was his resoluteness in the face of the social upheavals that the mounting opposition to the Vietnam War triggered. Jackson stood by the president and the premises of Cold War liberalism as both came increasingly under assault from liberals who considered the Vietnam War a mistake and the policy of vigilant containment the source of it. Despite his long-standing friendship with Bobby Kennedy, Jackson rebuffed his entreaty for support in the race for the 1968 Democratic presidential nomination when Kennedy entered belatedly as a candidate sympathetic to the New Politics wing of the Democratic Party. Instead, Jackson backed Vice President Hubert Humphrey, Johnson's handpicked successor. Jackson missed the spectacle of the Democratic Convention of 1968 in Chicago, which ended in bloodshed and riots televised across the nation. He could not escape, however, its political fallout. The upheavals of 1968 spelled the demise of Cold War liberalism's ascendancy in the Democratic Party for a generation. By the time Richard Nixon took the oath of office in January 1969, Henry Jackson had become his "favorite Democrat in the Senate."[11] Jackson was, by then, no longer just one of many, but a liberal distinguished from his brethren by his knowledge and competence. Increasingly, Cold War liberals identified him as their one great hope to recapture the Democratic Party and the presidency.

THE POLITICS OF THE INTERIOR COMMITTEE

When Jackson became chairman in January 1963, the Interior Committee concentrated mainly on the regional agendas of westerners, who dominated it: land and water resource issues, minerals, mining, and Indian affairs. Initially, Jackson's interest in the committee also arose from parochial concerns. He unabashedly used his position on the committee so that the Bonneville Power Administration under its jurisdiction would continue to have at its disposal abundant low-cost electrical energy: the magnet attracting industry to the Pacific Northwest. He always supported public power versus private power, federal dams versus private dams, multiple-use projects undertaken by the federal government versus single-use projects undertaken by private enterprise.

He also pursued, however, a national agenda that transcended such parochial concerns. He came to the Interior Committee with an appreciation for nature instilled in him by his boyhood camping trips in the Cascades with Bob Humphrey. His early approach to conservation issues largely derived from his hero, Theodore Roosevelt, who advocated the wise use of natural resources that balanced the preservation of the wilderness and recreational areas with the need for economic development. In 1957, Jackson co-sponsored the Wilderness Preservation System Bill, a forerunner of the Wilderness Bill that the Interior Committee reported and Congress passed in 1964. He urged that Americans must preserve "our national wilderness system" while "meeting, outside the wilderness reserves, all our needs for commodities and for developed recreational areas."[12]

During the Johnson presidency, Jackson's approach evolved beyond Theodore Roosevelt's version of traditional conservationism. He emerged as a leading advocate of government's implementing comprehensive plans to protect the air, water, wilderness, and wildlife. The Interior Committee reported and Congress passed a series of landmark bills between 1964 and 1968 that collectively left a "towering legacy" for which Henry Jackson "deserves enormous credit," according to then Secretary of the Interior Stewart Udall, a close friend and admirer of Jackson, notwithstanding their later differences over Vietnam and over the course of American foreign policy.[13] Those most intimately involved in the details and strategy of this legislation echoed Udall's assessment of Jackson's legacy in the areas of conservation and environment, which includes the following:

The Land and Conservation Act of 1964, establishing a special fund and financing scheme to help state, local, and federal agencies accelerate acquisition of land and water areas suitable for public parks and outdoor recreational use.

The Wilderness Act of 1964, establishing a National Wilderness Preservation System, placing 9.1 million acres of federal lands not yet commercially exploited immediately into the system, and designating another 52.1 million acres as later subject to review and placement into the system by the joint approval of the legislative and executive branches.

National Seashore Bills protecting the seashores and establishing national parks at Cape Cod, Massachusetts; Cape Lookout, North Carolina; Assateague Island, spanning 33 miles of the Virginia and Maryland coastline; San Juan Island, Washington; and Port Reyes, California.

The Water Resources Planning Act of 1965, establishing a water resources council to devise approaches for anticipating and redressing water problems of the future.

Redwood National Park, established in 1968 to protect millions of the world's oldest and tallest trees.

North Cascades National Park, created in Washington State in 1968 as part of a 1,191,000-acre region in northern Washington along the Canadian border and containing some of the most scenic wilderness in the world.

The Wild and Scenic Rivers Act of 1968, designed to preserve several wild and scenic rivers in their natural state.

The Colorado River Basin Project Act of 1968, authorizing the then largest reclamation project in American history in a single piece of legislation and thereby settling the dispute over the Central Arizona Project that had raged for decades.[14]

As chairman of the Interior Committee, Jackson discharged his responsibilities deftly, having learned a great deal during his first twelve years in the Senate watching his mentors Richard Russell and Clinton Anderson run the Armed Services and Interior Committees, respectively. Jackson brought other great strengths to his position as chairman of the Interior Committee besides a long apprenticeship. He had few peers in his capacity to master complex information and in his devotion to his job, which continued even after his marriage. He also had developed a clear and consistent agenda. Throughout his career, he attracted and retained a first-rate staff to work with him. Sterling Munro, who replaced John Salter as his administrative assistant, served Jackson brilliantly as perhaps the brightest and most effective administrative assistant of his day on Capitol Hill. He had an impressive mastery of and passionate interest in the resource, conservation, energy, and environmental issues that Jackson dealt with on the committee. Jackson usually hired his staff based on his assessment of their expertise and good judgment—not based on patronage. Bill Van Ness, Daniel Dreyfus, and Grenville Garside served as his principal advisers on his Interior Committee staff, which was notable for its knowledge, competence, and integrity. Jackson also wielded his great influence to ensure that the executive branch hired first-rate talent to work with him. He and Warren Magnuson prevailed on a reluctant Stewart Udall to appoint Charles Luce, director of the BPA, as undersecretary of the interior. To this day, Udall considers Luce the best appointment he ever made.[15]

Jackson's aptitude for knowing when and how to delegate authority to staff whom he trusted greatly amplified his impact. As Dan Dreyfus explained, the clarity and constancy of Jackson's views made it easy "to understand Scoop well enough to act as he would. Once you made the grade, you could operate in his name and be assured of his support. You could always get to him if you needed him."[16] Jackson also had an instinct for interpreting the mandate of his committee assignments expansively and the skill to carry it off without provoking the wrath of his fellow members. Many of the initiatives he took on the Interior and Government Operations Committees really belonged jurisdictionally under the Environmental and Public Works Committees.

Jackson could be intensely partisan, Dreyfus commented, but also had "a rare ability to deal with people of diverse philosophical points of view." His bipartisanship and reputation for integrity proved to be huge assets, not only in foreign policy, but also on the Interior Committee, where regional and economic interests usually trumped party splits. Senators Mark Hatfield, Republican from Oregon; Ted Stevens, Republican from Alaska; Bill Bradley, Democrat from New Jersey; Edmund Muskie, Democrat from Maine; Sam Nunn, Democrat from Georgia; George McGovern,

Democrat from South Dakota; Barry Goldwater; and others who served with Jackson on committees where he outranked them, all gave Jackson high marks for his treatment of Republican and junior members of the committee. Senator Daniel Patrick Moynihan summed up best why so many of his colleagues often deferred to Jackson. "Scoop not only had unparalled mastery of the issues, but could be trusted. If he said it was so, it was so."[17]

Jackson's accomplishments on the Interior Committee required a great deal of his legislative skill, expertise, and sound judgment. Congressman Wayne Aspinall, Democrat from Colorado and chairman of the House Interior Committee, had a restrictive conception of the committee's role and jurisdiction, which conflicted with Jackson's. Also, Aspinall was more reluctant than Jackson to constrain private development by government regulation in the name of conservationism, recreation, or environmentalism.[18] Jackson had to reckon, too, with powerful private interests and their supporters in Congress. His assumption of the chairmanship of the Interior Committee coincided with the first stirring of an environmental movement. In 1962, Rachel Carson had published *Silent Spring*, predicting that an insidious combination of the drive for economic development and the introduction of noxious pesticides would lead to the extinction of many species of birds and the earthly dominance of insects invincible to such chemicals. This best-seller had a decisive influence not only on the thinking of a generation of environmentalists but on the outlook of millions of other Americans previously unaware of such issues.[19]

Congressional approval of legislation creating North Cascades National Park exemplified Jackson's talent for reconciling divergent interests, striking a sensible balance between conservation and development, and forging a legislative consensus. In 1963, he initiated a two-year study of the feasibility of establishing such a park, a study that was completed in December 1965. For the next year and a half, he brokered a series of compromises that resolved disagreements between the Agriculture and the Interior Departments over specific boundary lines and respective jurisdictions in the park. "Jackson also managed his local constituency beautifully," recounted Stewart Udall. "Jackson balanced things well. His colleagues and his constituents trusted him."[20] On February 11 and 12, 1966, Jackson presided over two days of field hearings in Seattle which heard 260 witnesses. He had to overcome mining and timber interests, which were averse to any restrictions on their operations, on the one side, and environmentalists averse to any commercial exploitation, on the other.[21] A believer in the compatibility and necessity of economic growth and conservation, he built a consensus for an agreement that satisfied the legitimate needs of both without sacrificing one on the altar of the other. The wilderness and recreation areas of the park excluded timber and mining operations but did not decrease the commercial timber stands suitable for cutting. As a concession to Washington State's many hunters, Jackson changed the status of the Lake Chelan area from a national park to a recreation area so that hunting there could continue (the law prohibited hunting in national parks). Stewart Udall called North Cascades National Park "a monument to Henry Jackson, which never would have been done unless he wanted it done."[22]

THE VIETNAM WAR

Jackson received less attention for his accomplishments on the Interior Committee than for his unapologetic defense of the U.S. commitment to Vietnam as the war escalated exponentially. By 1965, President Johnson and his principal advisers, all holdovers from the Kennedy administration, concluded that Kennedy's policy toward Vietnam had failed. The United States could not preserve the independence of the fragile regime in South Vietnam against a determined adversary such as Ho Chi Minh without committing large numbers of U.S. combat forces. Reluctant to embroil the United States in a protracted conflict that could jeopardize his Great Society, Johnson feared even more the domestic political reaction of losing South Vietnam. The president anticipated that a North Vietnamese victory would incite a replay of the lacerating debate over who lost China so costly to the Democratic Party in the late 1940s. He also accepted the premises of Kennedy's principal advisers about the importance of preserving a noncommunist South Vietnam for U.S. grand strategy. They all assumed that both major communist powers sought relentlessly to weaken the United States by encouraging wars of national liberation in places such as Vietnam. If South Vietnam fell to the communists, they anticipated the rest of Southeast Asia would eventually fall too, increasing the threat to South Korea, spelling potential trouble for Japan, and undermining the will of the American people and U.S. allies in Europe to resist communist aggression elsewhere.[23]

Henry Jackson never believed that the outcome of the Vietnam War would determine the outcome of the Cold War. Or as he put it, "The present struggle to counter the expansionist thrusts of the Communist powers will not be won if South Vietnam is successfully defended, nor will it be lost if South Vietnam falls." Nevertheless, he did deem America's defense of South Vietnam significant for deterring Soviet and Chinese aggression in East Asia, which aimed, in his view, to subjugate that entire region, notwithstanding the deepening of the Sino-Soviet split, which he duly noted:

> The Russians and the Chinese may not see eye to eye on whether and where and how much violence should be used to overthrow non-communist governments. I think that they do not agree about everything related to the waging of the Vietnamese struggle. But the Sino-Soviet quarrel is an argument between them over ends, not means. Both are whole-hearted supporters of wars of national liberation. Both are supporting the war in Vietnam—with resources, with diplomacy, and with propaganda. And while we should take advantage of their quarrel as we can, the only sure guide to our policy is to do what we must do to defend our interest. We will only confuse and mislead ourselves if we look to their differences to give us an easy way out.[24]

Jackson attributed the failure of the Chinese communists to create a puppet regime in Indonesia, "the sixth most populous country in the world," to the demonstration of U.S. resolve in Vietnam. "Indonesia was ready for takeover in October of 1965," he proclaimed repeatedly. "If it had not been for our presence, we know from good sources that the pro-western counter coup would never have taken place. Then you would have the Communists facing Mindanao and the Philippines and close to the shores of Australia."[25]

So Jackson loyally voted for the Gulf of Tonkin Resolution of August 1964 authorizing the president to escalate the war should the need arise. He supported Johnson's agonizing decisions in 1965 to send large numbers of U.S. combat troops to Vietnam and to initiate a bombing campaign in the North. He endorsed, too, the president's decision to limit American objectives to "preserving the independence of South Vietnam" without having any "designs on North Vietnam."[26] He rejected, therefore, the ideas of Barry Goldwater and other hawks that the United States must seek absolute victory. From the beginning, however, Jackson had serious disagreements with the Johnson administration about how to fight the war and about the assumptions underlying U.S. strategy, disagreements that placed him on the spectrum somewhere between the president and Barry Goldwater. The memory of how the protracted conflict in Korea had eroded Harry Truman's popularity instilled in Jackson an aversion to the strategies of graduated escalation so attractive to Johnson, McNamara, and those most responsible for conducting the war effort:

> When American and South Korean forces threw back the third Chinese Communist offensive in the spring of 1951, with staggering Chinese losses, the Communists indicated their willingness to negotiate. Our forces were ordered to halt their drive and we agreed to sit down with the Communists at the conference table. . . . Once this country let up its military pressure, the Communists took advantage of the lull in the fighting to build a strong defensive line, fourteen miles deep, and once they had built it, they knew we could renew hostilities only at the cost of heavy casualties. With their defenses secure, they proceeded to drag out the negotiations, trying to win at the negotiating table far more than they had been able to win on the battlefield.[27]

The North Vietnamese, Jackson predicted, would interpret graduated escalation as a signal of U.S. weakness rather than determination. To retain the support of the American people, on which the success of the war effort depended, Jackson stressed the importance of defining U.S. objectives clearly and intervening decisively to accomplish those objectives.[28]

He considered the Johnson administration's strategy flawed on both counts, flaws he blamed on Robert McNamara and the type of thinking he represented. Instead of the administration's limited and incremental bombing strategy, which he believed imposed too many restraints to achieve decisive results, Jackson pressed unceasingly but unsuccessfully for a full-fledged strategic bombing campaign directed at inflicting crippling damage on North Vietnam: targeting ports, sources of hydroelectric power, and sources of petroleum. He also pressed unsuccessfully for the early mining and blockading of Haiphong Harbor, which the Nixon administration later undertook with his backing in 1972.[29] At one point, he advocated an American landing just north of the demilitarized zone formally separating the two Vietnams to interdict supply lines running to the South from southern North Vietnam and Laos. He also criticized the Johnson administration for its excessive fear of provoking a Chinese intervention in Vietnam—a fear that, in his estimation, unduly constrained the U.S. war effort:

> A recurrent note in the discussion of Vietnam these past weeks has been concern that the war there is open-ended, that it may lead us in the direction of a general war with Asia. This is very unlikely. China has almost no nuclear capability today, and would risk devastation were it to initiate the use of nuclear weapons. It would be far more difficult for the Chinese Communists to deploy and supply massed forces in Vietnam than it was in Korea, because of the hard facts of geography, transportation, and climate.[30]

Disturbed by the administration's tendency toward excessive optimism in portraying the course of the war to the American people, Jackson counseled against understating the difficulties that lay ahead:

> To arouse great but unjustified expectations may quiet a few critics today, but it will only sharpen their doubts and disillusion tomorrow. The willingness of government officials to speak frankly about conditions and policies and requirements is the necessary foundation of public confidence. . . .[31]

Jackson made two more trips to Vietnam, in December 1965 and 1966. His conversations with General Westmoreland, the commander and chief of U.S. forces in Vietnam, and his tours of the battlefield fortified his convictions about the imperative of dramatically expediting the American escalation and expanding the bombing campaign:

> The central issue in Vietnam is this—what was exclusively a guerilla war has now become in many areas of Vietnam a regular war with engagements involving regimental size forces. In sum, the longer we delay in taking counter-steps, the longer the war will be, with great losses in blood and property. The communist game is to protract the conflict, hoping that in weariness, the United States will withdraw. Superior military force must be brought to bear if we are going to bring the conflict to a conclusion.[32]

While in Vietnam in December 1965, Jackson also visited a civilian hospital in Saigon run by Project Hope, where he met Dr. Haakon Ragde, a urologist born in Norway whose parents had immigrated to the United States when he was a young boy. Jackson asked Ragde if there was anything he needed for the hospital. He also encouraged him to relocate to Washington State after the war, lauding the many virtues of the Pacific Northwest. Initially, Ragde reacted with intense skepticism to what Jackson had to say. After graduating from the University of Virginia Medical School, he had practiced for a year in the Seattle area, which he thought "a terrible place because it rained all the time." Also, many politicians had promised Ragde help with the hospital without delivering on it. What impressed Ragde about Jackson was that he delivered on what he promised. Two weeks after making the request, Ragde received all the supplies he asked for and more. Eventually, Jackson also wore down Ragde's aversion to the Pacific Northwest. After the war, he did relocate to Washington State, practicing medicine at the University of Washington, serving as Henry Jackson's personal physician, working on his political campaigns, and becoming one of his closest personal friends.[33] While in Vietnam in December 1966, Jackson also displayed physical courage to match the courage of his convictions. He did not even flinch when a shell exploded during his tour of the destroyer, *Manley*, wounding three sailors.[34]

By the time Jackson returned from his trip to Vietnam in December 1966, the war had come to polarize the nation and the Democratic Party, demolishing the liberal Cold War consensus he embodied. Disillusionment with the war catalyzed the emergence of the New Left, a movement rooted in the sensibilities and concerns of an exploding, adversarial, youth-dominated counterculture hostile to Cold War liberalism in general and the American involvement in Vietnam in particular. This movement drew strength from a number of other sources: the idealism and activism generated by the civil rights movement of the 1960s; the unprecedented affluence of American society, which permitted so many young people the leisure and luxury to protest; and the revisionist assault in the academy on Cold War liberalism launched with the publication of William Appleman Williams's *The Tragedy of American Diplomacy*, which blamed the war mainly on American rather than Soviet aggression.[35] The arguments of revisionist historians simultaneously fueled the emergence of the antiwar movement and gained popularity thanks to it.[36] Tom Hayden and his co-founders of Students for a Democratic Society (SDS), the largest and most influential of the radical student organizations, embraced anti-anticommunism as a core doctrine at Port Huron, Michigan, in June 1962. As Al Haber, another co-founder, put it:

> Port Huron was the first time our politics surfaced. [The League for Industrial Democracy] could tolerate searching young minds but not a group of people who were four-square against anti-Communism, eight-square against American culture, twelve-square against sell-out unions, one-hundred-twenty-square against an interpretation of the Cold War that saw it as a Soviet plot and identified American policy fondly.[37]

The New Left identified Henry Jackson, of "Washington State and Boeing," as the archetype of the retrograde "bomber liberals" who had dangerously and needlessly perpetuated the arms race and the Cold War.[38]

The growing militancy of the antiwar movement manifested itself in a proliferation of marches and demonstrations that often ended in violence. Elite American universities erupted into battlegrounds of protest, beginning with the free speech movement in 1964 at Berkeley, where student rebels successfully defied the university's edict against all types of political activities on campus. The first "teach-ins" against the Vietnam War occurred in April 1965 at the University of Michigan, igniting the spread of such demonstrations across the nation's college campuses outside the South. Thousands of student protesters marched on the Pentagon in October 1967. The severity and violence of student demonstrations at Columbia University forced the shutdown of New York's most prestigious university in April 1968. The New Left also promoted as the new vanguard for the black struggle the Black Panther Party, founded in 1966. Spurning the integrationist and nonviolent legacy of Martin Luther King, Jr., the Panthers and other radical groups similarly disposed often encouraged and certainly did not condemn the mayhem and disorder that plagued many American cities during the middle 1960s, beginning with the riots in the Watts section of Los Angeles in August 1965 and culminating in the devastating riots in Newark and Detroit in the summer of 1967.[39]

Marrying later in life spared Jackson the fate of most parents of his generation who had older children confronting them with the adversary culture and the antiwar movement in their homes. His daughter, Anna

Marie, had just turned three years old in 1966, the year Henry and Helen became parents again, in April, with the birth of Peter, named after the senator's father. Jackson had little interest in the cultural icons of a younger generation that rebelled against the ethics and values of his own. When he heard the word Beatles he thought of crawling insects, not the world-famous rock group.[40]

What Jackson deplored was the politics of the antiwar movement and the violence it spawned. "The characteristic element of the New Left," he said, is "the rejection of authority. The mood is negative, even nihilistic."[41] He attacked the student protesters for their ignorance of what his generation had learned and experienced. He linked "the fallacies" of the "so-called peace movement to our American tendency to neglect the study of history." He urged that every student study "that fascinating but shameful decade when Hitler was building the German war machine while the democracies were preaching disarmament and neglecting their military preparedness." He called on "well-intentioned advocates of immediate withdrawal from Vietnam" to ponder that "the peace movement helped bring on World War II, not to prevent it." As in the 1930s, he insisted, "the true advocates of peace today" are those who understand that power must be used, with restraint but also with assurance, to keep the peace or to restore it.[42] Jackson also chastised the antiwar protesters for describing the United States as an immoral and sick society:

> The United States need apologize to no one for its policies in the years since World War II. We have responded to the needs of the poor and the hungry and the sick with a generosity unmatched in history. Good works are our preferred course of action, when the choice is up to us. We covet no one's territory. We have committed no act of aggression. We have aided independent people whose crime, in communist eyes, is that they dare defend themselves against aggression.[43]

He did not reserve his criticism only for the young. He blasted the "articulate minority of older persons for being no more constructive than the New Left it has egged on. Thirty is, after all, more of a state of mind than a birthday, and a good many persons who will never see thirty again are thinking, if not behaving as if they were adolescents." He excoriated "professors who are themselves often the worst offenders in selling the patent medicine remedies of the New Left or the Old Right, of the Black Militants or the Ku Klux Klan . . . , who no longer believe that truth must be an essential consideration in a college or university community." He decried as a "smear phrase" the allegation of the New Left and an increasing number of liberals that he was a creature of the military-industrial complex.[44]

Like most ordinary Americans of his generation, Jackson also called for the restoration of law and order that, in his view, the riots, student upheavals, and urban violence of the late 1960s dangerously undermined.[45] The United States, he emphasized, was a great nation "because—more than any other country in the world—we have judiciously and fearlessly protected the freedom and right to criticize, to oppose and to join with others to bring about change," and he condemned without distinction "extremists of the left or right" who acted as if the ends justified the means.[46] Extremism, he warned, threatened "the very heart of democracy. Impatient with the democratic process, what they propose is tyranny of the minority."[47]

Jackson's confrontations with the politics of the New Left and the antiwar movement extended to his own political party. As he and other hawks urged the president to do more to win the war sooner, a growing number of liberals such as Senators Fulbright, Church, and McGovern challenged both the practicality and the morality of American policy, not only in Vietnam, but throughout the world. A toned-down but still potent version of the New Left's critique of American foreign policy underlay the arguments of a growing number of these Democratic doves.[48] J. William Fulbright, chairman of the Foreign Relations Committee, led this group in the 1960s. A Rhodes scholar of aristocratic bearing, mordantly witty, sophisticated, and urbane, he had become the darling of the antiwar movement for his relentless criticism of U.S. involvement in the Vietnam War as the Johnson administration massively increased the number of U.S. troops there between 1965 and 1967 to a peak of 550,000. What fanned his reputation as America's most articulate and influential dove was the publication of his *Arrogance of Power* in December 1966. This widely heralded and well-known best-seller denounced not only the American involvement in Vietnam but also the globalist assumptions of NSC 68, which had guided U.S. foreign policy throughout most of the Cold War. Fulbright argued that the United States should get out of Vietnam, scale down its definition of strategic goals, reduce its responsibilities, break the viselike grip of the neurotic fear of communism that had distorted American foreign policy, and rely increasingly on the United Nations to mediate international disputes. The main threat to world peace was not the Soviet Union, he said, but the arrogance of American power that needed desperately to be constrained.[49]

Aspects of Fulbright's critique of U.S. foreign policy reverberated powerfully and widely: to the New Left and liberal doves of both parties; to isolationists of the Old Right, disciples of Senator Robert Taft, Republican of Ohio; to foreign policy realists such as Hans Morgenthau and George F. Kennan.[50] Such men tended to depreciate the importance of ideology as a source of behavior in international politics. They thus took a more relaxed view of the Soviet threat than the Truman generation of Cold Warriors reflected in NSC 68. Unlike Truman and Henry Jackson, moreover, they did not believe it necessary or desirable for the United States to promote and defend liberal democracy in geopolitical regions deemed vital.[51]

Neither Fulbright nor his critique of U.S. foreign policy appealed to Jackson. There were few colleagues in the Senate that he did not like. Notwithstanding their sharply divergent views on the war and America's role in the world, Jackson and Frank Church always maintained an excellent relationship and worked harmoniously together for years on the Interior Committee, where usually they saw eye to eye.[52] Notwithstanding their ongoing battles over Vietnam, American foreign policy, and the future direction of the Democratic Party, Jackson and George McGovern always maintained a respectful relationship, albeit less close than Jackson and Church. When Jackson and McGovern debated one another on a morning television talk show in May 1967, they disagreed agreeably.[53]

Fulbright was the exception to Jackson's rule. "The only thing that Scoop and Senator Fulbright agreed on," remarked Helen Jackson, "was where to buy wing-tip shoes in London." Indeed, the two men detested one another. In 1967, Fulbright denounced Jackson by name as "the congressional spokesman for the military-industrial complex," a charge that always infuriated him because it impugned his integrity. Jackson thought Fulbright arrogant and a hypocrite, who ostentatiously professed his sympathy for the victims of the so-called arrogance of American power, yet voted for the Southern Manifesto of 1956 and against every major piece of civil rights legislation that came before the Senate. Jackson also suspected that anti-Semitism accounted in part for what he perceived as Fulbright's long-standing hostility toward Israel. Fulbright's best biographer denies the merits of Jackson's suspicions but supplies evidence that attests to their plausibility. During his trip to Poland in 1927 on a break from his studies as a Rhodes scholar at Oxford, Fulbright recounted his horror at seeing "the squalid, filthy Jewish villages in Poland. Truly our animals are better fed, cleaner, and probably as intelligent." Jackson applauded the Johnson administration's strong backing of Israel during Arab-Israeli War of 1967 and its aftermath; conversely, Fulbright saw the Jewish state as a liability, not an asset, to U.S. interests in the Middle East. When Charles de Gaulle shifted French foreign policy from its traditional pro-Israeli to a pro-Arab orientation after 1967, Fulbright opposed the Johnson administration's decision to have the United States replace France as Israel's principal supplier of weapons.[54]

It baffled Jackson that a growing number of domestic liberals excoriated him as a villain and hailed Fulbright as a hero. Fulbright had a reactionary voting record on domestic issues that placed him just slightly to the left of Mississippi Senator James Eastland, an archconservative Southern Democrat. Since arriving in Congress in 1941, Jackson had voted straight down the line for every liberal domestic initiative that Fulbright had voted against. He responded to Fulbright's military-industrial complex epithet by publicly ribbing him: he threatened to embarrass Fulbright in his home state by coming down to conservative Arkansas and calling him a liberal. Their reciprocal enmity never ceased. The two men would clash bitterly on virtually every significant foreign policy and defense issue that confronted the nation until Fulbright lost his Senate seat in 1974.[55]

Jackson also felt the repercussions of the Vietnam War closer to home. By 1967, the war had precipitated a growing rift in the Democratic Party in Washington State and among its delegation of congressional Democrats. Congressman Brock Adams, representing the Seattle area, emerged as the leader of the legions of Washington State liberals opposed to the war. Senator Magnuson, too, had begun to waver. Although Magnuson declined to come out publicly against the war as long as his close friend Lyndon Johnson remained in office, there were signs that he was inevitably heading in that direction. His unexpectedly close race against Richard Christensen in 1962 had spurred him to hire a gifted administrative assistant (Jerry Grinstein) and a highly professional staff intent on transforming his image from a backroom, cigar-smoking, womanizing, hard-drinking insider to a paladin of progressive causes such as consumer protection. Always softer on the Soviet Union than Jackson was, Magnuson eventually would cast his lot with the New Politics wing of the Democratic Party on defense and foreign policy issues, a metamorphosis his staff did everything to encourage. Magnuson and Jackson would continue to cooperate on domestic issues, with stunning success for their constituents.[56] All this, however, was a significant change from 1964, when the newly elected congressional Democrats of Washington State, some of whom owed their victory largely to Jackson, deferred to him on almost everything. Journalist William Prochnau recalled their first lunch in the Senate cafeteria in January 1965 as guests of Henry Jackson. Obediently following him in line, they also felt compelled to order what he ordered: navy bean soup, the cheapest thing on the menu.[57]

Over the years, Jackson had received extraordinarily good coverage from the Seattle papers and the dailies in the small towns and cities of Washington State. The Vietnam War did not entirely change that, but it did lead to greater criticism and scrutiny of Jackson in the local press than he was used to receiving. Even some of Jackson's friends began to criticize him for his stand on Vietnam in particular and for his hawkishness in general. Gerald Hoeck, a former Marine himself, attempted futilely to convince him that the United States could not win a guerrilla war against North Vietnam. Stan Golub, his closest friend, was no more successful in convincing Jackson to soften his position on the war for expedient as well as moral reasons.[58]

Lyndon Johnson appreciated Jackson's steadfastness, if many antiwar liberals and some of Jackson's friends did not. Although the president rejected most of Jackson's advice on how to pursue the war more aggressively, he confided in him frequently. Johnson literally invited himself over to the Jacksons' for dinner twice—in November 1966 and March 1967—to discuss Vietnam. With just a few days' notice before each of the dinners, he instructed Jackson to invite five or six other couples to join them, including Chet Huntley, co-author of NBC's nightly news with David Brinkley, and Ray Scherer, also of NBC. Helen Jackson obliged graciously when "Scoop informed her sheepishly" of the president's plans. She remembered that Lyndon Johnson barely took a breath or let anyone else speak.[59] The president lamented in particular that nothing good was ever written about his Vietnam policy.[60] He did enjoy, however, playing with the children, particularly "the beautiful Anna Marie." In his written thank you to Helen and Henry for one evening, he asked them to give Anna Marie "an extra kiss—for me."[61]

During a brief lull in the president's conversation at the November 1966 dinner, Henry Jackson told him that he must do a better job of explaining the war to the American people. The president responded months later. He issued a public letter to Jackson released on March 2, 1967, outlining the rationale for and effects of the bombing of North Vietnam.[62]

NATO, THE SOVIET UNION, AND THE FIGHT FOR ANTIBALLISTIC MISSILES

Henry Jackson also participated prominently in the other major defense debates of the day. Although Russell and Stennis formally outranked him on the Armed Services Committee, they increasingly relied on him to take the lead on controversial issues.[63] Jackson had finally attained such prominence on foreign policy and defense issues through the confluence of his steady judgment, hard work, years of immersion in the details, diligent cultivation of a wide array of informed sources in the Pentagon, and superb staff. With the indispensable help of Dorothy Fosdick, the staff director, Jackson used the broad jurisdiction of the Subcommittee on National Security and International Operations of the Government Operations Committee, which he chaired, to venture across the entire spectrum of national security issues. The subcommittee conducted a series of highly regarded hearings that produced several well-received reports on subjects including the roles of American ambassadors, the Department of State, and the National Security Council.

When French President Charles de Gaulle announced that his country would withdraw all its forces from the NATO command structure in early 1966, Jackson commenced widely publicized hearings of the subcommittee, which underscored the importance of maintaining the NATO alliance.[64] Presidents Truman and Eisenhower wrote Jackson public letters that refrained from criticizing de Gaulle but insisted on the continued need for NATO to deter Soviet aggression.[65] President Eisenhower urged the United States to use "every possible influence . . . to cement together even more strongly the other nations of NATO, so that through their increased unity the subtraction of the French military forces will have the least possible effect." Former Secretary of State Dean Acheson and Secretary of Defense Robert McNamara headlined the group of prominent witnesses testifying in a similar fashion. Jackson himself assailed de Gaulle for his attitude toward NATO and his decision to undermine it:

> For years, Stalin, then Khrushchev, now Kosygin and Brezhnev have sought to split NATO. The oldest stratagem in the history of conquest is: divide and rule. It would be ironic—and tragic—were the Western nations to give the Soviet rulers what they sought in vain.[66]

De Gaulle's return to power in 1958 may have saved France from chaos but it guaranteed serious discord within the Atlantic Alliance, which he distrusted from the beginning because of British and American participation.[67] Jean-Francois Revel may have exaggerated, but not by much, in saying that de Gaulle's hatred of the United States became stronger than his fear of the Soviet Union. De Gaulle started off by treating the superpowers as equivalent threats: "We are happy to have you [Khrushchev] to help us resist pressure from the United States . . . just as we are very glad to have the United States help us resist pressure on the Soviet Union." From 1964 on, de Gaulle's foreign policy aimed mainly to weaken the United States rather than to deter the Soviet Union, the threat that gave rise to NATO in the first place. Ultimately, he blamed the American alliance for "smothering Europe" and "blocking an understanding" with a Soviet Union he no longer thought of as an evil or particularly dangerous empire.[68]

De Gaulle's challenge to the Atlantic Alliance upset Jackson far more than the course of events in South Vietnam, which he considered important but secondary.[69] The outcome of the Cold War hinged, in his view, on the alignment of Western Europe, "the greatest aggregation of resources in the world."[70] His argument restated the geopolitical logic that largely, though not exclusively, underlay President Truman's conception of containment: If, on the one hand, Western Europe remained firmly within the NATO alliance, the United States could not lose the Cold War in the short term and would inevitably win it in the long term. If, on the other hand, "absorption in the Soviet orbit, neutralization between East and West, or the dominance of Europe by any single hostile entity denied the United States access to the region's enormous resources, "the world balance of power would be turned against this country and our vital interests imperiled." Jackson granted that the Soviet Union had undergone important changes since 1947. Internal political and economic developments, he speculated, may have made the Soviet rulers less inclined "to run large risks for large gains." He attributed the Soviet Union's more cautious approach not to the regime's growing moderation but "to the strength, unity, and firmness of the Western countries."[71]

By every means at his disposal, then, Jackson endeavored not just to rebut de Gaulle but to stave off mounting pressure for substantial U.S. force reductions in Europe, which the French withdrawal from NATO had precipitated. In 1966 and 1967, Senator Mike Mansfield introduced the first two of his many resolutions calling for such reductions. Much of the support for them came from those such as their co-sponsor, Senator Fulbright, who stressed that the relaxation of East-West tension made possible a substantial reduction of U.S. forces permanently stationed in Europe. Support also came from those who stressed financial considerations: that now-prosperous European allies had not contributed their fair share, a more pressing concern as the U.S. balance of payments with Europe had started to deteriorate; and that a reduction in Europe would ease the costs and manpower needs of the Vietnam War.[72]

Jackson and John Stennis led the successful floor fights against both resolutions. They argued that it was penny-wise but pound-foolish to cut U.S. forces in Europe.[73] Stability, according to Jackson, still depended on "a substantial military presence in Europe. The main purpose of the American troop commitment is to leave no doubt that the United States would be involved, deeply involved, from the outset of any move against Western Europe." The United States, Jackson argued, ought to abandon the unrealistic force goals of the Kennedy administration's initial flexible response strategy: the capability "to meet and contain whatever conventional forces the Soviet Union could order into action. At the same time, however, nothing less than a force capable of containing a sizable but limited attack is adequate." Jackson conceived of "the real political and military function of allied conventional forces" as resisting and containing "a limited attack, thereby confronting the adversary with the choice of calling it off or enlarging it" with the risk of triggering a nuclear response.

He also issued a warning to the European allies of the United States that they had to do more. Otherwise, "it would be increasingly difficult to maintain the political support necessary" for the Atlantic Alliance "to stay the course."[74] Jackson and Mansfield would reprise this battle annually for many years to come.

Jackson thrust himself into the center of another controversial debate that would carry into the Nixon administration and resurge periodically thereafter: whether to build a large and expensive antiballistic missile (ABM). Again, he clashed with Secretary of Defense McNamara. Since the Cuban missile crisis in 1962, McNamara had moved the administration steadily away from the U.S. strategic doctrine that had governed since Truman's administration—that the robustness of America's nuclear deterrent rested on maintaining unassailable U.S. strategic superiority. McNamara proposed instead a nuclear strategy of assured destruction based on the acceptance of strategic parity with the Soviet Union. He defined assured destruction as the capacity for U.S. forces to destroy, "after a well planned and executed Soviet surprise attack on our strategic nuclear forces, the Soviet government and military controls, plus a large percentage of their population and economy (e.g., 30% of their population and 50% of their industrial capacity)." McNamara devised the concept of assured destruction to justify capping U.S. strategic forces at 1,054 intercontinental ballistic missiles (ICBMs) and 656 submarine-launched ballistic missiles (SLBMs). Such a cap, he believed, would also facilitate Soviet-American arms control agreements that would protect each side's capacity to inflict assured destruction on the other, a doctrine better known as MAD. He insisted that deterrence worked best when both sides could not protect themselves against devastating destruction.

For McNamara, the 17 to 1 advantage in deliverable nuclear warheads the United States possessed during the Cuban missile crisis did not yield any advantage because, by his reckoning, U.S. vulnerability to even a few Soviet warheads deterred the president from forcing a showdown. The secretary of defense predicted confidently that the Soviets would not even try to match U.S. nuclear capabilities, because there was no need. When the massive nuclear buildup that the Soviets initiated after the Cuban missile crisis confounded that notion, it did not cause McNamara any alarm or apparently provoke any second thoughts on his part. He thought that increased U.S. vulnerability to a Soviet second strike would increase mutual stability as long as the Soviets did not jeopardize the U.S. capacity to inflict assured destruction. He also thought the logic of assured destruction so compelling that the Soviets inevitably would come to embrace it, if they had not already.[75]

McNamara's embrace of assured destruction dictated his opposition to the idea of building an antiballistic missile defense. He did not believe that any conceivable ABM system could keep damage to acceptable levels in the event of a Soviet first strike. If, however, an aggressor launched a pre-emptive strike, an extensive ABM defense might preclude the victim from inflicting unacceptable damage in a retaliatory strike. Thus, strategic defense would create incentives for preemption rather than restraint. McNamara wanted, therefore, to discourage the Soviet Union from building an ABM system, which he viewed as destabilizing, expensive, and not cost-effective. His staff estimated that for every dollar the United States spent on an ABM, the Soviets could negate that effort by spending only one-third of a dollar on additional offensive missiles.[76]

As a corollary to assured destruction, McNamara also set forth a conception of the arms race that became a staple for a generation of arms controllers who urged the United States to practice unilateral restraint in building and deploying new types of weapons. An action-reaction phenomenon fueled the arms race, according to McNamara, whereby the buildup of nuclear weapons by either side necessarily triggers reactions by the other side. He characterized the Soviet military buildup by then under way not as a quest for superiority, but as a "reaction to our own buildup since the beginning of the decade." He argued that deploying ABM would set off an arms race that forebearance could avert. What he preferred was to "come to a realistic and reasonably riskless agreement" that would prevent such an arms race, leaving both sides more secure.[77]

By 1967, President Johnson leaned in McNamara's direction on ABM and nuclear strategy. On January 10 he announced in his State of the Union message that the administration had not yet decided whether to counter the Soviet Union's move to build an ABM defensive shield around Moscow, a program American intelligence sources had detected in the fall of 1966. A furthering of the race in either offensive or defensive weapons, he announced in his January 24 budget message, would "waste resources without any gain in real security for any side."[78] Throughout early 1967, Johnson and McNamara proclaimed that the United States would defer any deployment of the ABM, pending the outcome of Soviet-American arms-control negotiations and the scheduled June summit meeting between Johnson and Soviet Premier Alexei Kosygin in Glassboro, New Jersey.

Jackson disagreed vehemently not only with the administration's position on ABM, but also with the logic behind it. The Soviet Union's military buildup following the Cuban missile crisis came as no surprise to Jackson, who took it for granted that "the Soviet government would do all it can to reduce the American lead in nuclear weapons systems."[79] He rejected McNamara's notion that nuclear superiority no longer had any relevance. As he saw it, "international peace and security depend not only on a parity of power, but on a preponderance of power in the peacekeepers over the peace upsetters." The maintenance of American nuclear superiority was essential, in his view, to offset the preponderance of conventional forces the Soviet Union enjoyed in Europe.

Jackson rejected McNamara's action-reaction metaphor for explaining the arms race, and disputed the secretary of defense's assessment about the cost-effectiveness of ABM.[80] Although he realized that an ABM program at its rudimentary stage of development could not provide comprehensive population defense against a massive Soviet nuclear attack, Jackson believed that deploying a thin line of ABM defense while amply funding research and development of more advanced systems would enhance deterrence. First, it could provide effective defense against the possibility of an ICBM attack from Communist China, which raised this concern by announcing on June 18, 1967, that it had successfully exploded its first hydrogen bomb. Second, it would give protection to U.S. ICBM sites, making any conceivable Soviet first strike against them prohibitive. Third, it could serve as the basis for providing nationwide protection to the U.S. population should a technical breakthrough occur in the realm of strategic defense.

What strengthened the case for ABM even more, in Jackson's eyes, was the advent of strategic missiles with multiple independently targeted warheads (MIRVs). The United States had begun to deploy MIRVed ICBMs and SLBMs in the mid-1960s. Contrary to the contentions of many in the arms-control community that in the late 1960s the United States could have achieved a ban on MIRVs by proposing one, Jackson forecast that the Soviet Union determined to deploy them regardless of what the United States chose to do. What worried him about the combination of MIRV technology and the massive Soviet buildup in ICBM launchers was this: The attendant and vast expansion in the number of Soviet ICBM warheads would give Moscow first-strike capability against the U.S. ICBM force frozen by McNamara at 1,054 launchers. Jackson contended that ABM made the threat or actuality of such a preemptive Soviet strike against the U.S. ICBM force less likely by hopelessly complicating the task of any Soviet leader contemplating that option.

In late 1966, Henry Jackson, John Stennis, and John Tower initiated a major campaign to pressure the administration into deploying the U.S. ABM system. By the fall of 1967, the administration had reluctantly relented, having failed to achieve any breakthrough on arms control at the June summit at Glassboro. McNamara announced on September 18, 1967, that the United States would begin to deploy a thin missile defense system, as Henry Jackson had advised. Jackson reacted to the administration's decision by convening hearings of his Subcommittee on Military Applications of the Joint Committee on Atomic Energy (November 6–8, 1967).[81] He aimed to bolster the case for ABM, which still faced rough sledding in the Senate from doves such as William Fulbright, who opposed the ABM categorically as unworkable, unnecessary, provocative, and costly. Jackson would wage that battle on the floor of the Senate in 1968.[82]

MARRIED, HAPPY, AND MOVING ON UP

The tranquility and happiness of Jackson's domestic life during the late 1960s contrasted starkly with the mood of the nation. Marriage agreed with Mr. and Mrs. Henry Jackson. Henry found Helen everything he could have hoped for in a spouse: kind, gracious, devoted to him and the children, understanding of the rigors of his office and responsibilities. Helen found him to be a model husband: empathetic, unswervingly committed to his family, cheerful, and a paragon of integrity, albeit a thrifty one. Henry Jackson, the champion of big government, had no compunction about lavishly spending the taxpayer's money on domestic or defense programs. He had even less compunction about giving away his own money—as he did anonymously with all of the money he received for speeches—to charity for those in need. What always caused him anguish was spending his money on luxuries, a concept he defined by the standards of Everett in the 1930s. He was oblivious to Helen's periodic hints—subtle at first, bolder in time—that perhaps she could use some new clothes. He applied the same frugal standards to himself. Color-blind since birth, Jackson always dressed conservatively. He wore traditionally cut (Ivy League style) suits in some shade of dark blue or gray, or a blue blazer and gray flannel slacks with a matching striped tie that Helen chose for him. He purchased all of his attire off the rack from Leon at No-Label Louie's, a discount men's store in Washington, D.C.[83]

Henry Jackson never aspired to great wealth; nor did he attain it. For all his vaunted thriftiness, he and Helen lived comfortably in a style and on an income that ensconced them firmly in the upper middle class. They became members of the exclusive Chevy Chase Club in 1964. When they learned in the middle of 1965 that their second child was on the way, they decided that a family of four needed more room than their apartment at 2500 Q Street afforded. So they bought a house at 4934 Rockwood Parkway, a four-bedroom red brick Georgian Colonial located in the posh Spring Valley area of northwest Washington, D.C., which they moved into just before young Peter arrived in April 1966. Henry always referred to the house, later the home of Togo West, secretary of the army during the Clinton administration, as the most modest house in a very rich neighborhood. The Jacksons also decided they needed more room in Everett, where Henry, Helen, and Anna Marie lived in the family home, along with Henry's sisters Gert and Marie. In 1967, the Jacksons became the owners of an old mansion at 1703 Grand Avenue, where banker William A. Butler, a staunch Republican and then the most powerful man in Everett, had lived when Henry was a boy. The delicious irony of it struck Jackson, who remembered delivering newspapers on that very street and Butler's disdain for working-class Norwegians like his father. "I can just see old Bill Butler rolling over in his grave knowing that I bought his house," Jackson told Helen and his new neighbor, Harry Metzger.[84]

Henry Jackson still possessed energy in his fifties that made it difficult even for younger people to keep up with him. When Congress was in session, Jackson normally arose at 6:30 A.M., ate breakfast at 6:45, arrived in the office by 8:00, and then read the *New York Times*, *Wall Street Journal*, and *Washington Post* before immersing himself in meetings and legislative work. At noon, he generally dined in the Senate dining room, often with staff, distinguished guests, or constituents. He spent the rest of the afternoon doing more legislative work and making phone calls. Barring an urgent matter or a call from the president, at 5:30 P.M. he left for the gym, where he did as much lobbying of his colleagues as exercising. He returned home by 7:00 to eat dinner, to visit with the children and Helen, and to watch the evening news, unless congressional business or a reception he felt obligated to attend intruded. After dinner, he usually did more work in his home office, reading background papers and making more phone calls. His day ended about 10:30 P.M. On weekends, he always "hung around" waiting for the Sunday morning news programs to call, which they often did because he excelled in that format of television. The commentators valued his expertise, forthrightness, and willingness always to provide them with at least some information that was newsworthy.[85] Although the Jacksons entertained and went out on the town occasionally in Washington, D.C., they generally kept a low social profile commensurate with Henry's reputation for hard work and seriousness.[86]

When Congress was out of session, Jackson canvassed the state of Washington, speaking to and meeting with newspaper editors, civil groups, and constituents. His hometown of Everett took great pride in his success, and he took an equal measure of pride in his hometown, where he always looked forward to returning. He felt it was very important for his children to have roots there. When Congress was in session during the summer months, he often sent Helen, Anna Marie, and Peter ahead to Everett in June to avoid the sweltering heat and humidity of D.C. He relished appearing at every type of gathering in Everett, where he caught up on the local gossip, listened to people's problems, and dispensed advice. "Scoop would come home at Christmas, have an obligatory scotch and water, then ask what was happening around town and how everybody was doing," recalled Harry Metzger. "When my mother was dying, Scoop heard about it and came by to say he cared about what was happening: the Norwegian way. Helen adopted his sense of community. She was dedicated to staying here."[87]

Henry Jackson was not only a good husband and neighbor, but also a good father. He doted on daughter Anna Marie, who adored him. Little Peter also delighted him, although he was no modern father. Helen handled the chores of caring for the infant. Typical of many men who become fathers later in life, he had a weak grasp of some of the practical aspects of handling children.

It was always a struggle to make Henry Jackson take a vacation. One of the most memorable for Helen happened early in their marriage: she and Henry rode on horses through the rain forests of the Olympic Peninsula in Washington State. She fondly remembered camping trips in the Cascades with the Golubs and the Hoecks. The Jacksons also enjoyed vacationing in Hawaii, where Henry liked to swim and walk the beach, and visiting Helen's father and his wife Mary in Palm Desert annually. Wherever Henry Jackson was on vacation, however, he could never stand to be too far from a telephone to keep up on the political action. Swimming, walking, talking, and holding court exhausted the repertoire of his recreational endeavors. Friends cannot recall him picking up a tennis racket or a golf club. Having obtained the moniker Scoop for his capacity to get others to do his yard work, he lived up to that tradition as an adult. He left most of the mundane details of life to Helen.[88]

Jackson also continued to maintain a warm rapport with his staff, many of whom he treated as extended family. He took an active interest in their education, financial situation, and career development. Fancying himself an amateur physician, he also dispensed medical advice to anyone who would listen, including his own doctor. When muggers shot Senator John Stennis in D.C. in 1973, Stennis ordered the ambulance to take him to the hospital and the physician Jackson had recommended. Jackson also treated the lowest echelons of his staff with thoughtfulness. He always had an encouraging word for his pages and messengers, whose names and life stories he usually recalled to the minutest detail. Russ Brown recounted an episode that reveals much about the senator's character. During the summer of 1968, he had just started working for Jackson on his personal staff. Jackson inquired about his living arrangements. When Brown told him that he, his wife Linda, and their young child had not yet found suitable lodging, Jackson insisted that they stay with him until they did. "It was no imposition at all," Jackson said, "because Helen, Anna Marie, and Peter had already gone to Everett for the summer." He also insisted that the Browns stay in his bedroom, and he moved up to the guest room on the third floor.[89]

Chapter 10

That Year: 1968

Henry Jackson's rock solid family life served as his refuge from the tumultuous events of 1968, which wracked the nation. In his critically acclaimed memoir tracing the political journey of the generation of 1968, Paul Berman, once a major figure in the New Left, described the year as one of "utopian exhilaration." There was a belief, according to Berman, "that a superior new society was already coming into existence" and "that we ourselves—the teenage revolutionaries, freaks, hippies, and students together with our friends and leaders who were five or ten years older and our allies around the world—stood at the heart of this new society."[1] That is not how Henry Jackson remembered 1968.

The year started off badly and steadily got worse for Jackson's wing of the Democratic Party. On January 30, the North Vietnamese launched the Tet offensive, a series of attacks across South Vietnam. Even the capital city of Saigon and the American Embassy there came under assault. Tet caught the American military by surprise and seemed to demolish the optimistic claims of the administration and the Pentagon that the United States was slowly but surely winning the war. Although North Vietnam suffered enormous losses, from which it took years to recover, and gained little on the battlefield, the media portrayed Tet as a great defeat for the United States.[2]

The Tet offensive had a devastating effect on the Johnson presidency. By March 1968, Johnson's public approval rating had plummeted to 36 percent.[3] Support for his handling of the war had dropped even lower to just 26 percent, with dissatisfaction rising among hawks, who thought the United States was doing too little, and doves, who thought it was doing too much.[4] General Westmoreland had requested 205,179 more troops in addition to the 550,000 already deployed in South Vietnam. The coalition that had swept Johnson to his landslide victory of 1964 had fallen apart.

The Tet offensive had given a huge boost to the movement within the Democratic Party to oust Johnson, initiated in the summer of 1967 by Allard Lowenstein, a brilliant, polemical, liberal New York lawyer implacably opposed to the war. Lowenstein considered Robert Kennedy, who had come out in 1967 against the war his brother escalated, as the best bet to topple Johnson. In the fall of 1967, however, Kennedy had rebuffed Lowenstein's entreaties to run, thinking it was hopeless to challenge a sitting president by dividing the Democratic Party. Lowenstein tried several others before finding a willing challenger in Senator Eugene McCarthy of Minnesota, an old nemesis of Henry Jackson, who declared his candidacy November 30, 1967.[5] A loner, an intellectual, arrogant, and unpredictable, with indifferent work habits and a meager legislative record, McCarthy nevertheless passed the litmus test of the New Politics wing of the Democratic Party because he regarded the war as a calamity and Johnson's replacement as imperative. McCarthy's languishing campaign in New Hampshire took off in the weeks following the Tet offensive. He received 42.2 percent of the vote in the March 12 primary there, not enough to win but a stunning performance for an obscure senator against an incumbent president. The press interpreted McCarthy's strong showing in New Hampshire as a crushing repudiation of Lyndon Johnson. It was not, however, an unequivocal triumph for the New Politics wing of the Democratic Party. Polling data revealed that three out of five who voted for McCarthy did so because they were more hawkish than Johnson. They wanted to win the war or get out.[6]

The president encountered mounting opposition not only from the left wing of his party, but also from the political Right. The precipitous escalation in urban violence and the student rebellion sweeping elite college campuses mingled with Southern hostility toward Johnson's landmark civil rights legislation to create a climate congenial to the impending third-party presidential campaign of the populist race-baiter George Wallace, the once and future Democratic governor of Alabama. The enthusiasm Wallace evoked exemplified the steady drift of the once solid Democratic South away from the Democratic Party at the level of presidential politics.[7]

Meanwhile, the Republican Party had made a remarkable comeback since the Goldwater debacle in 1964 by legitimately stressing some of the same concerns that George Wallace exploited illegitimately: the flaws in Johnson's military strategy, which promised nothing but stalemate; the hubris of the Great Society, which promised too much and delivered too little; and the breakdown of law and order, which the Johnson administration had done too little to discourage. The Republicans recouped significantly in the off-year election of 1966, gaining forty-eight seats in the House and electing a new star on the horizon, Ronald Reagan, governor of California by one million votes over incumbent Pat Brown, a loyal supporter of the Great Society.[8] By March 1968, Richard M. Nixon, the likely Republican presidential nominee, appeared poised to make a political comeback even more remarkable than his party's. He appeared to have a very good chance of defeating Johnson in the 1968 presidential election, after recovering from a defeat in the California governor's race of 1962 that had then seemed to finish his political career.[9]

It was as a result of this national climate that the president made two fateful decisions in late March of 1968: vetoing the troop increases that Westmoreland requested; and announcing his withdrawal from the presidential race. Jackson had long chaffed at the persistent refusal of the Johnson administration to undertake the more decisive measures he recommended. He had criticized especially the on-again off-again bombing campaign that, as he saw it, repeated the mistakes of the Korean War. He thus opposed sending more troops to Vietnam or calling up the reserves unless the Johnson administration changed its basic strategy. He did not expect that to happen. So when the president's new secretary of defense, Clark Clifford, who had replaced McNamara in March, solicited the views of Jackson, Richard Russell, John Stennis, and Margaret Chase Smith, these four hawks strongly advised against escalation beyond the 550,000 Americans already stationed in Vietnam.[10]

Jackson had not defected to the antiwar wing of his party. Nor did he wish President Johnson to withdraw from the race. On the contrary, he told Joseph Califano, the secretary of health, education, and welfare, that the president should turn him loose against Fulbright. He savored the prospect of "tearing Fulbright's voting record to shreds on the application of Vietnam funds to the problem of the cities and the Negroes." Distressed "about what was happening to the Democrats around the country," he believed that "the Communists of the 1930s are coming out of the woodwork and that they are getting named convention delegates with only one aim—to tear apart the Democratic Party." Jackson confided to Califano, too, that "he had some serious problems in his own state of Washington" along these lines.[11]

President Johnson's withdrawal disturbed Jackson, who still thought him the best candidate to keep the Democratic Party and the country together. It exacerbated the party's disarray, as several contenders vied for the nomination. Senator Robert Kennedy was one of them. Just days after the New Hampshire primary, Bobby announced his candidacy for the Democratic nomination. This reversal of his previous decision to stay out angered Eugene McCarthy, who resented Kennedy's exploitation of his success and refused to withdraw from the race as Kennedy had expected. President Johnson, who detested Bobby Kennedy as much as Bobby detested him, had designated Vice President Hubert Humphrey as his preferred successor.[12]

One of the first of those Kennedy called to seek an endorsement, Jackson said no—despite their friendship. "You know I cannot support you on this one," he told a disappointed Bobby. "I have to stick with Lyndon and Hubert." Kennedy had lurched too far to the left for Jackson's liking, on the war, student unrest, and issues of law and order. Jackson just had too much of a commitment to the tenets of Cold War liberalism, which Johnson largely accepted, to abandon him. The president was "deeply grateful" to have Jackson's backing during his time of travail.[13] He invited Henry, Helen, Anna Marie, and Peter to celebrate Peter's second birthday in the Oval Office on April 3. The president gave Peter and Anna Marie a present of toys and engraved silver cups. The Jacksons thanked him profusely for his "generosity" and "thoughtfulness."[14]

The next day, the assassination of Martin Luther King, Jr., at a Memphis motel ignited yet another round of burning and looting in dozens of cities, including Washington, D.C. Henry Jackson attended King's funeral.[15] He had admired the slain civil rights leader and defended his legacy as he construed it: equality of opportunity under the law for all Americans. He deplored, equally, anyone taking the law into his own hands, whatever the reason. He saw no justification for the violence that black militants advocated and a growing number of New Politics liberals excused. He disagreed wholly with the Kerner Commission report of March

1968, which blamed white racism for the sharp rise in black rioting. Jackson granted the existence of racism. He deplored and strove to eradicate it. He rejected, however, the evolving notion that racism or anything else exempted individuals "from the responsibility for their own acts. No person, no group, regardless of their political or ideological identifications, has the right to urge violence or violate the law. And this is true whether it is the Klan, the Minutemen, the New Left, a political assassin, or a mob burning a ghetto or taking over a university."[16]

Jackson watched with apprehension as the Democratic presidential candidates devoured one another and the party during the primary campaign. Badly organized because of his late entry into the race, Kennedy's campaign had difficulty building momentum against either McCarthy or Humphrey. Kennedy and McCarthy divided the antiwar, New Politics vote in the few primaries in which they directly contested one another. Beyond that, primaries determined only 19 percent of the delegates chosen to go to the Democratic Convention in 1968. Local leaders and party bosses selected the preponderance of the delegates by procedures that gave Humphrey, the choice of labor and the party regulars, a commanding advantage. McCarthy had no realistic chance of winning the nomination. Kennedy's slender hope lay in delivering a knockout blow to McCarthy, then convincing delegates committed to Humphrey to switch to him on the theory that only he could win in the fall. Kennedy's loss to McCarthy in the Oregon primary in late May made the California primary of June 4 a must-win situation. Kennedy did win in California, by a narrow margin of four points, but he did not get the opportunity to make his pitch to the party regulars. He was shot in the kitchen of the Ambassador Hotel in Los Angeles as he prepared to leave his victory celebration. He died two days later. What possibility there was for the Democrats to reconcile at their party convention in August died with him.[17]

The assassination of Robert Kennedy stunned and saddened his old friend Jackson, whose eulogy paid glowing tribute to him as a "man of dogged determination, giant capacity, and great courage." Jackson also said that "the whole nation must take stock of the state of our society and the attitudes and conditions that turn people to the lie that wrong can be righted by taking the law into one's own hands." He emphasized that Americans "cannot live in a climate of extremism, of disrespect for the law, and contempt for the rights of others. People must understand that if there is to be basic change in our democratic institutions, they must be changed by democratic means."[18]

Jackson soon received another terrible blow. In the summer of 1968, he learned that his beloved sister Gert, recently retired after forty-five years of teaching, had terminal cancer. "Scoop was very broken up about it," remembered Stan Golub. "Scoop really revered her. . . . He called me immediately after he found out and was very broken up about it. He really loved her as much as any brother could love a sister." Jackson reminisced with Golub about "what a wonderful and generous person she was, to him and to others." Gert devoted much of her time helping school children who were having difficulties or whose families could not support them." Jackson passed on attending the Democratic Convention in Chicago to be with Gert, Helen, and the children in Everett.[19] He could not evade, however, the political fallout from this fiasco televised to millions of Americans.

Democratic delegates arrived in Chicago in late August 1968, their party already rent with strife. Humphrey's unstintingly liberal record on civil rights and economic issues did not satisfy the antiwar liberals and their supporters in the New Left, for whom his public support of the Vietnam War trumped all. Compounding his troubles, President Johnson threatened Humphrey with a withdrawal of support if he distanced himself from the policies of the Johnson administration, as he was increasingly inclined to do. Humphrey's acquiescence to the president made him look weak at a time when Democrats craved resolution. Antiwar liberals lacked the strength to block Humphrey's nomination but possessed more than enough to block all hopes of reconciliation and to envenom the internal politics of the Democratic Party for decades.[20] Outside the convention hall, more than 10,000 demonstrators poured into town led by SDS founder Tom Hayden, Abbie Hoffman, Jerry Rubin, and other radicals. Taunted, pelted by flying rocks, bags of urine, and bags of feces, some of the Chicago police lost control of themselves. A veritable police riot ensued, filling the television screens with lurid images of policemen beating multitudes of demonstrators to a bloody pulp with riot sticks.[21]

Inside the convention hall, things did not go much better. Humphrey looked helpless as the delegates waged a series of bitter fights over an antiwar platform that the McCarthy forces introduced and over the credentials of several delegations. Although the Humphrey forces managed to win most of the battles at the convention, the New Deal–Fair Deal coalition he and Jackson represented lost perhaps the most significant battle of them all.[22] The convention passed a resolution setting in motion the McGovern-Fraser Commission, which would fundamentally change the rules for choosing Democratic presidential candidates.[23] As Lawrence O'Brien, future chairman of the Democratic Party, observed, this commission was "clearly weighted toward the liberal wing of the party, rather than being representative of the party as a whole."[24] Although Humphrey received the nomination, the convention ended with his prospects for the fall campaign appearing bleak. Disgusted by the behavior of the Chicago police, and dissatisfied that Humphrey had not repudiated Johnson's policy on Vietnam, McCarthy spurned his calls for reconciliation. Humphrey left Chicago trailing Nixon in the polls by double digits in a three-man race, which included George Wallace.[25]

Throughout the fall of 1968, foreign policy and national security preoccupied Jackson as much as the plight of his political party. He complained that radicals at Chicago who railed against police brutality and the oppressiveness of American society remained conspicuously silent about the Soviet Union's brutal invasion of Czechoslovakia that occurred the week before the Democratic Convention. Publicly, he condemned the invasion as emblematic of Soviet intentions, as a refutation of the idea "that the Soviet Union was on an irreversible course toward more moderate behavior and that detente was here to stay." He warned ominously about the "deteriorating military balance" created by Moscow's massive expansion of its military capability:

> In past Soviet adventures, the strategic inferiority of Soviet power has set limits on the extent of the risks that Moscow was willing to run. It is disquieting to contemplate the still more dangerous range of risks that the Kremlin might accept in the future if it were confident of being closer to an equality or a superiority of overall deterrent strength. . . . Strategic parity with the Soviet Union is not good enough. The survival of our nation and our allies in freedom depends not only on parity in nuclear power, but on a margin of advantage in nuclear power.[26]

Privately, Jackson expressed his hope to Major General Edward Rowny, regarding the Soviet invasion, that "the intellectuals and others who have

believed for a long time that the Russians have changed will learn a lesson. The lesson of the Hungarian Revolution did not last long."[27]

Senate doves did not learn, however, the lesson that Jackson had in
mind for them. In the fall of 1968, he again led the floor fight that thwarted, for the time being, their renewed attempts to eliminate funding for
ABM. He rebutted the arguments of critics who claimed that the ABM
would unduly stimulate the arms race without protecting the United
States effectively against a Soviet military attack and would divert funds
from necessary social programs. Concern for domestic problems, he said,
"was no excuse for any of us losing our perspective on what comes first,
and what comes first in a dangerous world is the American nuclear deterrent, the first prerequisite of survival." Jackson assailed the critics of ABM,
too, for distorting and inflating the claims that proponents had actually
made for it. He never presumed that the Sentinel ABM could "deter a
large Soviet ballistic missile attack. . . . [W]e do not have the means for a
fully efficient missile defense against a numerically large and technically
advanced missile force such as the Soviet Union." What the Sentinel
ABM could do, however, was "provide damage denial against the early
missile threat from China and a limited degree of protection for American strategic forces against Soviet attack." He defended the deployment
and development of the Sentinel system as "crucial" for "our continuing
effort of development and experimentation to achieve, if we can, an effective defense against a full-scale Soviet missile attack."[28]

Jackson spent much of the fall of 1968 campaigning hard for the
Democratic presidential ticket nationally and for Senator Magnuson in
Washington State. After a dismal start, Humphrey staged a strong comeback that fell just short of giving him a plurality victory in a three-way
race. He finished less than a percentage point behind Nixon in the popular vote: 43.4 percent to 42.7 percent. Unlike John Kennedy, Humphrey
carried Jackson's state of Washington, where Magnuson also won easily.
The infinitesimal difference in the popular vote masked, however, the extent of the defeat the Democrats had truly suffered. Almost 57 percent of
the American electorate—the combined vote total of Nixon and Wallace—had voted for candidates who repudiated Lyndon Johnson's version
of Cold War liberalism and against the candidate who campaigned as its
champion. Humphrey's percentage represented a huge decline from the
election of 1964, in which Johnson had received more than 61 percent of

the vote. Polls also indicated that Nixon would have received most of the Wallace vote in a two-man race. In the Electoral College, Nixon defeated Humphrey by more than 100 votes, and the long-term trends were even more ominous for the Democrats. Nixon swept all the states west of the Mississippi except Hawaii, Washington, Minnesota, and Texas. He also made significant gains with northern urban ethnics, including Catholics who had voted for John Kennedy. Humphrey failed to carry any state in the once solid South except, narrowly, Texas. He carried most of the industrial Northeast, a Democratic bastion and the dominant region in American politics for much of the New Deal, but by 1968 rapidly losing people and political power to the Sunbelt, a region trending strongly Republican. In his seminal book *The Emerging Republican Majority*, published shortly after the election, Kevin Phillips predicted presciently that the Republicans could secure a majority in the Electoral College by winning the bulk of white middle-class voters and large numbers of urban ethnics; these had become the critical swing groups in American presidential elections.[29]

The election of 1968 signaled the end of the ascendence of the New Deal–Fair Deal coalition to which Henry Jackson belonged. It did not yet signal, however, the beginning of "a new Republican cycle comparable in magnitude," as Phillips grandiosely claimed.[30] The Democrats easily retained their control of both houses of Congress. Nixon had not sought a mandate; nor did he get one. In a campaign long on generalities and short on specifics even by the conventional standards of American presidential elections, Nixon had conveyed little more than a hazy antipathy toward the Great Society, a vague commitment to restore law and order, and his determination to achieve peace with honor in Vietnam by largely unspecified means. He realized more than anyone the precariousness of his political position. Having won only 43 percent of the vote in a nation still bitterly polarized, facing an even more liberal Democratic Congress and a hostile media that viewed his victory as an accident, Nixon realized he needed to generate bipartisan support. He thus asked several prominent Democrats to fill important positions in his administration.[31]

Henry Jackson was one of them. His staunch pro-defense record and the "impeccable quality of his study of the nation's foreign policy machinery" greatly impressed Nixon.[32] Forever resentful of the "eastern elite," Nixon also noted the greater affinity between Jackson's more modest social background and his own. After consulting with Senators Tower and Goldwater, key Republican members of the Armed Services Committee, who were "delighted with the idea," he settled on Jackson as "his first choice for secretary of defense, by far the best choice." Indeed, Nixon wanted Jackson to join his administration badly enough to offer him his choice of secretary of state or defense. Jackson formally received these offers in early December, while vacationing in Hawaii with Helen and the dying Gert, who had barely two months to live. He agonized over the decision, tempted by the opportunity of becoming secretary of defense but worried about the political consequences of the decision. For two weeks, he talked at length with friends and colleagues, weighing the pros and cons of Nixon's offer. Correspondingly, he raised the ante on the Nixon administration, which went to great lengths to satisfy his conditions. Concerned about his standing with Washington State Democrats, he insisted that the Nixon administration persuade Governor Dan Evans, a Republican, to appoint a Democrat to fill his seat. When Evans resisted, Nixon applied "maximum pressure" through his chief of staff, John Ehrlichman, formerly a practicing lawyer in Seattle. A reluctant Evans finally relented, but not before extracting a quid pro quo from Nixon: he would name Representative Tom Foley, a protege of Jackson's, to replace him and a Republican to replace Foley.[33]

Notwithstanding these efforts of the Nixon administration to lure him, Jackson turned down the offer. Ultimately, he heeded the warnings of Ted Kennedy and Dorothy Fosdick that becoming Nixon's secretary of defense would kill his standing in the Democratic Party and his chance of becoming president.[34] Fosdick, Gerry Hoeck, and others cautioned that there was a heavy dose of political calculation in Nixon's desire to have him join the administration. Nixon, they said, sought to neutralize Jackson as a potential rival for the presidency. As a Democrat in a Republican administration, Jackson also suspected that Nixon, whom he did not completely trust, would sacrifice him at the first sign of trouble, ending his political career. A senator of his stature could exert a tremendous influence on foreign policy and national security without sacrificing his presidential ambitions, which had become more intense. Besides, he felt a strong moral and practical obligation to fight for the heart and soul of his party. He still believed that the New Politics movement was an aberration, not a harbinger of things to come for the Democratic party.[35] So he informed

Nixon that he could do him more good "in the Senate because the antiballistic missile thing is coming up and I'm the only one that can bring along the Democrats."[36]

Jackson was destined to have more impact on the Nixon administration than on any of the Democratic presidents he served with. Nixon and his key advisers always took Jackson's advice seriously.[37] On foreign policy and national security, the relationship between Jackson and Nixon would begin, but not end, harmoniously. Jackson would become the most formidable foe not just of McGovern liberals in his own party, but of Richard Nixon and Henry Kissinger's policy of détente toward the Soviet Union. These battles would impel Jackson to embark on his first campaign for the presidency in 1972.

Chapter 11

Jackson's Ascent, the Party's Descent, 1968–1972

THE NIXON presidency heralded the emergence of Henry Jackson as one of the most powerful and influential members of the United States Senate. As chairman of the Interior Committee, he presciently warned of an impending oil crisis two years before the OPEC embargo occurred in October 1973.[1] Nationally, he became the leading advocate for keeping the Democratic Party true to the tenets of Cold War liberalism: an activist government at home and vigilant containment of the Soviet Union abroad. By general acclaim, his work and accomplishments in the Senate displayed a mastery of a greater number of important subjects than any other American legislator of his time could justifiably claim.

Inevitably, Jackson became a more controversial figure in American politics as his power and influence grew, especially in a country as bitterly divided over foreign policy and moral and cultural issues as the United States was from 1968 until the end of the Cold War. For those Democrats who deplored the tactics and outlook of the New Politics wing of the party, Jackson was a hero. For the antiwar left, which propelled George McGovern to the Democratic Party's presidential nomination in 1972, he was an implacable foe. For opponents of détente with the Soviet Union and neoconservative supporters of Israel, Jackson was a modern Winston Churchill, warning of the perils of appeasement. For the proponents of détente such as Henry Kissinger and William Fulbright, he was a dangerous alarmist, a grave threat to improved relations with the Soviet Union and a more tranquil international environment.[2]

He began the Nixon administration's tenure, however, as the darling of the Sierra Club. In 1969 he was the first politician ever to win the organization's coveted John Muir Award, and in 1970 he was the recipient of the Bernard Baruch Conservation Award for his record as an environmentalist. The presenters of the Muir award lauded Jackson "for the excellency of his contribution toward preserving unspoiled a living part of the American heritage of wilderness . . . and for leadership in conservation.[3] What earned Jackson these prestigious awards? Why did his environmental legacy fail to mollify liberal Democrats? These questions offer a useful point of departure for understanding the life and times of Henry Jackson during the polarizing presidency of Richard Nixon.

NATIVE AMERICANS, THE ENVIRONMENT, AND THE NEPA

Through his chairmanship of the Interior Committee, Henry Jackson fashioned path-breaking legislation during the Nixon administration in a variety of areas. He continued his work to improve the lives of Native Americans, shepherding to passage the Alaska Native Claims Act of 1971, which settled long-standing claims against the United States by Eskimos and other Native Americans. This act granted them $962.5 million and 40 million acres of land, provisions in accord with Jackson's inclinations to reach a more generous settlement than the Nixon administration or congressional conservatives wanted. Because of Jackson's insistence, this act also authorized the secretary of the interior to withdraw up to 80 million acres of public lands and to make recommendations to Congress for inclusion of lands in, or the creation of new units of, the National Park, Forest, Wildlife Refuge, and Wild and Scenic River Systems. Jackson also sponsored the Indian Education Act of 1972, which provided for significant and comprehensive improvements in school programs for Native Americans.[4]

Prompted by his desire to convert Fort Lawton in Seattle into a public park rather than auction this surplus federal property for private development, Jackson authored and prevailed upon President Nixon, who opposed the idea, to sign the Public Lands for Parks Bill of 1969, which authorized the donation or sale at discount rates of federal property to local and state governments for parks and recreational purposes. This bill thus eliminated the requirement that states or local governments buying surplus property must pay half of the appraised value. In the tradition of President Franklin Roosevelt, Jackson also authored legislation, enacted in 1971, creating the Youth Conservation Corps. This program provided summer conservation work for young people between fifteen and eighteen.[5]

The National Environmental Policy Act (NEPA) stands as Jackson's crowning achievement in the area of environmental policy. NEPA established the Council on Environmental Quality, the forerunner to the establishment of the Environmental Protection Agency. To ensure the infusion of environmental goals and policies into the ongoing programs of the federal government, Jackson and his staff conceived of and drafted NEPA's most important provision, Section 102, which required the federal government to supply environmental impact statements for all major federal actions. NEPA also spawned the enactment of analogous laws in many states. Environmental interest groups ever since have employed the environmental impact statement as a powerful weapon to block, modify, or delay projects they consider insufficiently sensitive to environmental concerns. The enactment of NEPA culminated three years of intense activity on Jackson's part to transcend the formidable barriers that the measure faced: public indifference, bitter turf wars between congressional committees and federal agencies, and the active opposition of the Nixon administration. The controversies over the Central Arizona Project and the Colorado River during the Johnson administration had convinced Jackson that the nation sorely needed comprehensive legislation to establish national priorities on the environment and to coordinate the activities of the federal government, whose constituent parts too often worked at cross-purposes.[6]

In 1967 and 1968, Jackson staged a series of hearings, using the conflict between federal agencies over Everglades National Park to illustrate the inadequacy of existing standards. The Department of the Interior and the National Park Service sought to acquire land for the Everglades National Park. Simultaneously, the Army Corps of Engineers and other federal agencies north of the Everglades planned to construct a series of huge canals and dikes in the vicinity of the park so that agricultural land could grow cotton and other products. This project would have drained off large amounts of water naturally flowing into the Everglades, endangering fish and wildlife. The activities of the Department of Transportation (DOT) added a third dimension to the problem. DOT had proposed building a super jet airport adjacent to the park, nominally for the use of Dade County in Miami but mainly to train pilots and test new aircraft. The airport would have sharply curtailed water flows to the Everglades and created noise inconsistent with the values of a national park.

Having established the factual circumstances of this morass, Jackson summoned the secretary of transportation, the head of the Army Corps of Engineers, and the secretary of the interior to appear together. "He had them each explain what they were doing," Bill Van Ness recalled. "It was obvious that they had little or no recognition that their programs were in conflict with one another." There was nothing in the budgeting or planning process in the federal government—even on multimillion dollar projects—that forced these federal agencies and their officials to face the conflicts their programs created. This was the root of the problem that Jackson sought to address: he wanted a mechanism to force federal decision makers at the lowest possible levels to identify objectives and conflicts before they committed funds and undertook irreversible actions. Van Ness has cited the findings of these hearings as the genesis of the environmental impact statement, which Dan Dreyfus, Jackson's longtime staff director on the Interior Committee, suggested to Jackson be modeled on a synthesis of the Fair Employment Act of 1946 and the interagency review process for the Bureau of Reclamation.

Curiously, there was little or no interest in NEPA among any national environmental organizations or developers. So Jackson did not have to deal with pressure from those lobbies. Nor did he have to deal with effective resistance coming from the Nixon administration. "The president's science adviser suffered fools badly and dismissed preemptorily the need for NEPA," Dreyfus recalled. "He thus managed to alienate even right-wing Republicans."[7] Jackson encountered more difficulty in finding a committee to report NEPA in the House. Wayne Aspinall, chairman of the Interior Committee of the House, declined because he believed NEPA did not fall within his jurisdiction, which he construed narrowly and strictly. After holding a series of seminars and workshops on environmental policy between the House and Senate, Jackson persuaded Democrat John Dingell, chairman of the House Merchant Marine and Fisheries Committee, to introduce it as a fish and wildlife bill.[8]

Finally, Jackson had to work out a compromise with Senator Edmund Muskie, chairman of the Senate Public Works Committee, who initially saw NEPA as a subversion of his issue: pollution control.[9] Muskie also objected to the "formal finding requirement" of the environmental impact statement as Jackson originally envisaged it. He had little faith in the capacity of federal agencies to issue reliable findings on the environment and feared that such findings would preempt legitimate challenges to them. Rather, he believed in the necessity of firm standards of pollution control for water, air, and solid waste. After protracted and bitter negotiations, Jackson accepted two major changes, which accommodated Muskie's desire to diminish the authority of the agency findings and to justify greater outside influence on them. The final bill required a "detailed statement" of environmental impact by a responsible agency official, rather than a formal finding. It also imposed the requirements that government agencies consult with environmental agencies in preparing their environmental impact statements and that such agencies make the statements widely available to the public.[10]

After NEPA became law, Jackson pushed hard but unsuccessfully for legislation to impose strict limits on strip mining. He and Congressman Morris Udall, Democrat from Arizona, managed the strip mining legislation through the Ninety-third and Ninety-fourth Congresses, but Presidents Nixon and Ford, respectively, vetoed it. For three years, Jackson also fought unsuccessfully to enact his National Land Use Policy Act, which would have established a national land-use policy. This legislation called for statewide planning to provide for a full range of land uses, including preservation, recreation, and industrial and residential development. It sought thereby to minimize controversies over power plant sitings and to encourage states to undertake advance planning for the protection of valuable national assets such as beaches and rivers. He managed this bill through the Senate during the Ninety-third and Ninety-fourth Congresses, only to have it die twice in the House due to the opposition of the Nixon administration and prodevelopment congressmen. Opponents argued that Jackson's bill would result in socialist planning inimical to free enterprise and that it would unduly encroach on the prerogatives of the states.[11] In the long run, though, his abortive land-use bill had a more lasting effect than its defeat in the House suggested. State legislators across the nation appropriated many of its key concepts, "enabling them to create a more comprehensive and workable method of land use and conservation," according to a study conducted by the Land Use Center of Pace University's School of Law.[12] For all these endeavors on behalf of the environment, Jackson received two additional national conservation awards: the medal of the American Scenic and Historic Preservation Society and the National Wildlife Federation's Legislator of the Year Award.

Yet Jackson did not long remain a popular figure in the eyes of the nation's burgeoning environmental movement. Nor did he derive any significant political benefits from the New Politics wing of the Democratic Party, for which environmentalism had become increasingly important. On the contrary, he clashed frequently and sharply with environmentalists in the years ahead. This rift opened up shortly after the enactment of NEPA. As author and pundit Ben Wattenberg, in the early 1970s a key adviser to Senator Jackson, put it: "Jackson was not an ecology freak who considered industry a villain or development an anathema. He was a balancer who believed in the possibility and necessity of reconciling environmental protection with robust economic growth."[13]

Jackson thus denounced what he called "environmental extremists who attribute all our nation's environmental ills to economic growth and to our large gross national product." For Jackson, no-growth advocates exemplified "the politics of the emotional binge" riddled with "a gloom and doom view of America that denied the existence of progress." He castigated "much of the recent environmental awareness" as "more anti-technology than pro-environment." Scorning "affluent middle-class Americans" who demanded "that factories be shut down, that automobiles be banned, that no growth policies be adopted, that we adopt a new national lifestyle rejecting the materialist philosophy," he went on to say: "Technology, like science, is morally neutral. It is man who controls technology for good or evil ends. Technology has freed man from 16-hour days and has closed sweatshops. It has eradicated disease and prolonged life. Our technological prowess may well contain the seeds of man's destruction, but it also contains the possibility of salvation."[14] He warned that the environmental movement seemed to lurch toward embracing an agenda insensitive to the aspirations of the poor. "The fundamental human rights of these people," he insisted, "cannot be traded-off to satisfy environmental goals. Achieving human goals and environmental goals will require balance and difficult decisions."[15]

At the same time, Jackson displeased many businessmen by what he repeatedly told them: that some elements of the business community had ignored their responsibilities for environmental management; that the business community henceforth must bear environmental regulation as a cost of doing business; and that Americans must insist "on the kind of investment in public and private sectors that achieves our social and economic goals of clean water, clean air, and clean land."[16] Regardless, he lost considerable support among environmentalists by backing a number of specific policies and programs that they opposed.

Environmentalists and their supporters, including the editorial page of the *New York Times*, criticized Jackson's handling of the confirmation hearings for former Republican governor of Alaska Walter Hickel, nominated by president Nixon as his first secretary of the interior. They urged the Interior Committee to recommend rejection of Hickel because "his intimacy with the oil companies and his insensitivity to Indian needs" made him "unqualified to be the nation's chief conservationist." Jackson disagreed. In his judgment a president must have "a wide latitude in his choice of those who will serve the country as members of his cabinet." His hearings had discovered no "proper grounds by which to negate the President's choice" of Hickel, who turned out to be far more sympathetic to the agenda of environmentalists during his brief tenure as secretary of the interior than they ever expected. Jackson thought it illegitimate to negate a presidential nomination because "we may not agree with the views of those selected by the President. . . ."[17]

Jackson also alienated many environmentalists by his strong support of Boeing's SST, a program also supported by a powerful coalition of the Nixon administration, the aviation industry, and organized labor. Proponents of government participation in this program argued that continued funding was necessary to ensure U.S. superiority in the aerospace industry. Jackson, Magnuson, and other regional spokesmen also warned that killing the SST would create massive unemployment in the Pacific Northwest, where the unemployment rate in the Seattle area had already reached 13.2 percent in 1971. Opponents attacked the SST mainly on environmental grounds. They charged that a fleet of SSTs would contaminate the atmosphere, cause atrocious noise, and generate dangerous fallout.[18] In rebuttal, Jackson offered tomes of expert assessments that dismissed these charges as spurious and that defended the environmental safety of the program. By an exceedingly close margin in both chambers, however, Congress handed Jackson a rare but serious defeat by voting in

March 1971 to halt further participation by the federal government in the construction of the SST. Afterward he had harsh words for environmentalists. He was "very much disturbed by the way the absolutists on the left are perverting the environmental movement into an attack on working people."[19]

Jackson's critics lashed back. They revived the moniker "Senator from Boeing" that he detested. Although he contributed to this unhappy outcome by allowing John Salter, by then a lobbyist for Boeing, to use his Senate office to conduct the airline's campaign for the SST, the imputation that Boeing owned Jackson was unfair.[20] He would have supported a program such as the SST no matter what company built it or where. Actually, he and Magnuson did less well in securing Department of Defense contracts for the state of Washington than in obtaining federal funds for other programs and services in the state. By 1971, Connecticut, a state with a slightly smaller population, had received three times the amount of money from defense contracts as Washington State.[21]

The fight over the SST strained Jackson's relationship not only with many environmentalists but with some of his liberal colleagues in the Senate, including Edward Kennedy, whose brother John had initiated the program. Three months before the final vote, Ted Kennedy came out against the SST, which he had once supported. This cost him the backing of Jackson and Magnuson in his battle to retain the leadership post as majority whip that he had won in 1969, defeating Russell Long of Louisiana. When Robert Byrd, Democrat from West Virginia, who voted for the SST, challenged Kennedy in January 1971, Jackson and Magnuson voted for Byrd. Kennedy lost. Jackson staffers remembered an irate Ted Kennedy storming out of Jackson's office and slamming the door after Scoop informed him that he was backing Byrd.[22] It took years for the two men to repair their relationship.

Jackson's longtime enthusiasm for nuclear power also angered many environmentalists. In his home state of Washington, the convertible dual-purpose reactor at Hanford that he had doggedly fought for proved to be leaky and dangerous. Consumer activist Ralph Nader singled out Hanford, the storage site for more than 50 percent of the accumulated radioactive nuclear waste in the United States, as a prime argument against nuclear power plants.[23]

Jackson's position on the Alaska pipeline controversy in 1973 exemplified his balancing approach to environmental issues. Business interests advocated a pipeline exempt from the requirements of NEPA. Environmentalists opposed a pipeline altogether. Mindful that the United States would desperately need oil from Alaska during an impending energy crisis, hopeful that the area contained huge reserves, and confident of the possibility of building a pipeline that would satisfy the legitimate concerns of environmentalists, Jackson successfully managed the bill through the Senate which authorized construction of such a pipeline. He helped thwart several attempts by environmentalists to abandon the Alaska project and support a trans-Canada pipeline to carry oil to the American Midwest; he contended that the Canadian option would take too long to negotiate and complete. He joined with the environmentalists, however, to oppose an amendment, which passed by just one vote, barring judicial review of environmental aspects of the Trans-Alaskan Oil Pipeline.[24]

Jackson did this despite his vexation with the Supreme Court and the regulatory agency for vastly inflating the requirements of the environmental impact statement. He had intended it to be a short document laying out the costs and benefits of a given project, rather than a labyrinthian process involving mountains of detail, which environmentalists used to block key projects such as the Alaska pipeline for years. The benefits of NEPA, Jackson calculated, outweighed this unintended defect—a defect he conceded impeded some legitimate as well as much illegitimate development.[25]

UNREPENTANT COLD WARRIOR

If some of Jackson's domestic views offended environmentalists and the New Politics wing of the Democratic Party to which they gravitated, his record on foreign policy and defense made them apoplectic. Their antipathy toward Jackson astonished Senator Gaylord Nelson, Democrat from Wisconsin, who experienced it during a speech he gave in Seattle in the early 1970s. When Nelson praised Jackson for his environmental legacy, including NEPA, the audience booed. When he asked why, antagonists responded that a true environmentalist could not support the type of foreign and military politics that Henry Jackson espoused.[26] It was certainly unfair, but not entirely so, for these critics to fixate on just one aspect of his record while slighting his unyielding liberalism on domestic issues. Jackson said himself that "the true test of a man is where he stands on national defense." In the eyes of many liberals in his own party, he stood on the wrong side. Dan Dreyfus recalled Jackson telling him often that national security had to take precedence over environmental concerns: "I believe that the men in the Kremlin wake up every morning and calculate whether they can do us in today. The key to our survival is always to make sure that their answer to the question is no." Typically, when Jackson was running for reelection at a controversial time, two or three of his aides pleaded with him to let John Stennis manage the armed services bill "so we could do something environmental." Jackson refused. There was no "environmental value," he said, "that would outweigh a nuclear exchange."[27]

The most venomous criticism of Jackson during the first two years of the Nixon administration arose from his stand on the Vietnam War and his staunch support of Nixon's Safeguard ABM system. Jackson believed that the United States had to wind down a war in Vietnam that had "absorbed too much of the time and energy and resources of this country." He did not support President Nixon's position on the Vietnam War as unequivocally as his critics alleged. He opposed Nixon's decision in May 1970 to send U.S. troops into Cambodia, which ignited a firestorm of domestic protest and precipitated the tragic killing of four students at Kent State University by panicked National Guardsmen.[28] In a confidential letter to President Nixon dated September 15, 1971, Jackson urged the president to pressure General Thieu to hold free and fair elections, lest "remaining Congressional support for an orderly winding down of the war" erode, "with tragic repercussions."[29] He made the letter public after Nixon implied at his press conference the next day that Jackson advocated applying pressure to topple Thieu the way the Kennedy administration had toppled Diem in 1963.

Jackson did endorse, however, the general premises of Nixon's Vietnam policy. He opposed the immediate and unconditional withdrawal of U.S. troops from Vietnam, which a growing number of liberal Democrats were promoting with mounting boldness and intensity. He insisted that "American disengagement from Vietnam must be phased and orderly, or our foreign policy problems would become more unmanageable than ever. . . . A disorganized and haphazard retreat in the face of the recalcitrance of North Vietnam would have fateful consequences for the future of this nation and of individual liberty."[30] Until the spring of 1975, he consistently voted against repeated congressional attempts to cut off funding for the war effort or to end the American involvement by a specified date.[31]

Many environmentalists and New Politics liberals also could not forgive him for the decisive role he had in floor managing Nixon's Safeguard ABM system through the Senate. When Nixon unveiled his plan to expand President Johnson's Sentinel ABM system from two to twelve sites, he stirred up a ferocious controversy that spanned more than a year and a half. Democratic Senators Fulbright, Symington, Kennedy, and Gore, joined by John Sherman Cooper, Republican from Kentucky, led the opposition. These opponents argued that an expanded ABM program, ostensibly to protect U.S. strategic retaliatory capacity, would paradoxically lead to the opposite result. It would stimulate an arms race and undermine the chances for progress in SALT talks then under way. Further, they marshaled a battery of prominent scientists who testified that the Safeguard system was neither cost effective nor technologically capable of reliably intercepting a sufficient number of incoming Soviet strategic missiles to enhance deterrence. In their view, too, social programs deserved a greater share of public money than ABM or any other high priced weapons systems.[32]

Jackson led the fight for Safeguard. He rejected the notion that the Soviets strove merely to achieve nuclear parity and embraced the American doctrine of mutual assured destruction. He presented a detailed study of the current Soviet leadership, concluding that the Soviet Union was still bent on hegemony rather than peaceful coexistence, as Americans understood the term.[33] He argued that Safeguard was more essential than ever because of the alarming pace and scope of the Soviet Union's strategic buildup, which McNamara and the doves had confidently predicted would not occur. Whereas the United States froze the number of its strategic ballistic missile launchers in 1970, the Soviets had more than doubled the number of their launchers since then, equaling U.S. levels by 1969 and surpassing them by 1970. Instead of developing small missiles like the Minuteman, the staple of the U.S. ICBM force, the Soviets built much larger standard missiles (the SS-11) and a huge supermissile (the SS-9) which, when armed with multiple warheads, made a dangerous counterforce weapon threatening to the survival of the U.S. ICBM force. The United States needed Safeguard, said Jackson, to prevent the Soviets from attaining this unilateral first-strike capability against U.S.

ICBMs, which would erode the credibility of U.S. commitment to NATO allies and dampen U.S. resolve in a crisis with the Soviets. He emphasized that the Soviets were working feverishly on an ABM system of their own. If the United States failed to go ahead with Safeguard, he forecast that it would weaken rather than strengthen the bargaining leverage of U.S. arms-control negotiators.[34]

Safeguard barely survived two crucial congressional votes in August 1969 and August 1970, respectively, which the administration would have lost without Jackson. A *Washington Post* editorial called him "far and away the most effective advocate of the Safeguard system as a defense of the U.S. land based missile deterrent." In an unusual closed, five-and-a-half-hour session of the Senate on July 17, 1969, just two weeks before the first crucial vote, Jackson jousted with Symington, Fulbright, and Cooper. He upstaged Symington by producing bigger charts than the Missouri senator's illustrating the precipitous expansion of the Soviet Union's strategic nuclear buildup.[35] He restated powerfully his standard case that Safeguard was technologically feasible, cost effective, and necessary to protect the credibility of the U.S. deterrent. As Paul Wolfowitz observed:

> Symington got hold of a Pentagon chart proving the ABM would not work. I talked with Albert Wohlstetter about how easy it was to make a chart that refuted Symington's. We came up with charts and delivered them to Senator Jackson. It was the first time in my life I met a U.S. Senator. What impressed me was that he insisted on understanding the results we got on the graphs. He sat on the ground in shirtsleeves with a twenty-nine year old graduate student to master them. He then called in Senators John Tower and Peter Dominick and went through it with them. It was clear from the reaction after the secret session that Jackson had scored a big win. When it came down to it, it was not the intellectual argument, but who you believed. . . . He spoke with such authority that when he really believed something on a defense issue, few members of the Senate were comfortable challenging him.[36]

Walter Mondale, then a first-term Democratic senator from Minnesota and an opponent of Safeguard, later noted that Jackson made the case for ABM during this closed session in terms that articulated and anticipated the strategy Ronald Reagan would follow in the 1980s. Jackson argued that the United States had "to bankrupt the Soviet Union by developing weapons systems that forced the Soviets to match us, or else that they would be a constant menace to us. His idea was slowly but surely to bring a collapse of the system through relentless U.S. pressure."[37] In the weeks before the second crucial vote, on August 12, 1970, Jackson reprised his argument for ABM in a series of clashes with Cooper, the co-author of the Cooper-Hart Amendment forbidding the expansion of the Safeguard system to new sites.[38]

The ABM debate also displayed Jackson's formidable skills as a parliamentarian and his exquisite sense of his colleagues. He knew just when to push and when not to push. If members had reasons to be left alone, he would leave them alone. Before the critical vote in August 1969, which passed the ABM by just one vote, various administration officials were beside themselves with uncertainty over what the independent-minded Senator Margaret Chase Smith, Republican from Maine, would do. They all recommended lobbying her strongly. Jackson told them to back off. "The worst thing you can do with Margaret would be to mount a campaign," he said. On the day of the vote, he rebuffed several efforts to push her. Finally, Smith voted for Safeguard. If she had gone the other way, Safeguard would have lost.[39]

Jackson also knew how and when to apply pressure. He spent hours making appeals to his friend Clinton Anderson after the New Mexico senator announced his support for the Cooper-Hart Amendment in August 1970. He told Anderson it was essential to the country's bargaining position to back the administration on the Safeguard vote. Anderson relented. During the vote on the Cooper-Hart Amendment, Jackson took the seat immediately behind Anderson. One person in their vicinity reported hearing Anderson turn to Jackson and ask him how to vote. Jackson answered: "Vote no."[40]

The ABM debate of 1969–70 symbolized the dramatic transformation since 1960 in the outlook of the Democratic Party on foreign policy and national defense. No longer were the Democrats the more hawkish of the two parties. For George McGovern, Eugene McCarthy, and a growing number of Northern Democrats, the ABM was not just a specific political issue. Their opposition to it was part of their larger argument against the policy of vigilantly containing the Soviet Union that Henry Jackson indefatigably defended. The breakdown of the voting on ABM indicated how popular their critique of Cold War liberalism had become among

Northern Democrats. In the Senate, virtually every Northern liberal voted against the Safeguard system, with three conspicuous exceptions: Henry Jackson; Gale McGee, Democrat from Wyoming; and John Pastore,
Democrat from Rhode Island, who retired in 1972. A coalition of Republicans and Dixiecrats supported it, a preview of the alignment that prevailed in Congress for the rest of the Cold War. The ABM debate opened
a sustained barrage on the American military and foreign policy commitments by Northern Democrats, who now considered that the prime danger to U.S. national security was the arrogance of American power rather
than the menace of Soviet communism. Henceforth, Jackson would have
to rely mainly on the support of conservative Republicans and Dixiecrats
in his struggle to ensure that the United States stayed the course that his
hero Harry Truman had set. At the end of the ABM debate, conservative
stalwart Barry Goldwater declared his desire to have Jackson "around for
many, many years to give us the kind of backing and assurance we need."[41]

The ABM vote also precipitated a split in the Washington State delegation. Magnuson joined with other Northern liberals to vote against it.
Prodded by his advisers, conscious of his image, always more optimistic
about cooperation with the Soviet Union than Jackson, and now with his
close friend Lyndon Johnson out of office, Magnuson felt free to cast his
lot with the New Politics wing of the party on foreign policy and defense
issues. His defection did not affect Jackson's collaboration with him on
domestic issues or their personal friendship.[42] It magnified, however,
Jackson's sense of isolation from many liberals within his own state.

For Jackson, the ABM debate had one unalloyed benefit. It provided
him the opportunity to hire Richard Perle, a brash, young expert on nuclear strategy and American foreign policy whose views were symbiotic
with Jackson's own. Perle and Jackson met by accident. In the spring of
1969 Perle attended a meeting in D.C. that included Albert Wohlstetter
of the University of Chicago; Paul Wolfowitz, one of his prize students
and a future undersecretary of defense; and former Secretary of State
Dean Acheson. To counteract the arguments "of people like Fulbright,
Symington, George McGovern, and others who were opposing ballistic
missile defense," they decided to form the Committee on Prudent Defense, which Acheson and Paul Nitze chaired. Wohlstetter then asked
Perle, a doctoral student at Princeton, to come to Washington for a few
days and conduct some interviews on Capitol Hill so he could draft a re-

port on the developing debate over the ABM. While in Washington, he met Dorothy Fosdick, who introduced him to Jackson. Perle received an offer from Fosdick ten days later for a position on the Permanent Investigations Subcommittee of the Committee on Government Operations. With an academic career in mind, he thought a year in the Senate would be good experience. So he accepted and left his research job in Cambridge, Massachusetts, expecting to work on his thesis in his spare time. Things did not turn out that way. Perle spent the next eleven years on Jackson's staff as his point man on foreign policy and defense issues.[43]

"Scoop was a surrogate father to Richard, whose own father died early," remembered Howard Feldman, a close friend of Perle's and Jackson's chief council on the Permanent Investigations Subcommittee between 1973 and 1982. "When Richard got married at our house, Scoop was the best man. It was quite a happening. Jim Schlesinger ended up in the swimming pool playing his harmonica."

Perle had eccentric work habits, which Jackson amiably tolerated. "You could not get him into the office," said Feldman. "He not only slept late, but perfected the art of answering the phone at home as if he was really alert." Perle often antagonized congressmen, members of the executive branch, and their staffs with his brashness, abrasiveness, and penchant for playing "hardball."[44] Those who disagreed with Jackson but liked him often blamed Perle for his controversial positions on national security and the Middle East, as did some of the more dovish members of Jackson's staff.[45] Without question, Perle had a major hand in devising and pushing some of Jackson's most important foreign policy initiatives. It is a mistake, however, to view Jackson as a captive or creature of Perle's will. When Perle arrived, Jackson already had a well-established record on national security and a greater knowledge of that subject than any member of the Senate. No member of his staff, Perle included, would have survived long without following his well-defined line.[46] Take, for example, Jackson's ardent support of Israel, which critics have sometimes ascribed to Perle's influence because of his Jewish background. Actually, the reverse was true. Raised in a secular home in southern California, Perle had no pronounced views on the Middle East when he joined Jackson's staff in 1969. Jackson and Dorothy Fosdick changed that. They lectured him incessantly about the imperative of maintaining a strong Israel and the greatness of the Jewish tradition.[47] Thus Perle became an intrepid champion of Israel by the work of these two Niebuhrian Protestant missionaries in the Russell Building of the United States Senate.

NIXON'S FAVORITE DEMOCRATIC SENATOR

While Henry Jackson proceeded to antagonize many members of his own party by his stand on Vietnam and his fight for Safeguard, he endeared himself to President Nixon, at least for a time. In the spring of 1970, addressing a Veterans of Foreign Wars convention in Seattle, Nixon gushed that Jackson was "a great credit to his party and to America."[48] Nixon even undercut Dan Evans, the Republican governor of Washington, by telling Jackson first of his decision to cancel the shipment of nerve gas across the state, thereby diffusing the local uproar over it. Jackson convened a press conference immediately to make this announcement, which garnered him the credit for stopping it. Nixon's solicitousness toward Jackson on the nerve gas issue frustrated Evans, who had publicly defended the president's initial decision and taken the heat for it despite his strong opposition to the idea privately.[49] Intent on making the 1970 election a referendum on his administration, the president campaigned aggressively to win control of the Senate. The administration worked hard to defeat Northern liberals across the nation, except for Henry Jackson. Senator John Tower, chairman of the Republican National Committee, declared that no national party funds would go to Jackson's opponents.[50]

Yet Nixon's approval did not make Henry Jackson a conservative, by any valid meaning of the term. For one thing, Nixon was not really a conservative either, a fact that his own dissimulations out of office did much to obscure. He employed conservative rhetoric while largely following liberal policies. Lyndon Johnson's Great Society expanded vastly on his watch, a result that the president expended almost no political capital to prevent. Declaring that "we are all Keynesians now," he imposed mandatory wage and price controls—Henry Jackson's favorite remedy for economic distress—to curb the rise in inflation after 1970.[51] As commentator Michael Barone has noted in his magisterial *Our Country*, the program of Nixon's favorite cabinet officer—former Texas Governor John Connally, secretary of the treasury for nine months in 1971—"brought more state direction to economic policy and did more to undercut the operation of free economic markets than anything done, except in war, by the Roosevelt, Truman, Eisenhower, Kennedy, or Johnson administrations."[52] Nixon even endorsed Affirmative Action, a policy that Jackson opposed because it contravened his belief in equality of opportunity as the Civil Rights Act of 1964 originally intended it. In 1969, George Shultz, Nixon's secretary of labor, promulgated the Philadelphia Plan, a model for subsequent affirmative action programs, which established goals (really quotas) for black membership in building trade unions.[53]

Jackson took more liberal positions than Nixon did on most domestic issues. He voted with Northern liberals to oppose the president's nominations of Clement Haynsworth and Harrold Carswell to the Supreme Court, on the grounds that they lacked the necessary qualifications. He criticized the administration's economic policy as insufficiently statist, activist, and generous to social programs. He advocated the imposition of more extensive and long-lasting wage and price controls than even Nixon would countenance. He blamed the administration for "a current rate of economic growth that is half of what it should be to keep pace with the normal growth of the labor force." He called for personal income tax cuts to "spur essential consumer spending" and a massive public works program "to create 500,000 new jobs in the public sector." He assailed as "ill-conceived, lacking in constructive content, and dangerous in the extreme" Nixon's New Economic Policy of 1971, which unilaterally abrogated fixed international exchange rates. He persisted in his advocacy of national health insurance.[54] Above all, he insisted on categorizing himself as a liberal, even if others did not.[55]

Temperamentally, Jackson and Nixon had little in common. Whereas the president was insecure, brooding, pessimistic, and prone to self-pity, Jackson had an unshakable self-confidence and a sober, albeit nonutopian, faith in the American people's ultimate judgment. Senator Moynihan hailed him as a Viking warrior who relished political combat but rarely held a grudge. Certainly neither Moynihan nor anyone who has worked for Nixon would ever say that about him. What Jackson and Nixon did share was an aversion to the counterculture and its values. They were both traditionalists on the moral and cultural issues that increasingly divided the nation after 1968. Jackson opposed abortion because he believed "life begins at conception." He therefore disagreed with the Supreme Court's decision in *Roe v. Wade* that cast aside the rights of the state to prohibit abortion. He defended the imperative for maintaining law and order as the very essence of liberalism, not its antithesis. He denounced "the absolutists on the left" for interpreting law and order as a code term for racism.[56]

Jackson also opposed forced busing to achieve racial balance in schools, except as a remedy for de jure (legally imposed) segregation. His own actions indicate that the best rather than the worst of motives inspired him to take this position.[57] He sent Anna Marie and Peter (until they reached junior high school) to the public school in his Spring Valley neighborhood, a school that was 30 percent black and had a black principal. Jackson supported voluntary busing of blacks to better schools, but thought that mandatory busing would hurt education and race relations. He predicted that it would lead to more segregation by spurring the flight from urban districts of white middle-class parents who legitimately wanted the best for their children. Based on his own experience as a child, he extolled the virtues of neighborhood schools, which he feared mandatory busing would destroy.[58]

He lambasted "extremists" for the resurgence of disorder on campuses, which Nixon's invasion of Cambodia had triggered.[59] The not-so-young radical Jerry Rubin epitomized everything Jackson objected to about them. Jackson spoke bluntly on college campuses about what he perceived to be the narcissism and self-indulgence of the student left: "It is fashionable to say that you are indeed the best generation that we have ever produced," he typically addressed student gatherings, "but I did not come here to tell you that, because I do not believe it." He opposed "a general or unconditional amnesty for those who refused service [in Vietnam] or fled in order to avoid the consequences to serve." He called it unfair "for those individuals who violated the law to be officially excused from penalty while others, often at the risk of life, accepted the obligation of service."[60]

For their part, student radicals detested Jackson. They pelted him with marshmallows during a speech he gave at Mankato State College in Minnesota on February 3, 1970. They heckled and booed him at his alma mater, the University of Washington, during his speech to celebrate the first Earth Day on April 22, 1970. This latter incident "really shook up" Bill Van Ness, who accompanied him, but not Jackson, who was unflappable about it. Eventually, the atmosphere on college campuses degenerated enough that Jackson would not allow Helen to accompany him there. "You could not believe the awful language these kids use, even the girls," he told her, shocked by it himself.[61]

THE 1970 SENATE CAMPAIGN

Henry Jackson faced no serious threat to his reelection in 1970, but he did encounter an angry challenge from the New Politics wing of his own party in Washington State. Presaging what Jackson would experience in 1972 and 1976 as a presidential candidate, on June 7, 1969, the Washington Democratic Council (WDC), an antiwar group composed mainly of supporters of Eugene McCarthy and Robert Kennedy, officially committed itself to defeating him. The leaders gave two reasons for this move:

—The Senator's positions on military spending and national priorities are diametrically opposed to those of recognized leaders of the Democratic Party, namely, Vice-President Humphrey, Senators Muskie, Kennedy, McGovern, McCarthy, Hughes, Mansfield, Fulbright, and National party Chairman Senator Harris.

—The Senator's voting record and his "deep concern for the quality of our environment" is negated by his commitment and activity to keep active and alive an industrial mood of cold war confrontation—and to feed the military industrial complex a lion's share of our national resources in the face of pressing domestic needs.[62]

Their effort received much encouragement from leading members of the peace movement in the Democratic Party nationally: Eugene McCarthy, John Kenneth Galbraith, and Allard Lowenstein, all of whom were eager for Jackson to lose.[63]

Despite the heated opposition to Jackson's reelection, the WDC did not have an easy time recruiting an opponent to challenge him. His trustworthiness, effectiveness, and diligence as a senator had accumulated an enormous reservoir of good will for him among rank-and-file voters. Even many of those skeptical of his views on foreign policy and defense were supportive of his stand on domestic issues and his scrupulous attentiveness to constituent services. The rules governing primaries in Washington State heavily favored the type of politician, such as Jackson, who attracted broad and deep bipartisan support. Because the state's voters could cross party lines in the primaries, any prospective opponent would have to expect many Republicans and independents to turn out for Jackson.[64]

Thus few established politicians wished to jeopardize their careers by running what was inevitably a losing race. Brock Adams, the liberal congressman from Seattle with views on foreign policy and defense congenial to the New Politics wing of the party, declined to run against Jackson, partly for these reasons. Governor Dan Evans, a popular liberal antiwar Republican, also considered Jackson too formidable to beat.[65] Whereupon, Carl Maxey, a forty-five-year-old black attorney from Spokane, resigned as chairman of the WDC to challenge Jackson for the Democratic nomination to the Senate.

Few men in American politics could match Henry Jackson for integrity. Carl Maxey came close. Born in Tacoma on June 23, 1924, he spent his first twelve years an orphan in Spokane's Children's Home, which closed in 1936, and spent the next year at the Sacred Heart Mission, a Jesuit Indian School in De Smet, Idaho, before returning to Spokane in 1937, where he graduated from high school. He attended Gonzaga College in Spokane and the University of Oregon before military service interrupted his studies. After World War II, he transferred back to Gonzaga, where he completed law school. A former NCAA boxing champion, he described himself as "originally a great supporter of Henry M. Jackson." In the 1940s, he admired Jackson, especially for liberalism on labor issues, although he harbored one major reservation about him even then: his strident advocacy of Japanese internment. While working as a waiter on the Great Northern Railroad in the summer of 1942 between semesters at the University of Oregon, Maxey anguished over seeing many of the Japanese Americans he liked transferred to Tule Lake.[66]

He soured on Jackson over time because he perceived him becoming "more and more of an apologist for the military establishment and for Israel's suppression of Arab rights." The Vietnam War not only catalyzed Maxey's embrace of the New Left but fueled his animosity toward Jackson. Maxey castigated Jackson for being a conservative, a defender of Nixon and the ABM, a perpetrator of the arms race, a paranoid anticommunist who unconscionably defended U.S. involvement in a lost, costly, unjust war in Vietnam, which also destroyed the Great Society and set back the cause of social justice at home. In his campaign, Maxey, to use his favorite boxing metaphor, pulled no punches. "Our destiny," he said on April 2, 1970, "is in the hands of fat-cat contractors, bellicose generals, and a Napoleonic little senator who can juggle bombs and ballots, conservation and nerve gas on a platform of the continued draft that kills your sons and brothers of your city."[67]

Maxey's message swayed the majority of delegates at the King County Democratic Convention. In March 1970, they repudiated Jackson by giving Maxey their endorsement. In May, the King County Democrats followed up by adopting a platform that repudiated Jackson's Cold War liberalism. It called, domestically, for legalizing marijuana, legalizing abortion, and protecting the ability of Black Panthers and other minority political organizations to exist "free from government harassment." It called, internationally, for withdrawing all U.S. troops from Southeast Asia by the end of 1970, for ending the sale of weapons to any Middle Eastern country (including Israel), and for reestablishing trade with Cuba. It called, in the area of "War and Peace," for suspending the production and deployment of ABMs and MIRVs and for rapidly reducing the size of American armed forces. Proponents hailed this platform as "an extremely relevant social document." Some others assailed it as "coming directly from Moscow and Hanoi."[68] Maxey himself dubbed the results of the King County Convention "a good right hook to Jackson's belly."[69]

The Maxey forces succeeded in embarrassing and angering Jackson at the state Democratic convention in Spokane in July 1970. Although the convention rules prohibited outright endorsement of any candidate, the delegates passed several antiwar planks and a pro-amnesty plank over Jackson's objection. Maxey's forces managed, with television cameras rolling, to disrupt Jackson's introductory speech for Warren Magnuson, the keynote speaker of the convention who gave him only a tepid endorsement amid the tumult in the hall. According to Prochnau and Larsen's eyewitness account, "Jackson, unhappy that Maggie hadn't given him ringing praise, had a look of frozen fury on his face as they left the stage, past backstage police wearing 'Pigs is Beautiful' sweatshirts."[70]

Maxey also "pulled no punches" during the primary campaign. Mocking Jackson's record as an environmentalist, he ran a campaign ad, which his wife Lou placed in the sports pages of the Seattle papers, with this inscription over the silhouette of a soldier marching to battle: "No Deposit, No Return. Is Vietnam Henry Jackson's Idea of Conservation? Vote for

Carl Maxey." He accused Jackson of being a closet Republican, "a captive candidate of the Nixon administration, a destroyer of the two-party system." He railed against Jackson for his backing of the ABM and Vietnam. He ripped him for raising groundless apprehensions about the Soviet Union, thus fostering a dangerous arms race.[71]

Maxey's campaign attracted national attention from sympathetic New Politics liberals or those who fancied themselves in that camp. Kitty Kelley, the gossip columnist who grew up in Spokane and became a reporter for the *Washington Post*, sent Maxey "every good thought for your success."[72] Eugene McCarthy arrived in Washington State to campaign for Maxey a week before the September 15 primary. "Jackson stands more with the Republicans on the militarization of American society than any other man," McCarthy said. "He is always on the side of those seeking more military power, and more, and more." McCarthy derided him as a senator "who would not feel safe without ICBMs in every city—except Seattle—and so many submarines in the water that they run into each other." He hesitated "to bring it up," because Henry may want to close other gaps. . . . We're falling behind the Indians in poison darts. We're short of catapults. We should be totally safe." Jackson reciprocated McCarthy's disdain. Telling reporters that "McCarthy was free to come" to campaign against him, he dismissed him as someone "having absolutely no standing in the Senate." Jackson said he was "very proud of the fact that during my term in the Senate, I opposed both McCarthys, Eugene and Joe."[73]

Jackson's chief strategist advised him to ignore rather than engage Maxey, whose attacks genuinely bothered him, despite his outward composure to the contrary. Jackson's campaign stressed his record on the environment and his stature in the Senate. It portrayed him as a moderate, the embodiment of the sensible center in American politics: for law, order, and social justice at home, for the prudent defense of America's vital interests abroad. Intent on conducting himself as a statesman above the fray, he rarely rose to Maxey's bait. Jackson won the September 15 primary overwhelmingly, with 87 percent of the vote.[74]

The campaign for the general election was equally successful for Jackson, whose popularity scared off all credible challengers. Indeed, in February 1970, a mortified C. Montgomery "Gummie" Johnson, chairman of the Republican Party in Washington State, discovered that some of the top Republican donors had contributed $250,000 to ensure Jackson's re-election.[75] Jackson demolished Charles Elicker, his Republican opponent, by getting 84 percent of the vote.[76] His margin of victory not only shattered the previous records for Washington State, but it also ranked the highest of any contested election for the Senate in 1970. The magnitude of his victory provided a powerful impetus for his decision to run for the presidency in 1972.

Chapter 12

Gearing Up for the 1972 Presidential Campaign

BY LATE 1970, national columnists such as Stewart Alsop had begun to speculate favorably about the possibility of Jackson entering the presidential race on the strength of his landslide reelection.[1] Jackson moved steadily in the same direction during the first nine months of 1971. He traveled to 32 states and 126 cities—from Boston to New York to Los Angeles, from Miami to Chicago—testing the waters and honing his message. He pronounced the Nixon administration's economic policies a failure, resulting in continued high levels of unemployment, renewed inflation, and sluggish growth. He denounced the "intolerant extremists who have come to despise America and who would destroy the Democratic Party if they took it over." He chided those Democratic leaders "who have bent over backward to pay homage to this fringe." He warned that the Democrats would suffer a catastrophic defeat in November 1972 if the party nominated someone sympathetic to the New Politics wing.[2] In contrast to the other potential Democratic candidates for the presidency as well as President Nixon, he argued that the Soviet Union would become even more dangerous because of the ominous increase in Soviet strategic power. He anticipated not Nixon's "era of negotiation," but an era of confrontation with Soviet power throughout much of the world.[3]

Jackson's preliminary foray into the arena of presidential politics evoked a mixed reaction. Liberal columnists such as Tom Wicker of the *New York Times* criticized the substance and tone of his message as shrill and counterproductive. James A. Wechsler, whom Jackson had defended against Joe McCarthy's attacks, dismissed him as "a symbol of the sterile slogans of another era . . . , the faithful representative of every interest and ideologue that sees mankind doomed to another decade or more of the balance of terror and preparedness as the only national salvation." Conversely, labor leaders and other columnists responded positively. Robert Thompson reminded Jackson's liberal critics that "Kennedy in 1960 stood for almost the identical issues for which Scoop Jackson now stands—a nuclear defense posture that would guarantee America's security and a domestic policy that would provide greater equality of social and economic opportunity for all citizens."[4]

Although Jackson waited until November 20, 1971, to declare his candidacy officially, he had already decided to enter the race by late summer. Meanwhile, he had assembled his team for the campaign. Notwithstanding his break with Jackson over defense and foreign policy issues, Magnuson agreed to be the honorary chairman. Sterling Munro, Jackson's venerable administrative assistant, would run the campaign. Hyman Raskin, a Chicago attorney active in the campaigns of Adlai Stevenson, John Kennedy, and Hubert Humphrey, would act as an adviser and as national field man. Gerry Hoeck, Jackson's media adviser for all of his previous Senate campaigns, would handle his media and advertising strategy. His best friend, Stan Golub, would serve as treasurer, just as he had done for all of Jackson's previous Senate campaigns. Brian Corcoran, Jackson's press secretary in the Senate, would serve in that capacity for the presidential campaign.[5]

Jackson also hired Ben Wattenberg as his chief strategist. A former speech writer for Lyndon Johnson, Wattenberg and his co-author Richard Scammon had created a sensation with the publication of *The Real Majority* in 1970, the moderate Democrats' answer to Kevin Phillips's *The Emerging Republican Majority*, which shaped Nixon's 1972 campaign strategy. Their book challenged Phillips's main thesis that the Republicans had displaced the Democrats as the national majority party in presidential politics by forging a coalition of white voters of the South and the Sunbelt, on the one hand, and Northern and Midwestern ethnic Catholics disaffected by the New Politics of the Democratic Party, on the other. Scammon and Wattenberg contended that traditional economic issues still favored the Democrats. As they saw it, however, this advantage alone would not suffice for the Democrats to remain the majority party or to recapture the White House. They argued that the Democrats must move back to the center on foreign policy and on what they dubbed the social issues: an amalgam of law and order, pot, pornography, permissiveness, and elements of the race problem.[6]

What drew Wattenberg to Jackson was that "the prescriptions laid down in *The Real Majority* fit him to a T: strong on law and order but still a liberal, egalitarian on economic issues, flintlike and strong on foreign policy." Wattenberg recounted the circumstances that brought them together this way: Many leading Democrats courted him heavily because of the notoriety of *The Real Majority*. In 1971, Senator Edmund Muskie, the widely acknowledged front-runner for the 1972 Democratic presidential nomination, asked Wattenberg to join his staff. He declined, he said, because "Muskie was moving with the speed of light toward the left." Although Muskie voted with Jackson in 1971 against Senator Mike Mansfield's perennial resolution to cut U.S. NATO forces deployed in Europe by half, he had endorsed the agenda of the New Politics wing of the party on most other contentious foreign policy and national security issues. Muskie also had adamantly opposed Nixon's Safeguard ABM and supported the Moratorium of October 1969, a massive demonstration against the Vietnam War held in D.C. and attended by hundreds of thousands of protesters from across the nation. Wattenberg perceived Muskie "as becoming part of the antiwar left and pandering to the radical elements of the environmental and civil rights movements." He decided "that it would be a rear guard action to try to bring Muskie back to the center." Then Wattenberg received a call from Jackson, whom he had never met, requesting a meeting. Jackson impressed him tremendously during their hour-long talk, which also included Sterling Munro. They agreed "totally." Both of them considered the defense and promotion of "democratic values against a remorseless Soviet adversary . . . the most important thing that the government could do." When Munro asked him "to come on board," Wattenberg accepted because he believed avidly "in the importance of Jackson's cause."[7]

In his excellent 1996 book *Divided They Fell*, Ronald Radosh called Jackson's 1972 campaign the "last great opportunity for the Democrats before Bill Clinton" to resurrect the center of the Democratic Party.[8] He is wrong about that. Jackson's 1976 campaign represented by far his best and certainly his last bona fide opportunity to win the presidency and reinvigorate his wing of the party. Several things conspired to make 1972 a particularly unpropitious year for Jackson's presidential run. In a crowded field of well-known candidates—Edmund Muskie, Hubert Humphrey, George McGovern, George Wallace, and the mayor of New York John Lindsay—Jackson started off as a virtual unknown to the American public. He had implacably alienated New Left Democrats, who by then had attained a prominent and potentially dominant position in the party. Allard Lowenstein; Frank Mankiewicz, former press secretary for Bobby Kennedy and a top adviser to the very dovish Senator McGovern; Senator Fred Harris, Democrat from Oklahoma; and Representative Shirley Chisolm, Democrat from New York, among others, greeted Jackson's impending candidacy with the threat of bolting from the Democratic Party should he win the nomination. The party would "be committing suicide" if it nominated Henry Jackson, declared Lowenstein. "There is no way for the Democrats to win if they pick a man who stands for the worst things that Nixon stands for."[9] What made 1972 even more difficult for Jackson's candidacy was that McGovern's catastrophic defeat still lay in the future. In 1976, the Democratic Party at least had to acknowledge the disaster inherent in moving precipitously to the left, making Jackson's warnings more compelling and more difficult for the New Politics wing to dismiss out of hand. Unlike 1976, moreover, paltry funding and poor organization plagued Jackson's 1972 campaign from the outset.

These problems specific to 1972 intersected with several other liabilities endemic to both of Jackson's presidential campaigns. There was, to begin with, the problem of his demeanor. Senator Moynihan insisted that "Henry Jackson had the charisma of competence."[10] Helen Jackson insisted that he had charisma, period.[11] Few others have positively associated charisma with Henry Jackson, whom the national media depicted as a presidential candidate the way comedian Mark Russell used to joke about him: If Henry Jackson gave a fireside chat, the fire would go out. His close friend and media consultant Gerry Hoeck conceded, "You could never make a speech maker out of Jackson." He and others hired countless media consultants who tried to improve Jackson's speaking style but could not. "You cannot change a Norwegian," said Hoeck, of Norwegian ancestry himself. "Giving a speech, Jackson got pompous. He got boring. He dressed up the language. Instead of speaking in plain English, he embroidered the language. He loved to use famous phrases again and again."[12] Ambassador Robert Strauss echoed Hoeck's assessment: "Scoop

Jackson was a great United States senator. He was a great man in many respects. I loved him. But the one thing he could not do was capture an audience of strangers."[13] In Jackson's campaigns for Senate, Hoeck had compensated for Jackson's shortcomings as an orator by using all voiceovers "with Jackson talking conversationally." In a national campaign, however, "the news media is with you day after day and determines what goes on television that night."[14]

During the 1972 campaign, Hoeck and others also decided that "they had to get Jackson out of those goddam clothes. He looked so old-fashioned and fuddy duddy." They wanted to get him "something new, something more modern." Hoeck found the appropriate tailor to spruce up Jackson's wardrobe, a Jewish supporter from Baltimore who had done all of the suits for the stylishly attired Vice President Spiro Agnew. Sterling Munro assigned Hoeck the unenviable task of informing Jackson. Flying back to Washington, D.C., from New York City with him, Hoeck finally summoned the will to tell Jackson that campaign staff had made arrangements for him to get some new suits, shirts, and ties. Jackson said nothing for a long while as he sat reading the *New York Times*. Finally, he said no. "He could not do that to Leon." Leon was the proprietor of No-Label-Louie's, where Jackson had bought all his clothes off the rack for years. Then Hoeck called Helen Jackson for help. After a long pause, she replied, "Good luck." Hoeck persisted. He instructed the tailor to make an appointment to see Jackson and to say that "he wanted to give Jackson some suits as a campaign contribution." After the meeting, Hoeck finally persuaded Jackson to accept them by appealing to his generous instincts: "You cannot turn him down, Scoop. He will be hurt."

The primacy of television and of primaries in post-1968 presidential politics badly hampered Jackson's bids for the Democratic nomination. Neither he nor any of the other declared candidates except McGovern understood that the McGovern-Fraser rule changes had fundamentally transformed the nomination process and altered the balance of power in the party to the detriment of traditional Democrats such as Henry Jackson. The new rules magnified the influence of activists who largely embraced the New Politics at the expense of traditional constituencies such as organized labor and party bosses more likely to back Jackson or a candidate like him.[15]

In both of his presidential campaigns, Jackson tended to view the Democratic primaries through the lens of his experience in Washington State.[16] That was a misleading analogy. Most of the Democratic presidential primaries did not permit crossover voting. Jackson therefore could not attract the substantial support from independents and Republicans that boosted his vote totals in his home state. Instead, he faced an electorate disproportionately composed of the very elements in the party that he opposed. In Washington State, the trust and affection voters felt for him had ripened slowly but steadily. In the onrush of presidential primaries, there would be no such opportunity.

Jackson and his campaign team recognized some, though not all, of these deficiencies. They hoped, however, that Jackson would emerge as a powerful contender by challenging the most important assumptions of the other leading Democrats in the race. They calculated that he had significant potential appeal in the West (his home base), in the South (because of national defense), with labor (because of his pro-labor record), and with Jews (because of his staunch support of Israel). Also, they noted that President Nixon, Republican Senator John Tower of Texas, and other leading Republicans assessed Jackson as the toughest potential Democratic nominee.[17] Jackson also received endorsements from several powerful Southern Democrats: Congressman Wilbur Mills, chairman of the House Ways and Means Committee; Senator John Stennis, chairman of the Armed Services Committee; and Senator Sam Ervin from North Carolina, chairman of the Judiciary Committee.[18] Although declining to endorse any candidate, Georgia Governor Jimmy Carter, whom the Jacksons had called on during a swing through the state in the spring of 1971, also named him as the type of Democrat the party should nominate.[19]

In an internal memorandum mapping out the grand strategy for the campaign, Wattenberg identified the intrinsic strength of the Jackson candidacy as his "authentic position, rather sharply different than the other candidates." He cautioned, however, about "one basic contradiction" that Jackson would have to resolve swiftly or else the candidacy would founder. To gain the support needed (in the polls and in the primaries) he would have to emerge nationwide as the candidate starkly different from the others; but to avoid the New Left veto that might well operate at the convention, "he shouldn't alienate the left-liberals." Wattenberg's advice was to attack the New Left. On economic issues, he predicted that all "Democrats would take an essentially similar tack"; so he saw little profit in making this the cornerstone of the campaign. International issues (Vietnam, American foreign policy, and national defense) "lacked political sex appeal," lamented Wattenberg, even though Jackson had taken a position that was right, different from any others, and "without question the central issue that Americans must face in the 1970s." He therefore counseled Jackson to concentrate on the social issues: law and order; opposition to busing; the defense of patriotism and the success of the American experiment in ordered liberty; a condemnation of elitism; and the affirmation of the virtues of American values. Although Jackson believed economic and foreign policy issues warranted higher priority for the campaign than Wattenberg did, he followed much of Wattenberg's advice.[20]

Jackson's presidential campaign fizzled. The media often ignored him to cover the better-known candidates, who clobbered him. On the right, the enormous popularity of George Wallace's populism preempted his support in the South. On the left, the antiwar message and unabashed New Politics liberalism of George McGovern excited the legions of partisan activists critical for winning the nomination under the new rules that McGovern himself had helped write. In the center, the better-known and better-funded Hubert Humphrey prevailed over Jackson in their battle for the diminishing cohort of traditional Democratic voters such as organized labor.[21]

Jackson's 1972 presidential run still has great significance, however, for what it reveals about the post-1968 Democratic Party. He fought tenaciously but in vain for positions on foreign policy and social issues that the preponderance of liberal Democratic activists, including the preferred candidate George McGovern, roundly repudiated.

THE DEMOCRATIC PRIMARIES

On November 19, 1971, Jackson formally announced his presidential candidacy before a row of television cameras in the historic Caucus Room of the Old Senate Office Building. He ascended the stage, kissed Helen there beside him, and declared himself the candidate who could achieve the nation's number one priority of putting "our people back to work." His address blended a defense of traditional New Deal–Fair Deal economics, and the policy of containment as Harry Truman had envisaged it, with an attack on the credibility of President Nixon and the extremism of the other Democratic candidates. Emphasizing the social issues, Jackson contended that most Americans "were fed up with people running down America. This society is not a guilty, imperialistic, and oppressive society. This is not a sick society. This is a great country . . . that is conscious of its wrongs and is capable of correcting them." Although Jackson had the entire New Politics wing of the party in mind for this general critique, he reproached in particular Edmund Muskie, the putative Democratic front-runner, for his reaction to the Attica prison killings in 1971. "A prison riot," Jackson said, "does not prove that there is something terribly wrong with America. This kind off talk is part of the problem and not part of the cure." He also chastised those "who wince at the public's demand for law and order . . . and say it is a code word for racism and repression." He said he shared the feelings of other Americans that the crime situation was out of hand: "Until we are prepared to acknowledge that law and order is a real problem, we just won't solve it."[22]

In his address and the press conference that followed, Jackson reiterated his standard refrain on foreign policy: American weakness leads to peril. American strength leads to peace. He did not believe that the nation should overextend itself "or get bogged down in more Vietnams . . . or play world cop." If, however, America pulled back from world responsibility, he warned, "We will surely be isolated in a more dangerous world. We will suffer—and so would our friends and allies, in Europe, in the Middle East, around the world." He contended "it would be a tragic error" if the United States reduced its troop strength in Europe by 60,000 as Senators Mansfield, McGovern, Fulbright, and their other dovish colleagues in the Senate had proposed. In a line that produced warm applause, Jackson claimed to be "neither a hawk nor a dove"; he just did not want his country to be a "pigeon." He sought instead for the United States "to be the wise owl." He conceded that he was "an underdog in the race." That was all right, he said, because his party, "the Democratic Party, has always been the party of the underdog: . . . the party of the little guy; the party of the plain people, the party of plain talk; the party of Kennedy and Johnson; and still the party of Harry Truman—who showed what an underdog could do for this country." He was running for president "so that American could work for all people."

The New Hampshire Primary of March 7, 1972, immediately recast the race for the Democratic nomination. After sending Foley and Wattenberg to tour the state and traveling there himself, Jackson decided against running in New Hampshire, where he expected Senator Muskie from neighboring Maine to win easily. Also, he feared his entry there would prompt an endorsement from William Loeb, the ultraconservative editor of the *Manchester Union-Leader,* which his leftist opponents would exploit."[23] All Jackson's calculations went awry, however, when Muskie self-destructed by appearing to cry while excoriating Loeb for attacking his wife and wrongly accusing him of making disparaging statements about French Canadians, a sizable voting bloc in New Hampshire's Democratic primaries. Although Muskie won the primary over George McGovern, 46 percent to 37 percent, the press interpreted the results as a victory for McGovern, who had done much better than expected, and a defeat for Muskie, who had done much worse than expected. This spin spelled the collapse of the Muskie campaign and the emergence of McGovern as the leading candidate of the Democratic Left.[24]

The Florida primary came next, a week after New Hampshire's. Jackson had planned to make his first major effort in Florida, a large, diverse state where he thought he had a genuine chance to win. Indeed, he needed a strong showing there to have any chance for winning the nomination. He had natural allies in the state's aerospace industry, where he was appreciated for his pro-defense record, and in the Jewish community, because of his championing of Israel. Mandatory busing was also a major issue in Florida, about which voters overwhelmingly agreed with him. In February 1972, Jackson had introduced a constitutional amendment in the Senate that would have guaranteed the right of parents to send their children to a neighborhood school. He argued that a constitutional amendment was the only plausible way to resolve this issue, because the courts had routinely ignored legislative restrictions on their discretion to order mandatory busing to achieve racial balance.[25]

Jackson's campaign did not take off in Florida as he had hoped. He finished third in the March 14 vote, with 13 percent. Humphrey finished second with 19 percent. George Wallace trounced them both with 42 percent. Polls indicated that Jackson might have won the Florida primary without Wallace in the race.[26] Unfortunately for Jackson, the presence of the stridently populist Alabama governor deprived any Northern Democrat of a realistic chance of winning any primary in the South. In a contest against just Humphrey, Muskie, and McGovern, Jackson's law and order, pro-military, and anti-busing stances might well have attracted significant support from Wallace voters throughout the region.

Jackson's campaign suffered, too, from the press coverage, not just in Florida, but nationally. The media often slighted him. The headlines of many a major newspaper omitted, for example, any mention of Jackson in announcing the results of the Florida primary. Jackson complained bitterly about a photograph that the AP and UPI syndicated nationally showing him talking to only one elderly lady and a boy with a bicycle. This image fed the widespread perception that his campaign had generated no excitement. A photograph taken from another angle showed, however, that the crowd actually totaled about two hundred.[27]

When the media did take notice, Jackson often received harsh treatment. Liberal commentators and many Democratic candidates railed against him particularly for his stand on busing, which they often equated with Wallace's.[28] This charge of pandering to racist sentiment galled Jackson, who had voted for every major piece of civil rights legislation in the post–World War II era.[29]

George McGovern accused Jackson of "embracing racism" by opposing busing—despite the hypocrisy of such a charge coming from him.[30] In a 1971 segment of the television program *Sixty Minutes,* CBS reporter Mike Wallace pointed out that the children of most of Washington's leading liberals who staunchly supported mandatory busing attended expensive private schools. McGovern, a resident of the District of Columbia, arranged for his daughter to go to one of the best public high schools in suburban Maryland.[31] An angry Jackson duly noted the irony of the situation. He reiterated that he was the only presidential candidate who had a child in the public schools of Washington, D.C.: "My daughter goes to a school with a black principal, she has a black teacher, and 30 percent of her classmates are black." He explained to Wallace that he sent Anna Marie to public school because he believed in public education: "She attends a good, integrated school." He would not rule out, however, sending his children to private school in the future should he deem it in their best interests—a perfectly honorable motive, as he saw it, for any American:

If my opposition to forced busing solely to achieve a racial balance means I'm a racist, then Senator McGovern is accusing 75 per cent of the voters of Florida—and, indeed, the great majority of all Americans—of racism. For the polls show that the overwhelming majority of the American people oppose forced busing. The polls also show that the overwhelming majority are for integration. I don't think that the Democratic Party will nominate a man who regards most of his fellow Americans as racist.

Jackson called McGovern the "first big mudslinger of this campaign. . . . Instead of accusing other people of racism, Senator McGovern ought to practice what he preaches. . . . Although he lives in the District of Columbia, he doesn't send his child to the District of Columbia schools. He pays extra tuition to send his child across state lines, to a white school in Maryland." McGovern's "reckless charge," Jackson admonished, evidenced a serious problem with "certain kinds of so-called liberals: If you disagree with them, they call you a racist."[32]

The press also criticized Jackson's refusal to reveal the identity of donors to his campaign, which he claimed would embarrass several high level officials of the Nixon administration who secretly supported him. Later investigations revealed that Leon Hess, chairman of the Amerada Hess oil company, contributed $225,000, or 20 percent of the total funds Jackson received. He had no knowledge of the source of this contribution, which Hess disguised under the names of pseudonymous donors. The gift was not illegal; nor did it secure Hess any undue influence with Jackson on the Interior Committee, as his hostility to the oil industry during the energy crisis proved beyond a doubt. Nevertheless, it looked suspect. The Jackson campaign also received a $10,000 from the Gulf Oil Corporation, an illegal contribution that Jackson denied soliciting and the campaign later returned.[33]

Jackson lashed out at a *New York Times* report insinuating that Boeing was engaged in a massive and illegal corporate effort to influence the election in Wisconsin on Jackson's behalf. It turned out that the effort amounted to a grand total of $299.62, which an overenthusiastic Boeing employee making $15,000 a year spent on a few ads for Jackson that ran in weekly newspapers and on small radio stations in northern Wisconsin. "If the *New York Times* is honest, I expect an apology," an angry Jackson said.[34] He did not get one. President Nixon wrote Jackson a private note calling "the editorial in the *New York Times* attacking you . . . one of the most outrageous items I have ever seen in any election campaign."[35]

Yet the Florida Primary campaign also revealed the sharp limits of the president's solicitude even for his so-called favorite Democrats such as Henry Jackson. The *New York Times* accusation looked mild compared with the outrage that the Nixon operatives would perpetrate on Jackson. While working on the president's reelection campaign, Donald Segretti sent out a letter on Muskie stationary falsely accusing Jackson of sexual misconduct:

> Senator Henry M. Jackson was involved with a seventeen-year old girl named Joan Cramer while he was a senior at Everett High School. The result was an illegitimate daughter, named Mary Ann Cramer, born February 7, 1929. He refused to marry the girl and after a paternity suit paid child support until September of 1937, when for $4,500 he settled with the mother. Prior to his marriage to Helen Hardin on December 16, 1961, he was arrested twice in Washington, D.C. as a homosexual. Once was May 5, 1955, and the second October 17, 1957. No charges were ever brought against him because of his position.[36]

Segretti later admitted he wrote the letter off the top of his head after having "two or three glasses of wine at the local pub," not expecting anyone to believe it.[37] Jackson described it as "the worst kind of filth" that he "had ever seen in his political career."[38] He did not believe that a man of Muskie's integrity could have sanctioned such a letter. He demanded an investigation, which eventually led to a six-month jail term for Segretti. The Watergate investigation subsequently revealed that the Nixon operatives also had placed Jackson's administrative assistant, Sterling Munro, on the White House enemies list, presumably to discredit Jackson. Even Jackson's sternest critics did not place much stock, however, in allegations of his ethical impropriety. Jackson had justly earned his reputation as one of the most honorable and incorruptible men in the Senate.[39]

The media was not all to blame for Jackson's failure to get out his message effectively during the 1972 campaign. He deserves much of the blame himself. He never understood the importance of television in modern campaigning. Former speaker of the House Tom Foley recounted a story that encapsulated Jackson's obliviousness on this subject: Campaigning in Wisconsin, Jackson canceled an appearance on the *Today Show*, the hugely popular NBC morning program, because it conflicted with a scheduled event at a bowling alley. Foley pleaded with Jackson to change his mind. "On television, Scoop, you can communicate with millions, not just with dozens."[40] Jackson would not budge. His favorite venue was the union hall or the small group without television cameras filming it. Gerry Hoeck remembered Jackson's extemporaneous speech at a Milwaukee brewery as his best performance of the 1972 campaign. Jackson excited the hall and "impressed the hell out of them by defeating every one of those large burly workers who challenged him to an arm wrestle."[41] Alas, no one outside the union hall saw it.

ANYBODY BUT MCGOVERN

After finishing a distant third in Florida, Jackson's campaign languished, strapped for cash and overshadowed by the contest waged among the three main contenders: Wallace, McGovern, and Humphrey. Actually, Wallace probably could not have won the nomination even if he had not been shot and paralyzed from the waist down while campaigning in Laurel, Maryland, on May 15. Outside the South, he had enough popularity to scare his rivals, but rarely to beat them. His segregationist views put him irredeemably beyond the pale for a national Democratic electorate predominantly liberal and integrationist in outlook. He won big in Michigan, where busing was controversial, and by a slender margin in Maryland, a border state. He carried no other states that were not part of the old Confederacy.[42]

In 1972, only a bona fide liberal had a plausible chance of winning the Democratic Party's nomination. That meant McGovern or Humphrey: a New Politics liberal or a traditional New Deal–Fair Deal liberal who, unlike Jackson, had muted his formerly hawkish position on foreign policy but not entirely abandoned it. McGovern's victories in the April 4 Wisconsin and April 25 Massachusetts primaries vaulted him into the position of front-runner. Although Humphrey won several primaries and roughly the same percentage of the total popular vote in the primaries as McGovern (McGovern, Wallace, and Humphrey each won roughly 25 percent to Jackson's 2 percent), he lacked either the first-rate organization or the cadre of fervent activists so crucial to amassing delegates in the caucus states under the new rules. McGovern essentially wrapped up the nomination in early June by winning California's winner-take-all primary by a 4 percent margin over Humphrey.[43]

Jackson did not win anywhere except the party caucuses in Washington

State. It was not easy even there. His campaign in his home state also encountered fervent opposition from the New Politics wing of the party, which still loathed him. In King County, the largest in the state, the McGovernites controlled fifteen of the seventeen legislative districts. Ultimately, the Jackson forces succeeded locally in doing what McGovern had done nationally in party caucus states across the nation: by out-organizing the opposition, they secured all fifty-two of Washington State's delegates to the national convention.[44]

Jackson regarded McGovern's impending triumph as an unmitigated disaster for the party. Although his dismal fifth-place showings in Wisconsin and Ohio ended the active phase of his national campaign, he stoutly resisted the inevitability of the McGovern candidacy by all means at his disposal right up until the Democrats nominated McGovern in July. It was Hugh Scott, Republican senator from Pennsylvania, who coined the phrase that "McGovern was the candidate of amnesty, acid, and abortion." It was Henry Jackson, who popularized it during a swing through Ohio in April 1972.[45] He tagged McGovern as "the chief traveling salesman" of the New Left establishment:

> The New Left Establishment calls for massive defense cuts. So does McGovern. The New Left Establishment favors forced busing to achieve racial balance. So does McGovern. The New Left Establishment favors amnesty for draft-dodgers and deserters. So does McGovern. The New Left Establishment chooses to be silent on the issue of Law and Order, and to attack the F.B.I. So does McGovern. The New Left establishment denounces American policy in Vietnam as "barbaric" and "immoral"— while not condemning Hanoi's aggression. So does McGovern.[46]

Jackson criticized Humphrey and Muskie for appeasing the New left Establishment—"indeed, he said, "Muskie seems to be knocking on their door for admission." He vowed to speak out against McGovern, lest "we produce in 1972 a Democratic version of the Republican catastrophe" of 1964.

The clash between Jackson and McGovern personified the fundamental differences between New Deal–Fair Deal liberalism and New Politics liberalism. Where Jackson held the Soviet Union responsible for the Cold War, McGovern trumpeted the argument of revisionist historians of American foreign policy who faulted American statesmen for instigating and perpetuating it by their vast overreaction to the Soviet threat.[47] Where Jackson backed President Truman avidly in his fight against the dovish Henry Wallace to control the Democratic Party in the 1940s, McGovern proclaimed himself a great admirer of Wallace, "who saw no reason for the breakdown in peacetime of the cooperative relations we enjoyed with the Russians while we were combatting Nazi Germany" during World War II. He believed that "both the domestic health of the nation and the peace of the world would have been better served by the hopeful and compassionate views of Wallace than the get tough policy of the Truman administration."[48] If, wrote McGovern, "we had listened to some of the things that Henry Wallace said, we might have avoided Korea and the Vietnam War."[49] Where Jackson saw Soviet communism as an ever present danger to the vital moral and geopolitical interests of the United States, McGovern envisaged the arrogance of American power as the main danger. McGovern believed that the United States would have to reject its "paranoid anticommunism" and accept a "world of diversity" where "we can get along with the Communists."[50]

Accordingly, McGovern called for sharp cutbacks in U.S. military capabilities and commitments that a horrified Jackson considered a perilous evisceration of American power: a reduction in the number of aircraft carriers from fifteen to six; cancellation of the navy's F-14 and the air force's F-15 fighter planes; a reduction of the U.S. garrison in Western Europe from 300,000 to about 130,000; withdrawal of all remaining U.S. troops from South Korea; removal of all U.S. ground and air forces from Southeast Asia; a reduction in the U.S. bomber force from about 600 to 200; an end to the ABM program; and a 30 percent reduction in spending for military research and development. For Henry Jackson, the Vietnam War did not discredit the policy of vigilant containment. The mistake of American involvement lay in not resolving the war sooner one way or the other—by escalation or withdrawal. For McGovern, the tragedy of Vietnam was not an aberration but the essence of a "Cold War paranoia" that consistently prompted American statesmen immorally and imprudently to back corrupt right-wing regimes in a misbegotten effort to eradicate communism.[51]

The chasm between Jackson and McGovern extended to some key domestic issues beyond law and order and busing. Jackson conceived of civil rights, properly understood, as equality of opportunity, as the drafters

of the Civil Rights Act of 1964 had intended. McGovern and his supporters at the Democratic Convention conceived of civil rights as equality of result, with women and minorities represented in precise mathematical proportion to their numbers in the population.[52] Jackson
championed the accomplishments and values of the traditional liberal establishment since Truman. McGovern challenged both. Although most
Northern liberals would shy away from moving as far to the left as Mc-
Govern did, most would end up closer to his position on the spectrum
than to Jackson's, particularly on foreign policy and on matters of race.[53]
The Middle East stands out as the exception to this general rule. Most
liberal Democrats remained closer to Jackson's position on Israel than to
McGovern's, Fulbright's, or much of the academic left, which placed the
greater blame for the Arab-Israeli conflict on Israel's intransigence.[54]

THE 1972 DEMOCRATIC CONVENTION

Jackson continued his fight to stop McGovern at the Democratic National Convention in Miami in July 1972. Supporters of Jackson and
Humphrey, southerners, and organized labor had banded together in an
abortive effort, called "Anybody But McGovern," to stem the McGovern
tide. Their hopes hinged on successfully challenging McGovern's claim
to all of California's 271 votes, in the winner-take-all primary, for just 44
percent of the vote to Humphrey's 40 percent. The McGovernites not
only staved off this challenge but managed to throw out the entire Illinois
delegation, including Mayor Richard J. Daley of Chicago, a Democrat of
the old school, on the grounds that this popularly elected delegation contained too few women and minorities. They seated an alternative slate
that essentially replaced Mayor Daley with Reverend Jesse Jackson as
head of the Cook County delegation.[55]

Even when Muskie and Humphrey formally bowed out, Henry Jackson
would not. He received 536 votes for the nomination on the convention
floor. I. W. Abel, head of the United Steelworkers of America, nominated him. Governor Jimmy Carter of Georgia seconded the nomination. A
former nuclear engineer in the navy who touted his service under Jackson's great friend Hyman Rickover, Carter had expressed his loathing for
McGovern in several conversations with Jackson in terms that even Jackson thought extreme. What happened just after McGovern received the
nomination irrevocably colored Jackson's view of Carter. Richard Perle

remembered that Carter called Jackson at 4 A.M. with this request: "Would
Scoop be willing to approach McGovern to help get Carter selected as his
vice president." A stunned Jackson "could hardly believe what he was
hearing." Carter had spoken of McGovern with nothing but contempt;
yet now he was willing to overlook all that in the hope of being selected."
Whatever respect Jackson had for Carter was out the window with that
one phone call," Perle said. "Scoop could not ever think of Carter again
without a certain feeling of revulsion."[56] McGovern also found it off-
putting that Carter solicited the vice presidential nomination so assiduously after saying such nasty things about him during the primary campaign.[57]

Jackson also strove at the Democratic Convention of 1972 to insulate
congressional candidates from the calamitous defeat he anticipated Mc-
Govern would suffer in the general election. The day after McGovern's
triumph, nine men representing the stop McGovern forces met at the
Fontainebleau Hotel to discuss ways to get the "party back on the track":
three assistants of Senator Jackson (Brian Corcoran, Sterling Munro, and
William Brawley); four associates of Senator Humphrey (Max Kampelman, Stanley Bregman, William Connell, and Mike Maloney); an official
from the AFL-CIO's political arm, COPE; and Robert Strauss, a former
treasurer of the Democratic Party with close ties to Lyndon Johnson and
the business community. Alarmed that Nixon's coattails might even imperil the Democrats' control of Congress, Jackson played a pivotal role in
forming the Committee for the Reelection of a Democratic Congress, a
special fundraising campaign for Democratic congressional candidates,
which Strauss agreed to chair.[58] Jackson arranged for meetings with
Strauss and major congressional leaders to ensure their cooperation.
Strauss managed to persuade them all—even Mike Mansfield, the Senate
majority leader, and Carl Albert, the Speaker of the House, who were usually averse to making major fundraising appeals—to appear at three major fundraising events, in New York, San Francisco, and Los Angeles.
Strauss raised a considerable amount of money for Democratic congressional candidates through the committee, which was "quite active all over
the country."[59]

The 1972 presidential campaign confirmed what Jackson foretold in
October: "McGovern would not carry more than the District of Columbia and Massachusetts. . . . Although millions of people dislike President

Nixon, they have a greater dislike for George McGovern."[60] President Nixon trounced McGovern, winning 61 percent of the popular vote. For most of the fall campaign, Jackson did little for McGovern beyond his initial endorsement just after the South Dakota senator received the nomination in July, a sore point with some of his more liberal constituents in Washington State, who complained about it. Finally, Jackson appeared with McGovern on October 30 at the Seattle Center, where he introduced the South Dakota senator and reaffirmed his support. It was a tepid gesture, at best. Jackson concentrated instead on reelecting a Democratic Congress, with excellent results. The enormity of Nixon's landslide had virtually no effect on the Democratic majorities in Congress. The Republicans picked up only a few seats in the House and actually lost a few in the Senate.[61]

By the end of 1972, Jackson appeared to have good reason to take solace in the outcome of the election. The Democrats had retained their control of Congress. He thus would retain his position as majority member on several key committees that provided his power base in the Senate. The enormity of McGovern's defeat also appeared to bode well for his goal of rebuilding the Democratic Party in his own image. In December 1972, the election of Robert Strauss as chairman of the Democratic party over his more liberal rivals—George Mitchell, Charles Manatt (powerful lawyer and future chairman of the party), and Lawrence O'Brien—appeared to presage a shift back from New Left politics to the mainstream of traditional liberalism. By actively backing Strauss while Humphrey remained on the sidelines, Jackson appeared to displace Humphrey as the leader of those trying to wrest control of the party away from the McGovernites. Of course, Jackson was not the only reason Strauss prevailed but a major reason. As Strauss himself put it:

> Without Scoop Jackson, I would never have been elected chairman of the Democratic Party. Without him . . . if I had everybody else [and] if I had done everything I did and more, I would not have been elected chairman of the National Democratic Party. Scoop Jackson was the difference.[62]

Jackson and Sterling Munro expended an enormous amount of time and energy on Strauss's campaign.[63] It was Jackson who convinced George Meany to support Bob Strauss, despite organized labor's distrust of a Texan who was a friend of big business and John Connally, the former Texas governor now turned Republican political adviser to President Nixon.[64] Alexander Barkan, head of COPE, tried to talk George Meany, president of the AFL-CIO, out of it at a meeting with Jackson. "How well do you know Bob Strauss?" Jackson asked Barkan. "He is part of a group of conservatives—the John Connallys and the Lyndon Johnsons—that we were constantly fighting," Barkan replied. Jackson assured Meany that Barkan did not know Strauss as well as he did: "Strauss was very flexible."[65] By the time of the final vote, which Strauss won by just three votes, Jackson had telephoned every Democratic governor lobbying them to back him. All eighteen of them voted for Strauss.[66]

In late December 1972, Jackson's cause received another boost. Ben Wattenberg, his chief strategist, had initiated the formation of the Coalition for a Democratic Majority (CDM), an organization dedicated to propagating the vision of Cold War liberalism that Jackson had run on in the 1972 primary.[67] Jackson thus had paved the way for another presidential run, in 1976, which he had plausible reason to hope would turn out much better than his dismal 1972 performance. In four years, Henry Jackson would be sixty-four years old, but a healthy, vibrant sixty-four with the appearance and stamina of a man much younger. He still thrived on the regular twelve to fourteen hour workday that being a prominent senator and a presidential aspirant required. Named National Father of the Year in 1971, he had a happy family and a supportive wife willing to make the sacrifices necessary for him to run.[68] His defeat in the 1972 Democratic primaries also freed him to concentrate on his duties in the Senate, where he would exert a decisive impact in the ferocious debate unfolding over the proper course and outcome of American foreign policy in the era of Nixon-Ford détente.

Chapter 13

Perils of Détente, Part I:
1968–1976

Throughout most of Nixon's first term, Henry Jackson generally supported the president's foreign and defense policies, often in defiance of intense pressure from liberal congressional Democrats who favored unilateral withdrawal from Vietnam and huge cuts in military spending. Jackson twice saved the administration's ABM program. He joined with the administration to fend off perennial attempts to reduce substantially and unilaterally the number of American troops deployed in Western Europe. In the summer of 1973, he came to the administration's rescue again by lobbying hard for full funding of the Trident submarine program, the most important component of the U.S. nuclear deterrent, which Congress approved narrowly. He backed the administration despite his preference that the navy not base the Trident in Bangor, Washington, because it would enrage his more liberal constituents. He changed his mind after two of his most trusted confidants in the Pentagon—Admiral Elmo Zumwalt, chief of naval operations, and Admiral Kinnaird Mc-Kee—convinced him that the Bangor site was the best for the country.[1]

Jackson's thinking about Communist China evolved, too, in essentially the same fashion as President Nixon's. Long advocates of vigilantly containing Chinese as well as Soviet communism, Nixon and Jackson both deemed this monolithic assessment of the communist threat outdated by the late 1960s as the Soviet Union replaced the United States as China's number one enemy. The 1969 border clashes between Soviet and Chinese forces along the Ussuri River north of Vladivostok underscored the permanence and bitterness of the Sino-Soviet split, which Jackson and the president believed should be actively exploited as a counterweight to Soviet expansionism. Consequently, Jackson approved of Nixon's endeavors to open up relations with China, culminating in the president's trip there and the signing of the Shanghai Communiqué in February 1972. In the Middle East, although Jackson and the administration sometimes disagreed on tactics, they were of the same mind on the strategic goal of American foreign policy: undermine the Soviet position in the Arab world both by frustrating the designs of radical Arab regimes that looked to Moscow for support and by rewarding moderate Arab leaders who turned away from the Soviets. Both Jackson and Nixon envisaged a strong Israel as a prerequisite for the success of this strategy.

By 1972, however, their differences loomed larger than their similarities. Jackson had become the most "implacable" and formidable critic of the administration's Soviet policies, according to Henry Kissinger, the president's national security adviser, future secretary of state, and co-architect of those policies. Jackson's admirers and the senator himself saw a parallel between his relentless campaign against détente during the 1970s and Winston Churchill's campaign against appeasement during the 1930s. In their eyes, both were determined to tell their resistant electorates about the implacability of their international adversaries and the imperative for democracies to resist them resolutely. Jackson's critics disparaged his "Churchill complex" as fallacious, dangerous, misleading, and an obstacle to better relations with the Soviets. In their eyes, Jackson epitomized the mentality that made the perpetuation of the Cold War a self-fulfilling prophecy. Even Jackson's sternest critics, however, acknowledged his effectiveness. Most informed observers would concur with Kissinger that Jackson did more than any other person in American politics to galvanize the support that stopped détente "in its tracks."[2]

THE ENIGMA OF NIXON AND KISSINGER

The 1970s was not a good decade for liberal democracies in general and for the United States in particular. The cumulative effects of the Arab oil embargo, the American defeat in Vietnam, the prodigious growth of Soviet military power, and the rising tide of dictatorial collectivism in the underdeveloped world dangerously eroded the self-confidence of the United States and its allies. Bitter polarization and enormous self-doubt over the U.S. role in the world envenomed American politics throughout the decade. This corrosive mood generated enormous domestic pressure for reducing defense spending and disengaging from U.S. foreign policy commitments.

In this period of intellectual and political ferment, President Nixon and Henry Kissinger devised and implemented their conception of détente as an alternative to both Jackson's approach and the approach of their liberal critics pressing for a substantial devolution of U.S. global responsibilities. A word of caution is necessary at the outset of this discussion. It is rarely easy to discern in their proper proportion the motives and circumstances underlying any substantial change in American foreign policy. The complexity, the penchant for secrecy, and occasional disingenuousness of Nixon and Kissinger make the difficulties of sorting out the inspiration, intent, and effects of détente especially daunting. In their memoirs, written after the collapse of détente, Nixon and Kissinger both insisted that Jackson and other hawkish critics misunderstood the true nature of the policy, which they say differed from what Jackson advocated only tactically. Their justification of détente, offered during the 1980s, criticized Jackson not for his overall assessment of the Soviet threat, which by then they largely granted, but for failing to recognize the formidable domestic impediments to conducting a more vigilant foreign policy, which made détente a necessity until America recovered from the trauma of Vietnam. Yet Nixon and Kissinger's postadministration attempts to reduce the debate with Jackson over détente merely to tactics contradict what they said publicly at the time, and often what they said privately. Furthermore, John Lewis Gaddis and other diplomatic historians favorably disposed to Nixon and Kissinger's policies defended them precisely on the grounds that they did signal a fundamental departure from the tenets of Cold War liberalism that Henry Jackson continued to champion.[3]

This book argues that Nixon and Kissinger's true motives for pursuing détente lie somewhere between what they said during the 1980s and what they proclaimed grandiosely in the 1970s. Certainly, Jackson had fewer and less fundamental differences with Nixon-Ford-Kissinger than he had with the Democratic Left after 1968 and would have with President Carter. Perhaps Jackson and his brethren really did overestimate somewhat the unwillingness of the American people to support more vigilant policies during the 1970s. For reasons that are partly self-serving, however, Nixon and Kissinger underestimated what was possible. What follows below first lays out my interpretation of both Nixon and Kissinger's framework of détente and Jackson's critique of it. It then delves into the particulars of the debate between Jackson, on the one side, and the Nixon and Ford administrations, on the other, with special emphasis on three landmark issues whose outcome Jackson affected decisively: The SALT talks and the SALT I Treaty of 1972; human rights and Jewish emigration; and the Middle East.

NIXON AND KISSINGER'S CONCEPTION OF DÉTENTE

The nineteenth-century European balance-of-power tradition deeply influenced the statecraft of Nixon and Kissinger. Both distrusted and deemphasized the ideological dimension of American foreign policy to a degree unmatched by their predecessors and their successors during the Cold War. Neither of them intended to abandon, but only to modify, the policy of vigilant containment Henry Jackson embraced. As they saw it, the diminished salience of ideology and the emergence of multipolarity, a world of five great power centers instead of just two superpowers, made a period of U.S. global retrenchment prudent. They believed, too, that domestic constraints made such a retrenchment a necessity as well as a virtue. Even after his landslide reelection in November 1972, Nixon faced a Democratic Congress increasingly hostile to defense spending and the maintenance of U.S. global commitments. From 1969 through 1977, U.S. defense spending declined 38 percent, while the massive Soviet military buildup proceeded unabated. Nixon and Kissinger assessed the Congress and the American people as hostile to any substantial American combat involvement anywhere else abroad.[4]

The policy of détente toward the Soviet Union and China marked a major shift in the perception of America's interests and the most efficacious framework for securing them. Soviet ideology and its threat had become, according to Nixon and Kissinger, relatively less important compared with traditional conceptions of the national interest. Whereas previous administrations and Henry Jackson had defined the Soviet Union as a relentless and implacable ideological adversary with unlimited aims, Nixon and Kissinger believed that it had evolved into a more traditional type of empire, dangerous and expansionist but with limited ambitions, thus making possible some type of long-term equilibrium. Similarly, Nixon and Kissinger regarded China as less communist and more Chinese in its foreign policy. Both saw the Sino-Soviet split as a promising opportunity to normalize relations with China and minimize the adverse geopolitical consequences of withdrawing from Vietnam.

Nixon and Kissinger spoke publicly about removing ideology as a reference point for identifying and measuring threats. "We have no permanent enemies," Kissinger announced in December 1969. "We will judge other countries, including communist countries . . . on the basis of their actions and not on the basis of their domestic ideology." Security within Nixon and Kissinger's framework required equilibrium, but not necessarily ideological parallels. Their deemphasis on ideology opened the conceptual door for their endeavors to improve relations with America's erstwhile communist adversaries. As Kissinger put it in reference to China, "the leaders . . . were beyond ideology in their dealings with us. Their peril had established the absolute primacy of geopolitics."[5]

Nixon and Kissinger also rested their foreign policy framework on the assumption that the era of bipolarity, with Soviet and American powers preeminent in international politics, had begun to draw to a close. In a new era of global and regional multipolarity, they anticipated that other regional surrogates could substitute for American power in order to meet more traditional threats to American geopolitical interests. The Nixon Doctrine, as this strategy came to be called, reflected the administration's determination to address what it perceived to be the limited resources and will to meet U.S. global commitments. To lighten U.S. foreign policy burdens and thus make them more acceptable to the American people, Nixon and Kissinger sought to transform America's role in resisting Soviet aggression from primary to supporting.[6]

Rapprochement with China illustrated in high relief the central premises of the Nixon Doctrine. By forging a relationship with China, Nixon and Kissinger hoped to enlist its aid in containing Soviet expansionism, pressuring North Vietnam to accept a peace compatible with American honor, and maintaining geopolitical equilibrium in Asia. In the Middle East, they designated the shah of Iran as the primary U.S. surrogate. The United States would supply the arms, while the shah would provide the ground troops and actual military presence to preserve the regional equilibrium. Thus they chose not to confront congressional and public opposition to containment directly, but to adopt a damage-limitation strategy aimed at sustaining American capabilities and commitments to the maximum extent domestic politics would allow. The changing distribution of world power, the apparent waning of ideology as a determinant of foreign policy, Nixon and Kissinger's downgrading of the Soviet threat from a Leninist to a "merely imperial" rival, and the apparent availability of regional surrogates for American power seemed to make possible what domestic politics made necessary. Both expected that our NATO allies would react positively to the administration's initiatives toward the Soviet Union. In West Germany particularly, the linchpin state of the NATO alliance, the Social Democrats under Chancellor Willy Brandt already had begun to pursue their version of détente, known as Ostpolitik, with an enthusiasm that alarmed avid defenders of NATO such as Henry Jackson.[7]

Through arms control, Nixon and Kissinger hoped to constrain the Soviet Union's prodigious military buildup. More broadly, the implementation of détente required engaging the Soviet Union in building a stable international equilibrium, one in which the Soviets had a stake in maintaining order and tranquility rather than undermining them. Through negotiations and agreements, Nixon and Kissinger hoped to change Moscow's approach to international politics by convincing Soviet leaders that it was in their interest to emphasize cooperation rather than competition with the West.

Nixon and Kissinger advocated linking progress among all these issues to induce cooperation and compromise. They intended this concept of "linkage" as an ordering principle for American foreign policy and as a source of leverage with the Soviet Union that would enmesh it in a web of economic interdependence and thus moderate Soviet external conduct and ambitions. The SALT talks and treaties became the major instrument for implementing this conception of détente. By May 1972, Nixon and Kissinger had negotiated two agreements, the SALT I Interim Agreement limiting offensive strategic delivery systems and the ABM Treaty, which they hoped would restrain the Soviet military buildup without significantly impairing U.S. capability to upgrade its own military structure when the domestic environment became more propitious for increases in defense spending.[8]

Not all of détente was conciliation. When the Soviet Union egged on the Arab countries after Egypt and Syria attacked Israel in October 1973, the United States responded vigorously. Kissinger's shuttle diplomacy following the 1973 war succeeded in isolating the Soviets in the Middle East. In Latin America, which both considered part of America's sphere of influence, Nixon and Kissinger encouraged the Chilean military's overthrow of Salvador Allende's Marxist regime. Nixon, Ford, and Kissinger also responded with unremitting hostility to the phenomenon of "Eurocommunism" in Western Europe during the 1970s. What Nixon and Kissinger say they intended was "hard-headed détente."[9]

JACKSON'S CRITIQUE OF DÉTENTE

Most Northern liberals in the Democratic Party welcomed détente, SALT, the ABM Treaty, the opening to China, deemphasis of ideology, recognition of the Soviet Union's paramountcy in Eastern Europe, and the more modest balance-of-power goals that flowed from the Nixon and Kissinger approach. Yet they rejected Nixon and Kissinger's corollary assumption that the United States needed to rely on authoritarian regimes such as Iran under the shah to prevent communism from spreading in its sphere of influence. They condemned the secrecy and amorality of the Nixon-Kissinger foreign policy, exemplified in their view by the administration's unabashed support of right-wing dictators, efforts to topple Allende, fruitless and costly prolongation of the Vietnam War, and general callousness toward human rights. Furthermore, many such liberals complained that Nixon and Kissinger had not gone far enough in seizing the opportunities for an even more cooperative relationship with the Soviet Union.[10]

That is not what Jackson objected to about détente. Although he agreed with liberal critics that Nixon and Kissinger's approach unduly slighted the ideological and moral dimensions of foreign policy, he disagreed with them on just about everything else they criticized about it. Jackson's critique of détente anticipated and inspired the conservative and neoconservative challenge to détente that reached its apotheosis with the presidency of Ronald Reagan.

Jackson had five principal objections to détente as Nixon and Kissinger conceived it. First, although well aware that the Soviet leadership no longer engaged in the rampant terror emblematic of Stalin's times, he still considered the Soviet Union a totalitarian state, a malevolent Leninist-driven entity with unlimited aims and ambitions, not the traditional great power that Nixon and Kissinger considered it. Contrary to Nixon and

Kissinger, he believed, very much as the great Soviet dissidents Andrei Sakharov and Alexander Solzhenitsyn did, that the Soviet Union's internal structure was the key to its international behavior. The United States would have major trouble with the Soviet Union, Jackson emphasized, as long as it was a totalitarian state, as long as a handful of people made decisions on everything from the size of the military budget to intelligence operations, and as long as there was no public opinion to bound the ambitions and actions of a small totalitarian leadership. Although he professed his support for a genuine relaxation of Soviet-American tensions based on genuine reciprocity, he argued that the Soviet leadership envisaged détente merely as a change in tactics rather than the abandonment of unremitting conflict with the liberal Western democracies. The Soviets, he insisted, pursued arms control, arms treaties, and increased trade as part of a grand strategy to establish hegemony rather than as a commitment to achieving a long-term equilibrium, which Nixon and Kissinger sought. Or as Jackson typically put it: "The Soviets have not changed. They still fear the exposure of their people to Western society; that remains a cornerstone of their totalitarian approach. . . . The Russians are like a burglar going down a hotel corridor, trying all the doors. When they find one that's unlocked, they go in."[11]

Second, Jackson had less confidence than Nixon and Kissinger that there were sufficiently robust alternatives to American power to protect vital U.S. interests in geopolitically crucial regions. After his trip to the Middle East in the fall of 1972, which included a stay in Iran, for example, Jackson expressed serious doubts about whether the shah's regime had the capacity to discharge the responsibilities of maintaining regional stability that the Nixon administration had assigned to it.[12]

Third, Jackson criticized Nixon and Kissinger for misreading the nature of American public opinion and misunderstanding the basis for conducting an effective foreign policy in a liberal democracy. He argued that their excessive optimism about the Soviet Union interacted synergistically with their excessive pessimism about the United States to undermine the basis for vigilantly containing the Soviet Union. The American people would have supported more defense spending, according to Jackson, had the president understood and told them forthrightly about the gravity of the Soviet military threat. As Jackson saw it, the Nixon administration's deemphasis on ideology thus demoralized domestic advocates of a strong national defense while simultaneously emboldening others to seek further and far-reaching reductions in U.S. commitments and defense capabilities.[13]

Fourth, unlike Nixon, Kissinger, or the legion of academics impressed by the permanence and stability of the Soviet regime, Jackson believed that the Soviet Union had encountered "current, long-term, deep-seated economic trouble" that made it quite vulnerable to sustained economic pressure. He viewed the Cold War as a struggle with a terminal point, which would end with the breakup of the Soviet Union and/or the collapse of its totalitarian system. The objective of American foreign policy, according to Jackson, ought to be to hasten that end with every means available within the bounds of prudence. He thus criticized Nixon and Kissinger for a trade policy that subsidized the Soviet military buildup and staved off the need to liberalize the economy and the regime.[14]

Jackson used his Permanent Investigations Subcommittee of the Government Operations Committee as a vehicle to conduct two investigations of the administration's 1972 grain deal with the Soviets, which he termed the "great grain robbery" for subsidizing the Soviet military-industrial complex at below-market rates while the American food prices soared because this massive sale of grain depleted domestic stocks.[15] In the spring of 1972, following a cold spell and drought in the Soviet Union that destroyed much of its crop, Secretary of Agriculture Earl Butz negotiated a deal with the Soviets to buy American grain. The United States agreed to facilitate it by providing the Soviet Union with $750 million in credit over a three-year period through the Commodity Credit Corporation. In July 1972, the Soviets signed contracts with officials of the Department of Agriculture to purchase a total of 7.5 million tons of wheat. The Department of Agriculture had no clue, however, that the Soviets had secretly negotiated contracts with several American grain export companies to buy more wheat. By August 1972, the Soviets had signed contracts to purchase 11 million tons of wheat, which amounted to almost the entire U.S. surplus and 25 percent of the U.S. crop. The U.S. wheat market skyrocketed: by early 1974 the price of a bushel of wheat was triple the August 1972 levels. American consumers paid the price. Under the auspices of the Permanent Investigations Subcommittee, Jackson conducted several studies and inquiries, concluding that strict controls were needed on the flow of critical technology to the U.S.S.R. He urged, too, that the United States retain an expansive definition of what constituted "critical" in order to confront the Soviets with the stark choice of either liberalizing their regime, so they could compete effectively, or falling further behind the Untied States technologically.[16]

Fifth, Jackson chastised the administration for not paying enough attention to the issue of human rights. Nixon reveals more about his own motives than Jackson's by dismissing Jackson's advocacy of Jewish emigration as a ploy to boost his presidential ambitions.[17] Jackson acted out of bedrock conviction. His support for Jewish causes had remained unswerving since the 1940s. There was no difference in the substance or intensity of his position on Jewish emigration before and after he ran for president in 1972 and 1976.

Also, Kissinger badly misses the mark by attributing Jackson's human rights policy partly to a (Woodrow) Wilsonian utopianism inimical to America's geopolitical interests.[18] Jackson's approach to statecraft rested on a synthesis of power and principles. Unlike Kissinger and many antiwar liberals, Jackson considered American ideals and self-interest largely complementary. It was not until 1979 that Jeane Kirkpatrick, a former Jackson Democrat later to become President Reagan's ambassador to the United Nations, articulated and popularized the critical distinction between authoritarian and totalitarian regimes, morally and practically justifying an American support for the former against the latter. Long before that, Jackson had already based his human rights policy on Kirkpatrick's distinction, with one variation, which the Reagan administration later applied in dealing with traditional authoritarian regimes in Chile, the Philippines, and South Korea during the 1980s. Like Reagan, Jackson was more willing than Kirkpatrick to pressure some of America's rightwing allies over human rights. He supported sanctions on the racialist regimes of South Africa and Rhodesia. He supported the 1963 coup to topple Diem in South Vietnam and incurred Nixon's ire by berating Thieu in 1971 for failing to hold promised elections there. Like Reagan and Kirkpatrick, Jackson considered communist regimes the most systematic and egregious violators of human rights. The duty of the American government to safeguard and encourage human rights in the Soviet Union arose, he thought, from both moral and practical considerations.

Totalitarian nations, especially geopolitically powerful ones, that invoked expansionist, universalistic ideology to repress their own citizens system-atically at home were likely to commit or threaten aggression abroad.[19]

KISSINGER AND NIXON'S HISTORICAL PESSIMISM

Nixon and Kissinger have vehemently denied the charge that historical pessimism affected their judgment about the imperative of détente.[20] Kissinger disputes in particular this account by Jackson's close ally Admi-ral Elmo Zumwalt of a conversation he had with Kissinger that did much to trigger Jackson's reservations about him:

> Kissinger feels that the United States has passed its historic high point like so many earlier civilizations. He believes the U.S. is on the down-hill and cannot be roused by political challenge. He states that his job is to persuade the Russians to give us the best deal we can get, recognizing that the historical forces favor them. He says that he realizes in light of history he will be recognized as one of those who negotiated terms fa-vorable to the Soviets, but that the American people have only them-selves to blame because they lack the stamina to stay the course against the Russians "who are the Sparta to our Athens."

Nevertheless, Zumwalt stands by it.[21] Furthermore, some of Kissinger's closest aides, such as Peter Rodman and Helmut Sonnenfeldt, grant that Zumwalt did not invent what Kissinger said to him. Many critical of Kissinger's pessimism have ascribed it to his experience as a German-Jew-ish refugee fleeing the Holocaust. As Sonnenfeldt points out, however, "It was hard to be an optimist no matter what your background if you were in Washington, D.C., in the 1970s. It was a time when one had reason to question the capacity of this country to sustain a role of global leadership." Rodman, too, acknowledged that Kissinger's moods about America's prospects "could get very low."[22]

What Zumwalt's account neglects is that Nixon often found Kissinger's pessimism congenial, especially as the Watergate crisis inexorably emas-culated his presidency. Nixon revealed this dimension of his personality later to me while I assisted him in preparing *Beyond Peace*. He originally contemplated grounding the domestic section of that book in the philos-ophy of Nietzsche and Hegel, whom he claimed to be reading with great sympathy and interest. Their moral relativism and exaltation of power, which appealed to Nixon, would have appalled Henry Jackson. In the end, Nixon decided to abandon Nietzsche and Hegel in favor of the arguments of Hamilton and Tocqueville. The experience convinced me, however, that Nixon had more in common philosophically and temperamentally with his secretary of state than with his fellow westerner, Henry Jackson.[23]

Unlike Nixon and Kissinger, Jackson expected that the United States would overcome its difficulties and prevail in the Cold War. His conviction that the United States could and should do more to contain the Soviet Union underpinned the grand design he unveiled at the high point of euphoria over détente in the summer of 1972, which transformed the debate and laid the groundwork for the restoration of American power that occurred in the 1980s.[24]

SALT I

Jackson's critique of the SALT accords reached in Moscow in May 1972 and his legislative response to them formed an integral part of his comprehensive strategy to challenge Nixon and Kissinger's policy of détente. The accords had two components. The ABM Treaty of indefinite duration required the advice and consent of two-thirds of the Senate. It precluded either side from developing comprehensive ABM defenses to protect its national population and territory. It allowed the Soviet Union and the United States no more than two ABM sites with 100 interceptors each: one deployed around the nation's capital; and the other deployed to protect a limited portion of the nation's ICBM launchers.

The five-year Interim Agreement (SALT I) required the approval of only the majority of Congress. It froze the number of U.S. ICBMs at 1,054 and Soviet ICBMs at 1,618. It limited the United States to 44 strategic nuclear submarines with 710 launchers and the Soviet Union to 62 strategic nuclear submarines with 950 launchers. It imposed no restrictions on strategic bombers, a category in which the United States enjoyed a significant advantage over the Soviet Union, despite the vast air defense system the Soviets maintained and strove assiduously to upgrade.[25] The United States and the Soviet Union also reached a number of other agreements at the Moscow Summit in May 1972 to promote trade and expand cooperation in the areas of science, technology, medicine, and pollution control. Finally, Nixon and Brezhnev signed an agreement that the Soviets had pushed for strongly, establishing a code of conduct that both sides agreed to follow in their mutual relations. Theoretically, it committed the United States and the Soviet Union mutually to refrain from waging the Cold War in the underdeveloped world.[26]

On June 1, 1972, the president proclaimed grandly to a joint session of Congress that the SALT I Interim Agreement and the ABM Treaty had ushered in a new era of international relations. These accords signaled, in his view, the convergence of Soviet and U.S. military doctrine based on the American concept of mutual assured destruction: "By giving up missile defense, each side was leaving its population and its territory hostage to strategic missile attack. Each side therefore had the ultimate interest in preventing a new war that could only be mutually destructive. Kissinger called the summit "one of the greatest diplomatic coups of all times!" Most of the Congress, the press, and the academy reacted to the accomplishments of the summit with Nixon and Kissinger's sense of euphoria. John Newhouse, author of a popular account of the SALT I negotiations, compared the SALT accords with the Congress of Vienna of 1815, which established an equilibrium that preserved peace among the great powers for nearly a century. No analogy could have pleased Kissinger more. The Congress of Vienna was not only the subject of Kissinger's doctoral dissertation, which later became his extraordinary first book, but also the model of statecraft he sought to emulate.[27]

From the outset, Jackson expressed considerable misgivings about SALT I.[28] He objected to the ABM Treaty because it did not permit enough launchers to blunt the Soviet Union's capacity to launch a devastating first strike that could destroy more than 90 percent of the U.S. ICBM force. Also, he had always favored deploying a limited ABM defense in the short term so that the United States might surmount the technical obstacles to developing a more comprehensive, cost-effective strategic defense system in the long run. After braving the hostility of his own party and liberal voters in Washington State by leading the successful floor fight to pass Nixon's ABM program, Jackson felt Nixon and Kissinger had let him down by acquiescing to ABM limits that rendered the program next to useless. He surmised that the Soviets had agreed to the ABM Treaty not because they had endorsed U.S. strategic doctrine, but because they wished to constrain a program in which the United States enjoyed a technological advantage. Thus he expected that the Soviets would continue their active research and development program for strategic defense surreptitiously while the United States unilaterally curtailed its program, hoping to induce reciprocal Soviet restraint.[29]

Jackson had an even more negative reaction to the SALT I Interim Agreement limiting offensive weapons. He charged that the agreement did not establish genuine parity, but conferred on the Soviets a significant nuclear advantage by giving them a monopoly in heavy ICBMs (313 to 0) and permitting them 50 percent more land- and sea-based missile launchers than the Americans. To the administration's rebuttal that U.S. technological superiority, particularly in MIRVs, offset the numerical disadvantages into which SALT I froze the United States, Jackson retorted that the Soviet advantages were permanent while U.S. advantages were transitory. Eventually, then, the Soviet numerical advantage in launchers codified by SALT I would translate into a huge Soviet advantage in the size and number of ICBMs.[30]

Jackson also warned that the SALT agreements contained dangerous ambiguities, a flaw he blamed on Nixon and Kissinger's undue haste to conclude them under the pressure of self-imposed public relations deadlines at the Moscow Summit. He concentrated his fire on the "outstanding example" of the provision in the interim agreement that sought to limit the extent to which the Soviets would be able to add to the throw weight, or explosive power, of their missile force. Although Kissinger claimed that the Soviet Union agreed not to convert launchers for light missiles into launchers for heavy ones, they refused to agree to a definition of the terms "light" and "heavy." Jackson worried, too, about the atmospheric efforts of the SALT accords on American defense efforts. After Kissinger and Admiral Thomas Moorer, chairman of the Joint Chiefs of Staff, briefed a group of pro-defense senators days before the Moscow Summit, Jackson dissented from their otherwise unanimous expectation that the unequal numbers of the offensive agreement would expedite the enactment of U.S. strategic programs necessary to redress them. He correctly forecast that the mere existence of the treaties would diminish support for further strategic spending in the United States, while the Soviets would modernize their strategic forces to the maximum extent permissible and sometimes even beyond that by exploiting loopholes or by outright violations of the accords.[31]

In the political atmosphere of 1972, however, Jackson could not hope to defeat either the ABM Treaty or the Interim Agreement outright. Support for détente ran high, especially among liberal Democrats who dominated the Congress. Nixon's anticommunist reputation still inoculated him from criticism of being soft on the Soviets, despite the mounting apprehension his policies had raised among many conservatives. Jackson therefore decided to employ the same methods he had used so effectively in the ratification of the nuclear test ban treaty of 1963. He would support the agreements conditionally, but only after creating a public record about their controversial aspects and extracting concessions that would serve as the benchmark for evaluating future arms-control endeavors between the United States and the Soviet Union.[32]

Although John Stennis nominally chaired the Senate Armed Services Committee's hearings on SALT in June and July 1972, he and other members largely deferred to Jackson, who displayed a mastery of the subject that enhanced the credibility of the concerns he raised.[33] Jackson pressed and probed the secretary of defense, the chairman of the JCS, their respective SALT representatives, and the chief of naval operations for their assessments of the agreements. Always the good prosecuting attorney, he usually knew better than the witnesses the answers to his questions. Administration experts either conceded his argument or would be compelled to supply information for the record. As Richard Perle recalled, "Anybody that was watching the hearings was likely to see that Scoop was very much in command of the subject, and sometimes on the other side they were not."[34] Jackson did not stop there. When the Senate moved on August 7, 1972, to debate Senate Joint Resolution 241, providing congressional authorization to the Interim Agreement, Jackson submitted an amendment to the resolution bearing his name. This Jackson Amendment arose from his concerns that the Interim Agreement limited the United States to inferiority in intercontinental strategic nuclear delivery vehicles and granted the Soviet Union a preponderant advantage in throw weight. The amendment stated:

> The Congress recognizes the difficulty of maintaining a stable strategic balance in the period of rapidly developing technology; the Congress recognizes the principle of the United States–Soviet Union equality reflected in the anti-ballistic missile treaty, and urges and requests the President to seek a future treaty that *inter alia*, would not limit the Unit-

ed States to levels of intercontinental strategic forces inferior to the limits provided for the Soviet Union; and the Congress considers that the success of these agreements and the attainment of more permanent and comprehensive agreements are dependent upon the maintenance of a vigorous research and development and modernization program leading to a prudent strategic posture.[35]

Although its language was hortatory rather than mandatory, the amendment established concrete political guidelines that U.S. negotiators of any future SALT treaty could ignore only at their political peril. It was Fred Charles Ikle, then a member of the administration working for the Arms Control and Disarmament Agency (ACDA), who came up with the general idea for the Jackson Amendment in a conversation with Richard Perle about how to remedy the defects of the treaty process. It was Jackson and his staff, however, who implemented the idea and cleverly worded the amendment so that opponents faced the unsavory task of explaining why they opposed equality. This drove Kissinger and others crazy, according to Richard Perle, because they could not come up with an effective response.[36]

Senators William Fulbright, Edmund Muskie, Frank Church, Alan Cranston, and other liberals vehemently opposed the Jackson Amendment in the Senate. These critics tried to make the very complicated argument that equality had to be conceived in a larger sense and not system by system. They inveighed against the amendment as an obstacle to future arms control and as an incitement to a dangerous, costly and renewed arms race.[37] Their criticism of the Jackson Amendment to SALT I could not withstand the appeal of Jackson's simple but powerful argument for parity in numbers. Nor could they make a credible case that Jackson was simpleminded to those who had witnessed day in and day out his command of the details and generalities of national security policy. Finally, the administration grudgingly supported the amendment, which the Senate approved on September 11, 1972, by a majority of 56 to 35. Jackson relished needling Fulbright during this debate that he supported equality in all of its manifestations—an indirect reference to the Arkansas senator's segregationist record on civil rights.[38]

Jackson extracted several other significant concessions from Nixon and Kissinger on SALT. Partly to assuage him, the president purged the

ACDA of virtually everyone who had played a significant role in negotiating SALT I, including chief ACDA negotiator Gerald Smith, who also
attributes his dismissal to Kissinger blaming others for unpopular decisions that were often his own. Jackson and Kissinger also worked out another quid pro quo. In exchange for Jackson's acquiescence to the ABM
Treaty, which he did not like, the president appointed General Edward
Rowny, later President Reagan's chief arms negotiator, as the JCS representative to the SALT talks. Rowny had met Jackson in May 1952 while
teaching advanced tactics at Fort Benning, Georgia. He had paid a stiff
professional price for engaging in those discussions with Jackson. When
he returned to Washington, D.C., the secretary of the army gave him an
oral reprimand for teaching unauthorized tactics and proselytizing to
Jackson, which he had not done. "I was set back, silenced, and removed
from teaching," recalled Rowny. "I had no idea Jackson was going to talk
to the secretary of the army." Even so, Jackson and Rowny developed a
close friendship over the next two decades as the general's career flourished after that setback. Rowny would have preferred to remain in charge
of the task force to establish mutual, balanced force reductions between
the United States and the Soviet Union in Europe. When he learned that
Admiral Moorer, then chief of the JCS, did not want him as his deputy,
Rowny asked Jackson to relent. "You have set me back before, but I recovered. Now you are setting me back again." Jackson assured him, however, that "he was the right man for the job. He knew the strategic forces;
he spoke Russian." Rowny capitulated. "He just had such impeccable integrity and was so convincing by force of argument," said Rowny. "Jackson must have pulled the same type of stuff on other people he did on me.
He gave me lectures on duty, honor, and country. He sure knew how to
appeal to people."[39]

The loyalty and respect Jackson elicited from experts, his staff, and his
colleagues on both sides of the aisle contributed enormously to maximiz-
ing the breadth and depth of his influence on national policy. Because of
his vast knowledge and consistency, he had no reservations about giving
his staff considerable leeway. Because they knew where he stood, and had
confidence that he would back them to the hilt in the event of controversy, his staff could act decisively and confidently in his name. Senator Bill
Bradley, Democrat from New Jersey, observed insightfully in this regard:

Scoop's style illustrated another aspect of the modern Senate—the importance of staff. He surrounded himself with talented professionals and gave them his trust. They, in turn, were fiercely loyal to Scoop. They represented him in countless meetings with other Senate staffers, pushing his agenda in all of them. They always made sure he had the information he needed to be prepared. They amplified his voice and extended his reach. By watching how he gave credit to those who helped him, I saw his generosity of spirit demonstrated every day. Over the years, members of a senator's staff come and go. Yet, like old grads, they continue to think of themselves as Jackson staff. . . . Some senators are known as impossible to work for, because of their tempers, their work habits, or their egos. Scoop showed me how to motivate people to give 100 percent and keep them headed in a direction that supports the goals I've established.[40]

During a fall 1974 appearance on Martin Agronsky's television program in Washington, D.C., Richard Perle quipped that "Gerry Ford will be more careful with foreigners who drink vodka" after he hears the "likely congressional reaction" to his initiatives. The president called Jackson to express "his very strong objections to Perle's remarks." After pledging his highest regard for Ford's personal integrity, Jackson went on to defend Perle, taking full responsibility for his aide. He stressed that Perle's remarks "cast no unfavorable reflection on the president and were made in a light mood."[41]

Thus Jackson could have a broader and deeper impact than most legislators, who micromanaged their staffs and kept them on a short leash.[42] He also had an extensive network of academics, government officials, military people, lobbyists, and former staffers immersed in the Washington policy community upon whom he could call at a moment's notice. Annually, Jackson and his staffers would travel to Great Britain, usually staying at Claridges hotel in London, where they replenished their intellectual capital, conversing with many of the best Soviet scholars in the business (among them, Leonard Schapiro, Leopold Labedz, and Robert Conquest, author of the haunting *Great Terror*, the definitive account of the Stalinist purges of the 1930s, which Jackson considered must reading for anyone trying to understand the Soviet Union). Staffers Dorothy Fosdick,

Richard Perle, and Charles Horner kept Jackson in close touch with leading scholars in their fields: Russian experts Richard Pipes and Adam Ulam of Harvard, Robert and Suzanne Massie, and Robert Byrnes of Indiana University; China specialists Michel Oksenberg of Michigan, Dwight Perkins of Harvard, and Lucian Pye of MIT; Middle East authority Bernard Lewis of Princeton; and Japan authority Kenneth Pyle of the University of Washington.[43]

Chapter 14

Israel and the Cold War

JACKSON VIEWED Israel not only as a moral cause but also through the filter of the global struggle against communism. In his scheme of things, unswerving support of Israel meshed nicely with his antipathy toward the Soviet Union. He saw the Soviet ambition to dominate the Middle East, not the Israeli conflict with the Palestinians, as the basic threat to America's vital geopolitical interest in that oil-rich region. Rather than regarding American friendship with moderate Arab regimes and with Israel as a zero-sum game, he argued that a stable, secure, democratic, and militarily powerful Israel impeded Soviet penetration into the Arab World. For him nothing was so likely to facilitate Soviet policy in the Middle East as "a settlement based on Israeli withdrawal to the vulnerable borders of June 1967," which would guarantee that "the tensions and insecurity on which Soviet policy is based would continue to be exploited with tragic consequences for Arabs and Israelis alike."[1]

This is not how most of the first-generation Cold Warriors, other than liberal Democratic politicians such as Truman and Jackson, originally envisaged Israel's contribution to Soviet containment in the Middle East. George Marshall, James Forrestal, and Dean Acheson all had tried to talk President Truman out of supporting the creation of a Jewish state, precisely because they accepted the premise of State Department Arabists such as Loy Henderson that the very existence of Israel would fatally undermine the U.S. position among moderate Arab regimes.[2] Similarly, President Eisenhower and his secretary of state John Foster Dulles—Cold Warriors personified—continued to regard Israel more as a liability than as a strategic asset.[3]

By the late 1960s, this negative perception of Israel had largely abated among ardent Cold Warriors. Eisenhower, Dulles, and company grew disillusioned with the Arabists when the Soviet Union rather than the

United States received the credit in the Arab world for forcing the British, the French, and the Israelis to withdraw from the Sinai after the 1956 war. Also, Nasser and other radical Arab leaders angered U.S. statesmen by gravitating toward an alignment with the Soviet Union, notwithstanding assiduous American efforts to propitiate them. The Six-Day War of 1967 greatly raised Israel's standing among the huge majority of Americans, gratified that amid the frustrations of Vietnam an American ally had defeated a radical Arab coalition armed and abetted by the Soviet Union.[4] The evolution of William F. Buckley's *National Review*, the flagship journal for conservatives of the Cold War generation, illustrated this transformation. Originally mildly pro-Arab and anti-Israel, Buckley and his magazine had become staunchly pro-Israel by the early 1970s as the perception crystallized of Israel as a formidable barrier to Soviet ambitions in the Middle East.[5]

It is ironic that Jackson and the Nixon administration clashed so bitterly over the Middle East, for they held essentially the same outlook on America's goals and interest in the region. After momentarily flirting with the 1970 plan of his secretary of state, William Rogers, calling for an Israeli withdrawal to its pre-1967 borders in exchange for unspecified security guarantees, Nixon warmed to Kissinger's notion that a strong Israel served America's broader strategic interests. Indeed, the Nixon administration's policy in the Middle East offers the best evidence for Nixon and Kissinger's problematic claim that they practiced hard-headed détente. By demonstrating to the Arab world that only the United States had the leverage to broker a genuine peace with the Israelis, Nixon and Kissinger hoped to isolate the Soviet Union from the Middle East.[6] They fired, transferred, or demoted many of the old-line Arabists in the State Department, who were unreconciled to Israel's existence.[7] It was largely at the behest of the Nixon administration that the United States became Israel's main supplier of advanced weapons critical to its survival, and the Nixon administration also increased significantly the levels of military and nonmilitary aid the Jewish state received. During the Jordanian civil war of September 1970, Nixon and Kissinger tacitly collaborated with the Israelis to deter a Syrian intervention as King Hussein crushed the uprising of radical Palestinians that threatened the existence of his state. The Israeli leadership, especially Prime Minister Golda Meir, liked and respected Nixon. Kissinger maintained a close friendship with Simcha Dinitz, the Israeli ambassador to the United States during the 1973 Arab-Israeli War and the debate over the Jackson-Vanik Amendment. Despite their pro-Israeli orientation, Nixon and Kissinger believed that Israel's survival and American credibility with moderate Arab regimes hinged on the Israelis eventually trading land for a genuine peace. They strove to achieve a settlement incrementally on the theory that such a course eventually would encourage the forces of moderation on both sides.[8]

Jackson's devotion to Israel made Nixon and Kissinger's look tepid. It was Jackson who introduced into the debate the idea that "lasting peace in the Middle East lies in American support for a map of Israel with secure and recognized borders whose defense can be assured by the Israelis themselves." This precluded, in his view, the Israelis relinquishing the Golan Heights captured from Syria during the Six-Day War, because of the strategic importance of those mountains. Rather than considering the Sinai Peninsula essential for Israel's security, he expected that the Israelis would relinquish the Sinai eventually as the quid pro quo for Egypt accepting a durable peace.[9]

Jackson thus assailed the Rogers plan of 1970. Warning in 1970–71 that the Egyptians had begun deploying SAM antiaircraft missiles in the demilitarized zone around the Suez Canal, he accused the administration of laxity toward this violation of the disengagement agreement that the United States had hammered out between Egyptian and Israeli forces. He opposed any plan that would put American troops on the Golan Heights or any other sensitive areas of the territories Israel conquered in 1967. What made the Israeli-American relationship so robust and unique, he stressed, was that Israel could take care of any fighting itself.[10]

In 1970–71, Jackson also led the successful fight to secure congressional approval of military aid for Israel.[11] This authorization, which included F-4 Phantom jet fighters, had become bogged down in the Foreign Relations Committee because of the opposition of the chairman, William Fulbright, an Arabist of the old school who saw Israeli intransigence as the main problem for U.S. foreign policy in the Middle East. Again, Jackson infuriated the Arkansas senator by circumventing his committee. He pushed through the Armed Services Committee and the Congress a military procurement amendment authorizing the $500 million sale of Phantom jets and other military supplies to Israel. Like Jackson's,

Fulbright's attitude toward the Soviet Union shaped his views of the Arab-Israeli conflict, but in the opposite direction. Fulbright held the Cold War responsible for the Soviet Union's autocratic and repressive tendencies, which he reckoned a relaxation of tensions could ameliorate.[12] Jackson held the Soviet Union's totalitarian regime responsible for its relentless and insatiable expansionism, which he reckoned only American vigilance could deter. Fulbright saw Israel as a perpetual source of trouble. He assailed the Israelis for resorting to "Communist-baiting humbuggery" in an attempt to "manipulate" American policy in the Middle East.[13] Jackson saw Israel as a strategic bastion of the West. He commended the Israelis for defending Western trade routes and access to Middle Eastern oil against the surging tide of Soviet imperialism. Fulbright's scathing assessment of Jackson echoed what the Soviet Union had to say about him. Soviet Ambassador Anatoly Dobrynin told Jackson during a private meeting on January 14, 1973, that the Kremlin thought of him as the "number one cold warrior" dedicated to killing SALT I and détente.[14]

Powerful bonds of friendship, empathy, and affection for Israel buttressed Jackson's geopolitical convictions. He knew well all the major Israeli leaders of the ruling Labor Party. The late Prime Minister Yitzhak Rabin considered Jackson one of his "most cherished friends in the United States Senate." He first met Jackson in 1968 while serving as ambassador to the United States. Jackson immediately "captivated him" by his charm. "We small peoples must stick together, he said, because "only we can grasp the double struggle against external danger and great domestic difficulties." Jackson explained to a pleased but surprised Rabin that he identified with the Israelis because he could "never forget" his Norwegian origin. "The Norwegians have always been particular about protecting our independence from foreign invaders." Later, he told Rabin: "Just imagine. If Norway had instituted a law similar to the one now in force in the Soviet Union for Jews, my father would not have been able to emigrate to the United States, and I would not be an American citizen now."[15]

Rabin also credited Jackson for facilitating his close ties with much of the American military establishment. Jackson anticipated that Rabin, hero of the Six-Day War, and American military leaders would get on famously. These contacts greatly enhanced the cooperation Israel received from certain quarters in the Pentagon during the 1973 Arab-Israeli War.[16] Richard Perle described Jackson as "the closest thing Rabin had to a tutor in the ways of American politics." Jackson and Golda Meir not only agreed completely on security issues but were "enormously fond" of one another. To Jackson she was everything he admired—sensible, tough, down to earth. Meir treated Jackson in a maternal way. During their first meeting in Jerusalem in November 1970, Jackson lectured her that she must stop her chain smoking. "Stop worrying, Senator," she replied. "I will not die young."[17]

Jackson's second and third trips to the Middle East (1970 and 1972) fortified his conviction that Israel must be kept strong. What struck him most powerfully during the 1970 trip was the fragility of Israel's geographic position. He met with Prime Minister Meir, Defense Minister Moshe Dayan, the chief of staff of the Israeli Armed Forces, and General Yariv, chief of Israeli intelligence. The competence of the Israeli Army greatly impressed him. He flew by helicopter over the Sinai and Gaza, a ride that had several "hair-raising moments," according to Richard Perle, who took it less calmly than Jackson. Jackson also visited the Golan Heights, where he met with the commanding general of Israel's Northern Command. He followed the cease-fire lines along the Jordan, an area "of considerable terrorist activity and cross-border shelling."

Jackson's 1970 trip to Israel also brought him to Saudi Arabia and Iran. Having warned early of the impending difficulty of keeping oil flowing reliably from the Middle East, he had long wanted to visit Saudi Arabia. He almost had to abandon that trip, however, because the Saudis originally declined to grant Richard Perle (a Jew) and Dorothy Fosdick (a woman) visas. Shortly before the departure date, Jackson telephoned Joseph Sisco, the assistant secretary of state for Middle Eastern affairs: "If the visas are not here in twenty four hours, we will spend more time in Iran." Whereupon, visas for Perle and Fosdick arrived promptly. Jackson got on well with the Saudis, who treated him with great respect. The Saudis also seemed open to Perle. Several officials took him aside and said: "You write those Zionist speeches." They argued amiably until four in the morning. Jackson left Saudi Arabia more convinced than ever about the compatibility of maintaining good relations with the Israelis and the moderate Arab regimes. He had a less favorable reaction to his experience in Iran. Although he considered the shah infinitely better for Iranian and American interests than the plausible alternatives, it concerned him that "nobody else but the shah would take any responsibility for answering any of his questions." He left Iran troubled by its political structure and worried about its long-term stability.[18]

FREEDOM OF EMIGRATION: THE JACKSON-VANIK AMENDMENT

The Jackson-Vanik Amendment to the U.S. Trade Act combined Jackson's commitment to the political well-being of the state of Israel with his antipathy toward the Soviet Union. Although he did not originate the idea of conditioning the grant of most favored nation (MFN) status to the Soviet Union on its respect for the right to emigrate, he became its champion and driving force in Congress. What inspired the amendment was the surge in pride among Soviet Jews following Israel's victory in the Six-Day War of 1967. Soviet discrimination against its Jewish citizens increased as many more of them then demanded to emigrate. Israel's open-door immigration policy for Jews created enormous pressure on the Soviet regime because it gave as many Jews as wanted to leave the Soviet Union a place to go. After a period of slowly increasing the number of Jews allowed to leave, the Soviets cracked down in the summer of 1972 by imposing an "education tax," purportedly to recoup the investment made in educating these emigrants, but really to discourage the entire enterprise of emigration. This notorious tax formally targeted all prospective emigrants but hit Soviet Jews especially hard because they tended to have substantially more education than other segments of the population. Meanwhile, the Nixon administration began lobbying Congress to approve a series of trade agreements that the president had concluded extending MFN and authorizing more subsidized lending to the Soviet Union. Jackson took full advantage of this opening. On October 4, 1972, he introduced legislation that denied these concessions to nonmarket economies unless they respected the right of their citizens to emigrate. The Jackson-Vanik Amendment applied to everyone regardless of race, religion, or national origin, and did not affect nonsubsidized trade or commercial lending between the United States and the Soviet Union.[19]

The amendment greatly alarmed Nixon and Kissinger. They feared it could wreck the complex web of interlocking arrangements on which, in their view, the success of détente depended. Reluctant to jeopardize the unprecedentedly high levels (for a Republican) of support he expected to receive from Jewish voters against his Democratic opponent George McGovern, the president determined to defer the brewing controversy with

Jackson until after the November election. On September 30, just after the signing ceremony for the SALT accords, Nixon and Jackson discussed the amendment privately at the White House. They reached a tactical compromise: the president would not try to stop Republican senators from supporting the amendment in exchange for Jackson's promise not to make Jewish emigration a partisan issue during the presidential campaign. Nixon calculated that the Jackson amendment would die in the Senate at the end of the session, perhaps forever. Also, he counted on Wilbur Mills, the powerful Democratic chairman of the House Ways and Means Committee, and his allies in the American business community to kill the amendment in the House, should the Senate pass it during the next congressional session.[20]

The president had badly underestimated Jackson's prowess as a legislator. Jackson had crafted the legislation carefully to ensure maximum bipartisan support. Conservatives and labor leaders, particularly AFL-CIO president George Meany, rallied to Jackson-Vanik to strike a blow at a policy of détente they regarded as immoral and imprudent. The cause of Jewish emigration appealed greatly to many antiwar liberals, notwithstanding their enthusiasm for détente in its broader aspects.[21] The Jackson-Vanik Amendment elicited overwhelming support not just from American Jews, but from Americans of Eastern European descent whose ancestral homelands were captive nations of the Soviet Union. In addition, Jackson had the unstinting support of Andrei Sakharov and other leading Soviet dissidents with whom he maintained close contacts.[22] By November 1972, he had secured seventy-two sponsors for the amendment in the Senate, a strong base from which to renew his efforts in the next congressional session.[23]

Jackson reintroduced Jackson-Vanik in March 1973 as an amendment to the president's comprehensive trade bill, which included provisions to expand the president's authority to negotiate trade concessions with foreign governments and to allow him to grant the Soviet Union MFN status. "We proposed to deny the benefits of our abundant economy—most favored access to our markets, credits, credit guarantees, and investment guarantees—to any nonmarket economy that denies its citizens the right or opportunity to emigrate or imposes more than normal taxes on emigration," Jackson declared. "In so doing, we are upholding our traditional commitment to individual liberty—a commitment that was enshrined

Israel and the Cold War

in the Universal Declaration of Human Rights unanimously adopted by the United Nations more than 25 years ago. That declaration affirms the deep conviction of the American people that everyone has the right to leave any country, including his own, and to return to his country."[24]

Nixon flew into a rage that displayed his worst side. In one of the few White House meetings of the time not devoted almost exclusively to the Watergate crisis metastasizing around him, he called Jackson irresponsible for "sacrificing disarmament and cooperation unless the U.S.S.R. disavows its Jewish policy." He complained that "the Soviet Union would have to change their system if they, by treaty," gave in to Jackson's demands. He also ranted about "professional Jews" backing Jackson-Vanik: "I am not a professional Quaker and they hate me for it." He threatened "that a storm will hit American Jews if they are intransigent." It could "lead to antiSemitism." He would "lay it out on TV" that there will be "no summit on account of this."[25] So began a ferocious two-year debate with Jackson, the Nixon and Ford administrations, and the Kremlin the main protagonists.

DEBATE OVER JACKSON-VANIK, PHASE I (1973)

Finally realizing that they could not stop Jackson-Vanik from passing in the Senate, where Jackson had amassed an unassailable coalition, Nixon and Kissinger shifted their attention to persuading the House to block it. They also pressed the Jewish community to drop or at least moderate their support for the amendment, remembers Manny Weiss, a devoted aide to Senator Jackson who worked intensely on the issue.[26] This strategy probably would have succeeded but for Henry Jackson.

Critics of the amendment such as Senator Fulbright and President Nixon have confused cause and effect by attributing its passage to the baleful influence of the Jewish lobby in American politics.[27] Actually, Jackson led the Jewish community on Jackson-Vanik: the Jewish community did not lead him. The state of Israel then had neither the inclination nor the leverage to risk promoting a showdown with the Nixon administration over Jackson-Vanik. As Natan Sharansky and other dissidents who revere Jackson point out correctly but without sufficient appreciation of the circumstances that accounted for it, the Labor governments of Israel did not consider Jewish emigration from the Soviet Union a realistic or high priority. Historically, they thought in terms of freeing tens or hundreds of Soviet Jews by quiet diplomacy—a far cry from the several hundred thousand to a million Soviet Jews that Jackson had in mind.[28] Some Labor officials, such as Ambassador Dinitz, were receptive to the brutally direct argument of Nixon and Kissinger that Israel could not bear the onus of subverting détente that passage of the Jackson-Vanik Amendment would place on it.[29] True, the Israeli government rebuffed Nixon and Kissinger's repeated entreaties to instruct the Jewish community in the United States not to pressure Congress. "I cannot tell Jews of the United States what to do with their brethren in the Soviet Union," Rabin replied to Kissinger. "Nor could I possibly take any step that would be interpreted as stabbing Senator Jackson in the back." Nevertheless, Prime Minister Meir adopted a low profile on the amendment, which belies the idea that the Israelis manipulated this issue.[30]

The American Jewish community also anguished more over Jackson-Vanik than the public image suggests. Some of its key leaders argued that Jackson-Vanik could hurt Israel's relations with the pro-Israel Nixon administration and threaten the modest increases in Jewish emigration from the Soviet Union won by quiet diplomacy. In his September 25, 1972, address to the National Conference on Soviet Jewry, Jackson persuaded the delegates to defy the reticence of the Israeli embassy and the more cautious of the Jewish community leaders. The NCSJ voted to endorse the amendment.[31] Nixon and Kissinger then enlisted Max Fisher, president of the Council of Jewish Federations, and Jacob Stein, chairman of the President's Conference of Major Jewish Organizations, two of the top Republican campaign donors, to help the administration make its case against Jackson-Vanik.[32] They accepted Kissinger's argument that keeping the lines of communication open with the Soviets had yielded positive results: an end to the education tax, which the Soviets dropped in the spring of 1973, and the possibility that the Soviets might permit the emigration of up to 40,000 Jews per year. Yet neither they nor Kissinger could persuade Jackson to drop the amendment, despite persistent entreaties throughout 1973. During the 1973 Arab-Israeli War, Fisher, Stein, and Richard Maass, president of the NCSJ, tried one last time. They asked Jackson to back down following a meeting with Kissinger, during which he lectured them on the imperative of obtaining Soviet cooperation to end the crisis and ensure the peace. Jackson not only refused, but also told these Jewish leaders that they should be ashamed of themselves for the way the administration was using them.[33]

It took the House almost a year to debate and pass Jackson-Vanik. The administration and its supporters in the business and academic communities fought tenaciously against it. They conceded that the threat of Jackson-Vanik had served the useful purpose of increasing Jewish emigration, but they argued that its enactment would lead to a severe curtailment of emigration. They warned, moreover, that the amendment would complicate détente, could hurt American business, and constituted an unjustified interference in the internal affairs of the Soviet Union.[34]

Although most of the hard-line Sovietologists whose views on the amendment Jackson solicited were sympathetic to the dissidents, even they did not agree on whether his method would work. A majority of this group favored it on the grounds that it weakened the Soviet economy. Robert Conquest wrote Jackson that "the Russians have a perfectly good solution for their economic problems, in the form of not straining themselves to death in arms production. Why should we grant them trade privileges which amount, in effect, to subsidizing arms directed against ourselves?" Conquest added that "detente amounted to no more than giving the Russians a period—perhaps a decade, perhaps more, perhaps less—at the end of which they would hope to have reconstructed their economy, maintained their basic hostility, and improved their armaments position, so that they would be nice and fresh for another round of aggression. Obviously, any Western acceptance of such a package, as it stands, is suicidal lunacy. If they need our help, they should make concessions of real substance." Robert Byrnes, Leopold Labedz, Uri Ra'anan, Adam Ulam, and Leonard Schapiro responded to Jackson's inquiries in a similar fashion.[35]

Though Richard Pipes initially responded negatively to Jackson-Vanik, he changed his mind after he witnessed the chilling effect it would have on American economic loans and assistance to the Soviet Union. Jackson-Vanik also received the surprising endorsement of Hans Morgenthau, the dean of foreign policy realists, whose classic *Politics among Nations* scorned the U.S. tradition of mixing moralism with foreign policy. He wrote Jackson that "for the Soviet Union as for all Communist governments, foreign trade is not a commercial transaction for profit but a political act performed for national power. As the Soviet Union seeks political advantage from a trade agreement, so ought the United States. . . . To do otherwise would only confirm the Soviet leaders in their often repeated conviction that their desire for profit will doom the capitalists." On the other side, Sovietologists Elliot Goodman, Leon Goure, and John A. Armstrong all expressed doubts to Jackson about whether the amendment would work better than the alternative of not linking trade with human rights. George Kennan and many of the more soft-line Sovietologists, who no longer classified the Soviet Union as a totalitarian regime, expressed their hostility toward Jackson-Vanik publicly.[36]

The opponents proved no match for Jackson. On December 13, 1973, the House passed Jackson-Vanik by a margin of 319 to 80. Jackson demolished the pillar of the president's strategy by persuading Wilbur Mills to change his mind on the amendment. Mills had a Jewish aide named Tony Solomon who was dead set against the amendment, Richard Perle later explained. It was Solomon who had told Nixon that there was no way it would get through the Ways and Means Committee Mills chaired. He was wrong. In New York City, Jackson and Perle had met David Hermann, a semi-retired footwear manufacturer and spokesman for the industry, who knew Mills and Solomon well because footwear manufacturers frequently went to the Ways and Means Committee for protection against foreign competition. Jackson had given a speech at a dinner organized by Hermann's wife Rose. Afterward, Jackson and Perle asked him if he would help them out with Wilbur Mills. Hermann agreed, but insisted that Perle must brief him thoroughly first. In April 1973, Perle spent an entire morning before his meeting with Mills going over books and elaborate talking points with Hermann. Then Perle returned to his office and eagerly awaited Hermann's report on his lunch with Mills. Hermann called him at around 1:45 P.M. "I want you to hear this," he told Perle. Mill's secretary then came on the line and read him a statement that Mills would issue, heartily endorsing the Jackson-Vanik Amendment. An ebullient but stunned Perle asked how he did it. "Oh, I set aside what you gave me," Hermann replied. "I said to Wilbur that during the Hitler period, we stood by. . . . This may be another case. We have to get these people out." Mills turned to his secretary, said take this down, then dictated his endorsement on the spot.[37]

Jackson's campaign to sway the House received an enormous boost from the great Soviet dissident Andrei Sakharov, who called Jackson "our champion." On September 14, 1973, Sakharov issued an open letter urging Congress to pass the Jackson-Vanik Amendment. He denied that the amendment represented unjustified interference in the Soviet Union's internal affairs. The Soviets, he stressed, "must accept basic principles of conduct, among them respect for the right to emigrate as proclaimed in the 1948 Charter in the Universal Declaration of Human Rights." The amendment was, according to Sakharov, "simply a defense of international law, without which there could be no mutual trust." He ended with a stinging rebuke to the notion that quiet diplomacy would suffice:

> The abandonment of a policy of principle would be a betrayal of the thousands of Jews and non-Jews who want to emigrate, of the hundreds in camps and mental hospitals, of the victims of the Berlin Wall.
>
> Such a denial would lead to stronger repressions on ideological grounds. It would be tantamount to total capitulation of democratic principles in the face of blackmail, deceit and violence. The consequences of such a capitulation for international confidence, detente and the entire future of mankind are difficult to predict.
>
> I express the hope that the Congress of the United States, reflecting the will and traditional love of freedom of the American people, will realize its historical responsibility before mankind and will find the strength to rise above temporary partisan considerations of commercialism and prestige.
>
> I hope that the Congress will support the Jackson Amendment.[38]

DEBATE OVER JACKSON-VANIK, PHASE II (1974)

After the House approved Jackson-Vanik in December 1973, Kissinger altered his strategy. He sought to broker a compromise that would satisfy all in a protracted series of three-way negotiations—involving the administration, Congress (led mainly by Jackson), and Anatoly Dobrynin, the Soviet ambassador—which dragged on for most of 1974. This "dialogue," Kissinger commented ruefully, made him "long for the relative tranquility of the Middle East."[39] One reason was that Jackson and Kissinger continued to disagree on fundamental issues. Another reason was the mounting personal animosity between the two men that aggravated those differences. According to Peter Rodman and others, Jackson struck a raw nerve in Kissinger with his charge that the secretary of state,

Jewish himself, had insufficient concern for the plight of Jewish refugees and the security of Israel.[40] According to Richard Perle, the secretary of state's habitual duplicity offended the earnest and steadfast Jackson. "Kissinger was basically an honorable person," said Perle, who unlike Jackson grew fond of Kissinger in later years. "Kissinger was, however, capable of tactical misrepresentation, although he was very clever about the misrepresentation. He could avoid in a certain sophistic way the technical lie. But he could leave a very misleading impression. I am sure he considered that fair play."[41]

Kissinger's diplomacy during the 1973 Arab-Israeli War intensified Jackson's already strong distrust of him. The decision of Egypt and Syria to attack Israel on October 6 came as a complete surprise. Israel, the United States, and the Soviet Union all expected the Israelis to win as quickly and decisively as they had in 1967. Distracted by the Watergate crisis, Nixon left the day-to-day management of American foreign policy during the war largely to his secretary of state and national security adviser Henry Kissinger.[42] Kissinger wanted the Israelis to win a partial, not total victory. The latter outcome, he thought, would diminish the prospects for reaching a long-term resolution of the Middle East conflict by radicalizing the Arab world and increasing Israeli intransigence. Direct American intervention on the side of the Israelis, he believed, could have major adverse effects on the détente process with the Soviet Union; whereas a partial Israeli victory would improve the chances for settlement by allowing President Sadat of Egypt to save face, by convincing the moderate Arabs of the futility of the military option against Israel, and by demonstrating to the Israelis their utter dependence on American good will as an inducement to moderate their demands in peace negotiations with the Arabs. "The best thing that could happen to us," Kissinger remarked to Secretary of Defense James Schlesinger on October 7, "is for the Israelis to come out ahead but to get bloodied in the process."[43]

In the first days of the war, Kissinger still rated Israel's military capabilities so highly that he expected the main problem to be preventing a total Israeli victory. He decided therefore that the United States should delay providing Israel with substantial assistance in supplies and equipment. Initially, Israelis contributed to that decision by their arrogant expectations that they would demolish the Egyptian and Syrian armies as soon as they fully mobilized. If the Israelis were right, then it served no good purpose to incur the diplomatic fallout of providing them with massive amounts of equipment.[44] But Kissinger and the Israelis had miscalculated. Israel's overconfidence soon turned to panic when the Egyptians repulsed the Israeli counteroffensive in the Sinai on October 8 and 9. Israel's simultaneous counteroffensive on the Syrian front did better but not enough to allow for reallocation of forces to the Egyptian front. The Israelis also suffered heavy and unanticipated losses in aircraft and armor that only the United States could replenish.[45] After initially trying to discourage the Arab attack based on their estimates that it would fail miserably, the Soviets shed their tactical circumspection once it appeared the Arabs might win. They pressed for a cease-fire that would consolidate the Egyptian and Syrian gains on the battlefield, urged other nonbelligerent Arab nations to join the war, commenced a massive airlift to resupply the Egyptian and Syrian armies even as the United States still refused to resupply the Israelis, and undertook a major naval buildup in the Mediterranean while placing several airborne divisions on alert.[46] With their resources running dangerously low, the Israelis faced the grim prospect of a war of attrition that they would surely lose unless the United States initiated a massive airlift of supplies and equipment to match that of the Soviets. The Israeli government submitted an urgent request to Kissinger on October 9 for huge quantities of arms and equipment. Lest the United States underestimate the danger Israel was in, Prime Minister Meir offered to come to Washington to make this request in person.

Kissinger continued to stall the resupply until October 12. Still convinced that the Israelis could win a partial victory without substantial American aid, he did not want to antagonize the moderate Arab states or the Soviet Union. Instead, he sought to devise a way for the United States to supply the Israelis modestly and without an official American presence. Rather than allowing the U.S. air force to fly in equipment, Kissinger agreed first to allow unmarked Israeli aircraft to pick up supplies. Then he tried to arrange for the chartering of private aircraft to do it, an option the private companies refused.[47] All the while, he dissembled to the Israeli government and to the American press, pledging his support for immediately supplying Israel to make up for its war losses and blaming Secretary of Defense Schlesinger for holding it up. Prime Minister Meir wrote Nixon directly on October 12 to underscore the perilousness of Israel's predicament and the need for a massive American airlift without further delay. Ambassador Dinitz made a similar plea to Kissinger the same day, with a veiled warning of making the matter public to Israel's friends on Capitol Hill should the delay continue.[48] Kissinger had no desire to jeopardize Israel's existence. Once he realized the situation Israel faced, he changed his mind about the airlift.

It was not soon enough for Henry Jackson. Totally committed to Israel's military preeminence, he derided Kissinger's strategy of trying to calibrate a limited Israeli victory as a dangerous game that brought Israel to the threshold of defeat. He seethed as Kissinger continued to lie blatantly about his role in stalling the airlift. He knew better. The Israeli Embassy kept in constant touch with Jackson through Richard Perle, who had heard the Israelis make phone calls to Kissinger that directly contradicted the secretary of state's version of events.[49] Jackson also had received a blow-by-blow account of Kissinger's maneuverings from his allies James Schlesinger and Admiral Elmo Zumwalt. On October 11, Zumwalt did something he said he would not have done had he been sure that "Richard Nixon rather than the unelected, unaccountable Henry Kissinger was making national policy about the war." He informed Jackson that he believed "Israel would lose the war if the United States did not get the equipment aloft at once."[50] Jackson met with President Nixon that day, exhorting him to act. Nixon did not need much persuading. The United States could not tolerate, in his view, a Soviet-backed coalition inflicting a catastrophic defeat on a de facto American ally. Nixon thus made a decision critical to Israeli success. He ordered Schlesinger and Kissinger on October 13 to make sure that Israel immediately obtained all the American arms it needed, including from American reserve stocks of equipment if necessary.[51]

When the airlift got under way the next day, Jackson became heavily involved in that, too. The United States needed to use the Azores because all the NATO allies except Portugal had turned down U.S. requests to use their territory for refueling U.S. transports to Israel, for fear of offending the Arabs. The Portuguese had still not formally approved the request even as the first convoy of cargo planes took off for the Azores. They had a price. There was a piece of legislation pending in the Senate that was highly critical of Portugal's colonial rule in southern Africa. The Portuguese would grant landing rights only if the bill died in conference, which it did with Jackson's help. He rounded up enough senators to quash the bill so the administration could give the Portuguese the assurance they demanded. On October 18, Jackson also cosponsored a resolution, which the Senate passed overwhelmingly, urging "decisive action to assure that essential military equipment be transferred to Israel on a time scale and in whatever quantities are required to enable Israel to repel Syrian and Egyptian aggression."[52]

On October 25, Nixon put U.S. nuclear forces on alert when the Soviets threatened to intervene unilaterally as the war shifted in Israel's favor. The Israeli armed forces had by then defeated the Syrians decisively, crossed to the west side of the Suez Canal, and encircled the Egyptian Third Army. Schlesinger and Zumwalt kept Jackson apprised of the deliberations over the nuclear alert, which caused the Soviets to back down in exchange for the U.S. enforcing the October 22 cease-fire on the Israelis.[53] Jackson held Kissinger responsible for accepting such a cease-fire sooner or later, which forced the Israelis to draw back from encircling the Egyptian Third Army. In this case, however, Nixon had made the decision that Jackson so disliked. Kissinger would have preferred to delay implementation of the cease-fire for a few additional days to permit the Israelis to improve their military position. In Moscow to negotiate the cease-fire agreement, he had intended to slow the pace by claiming he lacked full authority to reach an agreement. Nixon undercut him by cabling Brezhnev with the assurance that Kissinger had such authority. The secretary had no choice but to reach a prompt agreement.[54]

The 1973 Arab-Israeli War turned out largely the way Kissinger had hoped it would, whether by luck, design, or probably a combination of the two. As Professor Nadan Safran, author of one of the best accounts of Israeli foreign policy, assessed the results:

> Israel was able to improve its military position a great deal and was grateful to Kissinger even though he barred them from complete victory. The Egyptians saw him as one who saved them from total defeat, even though he had helped place Israel in a position to put them under such threat. Finally, although these additional gains were scored at the expense of the Soviets, the structure of detente remained essentially intact.[55]

Ultimately, Kissinger succeeded in detaching Egypt from the radical Arab coalition. With his vaunted shuttle diplomacy, he also negotiated a military disengagement between Israel and Egypt that spawned the separate peace between the two countries that was consummated during the Carter administration. Even some members of the Jackson circle such as Paul Wolfowitz concede, in retrospect, that this treaty largely vindicated the Egyptian-Israeli aspect of Kissinger's diplomacy during the 1973 war.[56]

Jackson did not concede even that. He proclaimed the war "a disastrous example of this version of detente." Although he "strongly backed the decision to place American forces on nuclear alert," he chastised the administration "for a whole week of equivocation when we sent out the wrong signals to the Soviets." Although aware that the Soviets were initially "against the coordinated attacks by Egypt and Syria," he blasted them for not notifying the United States of what "they knew was coming." He also blasted Kissinger. "Without Soviet support and material encouragement, without Soviet training and equipment, without Soviet diplomatic and political backing, the war would never have been started," Jackson declared. "And yet Dr. Kissinger . . . comes before the American people to say that Soviet behavior had been moderate and not irresponsible. I cannot agree." When, he added, the Soviets discovered after a couple of days of fighting, much to their surprise, that the Arabs were doing very well, they showed their true colors by pouring "all this stuff in because the Israelis" were reeling and the United States was "not moving anything" to resupply the Israelis. "Where in all this lies detente?" he asked rhetorically.[57]

Jackson described his conversations with Kissinger during the October War as "warm and friendly," but in private the administration complained about the "abrasiveness" of Jackson's staff and the senator's lack of proportion.[58] Jackson, for his part, pounded away at Kissinger's lack of credibility and the administration's naive enthusiasm for achieving lasting agreements with Moscow before the Soviets liberalized their society.[59] Nixon delivered an address in Annapolis, Maryland, just before departing for the Moscow Summit of 1974, that criticized Jackson by name for meddling in the internal affairs of the Soviet Union, which, according to the president, were none of our business. Jackson called Nixon's criticism of him "nonsense." The Soviet Union, he declared, had an obligation to live up to the provisions of the United Nations charter, which it had signed freely. "It was a mistake," he said, for the president to proceed with the summit meeting while under the threat of impeachment (which, two months later, would force Nixon to resign). Expecting that the Soviets would attempt ruthlessly to take advantage of the president's domestic travails, Jackson worried that while at the summit a desperate Nixon might sign a bad arms control agreement rather than accept no agreement at all.[60]

Jackson thus maneuvered to constrain the president's options. On January 29, 1974, he offered Nixon a detailed alternative to the SALT I formulas, which he deemed gravely deficient. By reducing the strategic forces of both the Untied States and the Soviet Union to total aggregate levels of 1,760 strategic launchers, Jackson maintained that "we could achieve stability at a lower level of armament and expenditure." By negotiating a formula providing for equal throw weight, he added that "we could go quite far in diminishing the importance of MIRV as a destabilizing factor." Nixon responded politely but vaguely to Jackson's proposal. Keeping the pressure on the administration, Jackson commenced closed hearings of the Subcommittee on Arms Control on Wednesday, June 19, just a week before the president's departure. Through his exhaustive questioning of Pentagon officials and other experts, most notably his old friend Paul Nitze, who a month later would resign from the SALT team in protest over Kissinger's methods, Jackson established that the administration had often failed to solicit or had ignored the advice of the JCS and other professional advisers. He thereby succeeded, according to Zumwalt, in warning a "significant portion of the Senate . . . against the possibility of hanky panky in Moscow." In the end, Nixon declined to sign an agreement at the summit that accommodated the Soviet position on SALT, a firmness that the Jackson forces interpreted as a victory of their side over Kissinger.[61]

Jackson also moved to circumscribe the president's room to maneuver on the issue of Soviet emigration. Two days before the Moscow Summit, he criticized the administration for making insufficient progress on the issue and urged the president to be steadfast. Kissinger's years of sobering encounters with Jackson had convinced the secretary of state by this time that he was "up against a master psychological warrior."[62] In March 1974 Jackson had rejected Kissinger's proposed compromise that Congress would grant the Soviets MFN and establish a mechanism for reviewing Soviet emigration practices at regular intervals.[63] Initially, he demanded that the Soviet Union give a written guarantee of 100,000 exit visas annually, a figure he later reduced to 75,000. In October 1974, he agreed to a bottom-line figure of 60,000 but would go no lower than that.[64] The

Soviets first offered to give oral but not written assurances for 35,000 exit visas annually. Brezhnev agreed at the Moscow Summit of 1974 to make the number 40,000 to 45,000 annually.[65]

Throughout the late summer and early fall of 1974, protracted negotiations ensued in an effort to bridge the impasse. Kissinger found Jackson so difficult that he judged Soviet Foreign Minister Gromyko "to be the easier party."[66] Senators Abraham Ribicoff, Democrat from Connecticut, and Jacob Javits, Republican from New York—the two other members of Jackson's congressional negotiating team, who were both Jewish—consistently inclined to take Kissinger's rather than Jackson's side of the dispute for fear of jeopardizing détente. Left to their own devices, they would have resolved the matter largely on the administration's terms. Jackson would not let them, although they constrained his discretion, too.[67]

After lengthy discussions involving Jackson, Javits, Ribicoff, Dobrynin, Gromyko, and President Ford, who had replaced Nixon on August 9, the deadlock appeared to be broken in the fall of 1974.[68] Jackson and Kissinger signed two letters in the White House on October 18 that set forth the terms for this compromise agreement. Jackson agreed to include a waiver provision in the Jackson-Vanik Amendment, whereby the president could grant nonmarket economies MFN unconditionally for eighteen months. Thereafter, Congress would have to approve any further extension by concurrent resolution. The Jackson letter declared that the Soviets would have to meet or exceed Jackson's "minimum standard of compliance" of 60,000 emigrants a year to receive a waiver. Although Kissinger's letter did not refer to concrete numbers, he left Jackson with the strong impression that the Soviets had agreed to the 60,000 figure. Perle released both of these letters to the press later in the month. On December 13, the Senate passed the Jackson amendment to the trade bill by a vote of 88 to 0. On December 18, the House approved it by a vote of 323 to 36. Correspondingly, Congress passed the Stevenson amendment put forward by Adlai Stevenson, Jr., Democrat of Illinois, that capped all U.S. import-export bank loans to the Soviet Union at $300 million. This amendment, Stevenson announced, "reflects [Jackson's] concerns as well as a prodigious amount of his time and effort."[69]

The compromise on Jackson-Vanik soon unraveled. Gromyko wrote Kissinger an angry letter on October 26, 1974, objecting to the Kissinger-Jackson exchange of October 18 as "a distorted picture of our position and what we told the American side on the matter." The Soviet Union, he grumbled, declined resolutely to treat the numbers mentioned as assurances. Kissinger concealed this letter from Jackson and the Congress for the next two months, perhaps hoping to salvage the compromise before the Soviet Union went public with its complaints. In his December 3 testimony before the Senate Finance Committee, Kissinger did say that the Soviet Union had undertaken no commitment "either in form or substance on the issue of immigration." He portrayed his October 18 letter to Jackson as a clarification of Soviet emigration practices that President Ford and the Soviet leaders had given him. Jackson's reply of October 18, Kissinger explained, contained interpretations and clarifications "which were never stated by Soviet officials." Kissinger expected the emigration rate to correspond with the number of applications.[70]

On December 18, the Soviet Union publicly released the text of the Gromyko letter to Kissinger, along with a public statement denying the claim that the Soviets had given specific assurances that emigration would increase in exchange for American trade concessions. On December 25, President Ford received a stern letter from Brezhnev declaring the Jackson and Stevenson amendments unacceptable. On January 3, Ford reluctantly signed into law the trade bill with Jackson-Vanik attached because he needed the general authority to conduct trade negotiations with other countries that it provided.[71]

Not everybody greeted the enactment of Jackson-Vanik with huzzahs. On January 14, 1975, Kissinger announced at a press conference that the Soviets had rescinded their agreement to the trade deal. He blamed Henry Jackson for ruining it. Jackson antagonist William Fulbright and the editorials of many newspapers joined in this criticism. The *Chicago Tribune* opined that the Soviet disavowal of the trade agreement "was more of a blow to Senator Jackson than it was to the bill. Mr. Jackson had been tripped up by his own eagerness for publicity to fuel his campaign for the Presidency." Mike Padev, the foreign editor of the *Arizona Republic*, denounced the amendment as "Senator Jackson's monumental Soviet fiasco." The *Des Moines Register* editorial page pronounced that Jackson had outsmarted himself.[72]

The charge of subordinating the national interest to his presidential ambitions stung an angry Jackson especially hard. He complained that Kissinger had deceived the entire Congress by not disclosing the

Gromyko letter of October 26. As late as December 18, the day the Soviets released the Gromyko letter, the State Department had assured Jackson that the understandings contained in the Kissinger-Jackson letters of October 18 remained unchanged. By Perle's admission, however, Jackson would have pushed forward with the amendment even had he known about the contents of the October 26 letter. It was the Soviets, Jackson insisted, who had reneged on a good faith accommodation achieved on October 18.[73] The Jackson people attributed the Soviet decision to scuttle the October 18 compromise to the Stevenson amendment, the implications of which the Kremlin did not fully grasp until December 1974.[74] This is partly true, but an evasion. Jackson heartily endorsed the Stevenson amendment.

Later, Kissinger and his defenders maligned the Jackson-Vanik Amendment not only for undermining détente, but also for hurting the cause of Jewish emigration.[75] This is not an unreasonable inference to draw from the statistics on Jewish emigration from the Soviet Union, but it is not irrefutable. From October 1968 through 1970, total Jewish emigration numbered only 4,235. That number increased to 13,022 in 1971; 31,681 in 1972; and 34,733 in 1973. Thereafter, the numbers dropped significantly below the 40,000 to 45,000 that the Soviets had agreed to as an informal benchmark at the Moscow Summit of 1974: 20,628 in 1974; 13,221 in 1975; 14,261 in 1976; and 16,736 in 1977.[76] Critics of Jackson-Vanik cite this data as evidence that Kissinger was right and Jackson wrong about the virtues of quiet diplomacy to facilitate Jewish emigration.[77]

Yet there was no steady or reliable progress in Jewish emigration before the Jackson amendment. On the contrary, the Soviets had always behaved capriciously on emigration. Indeed, they had tried every conceivable method to stop it: the education tax, the infamous Leningrad trials and other trials of dissidents, releasing some leaders while incarcerating others. Without the Jackson-Vanik Amendment to make it an issue, Jewish emigration could have stopped completely; whereas the amendment gave the Soviets a huge incentive for relaxing restrictions on Jewish emigration when they desperately wanted something. Jewish emigration reached 51,320 in 1979, for example, as the Soviet Union stepped up its lobbying campaign for the abortive SALT II agreement. It declined to 21,471 in 1980 after the SALT II had stalled in the Senate. Eager to obtain American aid and good will as the Soviet empire unraveled, Gorbachev and

Yeltsin permitted far higher levels of Jewish emigration than they might have otherwise because Jackson-Vanik symbolized how important the United States regarded the issue. Jewish emigration from the Soviet Union climbed to 71,217 in 1989 and more than doubled, to 213,042, in 1990. The levels remained unprecedentedly high in subsequent years after the Soviet Union collapsed: 179,720 in 1991; 109,366 in 1992; 104,713 in 1993; 96,689 in 1994.[78] Jackson and organized labor also turned out to have sounder commercial instincts than the Republican presidents of the 1970s or their allies in the business community clamoring to grant the Soviet Union MFN and to give it more credit. When West Germany and other Western European nations, free from the restraints of the Jackson-Vanik and Stevenson amendments, pursued the kinds of economic policies Nixon and Kissinger had advocated, all they received was a mountain of debt that the Eastern bloc nations could not pay. These loans, commercial credits, and transfers of technology ended up subsidizing rather than liberalizing a Soviet regime that defined the West as its mortal enemy.[79]

Leading Soviet dissidents of all religious backgrounds still unanimously regard Jackson-Vanik as vital to their cause, as a chisel that helped crack the Soviet empire. Soviet ambassador Dobrynin suggests unintentionally that they were right to do so. The most important reason for the Kremlin opposing Jackson-Vanik "was not often heard," Dobrynin wrote in his memoirs. "In the closed society of the Soviet Union, the Kremlin was afraid of emigration in general (irrespective of nationality or religion) lest an escape hatch from the happy land of socialism seem to offer a degree of liberalization that might destabilize the domestic situation."[80] Jackson personally intervened on behalf of hundreds of courageous individuals, who looked upon him as their hero: Andrei Sakharov and Elena Bonner, Alexander Solzhenitsyn, Simas Kurdirka, Vladimir Bukovsky, and Natan Sharansky, to name just a few.[81] In the words of Sharansky himself:

> Each time when I hear the name of Henry Jackson I am inevitably reminded of the 51 volumes of my criminal case. . . . Prior to my trial, while reading all these volumes from my so-called case, I could find there names of my fellow "official accomplices." . . . But among those names, there was one name mentioned not just once, not just dozens, but hundreds of times, the name of the man who was singled out at the head of this plot, as my closest and most important comrade in crime. It was the

name [of a person] whom I never met, whom I never spoke with on the telephone, but whose very name symbolized for us all the best that was in the West and all the people in the West who came to our support when we needed it in our struggle. . . . It was the name of Senator Henry Jackson.[82]

Although détente survived in the short run, the Jackson Amendment eventually succeeded in its larger purpose of reminding the American people of the intimate linkage between Soviet tyranny at home and the threat the Soviets posed to the free world abroad. "Jackson-Vanik certainly established what type of regime the Soviet Union really was," said Senator Moynihan. "You were in a jail which you could not escape."[83] Kissinger himself acknowledged that Jackson-Vanik was "a tactically brilliant stroke . . . of public pressuring the Soviet Union."[84] Soviet Ambassador Dobrynin agreed that "no other single question did more to sour the atmosphere of detente than the question of Jewish emigration." The Soviet ambassador paid this compliment to Jackson's skill if not his judgment:

> A vitriolic but politically sophisticated campaign to promote free emigration from the Soviet Union . . . [was] led by Senator Henry (Scoop) Jackson, a conservative Democrat from the state of Washington with strong presidential ambitions and a long record as an opponent of the Soviet Union. The opposition [to détente] coalesced around a request by Nixon in the spring of 1973 for Congress to grant the Soviet Union "most favored nation" trading status. . . . Liberals wanted to make our MFN status dependent on Moscow lifting all restrictions on emigration from the Soviet Union. Conservatives were against granting MFN status simply because they were against detente as such. All this prompted a debate that blighted U.S.-Soviet relations ever after.[85]

HENRY JACKSON AND CHINA

Henry Jackson's zealous advocacy of strengthening ties to Communist China (PRC) constituted the third major component of his grand strategy to revive the policy of vigilant containment against the Soviet Union. By 1969 the deepening Sino-Soviet rift had persuaded him that China no longer saw the United States as its main enemy. He believed that Beijing now pursued a pragmatic rather than a revolutionary foreign policy geared to containing the Soviet threat the PRC deemed paramount. Accordingly, he became a leading proponent of improving Sino-American relations even before Kissinger's secret trip to China in 1971. In February 1969, Jackson delivered a major address urging that U.S. policy toward Communist China should aim to increase the chance of more normal relations if and when Beijing was willing to reciprocate. He called specifically for the resumption of U.S.-Chinese ambassadorial talks, which occurred a year later in Warsaw, Poland. In early 1971, he joined those who urged that the PRC join the United Nations. In February 1973, he called for prompt diplomatic recognition of the PRC and severing all diplomatic ties with Taiwan. Jackson also established close ties with the Chinese liaison office that opened in Washington, D.C., in 1973.[86]

The Chinese reciprocated Jackson's enthusiasm. They saw him not only as a serious contender for the presidency in 1976 but also as the leading opponent of the policy of détente, which they opposed with equal ardor. In the spring of 1974, the PRC invited Jackson to visit China.[87] He made the first of his four official trips there in July. The Chinese gave him a warm welcome, and he got on famously with Vice Premier Deng Xiaoping, with whom he had several one-on-one conversations. He, Deng, and the other Chinese leaders with whom he met concurred on the dangers of détente and the need for greater resistance to Soviet expansionism. Like Jackson, Deng often compared détente with the British appeasement of Germany during the 1930s. Henry and Helen Jackson also met with Premier Zhou Enlai, who was terminally ill with cancer. It was the highlight of the trip for Jackson, who ironically had worried until then that the Chinese had fobbed him off on lower level officials such as Deng. Jackson noticed that Zhou was short of breath, his hands shook, and his color was bad. Zhou pointed to his chest and said that it was his heart. Helen Jackson noticed a protrusion in his abdomen and sensed the smell of death. His physical deterioration did not affect his lucidity. Zhou conveyed Mao's regrets that he could not meet with Senator Jackson. The Chairman had said, however, that "it was important for him to do so." Zhou emphasized the lack of trustworthiness of the Soviets and the Soviet threat to NATO. He commended Jackson for resisting Senator Mike Mansfield's efforts to reduce American troop commitments in Europe.[88]

Jackson left China even more convinced that "the Chinese have a rather realistic view of the geopolitical situation on the Eurasion landmass . . .

and the expansionist and unrealiable nature of the Soviet Union." Upon his return to the United States, he counseled the Nixon administration to set aside its declared policy of evenhandedness toward the Soviet Union and China and of trying to improve relations with both. He thought the United States should lean heavily toward China in order to put more pressure on the Soviets. "We must grasp this moment in history," he proclaimed, "when geopolitical considerations have brought us together—to build a web of relations which will promote peace, especially as China moves ahead to become a nuclear and industrial power."[89] In this case, Jackson's criticism of the administration exaggerated the real differences between them. Nixon and Kissinger also strove to employ China as a geopolitical counterweight to the Soviet Union, notwithstanding their public rhetoric portraying their policy as evenhanded.[90]

Jackson's China policy offended many of his closest allies in the battle over détente who found the Chinese version of communism no less repugnant than the Soviet one. Jackson rejoined that the United States had a powerful strategic interest in joining with the PRC to oppose a Soviet Union that was militarily very powerful and geopolitically very aggressive. So he was willing to downplay the flagrant disregard of human rights in the PRC to enlist its support against the greater danger. He also thought that, in due course, the PRC would evolve in a more benign direction. At that point, he did not regard the PRC as a nation with imperial ambitions. Deng Xiaoping also impressed him greatly.[91] Norman Podhoretz, the neoconservative editor of *Commentary* and a great admirer of Jackson, accepted the senator's geopolitical logic but doubted whether propitiating the Chinese contributed any more to containment of the Soviet Union than treating them with benign neglect. He observed that the number of Soviet divisions pinned down on the Chinese border did not increase significantly after Kissinger and Jackson went to Beijing. Podhoretz borrowed one of Jackson's main arguments against détente with the Soviet Union in raising doubts about the policy of befriending China that Jackson advocated: namely, that closely aligning with a brutal communist regime deprived the Soviet-American conflict of the moral significance necessary to sustain the will of the American people to wage it.[92] William F. Buckley's *National Review*, usually in lockstep with Jackson on Soviet affairs, echoed Podhoretz's criticism of his stand on China: "The People's Republic, in fact, is a far more totalitarian state than the Soviet

Union, against whose repressive policies the Senator has made it his trademark to thunder."[93]

In retrospect, the geopolitical necessity for some kind of rapprochement with China during the 1970s seems overwhelming, in spite of the legitimate apprehensions Jackson's critics on the conservative side raised. What those critics did discern correctly is that more than geopolitics spurred Jackson to crusade for closer ties with the PRC. From his boyhood in Everett, Jackson had always admired the Chinese, a sentiment inspired by the novels of Pearl Buck and by his own experiences in Washington State. The marvelous reception he received in the PRC enhanced his favorable attitude toward the regime. In contrast to the Russians, whom he found heavy and ponderous, he genuinely liked the Chinese, their sense of humor, and the elegance of their geopolitical analysis. He had a soft spot for them, and it inclined him to gloss over many PRC brutalities for which he would have criticized the Soviet Union or other regimes.[94] Jackson's position on China grew softer over the years. By 1980, he had embraced the popular but dubious notion that the PRC could have been an ally rather than an adversary in Asia from the beginning had we listened to the advice of the China hands in the State Department rather than demonizing the PRC as a hostile, ideologically driven regime aligned with the Soviet Union. Jackson thus told his daughter Anna Marie in May 1980:

> The great tragedy of the McCarthy period was our failure to understand China. The result was that we were not able to listen to our scholars or experts on China, the people who understood that our long-term interest was with the PRC, not with Chaing Kai Shek or Taiwan. Korea might not have happened. Vietnam might not have happened. The greatest mistake in American diplomacy and intelligence during this century was our failure to understand mainland China, the fact that while they were Communists, they were not Russians. This was a major error in U.S. policy—Had we understood China properly and had not had the McCarthy hysteria, Vietnam would never have happened. China would have been our ally in that part of the world.[95]

The squalidness of Mao's life so painstakingly detailed in Dr. Li Zhisui's biography of him would have shocked Jackson, who remained uncharacteristically obtuse about the dark side of the PRC until the day he died.[96]

Chapter 15

The Ford Administration

THE BATTLE OVER détente between Jackson and Kissinger carried all the way through President Gerald Ford's abbreviated term in office. Jackson and the president had known each other since Jackson's days in the House of Representatives, and they had a good rapport and mutual respect for one another.[1] Ardently anticommunist, internationalist, and pro-defense during his quarter century as a congressman from Michigan, Ford's core convictions on these issues were more conservative than those of the more pragmatic Nixon. He also understood far better than his predecessor the importance of consulting with Congress on foreign affairs, especially with the legislature reasserting its prerogatives to rein back the so-called imperial presidency.

But Jackson regarded Ford as only a caretaker president unable to cope with the serious troubles that beset the nation: the severe economic crisis precipitated by the Arab oil embargo and the quadrupling of oil prices after the 1973 Arab-Israeli War; the erosion of the public's faith in American political institutions exacerbated by the Watergate crisis; and the humiliation and recrimination brought about by the final collapse of America's South Vietnamese ally in May 1975.[2] Retaining Kissinger as his secretary of state, Ford decided largely to follow the course of détente he had inherited from Nixon. He also enjoyed a much better personal relationship with Kissinger than Nixon had, for there was little fondness or trust between those two despite their common outlook on foreign affairs. Even while in the Congress, Ford did not have a good relationship with secretary of defense James Schlesinger, Jackson's closest ally and Kissinger's most relentless critic within the administration. The Ford-Schlesinger relationship deteriorated precipitously after Ford became president.[3] All this spelled difficulty for the president's political though not personal relationship with Henry Jackson.[4]

President Ford sided with Kissinger in the battle over Jackson-Vanik, which his administration lost. Jackson also objected strenuously to the Vladivostok Agreement that the president and Brezhnev concluded in late November 1974 after two days of talks in that major Soviet port city on the Pacific—the eastern terminus of the Trans-Siberian Railway. Envisaged as the framework for a SALT II Treaty, the agreement imposed equal ceilings of 2,400 intercontinental delivery vehicles and limited each side to 1,320 MIRVed vehicles. It imposed no constraints, however, on Soviet heavy missiles, forward-based systems, or missile modernization.[5]

Jackson castigated the Vladivostok Agreement for sanctioning a ten-year arms buildup, for authorizing "astonishingly high MIRV levels," and for legitimizing "the massive continuation of Soviet arms expenditures." Considering, continued Jackson, that the administration has requested unlimited authority to extend low-interest, subsidized loans to the Soviets, "we will end up under Vladivostok subsidizing the Soviet strategic weapons program as well as financing our own." Its results, he said "could also be a massive Soviet proliferation of and advantage in strategic warheads, . . . since the Soviet missiles that can be equipped with MIRVs have 3, 4, or even 6 times the payload of the U.S. missiles that can be so equipped." Jackson also objected to the exclusion of the Soviet Union's new Backfire bomber from aggregate ceilings and any constraints on the number or range of U.S. cruise missiles that Secretary of State Kissinger conceived of merely as a bargaining chip to trade away. The United States possessed a significant advantage in this category of nuclear missiles that were subsonic, relatively inexpensive, highly accurate, and capable of delivery from land, sea, or air. Again, Jackson called for obtaining equal ceilings at sharply reduced levels rather than agreeing to "an arms buildup agreement." Jackson kept his vow to "conduct extensive hearings on the Vladivostok Agreement that will enable the American people to make their own judgement—as I have made mine—to insist on strategic force reductions in a SALT II agreement."[6]

With the collaboration of Secretary of Defense Schlesinger, who had criticized the agreement largely on the same grounds, Jackson led the coalition in the Senate that managed to shelve a vote on the ratification of SALT II for the remainder of the Ford presidency. Jackson and Schlesinger attacked not only the specifics of the Vladivostok treaty but also Kissinger's entire approach to arms control, including SALT I. In hearings before the Subcommittee on Arms Control on March 5, 1975, they contended that Kissinger's technique of substituting unilateral U.S. interpretations for signed Soviet promises was the worst possible way to enter an agreement.[7]

Jackson assailed at great length the wording of the provision in the SALT I agreement that sought to limit sharply the extent to which the Soviets would be "able to add to their throw weight, or the explosive missile power of their missile force." The administration had acquiesced to Soviet deployment of the SS-19 ICBM, which greatly exceeded the U.S. definition of heavy missile, despite assurances to Jackson during the SALT I hearings that it would not do so. Jackson also charged that the administration had not investigated vigorously the testing and deployment of certain types of radar that might (and, as it turns out, did) constitute a serious violation of the ABM agreement. "A fully informed President could not have said, without qualification, as did President Ford on June 25th, 1975, that the Soviet Union has not violated the SALT Agreement nor used any loopholes," insisted Jackson. "This statement is false. . . . The lesson is clear. Any SALT II agreement must be precise."[8]

Schlesinger's collaboration with Jackson in opposition to détente was a major reason, though not the only one, that Ford fired him on November 2, 1975. On the same day, the president, who had never liked Kissinger holding the dual positions of national security adviser and secretary of state, relieved him of the former.[9] Jackson and Ronald Reagan, the former two-term Republican governor of California who was challenging Ford for the 1976 nomination largely on an anti-détente theme, pilloried the president for purging Schlesinger.[10] Jackson threatened to oppose the confirmation of Donald Rumsfeld, Ford's staff coordinator, who was chosen as Schlesinger's replacement. Rumsfeld's confirmation hearings before the Armed Services Committee produced several acrimonious exchanges between the two men before Jackson grudgingly relented.[11] Rumsfeld's performance as secretary of defense dispelled Jackson's fears that he was soft on the Soviets. In some ways, he turned out to be even more hawkish than Schlesinger. Paul Wolfowitz remembered, for example, that Rumsfeld stood up to Kissinger in January 1976 even more firmly than Schlesinger had done to thwart the secretary from accepting Soviet demands for tight constraints on U.S. long-range cruise missiles.[12]

By January 1975, Jackson had broken with the administration over the war in Vietnam, which the senator until then had backed staunchly in defiance of the liberal critics within the Democratic Party. He opposed President Ford's request for $300 million in military aid to South Vietnam. In his public justification for this decision, he stressed that no further aid could save a corrupt South Vietnamese regime that "lacked the determination, leadership, and direction to fight." The war had already drained precious resources from the more important strategic forces in Europe and the Middle East, Jackson explained. It was, in his view, high time to jettison the lost cause of the Thieu regime.[13]

Jackson's public rationale accounts partly but not entirely for this reversal of his long-standing views on Vietnam, a reversal that angered many conservatives; and even some of Jackson's great admirers such as Wolfowitz attributed his opposition to Vietnam aid partly to the expedience of his presidential campaign.[14] They were right. The reversal came only after a vigorous internal debate among the Jackson staff. Dorothy Fosdick and Brian Corcoran argued that opposing Ford on Vietnam aid might help mute the opposition of doves in the party to his presidential candidacy. Richard Perle argued that Jackson should back the president. In the end, "these political realities," as Perle called them, prevailed. A desire to propitiate the liberals in his party accounts partly, too, for Jackson's 1975 vote against the administration's request for aid to the noncommunist side in Angola, although it coincided with his convictions as well: he never regarded southern Africa as crucial for the outcome of the Cold War. He also abhorred the racialist regime of South Africa that was backing the anticommunist rebels.[15]

The final collapse of South Vietnam in April 1975 embroiled Jackson in yet another running argument with the administration. Based on information he had received from Admiral Zumwalt, Jackson accused the executive branch of misleading "a foreign government and the United States Congress about U.S. commitments to South Vietnam in 1972–3."[16] Zumwalt alleged that, unknown to the American Public or the Congress, President Nixon had made a secret agreement with South Vietnamese President Thieu promising that America would respond vigorously in the event of any major truce violations and would replace equipment used up by the South Vietnamese Army. Thieu, claimed Zumwalt, had demanded this pledge as his price for going along with a very unfavorable truce that had left the enemy intact in his country, in the south.[17]

Jackson's and Zumwalt's charges compelled the Ford administration to acknowledge that Nixon and Thieu had made confidential exchanges in which the United States had pledged to respond with "full force" and "take swift and severe retaliatory action" if North Vietnam violated the 1973 Paris Peace Accords. White House spokesmen argued, however, that what the Nixon administration had said privately matched what it had said publicly. Jackson disagreed. "There is a fateful difference," he countered, "between the administration publicly expressing a desire to retain certain options in the event of North Vietnamese violations of the Paris accords, and the president secretly committing the United States to exercise one or more of these options."[18] The issue went "to the very integrity of our foreign policy," Jackson declared. "A bipartisan foreign policy must begin with the kind of openness between the legislative and executive branches that is the heart of any such policy."[19]

On July 2, 1975, President Ford precipitated another major confrontation with Jackson by announcing that he would not meet with the Nobel Prize-winning author Alexander Solzhenitsyn, on the advice of the National Security Council. The president, vice president, Secretary of State Kissinger, and the leaders of the House and Senate also turned down an invitation to an AFL-CIO banquet that George Meany held in Solzhenitsyn's honor. Henry Jackson, Secretary of Defense Schlesinger, and Daniel Patrick Moynihan, then the U.S. ambassador to the United Nations, did attend. The administration spurned Solzhenitsyn because of his hostility toward détente.[20]

This episode indeed epitomized the fundamental differences between Jackson and Kissinger over how to conduct U.S. foreign policy. It was Kissinger who convinced Ford that the president should not invite the exiled Soviet writer to the White House.[21] Many of the president's advisers, including Brent Scowcroft, Kissinger's eventual replacement at NSC, seconded Kissinger's recommendation and the logic behind it.[22] Kissinger considered Solzhenitsyn's three-volume *Gulag Archipelago*, which chronicled the grotesque horrors of the Soviet regime under Stalin, a great moral event. He even showed it to President Ford. When, however, Peter Rodman and some of his other aides suggested that the administration use the *Gulag* to generate support for a strong foreign policy among liberals rediscovering their anticommunism, Kissinger refused, dismissing the idea as too provocative. If the administration whipped up support for an ideological crusade, he feared it could not turn it off again. Kissinger was, according to Rodman, "congenitally distrustful of ideological movements, even our own." He warned publicly that the symbolic meeting between the president and Solzhenitsyn could disadvantage the U.S. government. "If I understand the message of Solzhenitsyn, it is that the United States should pursue an aggressive policy to overthrow the Soviet system," Kissinger remarked at a news conference in Milwaukee. "If his views became the national policy of the United States, we would be confronted with a considerable threat of military conflict. . . . I believe that the consequences of these views would not be acceptable to the American people." Kissinger especially did not want to risk sabotaging the upcoming Helsinki Summit, scheduled for late July, where the administration expected to conclude a major agreement with Brezhnev.[23]

Jackson scolded Kissinger for distorting Solzhenitsyn's views: "If Kissinger and Ford had met with Solzhenitsyn rather than cowering with fear of the Soviet reaction to such a meeting, they would have learned that all Solzhenitsyn is asking for is a detente without illusions, for an American-Soviet relationship that promoted the cause of human rights and genuine peace."[24] Jackson, along with Jesse Helms, a conservative Republican senator from North Carolina, and Clifford Case, a liberal Republican senator from New Jersey, invited Solzhenitsyn to address a group of members from both houses of Congress in the Senate office building.[25] Solzhenitsyn inveighed upon them not to forget "that the tender dawn of détente was precisely the time when the starvation rations in the prisons and concentration camps in the U.S.S.R. were even skimpier, while in recent months when more and more Western speechmakers were pointing to the beneficial consequences of detente, the Soviet Union put the finishing touches on an even more novel and important improvement in its system of punishment." For freedom to triumph over Soviet tyranny, Solzhenitsyn declared, the United States "will have need not only of exceptional men, but of great men."[26]

The uproar over Solzhenitsyn set the stage for the next major confrontation between Jackson and the administration. From July 30 to August 1, 1975, President Ford attended the Conference on Security and Cooperation in Europe (CSCE), held in Helsinki. The Soviets had long pushed for such a conference, to which various American administrations had responded coolly. The Ford administration changed its mind, however, once the Soviets signed on to a new agreement on the status of West Berlin and expressed their willingness to begin mutual and balanced force reduction (MBFR) talks in Vienna.[27] The president also hoped thereby to placate America's West German allies. The ruling Social Democrats in West Germany were more intent than ever on engaging in Ospolitik, a version of détente far more conciliatory to the Soviets than Kissinger's.[28]

The thirty-five participants to the conference signed agreements (the Helsinki Final Act) specifying their commitments in three significant areas ("baskets"): security, economic, and cultural cooperation. The United States and the other signatories recognized the postwar boundaries of Europe, dividing it into east and west. In exchange, the Soviets agreed to basket three, pledging them to respect basic principles of human rights such as freedom of movement and exchange of ideas. President Ford hailed the results as a great victory for American foreign policy.[29] Conservatives, Cold War liberals, and dissidents such as Solzhenitsyn excoriated the president for signing the Helsinki Final Act, which, in their eyes, legitimized the Soviet Union's domination of Eastern Europe.[30] "The European Security Conference," Jackson complained, was "yet another example of the sort of one-sided agreement that has become the hallmark of the Nixon-Ford Administrations. . . . For three decades, the Soviets have sought formal Western recognition of their domination of Eastern Europe, just as they have sought international recognition of their conquest of the Baltic states. The President's signature on the CSCE declarations will be invoked by the Soviets as a sign of the West's retreat from this crucial point of principle." Jackson complained, too, "that the CSCE pronouncements dealing with human rights were so imprecise and so hedged as to raise considerable doubt about whether they can and will be seriously implemented. Unless the government of the United States makes it absolutely clear that it is committed to implementing in full the provisions of the freer movement of people and ideas, it is doubtful that anything will be salvaged from them."[31]

Ultimately, the Final Act had results unanticipated by its most ardent defenders and its sharpest critics. The Soviet Union and the government of West Germany did indeed see it as legitimizing the Soviet postwar domination of Eastern Europe.[32] The Ford administration also had little faith in the efficacy of basket three's human rights provisions, as it demonstrated graphically just weeks before by rebuffing Solzhenitsyn in order to placate Moscow. Confounding expectations on all sides, however, the human rights provisions of Helsinki helped bring about the demise not only of the Soviet empire in Eastern Europe, but also the Soviet regime itself. A courageous group of Eastern bloc activists, dissenters, and democrats employed these provisions with courage and imagination to undermine the ideological and political structure on which Soviet tyranny rested. Under successive administrations that rejected the Nixon-Kissinger-Ford passive approach to human rights, the United States regained the will and confidence relentlessly to press the Soviets to live up to the principles of basket three.[33] Natan Sharansky, one of those courageous dissidents who spent years in a Soviet gulag for demanding that the Soviet Union permit him to practice his faith, insists that Henry Jackson was instrumental to the felicitous consequences of Helsinki's human rights provisions:

> Jackson understood that you cannot deal with the Soviet Union by ignoring the issue of human rights. You cannot ignore the nature of the Soviet Union. You have to understand that if you want serious, real agreements which are based on trust, lasting agreements, you must demand from the Soviet Union that they change their behavior. We see the idea of linkage so clearly in the Helsinki Act—there must be parallel progress in the first, second and third baskets—in arms negotiations, economic cooperation, and in human rights. This idea could not have been so powerfully expressed in the Helsinki Agreement had there not been all those discussions for many years before the Jackson Amendment, about the legitimacy and nonlegitimacy of such linkage.[34]

All this did not become apparent until a decade after the divisive détente debate of the 1970s. What had become apparent by January 1976 was Jackson's remarkable success in galvanizing a nascent but potentially powerful coalition against détente, which identified him as their leader. He belonged, to be sure, to a dwindling remnant of the Democratic Party. As his failed presidential bid of 1976 would demonstrate, the liberal Left ascendant within the party continued to disparage his anticommunist internationalism and suspicion of the Soviet Union. The controversial Kissinger remained enormously popular with the American public at large. There were, though, some positive signs on the horizon. Jackson had commenced the daunting task of rebuilding the anticommunist coalition with the Jackson Amendment to SALT and the Jackson-Vanik Amendment to the Trade Act of 1974. William Buckley's conservative *National Review* remained vigilantly anticommunist. Ronald Reagan's surprisingly strong challenge to President Ford in the 1976 Republic primaries indicated that opposition to détente ran deep in a growing segment of a renascent conservative movement.[35]

The neoconservatives, a small but influential group of traditional Cold War liberals who rallied to Jackson, mounted a sustained defense of the policy of vigilant containment that he advocated and a sustained attack on the policy of détente that he criticized. Norman Podhoretz, editor of the American Jewish Committee's *Commentary*, stands out as the most important of the neoconservative intellectuals in the area of foreign policy. Distressed that revulsion against the Vietnam War had discredited the entire policy of containment among many liberals, incensed by the growing hostility toward Israel from the left typified by the anti-Zionist campaign of the Communist-Arab-African coalition at the United Nations during the 1970s, this former dissenter on the Vietnam War transformed *Commentary* into a bastion for anticommunist intellectuals seeking to restore anticommunism as a prominent part of U.S. foreign policy. Jackson's visceral anticommunism and antitotalitarianism thus brought him into the orbit of Jewish neoconservatives despite the subtle but important distinction in their outlook. The senator viewed the threat to Israel as a manifestation of the totalitarian threat he considered paramount. Some neoconservatives viewed Soviet totalitarianism as the threat to Israel they considered paramount.[36]

Podhoretz's close friend Daniel Patrick Moynihan gained for these neoconservative views a wide public hearing during his brief but memorable tenure as American ambassador to the United Nations from June 1975 to March 1976. Convinced that the United States must defend liberal democracy defiantly against the ferocious anticapitalist, antidemocratic assault of third world and communist regimes, Moynihan did so with gusto in a series of *Commentary* articles and U.N. speeches.[37] Virtually all the prominent neoconservatives, including Moynihan, would back Jackson for president in 1976.[38] As Podhoretz put it, "Jackson was appealing because he represented the halfway house to which we retreated, moving

away from the left. Scoop not only was the guy who was right about foreign policy. We also looked on him as the potential savior of the Democratic Party."[39]

Jackson also could draw upon a burgeoning group of outside experts
who regarded him as the most persistent and credible critic of détente. In
1976, George Bush, director of the CIA, convened a group of outside experts, known as Team B, to conduct a study of Soviet strategic intentions
as an alternative to what the inside intelligence community (Team A) had
done. Professor Richard Pipes of Harvard headed Team B, which also included Paul Nitze, Paul Wolfowitz of the Arms Control and Disarmament Agency, and Seymour Weiss, former director of the State Department's Bureau of Political-Military Affairs. All four had long-standing and
close ties with Senator Jackson.[40] Albert Wohlstetter, another longtime
member of the Jackson circle, acted as a major catalyst for Team B's formation. In 1974, he had published a series of articles in *Foreign Policy*
demonstrating that the U.S. intelligence community had systematically
underestimated Soviet strategic offensive capabilities. Team B rejected
the assumption of Team A, most liberals, and the Nixon administration
that the Soviets had embraced the American doctrine of MAD based on
nuclear parity. On the contrary, this group concluded that the Soviet
Union sought to achieve a nuclear war-fighting, war-winning capability
against the West. Much of the press reacted negatively to Team B's purportedly confidential report, the basic content of which it obtained by
leaks.[41] Jackson hailed the report, which affirmed his basic position. He
not only praised George Bush for his role in forming Team B, but he also
urged him to stay on as CIA director for the Carter administration.[42] Neither Carter nor Bush had any interest in that proposition.

In November 1976, Nitze and another close confident of Jackson's, Eugene Rostow, professor of law at Yale University, spearheaded the formation of the Committee on Present Danger, a bipartisan organization composed of 60 percent Democrats and 40 percent Republicans directed at
restoring "the strength and coherence of American foreign policy."[43]
Prominent Jackson supporters, advisers, and admirers from both sides of
the aisle predominated: Jeane Kirkpatrick, Georgetown University professor of government; Admiral Elmo Zumwalt; Max Kampelman; David
Packard, undersecretary of defense during Nixon's first term; Lane Kirkland, secretary-treasurer of the AFL-CIO; Richard Pipes; Richard Allen,

formerly Nixon's deputy assistant for international economic affairs; and Norman Podhoretz. "The principal threat to our nation, to world peace, and to the cause of human freedom," read the committee's policy statement, "is the Soviet drive for dominance based on an unparalleled military buildup. The Soviet Union has not altered its long-held goal of a world dominated from a single center—Moscow."[44]

Passions still run deep in the controversy over the policy of détente, which unraveled during the 1970s. William Fulbright, whose defeat in the Arkansas Democratic primary of 1974 Henry Jackson's Washington staff celebrated, exonerates the Soviet Union from any responsibility for subverting détente. Instead, he blames Jackson for intervening "to destroy it."[45] The revisionist Kissinger of the 1980s and the 1990s knows better than to exonerate the Soviet Union. As he concedes, the 1970s witnessed an "extraordinary surge in the expansionism on the part of the Soviet Union," confident that the correlation of forces had shifted in its favor.[46] It was then that collapse of Indochina, which the North Vietnamese consummated with Soviet arms, intensified the agonizing self-doubt and polar divisions over the proper course of American foreign policy. It was then that the Soviet military embarked on the most massive peacetime military buildup in history that consumed one quarter of the nation's GDP just as the United States slowed down its defense programs considerably in the hope of inducing the Soviets to reciprocate. It was then that the Soviets established themselves in Aden, Angola, Ethiopia. It was then that the virulently anti-American block of third world and communist regimes encouraged by the Soviet Union reached the peak of its influence at the United Nations. It was then that the collapse of the shah in Iran and the humiliating hostage crisis there a year later seemed to have sunk the United States to the nadir of its post–World War II international position. It was then that the Soviet Union escalated the Cold War by invading Afghanistan.[47]

As the revisionist Kissinger of the 1990s concedes, too, the Reagan years demonstrated that a bolder policy toward the Soviet Union, almost identical to what Henry Jackson advocated, "had much to recommend it." Kissinger argues, however, that such a policy could not have succeeded in his day, with the United States still recovering from Vietnam. He maintains that his conception of détente could have averted or ameliorated the dangerous erosion of America's geopolitical position during the 1970s had

Jackson's crusade and the Watergate crisis paralyzing the Nixon presidency not worked in tandem to undermine the Nixon administration.[48]

There is some merit in Kissinger's argument that Jackson overestimated the realm of the possible given the domestic constraints the administration faced. Doubtless, the Watergate crisis also did weaken the abilities of the Nixon and Ford presidencies to manage détente. Doubtless, too, the Nixon-Ford-Kissinger version of détente was more tough-minded than either President Carter's version or what the Jackson forces admitted at the time. Yet Jackson was also right that Kissinger underestimated the realm of the possible because of his congenital pessimism about America's prospects. Nixon and Kissinger bear a large measure of responsibility for the potency of antidefense sentiment in the nation during the 1970s, which their later writings deplore, and which Henry Jackson resisted stoutly. They underestimated American power and the capacity of the nation to recover its self-confidence in the aftermath of Vietnam. Many of their actions also had the same enervating effect on the pro-defense coalition that Henry Jackson led. During 1973–74, for example, Kissinger courted William Fulbright and other Senate doves assiduously while cutting off most contact with Jackson because of his criticism of the administration over détente and Middle East policy.[49] Even a secretary of state less shrewd than Kissinger should have known that abandoning Jackson for Fulbright, the paladin of New Left sensibilities on matters of foreign policy, would hurt any attempt to rally American people to support the policy of boldness the revisionist Kissinger professes to prefer.

Perhaps Kissinger did know. The record indicates that Nixon and Kissinger took much of their extravagant rhetoric about détente more seriously than their later writings imply. They really did seem to believe that the Soviet Union had become a traditional imperial power rather than a revolutionary and totalitarian one. They did strive to reassure the Soviets through arms-control agreements and the expansion of trade, which they anticipated would moderate Soviet ambitions by giving them a stake of self-interest in cooperating with the United States. Kissinger said so himself: "Over time, trade and investment may leaven the autarchic tendencies of the Soviet system, and by gradual association of the Soviet economy and the world economy, foster a degree of interdependence that adds an element of stability to the political equation."[50] What he did not grasp was that entangling trade arrangements could not constrain Soviet ambitions or create pressure to liberalize the system so long as the Soviet Union remained a totalitarian regime. Jackson understood that détente had very different meanings for the Soviet Union and the United States. Historian Martin Malia sums it up best: "For the West détente was a gradual way to transcend the Cold War; for the East it was a gradual way to win it." International trade did not hasten, but delayed, the regime's demise by allowing a declining Soviet economy to enter into "a parasitical economic relationship" with the West, just as Jackson had said it would.[51] Even before the Watergate crisis, the Soviet Union had already perceived détente as a shift in the correlation of forces in its favor and as a sign of American weakness that the emasculation of the Nixon presidency exacerbated.[52]

Henry Jackson exhibited the persistence, strength of character, knowledge, and legislative talent to challenge the conventional wisdom that détente was desirable, possible, and the best the United States could do. Through exhaustive hearings and key pieces of legislation, it was he, not Kissinger, who did more than anybody else in American politics during the 1970s to make possible the policy of boldness during the 1980s that the secretary of state now defends. Fulbright and Kissinger are right about one thing. Despite his assurances that he would have supported a genuine détente, Jackson did truly intend to subvert that policy during the 1970s. What impelled him was the belief that the Soviet regime must collapse before a genuine détente could occur.[53] Few legislators in American history have ever succeeded so brilliantly in redirecting American foreign policy. Although many of Kissinger's conclusions are debatable, his assessment of Jackson's importance is right on the mark:

All this [criticism of détente] might have remained inchoate sniping but for the emergence of a formidable leader able to unite the two strands of opposition and direct them to concrete issues that lent themselves to legislative intervention in foreign policy. Senator Henry M. Jackson of the state of Washington was a mainstream Democrat, popular with the labor movement for his progressive views on domestic policy; he had earned his spurs on the conservative side because of his staunch advocacy of a strong national defense and his courageous support of two administrations in the Vietnam war.

. . . Solid, thoughtful, stubborn as could be expected from the combination of Scandinavian origin and Lutheran theology, Jackson mastered problems not with flashy rhetoric or brilliant maneuvers but with relentless application and undeflectable persistence. He had carefully studied Soviet strategy and tactics; he was convinced that their goal was to undermine the free world, that any agreement was to the Soviets only a tactical maneuver to bring about our downfall more surely.

. . . Jackson was not a man to welcome debate over firmly held convictions; he proceeded to implement his by erecting a series of legislative hurdles that gradually paralyzed East-West policy. He was aided by one of the ablest—and most ruthless—staffs that I encountered in Washington.[54]

Chapter 16

Not in the Cards: The 1976 Presidential Campaign

O N FEBRUARY 7, 1975, Henry Jackson formally declared his presidential candidacy for a second time before an audience of about two hundred at the National Press Club in Washington, D.C. He pledged "to conduct a campaign not of rallies and slogans, but a campaign of proposals and issues." He called President Ford an "honest and honorable man, a decent man," who had nevertheless failed on the critical issues of the "deepening economic recession, mounting inflation, the energy crisis, and foreign policy." He intended to pursue the nomination by spending the majority of his time "not on the road, but on the job." He would run for president "on the basis of effective programs and solid accomplishments in the United States Senate." He proclaimed himself the candidate most capable of using "the political process to get the country moving again." On the same night, the Jackson campaign announced his candidacy to the American people in a five-minute documentary created by movie producer David L. Wolper which opened with the senator rising to the applause of an audience of 1,100 people at the Century Plaza Hotel in Los Angeles, then showed the beginning of his speech, and concluded with filmed highlights from the senator's thirty-four-year career in Congress.[1]

HIGH HOPES

The Washington Press Club speech and the documentary attracted much attention from the national press. Indeed, it appeared to many informed observers that Jackson was the front-runner for the 1976 presidential nomination. There were no skeletons in his closet. He was a model of integrity in his public and private life. He had a loving family devoted to his

success as a presidential candidate. Sixty-four years old, he was physically healthy and robust. He rarely missed his daily workout in the Senate
gym while Congress was in session. His son, Peter, usually accompanied
him on Saturday mornings for a swim. For his pending presidential run,
Jackson had slimmed down to a trim 170 pounds. He had required hos-
pitalization only twice since his back problem flared up in December
1954: for surgery to remove kidney stones in December 1974, and for cosmetic surgery to rectify a droopy eyelid in preparation for the campaign.[2]

Jackson also had compiled a remarkable record. Ralph Nader's Study
Group had recently designated him the "most effective senator" in the
U.S. Senate. Largely unknown to the American people while running for
president in 1972, he had solved that problem by February 1975, for his
prominence in the debates over détente and energy had generated an
enormous amount of publicity. Since 1973, he had appeared constantly on
the front pages of major newspapers, on nightly television news, and on
Sunday morning news programs: railing against the high cost of energy;
denouncing SALT, the Soviet record on human rights, and the Soviet
grain deal; and demanding a strong national defense and unswerving U.S.
backing of Israel. Several national polls showed that more than 60 percent
of Americans knew who he was, with his name recognition rapidly rising.
Still other polls showed that he offered President Ford his strongest potential challenge. Ford thought so, too. In November 1975, a Gallup Poll
reported Jackson running in a dead heat with Ford, with each getting
about 44 percent of the vote. A Gallup Poll also ranked Jackson as one of
the ten most admired people in the world for 1973 and 1974. Just days after he declared his candidacy, he appeared on the cover of *Time*, with the
caption "Scoop Out Front." *Newsweek, The New York Times, New York
Magazine, Esquire, New Republic, Atlantic Monthly*, and several other major publications also had previously or would soon run feature stories on
Jackson treating his front-runner status seriously, albeit for some as a
cause for alarm rather than celebration.[3]

Jackson would not have to face three of his most formidable potential
rivals, who had already announced their decisions not to run: Senators
Edward Kennedy, Walter Mondale, and Hubert Humphrey. Candidate
Jackson also appeared to enjoy a huge advantage over the contenders who
had declared or were likely to enter the race. Congressman Morris Udall,
a liberal Democrat from Arizona, would have to overcome the obstacle of

running for president from the House of Representatives, historically a graveyard of presidential ambition. Poor name recognition and financing also plagued the Udall campaign. Lloyd Bentsen, a first-term Democratic senator from Texas, had plenty of money but no record of legislative accomplishment. A defender of the big oil companies, the conservative Bentsen also had little appeal to traditional Democratic constituencies outside the Southwest. Fred R. Harris, the former Oklahoma senator, also lacked money and name recognition. Senator Birch Bayh, a left-of-center Democrat from Indiana, had the attributes of a formidable candidate: good looks, personal magnetism, an impressive legislative record, and organizational talent. Inhibited by his tough reelection campaign in 1974 and the breast cancer of his wife, however, Bayh delayed entering the race until October 1975, too late to mount a successful campaign under post-1968 rules governing the Democratic primary campaigns. Neither Terry Sanford, Democratic governor of North Carolina, nor Sargent Shriver, George McGovern's vice presidential running mate in 1972, had any plausible chance of winning the nomination. Yet those two left-of-center Democrats appeared strong enough to siphon off enough votes from Bayh and Udall so that Jackson could defeat the powerful left wing of his party. Milton Shapp, the Democratic governor of Pennsylvania and the first Jewish presidential candidate, was a nonentity as a candidate. He made Jackson look charismatic by comparison.[4] Governor George Wallace, Democratic governor from Alabama, began the 1976 campaign with more money and better name recognition than any other declared Democratic candidate, including Jackson. He remained popular enough to scare his rivals but not to win the nomination, because of his views on race, which a largely liberal Democratic Party could not abide. Crippled from the waist down by gunshot while campaigning in Maryland in May 1972, Wallace also suffered from chronic health problems that eroded even his core of support. Jimmy Carter, the former one-term Democratic governor from Georgia, had announced his candidacy in December 1974, two months before Jackson. Outside of his home state, however, he was virtually unknown, his campaign woefully short of money.[5]

Jackson had attained his advantage by starting early, planning intensely, and campaigning hard. Since the 1972 Democratic Convention, he had maintained a grueling pace, simultaneously discharging his duties as a powerful senator and a presidential aspirant. He canvassed the country on weekends and when the Senate was not in session, meeting with party leaders, courting organized labor and the Jewish community, and delivering hundreds of speeches, all without missing more than a few Senate votes. In 1974, Jackson traveled to twenty-seven states while leading the Senate with an astounding 99 percent attendance rating. In 1975, he went to thirty-eight states and still maintained his 99 percent rating.[6] Jackson also had taken the lead on some of the most time-consuming and important issues before the Congress: arms control, détente, human rights, national defense, and energy. His crucial role in electing Robert Strauss chairman of the DNC in December 1972 appeared to enhance his presidential prospects as well. Jackson expected that Strauss would manage his presidential campaign as a quid pro quo. When Strauss extricated himself from that commitment in July 1974 by persuading a reluctant Jackson that he would better serve the party by remaining at the DNC, Robert Keefe, Strauss's deputy at the DNC, became Jackson's campaign manager. Keefe had worked in the past presidential campaigns of Hubert Humphrey and Birch Bayh and as a political consultant to the AFL-CIO before joining the Jackson staff.[7]

By July 1974, with the Jackson Planning Committee housed just a few blocks from the senator's office in the Russell Building, Keefe seemed to have assembled a first-rate campaign team. He named Sterling Munro as his chief of staff; Walter Skallerup, a D.C. attorney, as the campaign treasurer; and Brian Corcoran, Jackson's press secretary, as head of the national press operation. The Jackson campaign had widespread and enthusiastic support from the Jewish establishment in Hollywood. Jackson received abundant advice, most of which he ignored, from some of the best producers, media consultants, and joke writers that the entertainment industry had to offer. Thanks to the game plan of Richard Kline, the fundraising coordinator for the campaign, Jackson also had early success in raising money, which seemed to put his opponents at a severe disadvantage. Kline staged $250-a-plate dinners for Jackson in major cities with large Jewish populations, reaping great dividends. By January 1, 1975, the campaign had raised $1.1 million based on the maximum individual contribution limit of $3,000 then pending in the Senate version of the campaign finance reform bill of 1974, before the new law limiting individual contributions to $1,000 came into effect. By the middle of 1975, the Jackson campaign had raised $2.3 million, vastly more than any other candidate but Wallace, who had raised $2.7 million. Jackson also had over $500,000 more in the bank than Wallace because the senator depended less than the governor, or his other opponents, on direct mail as a source of fundraising. It cost a great deal to make money with direct mail. For the Jackson campaign, it cost $1 dollar for every $1.50 returned in the mail. The Jackson campaign anticipated raising $7 to $10 million by February 1, 1976. Under the new federal campaign finance law, Jackson could also expect to receive matching funds of up to $5 million for primary expenses.[8]

The Jackson camp hoped that the end of the Vietnam War would mollify the bitter hostility antiwar liberals felt toward him. He softened some of his positions on national defense and foreign policy in order to broaden his appeal among Liberal Democrats, without sacrificing his core principles. In a major reversal he thus refused in February 1975 to back the administration's request for an additional $300 million in aid to South Vietnam, a regime he had championed for more than twenty years.[9] He also came out in favor of delaying construction of the B-1 strategic bomber, which the Pentagon pressed for as a replacement to the aging B-52. In January 1976 he recommended a $5 to $7 billion cut in the defense budget, an idea he dropped shortly after the campaign ended. In another gesture of conciliation to the left wing of his party, Jackson campaigned in 1974 for several prominent antiwar Democrats who had previously scorned him: Allard Lowenstein from New York; Abner Mikva from Illinois; Father Robert Drinan from Massachusetts; and McGovern's former campaign manager, Gary Hart from Colorado. He also joined liberal Democrats and liberal Republicans in denouncing President Ford's decision to pardon Richard Nixon in September 1974. Jackson appeared likewise to have achieved a partial reconciliation with Senator Edward Kennedy, who signaled that he no longer adamantly opposed Jackson's candidacy for president. One reason for that, as chairman of the Interior Committee and the Senate's foremost expert on energy, Jackson was the key figure in passing energy legislation. With the Northeast more dependent on foreign oil than any other region, Kennedy needed cooperation to protect Massachusetts from the higher costs of energy that Ford's program would entail. Kennedy and Jackson announced in late January 1975 their cosponsorship of a measure to delay the imposition of Ford's increase in the tax on oil imports.[10]

THE POLITICS OF OIL

Though conviction as well as expedience impelled him to focus on it, Jackson thought his prominent role in the energy debate would help propel him to the White House. An enthusiast of public power since the 1930s, Jackson during the 1970s transposed his deep suspicion of private power companies to the major oil companies. He believed that the answer to the energy crisis lay not with the private sector or the operation of the free market, but with an activist federal government creating incentives for increased production and conservation. An unflagging believer since World War II in the efficacy of wage and price controls, he fought against eliminating or reducing price controls on oil and natural gas, opposed any increase in tariffs on imported oil, and assumed that the oil companies' profits were so high that his program, inimical to free enterprise, would have no negative effect on the levels of domestic exploration and drilling.[11]

Most Americans also felt Jackson's sense of outrage over the skyrocketing cost of energy, which the OPEC cartel perpetrated by quadrupling the price of crude oil. Historian Paul Johnson has described this price revolution as "one of the most destructive economic events since 1945." For the United States and the other industrial democracies, the result was economic stagnation, inflation, and dramatic increases in unemployment. For the underdeveloped world, the result was even more catastrophic: economic decline, crippling debt, widespread famine and malnutrition. Jackson, almost alone among his colleagues, had warned repeatedly about the coming fuel shortages in the United States two years before the crunch emerged full blown. On June 13, 1972, he wrote President Nixon expressing "his increasing concern about the national security and foreign policy implications of growing American dependence on Middle Eastern oil."[12]

By the 1976 campaign, Jackson had introduced and played a pivotal role in the Senate's enactment of several key measures responding to the energy crisis. The Trans-Alaska Pipeline Bill of 1973 expedited the building of a 789-mile pipeline to carry oil from the North Slope fields to the southern port of Valdez for shipment by tankers to the American West Coast. By the 1980s, more than two million barrels a day flowed through this pipeline, which helped enormously to reduce the pressure from the OPEC cartel. As Daniel Yergin, author of *The Prize*, the authoritative study on oil politics, has observed, the Trans-Alaska pipeline made possible "the single most important new contribution to American energy supply since . . . discovery of the East Texas field in the 1930s." Jackson's Mandatory Allocation Bill required the president to allocate scarce fuels equitably across the country, giving priority to essential services such as hospitals and public safety. His Emergency Energy Bill provided the president with broad powers such as the right to ration gasoline and fuel oil. Jackson proposed a $20 billion program to develop new sources of energy such as coal, and the extraction of oil from shale, and more effective ways to harness solar, geothermal, and nuclear power. Jackson proclaimed, "We ought to be pushing energy research and development to make us self-sufficient in the next decade with the same urgency that we pushed the Manhattan project on atomic bombs in the 1940s and the space program in the early 1960s."[13]

Jackson had figured prominently in the enactment of legislation establishing the strategic petroleum reserve that provided a hedge against any further disruption of the world oil supply. He also pushed successfully for legislation setting fuel efficiency standards for the automobile industry. Enraged that the seven major oil companies had complied with Arab demands during the 1973 Arab-Israeli War to extend the oil embargo to the U.S. Sixth Fleet operating in the eastern Mediterranean, he secured overwhelming congressional approval for legislation making it a criminal act to deny supplies to the Department of Defense. "We are putting a stop to the major oil companies assisting foreign governments in cutting off oil supplies to our military forces," he declared. "This establishes, for the first time, a legislative standard by which we can judge the actions of American multinational corporations."[14]

In January 1974, Jackson garnered major headlines for his performance while chairing hearings of the Permanent Investigations Subcommittee on the energy shortage. In a crowded room filled with television cameras and reporters, he berated and humiliated executives representing the seven largest oil companies. Jackson accused them of making "obscene profits"—one of his most memorable epithets—at the expense of the American public. The oil companies "didn't have a chance," fumed the president of Gulf after the hearings, to defend themselves credibly in this forum against as savvy and experienced an interrogator as Henry Jackson.[15]

Despite the immediate benefits, Jackson's theatrics at the oil companies' expense hurt his presidential candidacy in the long run. His antipathy to markets and big oil antagonized moderate and conservative voters in the Southwest who had found his pro-defense views congenial.[16] It won him few converts among New Politics liberals, who still preferred Udall, Harris, Bayh, or even Carter as an alternative. Even some of his most unstinting admirers, such as Norman Podhoretz and George Will, have said that the energy crisis brought out the worst in him: an atypical and unflattering demagoguery.[17] There were a few other occasions on which Jackson uncharacteristically embarrassed himself as his presidential ambitions became manifest in 1974. During an investigation of organized crime on Wall Street, he unwisely gave credence to a dubious witness's unsubstantiated charge that Elliott Roosevelt, the son of President Franklin Roosevelt, had plotted the assassination of the prime minister of the Bahamas. While away from the Senate campaigning for president, Jackson had to apologize to colleagues on the Senate's Permanent Investigations Subcommittee for a botched publicity stunt: investigators acting on his behalf had announced their discovery of the location of Jimmy Hoffa's body, only to find out they were mistaken.[18] Neither of these blunders, however, had the visibility or impact of his haranguing of the oil executives. Bob Strauss tried to mitigate the damage Jackson's crusade against the oil companies had done to his campaign by arranging a meeting between the senator and prominent oil men to reach an acceptable compromise. The results ended up hurting Jackson politically, because he would not budge. "Scoop was a man of great character and principles who would not adjust his views to satisfy that constituency," Strauss explained. "He was unhappy to have those people there who might have helped him."[19]

The energy crisis also brought out the most serious flaws in Jackson's political philosophy to which he clung tenaciously notwithstanding the evidence. Although he deserves credit for his sensible approach to issues such as the strategic petroleum reserve and the Alaska Pipeline, his energy policies did more harm overall than good. It is now the conventional wisdom among economists that price controls are a bad idea. As Daniel

Yergin concluded in *The Prize*, price controls and rationing impeded rather than facilitated the necessary adjustments to the OPEC cartel that only free markets could undertake efficiently. What Jackson advocated exacerbated shortages and increased U.S. dependence on OPEC. Consider, for example, the untenable distinction he originally advocated between old oil drilled from existing wells and new oil currently under exploration. Congress imposed a $5.25-per-barrel price on old oil, significantly below the $13 per barrel that unregulated new oil fetched on the open market. In 1975, Jackson then proposed an overall price ceiling on all domestic oil not to exceed $7.66 per barrel, 59 cents below the existing average of $8.25 per barrel.[20] This scheme would have discouraged domestic exploration and production, encouraged domestic consumption, increased the importation of foreign oil from unstable Middle East oil-producing countries, and required a large bureaucracy to administer it.

DEMOCRATIC DINOSAUR

Jackson and his campaign did not fully fathom several other weaknesses lurking in his candidacy that the Democratic primaries of 1976 would baldly expose. All the media advice in the world could not make Henry Jackson telegenic as a presidential candidate when he had to work from a tight script rather than respond informally to probing questions, as on the Sunday morning news programs. Superb on *Meet the Press* and *Issues and Answers*, he performed poorly in television venues that had become critical for winning the nomination. "He was not relaxed on the campaign stump, except in Washington State, and terrible reading a speech," Richard Perle observed. "He could also butcher a line. I remember writing a speech for him in the early 1970s just after Earl Butz, secretary of agriculture, had been fired. Scoop was going down to give the speech to the AFL-CIO in Miami, a raucous gathering. I threw in the line: Thank god that we will not have Butz to kick around any more. Scoop, reading along in a wooden way, suddenly realized that the text in front of him was disrespectful to the secretary of agriculture. So he revised it on the spot." ABC television correspondent Barry Dunsmore, who covered Jackson's 1976 campaign, recalled that "as nice a man as Scoop Jackson was, he could put an audience to sleep faster than anybody I have ever seen. He had no public charisma. Jackson just could not stir up people."[21]

Henry Jackson's candidacy thus had some striking parallels with Senator Robert Dole's in 1996. Both of these self-made men came from modest backgrounds. Both excelled on the Sunday morning news programs, where they appeared frequently, but not on campaign television, where they came across as boring. Both gained their prominence in the Senate, an institution that rewarded skills different from those campaigning required. Confident in their abilities, adamant that old dogs like them could not learn new tricks, both resisted being manipulated. They chose to run for president as the men they were: effective senators, negotiators, and legislators rather than creatures of the media age. Both lacked the capacity to mobilize the public through the use of personal or charismatic power, an essential characteristic for effectively wielding executive authority in what political scientist Jeffrey Tulis has called the era of the "rhetorical presidency."[22]

Dole, however, represented the mainstream of his party, which allowed him to capture his party's nomination in 1996. By 1976, Jackson did not represent the mainstream of the Democratic Party. Unlike Dole, who possessed a mordant wit, which he sometimes displayed too much for his own good, Jackson had a reputation for humorlessness that was partly but not wholly unfair. Occasionally, he would poke fun at himself for his lack of charisma, as he did speaking at a California State Democratic Party dinner in late 1975. Onstage with most of the other Democratic presidential contenders, Jackson quipped that his dull ponderous speeches were intended to give the other candidates a false sense of security. "Then I'm going to strike when they least expect it. You see? Birch Bayh has already dozed off." It was more typical of Jackson, however, to find nothing amusing about a practical joke that his gregarious colleague Warren Magnuson played on him. Constantly lecturing the free-living Magnuson about the virtues of exercise and abstemiousness, Jackson once began doing pushups on Magnuson's floor to prove the point. Pretending to push a button on his intercom, Magnuson asked his secretary to send in William Allen, chairman of the Boeing Company. Jackson leaped to his feet, brushed himself off, and rushed to put on his coat. Magnuson and his staffers roared with laughter. A painfully earnest Jackson did not.[23]

It also did not help matters that Jackson neither relished nor had much experience running a seriously contested race. Richard Pipes of Harvard, a great admirer of Jackson and a staunch supporter of his presidential candidacy, gave this revealing account of what he witnessed during the Massachusetts primary in 1976:

> I observed him here at a victory rally in Massachusetts, a great triumph
> for him, and I could see that he really didn't relish the crowds. He was
> not a man who relished the crowds. He came out, the crowd cheered,
> but he did not have much rapport or derive much energy from the
> crowds. That showed me that he didn't really relish the political process.
> He had such a safe seat in Washington that he never really had a tough
> fight and did not really like them. He was not made for the rough and
> tumble of Presidential elections. He would have made a wonderful parliamentary leader in England, in that type of system: his party wins and
> then he becomes Prime Minister.[24]

Jackson personified the type of old-fashioned candidate who would have done much better running in an era of professional party conventions than in an open primary process.

Having married late, with children twenty years younger than those of his colleagues in the Senate, Jackson had virtually a tin ear for the new cultural ethos of the younger generation of activists within the Democratic Party. He abhorred the sexual revolution and considered homosexuality deviant. As a civil libertarian, he accepted that the right to privacy constrained the government from regulating homosexual conduct, but did not think that gays were entitled to protection under the Civil Rights Act or to equal rights in all spheres such as serving in the military. "Scoop was late to understand these new tensions and issues, because homosexuality was totally alien to him," Ben Wattenberg opined. "I remember Jackson making the remark that gays were sick. I talked to Sterling about it and told him to talk to Scoop. Sterling said for me to tell him." Also, Jackson believed passionately in the idea of America as a melting pot. He had little sympathy for the first rumblings of multiculturalism, gender, and racial politics stirring in the New Politics wing of the Democratic Party. While serving as the Senate's representative on the U.S.–Puerto Rico Commission on the status of Puerto Rico, he delivered many a lecture on the imperative of keeping English alone the official language of the United States, lest the nation break apart.[25]

A 1975 episode reveals the cultural chasm between Jackson and the younger generation of Democrats. Robert Redford, the most popular matinee idol of the decade, once visited Jackson's office while making the rounds on Capitol Hill on behalf of an environmental cause. Female employees swooned as Redford walked into the front office, recalled staff members Elliott Abrams and Julia Cancio. The actor wanted to see whether the senator was available. When a staffer ran in to the inner office where the personal and appointments secretaries sat, Jackson overheard someone say: "Robert Redford is here. He just wants five minutes. Can you see him?" Jackson replied: "Robert Redford, who is he and who is he with?" Jackson had no exposure to rock music either. "I did not listen to anything radical," reminisced Peter Jackson, "mostly the Beatles, the Beach Boys, and Bob Dylan. Dad had absolutely no awareness about any of it."[26]

Jackson and his campaign never fully understood how much he remained out of step with the activists of his party, politically as well as culturally. Despite his auspicious start, his efforts to move the Democratic Party back to the center had largely failed by 1976. The Coalition for a Democratic Majority, the creation of which he had inspired, had an impressive membership but little impact on the direction of the party. Peter Rosenblatt, a co-founder of CDM, attributed this disappointing result to lack of money and organization. Midge Decter, a member of DCM's board, attributed it to a more fundamental problem: "It was clear that the Jackson and Humphrey forces were unbelievably naive. They did not comprehend what they were up against. They treated New Politics activists as a fringe, something that was going to pass. They could not see that a revolution had occurred. You could not appease these forces, as Humphrey people were especially inclined to do."[27]

Decter was right. Together, the huge Democratic victories in the congressional elections of 1974 and the outcome of the Democratic Party's mini-convention held the following month largely enshrined the transformation that McGovern forces had wrought in the party. In the aftermath of Watergate and Nixon's resignation, the Democrats had increased their substantial majority in Congress by gaining four seats in the Senate and forty-six in the House in 1974. The election also had accelerated the increasing tilt of the Democratic party toward the views of young, culturally liberal, proenvironmental, antiwar members hostile to the military and American assertiveness abroad. This constituency, which was vital to winning the party's presidential nomination, tended to disdain and distrust Cold War Democrats such as Henry Jackson. Although these Democrats pushed intently for expansion in the size and scope of government while in office, they preferred not to draw attention to this dimension of their thinking the way the unabashed New Dealer–Fair Dealer Jackson always did. Instead, they focused their campaign rhetoric on the imperative of constraining the abuses of power at home and abroad in an age in which Vietnam and Watergate had disillusioned many Americans about the capacity of their government to solve problems. They emphasized group rights and equality of results rather than individual rights and equality of opportunity. They were, historian and commentator Michael Barone has summed up, more dovish on foreign policy and more liberal on cultural issues than traditional Democrats such as Henry Jackson, who steadfastly opposed détente, a substantial devolution of American responsibilities in the world, major cuts in the defense budget, Affirmative Action, busing, and abortion.[28]

During the 1976 presidential primaries, Jackson scoffed at the rhetoric of his rivals who railed against the evils of big government. "I don't buy the idea that because something is big it's bad," he said. "You can't have a national health program or have Washington take over $19 billion in welfare cost . . . unless it's a big one." He also decried the antigrowth mentality increasingly prevalent among the new breed of Democratic liberals. In early April 1976, he declared: "The view that America's material prosperity is so great that the goal of economic growth may be abandoned suggests a cruel betrayal of the hopes of millions of Americans for a better life. If we are to eliminate poverty, guarantee equal education opportunity, provide adequate health care for all Americans, build millions of new homes for young families now unable to afford them and secure full employment with decent wages, economic growth is absolutely essential. Indeed the age of abundance and of greater individual opportunity is just beginning."[29]

The Americans for Democratic Action issued a scurrilous report on Jackson's voting record in 1975, which evidenced the antipathy many liberal Democrats still felt toward him. Making no attempt to reexamine the record of any other senator during a twenty-year period, the ADA grossly distorted Jackson's very liberal record in an effort to cast him as a domestic as well as a foreign policy conservative. His staff released a rebuttal, demonstrating his voting record on domestic affairs to be among the most liberal in the Senate. Regardless, Joseph Rauh and other leaders of the ADA would not forgive Jackson for his record on foreign policy and national defense. Even though wary of Jimmy Carter, this powerful group of Democrats found Henry Jackson the most unacceptable of the candidates other than George Wallace.[30]

The Democratic mini-convention of December 1974 in Kansas City largely ratified the McGovern rules change in the party's nomination process.[31] A wary Bob Strauss persuaded an even more wary Henry Jackson to accept a nominal compromise that Jimmy Carter pressed for to abolish in theory quotas for selecting delegates, but implicitly endorsing them in practice by requiring "affirmative action" to achieve racial and gender diversity. Strauss meekly defended the results as not good but better than they could have been given the strength of the New Politics wing of the party:

> We were trying to get out of Kansas City with our lives. I told the Jackson people about the compromise on quotas late that night. I knew they would not like it. I knew that Mayor Daley would not like it. He had left the convention ill and gone to his hotel. I called him there. He said he did not like it. I said that I "did not like it either, Mr. Mayor. I feel like a second story burglar who has just got his hands on two-thirds of the jewelry. The police sirens are coming . . . he wants to get out with what he has his hands on, to get out alive." Daley replied that he would be over in a half an hour and hold the ladder for me.[32]

Carter biographer Peter Bourne described this compromise as "a camouflaged but significant blow to Jackson's presidential prospects."[33]

Elementary demographics also conspired against Jackson's efforts to revive the New Deal–Fair Deal coalition, on which the Democratic Party's electoral dominance had hinged from 1932 to 1968. Since the early 1960s, political power in presidential elections had shifted away from the largely Democratic ethnic, urban, and industrial Northeast and Midwest to the largely Republican and suburban sunbelt of the South and West. Even within the Democratic Party, suburbanites and their concerns had widely displaced the core New Deal–Fair Deal constituencies of self-consciously ethnic voters and organized labor as the most important segments of the electorate. Labor union membership as a percentage of the work force had declined steadily since its peak in 1952. Furthermore, the new generation of union leaders and the expanding public-sector unions often had different priorities and agendas than either the viscerally anticommunist AFL-CIO under George Meany or Henry Jackson, who entertained a similar outlook. Nor could organized labor deliver the votes in an era of voter independence and split-ticket voting the way the labor bosses once did. "My wife, a prominent labor lawyer who authored several speeches for Scoop, tried to warn him that the labor movement too had become a microcosm of the whole restructuring of American politics," remembered Howard Feldman. "Neither he nor his campaign advisers ever really understood that the monolithic bloc voting they banked their strategy on did not happen anymore."[34]

All this posed a serious problem for Jackson, who counted on considerable backing from organized labor to offset his weaknesses among other constituencies hostile or indifferent to his candidacy. To make matters worse, in early 1975 he had a falling out with George Meany. His visit to Communist China in July 1974 irritated the old anticommunist labor leader. In addition, his endorsement of the 1974 trade bill after forcing through the Jackson-Vanik Amendment also angered Meany, who wanted Jackson to vote against it. Meany and Alexander Barkan, the top AFL-CIO operative, also felt that Jackson did not stand firmly enough against the New Politics activists at the Democratic mini-convention in Kansas City. On February 12, 1975, Jackson wrote to Meany expressing his exasperation over the labor leader's charge that he had not dealt stringently enough with communist countries. "What is unique about Jackson-Vanik," he insisted, was that "he and his colleagues had driven a hard bargain" so that the Soviets could not get away this time "with going back on their word and violating agreements." By 1976, Meany and Jackson had partly but not totally repaired the rupture between them.[35] Neither Meany nor organized labor would back Jackson with the intensity that he expected. One reason had nothing to do with Jackson. For most major union leaders and their rank and file, Hubert Humphrey remained far and away the first choice. They thought of Jackson as the bridesmaid. Labor would not commit its full resources to Jackson so long as Humphrey, who formally declared himself a noncandidate, dangled the possibility of changing his mind, which he did repeatedly at critical junctures of the 1976 campaign.

History also did not favor Jackson's mounting a successful presidential campaign from the Senate. The Democratic presidential campaign of 1960 in which four senators ran—Kennedy, Johnson, Symington, and Humphrey—is the exception to the rule that senators in office rarely win either the presidential nomination or the general election. Dole, McGovern, and Goldwater accomplished the former. Only Kennedy and Warren G. Harding accomplished the latter. The post-68 rule changes in the nominating process for both parties raised these prohibitive odds for sitting senators such as Henry Jackson, who tried to run without relinquishing most of his time-consuming and enormous responsibilities in the Senate. Neither he nor any other sitting senators could easily compete in the age of weak parties and primaries with candidates who campaigned to the exclusion of all else. Since 1968, governors and ex-governors such as Ronald Reagan, Bill Clinton, and Jimmy Carter have made the most successful presidential primary candidates and the most successful nonincumbent presidential candidates, partly because they have the time and energy for the essential tasks, which sitting senators do not.

In November 1975, Bob Keefe acknowledged that Jackson had taken "a political risk in deciding to devote" himself "substantially to his work in the Senate rather than spending all of his time campaigning from state to state." The senator believed, Keefe said, "that it would have been improper and a political disservice to the nation if he had abandoned his major responsibilities in the Congress."[36] Jackson also miscalculated that campaigning while in the Senate would improve his chances to win the nomination by keeping him in the national spotlight. He gave Jimmy Carter more than a year's head start by waiting until January 1, 1976, before beginning his full-time campaign for the presidency. Despite his early status as front-runner, which beguiled his supporters, Jackson probably could not have won his party's nomination in 1976 even if his campaign had had a sound strategy and had run perfectly. Neither his message nor his persona fit the mood of the Democratic Party at a time when disillusionment with government ran high, the country still reeling from the humiliation of defeat in Vietnam and the resignation of a president. "The Democratic Party's primary voters were not going to elect an anti-Soviet hard-liner in 1976," mused Senator Moynihan.[37]

An incident early in the campaign exemplified how his reputation as a Cold Warrior continued to dog Jackson among liberal Democratic voters. Based on information leaked by the House Committee on Intelligence, major news media including CBS News and UPI reported in January 1976 that Jackson had intervened three years earlier on behalf of the CIA when it sought to block a congressional investigation of operations in Chile. An angry Jackson denounced the accusation as "McCarthyism in its purest form."[38] He insisted that "there was absolutely no evidence whatsoever connecting him to CIA skullduggery." There was indeed no credible evidence that he had done anything improper. In February 1973, Jack Maury, a congressional liaison officer for the CIA, had met with Jackson to talk about a problem the CIA was having with the Subcommittee on Multinational Corporations of the Foreign Relations Committee, chaired by Frank Church. Normally, Maury would have taken this problem to Senator Stennis, chairman of the Armed Services Committee and its CIA oversight committee, but Stennis had just been shot and critically wounded while being robbed near the Capitol.[39] While Stennis was convalescing, Jackson simply advised Maury that Senator John McClellan of Arkansas, chairman of the Appropriations Committee, who also chaired its CIA oversight committee, was the proper person to deal with Senator Church, whom he described as a "highly reliable and dependable person." During a dinner party at his house in May that included Senator Symington, Jackson also advised Richard Helms, U.S. ambassador to Iran and former director of the CIA, who had been called to testify before the Church committee, to lay out all the facts as he knew them. He strongly advised, too, that Helms testify in open public session. Helms asked for no suggestions, and Jackson gave none, about the substance of his testimony. The ambassador did express his concern that the Nixon administration was trying to implicate him falsely in open session.[40]

On other occasions, Jackson had also expressed concern that the investigations of the CIA must not get out of hand. He supported reforming the CIA, not destroying it, as he worried some were out to do. He disagreed with Church on many policy matters, but thought the Idaho senator had conducted his proceedings fairly.[41] Beyond that, Jackson had no other involvement in the flap over the CIA. Yet this was precisely the type of story that he wished to avoid as he sought to persuade liberal Democrats to support or at least not stridently oppose him.

Jackson had the misfortune of being the consummate insider in the year of the outsider. In 1976, Ronald Reagan nearly defeated President Gerald Ford for the Republican nomination by running on an anti-Washington theme. Jimmy Carter managed to win both the Democratic nomination and the presidency by running on the same theme. But what utterly doomed Jackson's uphill battle for the presidency in 1976 were the dynamics of the campaign itself. Candidate Jackson had a poor strategy, bad luck, and made many mistakes. Candidate Carter had an excellent strategy, first-rate luck, and ran a nearly flawless campaign.

As diplomatic historians have noted, statesmen and generals often prepare to fight the previous war rather than adapt to changing circumstances.[42] This adage applies nicely to Henry Jackson's campaign strategy, which reflected a misunderstanding of the profound changes that had occurred in the nominating process. Like most of his fellow Democratic candidates in 1976, Jackson assumed that his main task was to position himself as the candidate who could defeat George Wallace, whose formidability as an opponent he and others vastly overestimated, based on the 1972 campaign when the Alabama governor had run so strongly. Like them and like Bob Strauss, too, the Jackson campaign woefully underestimated Carter's appeal as a presidential candidate and his potential to stop Wallace in the South more effectively than anybody else. Unlike Carter, Jackson and his advisers failed to grasp that generating the money and momentum necessary to wage a successful campaign depended on getting off to a fast start in the delegate-poor but media-rich early primaries. Initially, they operated on the archaic premise more appropriate for pre-1968 campaigns that Jackson could lie low in such early primaries while concentrating his efforts on the large industrial states that came later. The big boost to his campaign, Jackson reckoned, would come with strong victories in the crucial New York primary of April 6 and the Pennsylvania primary of April 27.[43]

By following this course, the Jackson campaign also sought to dispel the senator's "serious image problem as a loser that the 1972 campaign" had left him. "Our strategy was to make sure that he did not lose," Bob Keefe explained. "We made only a minimal effort in Iowa, the first caucus state, because he would have done badly there." Keefe added that this fear of being branded a loser also accounted for the Jackson campaign's decision to stay out of the New Hampshire primary: the nation's first, scheduled for February 27, 1976. In early 1975, Jackson had traveled to New Hampshire with Tom Foley and Ben Wattenberg, where they met with a group of his purported supporters. Jackson worried that these backers were so conservative that they would tarnish his image with liberals even more.[44]

Jackson made the right decision in skipping dovish Iowa. He blundered, however, in skipping New Hampshire, with a Democratic electorate composed of a proportionately large number of Irish and French Canadian working-class voters who would have found Jackson more appealing than the alternatives. At a minimum, his active presence there probably would have taken enough votes away from Carter, his most formidable opponent, to make Udall rather than the Georgia governor the winner. Nor would this have detracted from Jackson's efforts in Massachusetts, the next primary, scheduled for a week later, where Jackson determined to make his first strong bid. New Hampshire and Massachusetts not only are neighboring states, but they also share the same television markets. In fairness to Keefe, the decision to stay out of New Hampshire drew into bold relief the basic vulnerability of Jackson's position, which would have daunted even the most gifted of campaign strategists. Jackson had a relatively narrow base of support within the Democratic Party and a slender margin of error. A Udall victory in New Hampshire would not have produced an unalloyed benefit from Jackson's standpoint. On the one hand, it would have slowed Carter's momentum, which was spurred by the lavish media attention he received from his twin victories in Iowa and New Hampshire. On the other hand, it might have produced a surge for the Arizona congressman that could have swept him to victory over Jackson in Massachusetts the following week. Such a loss also might have devastated the Jackson campaign.

What Jackson and his advisers should have recognized from the outset, but did not, was the paramount importance of stopping Carter first rather than Udall. The Carter campaign grasped more astutely than Jackson or his other competitors the mood of the Democratic electorate and the revolution occurring in the nominating process. Hamilton Jordan, chief of Carter's campaign staff, had devised a brilliant strategy, which Carter would execute brilliantly in the 1976 Democratic primary campaign. Carter had spent 1974 and 1975 consolidating his southern base, boosting his name recognition, assiduously recruiting supporters from every state, and mastering the rules that would govern the delegate selection process. He then expected to break out of the pack by winning the Iowa caucus on January 19, 1976, and the New Hampshire primary of February 27, which he did. These small states were tailor-made for the arduous retail campaigning and small-group encounters with unfamiliar voters at which Carter excelled. The former Georgia governor had the time and the talent to make the most of this opportunity. With the money and publicity produced by his early victories, he then planned to knock Wallace out of the race by defeating him in Florida. This would not only establish his dominance in the South, Carter strategists calculated, but would create an unstoppable momentum for him to win the large industrial states, making his nomination inevitable. As Peter Bourne, Jules Witcover, and others have noted, the particular circumstances in the election of 1976 greatly facilitated the smashing success of Carter's strategy. The new rules abolishing winner-take-all primaries made it crucial to enter every primary and file delegate slates in every state, something that the Carter, but not the Jackson, campaign was quick to do. The change in the campaign finance laws, providing federal matching funds and limiting the maximum individual contribution to $1,000, helped candidates such as Carter, who had few wealthy backers, and hurt candidates such as Jackson, who had many willing to give large sums to his campaign.[45]

Carter's anti-Washington theme and demonstrative religiosity also reverberated strongly among Democratic primary voters in 1976, as faith in American institutions plummeted in the immediate aftermath of Vietnam and Watergate. Henry Jackson, the quintessential Cold War liberal and powerhouse of the U.S. Senate had neither the credibility nor the inclination to capitalize on this mood of discontent. Instead, he touted his own long experience in Washington as an asset that distinguished him from Carter. "I know there are candidates who say they've never been to Washington, and they brag about it," Jackson remarked. "I am not one of them."[46]

Carter also benefited significantly from the protean quality of his campaign, abetted by an absence of a well-established record on national issues as a one-term governor from a small state. Compare that with Jackson, who in 1976 had been in public life longer than any other presidential candidate of either party. Having served thirty years in the Congress, he had a detailed public record on controversial issues, which left him little room for evasion. Temperamental differences between the two men speak well of Jackson, but actually helped Carter during the primaries when first impressions largely determine all. Carter created a wonderful first impression without sharply defining himself, attracting even voters unsure of his ultimate positions. That impression wore off with many Americans as they got to know him. As Barry Dunsmore, who covered both men extensively but largely agreed with Carter philosophically, put it: "Jimmy Carter loves the people, but hates people. He was an extremely testy character who disliked anybody who challenged him." Though he could not turn on the charm for television cameras, Jackson was genuinely well liked and was always friendly with people, even those who disagreed with him. "He was extraordinarily forgiving, even when you did not write flattering things about him," said Dunsmore. "Carter would carry his bags on the campaign trail and make a big thing of it. Jackson would carry his and yours and make nothing of it at all."[47]

There were, indeed, few men in American politics more decent, genuine, literal, or blunt than Henry Jackson. He relished letting people know where he stood, whether or not they approved of it. He insisted on being the same person, whether he talked on television, to constituents, to legislators, to presidents, to Soviet dictators or dissidents. He had trouble winning over a crowd unfamiliar with him. His popularity ripened slowly as people got the chance to know him. Carter thus succeeded in the primaries by offering all things to all people in a way that the stolid, well-known, and implacably consistent Jackson could not. Ben Wattenberg recalled that Jody Powell, Carter's press secretary, told him at the bar of the Parker House Hotel during the Massachusetts primary campaign, "You may beat us in Massachusetts, but we will beat you in the South because we are going to take votes out of your well." When the campaign returned north after the southern primaries, complained Wattenberg, Carter veered sharply to the left without paying a political price for his abrupt switch.[48]

Conservative southerners initially identified Carter as one of their own, a judgment they would sorely regret by 1980, when they deserted him in droves for Ronald Reagan. Despite Carter's previous hostility to busing and a spotty early record on civil rights, black voters backed him overwhelmingly, impressed by his heartfelt evolution toward the very liberal side on civil rights questions. Although the New Politics wing of the party distrusted him for his previous support of the Vietnam War and his more conservative rhetoric on economics, some of those Democratic voters gravitated toward supporting him early on because they identified him as the progressive with the best chance of stopping Wallace. Generally,

New Politics liberals also considered the then inchoate but moralistic foreign policy sensibilities of Carter infinitely more palatable than those of Jackson, who stood for everything they detested. Frank Mankiewicz, McGovern's former campaign manager, and Ann Wexler, a liberal activist prominent in the McGovern campaign, and others from the New Politics wing eventually jumped on Carter's bandwagon.[49]

There were some disturbing signs even before the primaries commenced that Jackson's campaign was not going as well as the senator had anticipated. His popularity in the public opinion polls remained stuck in the mid-teens in a multicandidate race. Most of the major news profiles of him running months before the primaries still depicted him as the epitome of dullness and as an apologist for the military-industrial complex. R. J. Apple, Jr., published a lengthy profile of him in the *New York Times Magazine* criticizing him for his inflexibility on Cold War issues. He wrote, too, that "Jackson's long identification with the system and his inability to excite voters are probably fatal handicaps." That article coincided with the publication of Peter Ognibene's pulp biography of Jackson that was in keeping with the writer's stated belief that the role of a political journalist ought to be that of an adversary. Ognibene acknowledged Jackson's hard work and decency but blasted him for his Cold War, pro-defense views.[50]

Some prominent Democrats pounded Jackson, too. His old nemesis Eugene McCarthy said in 1975 that it did not matter how much money Jackson raised: "Jackson is a little like an old Tin Lizzy that gets half-way up the hill, slips on the clutch, and starts smoking and spinning its wheels. . . . the harder it tries, the slower it goes." Senator Adlai Stevenson, Jr., from Illinois announced that "he might have trouble" supporting Jackson for the Democratic nomination. He complained that he "had major differences of opinion on military priorities and strategic questions." If Jackson's views "on military priorities persist," Stevenson predicted, "he could fail to generate the necessary support for the Democratic nomination." The Illinois senator did not "feel it was possible to maintain a sound economy and public confidence at the same time we're laying out billions of dollars on the military-industrial complex." Even the more sympathetic *Wall Street Journal* reported in late November 1975 that Jackson's campaign appeared to be drifting "without focus or fire, and the politicians talk about how drab and dull he seems on the stump."[51]

Chapter 17

The 1976 Democratic Primaries

THE EARLY EVENTS of the primary season surprised almost everyone except Carter and his advisers. His consecutive victories in Iowa and New Hampshire transformed this little-known governor into the instant front-runner and a veritable celebrity. With few exceptions, he initially received glowing coverage from the army of television and news journalists that flocked to him. An ebullient Carter looked to the Massachusetts primary as his opportunity to deliver a knockout blow to the other liberal candidates and to Jackson before moving toward a showdown with Wallace in Florida. Never imagining that Jackson could win Massachusetts, the Carter campaign worried mainly about preventing a Wallace victory, which would have badly damaged Carter's prospects for the upcoming primaries in the South.[1] Wallace saw the Massachusetts primary as his chance to stage an upset, enormously boosting his campaign nationally. He had run well there before, notwithstanding the state's reputation for liberalism. With controversy raging in the state over Federal District Judge W. Arthur Garrity, Jr.'s order to force busing in Boston's school districts and with a multicandidate field dividing the liberal vote, Wallace thought he might win. He did not.[2]

Henry Jackson was the one Carter should have worried about. The Jackson campaign had placed heavy emphasis on making a strong run in this, the first of the primaries in the delegate-rich, northern industrial states. The senator spent considerable time and money in Massachusetts disseminating his message to his political base: organized labor, white ethnics, and the Jewish community. In union halls across the state, he blamed the Ford administration for the high rate of unemployment and called for increased federal spending to alleviate it. In synagogues, he portrayed himself as Israel's most loyal defender in the American government. Everywhere, he stressed his long-standing opposition to forced busing. In a pointed attack on the abysmally unpopular Judge Garrity, he advocated placing school desegregation decisions in the hands of three-judge panels. He ran advertisements in the major Massachusetts newspapers proclaiming: "I am against busing."[3] This stand won him more votes than it lost him despite the disruption of his presentation at the Knights of Columbus meeting hall in the Charlestown section of Boston, where he was booed off the stage by antibusing extremists.[4] These protesters assailed Jackson because his alternative of a three-judge panel would not categorically preclude busing, but would only make it less likely in most cases. Jackson also ran as a middle-of-the-road Democrat, stressing his impeccable record on civil rights and criticism of Wallace as well as his opposition to busing. For more conservative Democrats, he offered a respectable alternative to Wallace on other issues: abortion, détente, defense, crime, and traditional values.[5]

Jackson had key endorsements from organized labor, prominent academics, and some popular politicians. Senator Moynihan not only endorsed him but came to Massachusetts the day after leaving his post as U.S. ambassador to the United Nations to campaign with him. In late 1975, Jackson had first connected with Moynihan during a campaign stop in New York. He had already mentioned that "it would be great to have Moynihan as his secretary of state." After their conversation at the U.N. Plaza, Moynihan drove Jackson to the Newark Airport to catch an airplane for his next campaign stop. In February 1976, Jackson reciprocated the favor. He sent a plane to fly Moynihan from New Haven, where he had just delivered a lecture at Yale, to Boston so that he could join him on the stump.[6]

The Massachusetts primary was the first time during the campaign that Jackson or any other candidates managed to shake Carter with their attacks on him. Jackson accused Carter of saying different things in different parts of the country. "In Pensacola and Jacksonville, he is for a strong national defense," Jackson said. "In Miami, he promises to cut the defense budget by billions. In Iowa, he promises to abolish legalized abortion. In New York, he promises to oppose a constitutional amendment for such change. In Atlanta, he writes letters to special interest groups promising support for a right-to-work law. In Florida, he promises audiences he would sign a repeal of the right-to-work law."[7] Jackson pounced on Carter not only for his proposal to cut the defense budget by 15 percent but also for his advocacy of eliminating the tax deductions allowed on home mortgages. The Jackson campaign broadcast commercials that savaged this stand, warning that it could destroy the housing industry. "If Jimmy Carter gets his way," Jackson told a news conference, "American home owners will pay $6 billion more in taxes . . . about 600,000 families in Massachusetts alone would pay about $600 a year more in income tax. . . . I don't think anybody who wants to raise taxes on the middle class is suitable for the Presidency."[8]

Feeling good about his prospects, Jackson predicted with uncharacteristic boldness that he would win the Massachusetts primary on March 2. "It may be dangerous for a candidate to predict victory in a race with so many other candidates," he said on February 26, "but I have never been more confident." Picked by many Massachusetts politicians to finish no higher than fourth place, he indeed finished first. He won 23 percent of the vote to Udall's 18 percent and Wallace's 17 percent. Carter finished a distant fourth with only 14 percent. While losing to Wallace in South Boston, Jackson carried working-class areas across the rest of the state. He also did very well among Jewish voters. Exhilarated by his victory in Massachusetts, Jackson said that "no Democratic candidate could win the nomination and the November general election without winning the big industrial states" like Massachusetts. "There is no secret about what we did here," he told his supporters. "We brought America back together again in this great Commonwealth, and we're going to bring it together again in all 50 states." Carried away by the euphoria of the moment, he predicted that "our next big victory will be New York State, which we are going to carry by a landslide."[9]

Alas, the media has never invested the Massachusetts primary—or for that matter the primaries of large states such as California held in June at the end of the race—with the significance of tiny New Hampshire's. It was therefore typical of American presidential campaigns that Jackson did not receive nearly the same boost from his victory in Massachusetts that Carter did from his successes in Iowa and New Hampshire, contests where comparatively few voters participated. As the race moved to Florida for the March 9 primary, the defects of his strategy began to show, and the campaign's belated efforts to correct them ultimately made matters worse. Carter's success and Wallace's slippage forced Jackson to abandon his initial start-slow, finish-strong strategy. If Jimmy Carter swept the southern primaries, Jackson would have a much more difficult time in the northern industrial states stopping the momentum of the moderate Georgia governor than defeating the fiery Alabama governor branded indelibly by his segregationist past. Jackson decided that he must make a strong showing in Florida, but he faced two popular governors from neighboring southern states with strong organizations and a flood of enthusiastic volunteers bused in from Georgia and Alabama. Dating back to his 1972 primary campaign, he had a potentially wide base of support in Florida among Jewish and Cuban voters centered in southern Florida and among those with ties to the state's aerospace and defense industry. He also had the endorsement of Democratic Governor Reubin Askew, who hated Carter. Nevertheless, he had almost no organization in the state because the campaign had neglected building one in the expectation that he would lie low until the northern industrial primaries. During 1974–75, Carter had spent seventy-five days campaigning in Florida. Jackson had spent just ten days there. Carter and Wallace campaigned hard across the entire state. Jackson concentrated his efforts in southern Florida. The Jackson campaign tried to compensate for its late start, previous neglect, and poor organization with money.[10]

The Carter campaign reacted to Jackson's victory in Massachusetts and his decision to come to Florida with a mixture of venom and alarm. By the admission of even his most stalwart admirers, Jimmy Carter did not take losing or criticism well.[11] Jackson had inflicted both on him. The Carter campaigners worried, too, that his defeat in Massachusetts could unravel their entire strategy, remembered Carter's pollster Patrick Caddell:

> [It seemed that] the whole thing, which twenty-four hours before had looked like it was about to be wrapped up, could fall apart within seven days. Now all of a sudden we had Jackson coming into Florida to cut us, and spend resources. We knew he couldn't win, but he could really screw us up. We could be out of the race, for all intents and purposes. The forty-eight hours after Massachusetts was just horrendous. We were off base, our candidate was off stride, and we were facing the crisis of our lives.[12]

Carter began lashing out at Jackson in Florida, charging that he won the Massachusetts primary by exploiting his opposition to busing, which the Georgia governor called "an emotional, negative issue that has connotations of racism." He accused Jackson of resorting to lies, distortions, and scare tactics to further his own presidential campaign. "He is not a dishonest man. He is not a bad man. But he wants to be president so much that he is departing from his usual truthfulness. . . . He is deliberately falsifying what I have said . . . just to scare people." An angry Jackson lashed back by accusing Carter of favoring a "weak defense" and stood by his criticism of Carter's plan to eliminate the mortgage interest tax deduction on private homes.[13]

Jackson's belated effort in Florida fell short. Carter won 43 percent of the vote to Wallace's 31 percent and Jackson's 23 percent. The results revived Carter's momentum, stopped Jackson in his tracks, and put Wallace on the ropes. Worse, Jackson reaped the worst dividends of his old and new strategies: he failed to stop Carter from winning in Florida and he spent $400,000 as a substitute for the organization he lacked. This ill-fated gambit sapped his campaign of the cash needed to mount an effective challenge in the northern industrial states, where he had to win to stay alive.[14]

Carter knocked Wallace out of the race during the two weeks following the Florida primary. On March 16, he defeated Wallace by 48 percent to 28 percent in the Illinois nonbinding preference primary. On March 23, he finished him off with a 54 percent to 35 percent win in the North Carolina primary. Jackson's nonexistent showing in Illinois epitomized the archaic thinking that plagued his campaign. Focusing myopically on winning delegates rather than recognizing that the perception of winning primaries becomes reality, the Jackson campaign decided to skip the state for fear of confronting Mayor Richard J. Daley, who ran an independent slate of delegates. It was a mistake. Carter won the nonbinding primaries and picked up 55 of the state's 155 delegates at stake.[15] Originally, Jackson had intended to make a major effort in North Carolina. His old friend Sam Ervin, Democrat from North Carolina who was widely popular for his performance as chair of the Senate Watergate committee, had endorsed him. Jackson decided to stay out of the North Carolina primary, however, after Ervin told him during his campaign swing through the state that his opposition to right-to-work laws "would kill him politically."[16]

The New York and Wisconsin primaries of April 6 came next. From the beginning, Jackson had insisted that his campaign would come together in New York, and several things seemed to stand in his favor at the outset. The delegate selection process in New York rewarded the enormous organizational advantage he enjoyed over any of his rivals there. The primary voting ballot did not identify the slate's delegates in the thirty-nine congressional districts with the presidential candidate they backed. This benefited Jackson, who had garnered the endorsements of many of the prominent local politicians and party bosses running to become delegates to the Democratic National Convention. Birch Bayh, better organized in New York than anyone but Jackson, had bowed out of the race. Morris Udall, a late starter in New York, initially chose to concentrate his scarce resources on defeating Carter in Wisconsin. At first, Carter chose not to make a major effort in New York.[17] Jackson also benefited from the fact that Jewish voters constituted a disproportionate share of the Democratic Party's electorate in New York. As the father of the Jackson-Vanik Amendment and Israel's most ardent defender in Congress, Jackson could expect to do well among the state's Jewish voters. Already, he had taken more than 50 percent of Jewish voters in Massachusetts and 61 percent in Florida.[18]

Yet Jackson had unwisely raised expectations by predicting after his victory in Massachusetts that he would win a landslide in New York. The media would impose a rigorous definition of "landslide" and interpret anything short of that as a defeat. A complex of mistakes, events beyond his control, and bad luck conspired to deny him the type of New York victory essential to reinvigorate his campaign. First, because of the significant cost of contesting the Massachusetts and Florida primaries, he was low on funds. Second, less than four weeks before the primary, New York enacted a couple of one-time exceptions to its law regulating primaries. It allowed the name of a preferred presidential candidate to be listed next to a delegate's name on the ballot, and it lowered the barriers for candidates to get on the ballot, which spurred the other candidates to make a greater effort than they had planned. Udall had begun to inherit most of Bayh's liberal support and organizational base. Poorly funded and distracted by Wisconsin, he had little hope of defeating Jackson but a good chance to cut substantially into his lead. Carter added to the mounting obstacles Jackson faced by deciding to contest for delegates in areas of upstate New York.[19]

Foreshadowing what would occur in Pennsylvania three weeks later, Hubert Humphrey also hurt Jackson by not ruling out his availability. Jackson thus failed in his attempts to merge uncommitted delegate slates of the Democratic organization with his own slates. He was trying to stave off a situation in which the Jackson slates and the uncommitted slates of the regular organization would compete for the same voter in twenty of the state's thirty-nine congressional districts. Most of the twenty independent slates were covert Humphrey supporters. Joseph Crangle, the Democratic Party boss of Eire County, whose influence extended to many upstate counties, rebuffed Jackson's repeated pleas to commit his three uncommitted slates to him. Crangle was an outspoken admirer of Humphrey.[20]

For three weeks, Jackson spent almost every waking hour campaigning in New York City and the surrounding suburbs, with a brief foray into Wisconsin that symbolized his sinking fortunes and Carter's dramatic ascent. While sitting with Moynihan in his hotel suite watching Morris Udall call himself a progressive rather than a liberal, Jackson, with a look of exasperation born of the hostility many liberals still felt toward him, said: "I may not be a liberal, but I am the only one in the race willing to call myself one." He was also the only one in the race pushing for national health insurance and brimming with faith in the capacity of an activist federal government to stimulate the economy and alleviate pressing social problems.[21]

Nevertheless, his domestic liberalism did not suffice for many liberals or for the antiwar heckler who spat on him later in the day as he descended the podium after delivering a speech at the University of Wisconsin. Jackson had flown with his entourage to Madison in an old DC-3 propeller aircraft the campaign had chartered for the primaries. The plane was parked right in front of the airport. When Jackson returned, he found it blocked by Carter's sleek 727 jet, which had arrived later in the day. Correspondent Barry Dunsmore described what happened next as a metaphor for the trajectory of the campaign: "A DC-3 does not have a reverse gear. . . . In order to leave the airport, the plane had to be moved. Reporters, secret service people, and the Jackson staff had to push it. The gleeful Carter people sitting in their 727 took pictures of Jackson's people pushing the plane."[22]

In the end, Jackson won a comfortable but not overwhelming victory in New York. He received 38 percent of the vote and 104 delegates to Udall's 25 percent and 70 delegates and Carter's 12.8 percent and 35 delegates. Jackson supporters felt let down by the results. The *ABC Evening News* titled its story on Jackson's New York performance, "When Is a Victory Considered a Defeat?" As Dunsmore, who covered this story for ABC, later put it:

> Jackson committed an unconscionable sin in the New York primary. In advance, he proclaimed that he was not only going to win, but he was going to win a landslide. . . . [W]hen given a chance to retract that, until the day of the primary, he insisted that he was going to win a landslide. When the poor man won, he was categorized as having lost by his own benchmarks despite having run a good solid campaign. Jackson never recovered from that. New York was the last primary he won.

Jackson also had the misfortune of having his victory celebration marred by NBC strikers picketing the Essex Hotel, the primary-night site for his campaign headquarters. Because the senator refused to cross the picket line, his rally had to be moved across the street to Central Park.[23]

Events in Wisconsin magnified the media's predisposition to slight or downplay Jackson's victory in New York. Carter got vastly more abundant and more favorable coverage, for staging a comeback in a race that two networks had initially projected for Udall, than Jackson had received for winning a much more significant state by a much greater margin. Furthermore, Carter likely would have lost Wisconsin, while Jackson perhaps would have won by a landslide in New York, had not the late change in New York's rules lured Udall to divert much of his attention and resources to that race. Even though Jackson had clobbered Carter by more than 25 percent in New York, and even though Carter had barely captured Wisconsin after nearly squandering a huge lead, the media depicted Carter as the winner and Jackson as a candidate on the ropes.[24]

JACKSON'S LAST STAND

Attention now turned to the April 27 primary in Pennsylvania, which Jackson defined as the crucial test of his candidacy. If he did not win there, he knew it was over. Pennsylvania had once seemed tailor-made for a Jackson victory over Carter. Labor unions had a huge impact on the politics of the Democratic Party in the state, which not only had a large blue-collar population but large numbers of traditionalist ethnic Democrats favorably disposed to candidates such as Jackson. The Jackson forces limped into Pennsylvania, however, desperately short of money for an all-out campaign. Only $100,000 was left of the nearly $6 million that had been in the bank in January. The Massachusetts, Florida, and New York campaigns had voraciously consumed the once ample resources. Jackson's lack of momentum and the turmoil within the campaign made it difficult to raise more money. Dick Kline, his chief fundraiser, who did such an excellent job securing him an initial financial advantage over his rivals, abandoned that role as he assumed greater responsibility in the political decision making. Fundraising atrophied as Kline's successors could not measure up to his example. Also, an impasse between President Ford and the Congress over the composition of the Federal Election Commission aggravated the cash crunch of Jackson and his rivals by suspending the disbursement of federal matching funds pending its resolution. With only a minimal media and advertising budget scheduled, Jackson lost precious days on the campaign trail soliciting financial contributions in person from small groups of supporters and by telephone from others to raise enough money for a strong effort in Pennsylvania.[25]

Friends and staffers urged Jackson to borrow. The Supreme Court had permitted use of the eligible federal matching funds, being held in abeyance, as collateral for loans that could be repaid once the flow of these funds resumed. Jackson also had the choice of obtaining a personal loan. He would not resort to either option.[26] His experiences during the Depression had instilled in him an aversion to debt of any kind. In his personal finances, he was as conservative as he was liberal in dispensing the public's money for domestic programs. Indeed, he was, to quote his good friend Sam Nunn, "tight as a tick" when it came to spending his own money for noncharitable causes. Walter Mondale described Jackson's 1961 Chevrolet as "something that ought to have been condemned."[27]

Jackson's personal circumstances and deeply ingrained frugality inhibited him from borrowing money for the Pennsylvania campaign. He was neither a wealthy nor a young man, he explained to his disappointed staffers. In 1973, the Jacksons earned $84,444.07. They gave $37,000 of it to the charity established in his sister Gertrude's name. In 1974, the Jacksons earned $77,671 and again gave a remarkable 44 percent of it to charity. In 1975, their income fell to $54,912 because presidential campaigning limited the amount Henry received from speeches and lectures to $7,700, all of which he gave to charity. In 1976, Henry and Helen Jackson had a combined net worth of $613,000: this included $118,000 in stock owned by Helen; a home in Washington, D.C., with an assessed market value of $142,489, on which they still owed $51,000; and a home in Everett, worth about $80,000. The Jacksons had an additional $76,900 in assets, including a $56,589 pension.[28] This was a solid but not enormous financial cushion for a senator in his situation. However much he wanted to be president, he "simply could not risk, at age sixty-four, the financial security of his wife and two young children."[29]

The Carter campaign also had just $100,000 going into the Pennsylvania campaign. With greater personal wealth than Jackson, however, and anticipating victory, Carter decided to borrow heavily on his personal assets. Advertising executive Gerald Rafshoon also arranged for a major loan to Carter and his campaign. (Although Carter's aggressive borrowing provoked complaints among Jackson staffers that he had broken the campaign finance laws, the Federal Election Commission later upheld the legality of those transactions.) Consequently, Carter outspent Jackson by more than three to one in Pennsylvania.[30]

Jackson badly needed organized labor to make an all-out effort for him, but it did not. In Pennsylvania more than anywhere else, labor preferred Hubert Humphrey, who not only declined to endorse Jackson unequivocally but signaled tantalizingly in the days before the primary that he might enter the race. Reporters frustrated Jackson and demoralized his potential supporters by increasingly characterizing him as merely a stalking horse for Humphrey.[31] Hence labor organized late, ineffectively, and unenthusiastically for Jackson, notwithstanding the AFL-CIO's annual report card on the Ninety-fourth Congress issued January 30, 1976, which showed him with the best cumulative voting record by labor's standards; and notwithstanding Carter's previous support for right-to-work laws, which labor denounced.[32] Jackson's close friend and personal physician Dr. Haakon Ragde, who traveled with him on the campaign, suspected that Humphrey already suffered from the incurable bladder cancer that killed him two years later. Although he felt that Humphrey had betrayed him, Jackson would not make his health an issue. He attributed Humphrey's quixotic behavior not to malice, but to an inability to cope with his mortality, a foible that Jackson did not judge harshly in retrospect. Tensions between the Jackson and Humphrey camps lingered on until the Minnesota senator died in 1978.[33]

Nor was it an unmixed blessing to have Mayor Frank Rizzo of Philadelphia publicly identified as one of Jackson's most enthusiastic backers in the state. The belligerent, polarizing, and corrupt mayor antagonized as many voters as he attracted. Jimmy Carter harped on Rizzo's endorsement of Jackson in the western part of Pennsylvania, where the mayor was very unpopular.[34] In the final days, Jackson also had to divert precious attention from the Pennsylvania campaign to deal with a bizarre and totally false charge levied against his two most trusted foreign policy aides by Vice President Nelson Rockefeller. The vice president told a private session in Georgia on April 15 that communists might have infiltrated Jackson's staff. Rockefeller accused Dorothy Fosdick and Richard Perle of harboring such sympathies. He invoked as one piece of "evidence" that Fosdick had served as Alger Hiss's chief assistant at the 1945 United Nations conference in San Francisco. Rockefeller did not even have this straight; Fosdick never worked with Hiss. She and Jackson had impeccable credentials as two of the toughest anticommunists and anti-Soviets ever to walk Capitol Hill. Even more damning to Rockefeller, Fosdick had known him for more than fifty years. Her father, Harry Emerson Fosdick, had been his family's minister at Riverside Church on the upper West Side of Manhattan.[35]

When Rockefeller's charge first became public in the *Atlantic Constitution* on April 21, spokesmen for Jackson just laughed. "I doubt that Nelson Rockefeller said any such thing," Jackson's deputy press secretary Gene Tollefson said when first asked for a reaction.[36] When Jackson found out that Rockefeller had really made the accusations, he exploded with righteous indignation. "The remarks attributed to you are obviously false and malicious," he wired Rockefeller on April 21 from the campaign trail in Pennsylvania. "I demand an immediate apology. . . . you have known Dr. Fosdick for many years, which makes your reported remarks about her all the more shocking. Dorothy Fosdick has been an outstanding public servant for over thirty years. . . . You have apparently made a general accusation against another unnamed staff member, which has the result that you have impugned the integrity of every member of my staff. . . . This kind of slur and vile innuendo has no place in this election campaign or in American life."[37]

Rockefeller refused initially to apologize because the session was off the record. In a tersely worded telegram to Jackson, he stated: "I have made no charge, and therefore there are none to be withdrawn." The national press blasted him for smearing Fosdick and Perle, and Jackson threatened to launch a congressional investigation of the matter. He conferred with Senate Majority Leader Mike Mansfield, who also issued a statement criticizing Rockefeller's comments and his refusal to apologize. Jackson told reporters that the Senate might insist that Rockefeller divulge "who gave him the information."[38] He and Richard Perle suspected that it was his old protege and close friend Henry Kissinger, whose policy of détente Jackson had excoriated for four years running. They also surmised that a desire to protect Kissinger and discredit his most outspoken congressional critic had motivated Rockefeller.[39] Nationally syndicated columnist George Will, a close friend of Jackson's and Fosdick's, commented, in that vein: "The most likely explanation of Rockefeller's exercise in slander is that he is serving his former servant Henry Kissinger, who is known to resent Dickie and Richard, as he resents all of the few remaining pockets of independent foreign policy judgment in government. It is a measure of Rockefeller's mind that he would try to peddle the idea that Jackson, of all people, is harboring a nest of Soviet sympathizers."[40]

Mansfield and Senate Majority Whip Robert Byrd challenged Rockefeller either to back up his statements or to apologize. Rockefeller relented in the face of this mounting pressure. He asked permission to address the full Senate, where he formally apologized on April 27 to the Senate and to Senator Jackson. He said that "there was no question" that he had made a mistake. Following Rockefeller's remarks, Jackson arose from the Senate floor to accept his apology. "On behalf of my staff and myself, this is the end of the matter."[41]

Back on the campaign trail, Jackson tried gamely to reverse the rising tide against him by campaigning nonstop across Pennsylvania. Saturday, April 10, was a typical day. He donned a miner's outfit outside of Pittsburgh in the morning, confronted protesters on the campus of Haverford College in the Philadelphia suburbs in the early afternoon, spoke to labor officials in Philadelphia later, before concluding his exhausting day with an evening appearance in Harrisburg.[42] He also intensified his attacks on Carter, pounding him for his vagueness on the issues and for supporting right-to-work laws. He and Udall assailed Carter, too, for his ill-advised remark that the federal government should not try to break down "the ethnic purity of white neighborhoods by assisting blacks or other minorities to move there"; and stressing his immigrant heritage, Jackson said that Carter's references to ethnic purity were "an insult to all Americans ... which raises questions of judgment."[43] Carter counterattacked. He accused Jackson of distorting his labor record. He told a group at a farm rally near Harrisburg, "Scoop Jackson is getting desperate." He complained that Jackson, Mayor Rizzo, and labor leaders had joined forces to lead a "Stop Carter Movement."[44] On April 25, two days before the primary, Jackson and Carter engaged in a heated and sustained exchange on right-to-work laws on ABC's *Issues and Answers*. On the final day of the campaign, Jackson defiantly predicted, in Johnstown, Pennsylvania, "I will win tomorrow, labor will win tomorrow, jobs will win tomorrow." He also appeared in Harrisburg, Philadelphia in a last-ditch effort to stave off defeat.[45]

It was not to be. Carter had too much money and momentum. Organized labor did not deliver for Jackson. Carter rolled to victory in Pennsylvania, winning 37 percent of the vote to Jackson's 25 percent, Udall's 19 percent, and Wallace's 11 percent. Jackson conceded that organized labor in Pennsylvania preferred Humphrey and that his campaign had failed to get its message across. Publicly, he reacted to this crushing defeat initially with a vow to persevere. He said he was changing his strategy and would go directly to the people instead of the "gimmickry and pressing the flesh" of the campaign.[46]

THE END OF THE LINE

Privately, Jackson and his staff had begun to contemplate withdrawing from the campaign even as they sped down to Washington, D.C., from Philadelphia the night of his defeat. It was not a happy trip. Exhausted and disappointed, Jackson complained that Humphrey, organized labor, Bob Keefe, and Dick Kline had let him down. He also complained that the press had treated Carter much more generously than it treated him on the campaign trail, especially by slighting his victories in Massachusetts and New York while inflating Carter's in the smaller states and caucuses. Ben Wattenberg and Sterling Munro urged him to remain in the race. So later did his daughter, Anna Marie, who hated to see her father give up his bid for the office he had worked indefatigably over the past five years to achieve. Wattenberg insisted that Carter remained vulnerable, despite his victory in Pennsylvania. Jackson, he believed, could pick up enough delegates to be a major force at the convention if Carter faltered, or to become Carter's vice president if he did not. Jackson not only dismissed the vice presidency idea vehemently but resorted to the rare use of profanity to scorn Carter. "I would not run with that blankety blank under any circumstances," he erupted.[47]

As Jackson saw it, Wattenberg's rosy scenarios were wishful thinking. The campaign, he pointed out, had no money or any plausible expectation of raising more after the loss in Pennsylvania. Jackson had no strategy of victory in any of the upcoming states, except for Washington. Although the successes of the late entrants into the 1976 Democratic primaries—Senator Frank Church and Governor Edmund (Jerry) Brown, Jr., Democrat of California—proved Wattenberg right about Carter's potential vulnerabilities, it is unlikely that Jackson could have exploited them. Both Church and Brown scored their victories over Carter in the West running against him from the left, not from Jackson's position on the spectrum. If these darlings of the New Politics wing of the party failed to stop Carter, notwithstanding their late surges, surely the archetypical Cold War liberal could not have done so with his battered campaign. Jackson also recoiled at playing the role of a spoiler, especially in a year when it appeared that the Democrats seemed poised to retake the White House by a large margin.

Over the next few days, the Jackson entourage rehashed these arguments in a series of meetings at his Senate office. Governor Ella Grasso, Democrat of Connecticut, pressed Jackson to campaign in her state regardless of his decision, which eventually he did, because her election as a delegate to the convention depended on him making at least a minimal showing there. He concluded, however, that his situation was hopeless. With the exception of fulfilling his obligation to Grasso in Connecticut, he would end any active campaigning for the nomination.[48] He flew home to Washington State, where he made that announcement on May 1, 1976, to several hundred supporters who gathered at the Washington Plaza Hotel ballroom in Seattle. Without bitterness or recrimination, he proclaimed that he was "proud to have made this race for the Presidency. We tried hard, we gave it everything we had, and we have no regrets." Since losing the Pennsylvania primary, Jackson explained, his campaign was no longer viable. "I do not have a personal fortune to enable me to go further," he said. "It would be unfair to ask my supporters to give more. I am a realist. I gave this campaign everything I had, and I believe I ran a good campaign for a long time." He thanked his many supporters at home and across the nation. "No state has done more for its native son than the State of Washington has done for me." Ending on a positive note, he announced his intention to run in 1976 for reelection to the Senate. His quest for the presidency was over. "I would not run for President under any circumstances," an exhausted Jackson told a group of reporters in the reception room of the U.S. Senate three days after his announcement in Seattle.[49]

Although Jackson bore his fate stoically in public, the strain of running a grueling campaign while faithfully discharging his responsibilities as a father and husband finally had taken its toll. He manifested his stress and exhaustion by losing his temper with his staff and colleagues more often and with more volubility than usual. He "tore the head off" of Don Donahue, his longtime assistant, for presuming to tell Helen of his decision to withdraw before he had done so. When, in June, Daniel Patrick Moynihan offered Elliott Abrams the job of managing his upcoming senate campaign in New York, Jackson blocked it. "The grounds Jackson offered— I was not cut out to be a campaign manager—may have been legitimate," Abrams recalled, "but I felt, and I think Pat felt, that I was the first defection and his defeat was still too raw." After Moynihan won in New York, running largely as a Scoop Jackson Democrat, Abrams joined his Senate staff. Charles Horner also left Jackson's staff for Moynihan's a few months later.[50]

Jackson's most precipitous eruption occurred during the waning hours of the congressional session. Senator Mike Gravel, Democrat from Alaska, was the object of his wrath. Jackson had helped Gravel raise funds and win election to the Senate in 1968. He expected that Gravel would be a big improvement over his predecessor, Ernest Gruening, in league with antiwar Democrats such as Fulbright. Yet, since his first days in the Senate, when Gravel promised Jackson he would vote one way and then voted another on the ABM, the two men had detested each other. Jackson had stymied Gravel's repeated attempts to get an appointment to the Joint Committee on Atomic Energy. In October 1976, Gravel tried to barter his way onto the committee: Jackson's support in exchange for Gravel's support for the Energy Research Development (ERDA) bill that Jackson had managed through the Interior Committee and the Senate. When

Jackson refused to deal, Gravel tied up the Senate in the early hours of the morning by forcing the clerk to start reading the complete text of the ERDA bill—over 150 pages. Jackson lit into Gravel. "I will not be blackmailed," he shouted. "You have no honor, you have no decency, you are a disgrace to the Senate."[51] A shocked Robert Byrd forced Jackson to withdraw his statements from the record. "I will withdraw them," Jackson replied. "But now the Senate knows" (about Gravel).[52]

BACK IN THE SADDLE AGAIN

Jackson's irascibility soon passed. The year ended with him having recovered his equilibrium. He was happy in his domestic life, confident, optimistic, and eager to work with a newly elected Democratic president buttressed by solid Democratic majorities in both chambers of the Congress. His failure as a national candidate had no adverse effect on his overwhelming popularity in Washington State. Even with his bashing of the oil companies and big corporations, which eroded his support among conservative Republicans who normally voted for him, Jackson won another landslide victory for the Senate in November 1976. He defeated George Brown, his Republican rival, winning 75 percent of the vote. His mere presence in the race deterred the most formidable Republicans in the state from entering. When it had appeared that Jackson might capture the Democratic presidential nomination, Governor Dan Evans and Attorney General Slade Gorton had seriously contemplated running against his likely successor as a Democratic candidate, liberal Congressman Brock Adams. But when Jackson announced his intention to run again, they wanted no part of such a race.[53]

At the July Democratic Convention in New York, Jackson also had the satisfaction of having his sympathizers prevail in the battle with the New Politics forces over the party's foreign policy platform. This document reflected "80 percent of Scoop's priorities and concerns."[54] It incorporated his view that the key element in American security was the Soviet-American strategic balance, that the trends in this balance were running in the Soviet Union's favor, and that the Soviets had gained more from détente as practiced than the United States had.[55] Although he harbored strong doubts about Carter's foreign policy instincts, many of his most important backers on those issues did not. Midge Decter and Elliott Abrams later remembered ruefully that they and most like-minded neoconservatives viewed him as more hawkish and more skeptical of détente than his Republican opponent, President Ford. They calculated that Carter's Annapolis background and his belated but seemingly warm embrace of Jackson's human rights plank would dispose him to side with them against the New Politics wing of the party.[56]

By year's end, Jackson had reason for optimism about his relationship with President-elect Carter. The two men appeared to have repaired significantly the breach widened by the bitter primary contest between them. *Seattle Times* reporter Richard Larsen described the Jackson-Carter interaction on the campaign trail as "frostily non-communicative."[57] Yet Jackson sought to discourage any efforts to stop Carter after his defeat in Pennsylvania. He applauded Humphrey's decision to stay out of the race and was the first of Carter's primary competitors to release his delegates and endorse Carter after the Georgia governor's victory in the Ohio primary. Years later Stewart Udall, manager of his brother Morris Udall's presidential campaign, still hailed Jackson for that magnanimous gesture. Despite having no interest in the vice presidential nomination and his harsh words on the subject previously, Jackson agreed to meet Carter in New York to discuss the possibility of being his running mate.[58] Carter had settled on interviewing Jackson and six other possibilities in person: Senator Mondale, his ultimate choice; Senators Church, Glenn, Muskie, and Stevenson; and Congressman Peter Rodino, Democrat from New Jersey, the chairman of the House Judiciary Committee.[59] Jackson joined Carter on the platform during the grand finale of the convention. A month after Carter's victory, the president-elect invited Jackson to his home in Plains, Georgia, for a series of meetings focusing on energy policy. He accepted Jackson's strong advice not only to create a Department of Energy but also to make his comrade-in-arms in the détente wars during the Nixon and Ford administrations, James Schlesinger, the head of it.[60]

When Carter took office in January 1977, Jackson remained at the peak of his influence in the Senate. As a leading member of the Senate Armed Services Committee, as chairman of the Government Operations Committee, and as the institution's foremost expert on national defense, he also could again expect to have a huge impact on the nation's military and foreign policy. As chairman of the Interior Committee, he could expect to have a significant influence in shaping the nation's energy policy, which

President-elect Carter had declared as his number one priority. As one of the most powerful and informed Democrats in Congress, he could expect the new Democratic administration to seek his advice and counsel often on major issues within the vast province of his expertise. The new president would have sizable majorities to work with in both the House (292–142) and the Senate (62–38).

The results of the next four years confirmed all of Jackson's expectations but one. His philosophy would not recapture the Democratic Party after all. Nor would the party recapture the presidency for the long term, as optimists who hailed the Carter victory predicted. Of the nine presidents from Roosevelt through Reagan with whom he served, Jackson would have the worst relationship by far with his fellow Democrat Jimmy Carter. He would become so disillusioned with Carter by 1979 that he would aid and abet Senator Ted Kennedy's challenge to the president in the 1980 Democratic primaries. By 1980, many neoconservative admirers of Jackson's foreign policy would become so disillusioned with Carter and the Democratic Party that they would permanently desert both for conservative Republican Ronald Reagan.

Chapter 18

Perils of Détente, Part II:
1977–1980

Pʀᴇsɪᴅᴇɴᴛ Cᴀʀᴛᴇʀ's relations with Henry Jackson and the rest of the Congress got off to a rocky start. He was determined to maintain his image as a Washington outsider, the theme of his successful presidential campaign, but having served just one term as governor of a state with a strong executive and a weak legislature, he had poor instincts about dealing with an assertive Congress and powerful legislators. His advisers spurned Washington insiders, especially those Carter had defeated in the Democratic primaries in 1976.[1] Former Speaker of the House Tom Foley remembered Hamilton Jordan, Carter's top aide, telling him that the administration did not have to cultivate Jackson because "we whipped his ass in the Pennsylvania primary." When Howard Feldman, his chief council on the Permanent Investigations Subcommittee, suggested calling Jordan about some matter several months into the Carter administration, an exasperated Jackson replied, "I have never talked to Hamilton Jordan. He has never shown any interest in conversing with me." "Carter never understood," according to Foley, "that it is the obligation of the winner to reconcile with the loser in Washington, D.C., not for the loser to reconcile with the winner, especially a loser as powerful in Congress as Henry Jackson."[2]

Neither Carter nor his top aides ever realized how much their success depended on the cooperation and good will of Henry Jackson. In the words of Senator Bill Bradley, Democrat from New Jersey, who served with Jackson on the Energy Committee:

Scoop . . . played the legislative game the way good generals fight wars: everything was planned; nothing was left to chance. Votes were lined up

in advance with meticulous personal lobbying. Outside groups were enlisted to lobby. Certain decided senators were asked to contact the other senators who were still uncertain about the issue at hand. For floor
debates Jackson prepared a battle book—that's what his staff called it—
in which every possible question was anticipated, mastered, and answered. He left as little as possible to improvisation, and then he went
out onto the floor and crushed his opponents.[3]

Senators Moynihan, Inouye, and Kennedy and other liberal Democrats
besides Jackson also found Carter's staff arrogant and aloof. It was, moreover, a common complaint among Democratic legislators, including Jackson, that Carter did not adequately consult with or cultivate key congressional leaders in formulating his major legislative initiatives. "Carter not
only had problems with Scoop, but just about every Senate leader," remembered Daniel Inouye. "He campaigned as an outsider. When you do
that, you campaign against the Congress. Consequently, there were very
few happy moments between the Democratic leadership and Carter."[4]

In February 1977, Carter started off by antagonizing Jackson and the
entire delegation of western senators by canceling nineteen western water projects in the middle of a drought. Congress not only reversed this
decision but unanimously approved an additional water bill that the president had opposed: Jackson's proposal to redistribute the scarce water supplies of the West. The administration did not "understand that Congress
had grown more independent and stronger as the natural fallout of Watergate," Jackson remarked in reference to the water projects. "The Senate . . . is a pretty powerful body these days." Vice President Mondale,
more astute than Carter about the ways of Congress and more sensitive
to the concerns of his former colleagues in the Senate, told the president
that he had blundered politically. He counseled a reluctant Carter not to
veto those measures.[5]

Personal differences exacerbated the growing estrangement between
Jackson and Carter that was evident by the end of 1977. As Secretary of
Energy James Schlesinger put it in wry understatement, "Jackson and
Carter had a very weak rapport," despite the efforts of both men early in
the administration to improve it. Helen and Anna Marie Jackson remembered fondly the private dinner that the entire Jackson family had with
the Carters at the White House on May 18, 1977. The president put the

children at ease by assuring them that fried chicken was meant to be eaten with their fingers. When eleven-year-old Peter Jackson stared uncomprehendingly at the finger bowl before him, the president joked that he had never seen one either before coming to the White House. Henry Jackson relished the occasion. He thanked Carter and his wife, Rosalynn, for inviting his family to dinner. He assured Carter that he would help him "in every way possible to be one of our great presidents." As a miffed Jackson later confided to friends and staffers, however, he and Helen never received another invitation to the White House from the Carter administration for either an official or a private dinner.[6]

Carter people blamed their estrangement on Jackson's jealousy that Carter, the outsider, had taken away the prize he felt he deserved.[7] The Jackson people blamed Carter and his aides, who they claimed "were down on Scoop and Helen" for inexplicable reasons. Bob Strauss attributed their mutual enmity to the inability of either man to transcend the lingering effects of their bitter primary battles. There is an element of truth to all of these explanations. Jackson did have grave doubts about Carter's capacity to govern. As Denny Miller, who replaced Sterling Munro in 1977 as Jackson's administrative assistant, observed, those doubts intensified as his image crystallized of Carter as a failed president who he feared would lead the Democratic Party to disaster in 1980. Carter's penchant for "wearing religion on his sleeve" also grated on Jackson, who preferred to express his own deeply held religious convictions in a more private way.[8]

It was far more typical of Carter than Jackson to personalize disagreements with his political rivals. "Carter was a man who loved humanity, but that did not mean he loved every human being," observed Zbigniew Brzezinski, Carter's hawkish national security adviser. "He has some strongly negative reactions to people with whom he should have had more rapport. Scoop was one of them." Stewart Udall, former secretary of the interior, sympathized strongly with "Scoop's negative reaction toward Carter" because of what happened to his brother, Morris. Carter was "very self-righteous and stiff-necked," said Udall. "He had the attitude that he did not owe anything to the old-timers like Jackson. He had a hidden scorn for his opponents. Eventually, he softened on Mo, but not on Scoop."[9]

There were, conversely, just a handful of senators who did not like and respect Henry Jackson: William Fulbright and Eugene McCarthy, who disdained him, and Charles Percy and Quentin Burdick, Democrat from North Dakota, who despised him.[10] Even at the beginning of his administration, Carter evinced his strong distaste for Jackson, even though Jackson largely backed him as a key committee chairman on his number one priority of passing the energy legislation he unveiled in April 1977. Indeed, Carter had a more favorable impression of Senator Russell Long, Democrat from Louisiana, an implacable opponent of his energy bill, than of Jackson, an active defender of it. On October 25, 1977, Carter thus wrote in his diary:

> Met with the congressional leaders for breakfast, and we discussed almost exclusively the energy legislation. I particularly wanted Scoop Jackson and Russell Long there, so that we could have it out among a group of Democrats concerning their differences, which are very deep and personal. I thought Russell acted very moderately and like a gentleman, but Scoop . . . was at his worst. . . . At the same time, he is supporting my positions much more than Russell is. . . . Long said he would recommit the bill to committee if the Jackson amendments pass, and Jackson said he would call for recommitment if his amendments fail. And of course, recommitting the bill in the Finance Committee would kill it.[11]

Nevertheless, Jackson helped to salvage a large portion of the president's energy program in the Senate, where opposition to it ran high. He did so despite misgivings about several important provisions of Carter's elaborate plan that he believed the administration had generated with undo haste.[12]

THE POLITICS OF ENERGY: THE CARTER YEARS

On January 20, 1977, the day he took office, Carter charged a small group of energy planners led by James Schlesinger to produce a comprehensive energy plan in ninety days. The primary goal of this April 20 energy package was to curb America's appetite for oil and natural gas and to use energy more efficiently. It contained a host of regulatory and tax measures, which the president advertised as striking a prudential balance between the demands of pro-consumer senators such as Jackson, who favored cheap energy and government regulation, and pro-oil and gas industry senators, who favored deregulation of energy prices and market solutions to the energy crisis:

—an increase in the gas tax, a tax on inefficient cars ("gas guzzlers"), and accompanying rebates for efficient autos.

—a crude oil equalization tax on all domestic oil production, increasing in three stages, ultimately to bring the price of all domestic oil to world market levels by 1980; a rebate to consumers of all revenues raised under this tax.

—the indefinite continuation of oil price controls on oil under current production; to simulate more U.S. exploration and production, the price of newly discovered oil would be allowed to rise starting in 1979.

—maintenance of price controls on natural gas in current production; price controls on new natural gas whether sold interstate or in the state where it was produced; the pricing of new natural gas equal to the energy equivalent amount of oil.

—doubling the strategic oil reserve program.

—tax incentives for companies switching from oil or natural gas to coal; tax penalties for those that did not.

The House passed Carter's energy program almost unchanged before the August 1977 congressional recess, a testament to the legislative skill of Speaker of the House Tip O'Neill, who steamrolled the opposition to it. Momentum bogged down, however, in the Senate, which, unlike the House, had not compiled a strong record of support for the types of energy policies that Carter proposed. Jackson, chairman of the Energy and Natural Resources Committee (the successor to the Interior Committee, which Congress renamed in 1977), and Russell Long, chairman of the Finance Committee, the two committees with jurisdiction, clashed fiercely over Carter's energy plan. Representing Louisiana, the heartland of the nation's oil and gas industry, Long objected that it did not provide adequate incentives to the industry for production. He gutted virtually all of the Carter plan's provisions for trying to induce energy conservation through tax penalties. His Finance Committee wrote an alternative bill in October, trying to induce additional energy production primarily through tax incentives to industry. Long and his allies on Jackson's Energy Committee, such as Senator J. Bennett Johnston, Democrat from Louisiana, also objected to the Carter plan's provisions that continued federal regulation over natural gas prices. Representing Washington State, the bastion of federally subsidized cheap power, Jackson continued to defend the efficacy of price controls and their compatibility with the increase in domestic production he also sought. He objected even to a gasoline tax at the pump as a way to discourage consumption, because it penalized consumers who relied on cheap energy.[13]

The deadlock on natural gas pricing, which pitted the senators from the energy producing states, who favored decontrol, against liberal northern Democrats, who opposed it, stalled action on Carter's energy program for nearly a year. Jackson contributed significantly to breaking the impasse. In a series of protracted negotiations that Secretary of Energy Schlesinger compared unfavorably to a "descent into hell," Jackson forged a shaky but bipartisan coalition on the Energy Committee in March 1978 in support of a compromise plan to end federal controls on new natural gas by 1985. House and Senate conferees narrowly approved it to save the president's package from total defeat, even though some supporters such as Jackson disagreed with deregulation on principle. In September 1978, Jackson also led the forces that defeated a last ditch effort by Senator Howard Metzenbaum, Democrat from Ohio, and James Abourezk, Democrat from South Dakota, to jettison the compromise they argued was a sellout of consumers. Finally, Congress approved a bill in October 1978 that substantially watered down Carter's original plan: it jettisoned, among other things, the gasoline tax and the domestic tax to raise the price of domestic crude oil to world levels. After the final vote, Jackson proclaimed, "I have given the best of my life for the last more than twelve months on the energy program—and 90 percent of that on the gas bill, working into the midnight oil."[14]

Henceforth, Jackson usually collaborated with the administration on energy policy, though not always. When the fall of the shah of Iran in January 1979 precipitated the second series of oil shocks, which lasted until autumn of 1979, Jackson opposed Carter's decision gradually to decontrol oil prices while enthusiastically backing his windfall profits tax on oil companies, which accompanied it.[15] He also saved Carter's gas-rationing plan from certain defeat by inducing the administration in the spring of 1979 to accept the compromise proposal of Senator Ted Stevens, Republican from Alaska, who wanted tighter restrictions on when rationing could be invoked. Stevens had introduced a resolution in May 1979 requiring certain findings before a president could use rationing authority. The administration deemed that resolution too restrictive. "The alternative to having a gasoline rationing plan ready in an emergency," Jackson declared, was "anarchy at the gas pump." By the summer of 1979, spurred by the termination of Iranian petroleum exports and the ensuing panic, the Carter administration also had come to embrace another measure that Jackson had long championed: legislation creating a huge synthetic fuels program to reduce American dependence on foreign oil.[16]

Jackson received much praise from both liberal and conservative members of Congress for conducting a series of thoughtful hearings in the spring and fall of 1980 on the geopolitics of oil. He drew a close link between U.S. economic problems, U.S. energy problems, and U.S. security problems. "Our access to oil imports will rest in no small part on the strength and credibility of our defenses," he concluded. "Our ability to maintain a strong defense depends on the strength of our economy and our industrial base. Whether we like it or not, these linkages between energy, the economy, and national security will govern national policy in the 1980s." His committee report, issued on November 10, 1980, recommended that the United States build up the Strategic Petroleum Reserve as rapidly as possible, develop plans in concert with its allies to mitigate the impact of an energy emergency, work in concert with its allies to ensure stability and resist Soviet advances in the Middle East, and vigorously support programs for increasing oil production outside the Middle East.[17]

Unfortunately, many of the measures Jackson advocated aggravated the adverse consequences of oil shocks and stifled an effective response to them. As Daniel Yergin trenchantly noted regarding the long lines at gas pumps across the United States in the spring and summer of 1979:

> Emergency regulations around the country made matters worse. Some states, in an effort to avoid running out of supplies, prohibited motorists from buying more than five dollars worth of gasoline at one time. The results were exactly the opposite of what was intended, for it meant that motorists had to come back to gas stations that much more frequently. Meanwhile, price controls limited the conservation response; and indeed, if gasoline prices had been decontrolled, the gas lines might have

disappeared rather quickly. At the same time, the federal government's own allocation system froze distribution patterns on a historical basis and denied the market the flexibility to move supplies around in response to demand. As a result, gasoline was in short supply in major urban areas, but there were more than abundant supplies in rural and vacation areas, where the only shortage was of tourists. In sum, the nation, through its own political immobilism, was rationing gasoline through the mechanism of gas lines. And, to make matters worse, gas lines themselves helped beget gas lines. . . . One estimate suggested that America's motorists in the spring and summer of 1979 may have wasted 150,000 barrels of oil a day waiting in line to fill their tanks![18]

Senator Ted Stevens observed in the same vein:

Scoop did not realize that domestic producers could not produce at the level he wanted at the price he was trying to establish. He had this old oil versus new oil concept that just could not work. People with the old oil would not produce to keep the market supplied. He did not understand that if you have free markets and prices rise, you will get more production. He wanted to regulate gas not only in terms of price; he also wanted to deny access of certain industries such as utilities to natural gas as a fuel. His reason was that he wanted the U.S. to preserve its domestic capability. He wanted us to be able to maintain a strong military. The military was the largest consumer of petroleum. I disagreed with Scoop's judgment . . . because the free market will bring us more energy at a lesser price. We are at Jackson's price today (1995). The military benefited from the lower cost and greater supply of petroleum that free markets produced.[19]

THE ENVIRONMENT AND DOMESTIC ECONOMIC POLICY

Jackson also cooperated with the Carter administration on environmental policy. Cecil Andrus, Carter's secretary of the interior, shared Jackson's balancing approach, which sought to reconcile economic growth with environmental protection. Jackson, Andrus said, was one of the "few and truly great statesmen in the United States Congress." Andrus credited Jackson above all others for the passage of the Alaska Lands Bill of 1980.

The bill more than doubled the size of the country's national park and wildlife refuge systems and nearly tripled the amount of land designated as wilderness in the country. During the months before the final vote, environmentalists and development interests had lobbied intensely on behalf of their competing positions. Environmentalists, on one side, sought greater protection for Alaska's wilderness areas, which would have largely thwarted any development. The Alaska state government, on the other, backed oil, timber, and mineral interests that sought access to the state's enormous natural resources. Jackson negotiated a compromise that satisfied enough moderates to overcome opposition from both sides. The final bill set aside 104.3 million acres into conservation units: more than developers wanted but less than the environmentalists had secured in the earlier House version of the bill. Instead of prohibiting logging, mining, hunting, and oil development entirely in those areas, the final bill employed varying degrees of restrictions on those activities, based on Jackson's multiple-use approach. It also completed the transfer of 44 million acres of land due to Alaska natives under the Alaska Native Settlement Claims Act of 1971 that Jackson had also sponsored.[20]

Jackson would become profoundly dissatisfied, however, with Carter's handling of the economy as interest rates and inflation soared while growth stagnated. He shared the grievances of liberals in his party such as Ted Kennedy that Carter pursued too conservative a fiscal policy. Again, Jackson called for the imposition of wage and price controls. He also pressed for more spending than Carter wanted on traditional Democratic social programs such as health. Carter accorded a higher priority than liberals of Jackson's ilk to curbing federal spending, even on social programs if necessary.[21] In staking out his critique of the administration, Jackson found himself in an utterly anomalous position within the Democratic Party. The very Democratic liberals with whom he basically agreed on economic matters largely supported Carter's foreign policy, which Jackson objected to vehemently. Jackson's foreign policy and defense positions drew their most unabashed support from conservative Republicans and fiscally conservative Southern Democrats who reviled Jackson's New Deal–Fair Deal domestic liberalism. On economic issues, he was closer to Ted Kennedy than to Carter. On social issues, he was more conservative than either Carter or Kennedy: tougher on crime, deeply skeptical of Affirmative Action, an opponent of busing and abortion. On foreign policy and defense issues, he had far more in common with Ronald Reagan by 1980 than with the vast majority of his party.

CARTER'S DÉTENTE: BRZEZINSKI'S VERSION VERSUS JACKSON'S

It is a tribute to Henry Jackson that even some of those with whom he battled fiercely have striven to mute the severity of their disagreements with him. In their memoirs, Richard Nixon and Henry Kissinger insisted, albeit unpersuasively, that their differences with Jackson were merely tactical. Similarly, in his memoirs and later interviews, Zbigniew Brzezinski claimed Carter took a tougher line toward the Soviets than either Jackson or the president's neoconservative critics aligned with him ever recognized. Brzezinski and his deputy at the National Security Council, General William Odom, credit Carter for initiating the military buildup that restored the robustness of American power and hastened the decline of the Soviet Union. In their eyes, President Reagan merely accelerated the Carter program.

Brzezinski and Odom rest their case, in part, on a series of presidential directives (PDs) that Carter issued to enhance the credibility and effectiveness of the U.S. Doctrine of Deterrence: PD-41, issued in September 1978, defining defensive capabilities such as strategic defense as part of the strategic balance; PD-53, issued in November 1979, enhancing U.S. capabilities to manage a protracted nuclear conflict by setting forth national goals for command, control, communication, and intelligence; and PD-59, issued in May 1980, expanding flexibility beyond preplanned options in the event of nuclear war. Brzezinski described PD-59 in particular as "marking an important new step in the evolution of American strategic thought. It gave greater targeting emphasis to Soviet military installations, Soviet industry, and intelligence facilities rather than population centers. It also called for the development of "look-shoot-look" strategic capabilities to identify and strike new and moving Soviet targets so that American planners would have meaningful choices beyond doing nothing or killing millions of innocent Soviet civilians.[22]

As more evidence of Carter's unflinching determination to resist Soviet expansion, Brzezinski also cited the president's decision in the spring of 1979 to proceed with the MX missile; his sanction in the fall of 1978 of several unprecedented clandestine programs for destabilizing the Soviet Union; his approval in 1980 of military aid for mujahedeen rebels in Afghanistan; his imposition in 1980 of the grain embargo on the Soviets; his establishment in March 1980 of the Rapid Deployment Force; and his public criticism of Soviet human rights abuses.[23]

Brzezinski's portrayal of the Carter administration's foreign policy thus was starkly at odds with Jackson's perception of it. He criticized Jackson, not Carter, for accentuating the demise of the liberal Cold War tradition within the Democratic Party. "The Jackson tradition was something I found quite congenial," remarked Brzezinski. "Ideological battles and human rights ought to be backed by power. But too many of Scoop's people and political allies went to work for Reagan with Scoop's tacit approval." Their defection, Brzezinski complained, not only left him "very much alone in the Carter administration, but also made it a foregone conclusion that we would be frozen out of the Democratic Party once Carter was defeated."[24]

I find Brzezinski's line of argument even less tenable than Kissinger's strained attempts to reduce his conflicts with Jackson to the realm of tactics. True, Brzezinski himself and Jackson had only tactical differences, except for the Arab-Israeli conflict, which Brzezinski blamed as much on Israeli as on Arab intransigence. As Soviet Ambassador Dobrynin stressed, Carter's support of prominent Soviet dissidents such as Sakharov and Sharansky also deeply disturbed the Soviet leadership. After the Soviet Union invaded Afghanistan, Carter did indeed display signally greater firmness toward the Soviet Union than he had during the previous three years. His speech on June 7, 1978, to the graduating midshipmen at the U.S. Naval Academy contained some stern rhetoric presaging his watershed change in his foreign policy. William Odom may be right to say that there were two Carters uneasily coexisting with one another: the deeply religious and idealistic Sunday school teacher with foreign policy inclinations close to the antiwar left; and the "leathery tough naval officer," an aspect of his personality he has almost "fully repressed" since he left the presidency.[25]

What highlighted this uneasy coexistence in bold relief was the unremitting tension between Brzezinski and Cyrus Vance, Carter's secretary of state. The renowned civil rights lawyer Morris Abrams, a mutual friend of his fellow Georgian, Carter, and Henry Jackson, described Vance as "the closest thing to a pacifist the U.S. had ever had as secretary of state, with the possible exception of William Jennings Bryan, who resigned over Woodrow Wilson's determination to enter World War I. In his memoirs, Carter's secretary of defense Harold Brown, who held views similar to Vance's during the first two years of the administration, but gradually moved closer to Brzezinski's thereafter, offered a similar assessment. Secretary Vance, according to Brown, "was persuaded that anything that involved the risk of force was a mistake." Perhaps Carter did manage, in Odom's words, to epitomize "in his own ambiguities the real ambivalence of the Democratic Party."[26]

Duly noting all of these caveats, Jackson rightly viewed the dovish side of Jimmy Carter's personality as the dominant inclination guiding his administration's foreign policy, especially for the three years before the Soviet invasion of Afghanistan. The Carter administration's actions on this score speak louder than Brzezinski's words. Discussing Carter's foreign policy nearly two decades after the fact, Senator Moynihan still erupted volubly over how the president "deliberately shut out" Jackson Democrats. "The Carter administration froze us out completely," averred former Jackson and Moynihan aide Elliott Abrams, who later found a home in the Reagan administration as an assistant secretary of state for human rights. In late 1976, the Coalition for a Democratic Majority, which Jackson and Moynihan co-chaired, presented a list of fifty-three candidates for office in national security affairs. The Carter administration rejected all but two, who received only peripheral positions. Former Senator Gale McGee became ambassador to the Organization of American States, and Peter Rosenblatt became the U.S. negotiator for Micronesian affairs. Rosenblatt believed that he and McGee secured these positions in spite of their connection with Jackson, "whom the Carter team regarded as a relic of a discredited Cold War past." Rosenblatt had connections with former members of the Johnson administration, who pushed his case. McGee, a former member of the Foreign Relations Committee, favored the Panama Canal Treaty, to which Carter assigned high priority.[27]

Instead, almost all of the political appointees to the Departments of State and Defense came from the New Politics wing of the Democratic Party largely associated with Senator McGovern's views. So did Andrew Young, Carter's U.N. ambassador, and Ted Sorensen, his nominee (subsequently withdrawn under pressure) to head the CIA. For his chief adviser on Soviet affairs, Secretary of State Vance chose Columbia professor Marshall Shulman, one of the most conciliatory and optimistic of all Sovietologists, whom Jackson assailed as the embodiment of flawed thinking about the Soviet Union. "You could really set Scoop off just by mentioning Shulman's name," remembered Professor Kenneth Pyle, who traveled twice to China with Jackson.[28]

Vance, his proteges such as Shulman, and in large measure Carter himself, spurned power politics and geopolitics in favor of a foreign policy based on human rights. They and the president tended to reject unilateral assertions of American power in favor of multilateralism and an enhanced role for international organizations such as the United Nations. Carter sought, moreover, to transcend what he called in his May 1977 speech at Notre Dame University "our inordinate fear of communism" by conciliating communist adversaries to a degree that Nixon and Kissinger in their most euphoric moments never thought prudent. In that speech, wrote his admiring biographer Peter Bourne, Carter effectively renounced "the fundamental pillars on which American foreign policy had been based since World War II."[29]

The early policies of the Carter administration substantially reflected the outlook of William Fulbright and anti-Vietnam War critics that the arrogance of American power rather than communist expansionism was the main problem for American foreign policy. Carter favored, though did not achieve, the withdrawal of American combat troops from South Korea and early recognition of North Vietnam. The Carter administration initially took a relatively relaxed view as the Soviet Union intensified its aggression in the third world, which culminated in the fall 1979 invasion of Afghanistan—an event that deeply shook even President Carter, who admitted in a moment of painful candor that he learned more about Soviet motives from that event than he had ever known previously. Although Brzezinski counterbalanced this tendency to some degree, Carter's human rights policy largely inclined in the direction of Patricia Derian, the assistant secretary of state for human rights, who inverted what Jackson had in mind by focusing on the human rights depredations of America's authoritarian allies rather than America's communist adversaries. The Carter administration's human rights staff did not include anyone who approached human rights from Henry Jackson's perspective. Derian and her key personnel shared what Joshua Muravchik, author of the best book on Carter's human rights policy, termed a "McGovernite" or left-liberal view."[30] Thus, U.N. Ambassador Andrew Young appalled Jackson and others by commending the role of Cuban troops acting as Soviet proxies on the African continent as providing a certain stability and order.

Nor did Vance or Shulman favor strong human rights actions against the Soviet Union. Vance once told *Time* that Carter and Brezhnev held similar dreams and aspirations about the most fundamental issues," and Shulman, who classified the Soviet Union merely as authoritarian rather than totalitarian, argued that "the effort to compel changes in Soviet institutions and practices by frontal demands on the part of other governments is counterproductive." Both Vance and Shulman preferred quiet diplomacy as an alternative and believed that the imperative for both sides to reduce the dangers of nuclear war through arms control transcended Soviet-American disputes on other issues.[31] Both counseled Carter to avoid vigorous action that the Soviet leaders might regard as provocative or destabilizing. Muravchik summed up nicely the fundamental distinction between Jackson's and Carter's approach to human rights:

> To the Jackson Democrats, the human rights issue brought to mind primarily the victims of Communism, and they thought of it as a way of maintaining the ideological struggle against the Soviet Union at a time when the American people were losing their stomach for the policy of containment. On the other side, the McGovern Democrats had in mind primarily the victims of rightist governments. Raising this issue was to them a way of scaling back America's foreign entanglements.[32]

Depreciating the utility of military power in the nuclear age, Carter simultaneously strove to achieve deep cuts in Soviet and American arsenals, not only by formal arms-control treaties, but also by exercising unilateral restraint in weapons building in the hope that the Soviet Union would reciprocate. Thus the Carter administration delayed the development and deployment of the Trident submarine, cruise missiles, and the MX missile; shut down the Minuteman ICBM production sites; canceled the enhanced radiation weapon, sometimes called the neutron bomb; and scrapped the B-1 bomber—all programs Nixon and Kissinger initiated and considered vital to maintaining the U.S.-Soviet strategic balance.

Meanwhile, the Soviet Union continued its relentless, massive, and comprehensive military buildup in defiance of the Carter administration's optimistic expectations. As historian Patrick Glynn noted, the greatest surge in the Soviet Union's strategic nuclear buildup took place "*after* the signing of SALT I, when as part of a massive modernization effort, the Soviets deployed four new ICBMs, three new SLBMs, five new ballistic-missile submarines, and a new medium-range bomber." During the same period, as Glynn also noted, "the United States added significantly to its stock of deliverable warheads through MIRVing but deployed no major new systems." Furthermore, Carter responded only belatedly to Moscow's deployment of a new generation of intermediate-range missiles, the SS-20s, which had ignited neutralist sentiment in Western Europe by undermining the credibility of the U.S. nuclear guarantee to its NATO allies. At the urging of Chancellor Helmut Schmidt of West Germany, the administration finally committed the United States in 1979 to NATO's two-track decision whereby the alliance would deploy land-based cruise missiles and Pershing intermediate-range ballistic missiles (IRBMs) to offset this dangerous Soviet advantage.[33]

Defense spending during the first three years of the Carter presidency reflected the administration's optimistic assessment of the Soviet Union in keeping with Secretary of State Vance's point of view. It was President Ford, not Carter, who first proposed to reverse the 38 percent decline in U.S. military spending that had occurred between 1968 and 1976. By raising defense spending by a modest 3 percent annually during the first three years of his administration, Carter actually slashed $57 billion from the six-year program that the Ford administration had proposed and projected.[34] Defense spending as a percentage of both GNP and federal spending continued to decline over the same period. Carter proclaimed proudly, for example, that his FY 1979 budget was "$8 billion below the defense budget projected for 1979 by the previous administration." As the *Wall Street Journal* observed, Carter sought to meet his pledge of a 3 percent real budget increase by holding down spending in the base year rather than raising base-year spending substantially, as President Ford intended to do.[35]

Unlike Presidents Nixon and Ford, who wanted to spend more than Congress was willing to appropriate for defense, President Carter wanted to spend substantially less. He fought hard against determined efforts by Jackson and others to increase defense spending further.[36] In August 1978, he vetoed a FY 1979 military authorization bill that Jackson and Sam Nunn had sponsored, which provided funding for an additional nuclear aircraft carrier, for more tanks, and for more expenditure on research and development than the president thought necessary. In August 1979, Jackson, Nunn, and John Tower wrote the president endorsing the Joint Chiefs' recommendation of an annual increase of 5 percent, after taking inflation into account. They also pressed for a supplemental budget request for FY 1980 to compensate for the higher than anticipated levels of inflation, which had cut the promised 3 percent rate increase in defense spending to less than 1 percent in real dollars. The president resisted stoutly. In September 1979, Carter vetoed a resolution sponsored by Senators Jackson, Nunn, and Ernest Hollings, Democrat from South Carolina, which passed the Senate 55 to 42, calling for a real increase in defense spending of at least 5 percent. Jackson's impassioned plea for it persuaded several colleagues but not the president.[37]

Almost all of the measures that Brzezinski invokes as evidence of Carter's greater firmness toward the Soviet Union—the grain embargo, the boycott of the Olympics, PD-59, approving a 5.4 percent increase in the FY 1981 budget—occurred after the invasion of Afghanistan, in the middle of his difficult fight for reelection in 1980. Indeed, he endorsed just one major increase in defense spending before Afghanistan, and begrudged that: in December 1979, he belatedly agreed to raise defense spending by 4.5 percent as the price he would have to pay to win Senate support for his embattled SALT II Treaty. Notably, he made no effort to court the Jackson Democrats, whom his administration had systematically excluded from important foreign policy positions, until his electoral difficulties drove him to make several half-hearted attempts to do so in the spring of 1980. "The Carter FY 1981 budget came late," opined Richard Perle. "It was a throwaway budget, a political response to Reagan he probably would have abandoned had he won reelection."[38]

Carter's born-again hawkishness during the early stages of the 1980 presidential campaign contrasted sharply not only with the trajectory of his administration's foreign policy during its first three years, but also with his dovish foreign policy inclinations since leaving office.[39] Throughout the fall of 1980, he tried to depict Reagan as a warmonger whose hawkish policies—almost identical to Jackson's—would provoke a dangerous arms race, possibly war. Thereafter, he fiercely opposed the Reagan administration's military buildup, which Brzezinski credits him for initiating.[40] During the Gulf War crisis of 1990–91, Carter so opposed the use of American military force that he unsuccessfully lobbied other members of the U.N. Security Council to block a resolution sanctioning it. He has exhibited similar inclinations in other postpresidential forays such as his negotiations in North Korea with dictator Kim Il Sung, hailed by his admirers as neutralizing a conflict that could have led to war and condemned by his detractors as providing a cover for North Korea to continue its military nuclear program. Asked recently about his legacy as president, Carter expressed hope that the American people would remember him as a man of peace who did not "send American soldiers abroad" or "bomb anybody."[41]

Of course, a president's conduct out of office does not offer an infallible guide for assessing his conduct while in it. Unburdened by the responsibilities of power, ex-presidents often talk differently from when they governed. Nixon and Kissinger pursued much more conciliatory policies toward the Soviets than their postadministration writings tried to suggest. Conversely, Carter in office did not take quite as soft a line as his postpresidential actions would indicate. Taken as a whole, however, Carter's record on foreign affairs attests that Jackson's portrayal of it lay much closer to the mark than Brzezinski's.

THE DEMISE OF DÉTENTE

Jackson emerged from the outset as the most relentless and formidable critic of the Carter administration's foreign and defense policies. In 1977, when Carter signaled his intention to withdraw American forces from South Korea, Jackson lobbied against it. In 1978, when Carter announced his decision to forgo the neutron bomb, a weapon capable of devastating large tank formations without causing extensive collateral damage to the European countryside, Jackson and Sam Nunn cosponsored several failed measures to reverse it. Jackson had vigorously urged deployment of the neutron bomb, which he stressed could offset significantly the Soviet Union's overwhelming advantage over NATO in conventional weapons, thereby enhancing the robustness of U.S. deterrence against Soviet aggression and political intimidation in Western Europe. Jackson charged that Carter's decision not to deploy the weapon undermined the credibility of the American commitment to Western Europe's security just as the Soviets prepared to embark on the deployment of the SS-20 IRBM, making NATO even more vulnerable. Jackson also rebuffed several attempts by Secretary Vance and others to repeal the Jackson-Vanik Amendment. Until the invasion of Afghanistan, the administration successfully impeded Jackson's ongoing campaign, for which he used the Government Operations Committee as a forum, to impose much tougher and more comprehensive restrictions on the export of critical technology to the Soviet Union. Jackson castigated, in particular, the Carter administration's decision to acquiesce to the East-West natural gas pipeline that he feared would make the Western Allies dangerously dependent on the Soviet Union.[42]

SALT II: THE WARNKE NOMINATION

The struggle between Jackson and Carter over SALT II stands out, however, as the most significant of them all. Patrick Glynn refers to the hearings of 1979, which Jackson dominated, as the defense debate of the decade:

> The SALT II hearings of 1979 had roughly the same relation to the election of 1980 that the Lincoln-Douglas debates of 1858 had to the election of 1860. They were both a preview and a clarification of the questions that would determine the country's strategic, if not moral, fate. The SALT II debate pitted one against another two fundamentally opposing views of foreign policy and national security; one that emphasized . . . the importance of unilateral restraint, and the primacy of negotiations; and another that emphasized the enduring relevancy of force, the continuing problem of Soviet expansionism, and the primacy of the balance of power. The very fact that such a debate took place could not help but alter perceptions. . . . The hearings provided the first chance for the critics to present a detailed case against the treaties to the widest possible audience.[43]

This titanic struggle began in February 1977 with Carter's nomination of Paul Warnke as his chief negotiator to the arms talks with the Soviet Union. Warnke epitomized the sensibilities of the New Politics wing of the Democratic Party that Jackson detested: he had not only worked for Robert McNamara as one of the Whiz Kids in the Pentagon during the late 1960s, but also served as the principal adviser to Senator McGovern on national security issues during the 1972 presidential campaign. Warnke saw arms races as the primary source, not a symptom, of political conflict, which arms control and unilateral restraint could alleviate. He saw the United States, not the Soviet Union, as the main culprit, for initiating and perpetuating a dangerous arms race that left both superpowers more insecure. He also dismissed the operational significance of nuclear superiority so long as either superpower maintained a minimal nuclear deterrent. Warnke believed that the Soviet Union armed prodigiously not because it sought relentlessly to subjugate the West, but because the "giddy heights" of American defense expenditure had given it no choice. In his landmark 1975 article published in *Foreign Policy*, "Apes on a Treadmill," Warnke had encapsulated the essence not only of his outlook, but also that of a generation of like-minded American arms controllers:

> I would not like to see the SALT talks stop. . . . But if we must accept the insistence that the momentum of our strategic weapons programs must be maintained in order to bargain effectively, the talks have become too expensive and a luxury. . . . Insofar as formal agreements are concerned, we may have gone as far as we can go. . . . We should, instead, try a policy of restraint, while calling for matching restraints from the Soviet Union. . . . The chances are good . . . that highly advertised restraint on our part will be reciprocated. The Soviet Union, it may be said again, has only one superpower model to follow. To date, the superpower aping has meant the antithesis of restraint. . . . It is time, I think, for us to present a worthier model. . . . We can be the first off the treadmill.[44]

Warnke glided through his confirmation hearings before the dovish Foreign Relations Committee barely scathed, despite glaring contradictions, which he stubbornly denied, between the tougher line he took during his testimony and his previous public record.[45] Warnke encountered sterner resistance, however, before the Senate Armed Services Committee. Jackson led the attack. Exhaustively quoting Warnke's own works against him, he exposed glaring inconsistencies between Warnke's record and judgments over the years and his testimony during his confirmation hearings. Jackson's probing and grilling forced Warnke to acknowledge that he had actually opposed programs and deployments he had told the Foreign Relations Committee he merely questioned.

JACKSON: Just to set the record straight, and setting aside for the moment your current view on these prior recommendations, I want to read a list of programs on which you have made recommendations in the past. When I have completed the list, which runs to 13 items, I would like you to tell the committee whether I have accurately summarized your recommendations of U.S. programs. You recommended:

(1) Against the B-1.

(2) Against the Trident submarine and the Trident II missile.

(3) Against the submarine-launched cruise missile.

(4) Against the AWACS program.

(5) Against the development of a mobile ICBM, by the United States.

(6) Against MIRV deployment.

(7) Against improvements to the U.S. ICBM force, including improved guidance and warhead design.

(8) Against the development of the XM-1 tank and for reductions in the procurement of the M-60 tank.

(9) For the reduction of U.S. tactical nuclear weapons in Europe from 7,000 to 1,000. I believe you said a moment ago that you did not recommend a reduction of nuclear weapons in Europe.

(10) For the withdrawal of some 30,000 troops from NATO without waiting for the conclusion of the MBFR agreement.

(11) For holding the army at 13 rather than 16 divisions, after improved efficiency made creation of three new divisions possible within existing manpower ceilings.

(12) For a $14 billion cut in the defense budget in fiscal year 1974 and an $11 billion cut in fiscal year 1975.

(13) For reduction in fiscal year 1975 dollars of 3 percent per year in the defense budget, with the result that, applied to the fiscal year 1978 budget, the total amount would result in cuts of some $26 billion from the Carter recommendations to Congress.

MR. WARNKE: Yes sir, Senator, that is absolutely correct.[46]

Behind the scenes, Jackson assembled a group of prestigious experts to fortify the opposition. Paul Nitze, co-chairman of the Committee on the Present Danger (CPD), an organization filled with Jackson Democrats and future Reagan Republicans who collaborated closely with Jackson throughout the Carter administration, testified against Warnke before the

House Armed Services Committee. Eventually, the Senate voted to confirm Warnke, but by only a 58 to 40 majority—less than the two-thirds majority necessary to ratify a SALT II treaty. Privately, Jackson expressed satisfaction at this outcome but alarm that Carter could have nominated a man with Warnke's views.[47]

RISE AND FALL OF THE MARCH 1977 PROPOSALS

Despite their clash over Warnke and despite the leftward tilt of Carter's foreign policy appointments, Jackson had not given up hope on the president in early 1977. He therefore decided to take his case to him directly. Carter's initial response seemed to confirm Jackson's belief that he had an open mind about arms control. The closeness of the Warnke vote had put Carter on notice about the danger of arousing Jackson's opposition; any SALT II treaty the administration proposed would likely die in the Senate without his support. To propitiate him, Carter designated Jackson's trusted confidant General Edward Rowny as the military's observer to the SALT II talks, which would give the senator his usual steady flow of inside information on their course.[48]

Carter also solicited Jackson's views. On February 4, 1977, the president and Jackson discussed SALT over breakfast at the White House. On February 15, Jackson followed up by sending the president a detailed twenty-three-page memorandum on the subject, which he and Richard Perle had drafted.[49] The Jackson-Perle memorandum opened with a criticism of the Nixon-Ford-Kissinger approach for neglecting the "obvious truth . . . that not all negotiable agreements are in our interest; that some agreements may be worse than none; that the failure to obtain an agreement now does not necessarily foreclose the possibilities of doing so in the future." Part two of the memorandum stated what a sound SALT agreement should *not* do:

* impair our security by increasing the vulnerability of our strategic forces, or decreasing their controllability, or the credibility that they could and would be responsibly used if necessary to defend against attack;

* foreclose promising programs and approaches for maintaining the equilibrium of regional force balances or enhancing our ability to deter conventional attacks by conventional means;

* fail to permit adequate verification that can be demonstrated clearly and without compromising our sources and methods of intelligence collection;

* discourage research and development, especially with respect to weapons whose deployment is constrained or banned;

* leave the United States vulnerable to the rapid acquisition of a significant Soviet advantage if the agreement is abrogated or violated;

* increase the vulnerability of our allies (or other nations whose resistance to Soviet military pressure is important to us), either by impairing our ability to assist in their defense or by channeling the growth of Soviet military capabilities into regional or conventional forces;

* confer or legitimize an impression of Soviet superiority that could be exploited to our political disadvantage;

* alter the terms of what must be assumed to be a continuing competition in a direction adverse to the United States, by prohibiting new systems that could achieve reduced vulnerability and greater controllability or counter Soviet systems unconstrained by agreement;

* foster illusions that we or our allies can reduce our defense effort or that the strategic and conventional military balances are self-maintaining;

* establish harmful precedents for future agreements or prematurely limit U.S. systems so as to reduce Soviet incentives for future limitation on their own forces.

Part three of the memorandum set forth the principles that any SALT II agreement "must include":

* substantial, immediate, and reciprocal reductions in the number of MIRVed ICBMs on both sides to reduce the growing Soviet threat to the survivability of U.S. land-based ICBM forces;

* no constraints on U.S. or allied options for deploying cruise missiles, as a means of strengthening our theater nuclear, or most importantly, our conventional posture, in the face of growing Soviet theater nuclear capability;

* freedom to deploy mobile missiles;

* the elimination of the permanent Soviet advantage in heavy missiles that SALT I established;

* a rigorous and precise definition of what constitutes a heavy missile so that missiles such as the Soviet SS-19 ICBM clearly falls within that category;

* timely and adequate consultation with our allies on all measures which affect their interest;

* the inclusion within the SALT limits of the Soviet Backfire bomber and launchers such as the Soviet SS-20 IRBM, capable of launching ICBMs;

* no linkage between measures required for adequate verification of SALT limitations and substantive U.S. concessions on wholly unrelated substantive matters.

The Jackson-Perle memorandum concluded with an extensive critique of past U.S. negotiating tactics on SALT, which it counseled the administration not to repeat. The U.S. negotiators must cease excluding "reasonable demands on the strength of a priori judgments that they are likely to prove non-negotiable."

Jackson elaborated on his proposal in a series of subsequent meetings with Carter, Secretary of State Vance, Secretary of Defense Brown, and National Security Adviser Brzezinski.[50] Many, though not all, of Jackson's suggestions found their way into the president's proposals that Vance took to Moscow in March 1977. Following Jackson's advice, Carter called for sweeping reductions in the missile and bomber ceilings that the Ford administration and the Soviets had tentatively agreed to at Vladivostok in November 1974. The president proposed cutting the Vladivostok levels of 2,400 missiles and bombers to 1,800–2,000, plus a 15 percent reduction in the number of delivery systems carrying MIRVed missiles from 1,320 to 1,100–1,200, with a 550 subceiling on MIRVed ICBMs.

To Jackson's dismay, the administration proposed a limit of 2,500 kilometers on the range of air-launched cruise missiles (ALCMs) deployed on heavy bombers and a limit of 600 kilometers on the range of other types of cruise missiles.[51] Jackson and Brzezinski engaged in a series of sharp private exchanges on this and other points of disagreement between the Jackson and Carter proposals. Jackson complained that the 600-kilometer range limit foreclosed important U.S. and allied theater options and could not be verified. He disapproved of the administration's provision that would force the United States to forgo the MX mobile ICBM necessary to redress the 2 to 1 advantage in MIRVed ICBM reentry vehicles the Soviets retained under it.[52]

Nevertheless, Jackson publicly commended the Carter proposals of March 1977 as a step in the right direction. He encouraged the president to remain steadfast when the Soviets summarily rejected all these proposals. On May 20, 1977, the president sent Jackson a private note outlining his priorities for SALT II, most of which he ultimately would not achieve: sharp reductions of the Vladivostok ceilings; limits on the Soviet Backfire bomber; nondeployment of mobile ICBMs; adequate measures for verifying the conversion of SS-20 IRBMs to SS-16 ICBMs; and not counting B-52s with ALCMs as MIRVed systems.[53]

There were signs, however, that the Carter-Jackson rapprochement on SALT would not survive for long. In May, Carter decided to jettison the March proposals in favor of Vance's new three-part structure that Vance unveiled to the Soviets in May. Part one called for an interim agreement, running for eight years, that would restore the Vladivostok ceilings of 2,400 strategic launch vehicles and 1,320 MIRVed systems. It permitted the Soviets 180 heavy missiles (SS-9s and SS-18s), a number significantly higher than in the March proposals, and raised the March subceiling of 550 MIRVed ICBMs, which the Soviets had objected to vituperatively, to 820 MIRVed ICBMs for both sides. The second part called for a three-year protocol banning the testing or deployment of new ICBMs, including mobile ICBMs. It also prohibited the testing or deployment of sea-launched and ground-launched (though not air-launched) cruise missiles. The third part set forth the guidelines to govern the agreement, which would come into effect after the expiration of the three-year protocol.[54]

With Jackson's encouragement, the Committee on the Present Danger blasted Vance's May proposals in an extended public statement issued July 6, 1977.[55] Eugene Rostow, Paul Nitze, Elmo Zumwalt, Joseph Fowler, and Jeane Kirkpatrick, all leading members of CPD, soon received telegrams from Secretary of Defense Harold Brown informing them of the president's displeasure with their statement and inviting them to the White House to discuss it. Rostow described the president's August 4 meeting with them scathingly as "a farce" that signaled the permanent es-

trangement between Carter and those who viewed the Cold War the way
Jackson and Rostow did:

> We had quite an impressive group in terms of experience and outlook,
> people who did not have an ounce of partisanship and who believed in a
> bipartisan foreign policy. We listened to Carter, but did not know what
> to make of it. We were stunned. The President was so disconnected. We
> suddenly realized that he was not really interested in our views but was
> asking us to support him. Joe Fowler, . . . a man very active in Christian
> laymen's groups, said to him in a very Southern voice: "Thank you very
> much Mr. President. We assure you we wish you well. If you come
> around to our point of view, we will support you." Carter just did not re-
> alize who he was dealing with. Carter was McGovernism without Mc-
> Govern.[56]

Admiral Zumwalt gave a similar account: "Carter heard us, but he just did
not listen. He had already made up his mind."[57]

Jackson, too, had grown steadily more apprehensive about the direction of Carter's foreign and national security policy. By October 1977, the
Carter administration faced a concerted attack—which again Jackson
led—on its approach to SALT II. Jackson summoned Secretary Vance to
appear before the Senate Armed Services Committee on October 15,
where he and his colleagues subjected him to a grueling three hours of
questioning on the entire range of compromises that Carter announced
had brought the United States and the Soviet Union within sight of an
agreement (essentially a recapitulation of Vance's May 1977 proposals but
with a reduction in the aggregate number of delivery systems from 2,400
to 2,200). Such an agreement, said Jackson, would give the Soviets enough
accurate MIRVed ICBMs to destroy the entire U.S. ICBM fleet with only
a fraction of the Soviet force. By his reckoning, U.S threats to retaliate
against such an attack with SLBMs and bombers would lack credibility,
because those weapons were not accurate enough to destroy the military
targets, only population centers. Thus, continued Jackson, the ability of
the remaining Soviet ICBMs to strike U.S. cities would inhibit the United States from retaliating against Soviet cities in the event of a Soviet preemptive attack against U.S. ICBMs.[58] Although Jackson never expected
the Soviets to launch a first strike against U.S. ICBMs, he feared the po-

litical consequences to the NATO alliance of allowing this asymmetric window of vulnerability to materialize. He also charged that the advantage of the Carter-Vance alternative fell far short of either the March 1977 proposals or previous Carter administration statements on what a new SALT treaty should accomplish. He doubted, moreover, that the United States could adequately verify key provisions of the administration's agreements.[59]

The administration counterattacked. Several officials accused Perle of unscrupulously fomenting doubt about SALT II by systematically leaking partial information to the press.[60] Calling the March 1977 proposals unrealistic, the administration and its supporters attempted to sell the new agreements as a major improvement over the abortive Vladivostok agreement of November 1974. The Soviets, they argued, had made significant concessions, including renunciation of their advantage in the number of strategic nuclear delivery systems that SALT I had permitted.[61] The administration would need an additional eighteen months to work out the final details of the SALT II agreements with the Soviet Union. In the interim, supporters of the administration and their opponents—with Jackson at the helm—girded themselves for a ratification debate whose battle lines had been fixed by the end of 1977. "It is high time," declared Jackson, "that we stopped the dangerous practice of entering into unequal deals with Moscow in the misguided notion that Soviet leaders would reward our generosity with restraint in international affairs."[62]

Henceforth, the Carter-Jackson relationship would become steadily more adversarial, even on the rare occasions when they did agree on a foreign policy or defense issue.[63] Jackson remained uncharacteristically reticent during the acrimonious debate over the Panama Canal Treaty, which the Senate approved in the spring of 1978. Correctly anticipating a close vote, Carter employed his usual tactic when he wanted something from Jackson. He sent James Schlesinger to lobby him. Jackson told Schlesinger not to worry. He would vote for the treaty but "wanted to make Carter sweat." Periodically, Jackson voiced his frustration that Carter was the only president with whom he had served who largely disregarded him. "It is hopeless to raise my concerns with Carter," Jackson said to Richard Perle. "He will just staff it out to the Vance crowd." Despite the large areas of convergences between their views, Jackson discounted the more hawkish Brzezinski as a potential ally because he and Perle considered him bureaucratically ineffective as well as a lonely voice in the administration. "Scoop and I had high regard for Zbig," Perle said, but "David Aaron, Zbig's deputy, a former Mondale staffer, ran rings around him. Zbig lost on every issue except for aid to Afghanistan."[64]

Chapter 19

Human Rights, SALT, and Linkage

THE JACKSON-CARTER debate over SALT II lay at the center of the larger debate simultaneously unfolding over human rights, détente, the Middle East, China, and America's role in the world. So it is necessary first to analyze Jackson's role in this larger debate before returning to his pivotal role in the final stages of the SALT II debate, which would climax in the summer and fall of 1979.

It was Jackson, not Carter, who first established human rights as a central focus of American foreign policy by campaigning successfully for the passage of the Jackson-Vanik Amendment on freedom of emigration. Jackson had criticized the Nixon and Ford administrations unceasingly for defining America's self-interest too narrowly without sufficient reference to American ideals. Throughout the Carter presidency, Jackson continued to assail the Soviet Union on human rights. He remained the world's most stalwart champion of all the leading Soviet dissidents: Andrei Sakharov; his wife, Elena Bonner; Ida Nudel; Natan Sharansky (Anatoly Shcharansky); Yuri Orlov; Vladimir and Maria Slepak; Viktoras Petkus; Naum Meiman; Oleksa Tykhy; Mykola Rudenko; Viktor Brailovsky; Alexander Podrabinek; Mikhail Kukobaka; and Mustafa and Reshat Dzhemilev.[1] Jackson also remembered the unheralded victims of Soviet repression. He was one of the few members of the U.S. Congress to retain a full-time staffer devoted solely to aiding dissidents around the world. In response to the 1978 Soviet trials of Alexander Ginzburg, Yuri Orlov, and Natan Sharansky, he urged President Carter unsuccessfully to disapprove of the license request of Dresser Industries to build a multi-million-dollar plant in the Soviet Union for turning out oil drilling bits crucial for the further development of Soviet energy resources. Later, he urged the Helsinki Review Conference to give special attention to the fate of Soviet and Eastern European members of groups formed to monitor compliance with the 1975 Helsinki accords.[2]

Jackson also declined to visit the Soviet Union as a guest of the government unless he could meet with Sakharov. The Soviet leaders considered Jackson "the key figure in the battle for the eventual Senate ratification of SALT II," recounted Soviet Ambassador Dobrynin. Carter had suggested to Dobrynin that the Soviets make an effort to win over Jackson. They took his advice. In November 1977, Dobrynin delivered to Jackson the official Soviet invitation for the senator to visit the U.S.S.R. He met Jackson for dinner on December 5 at the senator's home in Washington, D.C., where they discussed the details. They decided that Jackson would visit the Soviet Union in March 1978. Jackson requested a meeting with Brezhnev, which Dobrynin assured him could be arranged. Dobrynin and Jackson later offered conflicting accounts of why the visit did not take place. According to the Soviet ambassador, Jackson and Richard Perle insisted that the Soviets permit the senator a meeting with prominent dissidents, which the Western press would cover. According to Jackson's memorandum of the conversation, he insisted on a private meeting with just Sakharov and a few other prominent dissidents as a condition of his visit. According to Perle, Jackson would not budge from these conditions, which he acknowledged would irritate Brezhnev. The Soviet Union responded by canceling the visit with this official reply: "Even mere considerations of tact seem to show the irrelevance of a situation where the senator makes his trip to the Soviet Union dependent on our agreeing to his meeting with a group of persons defiantly opposed to our system." In his public statement Jackson expressed regret "that the Soviet leadership regarded private discussions as any obstacle" to his visit.[3]

Jackson criticized Carter not for his emphasis on human rights but for the way his administration went about promoting them. Jackson had two principal objections to Carter's human rights policy. First, he faulted Carter for what he perceived to be the administration's selective application of human rights sanctions against less repressive right-wing authoritarian allies while slighting the violations of more repressive left-wing totalitarian adversaries such as the Soviet Union. Jackson construed what he saw as the administration's skewed priorities partly as a pretext for imprudently abandoning the policy of vigilant containment and scaling back U.S. foreign commitments. As Richard Perle observed:

> Jackson was much closer to Jeane Kirkpatrick's conception of human rights than to Carter's. First of all, Scoop thought it was important to distinguish between the denial of human rights in authoritarian rightwing dictatorships and the denial of human rights by the Soviet Union, which developed its policies into a theory of the proper relationship between the citizen and the state. The Soviets were not apologetic about human rights. Contrast that to the dictatorships where human rights were abused, but there was no philosophical defense of it or an all-powerful state apparatus that repressed human rights comprehensively in all aspects of life. Nobody justified such repression as the right and proper relationship between generals and citizens. It was an abuse. Everybody understood it to be an abuse. So it was perceived as illegitimate, something that would eventually go away. In the Soviet case, however, there was a whole doctrine developed to defend what they were doing. Beyond that, most of the nasty regimes that had become the focal point of Carter's concerns were not menacing anyone or trying to export their doctrines beyond their own borders. They were not trying to impose by force a world of like-minded regimes.[4]

Jackson thus assailed the Carter administration for jeopardizing human rights by undermining U.S. allies while emboldening U.S. adversaries:

> Many share my continuing dismay at the American policy on human rights that finds it convenient to criticize the petty dictatorships, with which the world unhappily abounds, but inconvenient to speak out about the Soviet system that inspires repression around the world.
>
> Thus it is that the Administration speaks more about the abuses of human rights in Chile, the Philippines, Argentina, and Guatemala, while speaking less about violations of human rights in the Soviet Union. So the Administration brings home our Ambassador from Korea because the liberties of Koreans have been violated, but finds it impossible to summon our Ambassador from Moscow when the freedom of so many Soviet citizens are trampled.

For too many officials, the intensity of the struggle for human rights abroad is inversely related to the power of the offender. We even have certain officials who subscribe to a unique arithmetic: they think if a human rights standard is a good thing, then a double standard must be twice as good.

Only with sensible priorities can we hope to forge an effective policy out of the impulse to support the cause of international human rights. Only by reasserting our concern at the denial of basic rights in the Soviet Union can we make credible our concern about basic rights elsewhere.[5]

Second, Jackson faulted the Carter administration for slighting the imperatives of power and geopolitics in pursuit of its ideals.[6] He thus described the "unsettling mixture of moralism, malaise, and retrenchment" that, in his mind, evoked contempt for U.S. weakness—a perception crystallized dramatically by the Carter administration's apparent impotence in responding to the Iranian hostage crisis of 1979–80:

> The President often says he is a reader of Reinhold Niebuhr. I urge him to take to heart these words of that distinguished theologian: "There has never been a scheme of justice which did not have a balance of power at its foundation. If the democratic nations fail, their failure must be partly attributed to the faulty strategy of idealists who have too many illusions and realists who have too little conscience."
>
> . . . Each of us must help stop the slide to weakness and surrender. Only a strong American can stand up to the Soviet Union, safeguard the interests of our friends and allies, combat terrorism, champion basic human rights, and conduct wise and steady diplomacy. Nothing would do more to hearten our friends and allies abroad. Nothing would do more to give hope to those in the U.S.S.R. who are resisting Soviet oppression and aggression. And nothing would do more to assure that the free peoples of the world—and not the tyrant—will inherit the future.[7]

Initially, Jackson had little to say about Carter's policy toward Nicaragua that so disturbed Jeane Kirkpatrick and other neoconservatives who assailed it for playing a major role in the 1979 overthrow of the Somoza dictatorship, a brutal though loyal ally of the United States. The Carter administration's defenders replied that Somoza was responsible for his own downfall. Whether Somoza would have fallen but for U.S. pressure will always remain uncertain. There is no doubt, however, that the administration not only wanted Somoza gone but used its influence to overthrow him by active measures such as suspending U.S. aid to him. There is also no doubt that the administration initially took a benign view of the Sandinista revolutionaries who overthrew him.[8]

Jackson did blast the administration for its "weak and vacillating" reaction to the Iranian Revolution that brought down the shah of Iran in February 1979. In that case, the upper echelons of the administration feared that result and did not intend it. Furthermore, a sick and dying shah had perhaps lost the will to undertake the only course of action that could have saved his regime: a brutal suppression of the Ayatollah Khomeini's fundamentalist mobs. Nevertheless, Carter's human rights policy did embolden the shah's fundamentalist opposition and weakened his already precarious resolve.[9] As Brzezinski himself concluded, "Iran was the Carter Administration's greatest setback. . . . But my pained belief is that more could have been done by us on the American side." Brzezinski criticized the State Department, particularly, for discouraging the Iranian military from undertaking a coup that he favored as the only plausible way to avert the triumph of the militant mullahs. Cyrus Vance affirmed in his memoirs that he and his advisers at the State Department indeed opposed such a coup.[10]

Despite his mounting doubts about the stability of the shah's regime, Jackson considered it infinitely more palatable, geopolitically and morally, than any of the realistic alternatives. He appreciated that the shah was pro-American, anti-Soviet, and more tolerant of dissent than his successors, and that Iran was the least hostile to Israel of any of the Middle Eastern states, except for Egypt after President Sadat's trip to Jerusalem in 1978. Like Princeton professor Bernard Lewis, the Middle East expert on whom he relied the most, Jackson thought that the administration had erred badly by putting public pressure on the shah, because "it conveyed to the Iranian public that we were going to dump him." Jackson described the Ayatollah as "another Hitler" and the loss of Iran as an adverse "shift in the balance of power of historic proportions." In February 1979, he warned that the Ayatollah's Iran "would become a base of operations of the PLO and a significant source of strength for radical Arab regimes. This . . . shift means increased danger for Israel, increased pressure on

President Sadat, and a decrease in the security of oil supplies for the United States and its allies in Europe and elsewhere.[11]

Jackson viewed the Soviet union as the prime beneficiary of the Iranian Revolution. "In the absence of countervailing force," Jackson declared, "the Soviets would step up the process of encircling and intimidating America's allies in the region: Pakistan, Turkey, and Saudi Arabia, which shipped over 9½ billion barrels of oil . . . to the United States and its allies." He criticized the administration for its lack of understanding and will to "fashion an alliance of states prepared to resist the encroachments of the Soviets and their friends." For Jackson, "it was high time to stop repeating the silly cliché that we cannot be the world's policemen, and to begin to think about our future in a world without a cop on the corner." The loss of the American monitoring sites in Iran, he added ominously, rendered the prospective SALT II agreement unverifiable.[12]

Jackson also attacked the administration for its "complacency" in the face of the Soviet Union's escalating military involvement through its Cuban proxies on the Horn of Africa.[13] Having earlier succeeded in imposing its clients as the rulers of Angola, the Soviet Union had switched its allegiance from Somalia to Ethiopia as the leftist junta in power there since the 1974 death of pro-Western Haile Selassie had become ardently pro-Soviet. The Soviets provided money and airlifted twelve to fifteen thousand Cuban troops to Ethiopia to assist that regime in its border war with Somalia, which erupted in 1977 over contending claims to the Ogaden region. Like Carter's national security adviser, Zbigniew Brzezinski, Jackson saw the expansion of Soviet influence in the Horn of Africa coupled with the expansion of Soviet influence in South Yemen as part of an "arc of crisis" gravely menacing to the American position in the Middle East.[14] He depicted Soviet activities in South Yemen, the Horn of Africa, and Afghanistan as "a clear attempt to encircle the oil producing areas on which the West depended."[15] Brzezinski, Jackson, and a growing contingent in Congress all pressed the president to back the Somalis, who had requested American aid; more broadly, they favored making progress on SALT contingent on the Soviet Union's curtailing its mounting geopolitical offensive in the third world.[16] Brzezinski later remarked that "SALT lies buried in the sands of Ogaden." Again, President Carter and Secretary Vance resisted these entreaties for a sterner policy. Until

1979, they both strove to insulate progress on SALT II from Soviet activities in Africa or elsewhere in the third world.[17]

For Jackson, the Egyptian-Israeli Peace Treaty of 1979 stood as one of the few great accomplishments of the Carter administration. He heralded the treaty for removing Israel's most dangerous military threat and for establishing a foundation for a joint American-Israeli-Egyptian strategic partnership to resist Soviet predations in the Middle East. Nevertheless, he gave Israeli Prime Minister Begin and Egyptian President Sadat rather than Carter the main credit for that agreement, which was immensely beneficial to both sides and to their American ally. Indeed, he believed that Sadat and Begin came together in the first place as a benign but unintended result of Carter's poor judgment.[18]

No episode better illustrated Carter's naïveté to Jackson than the president's initial desire in the fall of 1977 to revive Soviet influence in the Middle East, which Kissinger's diplomacy had deliberately succeeded in diminishing. Intent on improving relations with the Soviet Union, assuming the fundamental compatibility between Soviet and American goals in the Middle East, Carter and Vance initially drove hard to achieve a comprehensive settlement to the Arab-Israeli dispute with active Soviet cooperation. The United States and the Soviet Union thus issued a joint communiqué on October 1, 1977, calling for an international conference under the joint chairmanship of the two countries that would also involve Syria and the PLO. Essentially, Carter and Vance proposed to restore the 1967 borders and to lay the basis for an independent Palestinian state on the West Bank in exchange for the Arab nations' making peace with Israel.[19]

Jackson joined the ferocious attack on the administration that ensued from devotees of Kissinger's incremental approach and from Israel's supporters in the United States. He continued to regard unswerving U.S. support for Israel as not only a moral but a strategic imperative, and to insist that the maintenance of a strong, secure, militarily powerful Israel impeded rather than facilitated Soviet penetration of the Middle East. He continued likewise to oppose complete withdrawal to the 1967 borders and the creation of a Palestinian state as a strategic nightmare for Israel that the Soviets would ruthlessly exploit. A U.S.-Soviet cosponsored

Geneva conference, Jackson thought, would hold American and Israel hostage to the "positions of the most inflexible and irredentist views of the PLO (or PLO surrogates), the Syrians, and the Soviets," who as always would foment the most radical Arab demands to undermine the United States in the Middle East. Such a course, contended Jackson, would subordinate "the more readily solvable dispute between Egypt and Israel to the intractable differences between Israel and the Palestinians, between the Palestinians and Syrians and the Jordanians. Insistence on a comprehensive settlement will assure that there will be no settlement at all."[20] Jackson; Moynihan; Senator Clifford Case, Republican from New Jersey; Senator Richard Stone, Democrat from Florida, and Professor Lewis met just after the issuance of the joint communiqué to discuss what to do about it. If they opposed the communiqué publicly, Carter threatened to ask the American people "to choose between those who supported the national interest and those who supported a foreign interest such as Israel."[21]

Begin and Sadat also reacted with horror to the Carter administration's October joint communiqué and the reasoning behind it. Lewis and Jackson both surmised that President Carter so frightened both men that they preferred meeting with each other than dealing with the Soviet Union and the regimes of their radical Arab supporters at Geneva. Throughout the negotiations at Camp David between Egypt and Israel, Jackson advised the president to "encourage rather than discourage a separate Egyptian-Israeli deal that deferred the resolution of issues surrounding the West Bank for subsequent negotiations among the affected parties." Although Jackson's arguments did not persuade him, political necessity compelled a reluctant Carter ultimately to settle for an Egyptian-Israeli peace treaty largely along the lines Jackson advocated.[22]

Jackson did share the president's high regard for the strategic vision and courage of Anwar Sadat. During a short trip to the Middle East in November 1978, which also took him to Israel, Jackson visited the Egyptian president at his villa on the Nile, where they conversed at length. Sadat told Jackson that he saw the possibility of cooperating with Israel on matters of defense to stop Soviet aggression in the region and conceived of a special role for himself in Africa opposing Cuban-Soviet activities. Jackson returned to the United States ebullient that he and Sadat had basically the same conception of the Soviet threat and the vigilant means necessary to combat it. A month earlier, Jackson had introduced a resolution calling for a new Marshall Plan for the Middle East, which would lead to "full economic partnership with the Israeli and Egyptian people and all those in the Middle East who are willing to live in peace. He stressed the desirability and possibility of nurturing "a de facto alliance among Israel, Egypt, and Saudi Arabia—countries with a common interest—in a stable and secure peace to counter Soviet influence in the Middle East."[23]

Even so, Jackson had stricter limits than the president, or many of his colleagues in the Senate, on the price he would pay for Saudi cooperation, especially if he perceived it to be at Israel's expense. He thus opposed unsuccessfully President Carter's May 1979 decision to sell advanced F-15 fighters to the Saudis. "Without meeting the real security needs of Saudi Arabia which are internal," Jackson intoned, "the transfer of F-15s to that country will have a profound and destabilizing effect on the delicate balance between Israel and her neighbors. . . . Possession of the F-15 in the hands of the Saudis will erode the basis on which Israel had thus far maintained a military balance in the region—the man-for-man superiority of its highly trained air force." Jackson favored withholding the planes until the Saudis gave "us hard evidence of their willingness to support a reasonable peace plan. . . . Rather than reminding the Saudis they desperately need Western support to guarantee stability in the Persian Gulf, we act as if the only linkage was that produced by the Western need for Saudi oil."[24]

Jackson, Israel's best and most powerful friend in Congress, had forged very close relationships with the leaders of Israel's long ascendant Labor Party, especially with Prime Minister Golda Meir and her successor, Yitzhak Rabin. He did not have as close a relationship with Prime Minister Menachem Begin, the leader of the Likud coalition, which had defeated the ruling Labor Party in the Israeli election held in the spring of 1977. "Jackson spoke a different language than the Likud people," recalled Richard Perle. "Scoop talked about security, not biblical entitlement or historical destiny, as Begin did. His point was defensible borders." When Begin first met with a group of U.S. senators during his first visit to the United States, Jackson saw that the Israeli prime minister was losing the audience discussing Judea and Samaria, the biblical names for the West Bank. "Scoop told me to get a map," said Perle, who "ran huffing and puffing to get it. When Scoop laid out the map, he transformed the meeting in thirty seconds to a discussion of the security of the West Bank."[25]

Jackson would become steadily more critical of Begin. On the one hand, he agreed with him that "there is no way the state of Israel can survive unless there is an arrangement by which they can defend the West Bank. If you go back to the situation prior to 1967, all of Israel was in artillery range." On the other hand, he called Begin's "intransigent position" on the West Bank settlements juridically right but politically unsound. Begin was "not discussing the right issue," Jackson proclaimed. "We should instead focus on the fundamental question of defensible borders. If Begin would get on the tube and point to the map and say, look folks, the issue is this: Can my country survive if we grant independence to the PLO, which is working hand and glove with the Russians? Israel would have unquestioned support." What Jackson proposed was for "the Arabs on the West Bank to have a full government short of national security requirements and foreign policy."

In Jackson's eyes, the creation of an independent state would be the worst of all possible worlds for the Israelis and the United States. He portrayed the PLO officials he expected would run such a state as terrorists and Soviet agents. "Immediately after they get independence, they could turn around and enter into an alliance with the Russians and [then] the state of Israel comes to an end." Jackson envisaged the PLO as part of a global Soviet-sponsored campaign of terror aimed at "the disintegration of democratic societies through undermining the confidence of their citizenry in their governments." He acknowledged that individual terrorist movements such as the PLO, the Baader-Meinhof gang in West Germany, the IRA in Ulster, the Red Brigades in Italy, and hosts of other terrorist groups in the Arab world, Africa, and Latin America, had indigenous motivations for their violence apart from the Soviet Union's conspiracy to destabilize legitimate states. Yet he insisted that many such groups, including the PLO, benefited enormously from Soviet support. The Soviets, he pointed out, had trained many of the PLO's expert terrorists from their military academy at Simferopol in the Crimea. Over the years, Jackson had received several death threats, including from the PLO. Before leaving for China in August 1979, he instructed his house sitter, Adam Garfinkle, then a consultant for him on SALT II and more recently the executive editor of the foreign policy journal *The National In-*

terest, to keep the blinds drawn because the "PLO had just threatened him again."[26]

In May 1979, Jackson accepted an invitation from Benjamin Netanyahu, the future prime minister of Israel, to attend the Jonathan Institute's Jerusalem Conference on International Terrorism. The institute bore the name of Netanyahu's late brother Jonathan, the lieutenant colonel killed in the heroic rescue of hostages at Entebbe. Jackson and his family arrived in Israel on June 28, 1979, for a ten-day visit that included a whirlwind of events besides his keynote speech at the conference: a two-day stint on the Kfar Blum Kibbutz in northern Israel; talks with Prime Minister Begin, Defense Minister Moshe Arens, and Rabin; a visit to the Holocaust memorial at Yad Vashem; and the awarding to Jackson, and also Henry Kissinger, of an honorary degree from Hebrew University in Jerusalem. Senator John McCain, Republican from Arizona, accompanied Jackson on several trips in his former capacity as the naval liaison officer to the Senate. He never forgot the hero's welcome the Israelis gave Jackson and his family: "After we left the airport, we saw this crowd of seven or eight hundred people, all of whom wanted to get closer. They shouted: God bless you, Scoop. Helen and Scoop got out of the car to talk to Avital Sharansky."[27]

In his commencement address at Hebrew University in Jerusalem on the afternoon of July 2, Jackson even complimented Henry Kissinger, who had apologized to him earlier for not disclosing Gromyko's letter of October 26, 1974, indicating that the Soviet Union would not comply with the Jackson-Vanik Amendment passed in December 1974. Jackson, forever wary of Kissinger, nevertheless found his approach significantly less wanting or dangerous than Carter's "abhorrence of power and misunderstanding of it." In his keynote address to the Jonathan Institute that evening, Jackson exhorted the democracies to unite firmly against the primary supporters of international terrorism: "the Soviet Bloc and the radical Arab camp."[28]

JACKSON AND CHINA

Jackson was almost as popular with the leadership of the PRC as he was with the Israelis. Vice Premier Deng Xiaoping held him in especially high regard. They had got on famously during Jackson's first trip to China in 1974. Their relationship flourished during the Carter administration.

Fully rehabilitated from the vilification campaign that had forced him to leave Beijing in 1976, Deng found Jackson's assessment of the Soviet threat and his prescriptions for dealing with it strikingly congenial. Jackson envisaged the PRC as an essential counterweight to the Soviet Union, as a potentially significant source of stability in Asia, as a potentially significant source of energy that could reduce U.S. dependence on Middle Eastern oil, and as an alluring market for American goods. He envisaged China's strength as a supplement to, but not a substitute for American power in the Pacific, which he still deemed critical to the security of "Japan, South Korea, all the Pacific islands down through the Philippines, and to the resolve of the ASEAN-nations in resisting soviet pressures."[29]

Jackson criticized the Carter administration's declared policy of "evenhandedness" toward the Soviet Union and China, which moved it, until the summer of 1979, to resist granting the Chinese MFN status unless the Soviets received the same treatment. He considered the chief proponents of evenhandedness to be Secretary Vance and Marshall Shulman, who feared that a pronounced U.S. tilt toward China would antagonize the Soviet Union and thus imperil SALT II and détente. Jackson did all he could to prod the president to abandon evenhandedness in favor of NSC adviser Brzezinski's preferred course of tilting U.S. policy strongly toward China.[30]

The PRC assiduously courted Jackson. At its invitation, Jackson visited China a second time, from February 12 to 20, 1978. He had "frank and friendly conversations" in Beijing with many of China's top leaders: Vice Premier Deng Xiaoping; Foreign Minister Huang Hua, and many other high officials.[31] Jackson and Deng agreed heartily on almost everything, except for the presence of U.S. forces in Korea, which Deng opposed, and the establishment of an independent Palestinian state, which Deng supported. Each took great pleasure in the deep distrust of the Soviet Union that the other conveyed with vehemence. Both stressed the large measure of complementarity between Chinese and U.S. interests around the world. Deng not only assured Jackson that the PRC would comply with Jackson-Vanik, but also reiterated the PRC's strong backing for a credible NATO, for American bases in Japan and the Philippines, and for robust U.S. efforts to resist Soviet expansionism in the Middle East and the Horn of Africa. Both men called for stronger U.S.-China ties and a united front against Moscow.[32] During his visit, Jackson and his entourage also traveled extensively to observe China's energy development. They took trips through Shandoing Province to the Shengli oil fields, to petro-chemical complexes south of Beijing and in Shandoing Province, and to the Hongshan coal mine (also in Shandoing).

Throughout 1978, Jackson pressed President Carter and Vance "to give the relationship with the People's Republic of China a higher priority." Jackson counseled the president, in a private memorandum dated October 13, 1978, to normalize relations with the PRC and grant it MFN status expeditiously. Normalization did finally occur on January 1, 1979, thanks largely to the initiative and maneuvering of Brzezinski, who also mentioned to the president that this initiative might soften Jackson's expected opposition to SALT II. (It did not.) During his first visit to the United States in February 1979, Deng Xiaoping sent the Carter administration an intentional message by lavishing special attention on Jackson, whom he considered the Senate's most influential critic of détente and advocate of closer U.S.-China ties. Deng concluded his U.S. trip with a stop in Seattle, where he and Jackson talked privately for over an hour. Jackson also delivered the introductory address for a Seattle dinner held in Deng's honor and escorted the Chinese premier on his tour of the Boeing aircraft plant.[33]

U.S. normalization of relations with the PRC did not end the battle still waging between advocates of "evenhandedness" versus the pro-PRC approach. In March 1979, Vance and Treasury Secretary Michael Blumenthal proposed to take Jackson on by granting MFN status to both the PRC and the Soviet Union. Vice President Mondale recognized, however, that Jackson's opposition to MFN for the Soviets was too powerful to surmount. The president accepted Mondale's advice to defer the matter. For the next several months, Vance and the "evenhandedness" contingent fought a rear-guard action. They did not oppose granting China MFN outright, but sought to delay it. The Carter administration reached a final agreement with the Chinese in July 1979 on a trade bill that would lower duties on some Chinese goods as much as 50 percent or more. The administration declined to submit it to Congress until the fall of 1979 in the hopes of arranging for the extension of similar benefits to the Soviet Union. Jackson ripped the administration for the delay. "Basic Soviet policies constitute a real threat to our interests and those of our allies," he declared. "Basic Chinese policies do not. Does that mean that if we make the same arrangements with the Chinese who are not threatening us, we have to make the same arrangements for the Soviets."[34]

Jackson visited China for the third time from August 7 to 25, 1979. He met again with top Chinese leaders. He largely accepted their defense of the PRC's winter 1979 incursion into Vietnam, which Deng and others told him was compelled by Vietnam's treatment of its Chinese minority and Vietnam's apparent belief that its treaty of friendship with the Soviet Union freed it to pursue its goals in Southeast Asia with impunity. In their conversations, which lasted for more than three hours, Deng and Jackson continued to emphasize the common interest that the PRC and the United States, Japan, and the NATO nations had in thwarting the "hegemonist policy of the Soviet Union." "It was imperative," they agreed, for the Carter administration not to create self-defeating linkages between U.S. efforts to assist China and U.S. global strategic posture vis-à-vis the Soviet Union. Deng also reiterated his previous assurances to him and Carter on China's compliance with Jackson-Vanik. "I will allow 10 million Chinese to emigrate if the Congress wants it," quipped Deng.[35]

Aware that Vice President Mondale would arrive in China the next day, Jackson blistered the evenhanded approach at a press conference he held on the day of his departure. "That will give Fritz [Mondale] something to respond to when he shows up," a beaming Jackson chortled to Kenneth Pyle, who had accompanied Jackson to the PRC, on the bus ride to the airport. Mondale reassured Deng during his visit that the administration would submit the trade agreement with China to Congress before the end of 1979. Congress passed the bill in January 1980. Henry Jackson testified before the Commerce Committees of the House and the Senate in support of this agreement. He argued that China had indeed complied sufficiently with Jackson-Vanik to warrant a presidential waiver of its provisions and a conditional grant of MFN.[36]

There was more, however, to Jackson's enthusiasm toward the PRC than the hardheaded geopolitical calculation that initially inspired it. Professor Pyle admitted that Jackson had a Pearl Buck type of euphoria about China that reinforced his positive image of the PRC. "He had a splendid rapport with Chinese leaders and a fascination with Chinese society," remarked Pyle. The thrifty Jackson had no interest in shopping, the Beijing opera, or other cultural events that lured the average tourist. What he enjoyed most was visiting military bases, petroleum facilities, and communes in the remotest part of the country. He particularly enjoyed his tour of Chinese military facilities in Xinjiang, facing the Red Army units deployed across the border in Mongolia.[37]

Occasionally, Jackson prodded the Chinese about human rights. He also objected to the PRC leadership's habit of still calling the United States "hegemonists." He did so, however, with a circumspection and infrequency starkly at variance with his treatment of the Soviet Union on these subjects. "Jackson believed that human rights had to be secondary regarding China, given the death struggle the U.S. was engaged in with the Soviet Union," explained Pyle. During this period, moreover, Jackson could and did point out that China's domestic policies were becoming more liberal. Yet Jackson's enthusiasm for the PRC certainly strayed well beyond the outer bounds of prudence when he insisted, in defiance of what the Soviet archives have revealed, that the PRC could have been "our ally in Asia from the beginning had we understood China properly."[38] What Jackson appreciated most about the PRC in the summer of 1979 was that it supported his endeavors to derail détente and SALT II.

SALT II: THE RATIFICATION DEBATE

The acceleration of Soviet expansionism in Africa, East Asia, and the Middle East had strengthened considerably the forces opposing SALT II, which Henry Jackson would lead. On May 9, 1979, the Carter administration and the Soviet government announced the conclusion of the SALT II negotiations. Carter and Brezhnev signed the agreement at a summit meeting in Vienna held June 15 through 18. SALT II imposed limits on intercontinental missiles and bombers that would run until 1985. It permitted both sides 2,250 intercontinental delivery systems. No more than 1,320 of these could carry missiles with multiple warheads (MIRVs) or long-range cruise missiles (ALCMs). No more than 1,200 of this 1,320 could be MIRVed intercontinental ICBMs and MIRVed SLBMs. No more than 820 of the 1,200 could be MRIVed ICBMs.

The three-year protocol to the SALT II agreement, effective through 1981, prohibited the testing or deployment of mobile ICBMs such as the pending U.S. MX missile or ground-launched or sea-launched cruise missiles with more than a 600-kilometer range. The protocol also would delay NATO's deployment of 1,600-kilometer cruise missiles to offset the

Soviet SS-20 IRBM, with a range of 5,000 kilometers left uncovered by any provision of SALT II.[39]

President Carter hailed SALT II as "the most detailed, far-reaching, comprehensive treaty in the history of arms control." Although the treaty would not "end the arms competition," the president promised that it would make the competition "safer and more predictable" and would reduce "the danger of nuclear war."[40] The SALT II treaty, he claimed, also "preserved our options to build the forces we needed to maintain the strategic balance." Simultaneously, the administration mounted a massive lobbying campaign to generate the public support needed to surmount the formidable opposition the SALT II faced in the Senate. By this time, the president had already written off Henry Jackson as a potential ally in securing ratification of SALT II, and had already told Vance that Jackson would oppose any treaty the "Soviets were likely to sign."[41] The president believed, however, that he would prevail regardless of what Jackson chose to do. He was wrong.

Senate support for Carter's approach to SALT had grown increasingly precarious since the narrow confirmation of Paul Warnke in February 1977.[42] Henry Jackson had led the fight against Warnke, whom the president had since replaced with General George Seignious in an effort to broaden the base of support for the treaty.[43] Even in 1977, it was unlikely that the president could have secured Senate passage of any SALT II with Jackson in opposition. Furthermore, Jackson would have significantly more help by the summer of 1979 than he had in 1972 when he singlehandedly created the legislative record and criteria by which to measure the adequacy of future SALT agreements. Ronald Reagan, the frontrunner for the 1980 Republican nomination, had excoriated SALT II and pledged to make Carter's foreign policy a major issue in the campaign.[44] Reagan derived many of his arguments and much of his information from Jackson's public remarks, which he often cited in his radio commentaries.[45] When Reagan began calling Jackson's home increasingly in the late 1970s for permission to quote him, a bemused Jackson replied "Of course." What he had said was in the public record.[46] Reagan corresponded with Jackson, thanking him for the "helpful materials" Jackson had sent him. He hoped that Jackson's colleagues in the Senate would "see the wisdom in the points" Jackson had "raised about SALT II."[47]

The Committee on Present Danger; Senator Sam Nunn, who had often worked in tandem with Jackson on the Armed Services Committee;
and several prominent Republican senators also had joined forces with
Jackson, their acknowledged leader. Eugene Rostow, chairman of the Policy Committee of CPD, served as the conduit for organizing "the cabal
to kill SALT II." Just after the Carter announcement of May 9, he and
Senator John Danforth, Republican of Missouri, a former student of his
at Yale Law School, met to discuss how to proceed. Danforth advised Rostow to get together a group consisting of the "key movers and shakers" in
the Congress. "Whatever else you do," Danforth told Rostow, "you get
Scoop Jackson from the first day. . . . We will all follow Scoop. He is the
only person who occupies this position in the Senate." Rostow promptly
arranged for a meeting at the offices of CPD which Jackson; Senate Minority Leader Howard Baker, Republican from Tennessee; John Tower;
John Danforth; and Sam Nunn attended. They asked CPD to provide information against SALT II. Collectively, these five senators represented a
broad political spectrum that encompassed the views of more than the
one-third of the Senate necessary to defeat the treaty. The administration
especially could not afford to lose Baker, whose support had been crucial
for winning ratification of the Panama Canal Treaty. Baker attributed his
decision to oppose SALT II largely to Jackson, though his presidential
ambitions for 1980 certainly influenced it, too. "The first thing I did when
SALT II came out, as I did in the Panama Canal debate, was to set up an
A team and B team in my own shop," recalled Baker. "I asked Scoop for
information. His office worked for several months to give me the best information. Scoop's staff was far superior to anything else we had seen.
That was my major factor in opposing SALT II."[48]

However much he opposed SALT II and the administration's foreign
policy, and however much he disliked Carter, Jackson would not compromise his core principles to win the debate. He rebuffed Perle's entreaties for him to disclose the contents of a confidential letter that Carter
had sent him in May 1977 outlining his administration's goals for SALT
II. Perle calculated that the actual treaty's failure to achieve any of these
goals would badly damage Carter's case before the Senate were the public to learn of it. Although he refused ever to betray a confidential communication or conversation with a president, Jackson considered Carter
fair game and felt the presidents' public record warranted withering crit-

icism.[49] He set the tone for the bruising ratification debate by charging the Carter administration with appeasement just three days before the president left for the Vienna Summit. Addressing CDM on June 12, Jackson expressed the sentiments of many hard-liners against SALT II in this lacerating condemnation of the treaty:

> To enter a treaty which favors the Soviets as this one does on the grounds that we will be in a worse position without it, is appeasement in its purest form. . . . Against overwhelming evidence of a continued Soviet strategic and conventional military buildup, there has been a flow of official administration explanations, extenuations, and excuses. It is all ominously reminiscent of Great Britain in the 1930s, when one government pronouncement after another was issued to assure the British public that Hitler's Germany would never achieve military equality—let alone superiority. The failure to face reality today, like the failure to do so then, is the mark of appeasement. In the areas of trade and technology, the right to emigrate and strategic arms, the signs of appeasement are all too evident.[50]

Jackson concentrated his fire on three provisions that, in his mind, constituted the most glaring among many inequities of SALT II: the Soviet Unions' retention of 300 heavy missiles (SS-18s), which the United States could not match; the exclusion of the Backfire bomber from the treaty's limits; and the moratorium the protocol imposed on cruise missiles and the deployment of the MX. He derided "as hopelessly naive" the administration's contention that the United States would be free to deploy whatever cruise missiles they might choose when the protocol expired in three years. "The West," he said, "will find it difficult to the point of impossibility to turn back the clock on temporary arms limitation and plunge ahead with new and previously banned weapons as though they had never been prohibited." Jackson wanted to avert "a replay of the neutron bomb story," which, he insisted, was "precisely what we will face three years from now if SALT II stops ground- and sea-launched cruise missiles at 600 kilometers." He also derided "the popular notion that U.S. military strength vis-à-vis the Soviet Union" no longer mattered in the nuclear age. "The real danger ahead is the Kremlin's political use of strategic superiority as an umbrella under which to pursue a series of probes to expand Soviet power and weaken the position of the United States," he warned. "Can we bargain confidently and stubbornly, can we stand up to

Soviet blackmail, can we hold our ground in crisis situations from a position of relative military weakness?"[51]

The tide seemed to be running the administration's way during the first week of the Foreign Relation Committee's hearings on SALT II, which commenced in early July 1979. Without a military authority of Jackson's stature in their ranks, the few declared opponents of SALT II on the committee found themselves at a severe disadvantage making their case against the combined weight of the Joint Chiefs' endorsement of the treaty, the administration's commitment to increasing military spending, and Secretary of Defense Brown's detailed justification of the military benefits of SALT II. Brown and General David Jones, chairman of the Joint Chiefs, argued that SALT II would constrain the Soviet military buildup while posing no obstacles to proceeding with the modernization of U.S. strategic forces.[52]

SALT II received intense and critical scrutiny from the Senate Armed Services Committee, which began its hearings on July 22. Again, Jackson and his allies upstaged the Foreign Relations Committee, which nominally had primary jurisdiction, by conducting by far the most important hearings on SALT II. Yet again, Jackson dominated the proceedings, with critical assists from Senators Tower and Nunn.[53] He clashed sharply with General Jones, whom he had long distrusted as a political general reflexively supporting SALT II to ingratiate himself with President Carter.[54] How could the JCS endorse the treaty, Jackson pressed Jones, when the administration had consistently disregarded the position the chiefs had taken on Soviet heavy missiles, cruise missiles, and Backfire bombers? How could Jones be confident that the administration truly would back the strategic programs on which the chiefs conditioned their support of SALT II, he asked skeptically, when the president had failed to initiate any new strategic weapons program in the preceding three years? Jackson extracted an admission from Secretary of Defense Brown that "in the past four years the Soviets have moved ahead more rapidly than we have moved ahead." He also refuted the administration's claim that SALT II complied with the Jackson Amendment to SALT I requiring equality in intercontinental strategic forces:

> As author of that amendment . . . I do not agree with the administration
> that the current treaty meets the test of that statute. This treaty is un-

equal in a number of respects, as you well know. It does not provide for equal missile throw weight. . . . My amendment requires . . . equality in numbers taking into account throw weight. The cosponsors and the opponents of the amendment understood that to be the intent of the language as shown by three different votes on the effort to change the meaning.

Jackson forced Secretary of State Vance to concede, too, that SALT II would allow the Soviet Union to deploy a fifth generation of more powerful, accurate, and reliable ICBMs.[55]

The three most effective witnesses against the treaty—Paul Nitze, General Edward Rowny, and Professor Richard Pipes of Harvard—also had long-standing and close ties with Jackson. Nitze testified that the strategic balance would continue to move against the United States if the Senate ratified SALT II without amendment. The Soviets, Nitze contended, would achieve meaningful nuclear superiority by the early 1980s, unless the United States promptly "took the most urgent steps to reverse the current trends." By the expiration of the SALT II treaty in 1985, Nitze forecast the Soviets would have "twice the area destructive capability, five times the hard target kill capability, three times the megatonnage, twice our throw weight, and a counterforce capability, which the U.S. could not match, to destroy 90 percent of U.S. ICBMs." He also criticized the administration for abandoning in March 1977 proposals that Jackson had inspired, proposals he called "a step in the right direction." He charged that the "unequal and one-sided accommodation by us" was the worst way "to assure the cooperation of the Soviet leadership toward world peace."[56]

General Rowny, named JCS representative to SALT II to placate Jackson, had since resigned from the army in protest over the concessions the administration was willing to make in its "zeal to reach agreement."[57] Rowny collaborated with Jackson aides Dorothy Fosdick, Richard Perle, and Frank Gaffney in preparing his answers to the questions Jackson wanted on the record.[58] He catalogued before the Armed Services Committee a long list of the concessions that resulted in an agreement that exacerbated "U.S. strategic inferiority" while making it "more costly" and difficult for the United States "to regain strategic parity."[59] To the argument of the treaty's proponents that the absence of an agreement on SALT would mark a return to the Cold War, Rowny responded that "a codification of Soviet strategic superiority will make Soviet leaders more aggressive and more adventuresome in supporting their surrogates in wars which are quite hot where they occur. Labelling our displeasure with the Soviet Union as a return to the Cold War plays into the hands of the Soviet Union."[60]

In his testimony, Professor Pipes challenged the administration's central premise "that the cause of arms limitation was so singularly important" that SALT ought to proceed on its own separate track, oblivious to the overall pattern of Soviet behavior toward the United States. SALT, Pipes argued, should "emphatically be linked to Soviet behavior," which "seen in its totality, suggests an ominous pattern of threatening hostility": the relentless anti-American hate propaganda inside the Soviet Union and in the third world; Soviet armed interventions in Afghanistan, Ethiopia, Vietnam, and the Caribbean; Soviet support of terrorism all over the globe; Soviet encroachments on Norwegian territory; the militarization of the Kuriles; and the building of military highways and railroads in Eastern Europe. The United States could not count on the SALT process enhancing security or reducing the danger of nuclear war, said Pipes, "until and unless the Soviet Union radically modifies its thinking and external policies." Instead, he recommended a "treaty similar to the March 1977 proposal, requiring deep cuts in the number of Soviet warheads that SALT II would allow to double."[61]

By fall 1979, Jackson and the opponents of the treaty had managed to transform the political dynamic that seemed initially promising for early ratification of SALT II. Their relentless campaign had put the treaty in deep trouble even before world events conspired to doom it. On August 31, the administration confirmed the charge of Foreign Relations Committee chairman Frank Church—a hero of the New Politics wing of the Democratic Party, but then facing a desperate reelection fight in his very conservative state of Idaho—that there were Soviet combat forces in Cuba.[62] Secretary Vance explained at his September 5 press conference, correctly we now know, that these forces, numbering from 2,000 to 5,000 troops and 40 tanks, did not substantially increase the Soviet presence in Cuba. Although he stressed that the brigade lacked the capability to threaten militarily the United States or any other Latin American country, Vance did say that its presence in Cuba "was a very serious matter" in violation of "long-held American policies." He insisted, moreover, that he would not be satisfied "with the maintenance of the status quo."[63] Carter also declared the status quo "unacceptable" on September 7.[64] In a complete reversal, however, the president announced on October 1 that the administration would accept the status quo after the Soviets refused even any cosmetic concessions in the configuration of the brigade. Carter flatly rejected the demands of Jackson, John Tower, other hard-liners, and the born-again hawk Frank Church that the administration withdraw SALT II from the Senate pending Soviet withdrawal of these forces.[65] "The greatest danger to American security . . . is certainly not the two or three thousand Soviet troops in Cuba," Carter insisted. "It is the breakdown of a common effort to preserve the peace and the ultimate threat of nuclear war."[66] This episode contributed materially to the erosion of the already dwindling Senate support for SALT II.

On November 9, the dovish Foreign Relations Committee voted to approve the SALT treaty by a tenuous margin of 9 to 6. The president then attempted to revive the flagging campaign for ratification by making a belated appeal to the hard-liners in the Senate. Having in September infuriated Jackson and Nunn by vetoing the Hollings Resolution, which called for a 5 percent rather than a 3 percent increase in defense spending, the president reversed course. He announced on December 12, that his FY 1981 defense budget would be 5.6 percent higher in real terms than his FY 1980 request.[67] This pledge impressed Sam Nunn enough for him not to oppose SALT II outright, though he did demand additional assurance from the president that he would follow through on this program. Jackson dismissed Carter's pledge entirely as a desperate attempt to save SALT II that did not reflect the president's genuine convictions. On December 20, the Armed Services Committee voted 10 to 0 with seven abstentions that "the SALT II Treaty, as it now stands" was "not in the national security interest of the United States of America." Jackson served as the main author of the committee's final report. All seven Republicans on the committee joined Jackson; Senator Harry Byrd, Independent from Virginia; and Howard Cannon, Democrat from Nevada, in opposing ratification. The remaining seven Democrats, including Sam Nunn, abstained.[68]

The Soviet invasion of Afghanistan on December 27, 1979, sealed the demise of SALT II. Bowing to political realities, Carter formally requested Senate Majority Leader Robert Byrd on January 3, 1980, to defer Senate action on the treaty. Carter later wrote, "Our failure to ratify the SALT

II treaty and to secure even more far-reaching agreements on nuclear arms control was the most profound disappointment of my Presidency."[69] Afghanistan marked a watershed for American public opinion precisely because the invasion seemed to confirm what Jackson had preached about the U.S.S.R. for decades. As early as 1956, he had warned, after his trip to Kabul, "the Soviets had built a highway through Afghanistan that would present the free world with another grave threat."[70] The Soviets, he said, "have concluded that they can crown a decade of détente by invading and occupying a sovereign state, that they believe the response of the West will be weak and insubstantial, because it has been just that." On February 4, 1980, Jackson issued this searing indictment of the decade of détente:

> The theory that has animated American Policy toward the Soviet Union over the last three decades and under three administrations—that the Soviets, lured by a series of cooperative agreements, would match our concessions and reward our restraint—is dangerously and demonstrably false. The Soviet invasion of Afghanistan has shown that detente for us was an illusion, and the Soviet "restraint" merely the absence of opportunity. And the political, economic and military policies developed to fit the theory that we have moved from confrontation with the Soviets to cooperation now lies in ruins. For a decade, the Soviets have watched our businessmen stream to Moscow, technology in hand. And they have watched as we rushed to OPEC, hat in hand, begging them to go easy on oil prices.
>
> The Soviets have seen our diplomats naively put forward proposal after proposal—on the Indian Ocean, on weapons in space, on conventional arms sales, on forces in Europe, on strategic arms control—based on the assumption that the Soviet leadership shares our desire for accommodation and a stable world order. They have heard our leaders tell the American people that manifestly unequal and unverifiable treaties favoring the Soviets are equal and verifiable and favorable to us. They have been told that restrictions would be placed on the importation of our energy extraction technology while, in fact, not a single license was denied in support of our announced policy. They have seen us stand by idly as their Cuban surrogates have marched over Africa bearing Russian arms and exploiting the instability of fledgling Third World governments.

They have heard no protest from us as they gave Castro ocean-going attack submarines and high performance ground-attack aircraft. They have listened as we called their combat brigade in Cuba unacceptable one week and acceptable the next. They have heard very little from us as their Vietnamese surrogates have pressed into Laos, into Cambodia, and threatened the borders of Thailand. What must they think of us in the Kremlin?[71]

Running against Jimmy Carter in 1980, Ronald Reagan would make the identical case in nearly identical terms. He, too, would call for a massive U.S. military buildup to negate the enormous Soviet military buildup of the 1970s. He, too, would condemn the SALT II treaty and the principles underlying it as fatally flawed. Paradoxically, it would take the election of this one-time Truman Democrat turned conservative Republican to pursue the policy toward the Soviet Union that Jackson had long championed—a policy that his fellow liberals in the Democratic Party had largely and increasingly repudiated since the tumultuous Democratic convention of 1968.

At the start of the 1980 campaign, Jackson had not yet reconciled himself to the idea of a Reagan presidency. He remained a fiercely partisan Democrat and a genuine liberal in most areas of domestic politics. He had decided, however, that the Democratic Party and the nation sorely needed an alternative to Carter, whom he regarded as a disaster. For the first time in his forty-year career in Congress, Henry Jackson would actively encourage a Democratic primary challenger to run against a sitting Democratic president.

Chapter 20

Anybody But Carter: The 1980 Presidential Election

THE 1970s ended badly not only for President Carter, but also for the nation. American decline during the decade seemed ominous, contrasting starkly with the spectacular growth of Soviet military capabilities and the steady expansion of Soviet global power. In the United States, double-digit inflation, interest rates in excess of 20 percent, oil shocks resulting in periodic gas lines, and slow growth seemed to menace the prosperity that many Americans had come to take for granted. The Iranian hostage crisis, which began on November 4, 1979, when the U.S. embassy in Tehran was attacked and fifty-two Americans were held captive, fueled the increasingly widespread perception among Americans that the United States had become impotent to resist brazen provocations abroad.[1]

Carter's political strength had plummeted correspondingly. His job approval rating stood at only 29 percent in June 1979. Throughout most of that year, polls showed him trailing Senator Edward Kennedy of Massachusetts, his prospective rival for the 1980 Democratic nomination, by a margin of two to one. A mid-September Harris Poll showed that 70 percent of Americans believed that Carter could not get elected.[2] Carter had alienated Cold Warriors with his foreign and defense policies. He had alienated much of the dominant liberal wing in his party by spending too little on traditional Democratic social welfare programs; his reluctance to endorse the sweeping $100 billion dollar health care plan that Kennedy proposed in May 1979 was only one example. He had alienated Henry Jackson—an avid supporter of the Kennedy health plan—on both counts.

The president's initial efforts to remedy his predicament worsened it. For twelve days in early July, he repaired to Camp David, secluded from the American public. He invited nearly 150 people to meet with him there for a reassessment of his presidency and style of leadership. His adviser Patrick Caddell persuaded him that the energy crisis was symptomatic of a more serious ailment besetting American society. America was, according to Caddell, "a nation deep in crisis . . . psychological more than material. . . . [It was] a crisis of confidence marked by a dwindling faith in the future." Caddell also advised the president that he should shake up his cabinet. The president concurred with his analysis. On July 15, he returned from Camp David to deliver what became infamously known as his "malaise speech." He told the American people that "a crisis of confidence . . . strikes at the very heart and soul and spirit of national will. . . . We've got to stop crying and start sweating, stop talking and start walking, stop cursing and start praying. The strength we need will not come from the White House, but from every house in America."[3] On July 16, Carter ordered all of his cabinet members to submit their resignations. He accepted four: Joseph Califano, secretary of HEW; Michael Blumenthal, secretary of the treasury; James Schlesinger, secretary of energy, who was eager to leave; and Brock Adams, secretary of transportation. Carter later rated his "malaise" speech as one of his best and his days at Camp David as "some of the most thought-provoking and satisfying of my Presidency."[4]

That is not how Henry Jackson and many others rated it. Jackson blasted Carter for blaming the deteriorating domestic and global situation on a "crisis of confidence" rather than incompetence of the administration, where Jackson placed the blame.[5] He emphatically rejected the notion, prevalent in the administration, that many adverse events besetting the nation were increasingly beyond the control of the United States to influence. "Too many have been selling America short. This is the greatest country on the face of the earth. We are rich in human and material resources. Our task is to marshal our resources at home and in concert with our allies to meet the challenges of today and tomorrow."[6] Jackson also complained that he had never seen an administration batter public confidence so badly. "The wholesale resignation of Carter's cabinet, made just two days after the President had asked the nation to avoid a crisis in confidence, left Capitol Hill in total bewilderment. No one understands it. Frankly we're beginning to have a case of battle fatigue," he said.[7]

Fearful that Carter would drag the Democratic Party down with him, Jackson declared on July 29, 1979, that the president ought to be prepared to drop out of the presidential race if he did poorly in the early primaries: "In all my years in Congress, I frankly never have observed a political situation as we face now. . . I think one has to be forthright on the fact that President Carter is in deep trouble. If he loses decisively in New Hampshire, Massachusetts and Florida, I don't see how he can be viable." Jackson predicted that Ted Kennedy would win the Democratic Party's nomination for president. Carter fired back at him: "Three or four years ago, when I was running for President—at that time, Mr. Jackson predicted he would be the next President. His judgment was not very good then." Undaunted, Jackson continued to encourage Kennedy to enter the race. In September 1979, he publicly challenged the president's claim that Kennedy could hurt the Democrats by splitting the party's vote. He told reporters that President Carter's weakness was the real problem for the party.[8] When Kennedy formally declared his candidacy on November 7, 1979, Jackson had already determined to take a more active role on his behalf. He sought, in so doing, to save the Democratic party from the catastrophic defeat he foresaw with Carter at the head of the ticket. He hoped that Kennedy would reassert the party's tradition of a robust foreign policy, the tradition of Presidents Truman, Johnson, and his brother JFK.[9]

POLITICS MAKES STRANGE BEDFELLOWS

There was, opined Bernard Lewis, no more eloquent testimony of Jackson's disenchantment with Carter than "Scoop's willingness to back Ted Kennedy against him." Since the late 1960s, Ted Kennedy had largely endorsed the foreign and defense policies of the New Politics wing of the party. Indeed, he had extolled the policies of the very people in the Carter administration whom Jackson had fiercely opposed: Cyrus Vance, Patricia Derian, Andrew Young, and Paul Warnke. As Richard Perle observed, however, Jackson always had "a soft spot for the Kennedys that went way back and overwhelmed his political differences with them."[10]

Jackson's treatment of Ted Kennedy had a paternalistic quality emblematic of how he had schooled a generation of younger senators in the ways of the Senate. Their relationship had recovered from its low point in February 1971, when the battle over the SST had generated ill will between them. Since then, Jackson and Kennedy had cooperated actively on energy policy. Kennedy had given labor in Massachusetts the green light to support Jackson in the 1976 primary there, which Jackson had won. Carter's malaise speech, which Jackson and Kennedy discussed, appalled them both.[11] Although Jackson opposed Affirmative Action and took a much tougher line on crime than Kennedy and most other liberal Democrats did, he agreed with them about virtually everything else on the domestic agenda. He still believed fervently not only in the New Deal but in much of the Great Society, which many Jackson Democrats had begun to doubt and later would repudiate. Throughout the late 1970s, Jackson's annual rating from the Americans for Democratic Action topped that of even Warren Magnuson, whom liberals revered.[12] Jackson and Kennedy also had in common their unwavering support for the concerns of organized labor. Longtime friend Doug Glant recalled, for example, that Jackson had refused to cross a picket line at the Four Seasons Hotel in Seattle even to attend the bar mitzvah party of the grandson of one of his closest friends.[13]

Jackson had few illusions about the difficulty and improbability of bridging the gap between him and Ted Kennedy on foreign and defense policy. He felt, however, "almost desperate . . . [and] that Kennedy was the last hope his wing of the party had."[14] Attorney Max Kampelman, a former legislative aide to Hubert Humphrey with long personal and professional ties to the late Minnesota senator, and an avowed Jackson Democrat, acted as liaison between the Jackson and Kennedy camps. Kampelman wrote Jackson on November 5, 1979, that a meeting with Kennedy that morning "had turned out quite well." He suggested that Jackson arrange "a session with some of the CDM [Coalition for a Democratic Majority] and the committee on the Present Danger luminaries who happened to be Democrats: . . . Gene Rostow, Bud Zumwalt, Paul Nitze, Richard Pipes, and Lane Kirkland. . . ." He conceded that it would "not be easy to affect" Kennedy, who "seemed vague and uncertain of himself in his stated skepticism of high technology defense systems." Kampelman urged Jackson to "talk with him about these issues as often as you can." Kennedy "obviously respects you . . . and needs you." Jackson could continue to count on Kampelman, he said, "with respect to this common objective we have. . . . [Y]our friends are many and have confidence in your judgment."[15]

Throughout November 1979, Jackson and Kennedy and their principal aides worked intensely to reach common ground. Kennedy asked

Richard Perle to suggest some experts to meet with him "to deal with some specific world struggle spots," and he and Jackson explored the possibility of more formal collaboration between them over dinner at Kennedy's home in Georgetown on November 26, 1979.[16] Jackson enthusiastically obliged Kennedy's request that Perle assist his chief foreign policy aide Jan Kalicki in drafting his speech to the Chicago Council on Foreign Relations on December 9, 1979. Kennedy was "delighted that Richard and Jan of our staffs will be working together closely in the months ahead," and Eugene Rostow of CDP also prepared a draft of a speech Jackson encouraged Kennedy to incorporate in his trademark foreign policy statement during the primaries against Carter.[17]

Kennedy did not follow through. By February 1980 it was apparent to all those involved except for Jackson himself that his wing and the Kennedy forces could not bridge the gap separating them on foreign and defense policy. Kampelman wrote Jan Kalicki a stinging critique of a speech that Kennedy delivered at Georgetown University on January 28, 1980, encapsulating this impasse from the standpoint of the Jackson Democrats. He assailed Kennedy for referring to Afghanistan as merely a regional crisis, for opposing draft registration, for opposing Carter's decision to permit the shah to enter the United States, for opposing economic sanctions on Iran, for opposing Carter's countermeasures in the Persian Gulf, and for characterizing the Persian Gulf problem as "the potential loss of a little gasoline." In Kampelman's judgment, Kennedy's Georgetown speech had squandered an enormous opportunity for "forging a united approach to the serious international crisis we face as the result of Soviet irresponsibility.[18] This speech also came on the heels of a disappointing meeting at Kennedy's house between the senator and a group of experts whom Jackson had invited to help coach him. "We talked about many things," recalled Bernard Lewis, a participant at the meeting. "In the early stages, Kennedy made a minimal contribution, but halfway through, checked out of the conversation and said nothing at all." Underwhelmed, Lewis asked Jackson on the car ride back whether "Kennedy was silent because he liked to listen or because he was ignorant." Kennedy added insult to injury by inaccurately quoting Lewis publicly days later during the course of an interview the senator gave in San Francisco about the shah. "I woke up in the morning, listened to the news, heard my name, and was horrified. I spoke with Jan Kalicki, who was evasive on this. When

I received a call from Moynihan on another matter, I told him: your colleague from Massachusetts invited me to dinner, screwed me, and left me to drown."[19] So ended the short courtship between Kennedy and Jackson Democrats.

THE DEFECTION OF THE JACKSON DEMOCRATS

Meanwhile, Kampelman and Vice President Mondale had failed in a final effort to broker a reconciliation between Jackson Democrats and the administration. Linked by their mutual admiration for Hubert Humphrey, the two men liked and respected each other. Mondale worried that Carter would lose the 1980 election without the support of this wing of the party.[20] At his behest, Carter decided to invite a group of CDM leaders to the White House. At Kampelman's behest, they accepted and met there with the president in January 1980.[21] Most of the major neoconservatives, all of whom considered Henry Jackson their champion, came: Jeane Kirkpatrick, Norman Podhoretz, Midge Decter, Ben Wattenberg, Elliott Abrams, Max Kampelman, Elmo Zumwalt, Austin Ranney, and Penn Kemble.[22]

The meeting was disastrous. Jeane Kirkpatrick described it as the last straw for the neoconservatives. "Most of us at the meeting already had important problems with Carter and his administration. Everybody there was unhappy with the Democratic Party and with Carter's approach to and analysis of the Cold War and the Soviet Union," she said. "Carter's more vigorous response to the invasion of Afghanistan had raised the hopes of CDM that he had a new realism in his assessment of the Soviet Union." Several members of the CDM group met shortly before the meeting with Carter to discuss how to approach it. They agreed that political scientist Austin Ranney, the most liberal and least contentious member of the group, would start. "Andy gave Carter a chance" to make amends, recalled Kirkpatrick. "He expressed concern about the President's approach to the Soviets, but hoped that Afghanistan had changed that." Carter dashed their hopes. He told them he had not changed his views on the Soviet Union at all.[23] The meeting ended forty-five minutes to an hour later without even muting the profound disagreements between them. When Carter left, Vice President Mondale asked the members of the CDM group to give him a few minutes. "Mondale was a decent, honorable, and competent man ... who understood us and addressed our concerns in a way that was much more meaningful to us," Kirkpatrick explained. By then, however, it was too late. Elliott Abrams, a former Jackson aide, summed up the universal reaction of those in attendance by pronouncing Carter "hopeless." Henceforth, their disdain for Carter and dislike of Kennedy would impel the neoconservatives to turn away from the Democratic Party and vote for Reagan.

The Reagan campaign and the candidate himself eased and expedited their journey by assiduously courting these neoconservative Jackson Democrats. Consider, for example, the case of Jeane Kirkpatrick. She thought Jackson "one of the two most important political people in my life," ran unsuccessfully as a Scoop Jackson delegate in Maryland in 1976, and did most of the analysis of the public opinion data for Jackson that year. Reagan had written her a glowing letter in praise of her article "Dictatorships and Double Standards." In March 1980, she received a phone call from Richard Allen, Reagan's top foreign policy adviser for the campaign and future national security adviser, asking her to meet with Reagan and a few others at the Madison Hotel on April 7. She agreed but gave no commitment to support Reagan. Fifteen minutes later, she received a call from Bernard Aronson at the Carter White House asking her to represent CDM's position in the Baltimore hearings of April 7 to thrash out the Democratic foreign policy platform for the convention. "Bernie, it is too late," she replied. "I already have a date." Kirkpatrick cites this episode as the moment of her transition. She discovered not only that she and Reagan held many important views in common, but also that he actually listened to her, unlike Carter and other liberal Democrats.[24]

Richard Allen played an important role in bringing "many of the neoconservatives across to Reagan," using the CPD, to which he belonged, as a conduit. He was not a Jackson Democrat but a Jackson Republican. "In the 1970s," said Allen, "Scoop Jackson was the last man at the bridge, defending it valiantly against Kissingerian pessimism and Carter's appeasement." He saw Jackson as a "great positive force, adept at playing defense and offense, an expert in weapons procurement, a true strategic thinker in the most fulsome sense." While an aide to President Nixon, he had even helped convince Nixon to offer Jackson the position of secretary of defense in 1968. Allen would have voted for Jackson against Republican Gerald Ford, had "he won the nomination in 1976."[25]

Foreshadowing things to come, Richard Perle left Jackson's office in

March 1980 to form a short-lived business partnership with John Lehman, author of Jackson's 1976 position paper calling for a restoration of U.S. naval power which, in their judgments, cutbacks and neglect had perilously eroded. With Jackson's assistance and blessing, Perle and Lehman would assume major positions in the Reagan administration, and have a major impact on its policies.[26]

THE DEMOCRATIC PRIMARIES AND THE CONVENTION

Kennedy's unwillingness to reassert the Truman tradition in foreign policy profoundly disappointed Jackson, though not enough to give up hope in the Democratic Party, as his neoconservative friends would increasingly do. Formally, Jackson maintained his neutrality throughout the primary campaign of 1980, in which Kennedy stumbled badly. As Moynihan observed, however, "Everybody in the Senate knew that Jackson wanted Kennedy to win and Carter to lose."[27] Jackson continued to blast the administration's foreign policy despite its change in tone since the Soviet invasion of Afghanistan. "We appear to be going from one crisis to another, with the Carter administration dispensing red-hot rhetoric at least once a week about the dire consequences about this or that or something else. Littered along the way are all of these strong positions, with no follow-through and no clear-cut policy," he added. "The tragedy is that we've ended up in a position where we're not credible either to the Soviets or to the weakest oil-producing states."[28]

What especially galled Jackson was the administration's "botched Iran rescue mission" on April 24, 1980. He thought it the height of folly to undertake a rescue of the hostages in Tehran with just eight helicopters when such a mission required at least six to be operational to have a minimum chance of success. The plan called for flying the eight helicopters to a remote desert site where cargo planes would refuel them and transfer assault teams before they moved several hundred more miles to a secret base closer to Tehran. The administration arrived at the number eight as a compromise between Brzezinski's staunch advocacy of the mission and Vance's categorical opposition. When three of the helicopters experienced mechanical difficulties, the president agreed to abort the mission on the commander's recommendation. Eight men died during the evacuation when an American plane and a helicopter collided. The president then announced the failure of the rescue mission to a stunned nation. Sec-

retary Vance resigned in protest because he opposed on principle any use
of force to resolve the hostage crisis. Jackson had disagreed with Vance on
a number of major issues, but "happened to agree with him on the Iranian mission. You just don't allow an operation of this magnitude, in terms
of world impact, to fail because of three helicopters."[29]

Jackson delivered his detailed diagnosis of the Democratic Party's
plight, whose cause ran deeper than Carter, in Chicago in an address to
the Cook County Democrats on May 22, 1980:

> The root of our problem is the widespread perception, by millions of
> Americans, that the Democratic Party is no longer what it once was: that
> it is no longer the Party of Roosevelt or Truman; that it has cut itself
> adrift from traditional Democratic constituencies; that it no longer of-
> fers a coherent and comprehensible program for social progress at home;
> that it no longer offers a clear view of the world or a strategy for pro-
> tecting America's interests. In domestic policy, we have been led in re-
> cent years by those who are seen to have no allegiance to the bedrock
> constituencies of the Democratic Party—and who therefore are inca-
> pable of defending the proven accomplishments of liberal government,
> or equally, or responsibly remedying its failures. When a large number
> of working people believe that the Democratic Party has reverted to the
> policies of Herbert Hoover, we are in trouble. . . . And how are the vot-
> ers to understand the Democratic foreign policy. In the decade of the
> 1970s, the Soviet Union was engaged in the most massive military
> buildup in peacetime history. Yet in 1972 and 1976 our presidential stan-
> dard-bearers campaigned for cuts in U.S. military spending. . . . What is
> the voter to think of the steadfastness of our party's foreign policy ob-
> jectives if our candidates warn us against "an inordinate fear of Com-
> munism" one day and, on another, admit that they had misjudged Sovi-
> et intentions in the world?[30]

Jackson warned that Ronald Reagan had made "a strong pitch to working
people who have been disenchanted with the administration's economic
policies and who are deeply worried by our nation's declining status in the
world." In yet another pointed attack on Carter's malaise speech and the
mindset it epitomized, Jackson in his Chicago speech counseled Democrats to stop "gagging on our own pessimism. Democrats must recognize
that even with all our problems, we are still the freest society in the world,

the most technologically advanced, the most economically resourceful and the most emulated. We need to remind ourselves of that fact and be damned proud of it! We are still the haven for the oppressed . . . a nation with a great untapped reservoir of will to get moving again."

Even when it became apparent that Carter would win the nomination, Jackson continued to pound away at him. He declined an invitation, which Magnuson accepted, to accompany Carter on a visit to Mount St. Helens after its eruption in May 1980.[31] Jackson also urged the defeat of a proposed convention rule that would guarantee Carter the nomination at the August Democratic National Convention in New York by binding the delegates to vote for the candidate to whom they were committed in the primary elections and caucuses. Carter arrived at the convention with nearly three hundred delegates more than he needed to win nomination on the first ballot. With the president reeling in the polls, Jackson called for an open convention that freed the delegates from their earlier commitments to either Carter or Kennedy.[32] In July 1980, some of Jackson's congressional allies and supporters even put together a group to explore the possibility of drafting him to be the nominee at the convention.[33] He neither encouraged nor discouraged the efforts to draft him, which had not the remotest prospect of success. He did not even attend the convention. "If they want me," he told a crowd at Seattle-Tacoma airport, "they can come and get me." Before the convention, Jackson did meet with Ted Kennedy, who had listed him as one of his seven potential vice presidential running mates. Jackson professed no interest in that possibility but did tell reporters that he preferred Kennedy to Carter.[34] It was all for naught. The Carter delegates remained loyal, defeated Kennedy's bid for an open convention, and renominated the president on the first ballot.

THE FALL CAMPAIGN

Publicly, Jackson refrained conspicuously from endorsing Carter, Reagan, or Independent John Anderson throughout September and much of October 1980. On October 2, he did issue letters to all three of the candidates asking for their views on the Jackson-Vanik Amendment.[35] Reagan responded with the most unequivocal endorsement of Jackson-Vanik and the assumptions underlying it:

> As President I would implement fully the letter and the spirit of the freedom of emigration provisions of the 1974 Trade Act. We would seek to

make it clearly understood that we would uphold the law, and that we will make no effort to modify the Jackson-Vanik Amendment. Fine words about human rights are one thing; action is another. The Congress took concrete action in passing the Jackson-Vanik Amendment; its effect has been blunted by holding out the hope to the Soviets that it might be modified or repealed.

I am proud indeed of the extraordinary bravery of those seeking to emigrate from the Soviet Union. The Soviet Jews in particular have shown the world what courage and determination to be free can mean even for men and women who could be imprisoned as a desire to emigrate. You have my assurance that I will work together with you in support of these brave people.[36]

Furthermore, the Reagan campaign actively courted Jackson to endorse the California governor against Carter. High-ranking campaign operatives Lyn Nofziger and William Casey, longtime admirers of Jackson, communicated with him through his Seattle friend Doug Glant, acting national campaign chairman of Business for Reagan-Bush. The subject of Reagan had come up between Jackson and Glant early in 1980 during one of their several lunches in the Senate dining room. Glant later told this story:

He was lord of the Senate in those days and always on a diet. Then the waitress would wink as she brought cornbread to the table. If he did not order it, it did not count. Scoop would put enough butter on the cornbread to sink a battleship. He started telling me that the Reagan campaign was not playing it right on Israel. That son of a bitch Carter, he said, did not know or care about Israel until he started running for President. Your guy is a longtime champion of Israel. Reagan was raising money for Israel even before it became a state in 1948. He ought to emphasize that fact.[37]

When Glant recounted his conversations to Casey and Nofziger, they instructed him to offer Jackson a cabinet post if he endorsed Reagan. Glant conveyed this offer during his next lunch with Jackson. "I know how you feel about Carter. The Reagan people know how you feel, too," Glant said. "If you come out for Reagan now, you will find a home." Jackson replied that this was not the first time a Republican had offered him a cabinet post. He then regaled Glant with the details of the Nixon offer in 1968 as a preface to turning him down:

> I did not say yes then. I will not say yes now. I have been a Democrat all my life. I will die a Democrat. I still believe in the New Deal. You guys are too hard on states rights and other things. I appreciate it, but no. You can tell them, though, privately, that I am flattered. I cannot come out publicly for Reagan, but will not support Carter publicly.[38]

Anticipating that the Democrats would hold on to their congressional majority, Jackson also calculated that he would have a greater impact on foreign and national security policy as a senior member of the Senate than as a Democrat in a Republican cabinet. Senator Inouye corroborated an essential aspect of Glant's story. Jackson told Inouye that Reagan had offered him a position, not in direct form "but through some intermediary."[39] Eugene Rostow also urged Jackson to come out for Reagan. "After a long period of official neutrality," he wrote Jackson on September 18, 1980, "I have decided to move publicly on the election. Carter is so appalling that the normal presumptions of party loyalty are no longer applicable." Rostow thought that Jackson's endorsement of Reagan could "well determine the outcome." Although Jackson would not go that far, he did instruct his administrative assistant, Denny Miller, to assure Jewish supporters who took their political cues from him that it was fine for them to contribute campaign money to and vote for Reagan.[40]

Meanwhile, liberals in Washington State howled at Jackson for not endorsing Carter. In late October, they finally prevailed on him to do so in a hanger at Boeing Field with Magnuson and Ted Kennedy at his side. "His body language testified eloquently to his low regard for Carter," recalled Glant. "He looked like he was taking Kaopectate when he endorsed him. Our Republican campaign operatives in Arlington had a good laugh over that one. It did Carter more harm than good."[41] Jackson had absolutely no regrets when Reagan trounced Carter by a landslide in November 1980.[42] Carter and too many Democrats had "misjudged the mood of the country," said Jackson. They had told the American people "that it was out of bounds for good Democrats to sound patriotic . . . and that to call America a great country was passe." Jackson credited Reagan with "pre-empting the historic stance of the Democratic party on issues of foreign policy and defense." Reagan had "struck at the very heart of our party—the tradition of Franklin Roosevelt and Harry Truman—champions of a strong and resolute America, leader of the Free World, proud of its greatness." Jackson noted his role and CDM's in the struggle on behalf of the "very themes that the Republican Party" in 1980 successfully appropriated against Carter:

—that a robust strategic equivalence with the Soviet Union is an essential foundation for a successful American foreign policy, one which will assure our national security and the safety of free nations;

—that a policy of detente and accommodation with the Soviets is transformed into a policy of retreat and appeasement when our leaders fail to insist that restraint must be reciprocal, that forbearance must be mutual;

—that no SALT II Treaty is preferable to an unsafe one that sanctions the massive buildup of Soviet strategic power, advantages them in critical respects, and continues provisions of great importance that we are unable to adequately verify;

—that one of the great cover-ups of this century is the effort by Western governments, which know better, to muffle the facts about Soviet-bloc support for international terrorism;

—that something is wrong with a policy on human rights that finds it convenient to criticize petty dictatorships, with which the world unhappily abounds, but inconvenient to speak out about the Soviet system, which inspires repression around the world;

—that Israel, structurally stable, militarily capable, and pro-Western in orientation, constitutes an indispensible Western asset in the Middle East;

—that the United Nations is out of hand and operating in many ways to undermine our basic national interests.[43]

Jackson had profound regrets, however, about the Democrats losing control of the Senate. He spent most of the fall campaigning hard for three Senate liberals in unsuccessful bids for reelection: George McGovern, Frank Church, and Warren Magnuson.[44] A perplexed William F. Buckley, the godfather of Reagan Republicanism, wondered how a "pillar of sanity" such as Henry Jackson could support Frank Church's bid "to resume his career as Neville Chamberlain."[45] That is because Buckley did not fully comprehend how loyal a Democrat Henry Jackson was. Although Church and Jackson disagreed fundamentally on foreign policy and defense issues, they had worked together very closely on domestic matters, particularly those dealing with the Pacific Northwest.

Magnuson's defeat shook Jackson most deeply of all. It ended an era in Washington State politics in which the two of them had operated as one of the most powerful Senate tandems in the nation. They had cooperated closely and amiably on all domestic issues, notwithstanding their open break on foreign policy and defense issues after 1968 when Magnuson joined the New Politics wing of the party. Together, they had amassed sixty-four years of Senate seniority by 1980. They had procured huge amounts of federal dollars for Washington State through Magnuson's chairmanship of the powerful Appropriations Committee, Jackson's chairmanship of the Interior and Energy Committees, and Jackson's prominence on the Armed Services Committee. "As Appropriations chairman," quipped Walter Mondale, "Magnuson had decided to be scrupulously fair. Half of the budget would go to the state of Washington and half would go to the rest of the country."[46] A combination of age, infirmity, and the changing demographics of the state finally caught up to the seventy-five-year-old Magnuson in 1980. The garrulous, hard-drinking, intensely partisan Magnuson had never enjoyed as broad or as deep a base of support as the sober, temperate, and hawkish Henry Jackson. By 1980, visible trouble walking and hearing contrasted starkly with the vigor of his fifty-four-year-old opponent, former state Attorney General Slade Gorton, who jogged constantly during the campaign to underscore the point.[47] Later, Jackson paid Magnuson this warm tribute;

> I have always considered it an honor and a privilege to serve with Maggie and have him as my colleague. . . . Our relationship was special. Few Senators from the same state—for whatever reason—work well together. Some do not even speak to one another. Maggie and I were different in that respect. We considered ourselves partners in the state of Washington. And our combined energies enabled us to succeed where others failed. There was no mystery or magic about it. Nor was it something we planned or agreed upon when I joined the Senate. Ours was a natur-

al relationship, never forced or contrived, and not something we had to work to maintain. This does not mean that we agreed on every problem or every approach to a problem. But we managed to disagree without being disagreeable. We talked and we listened. When a problem came up, Maggie and I did not write each other letters outlining our differences. Our offices were next door to one another, almost an extension of one another. He supported me and I supported him. I mention these things because they exemplified how Maggie operated in the Senate and succeeded in achieving so many of his goals. Maggie always knew there would be a tomorrow. In the Senate, today's opponents may be tomorrow's allies. . . .[48]

Following the election, rumors abounded in the press that Reagan was still considering Jackson strongly for a position as secretary of state or defense. The two men saw eye to eye on the growing danger of the Soviet threat, on the imperative of a robust response to it, and on the need to back Israel unswervingly.[49] The president-elect named Jackson to his transition team on foreign policy and defense.[50] Richard Allen, Reagan's chief foreign policy adviser, favored Jackson for the position of secretary of defense and touted his candidacy. So, too, did Eugene Rostow, Jeane Kirkpatrick, and Richard Pipes. Allen had cultivated them through the Committee on the Present Danger, which had provided much of the intellectual firepower behind Reagan's foreign policy ideas.[51]

Appearing on *Face the Nation*, Jackson himself proclaimed that he would help President-elect Ronald Reagan in every way he could, especially to get a bipartisan foreign policy program going again, and he counseled that "confronted with strength, the Soviets would not move." He predicted that, with a tough and realistic approach, the Reagan administration would have a "golden chance to provide for peace and avoid war." He considered it crucial for the president to choose "people who would send the right signal. It must be a signal of steadiness, of firmness, of strength, and of rationality."[52] On December 4, Jackson met with Reagan at Blair House to discuss his views.[53] The Democrats' loss of the Senate had by this time induced Jackson to have a change of heart about accepting a cabinet post with the Reagan administration, now that he faced the prospect of returning to Washington, D.C., in the minority without the prime chairmanships he had long held: Energy, the Permanent Investigations

Subcommittee of Government Operations, and the Armed Services Sub-committee on Arms Control.[54]

It was too late. Jackson had essentially missed his best chance for obtaining a cabinet post when he declined to endorse Reagan during the campaign. By November 1980, Reagan had already settled on Caspar Weinberger as secretary of defense. Those members of the transition team from the Nixon-Ford era backed former Secretary of the Treasury George Shultz for secretary of state. Richard Allen and Richard Perle also claimed that Reagan's longtime backers from California, known as the kitchen cabinet, disliked the idea of having a liberal Democrat such as Jackson participate in cabinet meetings as secretary of state.[55] For his part, Reagan thought Jackson would serve him better in the Senate than in the cabinet by forging bipartisan support for his defense buildup and foreign policy initiatives. The Jackson camp did succeed, though, in persuading Reagan to select the staunchly pro-Israel Al Haig rather than George Shultz as his first secretary of state. Jackson feared having two cabinet members (Weinberger and Shultz) who had served as high-ranking executives in the Bechtel Corporation, an organization with extensive ties and financial dealings in the Arab world.[56] Although Jackson proved to be right in viewing Weinberger, with whom he agreed on almost everything else, as inclining toward the Arab rather than the Israeli point of view on Middle East questions, he proved to be dead wrong about Shultz, who later emerged as one of the most pro-Israel secretaries of state the United States ever had.

A large and influential contingent of Jackson Democrats did secure prominent positions in the Reagan administration because of their association with Jackson and the congeniality of their outlook with Reagan's: Jeane Kirkpatrick as ambassador to the United Nations; Richard Perle as assistant secretary of defense; Elliott Abrams as assistant secretary of state for human rights; General Edward Rowny as the chief negotiator for the newly designated Strategic Arms Reduction Talks (START); Max Kampelman as U.S. negotiator to the Helsinki human rights talks in Madrid and later as chief U.S. arms negotiator; Paul Wolfowitz as assistant secretary of state for East Asian affairs; Richard Pipes as National Security Council adviser on Soviet affairs; Joshua Muravchik as Jeane Kirkpatrick's deputy at the United Nations. Perle brought two former Jackson staffers with him to the Department of Defense: Frank Gaffney and Doug Feith.

He had taken the job as assistant secretary of defense for policy rather than an important job that Haig intended to offer him based on Jackson's advice that he would get along better with Weinberger. He had pushed Jackson to lobby Reagan to choose John Lehman as secretary of the navy, which the president did after talking with Jackson.[57]

These disciples of and collaborators with Jackson would set in motion many of the policies of President Reagan that contributed mightily to winning the Cold War.[58] Paradoxically, Jackson's foreign policy ideas triumphed just as the peak of his power had passed. He would not live to see the collapse of the evil empire he worked so long and hard to bring about. By the end of 1980, he had reached the twilight time of his life and his career.

Chapter 21

Sunset, 1981–1983

IN JANUARY 1981, Henry and Helen Jackson returned to Washington, D.C., where they attended President Reagan's inauguration ceremonies. Jackson was now the senior senator from Washington State and the ranking Democrat on the Armed Services Committee, but he found himself in the minority for the first time in twenty-six years. His friend John Tower, Republican from Texas, became chairman of that committee, a position Jackson had long coveted in waiting behind first Richard Russell and then John Stennis. Even in the minority, Jackson retained a sizable reservoir of good will and significant influence because of the congeniality of his foreign policy and defense views with Reagan's and the scrupulousness with which he had treated Republicans on his committees while they were in the minority.[1]

The Reagan administration not only treated Jackson well (much better than Carter's had) but frequently solicited his views.[2] Jackson assisted the administration greatly in its successful campaign to secure congressional approval of Reagan's military buildup, and Assistant Secretary of Defense Richard Perle had a major hand in Reagan's decision to ban the sale of U.S. oil and gas equipment to the Soviet Union and to impose sanctions on foreign companies producing such equipment under American licenses.[3] This represented a major victory for Jackson, who during the 1970s had relentlessly pressed for tighter controls on the export of strategic technologies to the Soviet Union. Under the guidance of Assistant Secretary of State Elliott Abrams, the Reagan administration eventually pursued a human rights policy such as Jackson originally had envisaged and articulated during the 1970s. The administration applied its most unrelenting human rights pressure to America's totalitarian communist adversaries and also pressured privately authoritarian right-wing dictators such as General Pinochet of Chile to enact democratic reform.[4] Jackson

also came up with the idea for a Central America Commission to generate bipartisan support for the administration's policy of thwarting Soviet
efforts to destabilize Central America through its Cuban and Nicaraguan
proxies.[5]

The president's condemnation of the Soviet Union as an evil empire
and his unapologetic assertion of the moral superiority of democratic cap-
italism encapsulated what Henry Jackson had said and stood for in public
life for nearly four decades. Professor Richard Pipes of Harvard had significant input in drafting National Security Decision Directive 175
(NSDD 175), which the president signed in 1983, laying out his grand
strategy toward the Soviet Union, which mirrored Jackson's; NSDD 175
portrayed the Soviet Union as a system in the grip of a systemic crisis,
whose leaders had no choice short of war but to undertake drastic domestic reform.[6] Reagan's defense buildup sought not just to enhance deterrence, but "to contribute to the absolute decline of Soviet economic
power.[7] By committing the United States to developing advanced
weapons such as a strategic defense initiative (SDI), Reagan sought to exploit America's technological advantage over the Soviets, a major rationale for Jackson's advocacy of ABM and a major qualitative defense
buildup since the 1960s. Jackson thus endorsed the SDI, which the president announced in March 1983, though he had a more modest conception of it for the short term than Reagan did. Jackson stressed how SDI
could enhance deterrence by protecting U.S. ICBMs against a Soviet preemptive strike. Reagan stressed SDI's potential for providing comprehensive protection of the American population against nuclear attack, a
goal Jackson hoped SDI could achieve in the long term.[8]

All this mitigated but could not reverse the perceptible erosion of Jackson's power from its peak during the decade of the 1970s. Ironically, President Reagan and former Jackson Democrats in the administration rendered Jackson himself less essential by embracing much of his approach
to foreign policy and defense issues. Emblematic of his diminishing clout,
Jackson could no longer even save the job of his old friend Admiral Hyman Rickover, which he had done successfully for years. Secretary of the
Navy John Lehman, whom Reagan had chosen at Jackson's own behest,
laid the groundwork for Rickover's firing, which occurred on Friday, November 13, 1981. Jackson, the only member of Congress who fought to
retain Rickover, lost decisively.[9] For the remaining thirty-two months of

his life, Jackson thus moved from his accustomed role at center stage to a more supportive role in national politics.

Jackson never embraced Reagan's domestic agenda the way an increasing number of neoconservative Jackson Democrats would do. On the contrary, he remained to the end a partisan Democrat, an unswerving believer in an activist and regulatory federal government. He blasted Reagan's decision in 1982 to abolish all price controls on energy and natural gas, a decision that effectively ended the energy crisis.[10] Although Jackson gave Reagan "the benefit of the doubt" in 1981 by voting for the president's controversial tax and budget cuts, he campaigned for reelection in 1982 as an unbridled foe of "Reaganomics," which he denounced as a failure.[11] He also devoted much of his time to counseling Democrats on how to recapture the Senate and the White House.[12] He was now truly the last of the liberal Cold Warriors in the United States Senate.

DEFENSE AND FOREIGN POLICY

Henry Jackson saw as critical for the outcome of the Cold War the related battles over the deployment of Euromissiles (Pershing and ground-launched cruise missiles) to offset the Soviet SS-20 IRBMs and the Reagan defense buildup to redress the massive Soviet strategic buildup of the 1970s. For Jackson, the nuclear freeze movements in Western Europe and the United States and the outlook they reflected, which the Soviets did not create but actively fomented, loomed as the main obstacles to the implementation of these vital initiatives.[13] In the early 1980s, several states and hundreds of municipalities reacted to the Reagan military buildup by passing nuclear freeze resolutions, which Jackson believed would have locked America and Western Europe into a dangerous position of nuclear inferiority. The nuclear freeze movement also threatened to convulse the NATO alliance, particularly the politics of West Germany, NATO's linchpin state, where hundreds of thousands of demonstrators filled the streets in protest against Reagan's determination to fulfill the Carter administration's vacillating pledge to deploy the Euromissiles. If the West German electorate decided to choose leaders who supported the nuclear freeze and opposed the deployment of Euromissiles, it would kill the NATO decision to deploy the Euromissiles, gravely weakening the alliance and expanding Soviet influence in Western Europe at U.S. expense.[14]

Jackson thus urged President Reagan, during a private meeting at the White House in February 1981, to "launch a dramatic, sustained American peace offensive" so that the Soviets could not continue to "preempt the issue of peace." In a detailed letter to the president following up on their conversations, Jackson observed that "the Soviets were making headway with their peace propaganda among our allies in Europe." The administration, according to Jackson, should "make Moscow show its true colors by forcing the Soviets to respond and react to U.S. proposals . . . for far-reaching, innovative, serious mutual arms reduction—repeated, repeated, and repeated." He did not "foresee the Soviets initially welcoming such an effort but exhorted Reagan not to repeat the mistakes of the Carter administration by retreating "at the first Soviet objection." Such a genuine peace offensive "must be pressed month after month, year after year, if necessary," counseled Jackson. "It will clarify to our friends and allies our dedication to stabilizing nuclear arms reduction negotiations. At a minimum, it will put Moscow on the propaganda defensive. It keeps open the possibility of achieving over time real and significant steps in the direction of such a stabilizing disarmament at a time when the Soviet economy is in deep difficulty."[15]

In this case, Jackson's recommendations confirmed rather than shaped the president's own deeply held convictions. Reagan launched his own peace initiative in November 1981 by calling for the Soviets to remove all their SS-20 missiles in exchange for NATO forgoing deployment of any Pershing II or cruise missiles (the Euromissiles). Jackson "saluted" the president for offering this proposal, dubbed the Zero Option, which, among other things, would finally compel the Soviets "to put up or shut up."[16] Thereafter, Reagan stuck resolutely with the Zero Option, which Richard Perle originated, notwithstanding the initially hostile reaction from the Soviet Union, which was echoed by many American liberals. They complained that the Zero Option was unfair and unrealistic because it required the Soviets to give up a system that was already deployed in exchange for the West not deploying systems not yet in place. Although the Soviets even walked out of the Geneva Arms Control talks after the first deployment of the Euromissiles, the Zero Option did mollify a large enough segment of European and American opinion to blunt the impact of the nuclear freeze movement.[17]

Ultimately, the outcome of the battle over Euromissiles vindicated Reagan and Jackson. In 1983, West German voters inflicted a devastating defeat on Soviet grand strategy of the early 1980s by choosing the Christian Democrats, led by Helmut Kohl, who were intent on carrying out former Social Democratic Party Chancellor Schmidt's decision to deploy the Euromissiles, rather than the Social Democrats, who had turned against it. The Soviets thereby lost their last serious opportunity to unravel the NATO alliance. Eventually, Moscow accepted the Zero Option in the INF Treaty of 1987. As Jeffrey Herf, author of an outstanding study of the subject, concluded, the Soviets would have had no incentive to dismantle their SS-20s without the deployment of the Euromissiles. Richard Perle had not collaborated or consulted with Jackson in devising the Zero Option. He had no need to do so: "I had been trained by Scoop. Everything I knew I learned from him. I knew instinctively what he would think."[18]

In May 1982, Reagan also revived the approach to the SALT talks along the lines Jackson had called for during the 1970s. The president renamed the SALT talks the Strategic Arms Reduction Talks (START). Specifically, he proposed a significant reduction in the ballistic missile warheads of both sides, to 5,000 deployed on no more than 850 ballistic missiles (ICBMs and SLBMs combined). Throughout the Reagan presidency, Perle profoundly influenced the president's approach to START and effectively championed it within the administration in the face of unremitting liberal hostility. The START Treaty of 1991 once more vindicated the Reagan administration's arms-control strategy by achieving unprecedentedly deep cuts in both American and Russian strategic nuclear arsenals.[19]

Meanwhile, Jackson had launched his own peace offensive to blunt the burgeoning nuclear freeze movement, which was very popular in his home state, especially in Seattle.[20] By proposing in the spring of 1982 a joint U.S.-U.S.S.R. Consultation Center, Jackson sought to reduce the risk and assuage popular fears of an accidental nuclear war. He envisaged this joint consultation center as "kind of a live hot line" with two types of facilities: a jointly run central building with working areas for senior Soviet and American professional staffs; and adjacent "nationally operated buildings with secure communication links to their respective capitals, in which the staff of each side could confer in private." Nothing ever came of this proposal, notwithstanding the Reagan administration's positive

and polite response to Jackson, who lobbied hard for it.[21] Jackson did derive the political benefit, however, of softening his hawkish image as he
prepared to run for reelection in 1982.[22]

Jackson strove, too, to weaken mounting support for a nuclear freeze
in Congress. In March 1982, Senators Kennedy and Hatfield offered an
amendment to the FY 1983 Defense Authorization Bill (the Senate variant of the resolution that Representative Clement Zablocki, Democrat of
Wisconsin, offered simultaneously in the House) calling for a complete
and immediate nuclear freeze. Jackson and the Reagan administration rejected the freeze resolution's explicit premise that an unrestrained nuclear
arms race posed the greatest risk of nuclear war. "A nuclear freeze would
be heavily to the advantage of the Soviet Union, which has recently undertaken massive modernization," Jackson replied. "A freeze would cod-
ify present Soviet advantages, endorse the position that a balance currently exists, and reduce Soviet incentives to negotiate reductions. It
would prevent the United States from restoring strategic parity and thus
would undermine the credibility of our deterrent."[23] Jackson and Senator John Warner, Republican from Virginia, countered by introducing a
joint bipartisan alternative to the Kennedy-Hatfield amendment. The
Jackson-Warner Resolution called for "a verifiable nuclear forces freeze
at equal and sharply reduced levels of forces" rather than at "the in-
equitable and excessively high existing level." After sustained debate, with
Jackson at the forefront, Congress rejected resolutions for an immediate
freeze, which Jackson and the Reagan administration fought against
doggedly, in favor of the Jackson-Warner Resolution.[24]

Jackson also played an active role in working out the compromise that
saved the MX ICBM program from total cancellation. Reagan's two immediate predecessors had tentatively initiated the decision to deploy a
force of MX ICBMs, each carrying ten warheads, to offset the growing
Soviet capacity to destroy existing Minuteman ICBMs in their underground silos. Originally, the Ford administration, and more reluctantly,
the Carter administration, had advocated a basing mode for the MX
ICBMs that called for moving them at random among a total number of
launch sites large enough to exhaust the Soviet ICBM force if Moscow
fired two ICBM warheads at each U.S. launch site. The Reagan administration abandoned this plan, however, in the face of formidable opposition from a powerful coalition of liberals and Rocky Mountain state con-

servatives. Liberal arms controllers condemned the cost and complexity of this system. They also maintained that the MX was unnecessary, because the awesome destructive power of the existing U.S. strategic forces would deter any Soviet attack, regardless of the vulnerability of U.S. ICBMs to Soviet attack or any Soviet advantage in ICBM warheads. Many conservatives from the West objected to the construction of thousands of launch sites across sparely populated areas of Utah and Nevada that would make these areas a likely target in the event of a nuclear exchange. Despite Jackson's support for the administration, congressional liberals succeeded in killing President Reagan's first alternative plan for deploying the MX, which called for placing one hundred missiles temporarily in existing silos while the administration determined a permanent plan.[25]

Congress also killed, this time with Jackson's help, Reagan's second plan for deployment of the MX, announced in November 1982 and known as the "dense pack," which called for placing one hundred of these missiles close to each other at Warren Air Force Base near Cheyenne, Wyoming. Contrary to congressional liberal arms-control advocates, Jackson supported the MX but scoffed at the theory on which the dense pack rested—namely, that U.S. ICBMs deployed in this manner could not be wiped out in a single attack because incoming Soviet warheads would be so close together that the first few to explode would disable the rest of them (the "fratricide effect").[26] Instead, Jackson encouraged the administration to break the impasse over the MX by creating an independent commission to address this problem and to embrace its recommendations. The administration adopted that course of action.[27]

In January 1983, President Reagan deferred the question of the future of the U.S. ICBM force to a commission of seventeen distinguished experts, chaired by Brent Scowcroft, former national security adviser to Presidents Nixon and Ford. In April 1983, President Reagan endorsed the recommendations of the Scowcroft Commission to deploy one hundred MX missiles in existing silos while the Pentagon developed a new, smaller mobile missile invulnerable to a devastating Soviet first strike. By June 1983, Congress had narrowly approved funding for this plan. Jackson helped neutalize the fervent opposition in the Senate, led by Ted Kennedy and Gary Hart, Democrat from Colorado.[28]

Jackson also approved generally of the Reagan administration's policy toward the Middle East, a policy largely driven by four of his own core

assumptions: that Soviet expansionism, not the Arab-Israeli dispute, constituted the gravest threat to U.S. interests in the Middle East; that a stable, democratic, free, and militarily strong Israel constituted an enormous
strategic asset in a sea of authoritarian and often hostile pro-Soviet
regimes in the region; that staunch U.S. support for Israel did not preclude the U.S. from forging a regional coalition of moderate Middle Eastern regimes to contain Soviet power and influence; and that America's
most deeply held beliefs as well as geopolitical necessity dictated staunch
U.S. support for Israel.[29] Jackson did, however, quarrel with some of the
specifics of Reagan's Middle East policy.

In the fall of 1981, Jackson led the unsuccessful fight in Congress to
block Reagan's decision to sell AWACs radar aircraft and sidewinder missiles to Saudi Arabia. There were, in Jackson's view, better "realistic alternatives which would increase our security and help deter attack on Saudi Arabia, without courting the compromise or loss of a major U.S.
defense system, and without threatening our other friends and allies."
Jackson doubted whether the Saudis had either the will or the capability
to serve as America's linchpin in the Persian Gulf. He maintained that
ceding the Saudis sovereign control over AWACs would needlessly antagonize Egypt "just as we are striving to protect and build a continuing
relationship with Cairo." Highlighting the Saudis' antipathy toward Israel and their encouragement of the PLO's irredentism, he also warned
that the arming of Saudi Arabia would imperil Israeli security. Invoking
the example of Iran, Jackson also feared that the instability of the Saudi
regime could result in the loss, compromise, or misuse of the AWACs and
other American advance weapons systems. He proposed alternatively that
the United States clearly demonstrate its "determination to protect vital
Western interests with credible military force" by providing the Saudis
with AWACs protection and further support for their air defense programs.[30]

Always averse to sending American ground forces to the Middle East,
Jackson also opposed the Reagan administration's decision to deploy
American forces in Lebanon as peacekeepers in the wake of the Israeli invasion of that beleaguered country in the summer of 1982. Lebanon posed
"the most divisive situation that one could face in the Middle East," said
Jackson.[31] "This is going to be a long protracted problem and it's going
to take a long time before you bring stability . . . with the population one-

third Muslim, one-third Christian, with the Muslim world all split up between Shiites and Sunnis, and with a sizable Druze faction on top of all that. The Reagan administration made a mistake by sending U.S. soldiers in such an "open-ended matter," he said. "With a superpower playing a police role, the danger of Americans being killed, the danger of divisiveness that would accrue from those developments . . . are all too real. A superpower should not play that kind of role in a cauldron of trouble because sooner or later we are going to get hurt."[32] Events would confirm the prescience of his admonitions. In April 1983, terrorists bombed the U.S. embassy in Beirut, killing 67 Americans. In October 1983, they blew up the U.S. Marine barracks in Lebanon, killing 241 American troops, whereupon, President Reagan unceremoniously withdrew the remaining troops in February 1984 as U.S. enemies exulted in the administration's defeat.

Jackson also increasingly criticized the Begin government for policies he thought shortsighted and unwise. As he saw it, Prime Minister Begin and his defense minister Ariel Sharon had needlessly antagonized Americans of good will by harping on Israel's biblical claims to the West Bank rather than emphasizing the legitimate need for "secure and defensible borders." He chided the Israelis, too, for failing to consult the United States about their surprise invasion of Lebanon, unaware that they not only had informed Secretary of State Haig beforehand but had received the green light from him: "The Israelis have not consulted with our government on any of these matters to my knowledge. This can't continue and still have public support for the state of Israel. . . . Mr. Begin as a personality is hurting our relations with Israel."[33] In September 1982, when a contingent of Lebanese Christians allied with Israel murdered more than three hundred Palestinian civilians at a refugee camp in the Israeli zone of occupation, he expressed horror at these terrible atrocities "that Israel should have known were going on." He called on the Begin government to announce an inquiry comparable to the one after the 1973 Arab-Israeli War on their intelligence failure.[34] A combination of external pressure and domestic outrage prompted Begin to acquiesce. In February 1983, the Kahan Commission, headed by the president of the Supreme Court of Israel, reported the findings of the full and independent inquiry it had conducted on the massacre. It acquitted Israel of direct responsibility but held Defense Minister Sharon, the chief of staff, and two other senior officials indirectly responsible for the killings. The Israeli government removed Sharon as defense minister pursuant to the commission's recommendation, although he remained in the Begin government as a minister without portfolio. Jackson hailed this result and the selection of American-born Moshe Arens as Sharon's replacement.[35]

For all his differences with the Begin government, however, Jackson remained Israel's most stalwart defender in Congress. He defended the Israeli preemptive bombing of Iraq's nuclear facilities at Osirik in June 1981 as necessary to thwart Saddam Hussein from his goal of developing nuclear weapons.[36] He still opposed categorically any return to the pre-1967 borders, lest Israel utterly lack the geographic width and therefore the strategic depth to resist an Arab attack with a standing army of manageable proportions. Similarly, he remained unremittingly hostile to the idea of creating an independent Palestinian state under the PLO, "an organization dedicated by its very charter to the destruction of the Jewish State."[37] He also counseled his fellow Americans to retain their sense of proportion in criticizing Israel's controversial actions:

> Keep in mind a couple of central facts. Israel has 3,400,000 people and they face a hostile Arab world of 140,000,000 people. Israel is the only democracy in the Middle East. They are the strongest military power in the area. They have the finest air force in the world. Those facts have an enormous bearing on our ability to help bring peace to the Middle East and stability to the world in economic terms as it relates especially to oil. If Israel is gone, the real tragedy is that the crazies take over. I think we don't want to shoot ourselves in the foot here.[38]

During the first two years of the Reagan administration, Jackson also had reservations about the president's policy toward the People's Republic of China. The Chinese had less strategic significance in Reagan's grand strategy than in those of his predecessors or Henry Jackson. By and large, the administration believed, too, that Japan's democratic system made it a more compatable strategic partner than China, whose ambitions and repressive political system the president and his secretary of state, George Shultz, viewed warily.[39] Accordingly, Reagan initially showed considerable interest in upgrading U.S. relations with Taiwan and selling Taiwan advanced jet fighters. Jackson and the PRC believed that both those actions would violate the spirit and the letter of the Shanghai Communiqué of 1972, which recognized just one China with Taiwan as part of it. Jackson did not criticize the administration publicly, but he privately encouraged Secretaries of State Haig and Shultz, Secretary of Defense Weinberger, and Reagan to give the U.S. strategic relationship with the PRC priority over its relationship with Taiwan.[40] At the same time, he continued to make the case annually before Congress that the PRC had met the conditions for a waiver of the Jackson-Vanik Amendment and hence should receive MFN status.[41] He also pressed the administration to avail the PRC of American technology, particularly for developing China's vast energy potential, which he considered the key to its future. Jackson deferred his next visit to China until he felt comfortable with the administration's China policy and had something positive to report. The administration succeeded in reassuring him at least with the joint Sino-American Communiqué of August 17, 1982, governing U.S. arms sales to Taiwan, and with its decision in the spring of 1983 to relax technology transfers to China. Jackson, though not Reagan, interpreted the former as calling for the gradual but ultimate termination of U.S. weapons sales to Taiwan. In August 1983, Jackson would make his fourth and final trip to the PRC, carrying a letter from President Reagan to PRC leaders expressing the president's commitment to cooperative Sino-American relations.[42]

Jackson inflicted on the administration one of the few defeats it suffered on a defense issue during the early years of the Reagan presidency. With the Seattle-based Boeing Company and other commercial airlines that were mired in a deep slump lined up on Jackson's side, the Senate in May 1982 approved his amendment transferring funds earmarked for C-5 transport planes to buy surplus civilian Boeing 747 as a bargain alternative. Pork barrel concerns largely drove the bruising battle over the C-5, which pitted Jackson not only against the administration but also against his frequent collaborator Senator Sam Nunn from Georgia, where the Lockheed Corporation would produce these planes. The Boeing 747s, Jackson argued, offered a bargain alternative to building the more expensive C-5s. He thus tailored his successful appeal to the broad coalition of senators either alarmed by the cost of the Reagan buildup or representing districts with economically distressed industries hoping for similar help from the Reagan buildup.[43]

Past patterns of association and differences over domestic policy militated against Jackson and Reagan developing a truly close personal relationship, observed Elliott Abrams.[44] Reagan also could not come close to meeting "Scoop's standard" for knowledge on the issues, added his U.N. Ambassador Jeane Kirkpatrick. "What happens to people like Jackson, Hubert Humphrey, Lyndon Johnson, Bob Dole, and Sam Nunn—the strong and smart leaders of the Senate who have served a long time and are greatly respected by their peers—is that they become tremendously knowledgeable. They know more about the issues and develop a level of competence that surpasses the standard of any president." Dr. Kirkpatrick also stressed, however, that what separated Reagan and Jackson paled in comparison to what united them on foreign policy and national defense. Based on her close association with and great admiration for both men, she offered this definitive assessment of the Jackson-Reagan relationship:

> Jackson had great respect for Reagan because he was fundamentally right. They held some important views in common, above all, on the nature of the Soviet Union and Soviet intentions and what it meant for American foreign policy. In their views, this was absolutely the dominant foreign policy issue. Jackson respected Ronald Reagan for his seriousness about communism and Soviet expansion. He believed that Reagan had an understanding about the essence of the Soviet Union, an intellectual conviction.[45]

Jackson himself acknowledged the large measure of consistency between Reagan's foreign policy and his own. He publicly commended the president for "expressing a new resolve to stand up to the Soviet Union, talking more realistically about the adverse shifts in the strategic nuclear equation, launching the first steps to build up our conventional and strategic capabilities, including our naval forces, identifying international terrorism as a primary administration concern, and pledging continued American strength and concern for the stability of nations in Western Europe."[46]

JACKSON'S LAST CAMPAIGN

Henry Jackson turned seventy on May 31, 1982, as he prepared to run for his sixth term in the Senate. He and Helen had decided that it would be his last. Their children were growing up. In May 1981, Anna Marie had graduated from the Holton Arms School in Bethesda, Maryland, with

Jackson delivering the commencement address. She was now finishing her first year at Stanford, with her childhood adoration of her father undiminished. Even when he was very busy, she could still call him anytime for help on her homework, which he dispensed liberally, especially if the subjects were history and politics. Peter was now a sophomore at the St. Albans School in Washington. Like most teenage boys, he enjoyed needling his father for sport, usually for his hard-line views toward the Soviet Union. His father's reputation as a hawk had embarrassed the adolescent Peter among his more liberal peers and teachers. Jackson usually endured his son's provocations with patience and good humor. Jackson also had begun to devote considerable attention to furthering the University of Washington's School of International Studies as a world-renowned center for Chinese and Russian studies. He looked forward to teaching there after he retired at the end of his next term.[47]

Magnuson's defeat in 1980 had magnified Jackson's already powerful disposition not to take his reelection for granted. In March 1982, Democratic pollster Peter Hart met with Jackson and several of his closest campaign advisers—Sterling Munro, Ron Dotzauer, Brian Corcoran, Gerry Hoeck, and Joe Miller—to inform them that Jackson's political strength appeared to have eroded. "Hart told us that Scoop was no longer a 70 percenter in the state of Washington," recalled Dotzauer. "His numbers were not like the numbers of the Scoop Jackson of old." The National Conservative Political Action Committee (NCPAC) had targeted Jackson for defeat, notwithstanding the fact that his foreign and defense policies were indistinguishable from Reagan's.[48] "He has got a lot to answer for, you know, like his 100 percent AFL-CIO voting record," threatened Richard Viguerie, one of the leading figures of the New Right.[49] Jackson did not take NCPAC's efforts lightly. In 1978, the five liberal Democrats it targeted had lost: Warren Magnuson, George McGovern, Birch Bayh, Frank Church, and John Culver. Jackson also had irritated some conservative and moderate voters in Washington State by persuading President Carter to name Jack Tanner as a federal district judge. Tanner, Jackson's liaison to the black community during the 1976 presidential campaign, indeed proved to be a terrible choice. The American Bar Association rated him consistently as one of the worst judges on the bench.[50]

Jackson also faced opposition from the Left, vociferous in its criticism of his support for the Reagan buildup and his opposition to the nuclear freeze. His Republican opponents—Douglas Jewett, a thirty-six-year-old former King County prosecutor, and King Lysen, a Democratic state senator running as an independent—harped on these issues. They also tried to saddle him with responsibility for the ill-fated partnership between the Bonneville Power Administration (BPA) and the Washington Public Power Supply System (WPPSS), which subsidized the construction of nuclear power plants with the revenues generated by cheap hydroelectric power distributed by BPA. During the late 1970s, BPA administrator Donald Hodel and his successor, Sterling Munro, Jackson's close friend and former administrative assistant, argued that such a program was necessary to satisfy the Northwest's growing demand for electric power increases that existing hydroelectric power alone could not satisfy. By the early 1980s, construction problems and cost overruns on these nuclear plants had resulted in huge rate increases and default on WPPSS bonds. Jewett and Lysen made much of the fact that Jackson had helped establish the partnership between WPPSS and BPA and had drafted the Northwest Power Act of 1978 on his kitchen table.[51]

The campaigns of Jackson's opponents flopped completely. Peter Hart's polls had vastly underestimated the enormous popularity that Jackson still enjoyed in his home state. In November 1982, he won reelection with a whopping 69 percent of the vote. It had proved impossible to single him out for blame in the WPPSS fiasco. Local legislatures and private utilities, not Congress, had created WPPSS. Even if Jackson "may be guilty as sin" on WPPSS, opined one local commentator, "so was every member of the political establishment of Washington State."[52] Jackson also had managed to soften his hawkish image just enough by his call for a joint U.S.-U.S.S.R. command center to reduce the risk of nuclear war and by his sponsorship of an alternative to the Kennedy-Hatfield nuclear freeze resolution.[53] Having amassed a $1.9 million war chest, Jackson also waged a vigorous campaign, which included putting up 18,000 signs that just said "Scoop." Jackson's television commercials showed him with his family on the beach, talking about horrors of nuclear war and the environment.[54]

By 1982, Jackson also had achieved a partial albeit tenuous truce with the liberal wing of the state's Democratic Party, which had long reviled him. Although these New Politics liberals still abhorred his foreign and defense policies, their experience with genuine conservatives such as Ronald Reagan and Senator Slade Gorton, Republican from Washington

State, made him look tolerable by comparison. "Reagan's effect on Democratic Party unity has been tremendous," declared Washington State Democratic Party Chair Karen Marchioro, a longtime Jackson foe. "That will help Jackson no matter who the Republicans run," because "a lot of people are starting to think what it would be like to have no democratic senator from this state." She lamented that "it was not a pretty picture. Liberals are not going to announce that we were wrong all along and that Jackson is really a liberal. He is not. On foreign policy and defense, his record is irredeemable." Nevertheless, Marchioro appreciated that Jackson was "not voting with Reagan and Helms and Hatch like Gorton is."[55]

Jackson also benefited from the inexperience and incoherence of his main opponent, Doug Jewett, who put off more voters than he attracted by packaging himself as an unorthodox alternative, which left him outside the mainstream of both political parties. Typical of a Republican, he ran to the right of Jackson on fiscal policy. Typical of a New Politics liberal, he ran to the left of Jackson on foreign and defense policies. Many conservative Republicans remained loyal to Jackson because of his position on Cold War issues, even though they disagreed with him on domestic issues.[56]

The Jackson camp made the senator's denunciation of Reaganomics and the president's environmental policy the centerpiece of his campaign.[57] Befitting the last of the quintessential New Deal–Fair Deal liberals of the 1940s, Jackson championed the imperative for and the efficacy of a large activist federal government to promote the public welfare, social justice, and economic growth. He proposed massive federal jobs and construction programs to alleviate the effects of the deep recession that had begun in Carter's final year in office and worsened in the first two years of the Reagan administration. He called for a "major mid-course correction in the economic policies of the administration" because the Reagan plan was simply not working. "The President reminds me of a football coach whose team is behind 35–0 in the middle of the second quarter," declared Jackson at the Washington State Democratic Convention in June 1982. "He's called the same play 15 times and he's gained a total of six yards. And believe it or not, he doesn't want to change the game plan. Well, we're going to change the game plan for him in November." Jackson likewise ripped the Reagan administration for its abortive 1981 attempt to cut $88 billion from Social Security, for its proposed budget cuts to the Environmental Protection Agency, and for its plans "to gut the Wilderness Protection Act" by permitting the president to open wilderness areas for development unless the Congress passed a law to prevent it. James Watt, Reagan's controversial pro-development secretary of the interior, bore the brunt of many of Jackson's attacks on the administration.[58]

"Jackson genuinely enjoyed his last campaign," said Ron Dotzauer, his campaign manager. "It was still Scoop's idea of fun to meet with constituents across the state. He still had a fantastic memory for their names and faces." Dotzauer recalled with amusement how Jackson lived up to his reputation for being thrifty and a harrowing driving companion either as a passenger or behind the wheel:

> I picked him up to go to Bremerton for a Democratic Party picnic. We had to catch the Edmonds-Kingston Ferry. Just as we were getting close to the toll booth, Scoop told me. "Do not forget . . . I am a senior citizen. So get the senior citizen discount." We were the next car to get up to the window. Even without me doing anything, Scoop stuck his face out the window and announced, "I am Senator Jackson and I get a senior citizen discount." On the way home, he was in a hurry as usual. He told me he would give me senatorial immunity if I just stepped on the accelerator to get there. We passed Adele Ferguson, a reporter for the Seattle papers who did not like me because I helped get a county auditor elected she did not like. She later wrote an article saying that I jeopardized the senator's life by speeding to make the ferry back.[59]

THE CENTRAL AMERICA COMMISSION

In January 1983, Jackson began his sixth term in the Senate, totally unsuspecting that he had only nine months to live. He had gained a noticeable amount of weight around his middle, which Dorothy Fosdick joked about with him and among some of his staffers. His workout routine also had become less rigorous, remembered Peter Jackson, who regularly accompanied his father to the Senate gym on Saturday mornings while Congress was in session. "Dad just paddled around the pool and did more talking than exercising." Peter also sensed that his father had grown less patient with liberals who attacked his foreign and defense policies. "They just don't get it," Jackson told him increasingly.[60] In March 1983, Jackson perhaps manifested some of this frustration in an incident totally uncharacteristic of him; he shoved a man who refused to leave a "Senators only" elevator.[61] Yet he appeared generally to be his usual energetic and cheerful self, according to Helen Jackson, his colleagues in the Senate, and others who knew him well. Jackson had continued to pass with flying colors his annual physicals at Walter Reed Hospital in Bethesda. Tests showed that he suffered from no serious conditions whatsoever, other than his chronic back ailment, which he had incurred sitting for hundreds of hours through the Army-McCarthy trials of 1954.[62]

As he approached his seventy-first birthday in the spring of 1983, he entered the raging debate over U.S. policy toward Central America. The Reagan administration depicted the deteriorating situation in Central America as a classic struggle between East and West. It saw the Soviet Union and its Cuban proxy behind the revolutionary movements in Nicaragua and El Salvador and intent on spreading communism throughout Central America. Many liberal Democrats in Congress believed, conversely, that the Reagan administration vastly exaggerated the Soviet threat in Central America. They depicted these revolutionary movements, which some of them denied were even communist, as indigenous uprisings against injustice and American imperialism. They castigated Reagan's program for backing the government in El Salvador against the revolutionaries trying to overthrow it and for backing Contra rebels against the Sandinista government in Nicaragua for again putting the United States on the wrong side of history, in defiance of popular aspirations for freedom and social justice. By 1983, these clashing positions had culminated in a series of compromises that satisfied neither liberals in Congress nor conservatives in the administration as the crisis in the region mounted.[63] Jackson had not paid much attention to Central America over the years. He had concentrated instead on the Soviet Union, China, NATO, the Middle East, the strategic balance, and arms control. By the early 1980s, however, he had concluded that "current events in Nicaragua and Central America had enormous strategic implications for the United States." Appearing on *This Week with David Brinkley*, March 6, 1983, he identified the subversion of Mexico as the ultimate goal of the Soviets and their regional proxies. He emphasized not only the strategic importance of Mexico (constituting 76 percent of the land mass and 79 percent of Central America's population), but also the immense challenges confronting that nation, including a debt crisis that an international emergency package of August 1982 had barely alleviated: "Think of what the destabilization of the whole Central American isthmus, including Mexico, would weaken America's position in the world. Confronting hostile neighbors and the prospect of flooding refugees, any U.S. government would be faced with the demands to bring our troops home from Europe and to reduce our commitments in the Pacific. The credibility of our support for our friends in the Middle East could be eroded considerably," warned Jackson.[64]

Jackson's position on Central America lay closer to Reagan's than to the president's liberal Democratic critics in Congress. He assailed the Sandinistas in Nicaragua for betraying the revolution by "a Leninist power grab." He considered the Sandinista regime a Soviet and Cuban surrogate.[65] Jackson did fault the administration, however, for its inability to collaborate with organized labor in forging a bipartisan consensus and a sensible foreign policy approach toward Central America. Organized labor represented one of the last bastions of Cold War liberalism in the Democratic Party. After World War II, the labor movements of Western Europe had contributed significantly to saving those nations from communism. The Polish labor movement, Solidarity, and analogous movements elsewhere also would contribute enormously to freeing Eastern Europe from Soviet tyranny. Drawing heavily on the analogy of U.S. policy toward Western Europe under President Truman, Jackson defined the threat to U.S. interests in Central America broadly and the remedy comprehensively. The United States, he thought, needed to fashion a program that redressed the grueling poverty and social inequality exploited by communist revolutionaries while providing sufficient protection against communist aggression so that liberal reformers had a chance to succeed. "If we don't pay attention to the history of social and economic oppression in Central America," he said, "the military shield is bound to crumble."[66]

President Reagan's decision to create a bipartisan Central America Commission grew out of conversations Jackson had with his old friend, U.N. Ambassador Jeane Kirkpatrick, who shared Jackson's convictions about the great importance of the U.S. southern borders for "geomilitary strategic reasons." Over several breakfasts and lunches, she recalled, they talked about what was needed and how to package it to overcome "opposition among liberal Democrats and even some Republicans . . . to the notion that Central America was even an appropriate area of concern" for American foreign policy. They agreed that an adequate approach "substantively and politically salable to Congress would address the social, economic, political, and military problems simultaneously." What they both had in mind was a Marshall Plan for Central America. They decided that a bipartisan commission was the best shield for effective action. "Scoop took the lead among Democrats, while Kirkpatrick would take the lead among Republicans." She persuaded Senator Charles Mathias, Republican from Maryland, to cosponsor the resolution for a Central America Commission in the Senate and Jack Kemp, Republican from New York and another self-avowed Henry Jackson Republican, to cosponsor it with Mike Barnes, Democrat of Maryland, in the House.[67]

At the same time, Kirkpatrick took the issue to President Reagan and Judge William Clark, Richard Allen's replacement as national security adviser. Both responded enthusiastically to the Jackson-Kirkpatrick approach.[68] Reagan then met with Jackson and the other cosponsors of the resolution, which they unveiled in June 1983.

> Underlying the stalemate is the general reluctance of the American people to simultaneously embrace two hard facts: first, stability in Central America is of enormous strategic importance to the United States. And second, the chronic poverty, social injustices and human rights abuses in the region undermine stability. Embracing the first fact requires that we face the reality of Soviet and Cuban sponsored armed insurgencies. Embracing the second fact forces hard choices and confronts us with moral ambiguities with which no one is comfortable.[69]

Jackson declared that "a national bipartisan commission for Central America" offered a sensible first step "to achieving a comprehensive, coordinated Central American policy." He envisaged such a commission "drawing upon knowledgeable leaders from all sectors of American society, including Hispanic and religious communities, business, and especially labor." He commended the American trade union movement's "long record of continuing support for building democracy through labor organization efforts." Commentators hailed Jackson's resolution, which the Congress approved by an overwhelming bipartisan majority.[70]

Reagan not only named Jackson to the commission, but also took his advice in selecting some of the other members, notably Lane Kirkland, president of the AFL-CIO. Jeane Kirkpatrick recommended that Henry Kissinger chair the commission. She calculated that "we needed a very well-known person of great intelligence who would legitimate it."[71] Notwithstanding Kissinger's well-known historical disinterest in Latin America (expressed in his quip that Argentina was a dagger aimed at the heart of Antarctica), Kirkpatrick expected him immediately to understand the gravity of the problem once he focused on it: "Scoop was not happy about that. He felt that Kissinger had not played straight with him" during the Nixon and Ford administrations. Finally, Jackson relented. The night before leaving Washington, D.C., for Everett to prepare for his August trip to China, Jackson invited Kissinger and Kirkpatrick over for dinner: "It was a civilized and pleasant dinner which established a good basis for proceeding on the commission. There were not any problems, but Scoop still did not trust Kissinger."

In the long run, the triumph of democratic forces in El Salvador and Nicaragua confirmed Jackson's diagnosis of and prescriptions for the Central American crisis. In the short run, however, his death would destroy whatever remote change the Central America Commission had to create an enduring bipartisan consensus on how to deal with the region. Reagan's policy toward Central America remained a ferociously divisive and partisan issue for the remainder of his administration.[72] "Jackson may have succeeded in assuaging congressional opposition because of his expertise and stature," speculated Kirkpatrick. "Once Scoop died, Democrats who were inclined to agree with him and me on Central America and the Soviets broke off. . . . leading Democrats who were doing the right thing flaked off."[73]

Jackson reached one more milestone in the weeks before he departed, never to return, from Washington, D.C., bound for China via Everett. In July 1983, he drew a standing ovation from his colleagues for casting his 11,000th roll call vote in the Senate. Fittingly, he voted with the majority in the 50 to 49 defeat of an effort by Senate liberals to delete funds for nerve-gas production.[74]

JACKSON'S FINAL DAYS

Henry Jackson and his entourage arrived in China on August 15, 1983, for a two-week visit that brought him to several communes and facilities, including the large Daqing complex in the Northeast. In Harbin, the capital of Heilongjiang Province, he stopped in at a small church founded by the Lutherans, which had just reopened. "Scoop had his picture taken with his arm around the pastor," recalled Kenneth Pyle, who again accompanied Jackson and transcribed his conversations with Chinese leaders during this China trip.[75] Jackson spent more than twenty hours in discussions with Chinese leaders in Beijing and the Northeast. On August 27, he met for an hour and a half with Deng Xiaoping. He delivered to Deng a letter from President Reagan reassuring the PRC that he considered the strategic relationship between the two countries of great importance and that he highly valued Jackson's counsel. Deng found Reagan's letter "warm and with good desire; he wants to develop Sino-American relations." Transcripts of Jackson's conversations with Deng reveal that the Chinese still bristled over the Reagan administration's campaign position on Taiwan and were more skeptical of American motives generally.[76] "The Chinese were in a different mood," said Pyle. "The difference between the 1979 and 1983 visits was palpable. The Chinese treated us cordially, but Scoop did not get the effusive response in 1983 that he did in 1979."[77]

Pyle also noticed that Jackson was not as vigorous as he had been on the 1979 trip. He sensed that something was bothering Jackson, who seemed tired and overweight, and along with several members of his traveling party had acquired a deep chest cold and bad cough during the grueling train rides to northeastern China. His personal physician Dr. Haakon Ragde, who accompanied him on the trip, worried that his cold could turn into pneumonia and put him on antibiotics. After his return home to Washington State on August 28, Jackson still could not shake off the cough but seemed to recover. He felt somewhat better by Wednesday, August 31. So he decided to go to the office the next day.[78]

Thursday, September 1, began with the shocking news that the Soviet Union had shot down a Korean Air 747 passenger plane (KAL flight 007), killing all 269 people aboard. Jackson was outraged. Still coughing badly, he went in the morning to the University of Washington Medical Center for a meeting with Department of Surgery physicians who worried that the medical school would be forgotten now that Warren Magnuson was no longer in the Senate. Jackson assured the doctors that he would continue to be active on behalf of the hospital and the medical school. When he arrived at the office in the late morning, Ron Dotzauer greeted him with a list of callers anxious for his reaction to the Soviet attack on the Korean airline. He suggested that Jackson call a press conference. "Feeling under the weather and a little grouchy," Jackson thought about it for a few minutes before instructing Dotzauer to arrange a press conference at the Old Federal Office Building in downtown Seattle in half an hour.[79] Looking tired and drawn, apologizing to the press for being under the weather, Jackson proceeded to give his final sermon on the malevolence of the Soviet empire and the imperative of peace through American strength. Jackson castigated the Soviet attack on the Korean airliner as a "dastardly, barbaric act against humanity." Dotzauer rated Jackson's final press conference as one of the best he had ever seen Scoop give, "stylistically and substantively." Anticipating that the press would pester Jackson afterwards, Dotzauer arranged for them to go down the freight elevator, where he told Jackson that he had never heard him sound better. With a twinkle in his eye and a grin, Jackson replied: "You know, I was pretty good, wasn't I?"[80]

After lunch with Dotzauer and developer Kemper Freeman at the Seattle Athletic Club, Jackson returned to his office feeling poorly. He told Dotzauer he was going home for the rest of the day and canceling his schedule for the next morning. On the way, he stopped by Dr. Ragde's office for an X-ray. He thought he had pneumonia, but the X-ray showed nothing wrong. He went straight to bed as soon as he arrived home. When he twice turned down a plate of his favorite Finnish cookies the family's longtime housekeeper had just made, Helen "knew he was really feeling badly." He came downstairs briefly at around 5:30 P.M. to give Helen a pair of socks for darning. This request puzzled her. He had never before asked her to darn his socks, something his mother had done routinely for him as a boy.[81] Dr. Ragde and Denny Miller arrived at the Jackson home shortly after 7:00 P.M. with some strong cough syrup. When they entered the bedroom, they discovered Jackson lying in his bed unconscious, stricken by what Ragde first thought was a heart attack. He started cardiopulmonary resuscitation while Miller called for an ambulance.[82] Jackson was rushed to Providence Hospital, where doctors tried for more than an hour to revive him. They could not. Two Everett cardiologists, Dr. Kirk Pringle and Dr. Neil Smith, pronounced him dead at 9:25 P.M. Pacific Standard Time.[83] According to the autopsy report, it was a ruptured aorta, not a heart attack, that killed him. According to Ragde, "Scoop suffered from a degenerative disease afflicting the muscle in the aorta. His muscle was paper thin. He could have died at any time."[84] Jackson was seventy-one years old.

TRIBUTE TO AN INDOMITABLE VIKING WARRIOR

The news of Jackson's death evoked an outpouring of tributes. President Reagan called Mrs. Jackson to convey his condolences. "Nancy and I were deeply saddened to learn of the death of Henry Jackson," the president announced publicly. "He was a friend, a colleague, a true patriot, and a devoted public servant of the people. He will be sorely missed. . . ." In his television address to the nation on the Korean airline massacre, Reagan praised Jackson as "a wise and revered statesman . . . who probably knew the Soviets as well as any in American history."[85]

Jackson's colleagues in the Senate on both sides of the aisle expressed their admiration and affection for him. Senate Minority Leader Robert Byrd, Democrat from West Virginia, hailed Jackson "as a champion of a strong America, of a decent America, of a prosperous America, and of a just America."[86] Senator Robert Dole, Republican from Kansas, called him a "giant" in the Senate, and knew of no senator who did not have great respect for him. Former senator Warren Magnuson, Jackson's colleague of forty years in the Congress, marveled not only at Jackson's knowledge and grasp of foreign affairs but also at the immaculateness of his personal as well as his political life. There had never been one breath of scandal "in a half a century of public service," said Magnuson. "That's something, in this day and age." Senate Majority Leader Howard Baker called Jackson "a man of majestic stature, of strength and conviction; a man who could stand on the Senate floor and express the conscience of the Congress and the country; a man who could change the course of debate and shape and form the policy of a great nation; a man who was humble in the face of success and congratulations, and who was courageous and determined in the face of criticism and dissent; a man who knew who he was and where he was going and where he wished to take the country." Senator Sam Nunn placed Jackson in "the front rank of leaders in the Senate" and in the front rank of leaders in the history of the nation: "Upon the death of Harry S. Truman in 1972, Senator Jackson said of that great

American: 'With the passing of the years, his place in history—and in the hearts of his countrymen—is ever more assured.' With the passing of the years, the same will be said of our friend, Henry M. Jackson."[87]

Former secretary of state Henry Kissinger despaired that "America has lost a true patriot" in Henry Jackson. "We are much poorer today without him."[88] The Republican governor of Washington State, John Spellman, ordered all flags on state buildings to fly at half-mast for a week. On the weekend of September 2–4, more than four thousand mourners came to pay their respects at the Solie Funeral Home in Everett, where Jackson's body lay in state. Over 1,700 people attended a memorial service held for Jackson at the Memorial Coliseum in Everett on September 6, 1983.[89] More than a thousand people attended a separate memorial service for Jackson on the same day at the National Presbyterian Church in Washington, D.C. Ben Wattenberg, Grenville Garside, Lane Kirkland, Daniel Patrick Moynihan, Edward Kennedy, and George F. Will delivered the eulogies.

Wattenberg commended Jackson for contributing as much as anyone "toward shaping the policies and the power that kept freedom alive in this perilous era." Garside lauded him for practicing "the art of politics with vigor, enthusiasm, and hope right to the end." Kirkland heralded him for his decency, which placed him "steadfastly in the corner of the underdogs of American society, the oppressed of the world, and the wretched of the Earth."[90] Moynihan remarked in a similar vein:

> He lived in the worst of times, the age of the totalitarian state. It fell to him to tell this to his own people and to the world and he did so full well knowing that there is a cost for such truthtelling. But he was a Viking also. . . . Of all things human, the only emotion he never knew was fear; the only weakness he could never comprehend was the love of ease. . . . The American people have paid a price for not entirely wishing to hear him, but he forgave all, and why not? It was a life of true greatness.[91]

Ted Kennedy praised Jackson as a true friend who "was with me and with my family in the best and the darkest times. . . . His ties of affection reached across the political spectrum. George Will always seemed to agree with Scoop on national defense, and Scoop had such good sense that on domestic programs he always seemed to disagree with George."[92] George Will rhapsodized "unabashedly" that Henry Jackson was his hero:

Painted on the walls of the Senate reception room are portraits of five men who were selected by special committee a quarter of a century ago to constitute a kind of Senate hall of fame. The portraits are of Clay, Calhoun, Webster, La Follette, and Taft. There is no more space on the walls of that room, but there is a nonfunctional door. That door should be removed and the wall filled in and adorned with the portrait of a sixth Senator. A Senate hall of fame without Henry Martin Jackson is as unthinkable as Cooperstown without George Herman Ruth. . . .

Jackson was an anchor against weariness, wishful thinking and apostasy in his party and his country. He nurtured in this Republic something without which no republic can long endure: a sense that problems are tractable. To be in his presence was to experience the wholesome infection of a reviving spirit. This is especially remarkable because he, more than any contemporary, looked unblinkingly at and spoke uncomfortably about the terrors of our time. He taught less clear-sighted, less brave persons how to combine realism and serenity.

He missed the ultimate prize of our politics; perhaps be lacked the cracking temperament that marks persons who burn on the surface with a hard, gemlike flame. If his political metabolism seemed uncommonly calm, that is because he had the patience of a mature politician, a gift for planning, a thirst for detail, and a sense of ripeness in issues. He had a flame, but he had a depth in which he kept it. . . . There are those, and there are legions, who call themselves Jackson Democrats. I can say with absolute authority that there is such a thing as a Jackson Republican.[93]

Vice President George Bush, representing President Reagan; Chief Justice Warren Burger; Retired Rear Admiral Hyman Rickover; Retired Secretary of Defense James Schlesinger; Henry Kissinger; and sixty-five current members of the U.S. Senate headed the list of dignitaries who flew from Washington, D.C., to attend Jackson's funeral service in Everett on September 7, 1983. Warren Magnuson, Ted Kennedy, and Representative Tom Foley of Washington State, a member of Jackson's staff in the early 1940s, also delivered glowing tributes. After the service, Jackson was buried in the Evergreen Cemetery in Everett, near his father, mother, and four siblings.[94]

Posthumous accolades to Jackson accrued steadily over the next twelve months, although one such effort to memorialize him fizzled conspicuously. In a well-meaning but ill-advised tribute undertaken without adequate consultation, members of the Seattle Port Commission voted in September 1983 to rename Seattle-Tacoma International Airport the Henry Jackson International Airport. An ensuing firestorm of protest from residents of the town of SeaTac and the city of Tacoma forced the commission to reverse that decision. Their objection was not to honoring Jackson, but to the peremptory way it had been done. Tacoma residents felt strongly that the airport, located halfway between Tacoma and Seattle, should continue to bear the names of their municipalities.[95]

By and large, however, the public responded enthusiastically to the plethora of posthumous honors Jackson received. The University of Washington announced two weeks after his death that it would name its School of International Studies after him. The Henry M. Jackson Foundation was incorporated on October 5, 1983, to perpetuate his lifelong commitment to educational programs relating to international affairs, public service, the environment and natural resource management, and human rights. The Jackson Foundation has built an endowment of $25 million through a generous appropriation of $10 million by Congress and private contributions from thousands of donors. Helen Jackson, still a resident of Everett, Washington, continues to serve as the foundation's chairman of the board. A federal office building in Seattle also was renamed for Jackson.[96] In October 1983, President Reagan ordered the Trident submarine the USS *Rhode Island*, then under construction in Groton, Connecticut, renamed the USS *Henry M. Jackson*. The Jackson family attended ceremonies for the launching of the submarine on October 6, 1984.[97] In November 1987, Helen Jackson unveiled the bust of Henry Jackson in Washington, D.C., that now stands in the alcove of the Russell Building, where he maintained his Senate office.[98]

On June 26, 1984, President Reagan posthumously presented Henry Martin Jackson with the Medal of Freedom, the nation's highest civilian award. Helen Jackson accepted "this great honor the nation has bestowed on my husband" in a ceremony at the Rose Garden of the White House.[99] President Reagan's remarks on this occasion eloquently captured the essence of Henry Jackson's life and career:

Henry Jackson was a protector of the nation, a protector of freedom and its values. There are always a few such people in each generation. Let others push each new chic belief or become distracted by the latest fashionable readings of history. The protectors . . . go about seeing to it that the ideals that shaped this nation are allowed to survive and flourish. . . .

Henry Jackson understood that there is great good in the world, and great evil, too, that there are saints and sinners among us. He had no illusions about totalitarians, but his understanding of the existence of evil did not dishearten him. He had a great hope and great faith in America. He felt we could do anything. He liked to quote Teddy Roosevelt: "We see across the dangers the great future, and we rejoice as a giant refreshed. . . . [T]he great victories are yet to be won, the greatest deeds yet to be done."

. . . Henry Jackson absorbed within himself the three great strains of thought that go about making a noble foreign policy: the love of freedom, a will to defend it, and the knowledge that America could not and must not attempt to float along alone: a blissful island of democracy in a sea of totalitarianism.

Scoop Jackson was convinced that there was no place for partisanship in foreign and defense policy. He used to say, "In matters of national security, the best politics is no politics." His sense of bipartisanship was not only natural and complete—it was courageous. He wanted to be president, but I think he must have known that his outspoken ideas on the security of the nation would deprive him of the chance to be his party's nominee in 1972 and 1976. Still, he would not cut his convictions for the prevailing style.

I am deeply proud—as he would have been—to have Jackson Democrats serve in my administration. I am proud that some of them have found a home here. . . .

Scoop helped shape national policy on dozens of complex issues—on strategic planning and arms control, on the Soviet Union and Central America, on human rights, and Israel, and the cause of Soviet Jewry.

His support for Israel grew out of his knowledge that political decisions must spring out of moral convictions. It was not some grand geopolitical abstraction that made him back the creation of Israel; it was seeing the concentration camps firsthand at the end of the war. At Buchenwald, he saw the evil, as he said, "written on the sky"—and he never forgot.

He said the Jews of Europe must have a homeland. He did everything he could to strengthen the alliance between the United States and Israel, recognizing that we are two great democracies, two great cultures, standing together. Today, both nations are safer because of his efforts. . . .

Scoop was always at the side of the weak and forgotten. With some people, all you have to do to win their friendship is be strong and powerful. With Scoop, all you had to do was be vulnerable and alone. And so when Simas Kudirka was in jail in Moscow, it was Scoop who mobilized the Congress to demand his release.

When Baptists in the Soviet Union were persecuted, it was Scoop who went again to the floor of the Senate to plead their cause. When free trade unionists were under attack in Poland, Scoop worked with the American labor movement to help them.

A few years ago, he was invited to visit the Soviet Union. The invitation was withdrawn when he said he could not go without calling on Andrei Sakharov. If Scoop were here today, I know he would speak out on behalf of Sakharov—just as Sakharov, a man of immense courage and humanity, stood up in Moscow and hailed the Jackson Amendment as a triumph of "the freedom-loving tradition of the American people."

Scoop Jackson was a serious man. Not somber or self-important, but steady and solemn. He didn't think much of the cosmetics of politics. He wasn't interested in image. He was a practitioner of the art of politics, and he was a personage in the affairs of the world. But there was no cause too great or small for his attention. . . .

The principles which guided his public life guided his private life. By the time he died, dozens of young men and women had been helped through school by a scholarship fund he had established and sustained. No one knew the money came from Scoop, until a change in the financial disclosure laws many years later forced him to 'fess up. He had never told the voters; he'd never even told his own staff.

Other people were embarrassed when the disclosure laws revealed their vanities. Scoop was embarrassed when it revealed his virtue. . . .

In a eulogy for Scoop, it was pointed out that there's a room in the Senate where members of the public are greeted. And on the walls of the room are the portraits of five of the greatest U.S. Senators, men chosen by the members of the Senate to reflect the best that chamber ever knew. . . . I'm joining those who would suggest to the Majority Leader that the Senate make room and commission a portrait so that Scoop Jackson can be with his peers. And when it's all done and in place, I'd be very proud to be among those who would go to the Senate and unveil it, Republicans and Democrats alike, a bipartisan effort in memory of the greatest bipartisan patriot of our time.[100]

Jackson's Medal of Freedom bore this inscription:

Representative and Senator for more than four decades, Henry Martin Jackson was one of the greatest lawmakers in our century. He helped to build the community of democracies and worked tirelessly to keep it vigorous and secure. He pioneered in the preservation of the nation's national heritage, and he embodied integrity and decency in the profession of politics. For those who make courage and freedom their cause, Henry Jackson will always inspire honor, courage, and hope.[101]

Who deserves a better epitaph than that?

Chapter 22

The Jackson Legacy

AMERICA'S TRIUMPH over Soviet communism ranks as Henry Jackson's greatest legacy. No single event over the past fifty years has contributed more to U.S. security or to the cause of freedom generally than the collapse of the Soviet Empire. There are, of course, many heroes of the cold war entitled to acclaim: President Truman and his administration for laying out the strategy of vigilant containment; Truman's successors and much of Congress for implementing it; the American people for willingly sacrificing to support it; the dissidents behind the Iron Curtain for resisting Soviet tyranny in defiance of the risk; and President Reagan for his wise and successful strategy that mirrored Henry Jackson's own.

Nevertheless, Henry Jackson contributed enormously to ensuring that the United States fought and prevailed in this epochal struggle against Soviet totalitarianism. As former senator and White House chief of staff Howard Baker put it: "Jackson made sure we did not lose the Cold War during the 1970s so that Ronald Reagan could win it in the 1980s."[1] In the 1970s, that dismal decade, with pessimism and self-doubt running high in liberal democracies everywhere, Jackson radiated his sober but robust faith in the virtues of the American system and the essential decency of the American people. He exhorted his countrymen to stay the course of vigilantly containing the Soviet Union. His fight against and critique of the policy of détente as Presidents Nixon, Ford, and Carter practiced it laid the intellectual basis for President Reagan's successful policies of the 1980s, a judgment that many prominent Reaganites heartily endorse.[2] Instead of accepting the inevitability of accommodation to the Soviet Union's rising power and America's declining power, Jackson pressed for significant increases in American military spending and firm resistance to Soviet advances in the underdeveloped world. Instead of treating the Soviet Union and the United States as morally equivalent empires, or the

United States as the morally inferior of the two, Jackson strove to infuse American foreign policy with greater moral clarity and confidence about U.S. virtues and our adversaries' vices.

The Russian archives have roundly confirmed the approach of Jackson and Reagan. The Soviet Union was indeed an evil, repressive, expansionist empire driven by an illegitimate leadership's hostile ideology. The Cold War was indeed a moral as well as a geopolitical struggle in which the United States was on the right side of history.[3] As Boris Yeltsin told the U.S. Congress in 1992: "The world can breathe a sigh of relief. The idol of communism, which spread everywhere social strife, animosity and unparalleled brutality, which instilled fear in humanity, has collapsed."[4] The conciliatory policies proferred as an alternative to Jackson's and Reagan's approach prolonged rather than hastened the Soviet Union's demise.[5] The Soviets responded to such conciliatory policies pursued by the Nixon, Ford, and Carter administrations by intensifying their massive military buildup and their brazen interventionism in the underdeveloped world, culminating in the Soviet invasion of Afghanistan.[6] In that period of détente, many leading experts now estimate that the Soviets devoted as much as 70 percent of their industrial output to military or military-related purposes, while U.S. defense spending declined significantly.[7]

Conversely, Jackson's and Reagan's strategy of consciously exploiting Soviet vulnerabilities through relentless across-the-board pressure helped convince reluctant Soviet leaders that the U.S.S.R. could no longer outbuild or bully the United States as it had during the 1970s. On *Messengers from Moscow*, a four-part PBS documentary examining the history of the Soviet threat, senior Soviets—party, military, and KGB—testified that Reagan's rearmament program had a major impact on their policies. It helped confirm their feeling that their system, pushed to the breaking point, could not compete. Alexander Bessmertnykh, former foreign minister of the Soviet Union, and other former high-ranking Soviet officials have cited the Reagan defense buildup in general and his decision to go ahead with SDI in particular as vital factors accelerating the Soviet Union's collapse. In his memoirs, too, former secretary of state George Shultz, initially a skeptic about Reagan's enthusiasm for SDI, came to see Gorbachev's fear of SDI's potential as the driving force behind his willingness to accept deep and unprecedented cuts in the Soviet Union's nuclear arsenal.[8]

The evidence reveals, moreover, that many of Jackson's critics have exaggerated Gorbachev's contributions to ending the Cold War and underestimated those of American hard-liners.[9] The restoration of American power during the 1980s gave the Soviet Union no choice but to take the risk of choosing a reformer such as Gorbachev, who recognized that his country could no longer compete with a rejuvenated and more confident United States unless it liberalized at home and adopted a more conciliatory foreign policy abroad. Nor was Gorbachev a true democrat. He aimed to reform communism but not to abolish it.[10] His domestic reforms occurred as the regime began to implode under the cumulative weight of decades of U.S. containment of Soviet ambitions, Reagan's confrontational policies that intensified this external American pressure at a critical moment, and the inherent contradictions of the Soviet regime.[11] Whereas Gorbachev did not intend the breathtaking collapse of communism that his domestic reforms unwittingly unleashed, Jackson and Reagan strove for and did intend such an outcome. President Reagan even predicted it.[12] In a speech at Notre Dame in May 1981, he pronounced communism "a sad, bizarre chapter in human history whose last pages are even now being written."[13]

Equally, events have refuted the gloomy predictions of the declinists who argued that the United States could not afford the policy of vigilant containment that Henry Jackson championed. The Cold War ended and the post–Cold War era has begun with the United States in ascendance: technologically, politically, economically, and militarily.[14] Levels of U.S. defense spending, which so alarmed declinists, have plummeted from 6.5 percent of U.S. GDP in 1986 to 3.2 percent in 1997 thanks largely to the eradication of the Soviet threat.[15] The benign security environment the United States now enjoys owes much to the sanity of Henry Jackson's vision and his deftness at implementing it.

The wisdom of Jackson's perspective and his policy prescriptions for American foreign policy transcends the era in which he lived and the problems he confronted. His moral realism—a synthesis of power and principle blending geopolitics, a Judeo-Christian view of morality, and a belief in the possibility, though not inevitability or irreversibility, of evolutionary progress toward stable liberal democracy—still offers a more attractive framework for American foreign policy than any of the other three main contenders: the Wilsonian-Carterite multilaterism of the

Clinton administration, which underestimates the importance of power and overestimates the natural harmony of interests among states; the neoisolationism of Pat Buchanan on the right and Jesse Jackson on the left, a policy that was appropriate for the United States during its formative years when it was vulnerable and weak but which is inappropriate for the world's greatest power; and the conservative realism associated with the Nixon-Kissinger wing of the Republican Party, which laments America's legalistic-moralistic tradition in foreign affairs and attaches near exclusive importance to power.[16]

Jackson thus did not succumb to the most serious intellectual defect of conservative realism: that neither regime type nor ideology exerts a significant effect on the external behavior of states.[17] The depth of Jackson's anticommunism and his firm belief in democracy flowed naturally from his insight that the nature of regimes in power, the content of their ideologies, and the outlook of their leaders will profoundly influence their foreign policies. Unlike the realists, he grasped not only what the history of the twentieth century has demonstrated but also the policy prescriptions to derive from it. Whether Germany, Russia, or any other major power maintains a totalitarian, authoritarian, or liberal democratic regime will indeed make a significant difference to U.S. security. It is therefore consistent not only with U.S. ideals, but also with self-interest to promote the spread of stable, liberal democracy and respect for human rights when possible and prudent.

Jackson's emphasis on the enduring importance of power, the flawed nature of human beings, and the anarchical environment in which states operate inoculated him from the fallacies of the liberal democratic idealists and multilateralists. He understood that statesmen's choices in international politics often lie between the lesser of two evils. He believed that the United States could never escape from the imperatives of geopolitics. America would always have a vital interest in ensuring that no hostile power or combination of hostile powers achieved domination of Europe or East Asia, lest that power or combination of powers turn its vast resources against the United States. For Jackson, American power and overseas commitments to vital democratic allies would best ensure tolerable equilibrium in Europe and Asia, lest both these areas lapse into the historic rivalries that resulted in two horrendously bloody world wars. Geopolitics also dictated his conviction that the United States had a vital interest in preventing any aggressor from dominating the Middle East, the world's oil lifeline. Jackson's moral realism rested on a sound appreciation of the domestic requirements of conducting an effective American foreign policy. Neither unalloyed conservative realism nor utopian idealism will suffice to win and sustain requisite domestic support. Americans must believe that U.S. foreign policy is right and legitimate as well as in their interest.

Doubtless, Jackson's most important legacies lie in the areas of foreign policy and national security. Even so, his path-breaking environmental legislation such as NEPA, and the approach that informed it, have also withstood the test of time. Jackson rejected the false dichotomy of promoting economic growth or protecting the environment. He rightly insisted that the nation could balance both of those imperatives in a sensible way without unduly compromising either. Since the late 1960s, the United States has managed to improve significantly the environmental quality and environmental standards while simultaneously maintaining a dynamic, expanding economy.[18] There is no better example of the soundness of Jackson's vision in this area than the remarkable success of his own Washington State in reconciling rapid economic growth with protection of the scenic areas and the environment.

In addition, Jackson's approach to civil rights, civil liberties, and crime issues still has much to commend it. He opposed quotas and distrusted Affirmative Action not because he was a racist, but because he was not. He believed that rights inhered in individuals, not groups. He embraced the original and honorable premise of the civil rights movement that sought equality of opportunity, not equality of result. He opposed, too, the increasing propensity among post-1960 liberal elites to blame crime on societal injustice rather than on individual sin, and to stigmatize the term "law and order" as a cover for racism. He envisaged the vigilant defense of civil liberties and being tough on crime as necessary and complementary components of his political liberalism. With equal vigor, he fought both Joe McCarthy on the right and the radical elements of the antiwar movement on the left for acting as if the ends justified the means. He foresaw that liberal Democrats would continue to have difficulty winning presidential elections until they demonstrated in word and deed that being soft on crime was neither truly liberal nor compassionate.

Jackson's career offers a powerful refutation to the idea of term limits for members of Congress.[19] It took him longer than two terms in the Senate to attain the mastery of foreign policy and defense issues that made him such a decisive force in American politics during the 1970s. Term limits not only would deprive the nation of legislators of his stature and breadth of knowledge, but also would increase legislator's dependence on unelected and unaccountable staff, something that tends to proliferate on Capitol Hill. Jackson attracted and retained excellent people without ever becoming enslaved to them precisely because he always knew more than they did by dint of his diligence and long years of service.

Of course Henry Jackson had his faults. His enthusiasm for promoting closer ties between the United States and the PRC sometimes strayed beyond the sound geopolitical calculation that originally inspired it. His romantic attachment to China inclined him to downplay the human rights concerns that he pressed so staunchly against the Soviet Union and other totalitarian tyrannies. Also, Jackson excessively distrusted private markets. He never deviated from his sanguine belief, forged during his formative years in Everett, in the efficacy of government intervention in the economy and the need for and practicability of a massive welfare state. As historian and commentator Michael Barone has observed trenchantly, the New Deal–Fair Deal fiscal policies that Jackson advocated worked well between 1940 and 1965, a period when most job growth came from the big units of the economy: big government, big business, and big labor. Such policies proved problematic after the late 1960s, however, once small, private units emerged as the biggest generators of U.S. economic growth.[20] Jackson's response to the oil crisis of the 1970s exposed glaringly his fundamental misunderstanding of markets. As chairman of the Energy Committee, he made matters worse by pushing for such counterproductive measures as price controls on oil and natural gas.[21]

Jackson's liabilities do not diminish his evident greatness. Although he was not right about everything, he was right about what the United States needed to do to defeat the unprecedented threat that totalitarianism posed to freedom in the twentieth century. He was politically courageous, willing to take unpopular positions. He was a paragon of rectitude and integrity both in his professional and in his private life. He personified, in short, what the Founding Fathers hoped a senator could be.

Circumstances and the meaning of political categories have changed significantly since Henry M. Jackson first entered the Congress in 1941.

His Cold War liberalism, a compound of a vigilant foreign policy abroad and New Deal–Fair Deal economic policies at home, no longer commands the support of a major segment of the Democratic Party. Many liberals still agree with Jackson on economic issues. Many conservatives still agree with him on foreign policy and defense issues. There are, however, a dwindling number who agree with him on both, now that the heyday of the New Deal coalition and the cleavages in American politics that defined it have irretrievably passed.

The Jackson tradition in foreign policy and defense lives on most robustly in the Republican Party, where most of the prominent neoconservatives who originally identified themselves as Jackson Democrats during the 1970s found a home with Reagan during the 1980s. Though facing a serious challenge from conservative realists, libertarians, and isolationists, the foreign policy and national security views of this group remain widely popular and influential within the Republican Party. The Jackson tradition is alive, but hardly well, within the ranks of his own party. Although his New Deal–Fair Deal economic policies and his approach to environmental issues still appeal to a sizable constituency of Democrats, the mainstream of the party drifted even further to the left on foreign policy and defense issues during the 1980s. Without Jackson, neoconservatives no longer had an effective voice in the Democratic Party to make their case. Daniel Patrick Moynihan bitterly disappointed Norman Podhoretz, Midge Decter, Charles Horner, Elliott Abrams, and other neoconservatives who designated him as Jackson's natural heir.[22] By 1984, Moynihan's hard-line views on the Soviet Union and the danger of third world radicalism had softened considerably as he concluded that the Soviet threat had passed. He thus became a forceful and consistent opponent of the Reagan administration's defense program and Central America policy, which he had originally supported.[23] "The Soviet system was already finished by the early 1980s," commented Moynihan. "We did not have to go charging around Nicaragua or end up in debt."[24] Podhoretz, Decter, Horner, and Abrams probably give Moynihan too little credit by speculating that political calculation as well as conviction spurred his shift away from the Jackson tradition. According to this group, Moynihan shrewdly assessed the liberal trajectory of the Democratic Party and the political imperatives of surviving in a liberal state such as New York.[25] Whatever his motivation, his defection dealt a devastating blow to what remained of the Jackson tradition in his party. Conservative commentator Fred Barnes hit close to the mark by pronouncing the Jackson wing of the Democratic Party dead without Moynihan.[26]

During the 1980s, Sam Nunn of Georgia thus emerged as the most prominent, though not unequivocal, defender of the Jackson tradition among the Democrats. Nunn had a somewhat less stern view of the Soviet threat and America's defense requirements than either Henry Jackson or Ronald Reagan did. He opposed, for example, SDI and a broad interpretation of the ABM Treaty of 1972 that would have permitted its development. He also was significantly less liberal on economic issues than Jackson ever was. Like Jackson, however, Nunn also worked hard to move the Democratic Party back to the sensible center. He, Governor Charles Robb of Virginia, and other embattled moderates founded the Democratic Leadership Council (DLC) after the 1984 election for the same purpose that Jackson had co-founded CDM in 1972, albeit with a somewhat different focus and approach. The DLC adopted a less confrontationist posture toward the liberal wing of the party. It also concentrated mainly on domestic rather than foreign policy issues.[27] For all that, the DLC had as little effect on the trajectory of the Democratic Party during the 1980s as CDM did during the 1970s. Instead, liberal Democrats in Congress overwhelmingly supported the nuclear freeze, condemned Reagan's military buildup, derided the president's strategic defense program, assailed his confrontationist policies toward the Soviet Union, and opposed his policy in Central America.[28] Though to no avail, virtually all the major Democratic presidential candidates in 1984 and 1988 ran on this liberal critique of the Reagan foreign policy and defense program, a program that Henry Jackson had both inspired and supported.[29]

In 1992, hopes soared momentarily among some former Henry Jackson Democrats dissatisfied with President Bush's conservative realism in foreign policy, when the party nominated Governor Bill Clinton of Arkansas as its presidential candidate. Clinton had served as chairman of the DLC at the behest of Sam Nunn, who endorsed him early in his campaign. He ran in the primaries and in the general election against Bush as a New Democrat: tough on crime, promising an end to "welfare as we know it," defending free trade, and willing to take on Jesse Jackson. He chose as his running mate Senator Al Gore, Democrat from Tennessee, one of five Democratic senators who had voted for the Senate resolution to authorize President Bush's January 1991 decision to launch Desert Storm against Iraq.[30]

Through Representative Dave McCurdy, Democrat from Oklahoma, a backer of Contra aid during the 1980s, Clinton also actively courted neoconservatives who had defected to Reagan. Though most prominent neoconservatives, such as Jeane Kirkpatrick, Richard Perle, and Elliott Abrams remained loyal to the Republican Party in 1992, thirty-three moderate and neoconservative foreign policy experts endorsed Clinton in a half-page advertisement that appeared on August 17, 1992, in both the *New York Times* and the *Washington Post*.[31] The advertisement suggested that Clinton was more committed to spreading democracy and opposing communist governments than Bush. It hailed him for standing "by authentic democrats in the society of the former Soviet Union" and openly "stating his opposition to the brutal and archaic communist dictatorship in Beijing." Important signers of the advertisement included Paul Nitze; retired General William Odom; Richard Schifter, former assistant secretary for human rights under Reagan and Bush; Penn Kemble, a former adviser to Jeane Kirkpatrick and an ardent supporter of the Nicaraguan Contras; and Joshua Muravchik, formerly deputy to Kirkpatrick at the United Nations and currently a fellow at the conservative American Enterprise Institute in Washington, D.C. "Bill Clinton is reaching out to recapture the Harry Truman tradition," Muravchik said in August 1992; and a correspondent wrote: "For those Democrats who . . . trace their lineage to Henry M. Scoop Jackson of Washington State, Clinton represents the opportunity of a generation—a Democrat not afraid of engagement in the world."[32] Clinton also enlisted Muravchik and Kemble to help draft the major foreign policy address of his presidential campaign, which he delivered in Milwaukee on October 1, 1992.[33]

Muravchik, Odom, and several other signers of the August 17 statement endorsing Clinton soon repudiated it. President Clinton, they charged, reverted almost immediately and totally to the left liberalism that has dominated the foreign and defense policies of the Democratic Party since McGovern. "President Clinton's set of appointees in national security affairs held a deep aversion to the Brzezinski-Jackson tradition during the Carter years," said General Odom. "The President had taken a frontal lobotomy in foreign policy by appointing the Christophers, the

Tony Lakes, and the Strobe Talbotts and excluding people from the Jackson tradition and the Brzezinskis."[34]

There are still some irrepressible optimists, such as Ben Wattenberg and Robert Strauss, who have not written off the Jackson tradition in their own party.[35] This group also includes Senator Joseph Lieberman, Democrat from Connecticut, current chairman of the DLC. Thoughtful, informed, principled, and respected on both sides of the aisle, Lieberman may someday emerge as Jackson's true heir in the U.S. Senate. His political perspective largely mirrors that of Henry Jackson: a liberal on domestic issues; an opponent of Affirmative Action; a staunch advocate of vigilant internationalism and a strong military. Senator Lieberman confessed, however, that it will be an uphill battle "to reinvigorate the international aspects of the Jackson legacy in the Democratic Party."[36]

Henry Jackson personified a conception of America's role in the world that is at once realistic, humanitarian, moral, and tough. The integrity and decency that suffused his public and private life also offer other lessons well worth pondering as Americans debate the importance of character in politics. For the best of our political leaders, goodness and greatness are not mutually exclusive but synonymous. Henry Jackson possessed both of those virtues in abundance.

Notes

Prologue

1. An apt analogy can be drawn comparing Jackson with John Calhoun, Henry Clay, Daniel Webster, Robert La Follette, and Robert Taft—all dominant and controversial senators who were at once revered and reviled, never attained the presidency, but nonetheless had a decisive impact on history. See, for example, Irving H. Bartlett, *John C. Calhoun: A Biography* (New York: Norton, 1993); Robert Remini, *Henry Clay: A Statesman for the Union* (New York: Norton, 1991); idem, *Daniel Webster: The Man and His Time* (New York: Norton, 1997); Edward Newell Doan, *The La Follettes and the Wisconsin Idea* (New York: Rinehart, 1947); and James T. Patterson, *Mister Republican: A Biography of Robert A. Taft* (Boston: Houghton Mifflin, 1972).

2. See, for example, Jay Winik, *On the Brink: The Dramatic, Behind-the-Scenes Saga of the Reagan Era and the Men and Women Who Won the Cold War* (New York: Simon and Schuster, 1996). Although Winik is right about the influence of Jackson Democrats on Reagan, many of them have complained—in public and to me—that Winik often gets key details wrong. Among other things, he slights the monumental influence of CIA Director William Casey—also a great admirer of Henry Jackson—on Reagan and his foreign policy. The Winik book is thus important, but insufficient.

3. *Washington Post Book World*, Aug. 13, 1995, p. 1.

4. Literature on foreign policy tends to treat ideals and self-interest as mutually exclusive. On one side are the realists—classical and structural. Both types depreciate the importance of morality and democracy as means or ends of foreign policy, and concentrate on finite and fixed conceptions of the national interest. Whereas classical realists stress the deterring factor of flawed human nature, structural realists reach their conclusions about the limited importance or desirability of morality and democracy in foreign affairs from the premise that the systemic nature of world politics makes all states behave essentially alike, regardless of the type of regime or the character of its leaders. For American variants of realism, see George F. Kennan, *American Diplomacy, 1900–1950* (Chicago: University of Chicago Press, 1951), and Hans Morgenthau, *Politics among Nations: The Struggle for Power and Peace*, 6th ed., revised by Kenneth W. Thompson (New York: Knopf, 1985). For an excellent critical analysis of the realist tradition, see Michael Joseph Smith, *Realist Thought from Weber to Kissinger* (Baton Rouge:

Louisiana State University Press, 1986). For an excellent recent statement of classical realism that nevertheless fails to understand the successful synthesis of realism and idealism that Truman, Jackson, and Reagan all struck, see Walter A. McDougall, *Promised Land, Crusader State: The American Encounter with the World Since 1776* (Boston: Houghton Mifflin, 1997). For an excellent summary of the main tenants of neorealism, see Robert O. Keohane ed., *Neorealism and Its Critics* (New York: Columbia University Press, 1986).

Conversely, those who are idealists in foreign affairs have often depreciated the importance of power and stressed the basic harmony of interests among peoples and nations. For some examples of this school of thought, see Immanuel Kant, "Perpetual Peace" (1795) in Carl J. Friedrich, ed., *The Philosophy of Kant* (New York: Modern Library, 1949). On Thomas Jefferson's idealist pedigree, see Robert W. Tucker and David C. Hendrickson, *Empire of Liberty: The Statecraft of Thomas Jefferson* (New York: Oxford University Press, 1990); and Stanley Kober, "Idealpolitik," *Foreign Policy*, Summer 1990, pp. 3–24. Henry Jackson's emphasis on the importance of power and original sin as a limiting condition in international politics distinguished him from idealists. His outlook thus resembled that of Reinhold Niebuhr and Winston Churchill, who both argued for the imperative of blending ideals with self-interest in the conduct of foreign

policy. For an excellent statement of the type of synthesis Jackson personified, see Robert E. Osgood, *Ideals and Self-Interest in America's Foreign Relations: The Great Transformation of the Twentieth Century* (Chicago: University of Chicago Press, 1953). For a good introduction to Niebuhr's outlook, which many have mistaken for classical realism, see Reinhold Niebuhr, *The Nature and Destiny of Man*, 2 vols. (New York: Scribner's, 1943); Richard Wightman Fox, *Reinhold Niebuhr: A Biography* (New York: Pantheon, 1985); and George Weigel, "The Sensibility of Reinhold Niebuhr," *The National Interest*, Fall 1986, pp. 80–89. On Churchill's philosophy of statecraft, see Robert G. Kaufman, "E. H. Carr, Winston Churchill, Reinhold Niebuhr and Us: The Case for Principled Democratic Realism," *Security Studies* 5, no. 2 (Winter 1995): 314–53.

5. Quoted in Dorothy Fosdick, ed., *Henry M. Jackson and World Affairs: Selected Speeches, 1953–1983* (Seattle: University of Washington Press, 1990), p. 7. Dorothy Fosdick confirmed the soundness of my preliminary hypothesis that Niebuhr's outlook influenced Jackson deeply (interview with Dorothy Fosdick, May 23, 1991).

6. Charles Horner, "Human Rights and the Jackson Amendment," in Dorothy Fosdick, ed., *Staying the Course: Henry M. Jackson and National Security* (Seattle: University of Washington Press, 1987), pp. 100–128; Joshua Muravchik, *The Uncertain*

Crusade: Jimmy Carter and the Dilemmas of Human Rights Policy (Washington, D.C.: American Enterprise Institute, 1988), pp. 1–4; Kaufman interviews with Ben Wattenberg and Michael Novak, June 23, 1992.

7. William W. Prochnau and Richard W. Larsen, *A Certain Democrat: Senator Henry M. Jackson: A Political Biography* (Englewood Cliffs: Prentice-Hall, 1972), pp. 126–49; the only biography of Senator Jackson in print, this book is a solid and valuable journalistic account that stops at 1971, before Jackson's presidential runs and his political apotheosis as an opponent of détente.

8. There are, of course, some irrepressible optimists; Kaufman interview with Ben Wattenberg, March 14, 1995. (Though Mr. Wattenberg conceded disappointment, he had not given up on the possibility that Clinton might embrace the Jackson tradition.)

9. Prochnau and Larsen, *A Certain Democrat*, pp. 179–201; Kaufman interviews with Richard M. Nixon, Oct. 2, 1992, and Gerald Ford, Oct. 26, 1994.

10. Ben J. Wattenberg, *The First Universal Nation* (New York: Free Press, 1991), pp. 28–30.

11. Two excellent books make a complementary, although not identical, argument: Ben J. Wattenberg, *Values Matter Most: How Republicans or Democrats or a Third Party Can Win and Renew the American Way of Life* (New York: Free Press, 1995); Ronald Radosh, *Divided They Fell: The Demise of the Democratic Party, 1964–1996*

(New York: Free Press, 1996). Although I mostly agree with Radosh's thesis, I argue that he is wrong on some key particulars. Jackson's campaign of 1972 was not, as Radosh claimed, the last real chance to move the party back to the center. His 1976 campaign was a far more plausible and promising attempt.

12. For Henry Kissinger's assessment of Jackson and his importance, see particularly his *Years of Renewal* (New York: Simon and Schuster, 1999), pp. 92–135, 250–60; *Years of Upheaval* (Boston: Little, Brown, 1982), pp. 986–95; and *Diplomacy* (New York: Simon and Schuster, 1994), pp. 746–57. For Fulbright's comments, see J. William Fulbright with Seth P. Tillman, *The Price of Empire* (New York: Pantheon Books, 1989), pp. 31–34. For Bundy's views, see William Bundy, *A Tangled Web: The Making of Foreign Policy in the Nixon Presidency* (New York: Hill and Wang, 1998), p. 342.

13. For a definitive account reflecting this viewpoint, see Raymond L. Garthoff's *Detente and Confrontation: Soviet-American Relations from Nixon to Reagan* (Washington, D.C.: Brookings Institution, 1985, and his *The Great Transition: American-Soviet Relations and the End of the Cold War* (Washington, D.C.: Brookings, 1994). For a recent popular account reflecting this perspective, see CNN's *Cold War*, a 1998 television documentary, and Jeremy Isaacs and Taylor Downing, *Cold War: An Illustrated History, 1945–1991: Companion to the*

CNN TV Series (Boston: Little, Brown, 1998). For a trenchant critique of this series along the lines of the thesis of my book, see Gabriel Schoenfeld, "Twenty-Four Lies About the Cold War," *Commentary*, March 1999, pp. 28–35; and Charles Krauthammer, "Revolutionary Dreams," *Washington Post*, Jan. 1, 1999, p. A25. For an extended discussion of this series, pro and con, see "Left, Then Right, Through a Minefield: 'Cold War' on TV," *New York Times*, Jan. 9, 1999, pp. A17, A19. For a much better television series on the Cold War, which in my judgment gets it right by including extensive interviews of former Soviet officials, see PBS's documentary *Messengers from Moscow*, Parts 1–4, 1994, produced by Daniel Wolfe and Herbert J. Ellison.

14. Strobe Talbott, "Rethinking the Red Menace," *Time*, Jan. 1, 1990, p. 66.

15. For the most popular and cogently argued variant of this viewpoint, see Paul Kennedy, *The Rise and Fall of the Great Powers: Economic Change and Military Conflict from 1500 to 2000* (New York: Random House, 1987).

16. *Washington Post*, Jan. 2, 1998, p. A23.

17. *Washington Post Book World*, Aug. 13, 1995, p. 1.

18. Moynihan quoted in Memorial Addresses Delivered in Congress, *Henry M. Jackson: Late a Senator from Washington* (Washington, D.C.: Government Printing Office, 1983), p. 138; Will quoted, ibid., p. 227; Kauf-

man interview with Jeane Kirkpatrick, Dec. 28, 1996.

19. Quoted in Fosdick, ed., *Henry M. Jackson and World Affairs*, p. xi.

20. See John Lewis Gaddis, "The Tragedy of Cold War History," *Foreign Affairs*, Jan./Feb. 1994, pp. 142–54; Richard Pipes, "Misinterpreting the Cold War," *Foreign Affairs*, Jan./Feb. 1995, pp. 154–60; Douglas J. Macdonald, "Communist Bloc Expansion in the Early Cold War: Challenging Realism, Refuting Revisionism," *International Security*, Winter 1995–96, pp. 152–88. For a rebuttal, which I find unpersuasive, see Melvyn P. Leffler, "Inside Enemy Archives," *Foreign Affairs*, July/Aug. 1996, pp. 120–35.

1 The Everett Years

1. Kaufman interview with Peter Jackson (Henry Jackson's son), Jan. 13, 1996. (For a note on the interviewers referred to in this book, please see the beginning of the Bibliography.)

2. *Seattle Times*, Oct. 19, 1966, p. 4.

3. William W. Prochnau and Richard W. Larsen, *A Certain Democrat: Senator Henry M. Jackson: A Political Biography* (Englewood Cliffs: Prentice-Hall, 1972), pp. 82–83.

4. Robert E. Ficken and Charles P. LeWarne, *Washington: A Centennial History* (Seattle: University of Washington Press, 1988), p. 85; Kaufman interview with Bob Humphrey, Oct. 2, 1994.

5. For the definitive account of

Everett during this period, including the Everett Massacre, see Norman H. Clark, *Mill Town: A Social History of Everett, Washington, from Its Earliest Beginnings on the Shores of Puget Sound to the Tragic and Infamous Event Known as the Everett Massacre* (Seattle: University of Washington Press, 1970).

6. Interview with Bob Humphrey; Gaskin interview with Lloyd Solie.

7. *Seattle Post-Intelligencer,* March 16, 1975, p. 1; *Seattle Times,* March 15, 1977, p. A14.

8. Peter J. Ognibene, *Scoop: The Life and Politics of Henry M. Jackson* (New York: Stein and Day, 1975), pp. 34–35.

9. See, for example, Henry Jackson to Arthur Jackson, Jan. 15 and March 21, 1941; also Dr. R. K. Ghormley to Henry Jackson, April 7, 1942. These documents are in the Henry M. Jackson Papers, University Archives Division of the University of Washington Libraries, Seattle, Accession 3560–2, box 4, folders 9–12 (hereafter cited as HMJ 3560–2/4/9–12).

10. Kaufman interviews with Dr. Haakon Ragde, April 18, 1995, and Peter Jackson (note 1 above).

11. Gaskin interview with Osa Nurmi.

12. Gaskin interviews with Doris Closser and Margaret Deucy (Weberg); Kaufman interview with Helen Jackson, June 10, 1995.

13. Interview with Bob Humphrey.

14. Schmechel interview with Stan Golub, Dec. 26, 1986.

15. Quoted in *The Times of Israel and the World Jewish Review,* Aug. 1974, p. 22.

16. Gaskin interviews with Doris Closser, Lloyd Solie, and Alice Helema.

17. Kaufman interviews with Brian Corcoran, Sept. 6, 1994, and Helen Jackson (note 12 above); Schmechel interview with Golub.

18. Interview with Helen Jackson.

19. *One of Ours: Young Scoop Jackson: An Oral History of Senator Henry M. Jackson and Everett, Washington, from 1892 to 1940* (1989 video documentary produced by Thomas M. Gaskin, hereafter cited as *One of Ours*), Helen Sievers.

20. Anna Marie Jackson interview with Henry M. Jackson, May 1980.

21. Ibid. and Kaufman interview with Bob Low, Nov. 3, 1995 (reminiscing).

22. *One of Ours,* Ellen Repp, Fred Moore.

23. Jackson's report cards, which Helen Jackson kindly shared with this author at her home in Everett, reveal him to be a solid B or B-plus student, except in history, a subject for which he received straight As through college.

24. Gaskin interview with Dr. Edwin Chase.

25. Schmechel interviews with Leslie Cooper, Nov. 30, 1986, and March 13, 1987; Gaskin interview with Fred Moore.

26. Interview with Bob Humphrey.

27. Anna Marie Jackson interview with Jackson.

28. *One of Ours,* Lloyd Shorett; also Schmechel interview with Shorett, Dec. 4, 1987.

29. Kaufman interview with Doug Glant, Jan. 19, 1998.

30. Anna Marie Jackson interview with Jackson.

31. Schmechel interview with John Salter, Nov. 29, 1986.

32. Anna Marie Jackson interview with Jackson.

33. Interview with Golub.

34. Interview with Helen Jackson.

35. Anna Marie Jackson interview with Jackson.

36. Ibid.

37. Kaufman interview with Gerald Hoeck, April 2, 1995.

38. Ficken and LeWarne, *Washington: A Centennial*, pp. 113–14.

39. Interviews with Salter and Corcoran.

40. *One of Ours*, Solie and Moore.

41. Interviews with Bob Humphrey (bootlegging) and Cooper; *One of Ours* (corruption, tolerance policy).

42. Gaskin interviews with Stan Mitchell, Bob Humphrey, Verne Sievers, Osa Nurmi, Fred Moore, and Harold Griep.

43. Interview with Nurmi.

44. Kaufman interviews with Corcoran and Humphrey; Gaskin interviews with Moore, Nurmi, Verne Sievers, and Deucy (Weberg).

45. *One of Ours*.

46. *Everett Herald*, Sept. 14, 1938, p. 4.

47. Gaskin interview with Tom Stiger.

48. *One of Ours*. See also the more extended Gaskin interviews with Helen and Verne Sievers, Fred Moore,

Stan Mitchell, and the Schmechel interview with Leslie Cooper, March 13, 1987.

49. Henry M. Jackson to Shirley Bartholomew, April 10, 1946, HMJ 3560–2/46/5.

50. Gaskin interview with Phil Sheridan; Schmechel interview with Cooper, March 13, 1987.

51. *Everett Herald*, June 10, 1939, pp. 1, 10; *One of Ours*.

52. See, for example, Henry Jackson to Naomi Benson, Oct. 19, 1939, Ralph Corcoran to Clarence D. Martin, Oct. 12, 1939, and A. G. Edwards to Clarence D. Martin, Aug. 10, 1939, all in HMJ 356–1/1/1.

53. Interview with Verne Sievers.

54. *Everett Herald*, March 6, 1940, p. 8; March 27, p. 1.

55. Interview with Stiger.

56. *Everett Herald*, March 28, 1940, p. 1; March 29, p. 1; and March 30, p. 1; interview with Moore.

57. *Everett Herald*, March 26, 1940, p. 1; March 28, p. 1; and March 30, p. 1.

58. *Everett Herald*, June 25, 1940, p. 1; June 29, p. 1; July 1, p. 1; and Sept. 6, p. 1.

59. *Everett Herald*, July 10, 1940, p. 5; Aug. 9, pp. 1–2.

60. Gaskin interviews with Verne Sievers and Phil Sheridan.

61. *Everett Herald*, Aug. 16, 1940, p. 2.

62. *Everett Herald*, Oct. 1, 1940, p. 5; Oct. 28, p. 10; Oct. 31, p. 10; and Nov. 7, p. 6.

2 *Member of the House*

1. Kaufman interview with Gerald Hoeck, April 2, 1995; also recounted in Dorothy Fosdick, ed., *Staying the Course* (Seattle: University of Washington Press, 1987), p. 3.

2. HMJ 3560–2/43/13.

3. Kaufman interviews with Richard Larsen, April 20, 1995, and Bill Van Ness, May 20, 1995.

4. HMJ 3560–2/44/3; John Gunther, *Inside U.S.A.* (New York: Harper and Brothers, 1947), pp. 129–33.

5. HMJ 3560–2/30/3–9; Kaufman interview with Charles Luce, Sept. 18, 1996.

6. Sir Winston Churchill, *The Gathering Storm* (Boston: Houghton Mifflin, 1948).

7. Kaufman interviews with Hoeck, April 2, 1995; Van Ness, May 10, 1995; and Robert Low, Nov. 2, 1995.

8. Prochnau and Larsen, *A Certain Democrat*, p. 102 (lend-lease); Richard Overy, *Why the Allies Won* (New York: Norton, 1995), p. 15; Leslie M. Cooper to Jackson, Jan. 23, 1941, HMJ 3560–2/2/18; Jackson to Harry Wackter, June 9, 1941, HMJ 3560–2/56/26.

9. *Congressional Record*, 77th Cong., 1st sess., Dec. 9, 1941, vol. 77, pp. 9564–9965.

10. Jackson to Edward Allen, March 16, 1942, HMJ 3560–2/1/7.

11. Robert E. Ficken and Charles P. LeWarne, *Washington: A Centennial History* (Seattle: University of Washington Press, 1988), pp. 134–36.

12. Kaufman interviews with Richard Perle, Oct. 3, 1994; Hoeck, April 2, 1995; and George Weigel, Aug. 10, 1995.

13. Kaufman interview with Daniel Inouye, March 13, 1995.

14. *Congressional Record*, 78th Cong., 1st sess., Feb. 23, 1943, vol. 89, pp. 1239–40.

15. HMJ 3560–2156/31.

16. E. Harriet Gipson to Jackson, May 7, 1943, HMJ 3560–2/33/1a.

17. *Congressional Record*, 77th Cong., 2d sess., March 6, 1942, vol. 88, pp. A870–871; April 9, p. 3434.

18. *Seattle Times*, Dec. 7, 1966, p. 1; Kaufman interviews with Perle, Oct. 3, 1994, and Donald Donahue, Dec. 23, 1996; Sam Rayburn to Jackson, March 29, 1942, HMJ 3560–2/7–8.

19. Kaufman interview with Bob Humphrey, Oct. 2, 1994; Gaskin interview with Fred Moore.

20. Quoted in the *Saturday Evening Post*, July/Aug. 1974, p. 2.

21. Ibid.

22. Jackson to Elizabeth C. Kerr, April 3, 1944, HMJ 3560–2/54/26.

23. HMJ 3560–26 (tape 1), April 22, 1945.

24. Kaufman interviews with Perle, Oct. 3, 1994, and Low, Nov. 2, 1995; Schmechel interview with Stanley Golub, Dec. 26, 1986.

25. Kaufman interview with Haakon Ragde, April 18, 1995; L. June Evans to Phil Sheridan, Dec. 11, 1945, HMJ 3560–2/6/39; Henry Jackson to Peter and Marine Jackson, Feb. 2, 1946, HMJ 3560–2/4/14.

26. *Seattle Times*, Dec. 4, 1966, p. 44.

27. Ficken and LeWarne, *Washington*, pp. 130–32.

28. Michele Stenehjem Gerber, *On the Home Front: The Cold War Legacy of the Hanford Nuclear Site* (Lincoln: University of Nebraska Press, 1992), pp. 22–36.

29. Anthony Champagne, *Congressman Sam Rayburn* (New Brunswick: Rutgers University Press, 1984), pp. 151–55, 164; Kaufman interviews with Sam Nunn, March 14, 1995, and Bob Low, Nov. 2, 1995; Schmechel interview with John Stennis, March 7, 1987.

30. Schmechel interview with Sterling Munro, March 10, 1987.

31. Prochnau and Larsen, *A Certain Democrat*, pp. 105–6.

32. Michael Barone, *Our Country: The Shaping of America from Roosevelt to Reagan* (New York: Free Press, 1990), pp. 187–88 (strikes); *Seattle Times*, Nov. 4, 1946, p. 9.

33. Kaufman interviews with Low, Nov. 2, 1995 (thanking voters), and Joe Miller, June 18, 1996.

34. Kaufman interview with Julia Cancio, June 18, 1996.

35. For an excellent recent account that best conveys the incremental nature of the shift in American attitudes and policy toward the Soviet Union during the initial phase of the Cold War, see Wilson D. Miscamble, *George F. Kennan and the Making of American Foreign Policy, 1947–1950* (Princeton: Princeton University Press, 1992). On Stalin, see William Taubman, *Stalin's America Policy: From*

Entente to Detente to Cold War (New York: Norton, 1982), pp. 166–92.

36. John Lewis Gaddis, *Strategies of Containment* (New York: Oxford University Press, 1982), pp. 25–88; Melvyn P. Leffler, *A Preponderance of Power: National Security, the Truman Administration, and the Cold War* (Stanford: Stanford University Press, 1992), pp. 141–219.

37. Alonzo L. Hamby, *Man of the People: A Life of Harry S. Truman* (New York: Oxford University Press, 1995), pp. 397–403.

38. Graham White and John Maze, *Henry A. Wallace: His Search for a New World Order* (Chapel Hill: University of North Carolina Press, 1995), pp. 216–82; Herbert S. Parmet, *The Democrats: The Years After FDR* (New York: Macmillan, 1976), pp. 72–78.

39. Barone, *Our Country*, p. 209.

40. Parmet, *The Democrats*, pp. 80–83.

41. Hamby, *Man of the People*, pp. 452–66.

42. James Chace, *Acheson: The Secretary of State Who Created the American World* (New York: Simon and Schuster, 1998), pp. 274–79.

43. HMJ 3560–2/47/4.

44. Hamby, *Man of the People*, 404–16; Robert D. Kaplan, *The Arabists: The Romance of an American Elite* (New York: Free Press, 1993), pp. 85–87.

45. Anna Marie Jackson interview of Henry M. Jackson, May 1980. For the best critical account of President Roosevelt's softer views toward the Soviet Union, see Frederick W. Marks, *Wind Over Sands: The Diplo-*

macy of Franklin Roosevelt (Athens: University of Georgia Press, 1988). For the best defense of Roosevelt that still leaves this author unconvinced, see Gaddis, *Strategies*, pp. 3–24.

46. HMJ 3560–2/61/12–18.

47. *Congressional Record*, 81st Cong., 2d sess., April 19, 1949, vol. 95, p. 5465.

48. Jackson, "Jackson Day Address," State of Washington, 1946, HMJ 3560–2/67/4.

49. Jackson, "Speech on Behalf of Norwegian Independence Day," State of Washington, May 10, 1948, HMJ 3560–3/234/1.

50. Parmet, *The Democrats*, p. 79 (Wallace); *Seattle Times*, Nov. 2, 1948, p. 9 (election).

51. Kaufman interview with Gordon Culp, March 3, 1995.

52. Schmechel interviews with Sterling Munro, Dec. 30, 1986, and Jan. 19, 1987; interview with Low, Nov. 2, 1995.

53. Interview with Hoeck, April 2, 1995.

54. Kaufman interview with Joe Miller, June 18, 1996 (saloon, eleven o'clock news); *Everett Herald*, Jan. 19, 1947, p. 4 (not married).

55. *Seattle Times*, Sept. 3, 1983, p. A6 (prunes); Kaufman interview with Donahue, Dec. 23, 1996; Schmechel interview with Joel and John Merkel, April 13, 1987.

3 *The Cold War Becomes Colder*

1. *Congressional Record*, 81st Cong., 1st sess., Jan. 27, 1949, vol. 95, p. 472.

2. Richard Rhodes, *Dark Sun: The Making of the Hydrogen Bomb* (New York: Simon and Schuster, 1995), p. 363.

3. Jackson, "What Should the United States Do about the Atomic Bomb," *America's Town Meeting of the Air*, broadcast Oct. 15, 1949; *Congressional Record*, 81st Cong., 2d sess., Feb. 1, 1950, vol. 96, pp. 1315–16.

4. *Congressional Record*, 82d Cong., 1st sess., Oct. 9, 1951, vol. 97, p. 12867.

5. Lawrence quoted in "Biographical Data on Senator Henry M. Jackson of Washington," HMJ 3560–2/65/34; Truman quoted in Rhodes, *Dark Sun*, p. 363.

6. For the definitive account, see David Holloway, *Stalin and the Bomb* (New Haven: Yale University Press, 1994).

7. Kaufman interview with Richard Perle, Jan. 2, 1996.

8. Kaufman interviews with Kenneth Mansfield, May 31, 1995 (national security), and Perle, Jan. 2, 1996 (Rickover and Teller); Jackson, "Atomic Energy," Institute of Industrial and Legal Problems of Atomic Energy, Michigan University Law School, Ann Arbor, 1952, HMJ 3560–2/67/1 (generalists).

9. NSC 68: United States Objectives and Programs for National Security (April 14, 1950) (hereafter cited as NSC 68), in Ernest R. May, ed., *American Cold War Strategy: Interpreting NSC 68* (Boston: St. Martin's Press, 1993), pp. 25–31. For Jackson's views, see *Congressional Record*, 81st

Cong., 2d sess., Feb. 1, 1950, vol. 95, pp. 1315–16; ibid., 82d Cong., 1st sess., vol. 97, pp. 13129–30.

10. Paul H. Nitze, *From Hiroshima to Glasnost: At the Center of Decision: A Memoir* (New York: Grove Weidenfeld, 1989), pp. 93–100; Alonzo L. Hamby, *Man of the People: A Life of Harry S. Truman* (New York: Oxford University Press, 1995), pp. 508–14, 527–29.

11. John Lewis Gaddis, *Strategies of Containment* (New York: Oxford University Press, 1982), pp. 94–98.

12. Walter L. Hixon, *George F. Kennan, Cold War Iconoclast* (New York: Columbia University Press, 1989), pp. 73–80, 139–41.

13. Gaddis, *Strategies*, pp. 25–127. For another sympathetic portrayal of Kennan's conception of containment versus Truman's, see Melvyn P. Leffler, *A Preponderance of Power* (Stanford: Sanford University Press, 1992), pp. 312–60.

14. Hamby, *Man of the People*, pp. 534–37; Leffler, *Preponderance*, pp. 361–69.

15. Gaddis, *Strategies*, p. 10; Dean Acheson, *Present at the Creation: My Years in the State Department* (New York: Norton, 1969), pp. 354–57.

16. James T. Patterson, *Mr. Republican* (Boston: Houghton Mifflin, 1972), pp. 438–39.

17. For the best concise account of U.S. policy toward China during the final stages of the Chinese civil war, see Douglas J. Macdonald, *Adventures in Chaos: American Intervention for Reform in the Third World* (Cambridge: Harvard University Press, 1992), pp. 77–102.

18. James Chace, *Acheson* (New York: Simon and Schuster, 1998), pp. 217–24; Acheson, *Present at the Creation*, pp. 302–3, 306–7, 344–45.

19. Jackson to Mrs. Evelyn Jackson, Oct. 10, 1946, HMJ 3560–2/56/6 ("wholly in opposition"); to Mrs. Evelyn Twelker, July 5, 1951, HMJ 3560–2/56/22 (South Korea); to Alice Franklin Bryant, Dec. 14, 1950, HMJ 3560–2/32/31 (scale back objectives).

20. Jackson to Mr. Gordon Speck, Dec. 12, 1950, HMJ 3560–2/32/31.

21. *Congressional Record*, 82d Cong., 1st sess., Oct. 9, 1951, vol. 97, p. 12867.

22. Jackson speech, Oct. 1948, HMJ 3560–2/47/25.

23. *Congressional Record*, 82d Cong., 2d sess., June 5, 1952, vol. 98, p. 6783.

24. Ibid., 82d Cong., 1st sess., Sept. 18, 1951, vol. 97, p. 11805; Holloway, *Stalin and the Bomb*, pp. 294–319; *Congressional Record*, 82d Cong., 2d sess., June 5, 1952, vol. 98, pp. 6781–82.

25. There are several schools of thought on Truman's version of containment and the assumptions underlying it. Revisionist scholars assumed that the Soviet Union was a defensive entity, driven to aggression by historic insecurity and Western provocation that a more conciliatory U.S. policy could alleviate. See, for example, William Appelman Williams, *The Tragedy of American Diplomacy*, 2d ed. (New York: Dell, 1972); Walter La-

Feber, *America, Russia, and the Cold War, 1945–1992*, 7th ed. (New York: McGraw-Hill, 1993); Gar Alperovitz, *The Decision to Use the Atomic Bomb and the Architecture of an American Myth* (New York: Knopf, 1995). The writings of Daniel Yergin, Raymond Garthoff, Strobe Talbott, Richard Ned Lebow, and Janice Gross Stein are more nuanced, but sympathetic to this point of view. See, for example, Yergin, *A Shattered Peace: The Origins of the Cold War and the National Security State* (Boston: Houghton Mifflin, 1977): Garthoff, *The Great Transition* (Washington, D.C.: Brookings Institution, 1994); Strobe Talbott, "Rethinking the Red Menace," *Time*, Jan. 1, 1990, p. 66, and Lebow and Stein, *We All Lost the Cold War* (Princeton: Princeton University Press, 1994). Another group of scholars attributes the length and severity of the Cold War to the overreactions of both sides. See Gaddis, *Strategies*, and Leffler, *Preponderance*. Although both deny it, Gaddis makes a persuasive case that Henry Kissinger and Richard Nixon, statesmen steeped in the realist tradition, envisaged the Soviet Union as a traditional empire, with ideology the pretext not the source of its expansionist but limited aims. See also Henry Kissinger, *White House Years* (Boston: Little, Brown, 1979), pp. 3–150, *Years of Upheaval*, and *Diplomacy*, pp. 733–61.

26. This assumption underlies traditionalist and neotraditionalist interpretations of the Cold War. See, for example, Herbert Feis, *From Trust to Terror: The Onset of the Cold War, 1945–1950* (New York: Norton, 1970); Adam B. Ulam, *Expansion and Coexistence: Soviet Foreign Policy, 1917–73*, 2d ed. (New York: Praeger, 1974); Richard Pipes, *Survival Is Not Enough: Soviet Realities and American Foreign Policy* (New York: Simon and Schuster, 1984). A long and distinguished pedigree links totalitarian domestic structures to hyperaggressive and insatiable foreign policies. For the classics on this subject, see Hannah Arendt, *The Origins of Totalitarianism* (New York: Harcourt, Brace, 1951); Carl J. Friedrich and Zbigniew K. Brzezinski, *Totalitarian Dictatorship and Autocracy* (Cambridge: Harvard University Press, 1956); Jacob L. Talmon, *The Origins of Totalitarian Democracy* (New York: Praeger, 1960). For an excellent analysis of the concept of totalitarianism and its historical application to foreign policy analysis—the intellectual edifice of the traditionalist interpretation of the Cold War, see Abbott Gleason, *Totalitarianism: The Inner History of the Cold War* (New York: Oxford University Press, 1995).

27. *Messengers from Moscow*, Parts 1–4, produced by Daniel Wolfe and Herbert J. Ellison, PBS Documentary, Fall 1994; Steven Merrit Minor, "Revelations, Secrets, Gossips, and Lies," *New York Times Book Review*, May 14, 1995, pp. 19–21; Richard Pipes, ed., *The Unknown Lenin: From the Secret Archive* (New Haven: Yale University Press, 1996); Pipes, "Misinterpreting the Cold War," *Foreign*

Affairs, Jan./Feb. 1995, pp. 154–60; Douglas J. Macdonald, "Communist Bloc Expansion in the Early Cold War: Challenging Realism, Refuting Revisionism," *International Security*, Winter 1995–96, pp. 152–88. Based on recent revelations from the Soviet archives, John Lewis Gaddis has revised his original assessment. Now he too argues that hard-liners such as Henry Jackson were largely correct. See Gaddis, *We Now Know: Rethinking Cold War History* (New York: Oxford University Press, 1997). For his evolution from postrevisionist moral equivalence to placing the blame for the Cold War largely on the Soviet Union, see also Gaddis, *The United States and the Origins of the Cold War, 1941–1947* (New York: Columbia University Press, 1972); *The Long Peace: Inquiries into the History of the Cold War* (New York: Oxford University Press, 1987); *Russia, the Soviet Union, and the United States: An Interpretive History*, 2d ed. (New York: McGraw-Hill, 1990); and *The United States and the End of the Cold War: Implications, Reconsiderations, Provocations* (New York: Oxford University Press, 1992). For contra, the hard-liners, see Lloyd C. Gardner, *Spheres of Influence: The Great Powers Partition Europe, from Munich to Yalta* (Chicago: Ivan R. Dee, 1993); Melvyn P. Leffler, "Inside Enemy Archives," *Foreign Affairs*, July/Aug. 1996, pp. 120–35. I find Leffler's rebuttal to the hard-liners unpersuasive. Curiously, he does not even address the arguments of Richard Pipes, one of the foremost

Russian historians in the world. Also, he rests much of his argument on the conclusions drawn by Zubok and Pleshakov that Stalin had limited aims and ambitions. See Vladislav Zubok and Constantine Pleshakov, *Inside the Kremlin's Cold War: From Stalin to Khrushchev* (Cambridge: Harvard University Press, 1996). Notably, Robert Legvold, no hardliner himself, argues that a nuanced interpretation of the Zubok/Pleshakov book is consistent with that interpretation; Legvold, "Eastern Europe and Former Soviet Republics," *Foreign Affairs*, July/Aug. 1996, pp. 153–56. Also, R. C. Raack makes a persuasive case for viewing Stalin's ambitions as unlimited in his recent detailed archival study on Soviet foreign policy, *Stalin's Drive to the West, 1938–1945: The Origins of the Cold War* (Stanford: Stanford University Press, 1995).

28. Even some historians who depreciate the importance of ideology in Soviet thinking, a position with which I disagree, make the case that Stalin's paranoia precluded him from accepting volitionally a permanent settlement acceptable to the United States. For an excellent study along these lines, see Vojtech Mastny, *The Cold War and Soviet Insecurity: The Stalin Years* (New York: Oxford University Press, 1996).

29. Tony Smith, *America's Mission: The United States and the Worldwide Struggle for Democracy in the Twentieth Century* (Princeton: Princeton University Press, 1994), pp. 146–76;

Robert G. Kaufman, "A Two-Level Interaction: Structure, Stable Liberal Democracy, and U.S. Grand Strategy," *Security Studies* 5, no. 4 (Summer 1994): 696–701; Josef Joffe, *The Limited Partnership: Europe, the United States, and the Burdens of Alliance* (Cambridge, Mass.: Ballinger, 1987), pp. 186–88.

30. Sergei N. Goncharov, John W. Lewis, and Xue Litai, *Uncertain Partners: Stalin, Mao, and the Korean War* (Stanford: Stanford University Press, 1993). See, contra, Bruce Cumings, *The Origins of the Korean War* (Princeton: Princeton University Press, 1981). Cumings places the main onus on South Korea for initiating the war, but without the benefit of access to the Soviet and Chinese archives on which Goncharov, Lewis, and Litai drew heavily.

31. Hamby, *Man of the People*, pp. 584–98.

32. Richard Gid Powers, *Not without Honor: The History of American Anticommunism* (New York: Free Press, 1995), pp. 228–29, 232–33. For an excellent mea culpa exposing how much of the academic community blundered by romanticizing Mao and mistakenly viewing him as the preferred moral and geopolitical alternative to the Nationalists, see Ross Terrill, "Mao in History," *The National Interest*, Summer 1998, pp. 54–63.

33. Whatever doubt there ever was about this fact, the Soviet archives have removed it. See Harvey Klehr, John Earl Haynes, and Fridrikh Igorevich Firsov, *The Secret World of American Communism* (New Haven: Yale University Press, 1995).

34. Sam Tanenhaus, *Whittaker Chambers* (New York: Random House, 1997); Powers, *Not without Honor*, p. 195.

35. Allen Weinstein and Alexander Vassiliev, *The Haunted Wood: Soviet Espionage in America—the Stalin Era* (New York: Random House, 1999); Holloway, *Stalin and the Bomb*, pp. 222–23.

36. David McCullough, *Truman* (New York: Simon and Schuster, 1992), pp. 652, 759–60.

37. Michael Barone, *Our Country* (New York: Free Press, 1990), pp. 243–46.

38. Schmechel interview with Sterling Munro, Jan. 19, 1987.

39. *Seattle Times*, Nov. 4, 1950, p. E32.

40. Kaufman interview with Gerald Hoeck, April 2, 1995.

41. Kaufman interview with Brian Corcoran, Sept. 6, 1994; *Seattle Times*, June 21, 1996, pp. B2, B5; *Seattle Post-Intelligencer*, June 21, 1996, p. 8B.

42. *Liberty*, Feb. 1952, p. 10; C. N. Webster in the *Arlington Times*, undated HMJ 3560–2/48/11 ("best congressman"); Kaufman interview with Charles Luce, Sept. 18, 1996; *New York Times*, Oct. 5, 1952, p. 5 (Langlie).

43. Press release from the Office of Harry P. Cain, Dec. 21, 1950, HMJ 3560–2/48/18.

44. Prochnau and Larsen, *A Certain Democrat*, p. 120.

45. *Time*, March 20, 1950, p. 18;

"Political Scientists Rate U.S. Senators," Jan. 27, 1952, 3560–2/48/11.

46. *New York Herald Tribune*, June 14, 1947, p. 9.

47. Jackson, "Statewide Address," Everett, Washington, Nov. 1, 1952, HMJ 3560–12/10/25.

48. Quoted in the *Portland Oregonian*, Nov. 18, 1952, p. 1.

49. Joseph P. Miller, "First Political Junkie," manuscript, June 1995, pp. 8–9, 10.

50. Kaufman interview with Corcoran, Sept. 6, 1994; Bill Van Ness, May 2, 1995; and Dick Larsen, May 10, 1995; Schmechel interview with Sterling Munro, Jan. 19, 1987.

51. Statewide broadcast of Harry P. Cain, Oct. 14, 1952, HMJ 3560–12/11/23; *Seattle Post-Intelligencer*, Oct. 16, 1952, p. 8.

52. Kaufman interview with Hoeck, April 2, 1995.

53. Charles L. Fontenay, *Estes Kefauver: A Biography* (Knoxville: University of Tennessee Press, 1980), p. 219.

54. Barone, *Our Country*, pp. 254–55, 288–91.

55. Kaufman interview with Bob Low, Nov. 2, 1995.

4 The Eisenhower Years

1. Michael Barone, *Our Country* (New York: Free Press, 1990), p. 257.

2. William Smith White, *Citadel, the Story of the U.S. Senate* (New York: Harper, 1957).

3. Kaufman interview with Julia Cancio, June 18, 1995; Schmechel interview with Sterling Munro, Jan. 19, 1987.

4. Interview of Henry M. Jackson for the Lyndon Baines Johnson Oral History Project, HMJ 3560–10.

5. *Congressional Record*, 82d Cong., 1st sess., July 24, 1951, vol. 97, p. 7183.

6. Kaufman interview with Richard Larsen, May 3, 1995; Schmechel interview with Munro.

7. On Johnson, see Robert Dallek, *Lone Star Rising: Lyndon Johnson and His Times, 1908–1960* (New York: Oxford University Press, 1991), p. 432; Fulbright quoted in Randall Bennett Woods, *Fulbright* (New York: Cambridge University Press, 1995), p. 181.

8. HMJ 3560–3/67/1.

9. Schmechel interview with Eugene McCarthy, Feb. 1, 1988.

10. Kaufman interview with Robert Low, Nov. 2, 1995.

11. Stephen E. Ambrose, *Eisenhower: The President*, vol. 2 (New York: Simon and Schuster, 1984), pp. 160–68, 186–89.

12. Senate Committee on Government Operations, Subcommittee on Investigations, *State Department Information Hearings* (Washington, D.C.: Government Printing Office, 1954), pp. 253–81, 289–324.

13. Quoted in Thomas C. Reeves, *The Life and Times of Joe McCarthy* (New York: Stein and Day, 1982), p. 499.

14. Interview with Low.

15. *New York Times*, July 12, 1953, p. E3.

16. Quoted in Reeves, *Life and Times of Joe McCarthy*, p. 501.

17. Jackson commenting on CBS Radio, *Capitol Cloakroom*, Jan. 22, 1954.

18. Interviews with Gerald Hoeck, April 2, 1995, and Julia Cancio and Erna Miller, June 18, 1996.

19. Interview with Low; Jackson to Mr. and Mrs. Joseph Kennedy, March 26, 1954, HMJ 3560–3/1/39.

20. Richard Rovere, *Senator Joe McCarthy* (New York: Harcourt, Brace, 1959), pp. 204–21.

21. For a contemporaneous account of the trials that captures the mood well, see Michael Straight, *Trial by Television* (Boston: Beacon Press, 1954).

22. Reeves, *Life and Times of Joe McCarthy*, pp. 595–635.

23. Senate Committee on Government Operations, Subcommittee on Investigations, *Fort Monmouth Hearings*, 83d Cong., 2d sess., vol. 1, pp. 420–21.

24. Schmechel interview with Sterling Munro, Dec. 30, 1986.

25. Robert Kennedy to Jackson, June 2, 1954, HMJ 3560–3/257/22; Senate Committee on Government Operations, Subcommittee on Investigations, *Army-McCarthy Hearings*, 83d Cong., 2d sess., vol. 3, pp. 2616–17.

26. Larsen and Prochnau, *A Certain Democrat*, p. 154.

27. Quoted in the *Washington Evening Star*, June 12, 1954, p. A1.

28. Interview with Munro.

29. Barone, *Our Country*, p. 270 (polls); Rovere, *Senator Joe McCarthy*, 221–28 (censure).

30. *Seattle Times*, June 13, 1954, p. 1.

31. HMJ 3560–3/264/18, 3/1/45.

32. Kaufman interview with Helen Jackson, June 10, 1995.

33. Quoted in Reeves, *Life and Times of Joe McCarthy*, p. 668.

34. For an extended discussion on how McCarthy propelled anti-anti-communism, see Richard Gid Powers, *Not without Honor* (New York: Free Press, 1995), pp. 273–86.

35. Paul Douglas to Jackson, Aug. 6, 1954, Nov. 10, 1954, HMJ 3560–3/1/30.

36. Reinhold Niebuhr, *Christianity and Power Politics* (New York: Scribner's 1940), p. 104.

37. For the essence of Dorothy Fosdick's Niebuhrian approach to politics, see her *Common Sense and World Affairs* (New York: Harcourt, Brace, 1955); on Stevenson, see Porter McKeever, *Adlai Stevenson: His Life and Legacy* (New York: Morrow, 1989), pp. 164–66; *New York Times*, Feb. 10, 1997, p. B9 (lack of gumption).

38. Kaufman interview with Charles Horner, Dec. 9, 1994.

39. Kaufman interview with Dorothy Fosdick, May 23, 1991, and Low, Nov. 2, 1995.

40. Kaufman interview with James Schlesinger, Oct. 23, 1994.

41. Quoted in 1998 newsletter, *Henry M. Jackson Foundation*, p. 4.

42. Norman Polmar and Thomas B. Allen, *Rickover* (New York: Simon and Schuster, 1982), p. 19.

43. "Statement by HMJ (D. Washington) before the Senate Armed Services Committee," March 4, 1953, HMJ 3560/3/13/15.

44. Kaufman interview with J. Kenneth Mansfield, May 31, 1995.

45. Jackson to The Honorable Dan Kimball, Secretary of the Navy, Dec. 9, 1952, HMJ 3560–3/13/15; Jackson to Ed Guthman, March 19, 1953, ibid.

46. John Stennis to Jackson, March 13, 1953, ibid.

47. Kaufman interview with Gerald Ford, Sept. 26, 1994; Hyman Rickover to Jackson, Jan. 24, 1955, HMJ 3560–3/2/19.

48. Ambrose, *Eisenhower: The President*, 2:319–46.

49. John Lewis Gaddis, *Strategies of Containment* (New York: Oxford University Press, 1982), pp. 127–64.

50. Richard Smoke, *National Security and the Nuclear Dilemma: An Introduction to the American Experience*, 2d ed. (New York: Random House, 1987), pp. 85–103; Henry A. Kissinger, *Nuclear Weapons and Foreign Policy* (New York: Harper and Row, 1957).

51. Lawrence Freedman, *The Evolution of Nuclear Strategy* (New York: St. Martin's Press, 1981), pp. 93–119.

52. For the best discussion of the limited war theory as it evolved in the 1950s, see Christopher M. Gacek, *The Logic of Force: the Dilemma of Limited War in American Foreign Policy* (New York: Columbia University Press, 1994), pp. 124–57; on large conventional forces, see Richard

Smoke, *National Security and the Nuclear Dilemma* (New York: Random House, 1987), pp. 87–94.

53. Jackson, "Long Range Ballistic Missile Programs," July 30, 1954, HMJ 3560–6/3/24; CBS Radio, *Capital Cloakroom*, Jan. 22, 1954 ("grave calculated risk"); Jackson, "How Shall We Forge a Strategy for Survival," National War College, Washington, D.C., April 16, 1959, HMJ 3560–3/233/11 (15 percent of GNP); and "Peace Demands a Policy," American Society of International Law, Washington, D.C., May 2, 1959, HMJ 3560–3/234/10 (expand the economy).

54. Jackson to Charles E. Wilson, July 30, 1954, HMJ 3560–6/3/28; Jackson and Clinton Anderson to Dwight Eisenhower, June 30, 1955, ibid.; Charles Wilson to Jackson, Nov. 14, 1955, ibid.

55. Jackson, "The Race for Ballistic Missiles," Feb. 1, 1956, HMJ 3560–6/3/29.

56. Jackson, "Ballistic Seapower— Fourth Dimension of Warfare," U.S. Senate, May 27, 1957, HMJ 3560–6/3/45.

57. Dallek, *Lone Star Rising*, p. 529 (Johnson); *Congressional Record*, 84th Cong., 1st sess., July 13, 1955, vol. 101, p. 10478 (Kennedy).

58. Quoted in Michael S. Sherry, *In the Shadow of War: The United States Since the 1930s* (New Haven: Yale University Press, 1995), p. 214.

59. Ibid., pp. 214–15; Jackson, "How Shall We Forge a Strategy for

Survival," National War College, Washington, D.C., April 16, 1959, HMJ 3560–6/4/24.

60. Jackson, "Forging a National Strategy," Military Government Association, Washington, D.C., June 13, 1959, HMJ 3560–6/4/31.

61. Jackson, "Concerning the Polaris Missile System Program," July 26, 1960, HMJ 3560–6/4/43.

62. HMJ 3560–3/214/25.

63. See, for example, Robert S. McNamara, *Blundering into Disaster: Surviving the First Century of the Nuclear Age* (New York: Pantheon Books, 1986); Jerome H. Kahan, *Security in the Nuclear Age: Developing U.S. Strategic Arms Policy* (Washington, D.C.: Brookings Institution, 1975); Strobe Talbott, *Endgame* (New York: Harper and Row, 1979); Fred M. Kaplan, *Dubious Specter: A Skeptical Look at the Soviet Nuclear Threat* (Washington, D.C.: Institute for Policy Studies, 1980).

64. Ambrose, *Eisenhower: The President*, 2:598–99.

65. For the definitive accounts of this camapign of deception and its motives, see Arnold L. Horelick and Myron Rush, *Strategic Power and Soviet Foreign Policy* (Chicago: University of Chicago Press, 1963).

66. For the definitive account of this systematic underestimation of the Soviet missile-building program, see Albert Wohlstetter, "Is There a Strategic Arms Race?" *Foreign Policy*, Summer 1974, pp. 3–20, and "Rivals, But No 'Race,'" *Foreign Policy*, Fall 1974, pp. 48–81.

5 Khrushchev's Communism

1. Adam B. Ulam, *Expansion and Coexistence*, 2d ed. (New York: Praeger, 1974), pp. 559–71.

2. Ibid., pp. 590–604.

3. Steven T. Hosmer and Thomas W. Wolfe, *Soviet Policy and Practice toward Third World Conflicts* (Lexington, Mass.: Lexington Books, 1983), pp. 9–15.

4. Ibid., pp. 15–21.

5. Samuel P. Huntington, *The Clash of Civilizations and the Remaking of World Order* (New York: Simon and Schuster, 1996), p. 92; Bernard Lewis, *The Middle East: A Brief History of the Last 2,000 Years* (New York: Scribner, 1995), pp. 374–75.

6. Ulam, *Expansion and Coexistence*, pp. 584–89.

7. See Vladislav Zubok and Constantine Pleshakov, *Inside the Kremlin's Cold War: From Stalin to Khrushchev* (Cambridge: Harvard University Press, 1996), pp. 185–225. Even these authors call Khrushchev the last of the Soviet hierarchy who was a true believer. This author credits them for being half right. Khrushchev was a true believer, but not the last Soviet leader who had Lenin in his bones. The Leninist impulse ran strong in the Soviet leadership right up through Gorbachev. See Aleksandr Nekrich and Mikhail Heller, *Utopia in Power* (New York: Summit Books, 1986).

8. Adam B. Ulam, *The Communists: The Story of Power and Lost Illusions, 1948–1991* (New York: Scribner's

1992), pp. 177–80. For the classic analysis of the Sino-Soviet split during the 1950s, see Donald S. Zagoria, *The Sino-Soviet Conflict, 1956–1961* (Princeton: Princeton University Press, 1962).

9. Stephen E. Ambrose, *Eisenhower: The President* (New York: Simon and Schuster, 1984), 2:572–80.

10. Jackson, "Soviet-U.S. Summit Conference," U.S. Senate, May 19, 1960, HMJ 3560–6/4/59.

11. Jackson, "The Race for Ballistic Missiles," U.S. Senate, Feb. 1, 1956, HMJ 3560–6/3/29.

12. Jackson, "Raw Notes on Trip to Russia," HMJ 3560–3/230/23.

13. Jackson, "Raw Notes on Trip to the Middle East," HMJ 3560–3/230/23.

14. Jackson, "Israel Anniversary Celebration," April 1955, HMJ 3560–6/3/27; Statement by Henry Jackson, "Israel," March 20, 1956, HMJ 3560–6/3/31.

15. Jackson, "Middle East Peace and Stability," U.S. Senate, March 4, 1957, HMJ 3560–6/3/40.

16. Jackson, "Indo-China—the Key Conflict in the Defense of Southeast Asia," May 3, 1954, HMJ 3560–3/231/1; "Presenting the Report of the NATO Parliamentarians Conference," Nov. 17, 1958, HMJ 3560–6/4/11.

17. Jackson, "Peace Demands a Policy," American Society of International Law, May 2, 1959, HMJ 3560–6/4/26; "Defense Program, National Security Commission of the Ameri-

can Legion," Washington, D.C., Jan. 28, 1960, HMJ 3560–3/232/7.

18. Jackson, "Soviet Union," Ford Hall Forum, Boston, Massachusetts, March 10, 1957, HMJ 3560–3/230/23a.

19. For a splendid book that punctures the liberal myth about an uninformed Eisenhower that the president himself cultivated for political effect, see Fred I. Greenstein, *The Hidden-Hand Presidency: Eisenhower as Leader* (New York: Basic Books, 1982).

20. Jackson, "National Policy-Making in a Divided World," *The Proceedings of the American Society of International Law,* 1959.

21. Dwight Eisenhower to Lyndon Johnson, June 25, 1959; Jackson to Eisenhower, July 9, 1959; Eisenhower to Jackson, July 10, 1959, HMJ 3560–6/4/36.

22. Kaufman interviews with J. Kenneth Mansfield, May 31, 1995, and Grenville Garside, March 15, 1995.

23. Senate Committee on Government Operations, Subcommittee on National Policy Machinery, *Organizing for National Security,* vol. 1 (Washington, D.C.: Government Printing Office, 1961), pp. 12–45.

24. Ibid., pp. 1–37.

25. *Washington Sunday Star,* Sept. 24, 1961, p. 1.

26. Quoted in Grenville Garside, "The Jackson Subcommittee on National Security," in Dorothy Fosdick, ed., *Staying the Course* (Seattle: University of Washington Press, 1987), p. 52.

6 *Domestic Politics to 1961*

1. Kaufman interview with Ted Stevens, March 14, 1995; Schmechel interview with Ted Stevens, March 9, 1987.

2. Kaufman interview with Gordon Culp, April 4, 1995; Schmechel interview with Gordon Culp March 16, 1987.

3. Jackson, "Status and Prospects for Atomic Power Development," American Public Power Association, Seattle, Washington, May 38, 1959, HMJ 3560-3/324/33.

4. Kaufman interview with Charles Luce, Sept. 18, 1996; Schmechel interview with Charles Luce, Jan. 7, 1988.

5. For an excellent summary of the debate over Hells Canyon and its links to the Civil Rights Bill of 1957, see LeRoy Ashby and Rod Gramer, *Fighting the Odds: the Life of Senator Frank Church* (Pullman: Washington State University Press, 1994), pp. 71–91.

6. *Congressional Record,* 85th Cong., 2d sess., June 20, 1957, vol. 103, pp. 9828–31.

7. Kaufman interview with Luce; Schmechel interview with Sterling Munro, Jan. 19, 1987.

8. Ashby and Gramer do a splendid job of refuting this charge in *Fighting the Odds,* pp. 71–91.

9. Kaufman interview with Sam Nunn, March 14, 1996.

10. Interview of Henry Jackson, Lyndon Baines Johnson Oral History Project, HMJ 3560-10.

11. Herbert Brownell with John P. Burke, *Advising Ike: The Memoirs of Attorney General Herbert Brownell* (Lawrence: University Press of Kansas, 1993), pp. 218–26.

12. Robert Dalleck, *Lone Star Rising* (New York: Oxford University Press, 1991), pp. 517–28.

13. Jackson, "The Civil Rights Bill of 1957," HMJ 3560-3/232/25.

14. "Alice Franklin Bryant," HMJ 3560-12/14/40; "William Bantz," ibid., 14/39.

15. For the most recent and well-received foray into this type of analysis, see Anthony King, *Running Scared: Why America's Politicians Campaign Too Much and Govern Too Little* (New York: Free Press, 1997), pp. 188–91.

16. Kaufman interviews with Tom Foley, March 14, 1995; Norm Dicks, Aug. 5, 1995; and Lloyd Meeds, Aug. 8, 1995.

17. Harry McPherson, *A Political Education* (Boston: Little, Brown, 1972), p. 44.

18. Schmechel interview with Luce.

19. Kaufman interviews with Foley; Bill Van Ness, May 6, 1995; and Jason King, June 6, 1995.

20. Schmechel interview with Munro; Kaufman interview with Grenville Garside, March 15, 1995.

21. McPherson, *A Political Education,* pp. 39–40.

22. Schmechel interview with Munro.

23. Schmechel interview with Peggy MacDonald Heily, April 4, 1987.

24. *Seattle Magazine* 1, no. 2 (May 1964): 32–33.

25. Ibid., p. 32.

26. Schmechel interview with Munro.

27. Kaufman interview with Helen Jackson, June 10, 1995.

28. Kaufman interviews with Julia Cancio and Erna Miller, June 18, 1996; and with Van Ness.

29. Anecdote recounted by Sterling Munro in *Scoop;* Schmechel interviews with Peggy MacDonald Heily; and with Noreen Lydday Potts, Sept. 29, 1987.

30. Schmechel interview with Joel Merkel, April 13, 1987.

31. Kaufman interview with Joe Miller, June 18, 1996.

32. Kaufman interview with Gerald Hoeck, April 2, 1995; Theodore H. White, *The Making of the President, 1960* (New York: Atheneum, 1961), p. 52.

33. See, for example, *Congressional Record*, 84th Cong., 1st sess., July 13, 1955, vol. 101, p. 10478; ibid., 86th Cong., 2d sess., June 14, 1960, vol. 103, p. 11630.

34. Schmechel interview with Munro.

35. Kaufman interview with Hoeck; Schmechel interview with Munro.

36. White, *The Making of the President, 1960*, pp. 78–149.

37. Of Nixon's credible biographers, Jonathan Aitken has written the most favorable version. Even he conceded the polarizing aspects of Nixon's political and personal per-sonas that Kennedy exploited to great advantage in the 1960 campaign. See Jonathan Aitken, *Nixon: A Life* (Washington, D.C.: Regnery, 1993), pp. 274–306. See also Herbert S. Parmet, *Richard Nixon and His America* (Boston: Little, Brown, 1990), pp. 324–402. Parmet is the best of Nixon's biographers—not hostile, but no hagiographer either. He treats Nixon's character with a felicitous admixture of sympathy, balance, and frankness.

38. Michael Barone, *Our Country* (New York: Free Press, 1990), p. 327.

39. Quoted in the *Yakima Herald*, July 4, 1960, p. 1.

40. *Time*, July 4, 1960, p. 13; Press Release, "U.S. Senator Henry M. Jackson for Vice Presidential Committee," July 9, 1960, Sterling Munro Papers (endorsements).

41. *Seattle Times*, July 13, 1960, p. 1.

42. Kaufman interview with Hoeck; Schmechel interview with Edmund Muskie, Feb. 25, 1988.

43. Schmechel interview with Luce; Larsen and Prochnau, *A Certain Democrat*, pp. 190–92.

44. *Washington Star*, July 13, 1960, p. 13.

45. Kaufman interview with Hoeck.

46. Salter quoted in the *Seattle Argus* 22, no. 11 (March 12, 1965): 1.

47. Ibid., pp. 1–3.

48. Ibid; Kaufman interview with Robert Low, Nov. 2, 1995.

49. HMJ 2560–3/270/16.

50. Prochnau and Larsen, *A Certain Democrat*, pp. 192–95.

51. Jackson, "The Case for the Democratic Party," Oct. 15, 1960, HMJ 3560–3/232/22; "Campaign Speech," Hartford Connecticut, Sept. 24, 1960, HMJ 3560–3/232/14.

52. Jackson, "Campaign Speech," Kansas City, Missouri, Oct. 6, 1960, HMJ 3560–3/232/16.

53. Jackson, "Campaign Speech," National Press Club, Washington, D.C., Oct. 18, 1960, HMJ 3560–12/15.

54. Jackson, "The Case for the Democratic Party," Oct. 15, 1960, HMJ 3560–3/232/22.

55. Jackson, "Religion as a Campaign Issue," Washington, D.C., Sept. 15, 1960, HMJ 3560–12/15/19.

56. Ibid.

57. See, for example, John F. Kennedy, "Campaign Speeches and Writings," HMJ 3560–3/250/11–153 (144 speeches in all from the 1960 presidential campaign).

58. Barone, *Our Country*, pp. 318–35.

7 Henry Jackson and the New Frontier

1. Kaufman interview with Helen Jackson, June 10, 1995.

2. Kaufman interview with Julia Cancio, June 18, 1996; Schmechel interview with Peggy MacDonald Heily, April 11, 1987; *Roll Call*, Nov. 29, 1961, p. 8.

3. John Kennedy to Jackson, Dec. 16, 1961, White House Name File, box 1332, JFKL; interview with Helen Jackson.

4. Theodore C. Sorensen, *Kennedy* (New York: Harper and Row, 1965), p. 120.

5. Kaufman interview with Robert Low, Nov. 2, 1995.

6. Jackson to JFK, Dec. 6, 1960, HMJ 3560–12/20/8.

7. Robert J. Art, *The TFX Decision: McNamara and the Military* (Boston: Little, Brown, 1968), pp. 30–32.

8. Jackson, "The Political Authority and the Professional," U.S. National War College, Washington, D.C., April 29, 1964, HMJ 3560–6/5/47; "Executives, Experts, and National Security," U.S. Department of State, Foreign Service Institute, Arlington, Virginia, HMJ 3560–6/5/49.

9. Kaufman interview with William Prochnau, June 4, 1996.

10. Ibid.

11. Transcript, *Opinion in the Capitol: A Metropolitan Broadcasting Television Program*, June 7, 1964, HMJ 3560–3/230/36.

12. Jackson, Speech to the Democratic Convention, July 27, 1964, HMJ 3560–12/26/36.

13. Arthur M. Schlesinger, Jr., *Robert Kennedy and His Times* (Boston: Houghton Mifflin, 1978), p. 665; Jackson, Speech to the Democratic National Convention.

14. Jackson, "The U.S. in the U.N.: An Independent Audit," National Press Club, Washington, D.C., March 20, 1962.

15. Richard Russell to Jackson, March 23, 1962, HMJ 3560–6/50/30a; *Congressional Record*, 87th Cong.,

2d sess., April 4, 1962, vol. 108, p. 5910 (Tower); ibid., March 21, p. 4809 (Javits); Humphrey and Stevenson quoted in the *Seattle Times,* April 2, 1962, p. 4.

16. Adlai Stevenson to Jackson, April 13, 1962; Stevenson to Bob Tufts, April 12, 1962; and Stevenson to Dorothy Fosdick, May 1, 1962, in HMJ 3560–6/30/a.

17. Stevenson to Fosdick, May 1, 1962.

18. Daniel Patrick Moynihan, *A Dangerous Place* (Boston: Little, Brown, 1978).

19. *Public Papers of John F. Kennedy: 1962* (Washington, D.C.: Government Printing Office, 1963), pp. 254–55.

20. Quoted in Porter McKeever, *Adlai Stevenson: His Life and Legacy* (New York: Morrow, 1989), p. 510.

21. Richard Reeves, *President Kennedy: Profiles of Power* (New York: Simon and Schuster, 1993), pp. 449–50.

22. Michael S. Beschloss, *The Crisis Years: Kennedy and Khrushchev, 1960–1963* (New York: HarperCollins, 1991), pp. 396–98.

23. Douglas Brinkley, *Dean Acheson: The Cold War Years, 1953–1971* (New Haven: Yale University Press, 1992), pp. 148–55; Stephen Ambrose, *Eisenhower,* 2 vols. (New York: Simon and Schuster, 1984), 2:643.

24. Beschloss, *Crisis Years,* p. 491; Donald Kagan, *On the Origins of War and the Preservation of Peace* (New York: Doubleday, 1995), p. 467.

25. Barbara Tuchman, *The Guns of August* (New York: Macmillan, 1962);

Sidney Bradshaw Fay, *The Origins of the World War* (New York: Macmillan, 1928).

26. Beschloss, *Crisis Years,* p. 491.

27. Roger Hilsman, *The Cuban Missile Crisis: The Struggle over Policy* (Westport: Praeger, 1996), pp. 12–15, 39–44.

28. Anatoly Dobrynin, *In Confidence: Moscow's Ambassador to America's Six Cold War Presidents (1962–1986)* (New York: Times Books, 1995), pp. 72–73; Adam B. Ulam, *Expansion and Coexistence,* 2d ed. (New York: Praeger, 1974), pp. 666–78.

29. Kagan, *On the Origins of War,* pp. 466–86.

30. Reeves, *President Kennedy,* pp. 364–425.

31. For an edited but detailed account from the tapes of the actual conversations within the administration, see Ernest R. May and Philip D. Zelikow, eds., *The Kennedy Tapes: Inside the White House During the Cuban Missile Crisis* (Cambridge: Belknap Press, 1997).

32. Hilsman, *Cuban Missile Crisis,* pp. 109–10.

33. Robert Kennedy, *Thirteen Days* (New York: Norton, 1969), pp. 9–20.

34. Ibid., pp. 444–55.

35. *National Observer,* Feb. 11, 1963 in HMJ 3560–3/272/11.

36. Deborah Shapley, *Promise and Power: The Life and Times of Robert McNamara* (Boston: Little, Brown, 1993), pp. 187–201.

37. "Seven Assumptions that Beset US," *New York Times Magazine,* Aug. 4, 1963, in HMJ 3560–6/5/38.

8 The TFX Controversy and the "Senator from Boeing"

1. Robert J. Art, *The TFX Decision* (Boston: Little, Brown, 1968), pp. 157–66.

2. Deborah Shapley, *Promise and Power* (Boston: Little, Brown, 1993), pp. 201–11.

3. Ibid., p. 210.

4. *CQA: 1963*, pp. 1089–90.

5. Senate Committee on Government Operations, Permanent Subcommittee on Investigations, 88th Cong., 1st sess., *Hearings on the TFX Contract Investigation*, part 2, March 12, 13, 21, 27, and 28, 1963 (hereafter cited as *TFX Hearings*).

6. Ibid., pp. 445.

7. Kaufman interview of Richard Perle, Oct. 2, 1994.

8. Ibid.

9. Quoted in the *Seattle Times*, March 6, 1963, p. 1.

10. Senate Committee on Government Operations, Subcommittee on National Security and International Operations, Initial Memorandum, "Planning-Programming-Budgeting," 1967, pp. 5–9, in HMJ 3560–3/256/1.

11. Robert F. Coulam, *Illusions of Choice: The F-111 and the Problem of Weapons Acquisition Reform* (Princeton: Princeton University Press, 1977).

12. *Everett Herald*, March 5, 1963, p. 1.

13. *Washington Post*, May 5, 1963, p. 1.

14. *Everett Herald*, March 5, 1963, p. 1.

15. Quoted in the *Washington Sunday Star*, March 17, 1963, p. 1.

16. *TFX Hearings*, pp. 403, 445–46.

17. *Congressional Record*, 89th Cong., 1st sess., March 21, 1963, vol. 109, pp. 4695–98.

18. Ibid., p. 4698 (Lippmann); *Seattle Post-Intelligencer*, March 24, 1963, p. 9 (Pearson); *Detroit News*, March 15, 1963, p. 8.

19. Kaufman interviews with Richard Larsen, May 10, 1995, and Willam Prochnau, June 4, 1996.

20. Public Statement of William Allen, Sept. 8, 1964, draft in HMJ 3560–3/247/14.

21. Kaufman interview with T. A. Wilson, April 3, 1994.

22. Ibid.

23. Schmechel interview with Eugene McCarthy, Feb. 1, 1988.

24. Kaufman interview with Lloyd Meeds, Aug. 5, 1995; Schmechel interview with Brock Adams, June 29, 1987.

25. Michael Barone, Grant Ujifusa, and Douglas Matthews, *The Almanac of American Politics: 1974* (Boston: Gambit, 1974), p. 1068.

26. Kaufman interview with Tom Foley, March 14, 1995.

27. Ibid.

28. Quoted in the *Washington Post*, Aug. 2, 1963, p. 14.

29. *Public Papers of John F. Kennedy: 1963* (Washington, D.C.: Government Printing Office, 1964), p. 460.

30. Michael R. Beschloss, *The Crisis Years* (New York: HarperCollins, 1991), pp. 598–600.

31. Quoted in Richard Reeves, *President Kennedy* (New York: Simon and Schuster, 1993), p. 554.

32. Jackson, "Seven Assumptions that Beset US," *New York Times Magazine*, Aug. 4, 1963, HMJ 3560–6/5/38.

33. Kaufman interview with Richard Perle, Jan. 2, 1996.

34. Jackson, "Test Ban Treaty," U.S. Senate, Aug. 9, 1963, HMJ 3560–6/5/39.

35. *Washington Post*, Aug. 8, 1974, HMJ 3560–3/274/8.

36. William L. Neuman to the Editors of the *New York Times*, Aug. 5, 1963, HMJ 3560–3/202/1.

37. Jackson to James E. Carty, Aug. 23, 1963, HMJ 3560–3/202/1.

38. Jackson, "Test Ban Treaty," U.S. Senate, Aug. 9, 1963, HMJ 3560–6/5/39.

39. Jackson, "Test Ban Treaty," U.S. Senate, Aug. 15, 1963, HMJ 3560–6/5/40.

40. Ibid.

41. Jackson, "Test Ban Treaty," U.S. Senate, Sept. 13, 1963, HMJ 3560–6/5/41.

42. Kaufman interview with Brewster Denny, May 5, 1995.

43. Jackson, "Test Ban Treaty," U.S. Senate, Sept. 13, 1963.

44. Quoted in the *New York Tribune*, Aug. 26, 1963, p. 4.

45. *Congressional Record*, 89th Cong., 1st sess., Sept. 13, 1963, vol. 109, pp. 16957–70.

46. Thomas J. Schoenbaum, *Waging Peace and War: Dean Rusk in the Truman, Kennedy, and Johnson Years* (New York: Simon and Schuster, 1988), pp. 230–37.

47. For the best analysis of the domino theory, and one that recognizes its plausibility properly understood, see Douglas J. Macdonald, "Falling Dominoes and Systems Dynamics: A Risk Aversion Perspective," *Security Studies* 3, no. 2 (Winter 1993–1994): 225–53; and Douglas J. Macdonald, "The Truman Administration and Global Responsibility: The Birth of the Domino Principle," in Jack Snyder and Robert Jervis, ed., *Dominoes and Bandwagons* (New York: Oxford University Press, 1991), pp. 112–34.

48. Henry A. Kissinger, *Diplomacy* (New York: Simon and Schuster, 1994), pp. 626–27.

49. Stephen E. Ambrose, *Eisenhower*, 2 vols. (New York: Simon and Schuster, 1984), 2:614–15.

50. Reeves, *President Kennedy*, pp. 449–50.

51. Christopher M. Gacek, *The Logic of Force* (New York: Columbia University Press, 1994), pp. 158–219.

52. Stanley Karnow, *Vietnam: A History* (New York: Viking Press, 1983), pp. 215–69.

53. George C. Herring, *America's Longest War: The United States and Vietnam, 1950–1975*, 2d ed. (New York: Knopf, 1986), p. 67.

54. William J. Duiker, *The Communist Road to Power in Vietnam* (Boulder: Westview, 1981), pp. 198–228.

55. Dean Rusk, *As I Saw It* (New York: Norton, 1990), pp. 429–30.

56. Reeves, *President Kennedy*, pp. 635–52.

57. Robert S. McNamara, *In Retrospect: The Tragedy and Lessons of Vietnam* (New York: Times Books, 1995), pp. 96–97.

58. Rusk, *As I Saw It*, pp. 441–42.

59. For probably the definitive interpretation of the Kennedy administration's position on Vietnam, from the most reliable source, see Robert F. Kennedy, *In His Own Words: The Unpublished Recollections of the Kennedy Years* (New York: Bantam Books, 1988), pp. 393–425. Robert Kennedy said that there was never any consideration given to pulling out, but they had not decided about whether to escalate.

60. Karnow, *Vietnam*, pp. 395–426.

61. Jackson, "Raw Notes on Trip to Vietnam," Dec. 1962, HMJ 3560–3/231/1–2.

62. Ibid.

63. *Aberdeen Daily World*, Sept. 5, 1963, p. 1.

64. Timothy J. Lomperis, *The War Everyone Lost—and Won: America's Intervention in Viet Nam's Twin Struggles* (Baton Rouge: Louisiana State University Press, 1984), pp. 173–76; Guenter Lewy, *America in Vietnam* (New York: Oxford University Press, 1978), pp. 418–53.

65. On this point, see the debate between me and Stephen Walt. Stephen M. Walt, *The Origins of Alliances* (Ithaca: Cornell University Press, 1987); Robert G. Kaufman, "To Balance or To Bandwagon: Alliance Decisions in 1930s Europe," *Security Studies* 1, no. 3 (Spring 1992): 417–47; Steven M. Walt, "Alliances, Threats, and Grand Strategy: A Reply to Kaufman and Labs," *Security Studies* 1, no. 3 (Spring 1992): 448–82; Robert G. Kaufman, "The Lessons of the 1930s: A Reply to Stephen M. Walt," *Security Studies* 1, no. 4 (Summer 1992): 90–96.

66. See also Randall L. Schweller, "Bandwagoning for Profit," *International Security* 19, no. 1 (Summer 1994): 72–107.

67. Adam B. Ulam, *The Communists* (New York: Scribner's, 1992), pp. 230–36.

68. Jaspar Becker, *Hungry Ghosts: Mao's Secret Famine* (New York: Free Press, 1996).

69. For a startling firsthand account of Mao that should banish the myth of his moderation, see Dr. Li Zhisui, *The Private Life of Chairman Mao* (New York: Random House, 1994).

70. See Jeane J. Kirkpatrick, *Dictatorships and Double Standards: Rationalism and Reason in Politics* (New York: Simon and Schuster, 1982), pp. 23–138.

71. For the argument that American military intervention caused the Cambodian genocide, see William Shawcross, *Sideshow: Kissinger, Nixon, and the Destruction of Cambodia* (New York: Simon and Schuster, 1979). For the decisive rebuttal, see Kissinger, *Diplomacy*, pp. 735–48. For the longer version, see Kissinger, *White House Years* (Boston: Little, Brown, 1979), pp. 457–75, 484–509, 517–20; idem, *Years of Upheaval* (Boston: Little, Brown, 1982), pp. 335–69; Peter W.

Rodman, *More Precious than Peace: The Cold War and the Struggle for the Third World* (New York: Scribner's, 1994), pp. 451–78.

9 The Great Liberal Crackup

1. Kaufman interview with Dorothy Fosdick, May 23, 1991.
2. Schmechel interview with Barry Goldwater, March 14, 1988.
3. Jackson on *Opinion in the Capital*, Metropolitan Broadcasting, June 7, 1963; Robert Goldberg, *Barry Goldwater* (New Haven: Yale University Press, 1995), pp. 191–92.
4. Kaufman interview with Stewart Udall, Feb. 17, 1995.
5. Ibid.
6. Jackson on *Opinion in the Capital*, June 7, 1964.
7. John Kenneth Galbraith, *The Affluent Society* (Boston: Houghton Mifflin, 1958).
8. Richard Reeves, *President Kennedy* (New York: Simon and Schuster, 1993), pp. 452, 454.
9. Kaufman interview with Tom Foley, March 14, 1995.
10. Interview with Udall.
11. Kaufman interview with Richard M. Nixon, Oct. 2, 1992.
12. Jackson, "Address to the Bellingham Sportsmen," Sept. 7, 1957, HMJ 3560–3/233/43.
13. Interview with Udall.
14. Kaufman interviews with Bill Van Ness, May 10, 1995; Charles Luce, Sept. 18, 1995; and Daniel Dreyfus, Dec. 31, 1996.
15. Interview with Udall.
16. Interview with Dreyfus.
17. Kaufman interviews with Sam Nunn, March 14, 1995; Ted Stevens, March 14, 1985; and Daniel Patrick Moynihan, July 28, 1996. Schmechel interviews with Mark Hatfield, June 29, 1987; Bill Bradley, Nov. 24, 1987; Barry Goldwater, March 14, 1988; Edmund Muskie, Feb. 25, 1988; and George McGovern, June 30, 1987.
18. Interviews with Udall and Dreyfus.
19. Rachel Carson, *Silent Spring* (Boston: Houghton Mifflin, 1962); Gregg Easterbrook, *A Moment on the Earth: The Coming Age of Environmental Optimism* (New York: Viking, 1995), pp. 79–80.
20. Interview with Udall.
21. Senate Committee on Interior and Insular Affairs, *Hearings on North Cascades-Olympic National Park: Study Team Report of the Recreational Opportunities in the State of Washington*, 89th Cong., 2d sess., Feb. 11 and 12, 1966; Carsten Lien, *Olympic Battleground* (San Francisco: Sierra Club Books, 1991), pp. 323–29, 331–34.
22. Interview with Udall.
23. Irving Bernstein, *Guns or Butter: The Presidency of Lyndon Johnson* (New York: Oxford University Press, 1996), pp. 324–57; George C. Herring, *LBJ and Vietnam: A Different Kind of War* (Austin: University of Texas Press, 1994), pp. 1–13.
24. Jackson, "The Challenges of Vietnam," American Legion, Portland, Oregon, Aug. 21, 1965, HMJ 3560–4/231/4.
25. Jackson, "The Price of Power,"

Philadelphia, Feb. 25, 1966, HMJ 3560–4/231/45.

26. Jackson, "Facts and Fallacies about Foreign Policy," Boston College, May 4, 1965, HMJ 3460–4/231/7.

27. Ibid.

28. Jackson, "Vietnam," U.S. Senate, Feb. 16, 1966, HMJ 3560–4/231/47.

29. Jackson, "Vietnam," National War College, Washington, D.C., May 19, 1967, HMJ 3560–4/232/29.

30. Jackson, "The Duty of the Free and the Brave," U.S. Senate, March 10, 1966, HMJ 3560–4/231/32.

31. Jackson, "The Challenge of Vietnam."

32. Jackson, "Statement re Vietnam," Press Conference, Honolulu, Hawaii, Dec. 18, 1965, HMJ 3560–4/231/6.

33. Kaufman interview with Haakon Ragde, April 18, 1995.

34. *Seattle Times*, Dec. 7, 1966, p. 1.

35. William Appelman Williams, *The Tragedy of American Diplomacy*, 2d ed. (New York: Dell, 1972). For sympathetic accounts of the origins of the New Left and its impact on the antiwar movement, see Tom Hayden, *Reunion: A Memoir* (New York: Random House, 1988), pp. 73–241; Todd Gitlin, *The Sixties: Years of Hope, Days of Rage* (New York: Bantam Books, 1987), 88–282; and Paul Berman, *A Tale of Two Utopias: The Political Journey of the Generation of 1968* (New York: Norton, 1996), pp. 7–122. For a scathing account from a former leader of the movement, see David Horowitz, *Radical Son: A Generational Odyssey* (New York: Free Press, 1997), pp. 99–218. For the best and very critical assessment of the antiwar movement, see Adam Garfinkle, *Telltale Hearts: The Origins and Impact of the Vietnam Antiwar Movement* (New York: St. Martin's Press, 1995), pp. 117–48.

36. See, for example, Williams, *Tragedy of American Diplomacy;* Walter LaFeber, *America, Russia, and the Cold War,* 7th ed. (New York: McGraw-Hill, 1993); and Lloyd C. Gardner, *The Origins of the Cold War* (Waltham: Ginn-Blaisdell, 1970).

37. Quoted in Gitlin, *The Sixties,* p. 109–10.

38. Ibid., p. 92.

39. Horowitz, *Radical Son,* pp. 157–78.

40. Kaufman interview with Peter Jackson, Jan. 13, 1996.

41. Jackson, "Power and Responsibility," Methodist Council of Bishops, Seattle, Nov. 17, 1965, HMJ 3560–4/231/16.

42. Jackson, "Facts and Fallacies about Foreign Policy."

43. Jackson, "Foreign Policy," National War College, April, 1965, HMJ 3560–4/231/9.

44. Jackson, "The American Soldier: Servant of the Republic," Industrial College of the Armed Forces, Washington, D.C., June 10, 1969, HMJ 3560–4/233/8.

45. See, for, example, the highly acclaimed book by Dan T. Carter, *The Politics of Rage: George Wallace, the Origins of the New Conservatism, and the*

Transformation of American Politics (New York: Simon and Schuster, 1995), pp. 348–49.

46. Jackson, "The Authority of Reason," Seattle Pacific College, June 7, 1969, HMJ 3560/4239/10.

47. Jackson, "The Responsible Citizen," Washington, D.C., June 1968, HMJ 3560–4/233/1.

48. Randall Bennett Woods, *Fulbright: A Biography* (New York: Cambridge University Press, 1995), pp. 439–52; LeRoy Ashby and Rod Gramer, *Fighting the Odds* (Pullman: Washington State University Press, 1994), pp. 213–44.

49. J. William Fulbright, *The Arrogance of Power* (New York: Random House, 1966).

50. Hans J. Morgenthau, *Vietnam and the United States* (Washington, D.C.: Public Affairs Press, 1965); David Mayers, *George Kennan and the Dilemmas of U.S. Foreign Policy* (New York: Oxford University Press, 1988), pp. 276–84.

51. See Morgenthau, *Politics among Nations* (New York: Knopf, 1985); Kennan, *American Diplomacy: 1900–1950*.

52. Kaufman interview with Bill Van Ness, May 5, 1995.

53. Jackson and George McGovern on *ABC Scope*, May 13, 1967.

54. Kaufman interview with Helen Jackson, June 10, 1995 (wing-tip shoes); Woods, *Fulbright*, pp. 448–49 (military-industrial complex); Kaufman interview with Richard Perle, Jan. 2, 1996 (Israel); Woods, p. 34 (Poland), pp. 581–86 (Jewish state).

55. J. William Fulbright with Seth P. Tillman, *The Price of Empire* (New York: Pantheon Books, 1989), pp. 31–34; interview with Perle.

56. Kaufman interview with Shelby Scates, May 13, 1997; Schmechel interview with Brock Adams, June 29, 1987.

57. Kaufman interview with William Prochnau, June 14, 1996.

58. Kaufman interview with Gerald Hoeck, April 2, 1995; Schmechel interview with Stanley Golub, April 5, 1987.

59. Interview with Helen Jackson.

60. Ray Scherer to George Christian, March 25, 1967, WHCF Name File: Henry M. Jackson, LBJL.

61. Lyndon Johnson to Mr. and Mrs. Henry M. Jackson, March 11, 1967, WHCF Name File: Henry M. Jackson, LBJL.

62. Interview with Helen Jackson (must do a better job); "Letter to Senator Jackson Concerning the Bombing of North Vietnam," March 2, 1967, in *Public Papers of the Presidents of the United States: Lyndon B. Johnson, 1967* (Washington, D.C.: Government Printing Office, 1968), p. 267.

63. Schmechel interview with John Stennis, March 7, 1987.

64. Senate Subcommittee on National Security and International Operations, *Hearings on the Atlantic Alliance*, 89th Cong., 2d sess., April 27, May 17, June 21, and Aug. 15, 1966.

65. Dwight Eisenhower to Jackson, May 17, 1966; Harry Truman to Jackson, May 17, 1966, in *Hearings on the Atlantic Alliance*, Aug. 15, 1966.

66. Jackson, "The Will to Stay the Course," World Affairs Council, Seattle, Nov. 23, 1965, HMJ 3560–4/231/25.

67. Jean Lacouture, *De Gaulle, Ruler of France* (New York: Norton, 1991), pp. 363–86. Oddly, many American conservatives still admire de Gaulle, notwithstanding his pernicious impact on the NATO alliance and his propagation of the fallacy of moral equivalence between the U.S. and the U.S.S.R. For the best defense of this perspective, see Daniel J. Mahoney, *De Gaulle, Statesmanship, Grandeur, and Modern Democracy* (Westport, Conn.: Praeger, 1996).

68. Jean-Francois Revel, *How Democracies Perish* (New York: Doubleday, 1984), p. 260.

69. For a similar criticism of de Gaulle along these lines, see Raymond Aron, *Memoirs: Fifty Years of Political Reflection* (New York: Holmes and Meier, 1990), pp. 286–300, 347–48.

70. Jackson, "The Will to Stay the Course."

71. Jackson, "Floor Statement," U.S. Senate, Feb. 16, 1966, HMJ 3560–4/231/47.

72. U.S. Senate, *Hearings before the Combined Committees of Foreign Relations and the Armed Services Committee on the Subject of United States Troops in Europe*, 90th Cong., 1st sess., S. Res. 49 To Express the Sense of the Senate with Respect to Troop Deployment in Europe and Amendments Thereto S. Res. 83 Providing for Study and Reevaluation of United States-European Relations (Washington, D.C.: Government Printing Office, 1966), April 26 and May 3, 1967.

73. *CQA: 1967*, pp. 980–84.

74. Jackson, "The Will to Stay the Course."

75. Deborah Shapley, *Promise and Power* (Boston: Little, Brown, 1993), pp. 192–201.

76. Ibid., pp. 389–97.

77. Robert S. McNamara, "Remarks before United Press International Editors and Publishers," San Francisco, California, Sept. 18, 1967, Appendix 4 in Joint Committee on Atomic Energy, *Hearings before the Subcommittee on Military Applications on the Scope, Magnitude, and Implications of the United States Antiballistic Missile Program*, 90th Cong., 1st sess., Nov. 6–8, 1967 (Washington, D.C.: Government Printing Office, 1968), pp. 108–9 (hereafter cited as Joint Committee on Atomic Energy, *ABM Hearings*).

78. Quoted in *CQA: 1967*, p. 216.

79. Jackson, "The Duty of the Free and the Brave," U.S. Senate, March 10, 1966, HMJ 3560–4/231/32.

80. HMJ, "National Security: Basic Tasks," Hoover Institution, Palo Alto, California, Oct. 11, 1967.

81. Joint Committee on Atomic Energy, *ABM Hearings*.

82. Woods, *Fulbright*, pp. 519–25. For the extended debate, see *Congressional Record*, 90th Cong., 2d sess., June 19, June 21, June 24, 1968, vol. 114, pp. 17558–17767, 18208–26, 18379–85.

83. Interview with Helen Jackson.

84. Schmechel interview with Harry Metzger, Jan. 27, 1987.

85. Kaufman interviews with Grenville Garside, March 14, 1995, and Bill Van Ness, May 10, 1995.

86. Interview with Helen Jackson.

87. Interview with Metzger.

88. Interviews with Helen Jackson and Gerald Hoeck; Schmechel interview, with Stanley Golub, Feb. 18, 1987.

89. Interview with Stennis; Kaufman interviews with Julia Cancio and Erna Miller, June 18, 1996, and Russ Brown, Dec. 31, 1996.

10 *That Year: 1968*

1. Paul Berman, *A Tale of Two Utopias: The Political Journey of the Generation of 1968* (New York: Norton, 1996), p. 7.

2. For the classic statement of the gap between the actuality of Tet and how the American media portrayed it, see Peter Braestrup, *Big Story*, 2 vols. (Boulder: Westview Press, 1977; abridged ed., Yale University Press, 1983).

3. Herbert S. Parmet, *The Democrats* (New York: Macmillan, 1976), p. 250.

4. Michael Barone, *Our Country* (New York: Free Press, 1990), p. 434.

5. Ronald Radosh, *Divided They Fell: The Demise of the Democratic Party, 1964–1968* (New York: Free Press, 1996), pp. 75–86.

6. Barone, *Our Country*, p. 432.

7. Dan T. Carter, *The Politics of Rage* (New York: Simon and Schuster, 1995), pp. 324–70; Stephan Lesher, *George Wallace: American Populist* (Reading, Mass.: Addison-Wesley, 1994), pp. 387–428.

8. Robert Alan Goldberg, *Barry Goldwater* (New Haven: Yale University Press, 1995), pp. 246–47.

9. Stephen E. Ambrose, *Nixon: The Triumph of a Politician, 1962–1972* (New York: Simon and Schuster, 1989), pp. 118–47.

10. Mike Manatos to Lyndon B. Johnson, March 19, 1968, WHCF Name File: Henry M. Jackson, LBJL; Walter Isaacson and Evan Thomas, *The Wise Men* (New York: Simon and Schuster, 1986), p. 690.

11. Memorandum from Joseph Califano to LBJ, March 8, 1968, WHCF Name File: Henry M. Jackson, LBJL.

12. Arthur M. Schlesinger, Jr., *Robert Kennedy and His Times* (Boston: Houghton Mifflin, 1978), pp. 867–902.

13. Ibid. (seeks endorsement); Lyndon Johnson to Jackson, April 4, 1968, WHCF Name File: Henry M. Jackson, LBJL.

14. Helen Jackson to Lyndon Johnson, April 6, 1968, ibid.

15. Prochnau and Larsen, *A Certain Democrat*, p. 62.

16. Jackson, "We Must Dedicate Ourselves to Law and Justice," 1968, HMJ 3560-4/233/3.

17. Charles Kaiser, *1968 in America: Music, Politics, Chaos, Counterculture, and the Shaping of a Generation*

(New York: Weidenfeld and Nicolson, 1988), pp. 167–86.

18. Jackson, "We Must Dedicate Ourselves to Law and Justice."

19. Schmechel interview with Stanley Golub, Dec. 26, 1986.

20. Radosh, *Divided They Fell*, pp. 107–31.

21. Kaiser, *1968 in America*, pp. 238–41.

22. Theodore H. White, *The Making of the President, 1968* (New York: Atheneum, 1969), pp. 268–77.

23. Parmet, *The Democrats*, p. 280.

24. Quoted in Radosh, *Divided They Fell*, p. 136.

25. Ambrose, *Nixon: The Triumph of a Politician*, p. 183.

26. Jackson, "The Meaning of Czechoslovakia," Sept. 12, 1968, HMJ 3560–6/84.

27. Jackson to Edward Rowny, Aug. 29, 1968, HMJ 3560–4/4/14.

28. HMJ, "Sentinel Anti-Ballistic Missile System," U.S. Senate, Oct. 2, 1968, HMJ 3560–6/6/89.

29. Kevin P. Phillips, *The Emerging Republican Majority* (New Rochelle, N.Y.: Arlington House, 1969), pp. 27–42.

30. Ibid., p. 37.

31. Herbert S. Parmet, *Richard Nixon and His America* (Boston: Little, Brown, 1990), pp. 536–37.

32. Kaufman interview with Richard Allen, Oct. 24, 1996.

33. Kaufman interviews with Richard Nixon, June 13, 1993 (choice of state or defense); Helen Jackson, June 10, 1995 (formal offer); Gerald

Hoeck, April 2, 1995 (pros and cons); Dan Evans, Sept. 24, 1994 (Ehrlichman pressure); Tom Foley, March 14, 1995 (quid pro quo).

34. Kaufman interviews with Dorothy Fosdick, May 23, 1991, and Edward Kennedy, June 14, 1996; Christopher Matthews, *Kennedy and Nixon: The Rivalry that Shaped Postwar America* (New York: Simon and Schuster, 1996), p. 273.

35. Interview with Hoeck.

36. Parmet, *Richard Nixon and His America*, p. 537.

37. Kaufman interviews with Alexander Haig, Aug. 4, 1995; Peter Rodman, Aug. 5, 1995; and Helmut Sonnenfeldt, Aug. 3, 1995.

11 Jackson's Ascent, the Party's Descent

1. See Chapter 16 below. On the OPEC oil embargo, see Daniel Yergin, *The Prize: The Epic Quest for Oil, Money, and Power* (New York: Simon and Schuster, 1991), pp. 606–9.

2. Patrick Glynn, *Closing Pandora's Box: Arms Races, Arms Control, and the History of the Cold War* (New York: Basic Books, 1992), p. 264.

3. *Seattle Times*, March 16, 1969, p. 1.

4. HMJ 3560–4/266/8.

5. HMJ 3560–4/217/36.

6. Kaufman interview with Bill Van Ness, May 2, 1995.

7. Kaufman interview with Daniel Dreyfus, Dec. 31, 1996.

8. House Commitee on Science and Astronautics and the Senate

Committee on Interior Affairs, *Joint House-Senate Colloquium to Discuss a National Policy for the Environment* (Washington, D.C.: Government Printing Office, 1968).

9. Ross K. Baker, *Friend and Foe in the U.S. Senate* (New York: Free Press, 1980), pp. 219–20.

10. Interview with Dreyfus; Schmechel interview with Edmund Muskie, Feb. 25, 1988.

11. HMJ 3560–5/261/32/33; 3560–5/260/115–16.

12. John Nolan, Director of the Pace University School of Law Land Use Center, to Robin Pasquarella, Executive Director of the Henry M. Jackson Foundation, Jan. 3, 1995, Henry M. Jackson Foundation Papers, Seattle, Washington.

13. Kaufman interview with Ben Wattenberg, March 16, 1995.

14. Jackson, "American Federation of Labor–Congress of Industrial Organizations," Aug. 10, 1971, HMJ 3560–4/235/38.

15. Jackson, "Earth Day; Environmental Teach-in," University of Washington, Seattle, April 22, 1970.

16. Jackson, "The Environmental Responsibility of Business and Society," National Soft Drink Association, San Francisco, Nov. 18, 1969, HMJ 3560–4/233/23.

17. Reprinted in the *Congressional Record*, 91st Cong., 1st sess., Jan. 22, 1969, vol. 115, p. 1498.

18. *CQA: 1971*, pp. 129–40.

19. Jackson, "American Federation of Labor–Congress of Industrial Organizations."

20. Kaufman interview with T. A. Wilson, April 2, 1995.

21. Richard Reeves, "The Dawn of an Old Era: The Inevitability of Scoop Jackson," *New York Magazine*, Dec. 17, 1973, p. 53.

22. Kaufman interviews with Julia Cancio and Erna Miller, June 18, 1996.

23. Robert Scheer, "Why You Should Think About Scoop Again and Again and Again and Again," *Esquire*, Sept. 1975, p. 151.

24. Jackson, "Statement on the Alaska Pipeline," Nov. 12, 1973, HMJ 3560–4/260/51.

25. For the authoritative account on how the courts and the regulatory agencies interpreted the Environmental Impact Statement contrary to the way Jackson intended, see Daniel A. Dreyfus and Helen M. Ingram, "The National Environmental Policy Act: A View of Intent and Practice," *Natural Resources Journal: The University of New Mexico School of Law* (1978), pp. 243–62. Kaufman interviews with Bill Van Ness, May 5, 1995, and Dan Dreyfus, Dec. 31, 1996.

26. Kaufman interview with Gerald Hoeck, April 2, 1995.

27. Interview with Dreyfus.

28. Jackson, "Cambodia," May 1, 1970, HMJ 3560–6/7/72.

29. Jackson to Richard M. Nixon, Sept. 15, 1971, HMJ 3560–6/8/92.

30. Jackson, "America and the World," Commonwealth Club of California, San Francisco, March 5, 1971, HMJ 3560–4/235/37.

31. Jackson, "On U.S. Overseas

Troop Developments," U.S. Senate, June 7, 1974, HMJ 3560–6/10/141.

32. See, for example, *Congressional Record*, 91st Cong., 1st sess., vol. 115, pp. 19859–69, July 17, 1969; pp. 22841–43, Aug. 6, 1969.

33. Jackson, "Anti-Ballistic Missiles," U.S. Senate, July 17 and Aug. 6, 1969, HMJ 3560–6/7/26 and 29.

34. Jackson, "Anti-Ballistic Missiles," Aug. 5, 10, 11, 12, 13, and 19, HMJ 3560–6/7/85–90.

35. *Washington Post*, Aug. 12, 1970, p. 18 ("effective advocate"); July 18, 1970, p. 1 (secret session).

36. Kaufman interview with Paul Wolfowitz, Dec. 6, 1994.

37. Kaufman interview with Walter Mondale, Sept. 24, 1996.

38. *Congressional Record*, 91st Cong., 2d sess., vol. 116, pp. 27430–38, Aug. 5, 1970.

39. Kaufman interview with Richard Perle, Oct. 2, 1994.

40. *Albuquerque Journal*, Aug. 20, 1970, p. 1.

41. *Wall Street Journal*, Sept. 15, 1970, p. 1.

42. Kaufman interview with Shelby Scates, May 25, 1997.

43. Interview with Perle.

44. Kaufman interview with Howard Feldman, Dec. 18, 1996.

45. Schmechel interview with Cyrus Vance, Jan. 28, 1988 (controversial positions); Kaufman interview with Brian Corcoran, Sept. 6, 1994 (staff).

46. Kaufman interview with Grenville Garside, March 15, 1995.

47. Kaufman interview with Dorothy Fosdick, May 23, 1991.

48. *Wall Street Journal*, Sept. 15, 1970, p. 1.

49. Kaufman interview with Dan Evans, Sept. 26, 1994.

50. *Wall Street Journal*, Sept. 15, 1970.

51. Stephen E. Ambrose, *Nixon: The Triumph of a Politician* (New York: Simon and Schuster, 1989), pp. 458–59.

52. Michael Barone, *Our Country* (New York: Free Press, 1990), p. 492.

53. Ambrose, *Nixon: The Triumph of a Politician*, p. 474.

54. *Congressional Record*, 92d Cong., 1st sess., vol. 117, pp. 46141–42.

55. Jackson, "What it Means To Be a Liberal," University of Puget Sound, Tacoma, Washington, Aug. 14, 1970, HMJ 3560–4/235/37.

56. Kaufman interviews with Daniel Patrick Moynihan, July 28, 1996 (Viking warrior); Helen Jackson, June 10, 1995 (opposed abortion); "Civil Rights," San Diego Rotary Club, San Diego, California, May 20, 1971, HMJ 3560–4/235/47 (law and order).

57. CBS Television, *Sixty Minutes*, Nov. 14, 1971.

58. Jackson, "Statement at Washington, D.C. Press Conference re Constitutional Amendment on Busing," HMJ 3560–4/255/13; interview with Helen Jackson (neighborhood schools).

59. Jackson, "Perspectives on the American Revolution," Sons of the American Revolution; Washington Society, Washington, D.C., March 31, 1970, HMJ 3560–4/234/81.

60. Quoted in Laslo Pal's documentary, *Scoop* ("best generation"); Jackson, "Statement on Amnesty," Jan. 1972, HMJ 3560–4/195/14.

61. Kaufman interviews with Van Ness, May 2, 1995, and Helen Jackson.

62. "Resolution Passed by the Washington Democratic Council," Second Annual Meeting, HMJ 3560–12/30/27.

63. *Washington Post*, Dec. 28, 1969, p. B7.

64. Kaufman interview with Slade Gorton, Oct. 7, 1995.

65. Interview with Dan Evans.

66. Kaufman interview with Carl Maxey, April 26, 1995.

67. Ibid; *Seattle Post-Intelligencer*, April 2, 1970, p. 16 ("Napoleonic little senator").

68. *Seattle Post-Intelligencer*, May 10, 1970, p. 6.

69. Interview with Maxey.

70. Prochnau and Larsen, *A Certain Democrat*, pp. 316–17.

71. *Seattle Post-Intelligencer*, Aug. 13, 1970, p. 13; Carl Maxey, "Press Releases," Aug. 13 and Sept. 1, 1970, Carl Maxey Papers, Spokane, Washington.

72. Kitty Kelley to Carl Maxey, Aug. 5, 1970, Carl Maxey Papers.

73. McCarthy quoted in the *Seattle Post-Intelligencer*, Sept. 9, 1970, p. 1; Jackson in the *Washington Post*, Sept. 7, 1970, p. 1.

74. Interview with Hoeck.

75. *Seattle Post-Intelligencer*, Feb. 27, 1970, p. 1.

76. *Seattle Times*, Nov. 4, 1970, p. 1.

12 Gearing Up for the 1972 Presidential Campaign

1. *Washington Post*, Dec. 28, 1970, p. A19.

2. Jackson, "Democratic Women's Club of Florida," Miami, Oct. 9, 1971, HMJ 3560–4/235/51.

3. Jackson, "The Strategic Balance and the Nation's Safety," National War College, Washington, D.C., May 12, 1971, HMJ 3560–6/8/61.

4. *New York Times*, May 27, 1971, p. 19; *New York Post*, May 19, 1971, p. 13; *Seattle Post-Intelligencer*, May 27, 1971, p. 14.

5. Kaufman interview with Brian Corcoran, Sept. 6, 1994.

6. Richard A. Scammon and Ben J. Wattenberg, *The Real Majority* (New York: Coward-McCann, 1970).

7. Kaufman interview with Ben Wattenberg, March 16, 1995.

8. Ronald Radosh, *Divided They Fell* (New York: Free Press, 1996), p. 182.

9. *Washington Post*, Aug. 13, 1971, p. A11.

10. Kaufman interview with Daniel Patrick Moynihan, July 28, 1996.

11. *Portland Oregonian*, Oct. 11, 1971, p. 6.

12. Kaufman interview with Gerald Hoeck, April 2, 1995.

13. Kaufman interview with Robert Strauss, Oct. 26, 1996.

14. Interview with Hoeck.

15. Herbert S. Parmet, *The Democrats* (New York: Macmillan, 1976), pp. 285–305; Radosh, *Divided They Fell*, pp. 155–82.

16. Kaufman interviews with Brian Corcoran, Oct. 6, 1994, and Denny Miller, Oct. 2, 1994.

17. *Washington Post*, Aug. 5, 1971, p. A12; Richard Whalen, "Will The Real Majority Stand Up for Scoop Jackson?" *New York Times Magazine*, Oct. 3, 1971, p. 21.

18. *Oklahoma Journal*, June 5, 1971, p. 6; *Delta Democrat Times*, Dec. 21, 1971, p. 3.

19. *New York Times*, Feb. 2, 1972, p. 4.

20. Memorandum from Ben Wattenberg to Sterling Munro, HMJ 3560–12/36/24.

21. For the most vivid account, see Theodore H. White, *The Making of the President, 1972* (New York: Atheneum, 1973), pp. 70–133.

22. Jackson, "Announcement of Candidacy and Interview," Washington, D.C., Nov. 19, 1971, HMJ 3560–6/8/125.

23. Kaufman interviews with Tom Foley, March 14, 1995, and Ben Wattenberg, March 16, 1995.

24. White, *The Making of the President, 1972*, pp. 81–82.

25. Jackson, "Defense Campaign Speech," Pensacola, Florida, Jan. 27, 1972, HMJ 3560–5/9/54; "Busing Amendment," Feb. 14, 1972, HMJ 3560–6/9/64.

26. *Miami Herald*, March 19, 1971, p. 1.

27. Jackson to Hal Buell, Executive Newsphoto Editor, Associated Press, Feb. 14, 1972; Buell to Jackson, Feb. 24, 1972, HMJ 3560–12/32/19; *Los Angeles Times*, Feb. 10, 1972, p. 1.

28. See, for example, Anthony Lewis, "Senator Jackson's Strategy on Busing," in *New York Times*, March 13, 1972, p. 19; *Seattle Times*, March 17, 1972, p. 4.

29. Kaufman interview with Brewster Denny, May 2, 1995.

30. Quoted in Jackson's "Press Release," March 20, 1972, HMJ 3560–4/261/2.

31. *Sixty Minutes*, Nov. 14, 1971.

32. Ibid.

33. Daniel Yergin, "Scoop Jackson Goes for Broke," *Atlantic Monthly*, June 1974, p. 80.

34. *Milwakee Sentinel*, April 23, 1972, p. 1.

35. Richard Nixon to Jackson, April 5, 1972, President's Personal File, Subject: Henry M. Jackson, box 9, RMNPP.

36. "Citizens for Muskie Circular," HMJ 3560–12/38/27.

37. Quoted in the *Portland Oregonian*, Nov. 13, 1973, p. 1.

38. Quoted in the *Seattle Times*, Oct. 20, 1972, p. 1.

39. *Orlando Sentinel*, Aug. 15, 1971, p. 10A.

40. Interview with Foley.

41. Interview with Hoeck.

42. Michael Barone, *Our Country* (New York: Free Press, 1990), pp. 500–501.

43. White, *The Making of the President, 1972*, pp. 112–30.

44. Kaufman interview with Jason King, June 18, 1995.

45. Michael Barone, Grant Ujifusa, and Douglas Matthews, *The Almanac of American Politics: 1974* (Boston: Gambit, 1974), p. 1058.

46. Jackson, "McGovern Is Chief Travelling Salesman of the New Left Establishment," Columbus, Ohio, April 27, 1972, HMJ 3560–12/38/25.

47. George McGovern, *Grassroots: The Autobiography of George McGovern* (New York: Random House, 1977), pp. 40–41.

48. Ibid., p. 45.

49. Quoted in the *Washington Daily News*, April 27, 1972, p. 3.

50. Quoted in *Playboy*, July 1971, p. 54.

51. George McGovern, "Toward a More Secure America—An Alternative National Defense Posture," Jan. 19, 1972, HMJ 3560–12/38/21 (military cutbacks); "Cold War paranoia" quoted from George S. McGovern's mass-mailing fund appeal letter, 1971, no specific date, HMJ 3560–12/38/21.

52. White, *The Making of the President, 1972*, pp. 27–33.

53. Radosh, *Divided They Fell*, pp. 179–82.

54. McGovern, *Grassroots*, pp. 272–73.

55. Radosh, *Divided They Fell*, pp. 172–75.

56. Kaufman interview with Richard Perle, Oct. 2, 1994.

57. Schmechel interview with George McGovern, Sept. 30, 1987.

58. Kaufman interviews with Max Kampelman, Oct. 4, 1994, and Brian Corcoran, Sept. 6, 1994.

59. Interview with Strauss.

60. Quoted in the *Bremerton Sun*, Oct. 21, 1972, p. 1.

61. Parmet, *The Democrats*, pp. 304–8.

62. Interview with Strauss.

63. Schmechel interview with Sterling Munro, Jan. 19, 1987.

64. Kaufman interview with Robert Keefe, Aug. 6, 1994.

65. Schmechel interview with Alexander Barkan, Oct. 23, 1987.

66. *Baltimore News American*, Dec. 20, 1972, pp. A1, A5.

67. Interview with Wattenberg.

68. Jackson, "Father of the Year," 1971, HMJ 3560–4/260/231.

13 Perils of Detente, Part I

1. Kaufman interviews with Elmo Zumwalt, Dec. 3, 1994, and Kinnaird McKee, March 16, 1995; Jackson, "The Trident Program," U.S. Senate, Sept. 26, 1973, HMJ 3560–6/10/72; Memorandum, "Lines of Argument Against the McIntyre Amendment to Delay the Trident Program," HMJ 3560–6/50/27.

2. Henry A. Kissinger, *Diplomacy* (New York: Simon and Schuster, 1994), p. 747 (on Jackson); Eugene Rostow to Jackson, May 8, 1974, HMJ 3560–6/76/18; Jackson, "To the Pilgrims of Great Britain," London, Nov. 11, 1974, HMJ 3560–6/11/37 (on Jackson and Churchill). For a scathing criticism of the Cold War mentality, see Walter Isaacson, *Kissinger* (New York: Simon and Schuster, 1992), pp. 607–21.

3. Kissinger, *Years of Renewal* (New York: Simon and Schuster, 1999), pp.

92–135. Kissinger, *Years of Upheaval* (Boston: Little, Brown, 1982), pp. 980–95; Kissinger, *Diplomacy*, pp. 751–54; Richard M. Nixon, *Memoirs* (New York: Touchstone, 1990); Kaufman interview with Richard Nixon, June 11, 1993; John Lewis Gaddis, *Strategies of Containment* (New York: Oxford University Press, 1982), pp. 274–344; Stephen E. Ambrose, *Nixon: The Triumph of a Politician, 1962–1972* (New York: Simon and Schuster, 1989), pp. 439–67, 553–62; Robert D. Schultzinger, *Henry Kissinger: Doctor of Diplomacy* (New York: Columbia University Press, 1989). See, contra, William Bundy, *A Tangled Web* (New York: Hill and Wang, 1998), for an argument that Nixon and Kissinger remained too wedded to an ideological conception of the Cold War. My own research and personal experience with President Nixon had led me, however, to the opposite conclusion.

4. Gaddis, *Strategies*, pp. 294–304; Kissinger, *Diplomacy*, pp. 703–32.

5. Kissinger, *White House Years* (Boston: Little, Brown, 1979), pp. 7–309 (on China), quotations on pp. 162, 193.

6. Ibid., pp. 223–25; Gaddis, *Strategies*, pp. 298–99, 304–6.

7. Gaddis, *Strategies*, pp. 299–304; Dennis L. Bark and David R. Gress, *A History of West Germany*, vol. 2: *Democracy and Its Discontents, 1963–1988* (New York: Blackwell, 1989), pp. 158–72.

8. Kissinger, *White House Years*, pp. 820–21.

9. Kissinger, *Diplomacy*, pp. 733–61; interview with Nixon.

10. Isaacson, *Kissinger*, pp. 399–604; Seymour M. Hersh, *The Price of Power: Kissinger in the Nixon White House* (New York: Summit, 1983); William Shawcross *Sideshow* (New York: Simon and Schuster, 1979); Raymond L. Garthoff, *Detente and Confrontation* (Washington, D.C.: Brookings, 1985), pp. 325–485.

11. Jackson, "Detente and Human Rights," Yeshiva University, New York, June 4, 1973, HMJ 3560–6/10/31; "Detente: Some Reassessment," U.S. Senate, July 23, 1973, HMJ 3560–6/20/58; "Detente and SALT," Overseas Press Club, New York, April 22, 1974, HMJ 3560–6/10/122; and "Detente," July 1974, HMJ 3560–6/11/2. Kaufman interviews with Richard Perle, Oct. 3, 1994, Jan. 6, 1995, Jan. 2, 1996. Quotation from *The National Observer*, Nov. 10, 1973, p. 3.

12. Interview with Perle, Oct. 3, 1994.

13. Kaufman interviews with Norman Podhoretz and Midge Decter, Sept. 18, 1995; and Perle, Jan. 2, 1996.

14. Jackson quoted in *The National Observer*, Nov. 10, 1973; "Trade and Detente," Harvard University Business School, June 1, 1974, HMJ 3560–6/10/138.

15. Jackson, "Statement Opening Subcommittee's Hearings into the Sale of Grain to the Soviet Union," Oct. 8, 1974, HMJ 3560–6/17/20.

16. Senate Committee on Govern-

ment Operations, Permanent Subcommittee on Investigations, 93d Cong., 2d sess., *Sales of Grain to the Soviet Union* (Washington, D.C.: Government Printing Office, 1974); Jackson, "On Technology Transfer," U.S. Senate, June 7, 1974, HMJ 3560–6/10/142, and "On Technology Transfer to Eastern Bloc Countries," U.S. Senate, June 11, 1974, HMJ 3560–6/10/145.

17. Kaufman interview with Richard Nixon, Oct. 10, 1992.

18. Kissinger, *Diplomacy*, pp. 751–54.

19. Despite the many virtues of his analysis, Walter McDougall's stimulating conceptualization of American foreign policy fails to capture the compelling synthesis of realism and idealism that Truman, Reagan, and Henry Jackson personified: Walter A. McDougall, *Promised Land, Crusader State* (Boston: Houghton Mifflin, 1997); Jeane J. Kirkpatrick, *Dictatorships and Double Standards* (New York: Simon and Schuster, 1982), pp. 23–138; Kaufman interview with Jeane Kirkpatrick, Dec. 28, 1996; Peter W. Rodman, *More Precious than Peace* (New York: Scribner's, 1994), pp. 411–32 (Reagan).

20. Kaufman interviews with Richard Nixon, June 11, 1993; Alexander Haig, July 30, 1995; and Peter Rodman, July 30, 1995.

21. Elmo R. Zumwalt, *On Watch: A Memoir* (New York: Quadrangle, 1976), p. 319; Kaufman interview with Zumwalt, Dec. 8, 1974.

22. Kaufman interviews with Helmut Sonnenfeldt, July 29, 1995, and Peter Rodman, July 30, 1995.

23. Kaufman interviews with Richard Nixon, June 10, and July 8, 1993.

24. Kaufman interviews with Perle, Jan. 2, 1996, and Ben Wattenberg, March 18, 1995.

25. John Newhouse, *Cold Dawn* (New York: Holt, Rinehart and Winston, 1973), pp. 273–81.

26. Kissinger, *White House Years*, pp. 1246–57.

27. Ambrose, *Nixon: Triumph of a Politician*, pp. 548, 544 (quotations). For a representative sample of reactions, see HMJ 3560–6/49/16–19. On Kissinger's philosophy of détente, see Kissinger, *Diplomacy*, pp. 733–61, and *Years of Renewal*, pp. 92–135.

28. Jackson, "SALT Agreements," May 26, 1972, HMJ 3560–6/9/93.

29. Jackson on *Firing Line*, July 9, 1972.

30. Jackson, "SALT Accords," June 8, 1972, HMJ 3560–6/9/99, and "U.S. Senate and the Interim Agreement," U.S. Senate, Aug. 11, 1972, HMJ 3560–6/9/129.

31. Zumwalt, *On Watch*, p. 409.

32. Interview with Perle, Oct. 3, 1994.

33. Interview with Zumwalt, Dec. 6, 1994.

34. Interview with Perle, Jan. 2, 1996.

35. Jackson, "S.J.R. 241," U.S. Senate, Aug. 3, 1972, HMJ 3560–6/9/123.

36. Interview with Perle, Oct. 3, 1994.

37. Dorothy Fosdick, ed., "Legisla-

tive History of the Jackson Amendment, 1972 (Including the Full Record of the Congressional Debate on the ABM Treaty and the Resolution Authorizing Approval of the Interim Agreement on Offensive Weapons—August 3, 1972 through September 25, 1972)," pp. 1–239, HMJ 3560–28.

38. Interview with Perle, Oct. 3, 1994; Jackson, "For a Stable Strategic Balance (SALT)," U.S. Senate, Sept. 6, 1972, HMJ 3560–6/9/132.

39. Gerard Smith, *Doubletalk: The Story of the First Strategic Arms Limitations Talks* (New York: Doubleday, 1980), pp. 442–43; Kaufman interview with Edward Rowny, March 15, 1995.

40. Bill Bradley, *Time Present, Time Past: A Memoir* (New York: Knopf, 1996), pp. 69–70.

41. Jackson to Gerald Ford, Nov. 30, 1974, White House Subject File PR 16–1, box 149, GRFL.

42. Kaufman interviews with Stewart Udall, Feb. 14, 1995; John Danforth, April 30, 1995; Howard Baker, May 15, 1995; and Daniel Patrick Moynihan, July 28, 1995.

43. Kaufman interviews with Perle, Oct. 3, 1994; Michel Oksenberg, Nov. 17, 1994; Charles Horner, Dec. 6, 1994; Dwight Perkins, Sept. 25, 1995; Richard Pipes, Sept. 25, 1995; and Bernard Lewis, Nov. 4, 1995.

14 Israel and the Cold War

1. Jackson, "Israel's Own Security and Our Own," U.S. Senate, March 23, 1971, HMJ 3560–6/8/43.

2. Robert D. Kaplan, *The Arabists* (New York: Free Press, 1993), pp. 85–99.

3. Stephen Ambrose, *Eisenhower* (New York: Simon and Schuster, 1984), 2:356–70.

4. Peter W. Rodman, *More Precious than Peace* (New York: Scribner's, 1994), pp. 482–85; Nadav Safran, *Israel: The Embattled Ally* (Cambridge, Mass.: Belknap Press, 1978), pp. 417–19.

5. John B. Judis, *William F. Buckley, Jr.: Patron Saint of the Conservatives* (New York: Simon and Schuster, 1988), pp. 458–60.

6. Rodman, *More Precious than Peace*, pp. 486–94.

7. Kaplan, *The Arabists*, pp. 150–53, 167–72.

8. Kaufman interview with Peter Rodman, July 30, 1995.

9. Memorandum, Richard Perle to Jackson, Nov. 1974, HMJ 3560–6/1/1.

10. Jackson, "News Conference," American Embassy, Tel Aviv, Nov. 12, 1970, HMJ 3560–6/8/7, and "Israel and the Middle East," New York, April 28, 1971, HMJ 3560–6/8/54.

11. *Congressional Record*, 91st Cong., 2d sess., Sept. 1, 1970, vol. 116, pp. 14881–89; "Record of the Debate on the Jackson Amendment, 1971 to Appropriate $500 Million in Credits for Israel," U.S. Senate, Nov. 23, 1971, HMJ 3560–6/8/27.

12. Randall Bennett Woods, *Fulbright* (New York: Cambridge University Press, 1995), pp. 641–45.

13. Quoted in the *New York Times*, Feb. 8, 1971, p. 4.

14. Jackson, "Memorandum of a Conversation with Soviet Ambassador Dobrynin," Jan. 14, 1973, HMJ 3560–6/1/14.

15. Yitzhak Rabin, *The Rabin Memoirs* (Berkeley: University of California Press, 1996), p. 231.

16. Rabin, "Address in Honor of Henry M. Jackson," *Proceedings of the International Commemorative Conference on the Occasion of the Twentieth Anniversary of the Jackson-Vanik Amendment,* Jerusalem, Israel, Jan. 8–10, 1995.

17. Kaufman interview with Richard Perle, Jan. 6, 1995.

18. Kaufman interview with Richard Perle, Oct. 3, 1994.

19. Jackson, "Trade and Freedom (East-West Trade)," U.S. Senate, Oct. 4, 1972, HMJ 3560–6/9/146. The cosponsor of the amendment was Congressman Charles A. Vanik, Democrat from Ohio.

20. Kaufman interviews with Richard Nixon, Oct. 26, 1992, and Perle, Oct. 3, 1994.

21. Henry A. Kissinger, *Years of Upheaval* (Boston: Little, Brown, 1982), pp. 984–86.

22. See, for example, Alexander Solzhenitsyn to Jackson, July 7, 1974, HMJ 3560–6/1/36.

23. John Newhouse, *War and Peace in the Nuclear Age* (New York: Knopf, 1989), p. 236.

24. Jackson, "Jackson Amendment on Freedom of Immigration," U.S. Senate, March 29, 1973, HMJ 3560–5/10/11.

25. John Ehrlichman, "Notes of a Meeting with the President," April 18, 1973, box 14, folder 6, RMNPP.

26. Kaufman interview with Manny Weiss, Jan. 9, 1995; J. J. Goldberg, *Jewish Power: Inside the American Jewish Establishment* (Reading: Addison-Wesley, 1996), pp. 169–70.

27. Interview with Nixon, Oct. 26, 1992; Woods, *Fulbright*, pp. 641–45.

28. Kaufman interview with Natan Sharansky, Jan. 5, 1995.

29. Kaufman interview with Izo Rager, Jan. 7, 1995.

30. Rabin, *Memoirs*, pp. 230–33.

31. Paula Stern, *Water's Edge: Domestic Politics and the Making of American Foreign Policy* (Westport: Greenwood Press, 1979), pp. 30–33.

32. Thomas M. Franck and Edward Weisband, *Foreign Policy by Congress* (New York: Oxford University Press, 1979), pp. 186–89.

33. Kaufman interviews with Richard Perle, Jan. 2, 1996, and Manny Weiss, Jan. 9, 1995.

34. Stern, *Water's Edge*, pp. 85–89.

35. Robert Conquest to Jackson, June 4, 1973, HMJ 3560/6/40/18; Byrnes to Jackson, June 21, 1973; Schapiro to Jackson, June 6, 1974; Ulam to Jackson, June 11, 1973; Ra'anan to Jackson, June 5, 1973; Labetz to Jackson, June 6, 1973, HMJ 3560–6/40/18.

36. Kaufman interview with Richard Pipes, Sept. 26, 1995; Hans Morgenthau to Jackson, June 18, 1973, HMJ 3560–6/40/18; Goodman to Jackson, June 5, 1973; Armstrong to Jackson, June 9, 1973; Goure to Jackson, June 19, 1973, HMJ 3560–6/40/18; David Mayers, *George Kennan and*

the Dilemmas of U.S. Foreign Policy (New York: Oxford University Press, 1988), pp. 297–98.

37. Interview with Perle, Jan. 2, 1996.

38. Sakharov Open Letter, Sept. 14, 1973, HMJ 3560–6/10/63.

39. Kissinger, *Years of Upheaval*, p. 991.

40. Interview with Rodman.

41. Interview with Perle, Jan. 2, 1996.

42. Kaufman interview with Alexander Haig, Aug. 2, 1994.

43. Kaufman interview with James Schlesinger, Oct. 26, 1994.

44. Ibid.

45. Conor Cruise O'Brien, *The Siege: The Saga of Israel and Zionism* (New York: Simon and Schuster, 1986), pp. 521–23.

46. Safran, *Israel: The Embattled Ally*, pp. 480–81.

47. Interview with Schlesinger.

48. Safran, *Israel: The Embattled Ally*, pp. 480–81.

49. Interview with Perle, Oct. 3, 1994.

50. Elmo Zumwalt, *On Watch* (New York: Quadrangle, 1976), p. 435.

51. Interview with Haig.

52. Interview with Perle, Oct. 3, 1994; Jackson, "Military Aid to Israel," Oct. 18, 1973, HMJ 3560–6/10/83.

53. Kaufman interviews with James Schlesinger, Oct. 26, 1994, and Elmo Zumwalt, Dec. 6, 1994.

54. Interview with Rodman.

55. Safran, *Israel: The Embattled Ally*, p. 495.

56. Kaufman interview with Paul Wolfowitz, Dec. 9, 1994.

57. Jackson, "Middle East Peace," American Jewish Committee, Washington, D.C., Dec. 17, 1973, HMJ 356–6/10/92.

58. Jackson quoted in the *Seattle Post-Intelligencer*, June 2, 1974, p. 3; interview with Haig.

59. Jackson, "East-West Realities," March 1974, HMJ 3560–6/10/119.

60. Richard M. Nixon, "Attack on the Jackson Amendment," Annapolis, Maryland, June 5, 1974, HMJ 3560–6/10/140; Jackson on *Face the Nation*, June 9, 1974; Kaufman interview with Charles Horner, Dec. 6, 1994.

61. Jackson to Nixon, Jan. 29, 1974, HMJ 3560–6/57/7; Nixon to Jackson, March 8, 1974, HMJ 3560–6/57/7; Elmo R. Zumwalt, *On Watch* (New York: Quadrangle, 1976), pp. 504–5.

62. Kissinger, *Years of Upheaval*, pp. 992–97.

63. Richard Perle to Jackson, "Memorandum of Meeting with Dr. Kissinger," March 6, 1974; "memorandum of a Meeting with Dr. Kissinger," March 15, 1974, HMJ 3560–6/39/27.

64. Richard Perle to Jackson, "Memorandum of Meeting with President Ford," Sept. 20, 1974, ibid.

65. Raymond L. Garthoff, *Detente and Confrontation* (Washington, D.C.: Brookings, 1985), p. 454.

66. Kissinger, *Years of Upheaval*, p. 994.

67. Stern, *Water's Edge*, pp. 122–29.

68. President Ford, "Meeting with

Senator Henry Jackson," Oct. 11, 1994, Henry Kissinger and Brent Scowcroft Files, box 32, GRFL; Kaufman interview with Gerald Ford, Sept. 30, 1994; Kissinger, *Years of Renewal* (New York: Simon and Schuster, 1999), pp. 243–60.

69. "Jackson-Vanik Amendment and an Exchange of Letters between Jackson and Kissinger," Oct. 18, 1994, HMJ 3560–6/11/32; Stevenson quoted in Kissinger, *Years of Upheaval*, p. 997.

70. Gromyko to Kissinger, Oct. 26, 1974, HMJ 3560–6/40/1; Kissinger, "Testimony Before the Senate Finance Committee Concerning the Trade Act of 1974," Dec. 3, 1974, HMJ 3560–6/40/1.

71. Anatoly Dobryin, *In Confidence* (New York: Times Books, 1995), p. 337; interview with Ford.

72. Kissinger, Press Conference, Jan. 14, 1975, HMJ 3560–6/23/5; Woods, *Fulbright*, pp. 644–45; *Chicago Tribune*, Dec. 22, 1974, Sec. 2, p. 4; *Arizona Republic*, Dec. 26, 1974, p. 9; *Des Moines Register*, Jan. 19, 1975, p. 7.

73. Jackson, Press Conference, Jan. 15, 1975, HMJ 3560/6/40/2.

74. Perle to Jackson, "Memorandum," May 26, 1975, HMJ 3560–6/40/1.

75. William G. Hyland, *Mortal Rivals: Superpower Relations from Nixon to Reagan* (New York: Random House, 1987), pp. 108–9.

76. *Proceedings of the International Commemorative Conference on the Occasion of the Twentieth Anniversary of the Jackson-Vanik Amendment*, Jerusalem, Jan. 8–10, 1995.

77. Hyland, *Mortal Rivals*, p. 109.

78. Kaufman interviews with Richard Perle, Jan. 5, 1995; Charles Horner, Dec. 8, 1994; and Elliott Abrams, Dec. 8, 1994.

79. Interview with Pipes.

80. Dobrynin, *In Confidence*, p. 268.

81. For a sample of these efforts, see HMJ 3560–6/39/27 to 40/7.

82. Natan Sharansky, *The Henry M. Jackson Memorial Lecture*, Washington, D.C., Nov. 19, 1987.

83. Kaufman interview with Daniel Patrick Moynihan, July 28, 1996.

84. Henry A. Kissinger, *Diplomacy* (New York: Simon and Schuster, 1994), p. 753.

85. Dobrynin, *In Confidence*, pp. 334, 267.

86. Jackson, "Relations with the People's Republic of China," 1969–1973, HMJ 3560–6/10/100.

87. Robert S. Ross, *Negotiating Cooperation: The United States and China, 1969–1989* (Stanford: Stanford University Press, 1995), p. 70.

88. Jackson, "Transcripts of Meetings with Chinese Officials including Deng Xioping and Chou En Lai," July 2–5 1977, HMJ 3560–28/3/1.

89. Jackson, "On Closer Ties With China," *Los Angeles Times*, July 12, 1970, Part II, p. 7.

90. Kissinger, *Diplomacy*, pp. 733–62.

91. Kaufman interviews with Perle, Jan. 2, 1996, and Horner, Dec. 6, 1994.

92. Kaufman interviews with Norman Podhoretz and Midge Decter, Sept. 19, 1995.

93. Quoted in James Mann, *About Face: A History of America's Curious Relationship with China, from Nixon to Clinton* (New York: Knopf, 1999), p. 75.

94. Kaufman interview with George Weigel, Aug. 2, 1995.

95. Anna Marie Jackson interview with Henry Jackson, May 1980.

96. Kaufman interview with Gerald Hoeck, April 2, 1995. For an excellent analysis of how a generation of Sinologists and otherwise hard-headed statesmen romanticized Mao and his Communist regime, see Ross Terrill, "Mao in History," *The National Interest*, 1998, pp. 54–63.

15 The Ford Administration

1. Kaufman interview with Gerald Ford, Sept. 30, 1994.

2. Kaufman interview with Richard Perle, Oct. 3, 1994.

3. Gerald R. Ford, *A Time to Heal* (New York: Harper and Row, 1979), pp. 138–39, 321.

4. John Robert Greene, *The Presidency of Gerald R. Ford* (Lawrence: University of Kansas Press, 1995), pp. 120–24; interview with Ford.

5. William G. Hyland, *Moral Rivals* (New York: Random House, 1987), pp. 88–97.

6. Jackson, "On the Vladivostok Strategic Arms Agreement," Dec. 1974, HMJ 3560–6/11/50.

7. Senate Committee on Armed Services, Subcommittee on Arms Control, 94th Cong., 1st sess., March 6, 1975, *Soviet Compliance with Certain Provision of the 1972 SALT I Agreements* (Washington, D.C.: Government Printing Office, 1975), pp. 1–22.

8. Jackson, "SALT Debate," Dec. 28, 1975, HMJ 3560–6/11/170.

9. Ford, *A Time to Heal*, pp. 323–24.

10. Jackson, "The Schlesinger Firing," Nov. 3, 1975, HMJ 3560–6/11/144.

11. Senate Committee on Armed Services, 94th Cong., 1st sess., Nov. 12–13, 1975, *Nomination of Donald Rumsfeld to be Secretary of Defense* (Washington, D.C.: Government Printing Office, 1975), pp. 42–43.

12. Kaufman interview with Paul Wolfowitz, Dec. 9, 1994.

13. Jackson, "Vietnam Supplemental Aid Appropriation," Los Angeles, Jan. 26, 1975, HMJ 3560–6/11/56.

14. *Tacoma News Tribune*, Feb. 6, 1995, p. 8; interview with Wolfowitz.

15. Kaufman interviews with Richard Perle, Oct. 3, 1994, and Elliott Abrams, Dec. 6, 1994.

16. Jackson, "Secret Vietnam Agreements," U.S. Senate, April 8, 1996, HMJ 3560–6/11/72.

17. *Washington Post*, May 2, 1975, p. A4.

18. *Baltimore Sun*, April 10, 1975, p. A5.

19. Jackson, "The Need for Full Disclosure of Vietnam Documents,"

U.S. Senate, May 1, 1975, HMJ 3560–6/11/84.

20. Michael Scammell, *Solzhenitsyn* (New York: Norton, 1984), pp. 916–17.

21. *Los Angeles Times*, Part I, p. 8, July 17, 1975; Kaufman interviews with Helmut Sonnenfeldt, July 29, 1995, and Peter Rodman, July 30, 1995. The record and Kissinger's own aides refute his revisionist account of the Helsinki Conference, in which he claims that he not only comprehended Soviet vulnerabilities but pressed human rights concerns at Helsinki to exploit them. See Kissinger, *Years of Renewal* (New York: Simon and Schuster, 1999), pp. 635–63.

22. "Memorandum for Lieutenant Brent Scowcroft," June 26, 1975, HMJ 3560–6/38/1.

23. Interview with Rodman; Kissinger quoted in the *Los Angeles Times*, July 17, 1975, p. 7; Ford, *A Time to Heal*, p. 298 (Helsinki Summit).

24. Jackson, "Re: Kissinger's attack on Solzhenitsyn," July 17, 1995, HMJ 3560–6/11/112.

25. Jackson, "Solzhenitsyn Reception Invitation," July 10, 1995, HMJ 3560–6/11/109.

26. Alexander Solzhenitsyn, "Remarks at U.S. Congress Reception," U.S. Senate, July 16, 1975, HMJ 3560–6/11/109.

27. Ford, *A Time to Heal*, p. 299.

28. For the best account of Ostpolitik, see Timothy Garton Ash, *In Europe's Name: Germany and the Divided Continent* (New York: Random House, 1993), pp. 48–215.

29. Ford, *A Time to Heal*, p. 299.

30. Scammell, *Solzhenitsyn*, pp. 919–21.

31. Jackson, "Helsinki Summit," July 22, 1975, HMJ 3560–6/11/115.

32. Anatoly Dobrynin, *In Confidence* (New York: Times Books, 1995), p. 345–47; Ash, *In Europe's Name*, pp. 259–60.

33. William Korey, *The Promises We Keep: Human Rights, the Helsinki Process, and American Foreign Policy* (New York: St. Martin's Press, 1993).

34. Sharansky, *The Henry M. Jackson Memorial Lecture*, Washington, D.C., Nov. 19, 1987.

35. Richard Gid Powers, *Not without Honor* (New York: Free Press, 1995), pp. 340–43.

36. Kaufman interview with Daniel Patrick Moynihan, July 28, 1996.

37. Daniel Patrick Moynihan, *A Dangerous Place* (Boston: Little, Brown, 1978).

38. Kaufman interviews with Moynihan, July 28, 1996, and Irving Kristol, Aug. 2, 1995.

39. Kaufman interview with Norman Podhortez, Sept. 19, 1995.

40. Kaufman interview with Richard Perle, Jan. 2, 1996.

41. Paul H. Nitze, *From Hiroshima to Glasnost* (New York: Grove Weidenfeld, 1989), pp. 350–53.

42. George Bush to Jackson, Dec. 3, 1976, HMJ 3560–28/1/2.

43. Kaufman interview with Eugene Rostow, March 18, 1995; Nitze, *From Hiroshima to Glasnost*, pp. 353–54.

44. "How the Committee on The Present Danger Will Operate," in

Charles Tyroler and Max M. Kampelman, eds., *Alerting America: The Papers of the Committee on The Present Danger* (New York: Pergamon-Brassey's, 1984), pp. ix–xi.

45. William J. Fulbright, *The Price of Empire* (New York: Pantheon Books, 1989), p. 31.

46. Henry A. Kissinger, *Diplomacy* (New York: Simon and Schuster, 1994), p. 755.

47. Adam B. Ulam, *Dangerous Relations: The Soviet Union in World Politics, 1970–1982* (New York: Oxford University Press, 1983), pp. 83–144.

48. Kissinger, *Diplomacy*, p. 756. For Kissinger's most recent swipe at Jackson and neoconservatives, see his "Between the Old Left and the New Right," *Foreign Affairs*, May/June 1999, pp. 99–116.

49. Randall Bennett Woods, *Fulbright* (New York: Cambridge University Press, 1995), pp. 651, 669. Woods is right that the Jackson office celebrated Fulbright's defeat, but wrong about the specifics of the celebration. The Jackson office never would have broken out a case of whiskey as Woods claims. Kaufman interview with Richard Perle, Jan. 2, 1996.

50. Quoted in Martin Malia, *The Soviet Tragedy* (New York: Free Press, 1994), p. 376.

51. Ibid., pp. 377–78.

52. *Messengers from Moscow*, Part 4; Kaufman interview with Richard Pipes, Sept. 26, 1995.

53. Kaufman interview with Richard Perle, Jan. 5, 1995.

54. Henry A. Kissinger, *Years of Upheaval* (Boston: Little, Brown, 1982), pp. 984–85.

16 Not in the Cards: The 1976 Presidential Campaign

1. Jackson, "Presidential Candidacy," Feb. 7, 1975, HMJ 3560–5/261/61.

2. Kaufman interviews with Helen Jackson, June 10, 1995, and Haakon Ragde, April 15, 1995.

3. *Seattle Post-Intelligencer*, Nov. 6, 1973, pp. A1, A15 ("most effective senator"); Gallup and Harris Polls, 1975, HMJ 3560–12/43/14–15; Kaufman interview with Gerald Ford, Oct. 30, 1994 (on Jackson as opponent); *New York Times*, Nov. 24, 1975, p. 1 (dead heat); *Time*, Feb. 17, 1975 (cover); "The Year of Scoop Jackson," *Newsweek*, Jan. 7, 1974; R. J. Apple, Jr., "Puritan for President," *New York Times Magazine*, Nov. 23, 1975; Richard Reeves, "The Dawn of an Old Era: The Inevitability of Scoop Jackson," *New York Magazine*, Dec. 17, 1973; Daniel Yergin, "Scoop Jackson Goes for Broke," *Atlantic Monthly*, June 1974; Gwen Dobson, "The Big Scoop Around Washington," *Saturday Evening Post*, Aug./Sept. 1974; Stanley Karnow, "Jackson's Bid," *New Republic*, May 25, 1974; and Robert Scheer, "Why You Should Think About Scoop Again and Again and Again and Again," *Esquire*, Sept. 1975.

4. Jules Witcover, *Marathon: The Pursuit of the Presidency, 1972–1976* (New York: Viking, 1977), pp. 138–55.

5. Betty Glad, *Jimmy Carter, in*

Search of the Great White House (New York: Norton, 1980), pp. 216–21.

6. Jackson, "Presidential Campaign," Dec. 4, 1975, HMJ 3560–5/262/94.

7. Kaufman interviews with Robert Strauss, Oct. 26, 1995, and Robert Keefe, July 30, 1995.

8. "Financial Records and Fundraising, 1976 Presidential Campaign," HMJ 3560–12/43/21–23.

9. Jackson, "Vietnam Supplemental Appropriation," Jan. 26, 1975, HMJ 3560–6/11/56.

10. Jackson, "B-1 Bomber," Feb. 1, 1976, HMJ 3560–6/34/9, and "Defense Budget," Jan. 20, 1976, HMJ 3560–6/11/179; *Boston Globe*, Oct. 6, 1974, p. 26 (antiwar Democrats); Jackson, "Nixon Pardon," Sept. 10, 1974, HMJ 3560–5/261/5, and "Consumer Oil Prices," Jan. 28, 1975, HMJ 3560–5/261/56.

11. Jackson, "Oil and Energy Policy," HMJ 3560–5/261/50–51, 53, 107–8, 130–31, 135, and 262/241–50.

12. Paul Johnson, *Modern Times* (New York: Harper and Row, 1983), p. 669; Jackson to Richard Nixon, June 13, 1972, HMJ 3560–6/1/43.

13. Daniel Yergin, *The Prize* (New York: Simon and Schuster, 1991), p. 660; Jackson, "Energy Policy Legislation," Oct. 2, 1975, HMJ 3560–5/261/16.

14. Kaufman interviews with Richard Perle, Oct. 3, 1994, and Bill Van Ness, May 10, 1995; HMJ, "Energy," June 9, 1974, HMJ 3560–5/260/113.

15. Yergin, *The Prize*, p. 657.

16. Kaufman interviews with Robert Strauss, Oct. 30, 1995, and Charles Luce, Sept. 19, 1995.

17. Kaufman interviews with George Will, Dec. 6, 1994, and Norman Podhoretz, Sept. 19, 1995.

18. Kaufman interview with Sam Nunn, March 16, 1995; *Pasco* [Washington] *Tri-City Herald*, Feb. 18, 1976, p. 4.

19. Interview with Strauss, Oct. 30, 1995.

20. Yergin, *The Prize*, pp. 657–710; Jackson, "Oil Price Controls," HMJ 3560–5/262/58–62.

21. Kaufman interviews with Perle, Oct. 3, 1994, and Barry Dunsmore, Oct. 13, 1995.

22. Jeffrey K. Tulis, *The Rhetorical Presidency* (Princeton: Princeton University Press, 1987).

23. Jackson quoted in the *Seattle Times*, Oct. 12, 1975, p. A4; Kaufman interview with Gerald Hoeck, April 2, 1995.

24. Kaufman interview with Richard Pipes, Sept. 26, 1995.

25. Kaufman interview with Ben Wattenberg, March 18, 1995; James Schlesinger, "Uncharted Waters: America's Role in a Post–Cold War World," *Henry M. Jackson Memorial Lecture*, University of Washington, Seattle, Nov. 14, 1994.

26. Kaufman interviews with Elliott Abrams, Dec. 6, 1994; Julia Cancio, June 18, 1996; and Peter Jackson, Jan. 13, 1996.

27. Kaufman interviews with Peter Rosenblatt, Sept. 18, 1997, and Midge Decter, Sept. 19, 1994.

28. Michael Barone, *Our Country* (New York: Free Press, 1990), p. 538.

29. Quoted in the *Seattle Post-Intelligencer*, April 11, 1976, p. 1 (big government); *New York Times*, April 8, 1976, p. 30 (America's prosperity).

30. Steven Brill, "Is Henry M. Jackson a Liberal," Americans for Democratic Action Report, Aug. 1975, HMJ 3560–12/43/13; "The Truth About the Jackson Record," ibid.; Kaufman interview with Wattenberg, March 16, 1995.

31. Herbert S. Parmet, *The Democrats* (New York: Macmillan, 1976), pp. 310–14.

32. Interview with Strauss, Oct. 30, 1995.

33. Peter G. Bourne, *Jimmy Carter* (New York: Scribner's, 1997), p. 255.

34. Barone, *Our Country*, p. 561 (organized labor); Kaufman interview with Howard Feldman, Aug. 2, 1995.

35. *New Orleans Times-Picayune*, Feb. 15, 1975, p. 9 (Meany and Barkan); Jackson to George Meany, Feb. 12, 1975, HMJ 3560–6/1/29; *Portland Oregonian*, Feb. 23, 1976, p. 9 (Meany-Jackson rupture).

36. Quoted in the *New York Times*, Nov. 28, 1975, p. 4.

37. Kaufman interview with Daniel Patrick Moynihan, July 28, 1996.

38. *UPI Report*, Jan. 26, 1976; Jackson, "U.S. Central Intelligence Agency Activities," Jan. 26, 1976, HMJ 3560–6/11/185.

39. Schmechel interview with John Stennis, March 10, 1987.

40. Jackson, "CIA Leak," Jan. 26, 1974, HMJ 3560–5/2/165.

41. Kaufman interview with James Schlesinger, Oct. 30, 1994.

42. Ernest R. May, *"Lessons" of the Past: The Uses and Misuses of History in American Foreign Policy* (New York: Oxford University Press, 1973).

43. Interviews with Strauss, Oct. 30, 1995, and Keefe, July 30, 1995.

44. Kaufman interviews with Ben Wattenberg, March 18, 1995, and Tom Foley, March 14, 1995.

45. Bourne, *Jimmy Carter*, pp. 243–68; Witcover, *Marathon*, pp. 105–18.

46. Quoted in the *St. Petersburg Times*, Feb. 4, 1976, p. 18A.

47. Interview with Dunsmore.

48. Interview with Wattenberg.

49. *Atlanta Constitution*, Feb. 12, 1976, p. 6A.

50. Apple, "Puritan for President," p. 62; Peter J. Ognibene, *Scoop* (New York: Stein and Day, 1975).

51. McCarthy quoted in *Chicago Tribune*, May 30, 1975, p. 1; Stevenson in *Chicago Sun-Times*, April 8, 1975, p. 10; *Wall Street Journal*, Nov. 19, 1975, p. 1.

17 The 1976 Democratic Primaries

1. Jules Witcover, *Marathon* (New York: Viking, 1977), p. 248.

2. Stephan Lesher, *George Wallace* (Reading: Addison-Wesley, 1994), pp. 493–95.

3. *Lynn Daily Evening Item*, Jan. 31, 1976, p. 1.

4. *Seattle Times*, Feb. 13, 1976, p. A4.

5. *New York Times*, Feb. 12, 1976, p. 4.

6. Kaufman interview with Daniel Patrick Moynihan, July 28, 1996.

7. Quoted in the *Washington Post*, Feb. 18, 1976, p. A3.

8. Jackson, "Jimmy Carter Tax Plan," Feb. 26, 1976, HMJ 3560–5/262/140.

9. Jackson, "Presidential Campaign," March 3, 1976, HMJ 3560–5/262/143.

10. Kaufman interviews with Denny Miller, Oct. 3, 1994; Ben Wattenberg, March 18, 1995; and Bob Keefe, July 30, 1996.

11. Betty Glad, *Jimmy Carter* (New York: Norton, 1980), pp. 487–507.

12. Quoted in Witcover, *Marathon*, p. 252.

13. Carter quoted in the *Miami Herald*, March 4, 1976, p. 4 ("connotations of racism"), and *Washington Post*, March 12, 1976, pp. A1, A17 ("deliberately falsifying"); Jackson in *New York Times*, March 6, 1976, p. 10.

14. Interview with Miller.

15. Interview with Keefe.

16. Interview with Wattenberg.

17. *New York Times*, March 12, 1995, pp. 1, 17.

18. Jackson, "Massachusetts Campaign," HMJ 3560–12/47/11, and "Florida Campaign," HMJ 3560–12/46/32.

19. *New York Times*, March 12, 1976, pp. 1, 17.

20. Ibid., March 18, 1976, p. 3.

21. Jackson, "Itineraries: 1976 New York Primary," HMJ 3560–5/244/1–2; interview with Moynihan; Jackson, "National Health Plan," Jan. 13, 1976, HMJ 3560–5/262/110.

22. Kaufman interview with Barry Dunsmore, Oct. 13, 1995.

23. Interview with Keefe.

24. Kaufman interviews with Stewart Udall, Feb. 18, 1995, and Wattenberg, March 18, 1995.

25. Interview with Keefe.

26. Ibid.

27. Kaufman interviews with Sam Nunn, March 14, 1995, and Walter Mondale, Sept. 24, 1996.

28. Jackson, "News from the Jackson Campaign: Jackson Makes Public His Tax Returns," Feb. 17, 1976, HMJ 3560–12/443/21; *Money Magazine*, March 1976, pp. 36–37.

29. Interview with Wattenberg.

30. Glad, *Jimmy Carter*, pp. 264–65.

31. Steve Neal, "Pennsylvania: The Ward Heelers' Primary," *The Nation*, April 28, 1976, pp. 487–88.

32. Kaufman interview with Shelby Scates, June 28, 1997; Jackson, "AFL-CIO Presidential Endorsements," HMJ 3560–12/46/3.

33. Kaufman interviews with Haakon Ragde, April 18, 1995, and Max Kampelman, Oct. 4, 1994.

34. *Washington Post*, April 21, 1976, pp. A1, A3.

35. Ibid., April 24, 1976, p. A3.

36. *Atlanta Constitution*, April 21, 1976, p. 3.

37. Jackson to Nelson Rockefeller, April 21, 1976, HMJ 3560–6/1/35.

38. Rockefeller to Jackson, April 21, 1976, HMJ 3560–6/1/35; Jackson quoted in the *Seattle Times*, April 24, 1976.

39. Kaufman interview with Rich-

ard Perle, Oct. 3, 1994; *Time*, May 3, 1976, p. 19.

40. *Washington Post*, April 26, 1976, A9.

41. *Seattle Post-Intelligencer*, April 28, 1976, p. A1.

42. *Washington Post*, April 12, 1976, pp. A1, A18.

43. Jackson, "Jimmy Carter," HMJ 3560–12/46/13, and "Presidential Campaign," April 20, 1976, HMJ 3560–5/262/157.

44. Quoted in *Vancouver* [Washington] *Columbian*, April 16, 1976, p. 3.

45. *Olympia* [Washington] *Olympian*, April 26, 1976, p. 1.

46. *Seattle Times*, April 28, 1976, p. 1.

47. Interview with Wattenberg.

48. Ibid.

49. Ibid.; Jackson, "Withdrawal Statement," May 1, 1976, HMJ 3560–12/47/33; and *Seattle Times*, May 4, 1976, p. A15.

50. Kaufman interviews with Elliott Abrams, Dec. 6, 1994, and Charles Horner, Dec. 6, 1994.

51. Quoted in the *Seattle Argus* 83, no. 42 (Oct. 15, 1975): 10.

52. Kaufman interview with Daniel Dreyfus, Dec. 31, 1996.

53. Kaufman interviews with Slade Gorton, Oct. 25, 1995, and Dan Evans, Sept. 14, 1994.

54. Interviews with Wattenberg and Moynihan.

55. *Washington Post*, July 21, 1976, p. A9.

56. Kaufman interviews with Elliott Abrams, Dec. 6, 1994, and Midge Decter, Sept. 19, 1994.

57. *Seattle Times*, June 8, 1976, p. A21.

58. Martin Schram, *Running for President, 1976: The Carter Campaign* (New York: Stein and Day, 1977), pp. 4–5 (endorsed Carter); interview with Stewart Udall; *Spokane Spokesman Review*, July 11, 1976, p. 1 (running mate).

59. Peter G. Bourne, *Jimmy Carter* (New York: Scribner's, 1997), p. 331.

60. *Seattle Post-Intelligencer*, Dec. 16, 1976, p. 1; Kaufman interviews with James Schlesinger, Oct. 30, 1994, and Dan Dreyfus, Dec. 31, 1996.

18 Perils of Détente, Part II

1. Peter G. Bourne, *Jimmy Carter* (New York: Scribner's, 1997), p. 371.

2. Kaufman interviews with Tom Foley, March 13, 1995; Howard Feldman, Aug. 2, 1995; and Foley, March 14, 1995.

3. Bill Bradley, *Time Present, Time Past* (New York: Knopf, 1996), pp. 67–68.

4. Kaufman interviews with Daniel Inouye, March 13, 1995; Ted Kennedy, June 18, 1996; and Daniel Patrick Moynihan, July 28, 1996.

5. Jackson quoted in *Newsweek*, March 12, 1977, p. 16; Steven M. Gillon, *The Democrats' Dilemma: Walter F. Mondale and the Liberal Legacy* (New York: Columbia University Press, 1992), p. 192.

6. Kaufman interview with James Schlesinger, Nov. 13, 1994; Jackson to Jimmy Carter, May 23, 1977, "Social File: Henry Jackson," *JCL*; Kaufman

interviews with Denny Miller, Oct. 3, 1994, and Doug Glant, Oct. 30, 1996.

7. Kaufman interview with Zbigniew Brzezinski, Dec. 10, 1994.

8. Kaufman interviews with Denny Miller, Oct. 3, 1994; Robert Strauss, Oct. 30, 1995; and Helen Jackson, June 10, 1995.

9. Kaufman interviews with Brzezinski, Dec. 9, 1994, and Stewart Udall, Feb. 17, 1995.

10. Kaufman interviews with John McCain, Aug. 2, 1995; Joe Miller, June 18, 1996; Ted Kennedy; and Moynihan.

11. Quoted in Jimmy Carter, *Keeping Faith: Memoirs of a President* (New York: Bantam Books, 1983), p. 100.

12. Kaufman interview with Daniel Dreyfus, Dec. 31, 1996.

13. *CQA: 1977*, pp. 708–13.

14. Interview with Schlesinger; *CQA: 1978*, pp. 638, 647–60.

15. Jackson on *Meet the Press*, April 6, 1979.

16. *CQA: 1979*, pp. 632–50.

17. Kaufman interview with Ted Stevens, March 15, 1995; Schmechel interview with Bill Bradley, Nov. 24, 1987; "Statement of Senator Henry M. Jackson on the Release of the Geopolitics of Oil," Nov. 20, 1980, HMJ 3560–6/13/110; Staff Report, *The Geopolitics of Oil*, printed at the request of the *Committee on Energy and Natural Resources, the United States Senate*, November 1980 (Washington, D.C.: Government Printing Office, 1980).

18. Daniel Yergin, *The Prize* (New York: Simon and Schuster, 1991), p. 692.

19. Kaufman interview with Ted Stevens, March 14, 1995.

20. Kaufman interviews with Cecil Andrus, Feb. 18, 1995, and Denny Miller; *CQA: 1980*, pp. 564–74.

21. Jackson, "New Directions for Our Party," Cook County Democratic Dinner, Chicago, May 22, 1980, HMJ 3560–5/247/3; Bourne, *Jimmy Carter*, p. 375.

22. Kaufman interviews with Zbigniew Brzezinski, Dec. 8, 1994, and William Odom, Dec. 8, 1994; Brzezinski, *Power and Principle: Memoirs of the National Security Adviser, 1977–1981* (New York: Farrar, Straus, Giroux, 1983), p. 459.

23. Interviews with Brzezinski and Odom, Dec. 8, 1994; Robert Gates makes a similar case regarding Carter's approval of aid to the mujahedeen and secret initiative to destabilize the Soviet regime. See, for example, Robert M. Gates, *From the Shadows: The Ultimate Insider's Story of Five Presidents and How They Won the Cold War* (New York: Simon and Schuster, 1996), pp. 135–69.

24. Interview with Brzezinski, Dec. 8, 1994.

25. Richard Perle, Senator Moynihan, and Senator Nunn concur with my argument that Carter's foreign policy was much closer to the line of the New Politics wing of the Democratic Party than to Brzezinski's or Jackson's. Kaufman interviews with Richard Perle, Jan. 2, 1996; Sam

Nunn, March 14, 1995; and Moynihan, July 28, 1996; Anatoly Dobrynin, *In Confidence* (New York: Times Books, 1995), pp. 387–90; Carter, *Keeping Faith*, pp. 229–30 (June 1978 speech); interview with Odom.

26. Kaufman interview, Morris Abrams, Jan. 8, 1995; Brown quoted in Brzezinski, *Power and Principle*, p. 44; interview with Odom.

27. Kaufman interviews with Moynihan; Elliott Abrams, Dec. 8, 1994; and Peter Rosenblatt, Sept. 26, 1997.

28. Chalmers Johnson, "Carter in Asia: McGovernism without McGovern," *Commentary*, January 1978, pp. 36–39; Robert L. Schuettinger, "The New Foreign Policy Network," *Policy Review*, July 1977, pp. 95–119. Shulman set forth the dominant paradigm of the administration in his widely read article, "On Learning to Live with Authoritarian Regimes," *Foreign Affairs*, January 1977, pp. 325–38; Shulman not only argued that the Soviet Union was not totalitarian, but that Soviet communist expansionism no longer constituted a major threat to U.S. security. Jackson viewed the Soviet Union as a totalitarian regime as depicted by Pipes, Malia, and Odom, among others. See Martin Malia, *The Soviet Tragedy* (New York: Free Press, 1994); Richard Pipes, *Russia under the Bolshevik Regime* (New York: Knopf, 1993), pp. 240–81; William Odom, *The Collapse of the Soviet Military* (New Haven: Yale University Press, 1998); and Odom, "Soviet Politics and After: Old and New

Concepts," *World Politics*, October 1992, pp. 66–98. Kaufman interviews with Kenneth Pyle, May 4, 1995, and Richard Perle.

29. Bourne, *Jimmy Carter*, pp. 385–86.

30. Ibid. (Afghanistan); Joshua Muravchik, *The Uncertain Crusade* (Washington, D.C.: American Enterprise Institute, 1988), p. 10.

31. *Time*, April 24, 1978, p. 20; Shulman, "On Learning to Live with Authoritarian Regimes," pp. 333–34; Schmechel interview with Cyrus Vance, Jan. 28, 1988.

32. Muravchik, *Uncertain Crusade*, p. 4.

33. Patrick Glynn, *Closing Pandora's Box* (New York: Basic Books, 1992), p. 289; Jeffrey Herf, *War By Other Means: Soviet Power, West German Resistance, and the Battle of the Euromissiles* (New York: Free Press, 1991), pp. 45–66.

34. For an excellent critical assessment of the Carter administration's defense program along these lines, see Colin Gray and Jeffrey Barlow, "Inexcusable Restraint: The Decline of American Military Policy in the 1970s," *International Security*, Fall 1985, pp. 27–69.

35. U.S. Office of Management and Budget, *Budget of the United States: FY 1978–1982* (Washington, D.C.: Government Printing Office, 1979–83), hereafter cited as OMB, *Budget*. Carter quoted in OMB, *Budget: FY 1979*, pp. 5–6; *Wall Street Journal*, Jan. 24, 1980, p. 11.

36. *CQA: 1979*, p. 435.

37. Jackson statement, "On the President's Veto of the Department of Defense Authorization Bill," Aug. 18, 1978, HMJ 3560–6/12/178; Jackson, Nunn, and Tower to Carter, Aug. 2, 1979, HMJ 3560–6/1/41; Jackson, "Closing the Gap: Hollings Amendment to Budget Resolution," U.S. Senate, Sept. 18, 1979, HMJ 3560–6/13/33.

38. *CQA: 1979*, pp. 411–37; interview with Perle.

39. For some recent favorable accounts of Carter's foreign policy that also make the case that he was more dovish than Brzezinski claims, see David Skidmore, *Reversing Course: Carter's Foreign Policy, Domestic Politics, and the Failure of Reform* (Nashville: Vanderbilt University Press, 1996), pp. 26–51; Jerel A. Rosati, *The Carter Administration's Quest for Global Community: Beliefs and Their Impact on Behavior* (Columbia: University of South Carolina Press, 1987), pp. 39–150.

40. For an excellent account of the significant contrast between Carter's and Reagan's defense programs favorable to the latter, see Samuel F. Wells, "A Question of Priorities: A Comparison of the Carter and Reagan Defense Programs," *Orbis*, Fall 1983, pp. 641–66.

41. Douglas Brinkley, *The Unfinished Presidency: Jimmy Carter's Journey beyond the White House* (New York: Viking, 1998), pp. 333–43; Carter interview on *Larry King Live*, CNN, Nov. 18, 1997.

42. Jackson, "Neutron Bomb," U.S. Senate, July 13, 1977, HMJ 3560–6/12/136; Jackson, "Neutron Bomb," July 12, 1978, HMJ 3560–6/12/169; *Seattle Post-Intelligencer*, April 6, 1978, p. 3; Jackson to Cyrus Vance, July 13, 1977, HMJ 3560–6/1/48; Jimmy Carter to Jackson, July 26, 1977, HMJ 3560–6/1/41; Jackson, "Technology Transfer to the Soviet Union," U.S. Technological Policy Issues Conference, Washington, D.C., April 30, 1980, HMJ 3560–6/13/82.

43. Glynn, *Closing Pandora's Box*, p. 301.

44. Paul C. Warnke, "Apes on a Treadmill," *Foreign Policy*, Spring 1975, pp. 25–29.

45. Senate Committee on Foreign Relations, *Warnke Nomination*, Feb. 8 and 9, 1977 (Washington, D.C.: Government Printing Office, 1977).

46. Senate Committee on Armed Services, *Consideration of Mr. Paul C. Warnke to be the Director of the U.S. Arms Control and Disarmament Agency and Ambassador*, Feb. 22, 23, and 28, 1977 (Washington, D.C.: Government Printing Office, 1977), pp. 17–18.

47. Kaufman interview with Richard Perle, Oct. 3, 1994.

48. Interview with Vance; Cyrus R. Vance, *Hard Choices: Critical Years in America's Foreign Policy* (New York: Simon and Schuster, 1983), p. 51; Kaufman interview with Edward Rowny, March 14, 1995.

49. Jackson to Jimmy Carter, Feb. 15, 1977, HMJ 3560–6/1/41; "Jack-

son-Perle Memorandum," Feb. 15, 1977, HMJ 3560–12/113.

50. Carter to Jackson, March 31, 1977, HMJ 3560–6/1/41.

51. Perle memorandum to Jackson, "The March Proposals," April 29, 1977, HMJ 3560–6/57/8.

52. Jackson to Brzezinski, April 25, 1977; Brzezinski to Jackson, April 26, 1977; Jackson to Brzezinski, April 27, 1977, HMJ 3560–28/1/1.

53. Carter to Jackson, May 20, 1977, HMJ 3560–28/1/3.

54. Vance, *Hard Choices*, pp. 51–60.

55. Committee on the Present Danger, "Where We Stand on SALT," July 6, 1977, p. 5.

56. Kaufman interview with Eugene Rostow, March 16, 1995.

57. Kaufman interview with Elmo Zumwalt, Dec. 9, 1994.

58. Having only 2,100 warheads deployed on its 1,054 ICBMs, the United States lacked the reciprocal capability to destroy the entire Soviet ICBM force of more than 1,400 launchers, because it took two ICBM warheads for every ICBM silo to ensure a 95 percent kill probability of that silo. The Soviet Union had over 6,000 warheads deployed on its ICBM force, more than enough to launch a preemptive attack against U.S. ICBMs with warheads to spare for countercity attacks should the U.S. retaliate.

59. Jackson, "U.S. Senate, Armed Services Committee, Arms Control Subcommittee," Oct. 15, 1977, HMJ 3560–6/12/144.

60. Interview with Vance.

61. *Washington Post*, Oct. 28, 1977, p. A7; *San Francisco Chronicle*, Nov. 9, 1977, p. 9.

62. Quoted in the *Vancouver Columbian*, July 12, 1978, p. 8.

63. Interview with Perle, Oct. 3, 1994.

64. Kaufman interviews with Schlesinger, Nov. 12, 1994, and Perle, Oct. 3, 1994.

19 Human Rights, SALT, and Linkage

1. *Proceedings of the International Commemorative Conference on the Occasion of the Twentieth Anniversary of the Jackson-Vanik Amendment*, Jerusalem, Jan. 8–10, 1995.

2. Jackson, "The Madrid Conference and Soviet Immigration," U.S. Senate, Sept. 30, 1980, HMJ 3560–6/13/101.

3. Jackson, "Soviet Trip Cancellation," March 10, 1978, HMJ 3560–6/12/158; Anatoly Dobrynin, *In Confidence* (New York: Times Books, 1995), pp. 400–401; Jackson, "Notes of a Conversation with Ambassador Dobrynin," March 8, 1977, HMJ 3560–6/1–57; Kaufman interview with Richard Perle, Jan. 2, 1996.

4. Kaufman interview with Perle, Oct. 3, 1994.

5. Jackson, "The Balance of Power and the Future of Freedom," Washington, D.C.: April 24, 1978, HMJ 3560–6/13/78.

6. Jackson believed instinctively what Professor Samuel Huntington of Harvard has argued elaborately: that American power does have a signifi-

cant impact on the fate of liberty in the rest of the world; that, specifically there is a correlation between the decline of American power and the decline of liberty; and that, conversely, there is a positive correlation between the extension of American power and the extension of liberal democratic government. See Samuel P. Huntington, *American Politics: The Promise of Disharmony* (Cambridge, Mass." Belknap Press, 1981), pp. 246–62; idem, *The Third Wave* (Norman: University of Oklahoma Press, 1991), pp. 92–100.

7. Jackson, "The Balance of Power and the Future of Freedom."

8. For an account of U.S. policy toward Nicaragua highly critical of Carter's foreign policy from Jackson's perspective, see Robert Kagan, *A Twilight Struggle: American Power and Nicaragua, 1977–1990* (New York: Free Press, 1996), pp. 32–88. For accounts hostile to Jackson's point of view, see Robert Pastor, *Condemned to Repetition: The United States and Nicaragua* (Princeton: Princeton University Press, 1987); William M. LeoGrande, *Our Own Backyard: The United States in Central America, 1977–1992* (Chapel Hill: University of North Carolina Press, 1998).

9. For the definitive critical accounts of the Carter policy toward Iran, see Michael Ledeen and William Lewis, *Debacle: The American Failure in Iran* (New York: Knopf, 1981); Barry Rubin, *Paved with Good Intentions: The American Experience and Iran* (New York: Oxford University Press,

1980). For the best account defending Carter's policy, see Gary Sick, *All Fall Down: America's Tragic Encounter with Iran* (New York: Random House, 1985).

10. Zbigniew Brzezinski, *Power and Principle* (New York: Farrar, Straus, and Giroux, 1983), p. 354; Cyrus R. Vance, *Hard Choices* (New York: Simon and Schuster, 1983), p. 331.

11. Kaufman interview with Bernard Lewis, Nov. 6, 1995; Jackson quoted in the *Seattle Times*, Jan. 18, 1979, p. 5.

12. Jackson, "Iran and the Middle East: Past and Present," George Washington University, Feb. 25, 1979, HMJ 3560–6/13/5; Jackson on *Face the Nation*, Feb. 11, 1979.

13. Jackson, "The Balance of Power and the Future of Freedom."

14. Jackson to Carter, Nov. 16, 1979, HMJ 3560–6/1/41.

15. Jackson, "Interview with Michael Ledeen," 1978, HMJ 3560–6/12/189.

16. Jackson to Carter, Nov. 16, 1979, HMJ 3560–6/13/53.

17. Brzezinski, *Power and Principle*, p. 189; Vance, *Hard Choices*, pp. 91–92, 99–103.

18. Interviews with Perle and Lewis; Jackson to Jimmy Carter, "Memorandum on the Situation in the Middle East," June 29, 1978, HMJ 3560–6/12/171.

19. William B. Quandt, *Camp David: Peacemaking and Politics* (Washington, D.C.: Brookings Institution, 1986), pp. 111–41.

20. Jackson to Carter, "Memoran-

dum on the Situation in the Middle East."

21. Interview with Lewis.

22. Jackson to Carter, "Memorandum on the Situation in the Middle East"; Quandt, *Camp David*, pp. 291–339.

23. Jackson, "Memorandum of a Conversation with Sadat," Middle East Trip File, Nov. 1979, HMJ 3560–5/233/49; "On a New Marshall Plan for the Middle East," U.S. Senate, Oct. 12, 1978, HMJ 3560–6/12/187; "Encirclement in the Middle East," U.S. Senate, Jan. 23, 1979, HMJ 3560–6/13/2.

24. Jackson, "Proposed Middle East Arms Sale Package," U.S. Senate, HMJ 3560–6/12/166.

25. Kaufman interview with Richard Perle, Jan. 2, 1996.

26. Jackson quoted in *Washington Star*, June 17, 1980, p. 10 (PLO and Soviets); Jackson, "Terrorism as a Weapon in International Politics," Jerusalem Conference on International Terrorism, Jerusalem, July 2, 1979, HMJ 3560–6/13/27; Claire Sterling, *The Terror Network* (New York: Holt, Rinehart and Winston, 1981); Kaufman interview with Adam Garfinkle, Jan. 7, 1996.

27. Benjamin Netanyahu to Jackson, May 30, 1979, HMJ 3560–6/22/33.

28. Jackson, "Commencement Address: Hebrew University of Jerusalem," Mount Scopus, Israel, July 2, 1979, HMJ 3560–6/13/26; Kaufman interview with Perle, Jan. 7, 1995; Jackson, "Terrorism as a Weapon."

29. Jackson, "The U.S., China, and the 1980s," Sino-Soviet Conference, University of Washington, School of International Studies, Feb. 9, 1980, HMJ 3560–6/13/70.

30. Dorothy Fosdick to Jackson, "Memorandum on the Issue of MFN for the PRC," Jan. 29, 1979, HMJ 3560/28/1/1.

31. Jackson, "China Trip," Feb. 22, 1978, HMJ 3560–6/12/156.

32. Jackson, "Meeting With Deng Xiao Ping," Great Hall of the People, Beijing, China, Feb. 16, 1978, HMJ 3560–28/1/2.

33. Jackson to Carter, Oct. 13, 1978, HMJ 3560–6/1/41; Kaufman interview with Michel Oksenberg, Nov. 16, 1979 (SALT II); Jackson, "Deng Xiaoping Visit," Feb. 4, 1979, HMJ 3560–5/263/60.

34. Kaufman interview with Walter Mondale, Sept. 18, 1996; Brzezinski, *Power and Principle*, pp. 196–233 (MFN for China); Jackson, "Deng Xiaoping," Jan. 14, 1979, HMJ 3560–6/13/21.

35. Jackson, "China Trip, 1979," HMJ 3560–28/1/5–8; "Meeting with Deng Xiaoping," Great Hall of the People, Beijing, China, Aug. 23, 1979, HMJ 3560–28/8.

36. Kaufman interview with Kenneth Pyle, May 4, 1995; Gillon, *The Democrats' Dilemma*, pp. 246–47 (Mondale); Jackson, "China, Trade, and MFN," U.S. Senate, International Trade Subcommittee, Nov. 1, 1979, HMJ 3560–6/13/45.

37. Interview with Pyle.

38. Jackson, "Meeting with Deng Xiaoping," 1979; interview with Pyle.

39. "SALT II," HMJ 3560–6/23/19.

40. Ibid.

41. Jimmy Carter, *Keeping Faith* (New York: Bantam Books, 1983), pp. 261–62, 225.

42. Barry Blechman, "The New Congressional Role in Arms Control," in Thomas E. Mann, ed., *A Question of Balance: The President, the Congress, and Foreign Policy* (Washington, D.C.: Brookings Institution, 1990), p. 116.

43. Raymond Garthoff, *Detente and Confrontation* (Washington, D.C.: Brookings Institution, 1985), p. 818.

44. Carter, *Keeping Faith*, p. 265.

45. Kaufman interview with Edwin Meese, Oct. 5, 1994.

46. Kaufman interviews with Denny Miller, Oct. 3, 1994, and Helen Jackson, June 10, 1995.

47. Ronald Reagan to Jackson, Aug. 16, 1979, HMJ 3560–6/1/44.

48. Kaufman interviews with Sam Nunn, March 16, 1995; Eugene Rostow, March 14, 1995; John Danforth, June 6, 1996; and Howard Baker, June 17, 1995.

49. Jimmy Carter to Jackson, May 20, 1977, HMJ 3560–28/1/3; interview with Perle, Jan. 2, 1996.

50. Jackson, "The Sign of the Times," Coalition for a Democratic Majority, Washington, D.C., June 12, 1979, HMJ 3560–6/13/19.

51. Jackson, "Fear of Rejection of SALT II," U.S. Senate, June 19, 1979, HMJ 3560–6/13/25.

52. *CQA: 1979*, pp. 411–21.

53. Senate Committee on Armed Services, *Military Implications of the Treaty on the Limitation of Strategic Offensive Arms and the Protocol Thereto (SALT II Treaty)*, Parts 1–4, 96th Cong., 1st sess., July 23–26, 30–31; Aug. 1–2; Oct. 9–11, 16–18, and 23–24, 1979 (hereafter cited as *SALT II Hearings*).

54. Kaufman interview with Edward Rowny, March 14, 1995.

55. *SALT II Hearings*, Part 2, pp. 477–80.

56. Ibid., p. 878.

57. Ibid., p. 978.

58. Interview with Rowny.

59. *SALT II Hearings*, Part 3, pp. 977–80.

60. Ibid., p. 981.

61. Ibid., pp. 1321–22.

62. LeRoy Ashby and Rod Gramer, *Fighting the Odds* (Pullman: Washington State University Press, 1994), pp. 593–99.

63. Cyrus Vance, "The Soviet Brigade in Cuba," Sept. 5, 1979, HMJ 3560–6/28/27.

64. Carter, "Public Statement on Soviet Brigade in Cuba," Sept. 7, 1979, HMJ 3560–6/20/19.

65. Jackson, "Fortress Cuba," U.S. Senate, Sept. 11, 1979, HMJ 3560–6/13/32; HMJ, "Soviet Combat Forces in Cuba," Oct. 2, 1979, HMJ 3560–6/13/36; Jackson, "The Russians in Cuba and SALT," CBS broadcast, Oct. 10, 1979, HMJ 3560–6/13/37.

66. Jimmy Carter, "Soviet Troops in Cuba," Television Address to the Nation, Oct. 1, 1979, HMJ 3560–20/19.

67. *CQA: 1979*, pp. 436–37.

68. Jackson, *SALT II*, Dec. 20,

1979, HMJ 3560–6/13/57; Senate Committee on Armed Services, *Report on the Hearings on the Military Implications of the Proposed SALT II Treaty Relating to National Defense* (Washington, D.C.: Government Printing Office, 1980), pp. 16, 2–4, 17.

69. Carter, *Keeping Faith*, p. 265.

70. Jackson, "My 10,000 Miles through Soviet Russia," 1956, HMJ 3560–6/3/35.

71. Jackson, "Virginia General Assembly Address," Williamsburg, Feb. 4, 1980, HMJ 3560–6/13/68.

20 Anybody But Carter: The 1980 Presidential Election

1. Michael Barone, *Our Country* (New York: Free Press, 1990), pp. 581–82.

2. Peter G. Bourne, *Jimmy Carter* (New York: Scribner's, 1997), p. 450.

3. Steven M. Gillon, *The Democrats' Dilemma* (New York: Columbia University Press, 1992), p. 262.

4. Jimmy Carter, *Keeping Faith* (New York: Bantam Books, 1983), pp. 115, 121.

5. Jackson on *Face the Nation*, July 29, 1979.

6. Jackson, "Virginia General Assembly Address," Williamsburg, Feb. 4, 1980, HMJ 3560–6/13/68.

7. Quoted in the *Seattle Post-Intelligencer,* July 19, 1979, p. A1.

8. *Reuters*, July 29, July 25, and Sept. 12, 1979, A.M. Cycle.

9. Kaufman interview with Richard Perle, Jan. 2, 1996.

10. Kaufman interviews with Bernard Lewis, Nov. 6, 1995; Ted Kennedy, June 18, 1996; and Perle.

11. Interview with Kennedy.

12. *Seattle Times*, p. A11.

13. Kaufman interview with Doug Glant, March 18, 1997.

14. Interview with Lewis.

15. Kaufman interview with Max Kampelman, Oct. 4, 1996; Kampelman to Jackson, Nov. 27, 1979, HMJ 3560–6/1/22.

16. Ibid. (Kampelman letter); Kennedy to Jackson, Nov. 27, 1979, HMJ 3560–6/1/22.

17. Ibid. (Kennedy letter); Rostow, "Draft of a Basic Foreign Policy Speech for Senator Edward M. Kennedy," Jan. 23, 1980, HMJ 3560–6/25/38.

18. Kampelman to Kalicki, Jan. 30, 1980, HMJ 3560–6/1/22.

19. Interview with Lewis.

20. Kaufman interview with Max Kampelman, Oct. 3, 1994.

21. For an account that, typical of the book, gets many of the details wrong but the essence right, see Jay Winik, *On the Brink* (New York: Simon and Schuster, 1996), pp. 88–92.

22. Kaufman interviews with Norman Podhoretz and Midge Decter, Sept. 19, 1995; Elliott Abrams, Dec. 8, 1994; Elmo Zumwalt, Dec. 11, 1994; Ben Wattenberg, March 16, 1995.

23. Interviews with Kirkpatrick and Abrams.

24. Kaufman interview with Kirkpatrick; and with Joshua Muravchik, Jan. 11, 1996.

25. Kaufman interview with Richard Allen, Nov. 3, 1996.

26. Jackson, "American Seapower and the U.S. Navy," Feb. 18, 1976, HMJ 3560–6/12/11; Kaufman interview with Perle, Oct. 3, 1994.

27. Kaufman interview with Daniel Patrick Moynihan, July 28, 1996.

28. Quoted in the *Wall Street Journal*, May 13, 1980, p. 9.

29. Quoted in *Seattle Post-Intelligencer*, May 9, 1980, p. A1.

30. Jackson, "New Directions for the Democratic Party," Cook County Democratic Dinner, Chicago, Illinois, May 22, 1980, HMJ 3560–6/13/85.

31. *Seattle Times*, May 22, 1980, p. B6.

32. *Seattle Post-Intelligencer*, July 29, 1980, p. A1.

33. Kaufman interview with Harrison Dogole, March 19, 1995; *Seattle Times*, July 28, 1980, p. A1.

34. *Bremerton* [Washington] *Sun*, Aug. 11, 1980, p. 1.

35. Jackson, "Jackson-Vanik Amendment; Letters to the Candidates," Oct. 2, 1980, HMJ 3560–6/13/103.

36. Ronald Reagan to Jackson, Oct. 24, 1980, HMJ 3560–6/1/41.

37. Kaufman interview with Doug Glant, Sept. 18, 1996.

38. Ibid.

39. Ibid.

40. Rostow to Jackson, Sept. 18, 1980, HMJ 3560–6/1/35; Kaufman interview with Denny Miller, Oct. 3, 1994.

41. Interview with Glant.

42. Kaufman interview with Haakon Ragde, April 15, 1995.

43. Jackson, "Coalition for a Democratic Majority," Washington, D.C., Feb. 2, 1981, HMJ 3560–6/13/116.

44. Schmechel interview with George McGovern, Sept. 30, 1987.

45. *Seattle Times*, Oct. 13, 1995, p. A12.

46. Quoted in the *Seattle Post-Intelligencer, Seattle Northwest Magazine*, Feb. 8, 1981, p. 6.

47. Shelby Scates, *Warren G. Magnuson and the Shaping of Twentieth-Century America* (Seattle: University of Washington Press, 1997), pp. 269–82, 318.

48. Quoted in the *Seattle Post-Intelligencer, Seattle Northwest Magazine*, p. 8.

49. Kaufman interview with Richard Allen, Oct. 30, 1996.

50. *Seattle Post-Intelligencer*, Nov. 7, 1980, p. B1.

51. *The Economist*, Nov. 15, 1980, pp. 23–27.

52. Jackson on *Face the Nation*, Nov. 16, 1980.

53. *Seattle Post-Intelligencer*, Dec. 5, 1980, p. A1.

54. Kaufman interview with Peter Jackson, Jan. 12, 1996.

55. Interviews with Allen, Oct. 30, 1996, and Perle, Jan. 2, 1996.

56. Ibid; the *Economist*, Nov. 15, 1980, pp. 23–27.

57. Winik, *On the Brink*, pp. 122–23.

58. Ibid.

21 Sunset

1. Kaufman interviews with John McCain, Aug. 1, and Ted Stevens, March 14, 1995.

2. Kaufman interview with Denny Miller, Oct. 3, 1994.

3. Jackson, "Defense Authorization Bill," U.S. Senate, July 11, 13–18, 1983, HMJ 3560–6/14/66, 68; Kaufman interviews with Edwin Meese, Oct. 4, 1994, and Richard Perle, Jan. 2, 1996. For a detailed account of the huge impact of Henry Jackson Democrats such as Perle on President Reagan's foreign policy that is often wrong on the details but right in the essentials, see Jay Winik, *On the Brink* (New York: Simon and Schuster, 1996).

4. Peter W. Rodman, *More Precious than Peace* (New York: Scribner's 1994), pp. 411–14.

5. Kaufman interview with Jeane Kirkpatrick, Dec. 28, 1996; Jackson, "Central America Commission," U.S. Senate, June 15, 1983, HMJ 3560–6/14/62.

6. Kaufman interview with Richard Pipes, Sept. 26, 1995; Pipes, "Misinterpreting the Cold War: The Hard-Liners Had It Right," *Foreign Affairs*, Jan./Feb. 1995, pp. 154–57.

7. Peter Schweizer, *Victory: The Reagan Administration's Secret Strategy that Hastened the Collapse of the Soviet Union* (New York: Atlantic Monthy Press, 1994), p. 283.

8. Jackson, "Notes on Strategic Defense," April 1, 1983, HMJ 3560–6/61/7; interview with Perle.

9. Norman Polmar and Thomas B. Allen, *Rickover* (New York: Simon and Schuster, 1982), pp. 667–68.

10. Jackson, "Oil Glut Mirage," Feb. 24, 1982, HMJ 3560–5/264/70.

11. Kaufman interview with Peter Jackson, Jan. 13, 1996; "HMJ, Position Papers, 1982 Campaign," HMJ 3560–12/49/21–2.

12. Kaufman interview with Ron Dotzauer, Sept. 28, 1997.

13. Jackson to Ronald Reagan, March 24, 1981, HMJ 3560–6/49/24.

14. Jeffrey Herf, *War By Other Means* (New York: Free Press, 1991), pp. 1–14.

15. Jackson to Reagan, March 24, 1981.

16. Jackson, *KIRO TV News Interview*, Nov. 18, 1981.

17. For the standard liberal critique, see Strobe Talbott, *Deadly Gambits: The Reagan Administration and the Stalemate in Nuclear Arms Control* (New York: Vintage Books, 1984), especially pp. 57–77 on his negative appraisal of Richard Perle.

18. Herf, *War By Other Means*, p. 229; interview with Richard Perle.

19. For the standard liberal critique of Reagan's approach in general and Perle's influence on it in particular, see Strobe Talbott, *The Master of the Game: Paul Nitze and the Nuclear Peace* (New York: Knopf, 1988), pp. 221–394. For a more concise and, in my view, correct assessment of Reagan's arms control record, see Dinesh D'-Souza, *Ronald Reagan* (New York: Free Press, 1997), pp. 144–48.

20. Kaufman interview with George Weigel, Aug. 2, 1995.

21. Jackson to Ronald Reagan, April 28, 1982; Reagan to Jackson, May 11, 1981, HMJ 3560–6/49/24.

22. Interview with Dotzauer.

23. Jackson, "Floor Statement on Kennedy-Hatfield Nuclear Resolution," U.S. Senate, March 30, 1982, HMJ 3560–6/13/175.

24. *CQA: 1982*, pp. 112–24; Jackson, "Nuclear Arms Reduction," U.S. Senate, May 12, June 28, 1982, HMJ 3560–6/13/180 and 6/14/3.

25. *Congressional Quarterly Weekly Report*, July 23, 1983, pp. 1483–89.

26. Jackson, "MX Missile," U.S. Senate, Dec. 14, Dec. 16, 1982, HMJ 3560–6/14/31, 34.

27. Telephone Conversation between President Reagan and Jackson, Dec. 12, 1982, Jackson meeting with President Reagan, Dec. 14 and 17, 1987, Central File, "Henry Jackson," RWRL.

28. *Congressional Quarterly Weekly Report*, July 23, 1983, pp. 1483–89.

29. Jackson, "Middle East themes," Sept.–Dec. 1982, HMJ 3560–6/14/17; and "The Struggle for Human Rights and Decency," United Jewish Appeals Conference, Reno, Nevada, June 1983, HMJ 3560–6/14/65.

30. Jackson, "On the proposed Advanced Warning and Airborne Command System and F-15 Enhancement Arms Sales Package to Saudi Arabia," HMJ 3560–6/13/151.

31. Jackson on *Capitol Cloakroom*, CBS, Sept. 23, 1982.

32. Jackson on *Face the Nation*, Feb. 20, 1983.

33. *Capitol Cloakroom*, Sept. 23, 1982.

34. Ibid.

35. *Face the Nation*, Feb. 20, 1983.

36. Jackson, "Israeli Raid on Iraq's nuclear facilities," June 9, 1981, HMJ 3560–6/13/132.

37. Jackson, "Keynote Address B'nai B'rith Anti-Defamation League," Washington, D.C., June 8, 1983, HMJ 3560–6/14/61.

38. *Capitol Cloakroom*, Sept. 23, 1982.

39. James Mann, *About Face* (New York: Knopf, 1999), pp. 115–54.

40. Jackson, "Agenda and Meeting Notes," Alexander Haig, George Shultz, and Caspar Weinberger, 1982–83, HMJ 3560–6/1/59.

41. Jackson, "Jackson-Vanik Amendment Waiver Authority," U.S. Senate, International Trade Subcommittee, Aug. 10, 1982, HMJ 3560–6/14/8.

42. Kaufman interview with Kenneth Pyle, May 10, 1995.

43. *Congressional Quarterly Weekly Report*, May 15, 1982, pp. 1155–59.

44. Kaufman interview with Elliott Abrams, Dec. 8, 1994.

45. Kaufman interview with Jeane Kirkpatrick, Dec. 28, 1996.

46. Jackson, "Foreign Policy Address to CDM," Washington, D.C., June 23, 1981, HMJ 3560–6/13/139.

47. Kaufman interviews with Anna Marie Jackson, Oct. 26, 1994; Peter Jackson, Jan. 13, 1996; Kenneth Pyle, May 10, 1995; and Helen Jackson, June 10, 1995.

48. Interview with Dotzauer.

49. Quoted in *Spokane Spokesman Review*, Dec. 17, 1980, p. 9.

50. Kaufman interview with Donald Hellmann, June 14, 1995.

51. *Seattle Weekly*, Aug. 4, 1984, pp. 3–4.

52. Ibid.

53. *Seattle Post-Intelligencer,* Sept. 15, 1982, pp. A1, A7.

54. Interview with Dotzauer.

55. *Seattle Weekly*, Feb. 10, 1982, pp. 23–28.

56. *Seattle Times*, Oct. 25, 1982, p. C1.

57. Interview with Dotzauer; *Seattle Times*, Nov. 3, 1982, p. C2.

58. Jackson, "Keynote Speech to the State Democratic Convention," Spokane, Washington, June 12, 1982, HMJ 3560–12/51/17.

59. Interview with Dotzauer.

60. Interview with Peter Jackson.

61. *Washington Post*, March 18, 1983, p. E9; Kaufman interview with Norman Dicks, Aug. 4, 1995.

62. Kaufman interview with Haakon Ragde, April 10, 1995.

63. Robert Kagan, *A Twilight Struggle* (New York: Free Press, 1996), pp. 167–77.

64. Jackson, "A Stolen Revolution, Nicaragua," Washington, D.C., July 19, 1983, HMJ 3560–6/14/69.

65. Ibid.

66. Quoted in the *Wall Street Journal*, June 10, 1983, p. 11.

67. Kaufman Interviews with Jeane Kirkpatrick, Dec. 28, 1996, and Jack Kemp, Dec. 9, 1994.

68. Interview with Kirkpatrick.

69. Jackson, "A Jackson-Mathias-Barnes, Kemp Proposal," June 26, 1983, HMJ 3560–6/14/63.

70. Kagan, *Twilight Struggle*, p. 279.

71. Kaufman interview with Lane Kirkland, March 16, 1995; interview with Kirkpatrick.

72. Cynthia J. Arnson, *Crossroads: Congress, the President, and Central America, 1976–1993*, 2d ed. (University Park: Pennsylvania State University Press, 1993), pp. 53–227.

73. Interview with Kirkpatrick.

74. *Everett Herald*, Sept. 2, 1983, p. 1.

75. Interview with Pyle.

76. Ronald Reagan to Deng Xiaoping, Aug. 12, 1983, in *The China Policy of Henry M. Jackson: Staff Report to the Committee on Armed Services: United States Senate* (Washington, D.C.: Government Printing Office, 1983), p. 12.

77. Interview with Pyle.

78. Kaufman interview with Haakon Ragde, April 16, 1995.

79. Interview with Dotzauer.

80. Jackson, "Press Conference," Sept. 1, 1983, HMJ 3560–22/Video Tape-59.

81. Interview with Helen Jackson.

82. Kaufman interviews with Denny Miller, Oct. 3, 1994, and Haakon Ragde, April 16, 1995.

83. *Everett Herald*, Sept. 2, 1981, p. 1.

84. Interview with Ragde, April 18, 1995.

85. Ronald Reagan to Helen Jackson, Friday Sept. 2, 1983, "Henry Jackson Name File," RWRL; Reagan quoted in *UPI*, Washington News, A.M. Cycle, Sept. 2, 1983, and in the *New York Times*, Sept. 6, 1983, p. 15.

86. Quoted in Memorial Addresses

Delivered in Congress, *Henry M. Jackson: Late a Senator from Washington* (Washington, D.C.: Government Printing Office, 1983), p. 28.

87. Ibid., pp. 2, 24, 99, 208–9.

88. *Everett Herald*, Sept. 4, 1983, p. 12.

89. *Henry M. Jackson: Late a Senator*, pp. 407–13.

90. Ibid., p. 416 (Wattenberg); p. 418 (Garside); and p. 421 (Kirkland).

91. Ibid, pp. 422–23.

92. Ibid., p. 424.

93. Ibid., pp. 416–18.

94. *Everett Herald*, Sept. 8, 1983, p. 1.

95. *Seattle Times*, Sept. 15, 1983, pp. A1, A20.

96. Ibid., Nov. 19, 1983, p. A1.

97. Ibid., Oct. 7, 1984, p. A1.

98. *UPI*, B.C. Cycle, Nov. 20, 1987.

99. Quoted in "Remarks of the President at Posthumous Presentation of the Medal of Freedom to Henry Jackson, Rose Garden, Washington, D.C., June 26, 1984," Henry M. Jackson File, RRL.

100. Ibid.

101. Ibid.

22 *The Jackson Legacy*

1. Kaufman interview with Howard Baker, June 16, 1995.

2. Kaufman interviews with George Shultz, Sept. 19, 1994; Edwin Meese, Oct. 3, 1994; and Jeane Kirkpatrick, Dec. 28, 1996.

3. Richard Pipes, "Misinterpreting the Cold War," *Foreign Affairs*, Jan./Feb. 1995, pp. 154–60; Kaufman in-

terview with Richard Pipes, Sept. 26, 1995.

4. Quoted in the *Washington Post*, Jan. 30, 1995, p. A9.

5. See, for example, Raymond L. Garthoff, *The Great Transition* (Washington, D.C.: Brookings Institution, 1994). For a similar analysis along these lines, see Richard Ned Lebow and Janice Gross Stein, *How We All Lost the Cold War* (Princeton: Princeton University Press, 1994).

6. Pipes, "Misinterpreting the Cold War," pp. 154–60.

7. *Messengers from Moscow*, Part 4.

8. Ibid.; Dinesh D'Souza, *Ronald Reagan* (New York: Free Press, 1997), p. 173; George P. Shultz, *Turmoil and Triumph: My Years as Secretary of State* (New York: Scribner's, 1993), pp. 473–77, 753–73.

9. For a leading example of such an excessively flattering account of Gorbachev's role, see Strobe Talbott and Michael R. Beschloss, *At the Highest Levels: The Inside Story of the End of the Cold War* (Boston: Little, Brown, 1993); Jeremy Isaacs and Taylor Downing, *Cold War* (Boston: Little, Brown, 1998). For a rebuttal, see Gabriel Schoenfeld, "Twenty-Four Lies About the Cold War," *Commentary*, March 1999, pp. 28–36.

10. William E. Odom, *The Collapse of the Soviet Military* (New Haven: Yale University Press, 1998), pp. 88–222.

11. Richard Pipes, *Communism, the Vanished Specter* (New York: Oxford University Press, 1994).

12. Interview with Pipes.

13. Quoted in D'Souza, *Ronald Reagan*, p. 141.

14. Paul Kennedy, *The Rise and Fall of the Great Powers* (New York: Random House, 1987).

15. *Washington Post*, Jan. 2, 1998, p. A23.

16. For a prime example of the conservative isolationist impulse, see Patrick Buchanan, "America First—and Second and Third," *The National Interest*, Fall 1985, pp. 8–15; for a rebuttal, see Robert G. Kaufman, "Three Approaches to U.S. Foreign Policy," *Strategic Review*, Summer 1994, pp. 62–77.

17. Robert G. Kaufman, "A Two-Level Interaction: Structure, Stable Liberal Democracy, and U.S. Grand Strategy," *Security Studies*, Summer 1994, pp. 678–717.

18. For an excellent argument along these lines from someone sympathetic to the environmental movement, see Gregg Easterbrook, *A Moment on the Earth* (New York: Viking, 1995).

19. George F. Will, *Restoration: Congress, Term Limits, and the Recovery of Deliberative Democracy* (New York: Free Press, 1992). Mr. Will concedes that Henry Jackson is the best argument there is against term limits, but argues that the benefits will be greater than the cost of losing Jackson. Kaufman interview with George F. Will, Dec. 8, 1994.

20. Kaufman interview with Michael Barone, Aug. 3, 1995; Barone, *Our Country*, p. 661.

21. Contemporary liberalism still suffers from this defect. What characterizes all the leading recent attempts to rethink liberalism is an unsufficient appreciation of private enterprise and an excessive faith in the efficacy of strong government intervention in the economy. See, for example, E. J. Dionne, Jr., *They Only Look Dead: Why Progressives Will Dominate the Next Political Era* (New York: Simon and Schuster, 1996): Stanley B. Greenberg, *Middle Class Dreams: The Politics and Power of the New American Majority* (New York: Times Books, 1995); Stanley B. Greenberg and Theda Skocpol, eds., *The New Majority: Toward a Popular Progressive Politics* (New Haven: Yale University Press, 1997); and Michael Tomasky, *Left for Dead: The Life, Death, and Possible Resurrection of Progressive Politics in America* (New York: Free Press, 1996).

22. Kaufman interviews with Midge Decter and Norman Podhoretz, Sept. 19, 1995; Elliott Abrams, Dec. 8, 1994; and Charles Horner, Dec. 8, 1994.

23. John Ehrman, *The Rise of Neoconservatism* (New Haven: Yale University Press, 1995), pp. 165–71.

24. Kaufman interview with Daniel Patrick Moynihan, July 28, 1996.

25. Interviews with Podhoretz, Decter, Abrams, and Horner.

26. Fred Barnes, "The Death of the Jackson Wing," in R. Emmett Tyrrell, Jr., ed., *Orthodoxy* (New York: Harper and Row, 1987).

27. Kaufman interview with Sam Nunn, March 16, 1995.

28. Robert Kuttner, *The Life of the*

Party: Democratic Prospects in 1988 and Beyond (New York: Viking, 1987), p. 224.

29. Ronald Radosh, *Divided They Fell* (New York: Free Press, 1996), pp. 192–210.

30. Kaufman interview with Joshua Muravchik, Jan. 13, 1996.

31. *New York Times*, Aug. 17, 1992, p. A14; *Washington Post*, Aug. 17, 1992, p. A20.

32. Quotations from the *St. Louis Post Dispatch*, Aug. 20, 1992, p. 9.

33. Interview with Muravchik. For the best book on Clinton's foreign policy generally, which amplifies Muravchik's point, see William G. Hyland, *Clinton's World: Remaking American Foreign Policy* (Westport: Praeger, 1999).

34. Kaufman interview with William Odom, Dec. 10, 1994.

35. See, for example, Ben J. Wattenberg, *Values Matter Most* (New York: Free Press, 1995); Kaufman interview with Ben Wattenberg, March 16, 1995.

36. Kaufman interview with Joseph Lieberman, March 18, 1996.

Bibliography

Key to Abbreviations

CQA: *Congressional Quarterly Almanac.*
GRFL: Gerald R. Ford Library, Ann Arbor, Michigan.
HMJ: Henry Martin Jackson Papers, University of Washington Libraries, Seattle, Washington.
JCL: Jimmy Carter Library, Atlanta, Georgia.
JFKL: John F. Kennedy Library, Boston, Massachusetts.
LBJL: Lyndon B. Johnson Library, Austin, Texas.
RMNPP: Richard M. Nixon Presidential Project, National Archives, Suitland, Maryland.
RRL: Ronald Reagan Library, Simi Valley, California.
WHCF: White House Central File.

Interviews

This biography uses three different sets of interviews. The designation "Kaufman interview" refers to those conducted by the author. The designation "Schmechel interview" refers to those Donald A. Schmechel conducted as part of an oral history project sponsored by the Henry M. Jackson Foundation headquartered in Seattle, Washington. The designation "Gaskin interview" refers to those that Dr. Thomas M. Gaskin and his team conducted for the oral history *One of Ours: Young Scoop Jackson: An Oral History of Senator Henry M. Jackson and Everett, Washington, from 1892 to 1940* (video produced by the Institute for Media and Creative Arts, Everett Community College, 1989). Only the Kaufman and Schmechel interviews designate a specific date.

Books and Articles

Acheson, Dean. *Present at the Creation: My Years in the State Department.* New York: Norton, 1969.
Aitken, Jonathan. *Nixon: A Life.* Washington, D.C.: Regnery, 1993.
Alperovitz, Gar. *The Decision to Use the Atomic Bomb and the Architecture of an American Myth.* New York: Alfred Knopf, 1995.

Ambrose, Stephen E. *Eisenhower: The President.* Vol. 2. New York: Simon and Schuster, 1984.

———. *Nixon: The Education of a Politician, 1913–1962.* New York: Simon and Schuster, 1987.

———. *Nixon: The Triumph of a Politician, 1962–1972.* New York: Simon and Schuster, 1989.

———. *Nixon: Ruin and Recovery, 1973–1990.* New York: Simon and Schuster, 1991.

Arendt, Hannah. *The Origins of Totalitarianism.* New York: Harcourt, Brace, 1951.

Arnson, Cynthia J. *Crossroads: Congress, the President, and Central America, 1976–1993.* 2d ed. University Park, Penn.: Pennsylvania State University Press, 1993.

Aron, Raymond. *Memoirs: Fifty Years of Political Reflection.* New York: Holmes and Meier, 1990.

Art, Robert J. *The TFX Decision: McNamara and the Military.* Boston: Little, Brown, 1968.

Ash, Timothy Garton. *In Europe's Name: Germany and the Divided Continent.* New York: Random House, 1993.

Ashby, LeRoy, and Rod Gramer. *Fighting the Odds: The Life of Senator Frank Church* (Pullman: Washington State University Press, 1994.

Baker, Ross K. *Friend and Foe in the U.S. Senate.* New York: Free Press, 1980.

Bark, Dennis L., and David R. Gress. *A History of West Germany,* vol. 2: *Democracy and Its Discontents, 1963–1988.* New York: Basil Blackwell, 1989.

Barone, Michael. *Our Country: The Shaping of America from Roosevelt to Reagan.* New York: Free Press, 1990.

Bartlett, Irving H. *John C. Calhoun: A Biography.* New York: Norton, 1993.

Becker, Jaspar. *Hungry Ghosts: Mao's Secret Famine.* New York: Free Press, 1996.

Bernstein, Irving. *Guns or Butter: The Presidency of Lyndon Johnson.* New York: Oxford University Press, 1996.

Beschloss, Michael R. *The Crisis Years: Kennedy and Khrushchev, 1960–1963.* New York: HarperCollins, 1991.

Bourne, Peter G. *Jimmy Carter: A Comprehensive Biography from Plains to Postpresidency.* New York: Scribner's 1997.

Bracher, Karl Dietrich. *The Origins, Structure, and Effect of National Socialism.* New York: Praeger, 1970.

Bradley, Bill. *Time Present, Time Past: A Memoir.* New York: Knopf, 1996.

Braestrup, Peter, *Big Story: How the American Press and Television Reported and Interpreted the Crisis of Tet 1968 in Vietnam and Washington.* Boulder: Westview, 1977. New Haven: Yale University Press, 1983.

Brinkley, Douglas, *Dean Acheson: The Cold War Years, 1953–1971.* New Haven: Yale University Press, 1992.

———. *The Unfinished Presidency: Jimmy Carter's Journey beyond the White House.* New York: Viking Press, 1998.

Brownell, Herbert, with John P. Burke. *Advising Ike: The Memoirs of Attorney General Herbert Brownell.* Lawrence: University of Kansas Press, 1993.

Brzezinski, Zbigniew. *Power and Principle: Memoirs of the National Security Adviser, 1977–1981.* New York: Farrar, Straus, Giroux, 1983.

Buchanan, Patrick. "America First—And Second and Third." *The National Interest,* Fall 1985, pp. 8–15.

Bundy, William. *A Tangled Web: The Making of Foreign Policy in the Nixon Presidency.* New York: Hill and Wang, 1998.

Carson, Rachel. *Silent Spring.* Boston: Houghton Mifflin, 1962.

Carter, Dan T. *The Politics of Rage: George Wallace, the Origins of the New Conservatism, and the Transformation of American Politics.* New York: Simon and Schuster, 1995.

Carter, Jimmy. *Keeping Faith: Memoirs of a President.* New York: Bantam Books, 1983.

Chace, James. *Acheson: The Secretary of State Who Created the American World.* New York: Simon and Schuster, 1998.

Champagne, Anthony. *Congressman Sam Rayburn.* New Brunswick: Rutgers University Press, 1984.

Churchill, Sir Winston. *The Gathering Storm.* Boston: Houghton Mifflin, 1948.

Clark, Norman H. *Mill Town: A Social History of Everett, Washington, from Its Earliest Beginnings on the Shores of Puget Sound to the Tragic and Infamous Event Known as the Everett Massacre.* Seattle: University of Washington Press, 1970.

Coulam, Robert F. *Illusions of Choice: The F-111 and the Problem of Weapons Acquisition Reform.* Princeton: Princeton University Press, 1977.

Cumings, Bruce. *The Origins of the Korean War.* 2 vols. Princeton: Princeton University Press, 1981.

Dallek, Robert. *Lone Star Rising: Lyndon Johnson and His Times, 1908–1960.* New York: Oxford University Press, 1991.

Dionne, E. J., Jr. *They Only Look Dead: Why Progressives Will Dominate the Next Political Era.* New York: Simon and Schuster, 1996.

Doan, Edward Newell. *The La Follettes and the Wisconsin Idea.* New York: Rinehart, 1947.

Dobrynin, Anatoly. *In Confidence: Moscow's Ambassador to America's Six Cold War Presidents (1962–1986).* New York: Times Books, 1995.

Dreyfus, Daniel A., and Helen M. Ingram. "The National Environmental Policy Act: A View of Intent and Practice." *Natural Resources Journal: The University of New Mexico School of Law* (1978), pp. 243–62.

D'Souza, Dinesh. *Ronald Reagan.* New York: Free Press, 1997.

Duiker, William J. *The Communist Road to Power in Vietnam.* Boulder: Westview, 1981.

Easterbrook, Gregg. *A Moment on the Earth: The Coming Age of Environmental Optimism*. New York: Viking, 1995.

Ehrman, John. *The Rise of Neoconservatism: Intellectuals and Foreign Affairs, 1945 – 1994*. New Haven: Yale University Press, 1995.

Fay, Sidney Bradshaw. *The Origins of the World War*. New York: Macmillan, 1928.

Feis, Herbert. *From Trust to Terror: The Onset of the Cold War, 1945 – 1950*. New York: Norton, 1970.

Ficken, Robert E., and Charles P. LeWarne. *Washington: A Centennial History*. Seattle: University of Washington Press, 1988.

Fontenay, Charles L. *Estes Kefauver: A Biography*. Knoxville: University of Tennessee Press, 1980.

Ford, Gerald R. *A Time to Heal*. New York: Harper and Row, 1979.

Fosdick, Dorothy. *Common Sense and World Affairs*. New York: Harcourt, Brace, 1955.

Fosdick, Dorothy, ed. *Henry M. Jackson and World Affairs: Selected Speeches, 1953 – 1983*. Seattle: University of Washington Press, 1990.

———. *Staying the Course: Henry M. Jackson and National Security*. Seattle: University of Washington Press, 1987.

Fox, Richard Wightman. *Reinhold Niebuhr: A Biography*. New York: Pantheon, 1985.

Franck, Thomas M., and Edward Weisband. *Foreign Policy by Congress*. New York: Oxford University Press, 1979.

Freedman, Lawrence. *The Evolution of Nuclear Strategy*. New York: St. Martin's Press, 1981.

Friedrich, Carl J., and Zbigniew K. Brzezinski. *Totalitarian Dictatorship and Autocracy*. Cambridge: Harvard University Press, 1956.

Fulbright, J. William. *The Arrogance of Power*. New York: Random House, 1966.

Fulbright, J. William, with Seth P. Tillman. *The Price of Empire*. New York: Pantheon Books, 1989.

Gacek, Christopher M. *The Logic of Force: The Dilemma of Limited War in American Foreign Policy*. New York: Columbia University Press, 1994.

Gaddis, John Lewis. *The Long Peace: Inquiries into the History of the Cold War*. New York: Oxford University Press, 1987.

———. *Russia, the Soviet Union, and the United States: An Interpretive History*. 2d ed. (New York: McGraw-Hill, 1990).

———. *Strategies of Containment*. New York: Oxford University Press, 1982.

———. "The Tragedy of Cold War History." *Foreign Affairs*, January/February 1994, pp. 142–54.

———. *The United States and the End of the Cold War: Implications, Reconsiderations, Provocations*. New York: Oxford University Press, 1992.

———. *The United States and the Origins of the Cold War, 1941–1947*. New York: Columbia University Press, 1972.

———. *We Now Know: Rethinking Cold War History.* New York: Oxford University Press, 1997.

Gardner, Lloyd C. *The Origins of the Cold War.* Waltham: Ginn-Blaisdell, 1970.

———. *Spheres of Influence: The Great Powers Partition Europe, from Munich to Yalta.* Chicago: Ivan R. Dee, 1993.

Garfinkle, Adam. *Telltale Hearts: The Origins and Impact of the Vietnam Antiwar Movement.* New York: St. Martin's Press, 1995.

Garthoff, Raymond L. *Detente and Confrontation: Soviet-American Relations from Nixon to Reagan.* Washington, D.C.: Brookings Institution, 1985.

———. *The Great Transition: American-Soviet Relations and the End of the Cold War.* Washington, D.C.: Brookings Institution, 1994.

Gates, Robert M. *From the Shadows: The Ultimate Insider's Story of Five Presidents and How They Won the Cold War.* New York: Simon and Schuster, 1996.

Gerber, Michele Stenehjem. *On the Home Front: The Cold War Legacy of the Hanford Nuclear Site.* Lincoln: University of Nebraska Press, 1992.

Gillon, Steven M. *The Democrats' Dilemma: Walter Mondale and the Liberal Legacy.* New York: Columbia University Press, 1992.

Gitlin, Todd. *The Sixties: Years of Hope, Days of Rage.* New York: Bantam Books, 1987.

Glad, Betty. *Jimmy Carter, in Search of the Great White House.* New York: Norton, 1980.

Gleason, Abbott. *Totalitarianism: The Inner History of the Cold War.* New York: Oxford University Press, 1995.

Glynn, Patrick. *Closing Pandora's Box: Arms Races, Arms Control, and the History of the Cold War.* New York: Basic Books, 1992.

Goldberg, J. J. *Jewish Power: Inside the American Jewish Establishment.* Reading: Addison-Wesley, 1996.

Goldberg, Robert Alan. *Barry Goldwater.* New Haven: Yale University Press, 1995.

Goncharov, Sergei N., John W. Lewis, and Xue Litai. *Uncertain Partners: Stalin, Mao, and the Korean War.* Stanford: Stanford University Press, 1993.

Greenberg, Stanley B. *Middle Class Dreams: The Politics and Power of the New American Majority.* New York: Times Books, 1995.

Greenberg, Stanley B., and Theda Skocpol, eds. *The New Majority: Toward a Popular Progressive Politics.* New Haven: Yale University Press, 1997.

Greene, John Robert. *The Presidency of Gerald R. Ford.* Lawrence: University of Kansas Press, 1995.

Greenstein, Fred I. *The Hidden-Hand Presidency: Eisenhower as Leader.* New York: Basic Books, 1982.

Gunther, John. *Inside U.S.A.* New York: Harper and Brothers, 1947.

Hamby, Alonzo L. *Man of the People: A Life of Harry S. Truman.* New York: Oxford University Press, 1995.

Hayden, Tom. *Reunion: A Memoir.* New York: Random House, 1988.

Herf, Jeffrey. *War By Other Means: Soviet Power, West German Resistance, and the Battle of the Euromissiles.* New York: Free Press, 1991.

Herring, George C. *America's Longest War: The United States and Vietnam, 1950– 1975,* 2d ed. New York: Knopf, 1986.

———. *LBJ and Vietnam: A Different Kind of War.* Austin: University of Texas Press, 1994.

Hersh, Seymour M. *The Price of Power: Kissinger in the Nixon White House.* New York: Summit Books, 1983.

Hilsman, Roger. *The Cuban Missile Crisis: The Struggle over Policy.* Westport: Praeger, 1996.

Hixon, Walter L. *George F. Kennan: Cold War Iconoclast.* New York: Columbia University Press, 1989.

Holloway, David. *Stalin and the Bomb: The Soviet Union and Atomic Energy, 1939– 1956.* New Haven: Yale University Press, 1994.

Horelick, Arnold L., and Myron Rush. *Strategic Power and Soviet Foreign Policy.* Chicago: University of Chicago Press, 1966.

Horowitz, David. *Radical Son: A Generational Odyssey.* New York: Free Press, 1997.

Hosmer, Stephen T., and Thomas W. Wolfe. *Soviet Policy and Practice toward Third World Conflicts.* Lexington, Mass.: Lexington Books, 1983.

Huntington, Samuel P. *American Politics: The Promise of Disharmony.* Cambridge, Mass.: Belknap Press, 1981.

———. *The Clash of Civilizations and the Remaking of World Order.* New York: Simon and Schuster, 1996.

———. *The Third Wave: Democratization in the Late Twentieth Century.* Norman: University of Oklahoma Press, 1991.

Hyland, William G. *Clinton's World: Remaking American Foreign Policy.* Westport, Conn.: Praeger, 1999.

———. *Mortal Rivals: Superpower Relations from Nixon to Reagan.* New York: Random House, 1987.

Isaacs, Jeremy, and Taylor Downing. *Cold War: An Illustrated History, 1945–1991: Companion to the CNN TV Series* (Boston: Little, Brown, 1998).

Isaacson, Walter, and Evan Thomas. *The Wise Men.* New York: Simon and Schuster, 1986.

Joffe, Josef. *The Limited Partnership: Europe, The United Stats, and the Burdens of Alliance.* Cambridge, Mass.: Ballinger, 1987.

Johnson, Lyndon B. *Public Papers of the Presidents of the United States: Lyndon B. Johnson, 1963–1968.* Washington, D.C.: Government Printing Office, 1964–69.

Judis, John B. *William F. Buckley, Jr.: Patron Saint of the Conservatives.* New York: Simon and Schuster, 1988.

Kagan, Donald. *On the Origins of War and the Preservation of Peace.* New York: Doubleday, 1995.

Kagan, Robert. *A Twilight Struggle: American Power and Nicaragua, 1977–1990.* New York: Free Press, 1996.

Kahan, Jerome H. *Security in the Nuclear Age: Developing U.S. Strategic Arms Policy.* Washington, D.C.: Brookings Institution, 1975.

Kaiser, Charles. *1968 in America: Music, Politics, Chaos, Counterculture, and the Shaping of a Generation.* New York: Weidenfeld and Nicolson, 1988.

Kaplan, Fred M. *Dubious Specter: A Skeptical Look at the Soviet Nuclear Threat.* Washington, D.C.: Institute for Policy Studies, 1980.

Kaplan, Robert D. *The Arabists: The Romance of an American Elite.* New York: Free Press, 1993.

Karnow, Stanley. *Vietnam: A History.* New York: Viking Press, 1983.

Kaufman, Robert G. "A Two-Level Interaction: Structure, Stable Liberal Democracy, and U.S. Grand Strategy." *Security Studies,* Summer 1994, pp. 696–735.

———. "E. H. Carr, Winston Churchill, Reinhold Niebuhr and Us: The Case for Principled Democratic Realism." *Security Studies,* Winter 1995, pp. 314–53.

———. "To Balance or to Bandwagon: Alliance Decisions in 1930s Europe." *Security Studies,* Spring 1992, pp. 417–47.

———. "The Lessons of the 1930s: A Reply to Stephen M. Walt." *Security Studies,* Summer 1992, pp. 90–96.

———. "Three Approaches to U.S. Foreign Policy." *Strategic Review,* Summer 1994, pp. 62–77.

Kennan, George F. *American Diplomacy, 1900–1950.* Chicago: University of Chicago Press, 1951.

Kennedy, John F. *Public Papers of John F. Kennedy, 1961–1963.* Washington, D.C.: Government Printing Office, 1962–64.

Kennedy, Paul. *The Rise and Fall of the Great Powers: Economic Change and Military Conflict from 1500 to 2000.* New York: Random House, 1987.

Kennedy, Robert F. *In His Own Words: The Unpublished Recollections of the Kennedy Years.* New York: Bantam Books, 1988.

Keohane, Robert O., ed. *Neorealism and Its Critics.* New York: Columbia University Press, 1986.

Korey, William. *The Promises We Keep: Human Rights, the Helsinki Process, and American Foreign Policy.* New York: St. Martin's Press, 1993.

King, Anthony. *Running Scared: Why America's Politicians Campaign Too Much and Govern Too Little.* New York: Free Press, 1997.

Kirkpatrick, Jeane J. *Dictatorships and Double Standards: Rationalism and Reason in Politics.* New York: Simon and Schuster, 1982.

Kissinger, Henry A. *A World Restored: Metternich, Castlereagh and the Problems of Peace, 1812–1822.* Boston: Houghton Mifflin, 1957.

————. "Between Old Left and New Right." *Foreign Affairs*, May/June 1999, pp. 99–116.

————. *Diplomacy*. New York: Simon and Schuster, 1994.

————. *Nuclear Weapons and Foreign Policy*. New York: Harper and Row, 1957.

————. *White House Years*. Boston: Little, Brown, 1979.

————. *Years of Renewal*. New York: Simon and Schuster, 1999.

————. *Years of Upheaval*. Boston: Little, Brown, 1982.

Klehr, Harvey, John Earl Haynes, and Friderikh Igorevich Firsov. *The Secret World of American Communism*. New Haven and London: Yale University Press, 1995.

Kober, Stanley. "Idealpolitik." *Foreign Policy*, Summer 1990, pp. 3–24.

Kuttner, Robert. *The Life of the Party: Democratic Prospects in 1988 and Beyond*. New York: Viking, 1987.

Lacouture, Jean. *DeGaulle, Ruler of France*. New York: Norton, 1991.

LaFeber, Walter. *America, Russia, and the Cold War, 1945–1992*. 7th ed. New York: McGraw-Hill, 1993.

Lebow, Richard Ned, and Janet Gross Stein. *We All Lost the Cold War*. Princeton: Princeton University Press, 1994.

Ledeen, Michael, and William Lewis. *Debacle: The American Failure in Iran*. New York: Knopf, 1981.

Leffler, Melvyn P. *A Preponderance of Power: National Security, the Truman Administration and the Cold War*. Stanford: Stanford University Press, 1992.

————. "Inside Enemy Archives." *Foreign Affairs*, July/August 1996, pp. 120–35.

Legvold, Robert. "Eastern Europe and Former Soviet Republics." *Foreign Affairs*, July/August 1996, pp. 153–56.

LeoGrande, William M. *Our Own Backyard: The United States in Central America, 1977–1992*. Chapel Hill: University of North Carolina Press, 1998.

Lesher, Stephan. *George Wallace: American Populist*. Reading, Mass.: Addison-Wesley, 1994.

Lewis, Bernard. *The Middle East: A Brief History of the Last 2000 Years*. New York: Scribner, 1995.

Lewy, Guenter. *America in Vietnam*. New York: Oxford University Press, 1978.

Li Zhisui, Dr. *The Private Life of Chairman Mao*. New York: Random House, 1994.

Lien, Carsten. *Olympic Battleground*. San Francisco: Sierra Club Books, 1991.

Lomperis, Timothy J. *The War Everyone Lost—and Won: America's Intervention in Viet Nam's Twin Struggles*. Baton Rouge: Louisiana State University Press, 1984.

McCullough, David. *Truman*. New York: Simon and Schuster, 1992.

McDougall, Walter A. *Promised Land, Crusader State: The American Encounter with the World Since 1776*. Boston: Houghton Mifflin, 1997.

McGovern, George. *Grassroots: The Autobiography of George McGovern.* New York: Random House, 1977.

McKeever, Porter. *Adlai Stevenson: His Life and Legacy.* New York: William Morrow, 1989.

McNamara, Robert S. *Blundering into Disaster: Surviving the First Century of the Nuclear Age.* New York: Pantheon Books, 1986.

———. *In Retrospect: The Tragedy and Lessons of Vietnam.* New York: Times Books, 1995.

McPherson, Harry. *A Political Education.* Boston: Little, Brown, 1972.

Macdonald, Douglas J. *Adventures in Chaos: American Intervention for Reform in the Third World.* Cambridge: Harvard University Press, 1992.

———. "Communist Bloc Expansion in the Early Cold War: Challenging Realism, Refuting Revisionism." *International Security,* Winter 1995–96, pp. 152–88.

———. "Falling Dominoes and Systems Dynamics: A Risk Aversion Perspective." *Security Studies,* Winter 1993–1994, pp. 225–53.

Mahoney, Daniel J. *De Gaulle: Statesmanship, Grandeur, and Modern Democracy.* Westport: Praeger, 1996.

Malia, Martin. *The Soviet Tragedy: A History of Socialism in Russia, 1917–1991.* New York: Free Press, 1994.

Mann, James. *About Face: A History of America's Curious Relationship with China, from Nixon to Clinton.* New York: Knopf, 1999.

Mann, Thomas E., ed. *A Question of Balance: The President, the Congress, and Foreign Policy.* Washington, D.C.: Brookings Institution, 1990.

Marks, Frederick W. *Wind Over Sands: The Diplomacy of Franklin Roosevelt.* Athens: University of Georgia Press, 1988.

Mastny, Vojtech. *The Cold War and Soviet Insecurity: The Stalin Years.* New York: Oxford University Press, 1996.

Matthews, Christopher. *Kennedy and Nixon: The Rivalry that Shaped Postwar America.* New York: Simon and Schuster, 1996.

May, Ernest R. *"Lessons" of the Past: The Use and Misuse of History in American Foreign Policy.* New York: Oxford University Press, 1973.

May, Ernest R., ed. *American Cold War Strategy: Interpreting NSC 68.* Boston: St. Martin's Press, 1993.

May, Ernest R., and Philip D. Zelikow, eds. *The Kennedy Tapes: Inside the White House During the Cuban Missile Crisis.* Cambridge, Mass.: Belknap Press, 1997.

Mayers, David. *George Kennan and the Dilemmas of U.S. Foreign Policy.* New York: Oxford University Press, 1988.

Memorial Addresses Delivered in Congress. *Henry M. Jackson: Late a Senator from Washington.* Washington, D.C.: Government Printing Office, 1983.

Miscamble, Wilson D. *George F. Kennan and the Making of American Foreign Policy, 1947–1950.* Princeton: Princeton University Press, 1992.

Morgenthau, Hans J. *Politics among Nations: The Struggle for Power and Peace.* 6th ed., revised by Kenneth W. Thompson. New York: Knopf, 1985.

———. *Vietnam and the United States.* Washington, D.C.: Public Affairs Press, 1965.

Moynihan, Daniel Patrick. *A Dangerous Place.* Boston: Little, Brown, 1978.

Muravchik, Joshua. *The Uncertain Crusade: Jimmy Carter and the Dilemmas of Human Rights Policy.* Washington, D.C.: American Enterprise Institute, 1988.

Nekrich, Aleksandr, and Mikhail Heller. *Utopia in Power.* New York: Summit Books, 1986.

Newhouse, John. *Cold Dawn: The Story of SALT.* New York: Holt, Rinehart, and Winston, 1973.

———. *War and Peace in the Nuclear Age.* New York: Knopf, 1989.

Niebuhr, Reinhold. *Christianity and Power Politics.* New York: Scribner's, 1940.

———. *The Nature and Destiny of Man.* 2 vols. New York: Scribner's, 1943.

Nitze, Paul H. *From Hiroshima to Glasnost: At the Center of Decision: A Memoir.* New York: Grove Weidenfeld, 1989.

Nixon, Richard M. *Memoirs.* New York: Touchstone Books, 1990.

Odom, William E. *The Collapse of the Soviet Military.* New Haven: Yale University Press, 1998.

———. "Soviet Politics and After: Old and New Concepts." *World Politics,* October 1992, pp. 66–98.

Ognibene, Peter J. *Scoop: The Life and Politics of Henry M. Jackson.* New York: Stein and Day, 1975.

Osgood, Robert E. *Ideals and Self-Interest in America's Foreign Relations: The Great Transformation of the Twentieth Century.* Chicago: University of Chicago Press, 1953.

Overy, Richard. *Why the Allies Won.* New York: Norton, 1995.

Parmet, Herbert S. *The Democrats: The Years After FDR.* New York: Macmillan, 1976.

———. *Richard Nixon and His America.* Boston: Little, Brown, 1990.

Pastor, Robert A. *Condemned to Repetition: The United States and Nicaragua.* Princeton: Princeton University Press, 1987.

Patterson, James T. *Mr. Republican: A Biography of Robert A. Taft.* Boston: Houghton Mifflin, 1972.

Phillips, Kevin P. *The Emerging Republican Majority.* New Rochelle, N.Y.: Arlington House, 1969.

Pipes, Richard. *Communism, the Vanished Specter.* New York: Oxford University Press, 1994.

———. "Misinterpreting the Cold War: The Hard-Liners Had It Right." *Foreign Affairs,* January/February 1995, pp. 154–60.

———. *Russia under the Bolshevik Regime.* New York: Knopf, 1993.

———. *Survival Is Not Enough: Soviet Realities and American Foreign Policy* (New York: Simon and Schuster, 1984).

Pipes, Richard, ed. *The Unknown Lenin: From the Secret Archive.* New Haven: Yale University Press, 1996.

Polmar, Norman, and Thomas B. Allen. *Rickover.* New York: Simon and Schuster, 1982.

Powers, Richard Gid. *Not without Honor: The History of American Anticommunism.* New York: Free Press, 1995.

Prochnau, Willam W., and Richard W. Larsen. *A Certain Democrat: Senator Henry M. Jackson: A Political Biography.* Englewood Cliffs: Prentice-Hall, 1972.

Quandt, William B. *Camp David: Peacemaking and Politics.* Washington, D.C.: Brookings Institution, 1986.

Raack, R. C. *Stalin's Drive to the West, 1938–1945: The Origins of the Cold War.* Stanford: Stanford University Press, 1995.

Rabin, Yitzhak. *The Rabin Memoirs.* Berkeley: University of California Press, 1996.

Radosh, Ronald. *Divided They Fell: The Demise of the Democratic Party, 1964–1996.* New York: Free Press, 1996.

Reeves, Richard. *President Kennedy: Profiles of Power.* New York: Simon and Schuster, 1993.

Reeves, Thomas C. *The Life and Times of Joe McCarthy: A Biography.* New York: Stein and Day, 1982.

Revel, Jean-Francois. *How Democracies Perish.* New York: Doubleday, 1984.

Remini, Robert V. *Daniel Webster: The Man and His Time* (New York: Norton, 1997).

———. *Henry Clay: A Statesman for the Union* (New York: Norton, 1991).

Rhodes, Richard. *Dark Sun: The Making of the Hydrogen Bomb.* New York: Simon and Schuster, 1995.

Rodman, Peter W. *More Precious than Peace: The Cold War and the Struggle for the Third World.* New York: Scribner's, 1994.

Rosati, Jerel A. *The Carter Administration's Quest for Global Community: Beliefs and Their Impact on Behavior.* Columbia: University of South Carolina Press, 1987.

Ross, Robert S. *Negotiating Cooperation: The United States and China, 1969–1989.* Stanford: Stanford University Press, 1995.

Rovere, Richard. *Senator Joe McCarthy.* New York: Harcourt, Brace, 1959.

Rubin, Barry. *Paved with Good Intentions: The American Experience and Iran.* New York: Oxford University Press, 1980.

Rusk, Dean. *As I Saw It.* New York: Norton, 1990.

Safran, Nadav. *Israel, The Embattled Ally.* Cambridge, Mass.: Belknap Press, 1978.

Scammell, Michael. *Solzhenitsyn.* New York: Norton, 1984.

Scammon, Richard A., and Ben J. Wattenberg. *The Real Majority.* New York: Coward-McCann, 1970.

Scates, Shelby. *Warren G. Magnuson and the Shaping of Twentieth-Century America.* Seattle: University of Washington Press, 1997.

Schlesinger, Arthur M., Jr. *Robert Kennedy and His Times.* Boston: Houghton Mifflin, 1978.

Schoenbaum, Thomas J. *Waging Peace and War: Dean Rusk in the Truman, Kennedy, and Johnson Years.* New York: Simon and Schuster, 1988.

Schoenfeld, Gabriel. "Twenty-Four Lies about the Cold War." *Commentary,* March 1999, pp. 28–35.

Schram, Martin. *Running for President, 1976: The Carter Campaign.* New York: Stein and Day, 1977.

Schultzinger, Robert D. *Henry Kissinger: Doctor of Diplomacy.* New York: Columbia University Press, 1989.

Schweitzer, Peter. *Victory: The Reagan Administration's Secret Strategy that Hastened the Collapse of the Soviet Union.* New York: Atlantic Monthly Press, 1994.

Schweller, Randall L. "Bandwagoning for Profit." *International Security,* Summer 1994, pp. 72–107.

Shapley, Deborah. *Promise and Power: The Life and Times of Robert McNamara.* Boston: Little, Brown, 1993.

Shawcross, William. *Sideshow: Kissinger, Nixon, and the Destruction of Cambodia.* New York: Simon and Schuster, 1979.

Sherry, Michael S. *In the Shadow of War: The United States Since the 1930's* (New Haven: Yale University Press, 1995.

Shulman, Marshall D. "On Learning to Live with Authoritarian Regimes." *Foreign Affairs,* January 1977, pp. 325–38.

Shultz, George P. *Turmoil and Triumph: My Years as Secretary of State.* New York: Scribner's, 1993.

Sick, Gary. *All Fall Down: America's Tragic Encounter with Iran.* New York: Random House, 1985.

Skidmore, David. *Reversing Course: Carter's Foreign Policy, Domestic Politics, and the Failure of Reform.* Nashville: Vanderbilt University Press, 1996.

Smith, Gerard C. *Doubletalk: The Story of the First Strategic Arms Limitations Talks.* New York: Doubleday, 1980.

Smith, Michael Joseph. *Realist Thought from Weber to Kissinger.* Baton Rouge: Louisiana State University Press, 1986.

Smith, Tony. *America's Mission: The United States and the Worldwide Struggle for Democracy in the Twentieth Century.* Princeton: Princeton University Press, 1994.

Smoke, Richard. *National Security and the Nuclear Dilemma: An Introduction to the American Experience,* 2d ed. New York: Random House, 1987.

Snyder, Jack, and Robert Jervis, eds. *Dominoes and Bandwagons.* New York: Oxford University Press, 1991.

Sorensen, Theodore C. *Kennedy.* Harper and Row, 1965.

Sterling, Claire. *The Terror Network.* New York: Holt, Rinehart, and Winston, 1981.

Stern, Paula. *Water's Edge: Domestic Politics and the Making of American Foreign Policy.* Westport: Greenwood Press, 1979.

Straight, Michael. *Trial by Television.* Boston: Beacon Press, 1954.

Talbott, Strobe. *Deadly Gambits: The Reagan Administration and the Stalemate in Nuclear Arms Control.* New York: Vintage Books, 1984.

———. *Endgame: The Inside Story of SALT II.* New York: Harper and Row, 1979.

———. *The Master of the Game: Paul Nitze and the Nuclear Peace.* New York: Knopf, 1988.

Talbott, Strobe, and Michael R. Beschloss. *At the Highest Levels: The Inside Story of the End of the Cold War.* Boston: Little, Brown, 1993.

Talmon, Jacob L. *The Origins of Totalitarian Democracy.* New York: Praeger, 1960.

Tanenhaus, Sam. *Whittaker Chambers.* New York: Random House, 1997.

Taubman, William. *Stalin's American Policy: From Entente to Detente to Cold War.* New York: Norton, 1982.

Terrill, Ross. "Mao in History." *The National Interest,* Summer 1998, pp. 54–63.

Tomasky, Michael. *Left for dead: The Life, Death, and Possible Resurrection of Progressive Politics in America.* New York: Free Press, 1996.

Tuchman, Barbara. *The Guns of August.* New York: Macmillan, 1962.

Tucker, Robert W., and David C. Hendrickson. *Empire of Liberty: The Statecraft of Thomas Jefferson.* New York: Oxford University Press, 1990.

Tulis, Jeffrey K. *The Rhetorical Presidency.* Princeton: Princeton University Press, 1987.

Tyroler, Charles, and Max M. Kampelman, eds. *Alerting America: The Papers of the Committee on the Present Danger.* New York: Pergamon-Brassey's, 1984.

Tyrrell, R. Emmett, Jr., ed. *Orthodoxy.* New York: Harper and Row, 1987.

Ulam, Adam B. *The Communists: The Story of Power and Lost Illusions, 1948–1991.* New York: Scribner's, 1992.

———. *Dangerous Relations: The Soviet Union in World Politics, 1970–1982.* New York: Oxford University Press, 1983.

———. *Expansion and Coexistence: Soviet Foreign Policy, 1917–73,* 2d ed. New York: Praeger, 1974.

Vance, Cyrus R. *Hard Choices: Critical Years in America's Foreign Policy.* New York: Simon and Schuster, 1983.

Walt, Stephen M. "Alliances, Threats, and Grand Strategy: A Reply to Kaufman and Labs." *Security Studies,* Spring 1992, pp. 444–82.

———. *The Origins of Alliances.* Ithaca: Cornell University Press, 1987.

Wattenberg, Ben J. *The First Universal Nation.* New York: Free Press, 1991.

———. *Values Matter Most: How Republicans or Democrats or a Third Party Can Win and Renew the American Way of Life.* New York: Free Press, 1995.

Weigel, George. "The Sensibility of Reinhold Niebuhr." *The National Interest,* Fall 1986, pp. 80–89.

Weinstein, Allen, and Alexander Vassiliev. *The Haunted Wood: Soviet Espionage in America—the Stalin Era.* New York: Random House, 1999.

Wells, Samuel F. "A Question of Priorities: A Comparison of the Carter and Reagan Defense Programs." *Orbis,* Fall 1983, pp. 641–66.

White, Graham, and John Maze. *Henry A. Wallace: His Search for a New World Order.* Chapel Hill: University of North Carolina Press, 1995.

White, Theodore H. *The Making of the President, 1960.* New York: Atheneum, 1961.

———. *The Making of the President, 1968.* New York: Atheneum, 1969.

———. *The Making of the President, 1972.* New York: Atheneum, 1973.

White, William Smith. *Citadel, the Story of the U.S. Senate.* New York: Harper, 1957.

Will, George F. *Restoration: Congress, Term Limits, and the Recovery of Deliberative Democracy.* New York: Free Press, 1992.

Williams, William Appelman. *The Tragedy of American Diplomacy.* 2d ed. New York: Dell, 1972.

Winik, Jay. *On the Brink: The Dramatic, Behind-the-Scenes Saga of the Reagan Era and the Men and Women Who Won the Cold War.* New York: Simon and Schuster, 1996.

Witcover, Jules. *Marathon: The Pursuit of the Presidency, 1972–1976.* New York: Viking, 1977.

Wohlstetter, Albert. "Is There a Strategic Arms Race?" *Foreign Policy,* Summer 1974, pp. 3–20.

———. "Rivals, But No 'Race.'" *Foreign Policy,* Fall 1974, pp. 48–81.

Woods, Randall Bennett. *Fulbright* (New York: Cambridge University Press, 1995.

Yergin, Daniel. *A Shattered Peace: The Origins of the Cold War and the National Security State.* Boston: Houghton Mifflin, 1977.

———. *The Prize: The Epic Quest for Oil, Money, and Power.* New York: Simon and Schuster, 1991.

Zagoria, Donald. *The Sino-Soviet Conflict, 1956–1961.* Princeton: Princeton University Press, 1962.

Zubok, Vladislav, and Constantine Pleshakov. *Inside the Kremlin's Cold War: From Stalin to Khrushchev.* Cambridge: Harvard University Press, 1996.

Zumwalt, Elmo R. *On Watch: A Memoir.* New York: Quadrangle, 1976.

Index